STATELESSNESS

'Statelessness' is a legal status denoting lack of any nationality, a status whereby the otherwise normal link between an individual and a state is absent. The increasingly widespread problem of statelessness has profound legal, social and economic consequences but also gives rise to the paradox of an international community that claims universal standards for all natural persons while allowing its member states to allow statelessness to occur. In this powerfully argued book, Conklin critically evaluates traditional efforts to recognize and reduce statelessness. The problem, he argues, rests in the obligatory nature of law, domestic or international. By closely analysing a broad spectrum of court and tribunal judgments from many jurisdictions, Conklin explains how confusion has arisen between two discourses as to the nature of the international community. One discourse describes a community in which international law justifies a state's freedom to confer, withdraw or withhold nationality. This international community incorporates state freedom over nationality matters, bringing about the stateless condition. The other discourse highlights a legal bond of socially experienced relationships. Such a bond, judicially referred to as 'effective nationality', is binding upon all states, and where such a bond exists, harm to a stateless person represents harm to the international community as a whole.

Volume 49 in the series Studies in International Law

The University of Law

2 New York Street
Manchester
M1 4HJ

Studies in International Law
Recent titles in this series

For the complete list of titles in this series, see 'Studies in International
Law' link at www.hartpub.co.uk/books/series.asp

Statelessness

The Enigma of an
International Community

William E Conklin
With a Foreword by William Twining

·H A R T·
PUBLISHING
OXFORD AND PORTLAND, OREGON
2014

Published in the United Kingdom by Hart Publishing Ltd
16C Worcester Place, Oxford, OX1 2JW
Telephone: +44 (0)1865 517530
Fax: +44 (0)1865 510710
Email: mail@hartpub.co.uk
Website: http://www.hartpub.co.uk

Published in North America (US and Canada) by
Hart Publishing
c/o International Specialized Book Services
920 NE 58th Avenue, Suite 300
Portland, OR 97213-3786
USA
Tel: +1 (503) 287-3093 or toll-free: 1 (800) 944-6190
Fax: +1 (503) 280-8832
Email: orders@isbs.com
Website: http://www.isbs.com

© William E Conklin 2015
First printed in hardback, 2014

Hart Publishing is an imprint of Bloomsbury Publishing plc.

British Library Cataloguing in Publication Data
Data Available

ISBN: 978-1-84946-969-2

Typeset by Hope Services, Abingdon
Printed and bound in Great Britain by
TJ International Ltd, Padstow, Cornwall

For Annie

To refuse all admission to the foreigner and permit the native no opportunity of foreign travel is, for one thing, not always possible, and, for another, may earn a state a reputation for barbarism and inhumanity with the rest of the world.

Plato, *Laws*

There are others again who say that account should be taken of other citizens, but deny it in the case of foreigners; such men tear apart the common fellowship of the human race. When that is removed, liberality, goodness and justice are utterly destroyed.

Cicero, *On Duties*

Foreword

Official figures report that in 2011 there were 12 million stateless people in the world and that numbers are increasing. Other estimates put the figure much higher, especially in relation to migrant children whose births were never registered, internally displaced persons, nomads and other barely documented groups. The condition of statelessness, both potentially and in fact, can have terrible consequences – social, economic and psychological as well as legal. The problems have long been recognized, but nearly all attempts have failed. The problem of nationality is essentially a legal one requiring a legal solution, but the reformers have been asking the wrong question. This book argues that the main reason for this failure has been misguided deference to an outdated doctrine that states have a reserved freedom to grant or deny nationality, almost the last residue of state-centrism. Based on decisions of transnational, international and national tribunals the argument shows that this doctrine has been eroded and its rationale extinguished. There is now a basis for recognizing a right to nationality in international law that places a binding obligation on states and other actors to recognize and enforce this right. The main error in previous attempts to resolve this intractable problem has been a conflation of two conceptions of the idea of the international community – as a community of states and as a community of all natural persons.

The argument is straightforward. It is not just an aspiration, but based on a combination of persistent research and powerful theoretical analysis, grounded in the realities of the conditions of statelessness and the discourses about social communities and the idea of an international community. With a profound and wide-reaching argument the author shows why state-centric conceptions of law are inadequate for a conception of international community of individuals and groups and for international law itself as binding law.

Bill Conklin is outstandingly well qualified to take on this task. A distinguished jurist and legal philosopher and an international lawyer, he combines patient scholarship with deep commitment to resolving this intractable set of problems. The book has wider implications for ideas about a community, identity, citizenship, the changing position of the state and much else besides.

William Twining
Quain Professor of Jurisprudence Emeritus, University College London

Preface

This study was generated by a blind spot permeating the discipline of law. The blind spot has emerged because of a contingently accepted boundary between legal norms and what jurists have taken as extra-law or non-law. The boundary encloses legal space (or what jurists describe as 'jurisdiction') within which legal norms are identified. All binding legal norms have been signified inside the boundary of legal knowledge. It is because one cannot hypothesize a boundary without implicitly acknowledging what is external to that boundary that I assert that a blind spot permeates legal knowledge. What concerns me in this study is the boundary of knowledge about an international community. Although jurists have differed as to what sources are incorporated inside the boundary of international law, the boundary itself has separated the legal knowledge about rights, duties, rules and other norms within it from the non-legal knowledge outside it. The blind spot is that despite an implicit claim of knowing what lies external to the hypothesized boundary, the boundary itself has foreclosed one from acknowledging just such extra-legal phenomena. Stateless peoples have been left as persons and groups who cannot be recognized or protected because they remain outside the boundary of legal knowledge.

Statelessness has taken two forms. The one has concerned individuals and groups whose members lack any conferral of nationality by a state member of the international community. The other has involved persons conferred such nationality, though they lack effective recognition and protection by any state member of the international community. That this absence of state recognition or protection has been linked to the international community has rested upon a territorial-like bounded residuary of international law-making and law-enforcement. This residuary of norms has reserved the formal and effective incidents of nationality to state action although international norms have sometimes and arguably impacted remedies against the state after the state has withdrawn or restricted nationality on paper, or in effect. As a consequence of such a *domain réservé*, the state has become the subject of international law. International legal normativity has become the product of either the express or the implied consent of the subject state. Although this residuary has been somewhat narrowed since the Second World War, the international community has continued to reserve the conferral, withdrawal and restriction of nationality for the state. Aside from the legal consequences (assuming that 'legal' involves the 'inside' of the contingently presupposed boundary of international legal knowledge), the social, economic, and psychological consequences of the blind spot have been sharp and disturbing. This is documented in chapter three and other examples throughout my study.

As an example, and only as an example, of *de jure* and effective statelessness in common law states, it is often thought that constitutional and international legal doctrines ensure protection for indigenous inhabitants once a constitutional bill of rights is enacted or a treaty ratified. However, given the reserved space protecting the freedom of the state in matters of nationality, the state, institutionalized as the residuary of international law, has been accepted by the international community as the ultimate source of binding laws for indigenous inhabitants. Such a state authority has excluded the possibility that indigenous legal traditions, independent of the sovereign state and independent of the domestic legal discourse, could represent the identity and binding character of laws. Indigenous legal traditions have possessed a very different sense of 'law' than that entertained by the dominant state-centric international community. As an example, the accepted (European) sense of sovereignty and of property as an intellectual or cognitive possession has displaced the experiential attachment to land and to symbols accepted in pre-colonial and contemporary indigenous legal traditions. What jurists in the European tradition have taken as 'law' has especially highlighted rules, doctrines and other related concepts. This has excluded the embodiment as law of indigenous legal traditions once the cognitively authored rules have been expressly or impliedly willed by a state's institutions.

Against the above background concerning indigenous and other *de jure* or *de facto* stateless individuals and groups addressed in my study, my research took an abrupt turn after a lengthy sojourn. Until that moment, I had taken for granted that 'the law' relating to stateless persons was inscribed in treaties and international customary norms. As such and as outlined in my early chapters, I worked within a framework premised upon the need both to reform state nationality laws and to widen the scope of human rights treaty law. However, as my research progressed, four observations gradually dawned upon me.

For one thing, I came to appreciate more fully a now seemingly obvious point that statelessness would always exist, so long as the international community reserved the bounded domain of nationality for state action alone.

From this observation flowed a second one. As noted above, I had been assuming, as I had been taught, that both international and domestic laws comprise rules, principles, policies, rights and doctrines signified by treaties and *indicia* of customary international norms. I had taken such sources of law to be either self-standing or inter-related with other rules, doctrines and other concepts. I came to appreciate, however, that rights, rules and the like were normative or ideal-directed concepts as opposed to the lived experiences of social relationships enclosed by the boundary of legal knowledge.

This led me to a third observation: the social relations of *de jure* and in effect stateless persons had entered legal analysis *after* laws had taken form as concepts. Such concepts, in turn, had been tilted in favour of an international community which reserved to its member states a bounded territorial-like legal space within which the state was free to legislate and adjudicate in matters of nationality.

The possibility of law as rooted in social relationships independent of the state – the fruits of my research here being elaborated in my chapters six to nine – suggested, fourth, that a focus upon rights and rules in treaty and customary norms was misdirected. Instead, international law was a discourse. The rights and state duties were nested in a discourse. What I found, however, was not one international law discourse but two, the one nested inside the other like a Russian doll. The two discourses have been engaged in a dialectical struggle since the early modern international community, each discourse vying for recognition and enforcement. Within that discursive struggle the emphasis and prominence of one discourse has overlapped and often displaced the other throughout the nineteenth and twentieth centuries.

The dominant discourse, I found, had assumed the international community as constituted from an aggregate of the wills of individual states. Much as the proposition that the individual possessed a freedom to act as long as s/he did not cause harm to another individual had been taken for granted, I found that Grotius, Pufendorf, Vattel, Kant, Mill and other jurists of nineteenth and early twentieth century Europe had extended this sense of freedom to each state of the international community. In this dominant discourse, it made sense that the binding character of a nationality law would rest upon the allegiance of the individual to the state as adjudged and administered solely by state officials.

Inside the dominant discourse of international law, however, another competing discourse could be perceived. I found this counter inner discourse as taking form more or less contemporaneously, often being recognized in the same treaties and judgments as had the state-centric international legal discourse. In contradistinction to the dominant discourse, the legal bond in this inner discourse rested in the lived experiences of individuals and groups in their social relationships. Such lived experiences were determined by the freedom and territorial border of a state where one had been born or where one shared the dominant construct of bloodline as the basis of nationality conferred by the state. Indeed, what became pivotal was the place of one's social relationships – not the territory owned by a state where one was born or where an alleged bloodline was associated with the state's 'nation'. Such a place of lived experiences was independent of the territorial borders of states and independent of the territorial-like boundaries of familiar juridical concepts such as jurisdiction, rights and the like. Moreover, the very jurists who have been highlighted as the 'founders' of the dominant International Law discourse had also recognized this very different sense of a legal bond. They called this bond, 'sociability'.

Conscious of sociability as the legal bond in the inner discourse, I re-read the dominant discourse and found this second legal bond still vibrant to the present day. The challenge has been to re-examine a series of concepts long taken for granted as normatively linked with the state-centric international community: the identity and binding character of a law, evidence of the place of social relations, the role of experiential space and time, the nature of peremptory norms and state duties generally, legal objectivity, the legal subject and the nature of the 'international community as a whole'. This is just a beginning. If it is worthy of close study, I hope that my book will trigger future research which explores the possibility of a law where stateless persons will receive the recognition and protection to which they are due. Such a possibility, however, will require a very different sense of law than that which hypothesizes a territorial-like boundary of legal knowledge.

William E Conklin, FRSC
June 2015 Windsor
Canada

Acknowledgements

I began this effort some years ago, believing that statelessness could be understood in simple terms of legal rules and legal tests about a right to nationality. As the years passed, I found the task increasingly complex and demanding. In my endeavour, I have benefited from research assistants who continually brought me up to date with judicial decisions, treaties, studies and academic commentaries. I was aided in this respect by Shaoye Dai, Brendan Plant and Federica Paddeu, who helped me find Asian, African and Latin American materials, and by Ryan Fritsch, who helped me work through International Law Commission materials. Annette Demers, Kristi Thompson, Selma Eren and Vicki Leung, Windsor University librarians and library staff, were also enormously helpful in finding tribunal decisions, documents of international organisations, commentaries and statistical studies. Dany Theberge, Christa Yu and Amandeep Singh Hayer helped me prepare the manuscript for copyediting. I am grateful to Rachel Turner at Hart Publishing and especially acknowledge the enormous help that Lisa Y Gourd offered in copyediting the manuscript. The anonymous Hart referees raised important issues, which I attempted to address in my final draft.

I have benefited from the particular financial support of the Ontario Law Foundation. A grant from the Humanities Research Group at the University of Windsor released me from teaching for six months, and a grant from the Morris and Beverly Baker Foundation released me from teaching for twelve months. Without these grants, the manuscript would not have reached a publishable stage. Most importantly, during my summers and research leaves since 2000, I have found myself at the Lauterpacht Centre, Clare Hall College and the University Library of Cambridge University. I welcomed the environment at Cambridge, for there I found the essential peace and sociability needed to carry out this project. I remain solely responsible for any errors and omissions.

Cambridge
27 July 2013

Table of Contents

Introduction

A N ENIGMA PERMEATES what jurists have taken as an international community. The norms and institutions of the community claim a universality that is protective of all natural persons of the globe. And yet millions of natural persons lack membership in such an international community. Because such membership is left to state members to determine and because the state is the primary legal person of the international community, natural persons lacking a state are excluded from the protection of the international community. The enigma begs the question: why? Why do natural persons remain stateless despite claims of the universality of protection?

There have been various efforts to address such a 'why'. To take an example, the enigma would dissipate, it has been assumed, if the international community were constituted from civic – or what more recently has been called 'secular' – states rather than ethnic states. Jurists have also taken for granted that statelessness would be a thing of the past if only more states and more international instruments recognized more universal rules – and more rigorously detailed rules at that. As another alternative, the habitual residence of those who find themselves without membership in an international community has been offered as a means to erase their legal predicament and traumatic suffering. As a still other alternative, jurists advocate that the provisions of the six international human rights treaties must be taken more seriously. After all, all natural persons, including (presumably) stateless persons, possess human rights. In particular, several human rights treaties recognize the right to nationality. Although ratified by only a minimum of states, two other treaties have recognized the legal status of stateless persons and the nationality of all infants born on the territory of a state. Social science and legal studies increasingly expose the extent of statelessness. The texts of international organizations such as the UN High Commission for Refugees (UNHCR), charged as it is to protect persons lacking a state's nationality, clothe their reports with hope that their statistics will caution states to come to terms with what the UNHCR has described as 'the crisis' and 'the challenge' of our times.[1] Despite such

---

[1] UNHCR, 'Global Trends 2011: A Year of Crises' (Geneva, 18 June 2012), www.refworld. org/docid/4fdeccbe2.html; and UNHCR, 'Global Trends 2012: Displacement, the New

efforts, the enigma of statelessness in an international community claiming universal jurisdiction remains. So too the question remains: why?

The problem, I suggest, rests with the ethos of an international community.[2] One might better describe an ethos as a 'culture', widely understood as the shared assumptions and expectations of members of a community. An ethos/culture might be of a family, a village, a city, a province, a state, a profession or an international community. Needless to say, the traditional juristic focus upon a discrete rule or right, said to exist by the cutting and pasting of the rule or right from treaties, statutes, judicial precedents and *indicia* of customary norms, has rendered the ethos of an international community opaque. Statelessness exists by virtue of an ethos of a sense of a particular international community. This community has recognized and protected a special residuary within which each state member is free to enact and administer laws regarding nationality. No external legal or political entity – neither another state, nor an international organization nor a non-governmental organization – can interfere with such a freedom of a state to choose its members (and, by inference, the natural persons who are members of the international community). As a result, the job of addressing the consequences of some people living without nationality has fallen to international standards. This Introduction sets the background to the enigma of statelessness in an international community.

I. TWO COMMUNITIES

When we speak about a natural person's freedom, the natural person is believed to possess a bounded autonomy within which s/he may think, believe, express and act without external interference from others or from a state unless s/he causes harm to another individual's autonomy. Jurists have attributed a similar sense of freedom to each state member of an international community. Like the freedom of a natural person, a residuary of an international community represents a protected freedom left for each state member of the international community. The residuary entitles a state to enact and administer laws over all persons and objects within the boundary of the residuary. Article 2(7) of the UN Charter describes elements of the international community's residuary as 'essentially within the domestic jurisdiction of any state'. In a similar vein, Article 15(8) of the

---

21st-Century Challenge' (Geneva, June 2013), unhcr.org/globaltrendsjune2013/UNHCR%20GLOBAL%20TRENDS%202012_V05.pdf.

[2] By an ethos (*ēthos*), the *Oxford Canadian Dictionary* signifies 'the characteristic spirit or attitudes of a community, people, or system, or of a literary work etc'. *Oxford Canadian Dictionary*, Alex Bisset (ed) & Katherine Barber (ed-in-chief) (Oxford University Press, Don Mills, 2000). An *ethnos* concerns a context-specific and common cultural, racial or ethnic tradition of a group.

League of Nations Covenant deemed that some matters, being 'solely' within the internal jurisdiction of states, could not be the object of external scrutiny, even by the League's Council.[3]

Nationality is the primary matter of such residuary. As such, states have been free to choose their own members (and by inference, to choose the members of the international community). The legal consequence has been that those natural persons without nationality in any state member of the community find themselves in what various jurists have described as a 'legal vacuum',[4] 'legal black hole',[5] 'legal anomaly',[6] 'anomalous zone'[7] or a 'liminal legal zone.'[8] Early common law jurists had a term for this legal vacuum: *damnum absque injuria* ('loss without legal injury'). The US Supreme Court noted the legal phenomenon in 1935.[9] Without legal recognition as members of a state, stateless persons have been described as outsiders to a legal order, domestic or international; that is, they are 'international pariahs',[10] 'trapped' in 'legal limbo' as 'virtual non-persons',[11] 'without papers'[12] and 'outcasts from the global political system of states'.[13]

The international legal discourse has also privileged a second, very different sense of international community. This community has existed without such a residuary. It has been described as 'the international community as a whole'. Indeed, we had better speak of two international communities

[3] League of Nations Covenant, Treaty of Versailles, Part 1, Articles 1-26, in force 10 January 1920; and BFPS (British Foreign Service Cases) 112: B, 316, 28 June 1919. The League Council, however, could refer a dispute to the Assembly.

[4] *Amuur v France*, 17/1995/523/609, Council of Europe: European Court of Human Rights, 25 June 1996, para 50, www.refworld.org/docid/3ae6b76710.html.

[5] J Steyn, 'Guantanamo Bay: The Legal Black Hole', FA Mann Lecture at Lincoln's Inn Old Hall, London (25 November 2003) as cited in K Raustiala, 'The Geography of Justice' (2004–05) 73 *Fordham Law Review* 2501, 2501 (n 5) and 2547 (n 251).

[6] N Gelazis, 'An Evaluation of International Instruments that Address the Condition of Statelessness: A Case Study of Estonia and Latvia' in R Cholewinski, R Perruchoud and E MacDonald (eds), *International Migration Law: Developing Paradigms and Key Challenges* (The Hague, Asser Press, 2007) 291–92.

[7] GL Newman, 'Anomalous Zones' (1996) 48 *Stanford Law Review* 1997.

[8] L King-Irani, 'Exiled to a Liminal Legal Zone: Are We All Palestinians Now?' in R Falk, B Rajagopal and J Stevens (eds), *International Law and the Third World* (London, Routledge-Cavendish, 2008).

[9] *Alabama Power Co v Ickes* (1938) 302 US 464, 479.

[10] See, eg, *M/V Saiga (No 2) Case (Saint Vincent and the Grenadines v Guinea)*, 1 July 1999, International Tribunal of Law of the Sea, www.itlos.org/index.php?id=64, paras 63 and 83–84. See also *Molvan v Attorney-General for Palestine (The Asya)* [1948] AC 351, 370. Stateless persons are described as 'floating sanctuaries' with 'no internationally recognized right[s]': *United States v Marino-Garcia* (1982) 679 F.2d 1373, 1382 (11th Cir). This description is repeated in *United States v Pinto-Mejia* (1983), 720 F.2d 248 (2d Cir). As Oppenheim puts it, the stateless person lives as if in the open seas without the flag of a state. LFL Oppenheim, *International Law*, H Lauterpacht (ed), 8th edn (New York, David McKay, 1955) 668.

[11] UNHCR, 'The Problem of Statelessness has become a Live Issue Again' (1998) 112 *Protecting Refugees Magazine*.

[12] Economic and Social Council Ad Hoc Committee on Statelessness and Related Problems, Summary Record of 34th Meeting, 14 August 1950, E/AC.32/SR.3422, Proposed draft Convention relating to the Status of Refugees, Art 22 (identity Papers), 35.

[13] UNHCR, 'The Problem of Statelessness' (above n 11).

rather than one. Instead of reserving a residuary within which a state member is free to enact and administer laws regarding nationality, this second sense of an international community has been analytically independent of the choices of states. The 'international community as a whole' is more inclusive than the international community with a residuary.[14] Although James Crawford has opined that 'the international community as a whole' is not yet a legal entity,[15] my later chapters render such a view suspect in nationality matters.

The 'international community as a whole' has emerged, I argue, from a very different legal bond than that attributed to the international community with a residuary. The legal bond of the latter sense of an international community has been the natural person's allegiance to a state member. The international community as a whole, in contrast, has assumed a legal bond nested in the social relationships of natural persons. Both international and domestic legal discourses have described the legal bond of the international community as a whole as represented by an 'effective', 'vital' or 'genuine' nationality rather than as relying upon an individual's allegiance to a state. Although this sense of a legal bond as effective social relationships is widely associated with the leading International Court judgment of *Nottebohm* in 1955,[16] chapter six below retrieves such a view of a legal bond from the early nineteenth century to the present day.

Both senses of an international community may be manifested in the judgment of any one domestic or international judicial or quasi-judicial tribunal. Both senses of an international community may be represented by various provisions of a treaty or a commentator's treatise. Even human rights treaties, customary norms, shared domestic principles and opinio juris about such sources may arguably signify both senses of an international community. One shape of the international community may appear dominant during one epoch, while the other emerges in another. Even a single jurist may take one sense of an international community for granted in one essay and the other sense in another context.

The point is an analytic one: international law is constituted from two discontinuous legal discourses. The two shapes of international community are recognized in the two different discourses. The one discourse,

---

[14] The members of the international community now include the United Nations, the communities of Europe, Africa, the Americas and Asia, the International Committee of the Red Cross, the International Court of Justice, the committees of human rights treaties, the International Criminal Court and international arbitration tribunals. See J Crawford, 'Introduction' in J Crawford (ed), *International Law Commission's Articles on State Responsibility: Introduction, Text and Commentaries* (Cambridge, Cambridge University Press, 2002) 31–32 and 41; and ILC, 'Draft Articles on Responsibility of States for Internationally Wrongful Acts, with Commentaries', *Report of the ILC on the Work of its Fifty-Third Session*, UN Doc A/56/10 (2001), www.un.org/documents/ga/docs/56/a5610.pdf, 43.

[15] Crawford, 'Introduction' (ibid) 40.

[16] *Nottebohm (Liechtenstein v Guatemala)* (second phase), ICJ Rep 1955, 4 at 23 (also reported in 22 ILR 349), www.refworld.org/docid/3ae6b7248.html.

highlighting the international community as a whole, has existed inside the discourse that privileges an international community with a residuary. Although the latter shape of an international community has taken for granted a bounded residuary of which nationality is an incident, the international community as a whole has dissolved the boundary of the residuary. With respect to the international community with a residuary of law-making and law administration, one may possess a nationality in the residuary – and yet the national may not be protected by the state. In the latter case, the national is effectively stateless. Conversely, a natural person may lack a nationality in the residuary and yet possess an effective nationality in the international community as a whole. Although a territoriality has been believed to fix the boundary of the residuary, effective nationality rests with the place where one's social relationships have been experienced.

The two very different senses of an international community, each with its own sense of legal bond, impact upon how jurists have understood diverse legal issues involving stateless persons. Such issues have concerned the role of the judiciary, prolonged detention, expulsion, the admission of a natural person to a state's territory, forced internal migration, whether a stateless person has a country, the general relation of international standards to domestic laws and, most importantly, the obligatory character of a domestically enacted or administered nationality law or of an internationally recognized right to nationality. The social consequences of the determination of such issues have led to profound suffering.

II. WHO IS STATELESS?

Statelessness is not a recent phenomenon, having been recounted when the community of the Jewish faith was expelled from Judea to Babylon during the sixth century bce. Roman law left vast numbers of natural persons stateless until 212 ce, when Caracalla extended citizenship to all free persons of the Empire (excepting slaves).[17] Statelessness characterized slavery, so common in the Roman and early modern international (European) community. My effort concerns statelessness in the modern state-centric international community. Such a community arguably took form amongst the city-states of Renaissance Italy, subsequently being extended to France, Britain, Spain, the Netherlands and Denmark during the sixteenth century. By the late eighteenth century, a fundamental shift transpired in juristic accounts of this community. The freedom associated by jurists with a natural person's voluntary choice of her/his own nationality (a freedom hardly realistically practised, given the lack of communication and travel at the time) was also

[17] MI Finley, 'Empire in the Greco-Roman World' (1978) 25 *Greece and Rome* 14.

transferred to the state's law-making authority. The state came to possess the sole legal authority to confer, withdraw or withhold nationality from any natural person under its control.

The state's universal authority stemmed from a bounded *domain réservé*, initially elaborated in detail by Emerich de Vattel (1714–67).[18] Within such a domain, the state was free to choose whomever it desired for its membership. An international community emerged, to be sure. But the community was composed and constituted from the aggregate of the particular wills of states. The community protected the state's authority to exclude natural persons from a nationality. From the standpoint of a state, acting within its freedom, what mattered was the incident of nationality in the reserved domain. The ethos of such an international community is signified by Article 1 of the Convention Relating to the Status of Stateless Persons (1954).[19] Article 1 defines a stateless person as someone 'not considered as a national by any State under the operation of *its* law'.[20] Such a signification of a stateless person, immersed as it is in an ethos of an international community as the aggregate of the wills of states, has been interpreted in a manner that takes 'its law' as a state's law enacted inside the bounded residuary of the international community. The United Nations High Commissioner for Refugees (UNCHR) and commentators have followed suit.[21]

---

[18] E de Vattel, *The Law of Nations or the Principles of Natural Law*, G Fenwick (trans) (Washington, DC, Carnegie Institution, 1916) Book 2, ch 7 (paras 79–97), ch 9 (paras 116–30) and ch 10 (paras 131–39).

[19] Convention Relating to the Status of Stateless Persons (1954), 360 UNTS 117 (in force 6 June 1960) (23 signatories, 79 parties at date of writing).

[20] Ibid, vol 360, 117, Art 1 (emphasis added). See also Art 19 of the American Declaration of the Rights and Duties of Man ('Pact of San José, Costa Rica') (Bogota, 2 May 1948), (1953) 6 *Actas y Documentos* 297, reprinted in OAS, *Basic Documents in the Inter-American System* (1992), OEA/Ser.L.V/ii.82 doc.6 rev.1, 17, www.oas.org/en/iachr/mandate/basic_documents.asp. See also the *Dictionary of International Law and Diplomacy*, which in a similar vein defines a 'stateless' person as one whose state of nationality no longer protects or assists the national by operation of law: MJ Gamboa, *A Dictionary of International Law and Diplomacy* (New York, Oceana, 1973) 246.

[21] UNHCR, 'Statelessness Determination Procedures and the Status of Stateless Persons: Summary Conclusions' (December 2010), available at www.unhcr.org/refworld/docid/4d9022762.html. See also, eg, I Shearer and B Opeskin, 'Nationality and Statelessness' in B Opeskin, R Perruchoud and J Redpath-Cross (eds), *Foundations of International Migration Law* (Cambridge, Cambridge University Press, 2012); BK Blitz and M Lynch (eds), *Statelessness and Citizenship: A Comparative Study on the Benefits of Nationality* (Northampton, MA, Edward Edgar, 2011); A Edwards and C Ferstman (eds), *Human Security and Non-Citizens* (Cambridge, Cambridge University Press, 2010); D Weissbrodt and C Collins, 'The Human Rights of Stateless Persons' (2006) 28 *Human Rights Quarterly* 246; and C Sawyer and BK Blitz (eds), *Statelessness in the European Union: Displaced, Undocumented, Unwanted* (Cambridge, Cambridge University Press, 2011). Cf J Bhabba (ed), *Children without a State: A Global Human Rights Challenge* (Cambridge, MA, Massachusetts Institute of Technology Press, 2011).

III. THE EXTENT OF STATELESSNESS

The condition of de jure statelessness cannot be shoved under the carpet as an issue of mere academic interest. The UNHCR estimates that there are 12 million inhabitants of the globe who are stateless.[22] The crux of this statistic draws from the UNHCR mandate to associate a stateless person with the absence of a nationality by operation of domestic law. I shall use the phrase 'de jure statelessness' to describe such a determination.

The number of stateless persons may be substantially higher. For one thing, the figure of 12 million relies upon the capability and good will of states to provide information. The UNHCR emphasizes in several studies that the figure of 12 million is only an estimate based upon unreliable information because many states have not submitted records.[23] Only 64 states for 2011 and 72 states for 2012 provided information as to the numbers they considered lacking nationality within their jurisdictions. For another, the estimate includes those whose nationality is uncertain. A 2003 survey, based upon responses from 74 states, documented how difficult it was for states to recognize who was stateless.[24] For the 2011 figures, such populous states as India, Indonesia and the European Community (along with the Dominican Republic), did not submit records. Reporting states are generally from the northern hemisphere, and yet over 80 per cent of persons of concern to the UNHCR are from the southern hemisphere. In addition, although 3.5 million people are reported by states as stateless, the UNHCR has estimated that at least an additional eight million are stateless.[25]

[22] This figure is for 2011 and 2012. For 2012, see UNHCR, *Global Appeal 2013 Update*, www. unhcr.org/50a9f8120.html, 'Addressing Statelessness' 50. For 2011, see UNHCR, 'Global Trends 2011' (above n 1) 2; and UNHCR, *Global Appeal Update 2011*, www.unhcr. org/4cd917c99.html, 'Addressing Statelessness' 46. However, a different UNHCR summary indicates 10 million: UNHCR, 'Global Trends 2012' (above n 1) Annexes (Excel Tables), www.unhcr.org/globaltrends/2012GlobalTrends_0913.zip, 2.

[23] UNHCR, 'Stateless People Figures', www.unhcr.org/pages/49c3646c26.html. The Committee of the High Commissioner's Program (35th Meeting of the Standing Committee) has remarked on the 'millions' of stateless persons in UNHCR, 'Stateless: Prevention and Reduction of Statelessness and Protection of Stateless Persons', EC/57/SC/CRP.6 (14 February 2006), published in (2006) 25(3) *Refugee Survey Quarterly* 72–76, 73.

[24] 59.4% of all respondent state officials (of which 45.9% were from Europe) indicated that they had encountered problems recognizing stateless persons. UNHCR Department of International Protection, 'Final Report Concerning the Questionnaire on Statelessness Pursuant to the Agenda for Protection' (March 2004), www.unhcr.org/4047002e4.pdf. See also 'Preliminary Report Concerning the Questionnaire on Statelessness pursuant to the Agenda for Protection' (September 2003), www.unhcr.org/3ff00a182.pdf, para 23. See also Executive Committee of High Commissioner's Program (33rd Meeting of the Standing Committee), 'UNHCR's Activities in the Field of Statelessness: Progress Report', EC/55/SC/CRP.13/REV.1 (May 2001), reprinted in (2006) 25 *Refugee Survey Quarterly* 122.

[25] The reported stateless persons of 3,477,101 and 3,335,777 in 2011 and 2012 contrast with the estimate of 12 million: UNHCR, *Statistical Yearbook 2011*, 11th edn (Geneva, 8 April 2013), available at www.unhcr.org/516282cf5.html, Annex Tables 3, 7 and 12; and UNHCR, 'Global Trends 2012' (above n 1) Annexes (Excel Tables), 21. In 2004, the figure was estimated at 17 million: UNHCR, 'Stateless: Prevention and Reduction' (above n 23).

The estimate of 12 million stateless persons includes more than de jure stateless persons (that is, persons lacking a nationality by the operation of a state's law). For one thing, the Reports of the UNHCR state that the figure of 12 million includes natural persons who are categorized as 'de facto' stateless. The latter category is said to include 'persons who are unable to establish their nationality'.[26] De facto statelessness is a term traditionally associated with an absence of diplomatic protection. It is unclear whether de facto statelessness, for the purpose of the UNHCR studies, includes 'effective statelessness' as that term is elaborated in chapter six below. By effective nationality, de jure nationals remain legally, socially and economically unprotected by their state of nationality. Effectively stateless persons in this sense would seem to be excluded from the UNHCR statistic of 12 million stateless persons because the UNHCR studies distinguish the 'stateless persons' from categories of persons usually having de jure nationality: 'refugees', 'people in refugee-like situations', 'asylum-seekers', 'internally displaced persons' and 'various' others. It is difficult to suggest that a national is effectively protected by the state of nationality for the 42.5 million persons forcibly displaced worldwide.[27] In 2006, 7.4 million 'persons of concern' to the UNHCR were considered 'warehoused' (that is, refugees living in camps for more than a decade).[28] Warehousing impacts negatively upon access to public education, medical services, social security, employment and other social rights, aside from inequitable treatment with entitlements of nationals on the territory where warehoused. One could hardly be described as possessing an effective nationality if one were a warehoused refugee, one of the 35 million 'of concern' to the UNHCR, one of the 618,703 persons living in 'refugee-like' conditions or one of the tens of millions children with unregistered births and therefore with a likely absence of de jure nationality.[29]

The above studies suggest several points related to subsequent chapters. Many states simply do not possess the financial and administrative capacity to register or provide documentation of the nationality for all

---

[26] UNHCR, *Statistical Yearbook 2011* (ibid) Annex Table 1, fn 8. By de facto statelessness, the UNHCR may be adopting the longstanding signification of the lack of diplomatic protection of a national. However, the Report for 2011 defines a stateless person as 'persons who are not considered nationals by any state under the operation of its laws'. This category is said to include 'persons who are unable to establish their nationality'.

[27] For the radical increase of asylum applications, see UNCHR, 'Asylum Trends 2012: Levels and Trends in Industrialized Countries' (21 March 2013), www.unhcr.org/5149b81e9.html.

[28] UNHCR, 'Stateless: Prevention and Reduction' (above n 23).

[29] The studies of June 2013 estimate 35,844,480 'persons of concern'; one million (936,740) asylum seekers (pending cases); 10,500,241 refugees and 'people in refugee-like situations', of whom over 6.5 million (6,674,740) persons are assisted by the UNHCR, and over 17.5 (17,670,368) 'internally displaced persons assisted by the UNHCR'. 'Persons of concern' include refugees, asylum-seekers, internationally displaced persons, returned refugees, returned IDPs and 'others of concern' separate from 'stateless persons': UNHCR, 'Global Trends 2012' (above n 1) 12, Table 1. See also UNHCR, 'Global Trends 2011' (above n 1) 2.

habitual residents.[30] This is especially so during internal or inter-state warfare. The issue is pressing because a recent study records that children under 18 years of age constitute 46 per cent of refugees, 34 per cent of asylum-seekers and roughly 50 per cent of all persons of concern to the UNHCR.[31] In addition, by virtue of several human rights and stateless-ness treaties examined in chapter four below, state parties have under-taken to posit the criterion of nationality by law and by naturalization in terms of all births within their territories. This legal criterion, however, is somewhat reified vis-à-vis the demographics of such registration. For 2012, 40 million, or one third of all births on the globe, lacked registra-tion.[32] In 2007, 51 million children lacked birth registration throughout the globe.[33] Children may have been left abandoned and parents killed, unknown or having disappeared. If left unregistered at birth, such a child is de jure stateless unless or until subsequently naturalized by the state of birth.

The statistics about statelessness raise a further point. Legal formalism may suggest the absence or understating of the legal condition of stateless-ness in a state's territory. This may be so, we shall find in chapter three, because the laws are sometimes administered in a way to exclude inhabit-ants from naturalization. So too, states may lack the economic and adminis-trative facilities to register nationals. The latter point is especially pertinent because 'developing countries' host most refugees and internally displaced persons and, by inference, most stateless persons.[34]

In addition, statistics are more reliable for stateless persons who have crossed the territorial borders of their states of habitual residence and thereby become eligible for refugee status. The vast majority of stateless persons, however, do not cross territorial borders. The boundary of inter-nal jurisdiction hence risks silencing the voices of stateless persons even

---

[30] Executive Committee of High Commissioner's Program, 'UNHCR's Activities in the Field of Statelessness' (above n 24) para 2. For an analysis of migration generally, see C Dauvergne, 'Sovereignty, Migration and the Rule of Law in Global Times' (2004) 67 *Modern Law Review* 588.

[31] UNHCR, *Statistical Yearbook 2011: Trends in Displacement, Protection and Solutions* (Geneva, 8 April 2013), www.unhcr.org/516282cf5.html, 46–47. See generally UNHCR, 'Revised Background Note on Gender Equality, Nationality Law and Statelessness' (8 March 2013), www.refworld.org/docid/4f59bdd92.html.

[32] World Health Organization (WHO), 'Country Health Information Systems: A Review of the Current Situation and Trends' (Geneva, 2011), www.who.int/healthmetrics/news/chis_report.pdf, 1.

[33] UNICEF, *Progress for Children: A World Fit for Children – Statistical Review* (December 2007) No 6, www.unicef.org/progressforchildren/2007n6/files/Progress_for_Children_-_No._6.pdf, 42. The number is also cited by the Universal Birth Registration website at www.plan-international.org/birthregistration. This figure increased by over three million from 2005. See UNICEF, *The 'Rights' Start to Life: A Statistical Analysis of Birth Registration* (New York, UNICEF, 2005), www.unicef.org/publications/files/R55BirthReg10a.pdf, 3. See also the website of the Migration Policy Institute, www.migrationinformation.org/datahub/comparative.cfm.

[34] UNHCR, *Global Report 2012*, available at www.unhcr.org/gr12/index.xml, 62.

in the context of statistics. As an example, the trafficking and slavery of women and children often lack statistical signification because though nationality may have been conferred, their documentation is frequently confiscated by the traffickers and slave owners.

A further point is appropriate. Although the focus upon the territory of birth may have been appropriate when introduced into the international law discourse, present-day large-scale migration suggests that the territory of birth is an unrealistic criterion for nationality. In 2011, the foreign-born population of the (presently 34) state members of the Organisation for Economic Co-operation and Development (OECD) had reached 111 million, an increase of 25–30 per cent from 2001.[35] More generally, migrants grew on the globe from 75 million in 1965 to 150 million in 2000, and then to 232 million in 2012.[36]

Multilateral treaties offer an alternative to birth as the criterion of nationality: namely, habitual residence. Habitual residence, however, suggests a fixity of residency. The large-scale migration of individuals and groups, despite technological advances of communication, renders such a fixity suspect. In addition, as documented below in chapter three, large numbers of nomadic and travelling groups characterize life throughout the globe today.[37] In addition, although domestic laws may guarantee equal treatment for all habitual residents, members of indigenous groups may lack effective legal and social protection experienced by other habitual residents. The problem, we shall find, is that the human rights treaties and customary international norms have been read against a deeper and more pervasive cultural assumption than any such texts state: namely, the incorporation of a state's reserved domain into the international community.

---

[35] Organisation for Economic Co-operation and Development (OECD), 'Recent Developments in International Migration Movements and Policies' in OECD, *International Migration Outlook 2013* (OECD, 2013), dx.doi.org/10.1787/migr_outlook-2013-en, 36.

[36] See UN, 'International Migration and Development: Report of the Secretary-General', UN Doc A/68/190 (25 July 2013), daccess-dds-ny.un.org/doc/UNDOC/GEN/N13/408/48/PDF/N1340848.pdf?OpenElement, para 1.1. For 2013 figures, see International Organization for Migration (IOM), 'World Migration Report 2013: Migrant Well-Being and Development' (Geneva, 2014), www.iom.int/cms/wmr2013, 55–68. For 2012 figures, see the 'Data Hub' on the Migration Policy Institute (MPI) website at www.migrationinformation.org/datahub/index.cfm. For the 2010 figures, see MPI, 'Top Ten Countries with the Largest Number of International Migrants' (2010), www.migrationinformation.org/datahub/charts/6.1.shtml. For earlier figures, see UN Department of Economic and Social Affairs (UNDESA), 'Trends in International Migrant Stock: The 2008 Revision', POP/DB/MIG/Stock/Rev.2008 (July 2009), www.un.org/esa/population/migration/UN_MigStock_2008.pdf; and International Organization for Migration, *World Migration Report 2003: Managing Migration – Challenges and Responses for People on the Move* (Geneva, IOM, 2003) 4–5.

[37] 268 million members of pastoral groups, lacking a fixed place of habitation, are estimated to inhabit the globe. See below ch 3, s IIIB (121–25).

IV. EFFORTS TO ERADICATE STATELESSNESS

Efforts to understand and eradicate statelessness are not new. Analytic and empirical studies of statelessness have taken several distinct approaches. Each approach takes the residuary of the international community for granted. To begin with, one does not infrequently read of the cause of statelessness as the 'Tamil problem', the 'Palestinian problem', the problem of 'the wandering gypsy', 'the Jewish problem' and the like.[38] Even eminent jurists attribute the stateless condition of natural persons to their own doing.[39] Edward Said has made us aware that statelessness has too often been believed to be 'a temporary nuisance that, given time and effort (and punitive violence from time to time), will finally go away'.[40] No one state, it is often believed, can be considered blameworthy of the condition of a stateless person.[41] Even an early UN Secretary General assured the public at one point that the cause of statelessness had 'dried up'.[42] The enigma of statelessness is far too complicated to attribute it to the victims themselves or to imagine that it might disappear on its own.

A. The Ethnic Versus Civic State

One approach has attributed statelessness to ethnic nationalism. Hannah Arendt and Margaret Somers have especially decried how the conquest of the state by the ethnic nation has factored into the stateless condition.[43] Along with Arendt and Somers, Charles Taylor has especially advocated the need for a civic, as opposed to an ethnic, state.[44] In a similar vein, Catherine Dauvergne has argued that the state must become 'unhinged' from the ethnic nation because of economic globalization and migration.[45]

---

[38] H Arendt, *The Origins of Totalitarianism* (New York, Harcourt Brace Jovanovich, 1979 [1951]) 289–90; H Arendt, *Eichmann on Trial* (London, Penguin, 1963) 167 and 240; and J-P Sartre, *Anti-Semite and Jew*, George Beck (trans) (New York, Schocken Books, 1976).

[39] Eg, M Hudson, 'Report on Nationality, Including Statelessness' in *ILC Yearbook* 1952, UN Doc A/CN.4/50 (21 February 1952) vol II, 41.

[40] E Said, *Orientalism* (New York, Vintage Books, 1979) 49.

[41] *Kalderas Gipsies v Federal Republic of Germany*, App nos 7823/77, 7824/77, 11 DR 221, (ECHR), 6 July 1977, 11 *Decisions and Reports* 221, para 38.

[42] P Weis, 'Legal Aspects of the Convention of 25 July 1951 relating to the Status of Refugees' (1953) 30 *British Yearbook of International Law* 478.

[43] Arendt, *The Origins of Totalitarianism* (above n 38); and M Somers, *Genealogies of Citizenship: Markets, Statelessness and the Right to Have Rights* (Cambridge, Cambridge University Press, 2008).

[44] C Taylor, 'Nationalism and Modernity' in R McKim and J McMahan (eds), *The Morality of Nationalism* (Oxford, Oxford University Press, 1997); and C Taylor, 'Nationalism and Modernity' in JA Hall (ed), *The State of the Nations* (Cambridge, Cambridge University Press, 1998).

[45] C Dauvergne, *Making People Illegal: What Globalization Means for Migration and Law* (Cambridge, Cambridge University Press, 2008) 182–85.

Impartial judges, independent of the executive arm of the state, would represent the rational and self-interested will of the civic state. All that is needed is the replacement of the ethnic nation by the civic state.

The displacement of the ethnic nation by the civic state would leave statelessness unabated, however. The civic state would still remain free to confer, withdraw or withhold nationality as a feature of the residuary of the international community. The civic state would remain a member of the same international community that has reserved its own membership to the laws of state members. One of the two instrumental criteria of nationality has been *sanguinis* or bloodline of the parents. Ironically, with such a criterion, officials would be encouraged to withhold or withdraw nationality if an individual lacked the dominant ethnicity of the nation-state. The civic state would still possess a bounded jurisdiction within which the state would remain free to choose its own members. Such laws would be exclusionary of international standards. The boundary of the jurisdiction would exclude as well as include individuals.

B. Codification

A second approach to reducing or eradicating statelessness has urged the codification of international rules. Such rules have generally aimed to resolve conflicts in the domestic laws of two or more states.[46] The Economic and Social Council's AD Hoc Committee on Statelessness and Related Problems expressed as early as 1950 that 'either Governments could be asked ... to amend their legislation in such a way as to abolish the causes of statelessness, or those causes could be removed by preparing an appropriate convention.'[47]

The UNHCR has accepted that stateless persons could be protected by states legislating formal procedures to determine who is stateless and by integrating such legislated procedures into existing administrative procedures.[48] The International Law Commission (ILC) has more recently taken for granted in its draft rules for state succession that statelessness could be prevented by codifying international rules guiding states in nationality

---

[46] DP O'Connell, *The Law of State Succession* (Cambridge, Cambridge University Press, 1956) 245 and 258.

[47] UNHCR Ad Hoc Committee on Statelessness and Related Problems, 'Summary Record of 27th Meeting' (13 February 1950) UN Doc E/AC.32/L.32, para 25, also reprinted in (1952) 29 *British Yearbook of International Law*14. The Committee was established as documented in Economic and Social Council, GA Res 248 BCIX, 8 August 1949, UN Doc A/CN 4/50, 14. For an overview of the documents, see UN Economic and Social Council, 14th session, Doc E/2230, A/CN.4/56 (New York, 1952).

[48] UNHCR, Statelessness Determination Procedures and the Status of Stateless Persons ('Summary Conclusions') (December 2010), www.unhcr.org/refworld/docid/4d9022762.html.

matters.[49] A related feature of recent studies has urged the expansion of the scope of existing international rules protecting stateless persons.[50] The ILC has continued to focus upon codification of rules needed to diplomatically protect nationals.[51] Although Article 1(A)(2) of the Refugee Convention (1951) provides that a refugee includes a person lacking nationality who finds her/himself 'outside the country of his former habitual residence',[52] refugee protections may arguably extend to a stateless person without crossing the territorial border of her/his habitual residence.[53] Let us examine several different ways in which codification efforts have tried to eradicate statelessness.

1. A Coded Proscription against Withdrawal of Nationality

One codification effort has proscribed any state from denaturalizing its nationals. As early as 1906, a pan-American treaty established that a denaturalized 'native' could regain nationality after two years residency.[54] Denaturalization was forbidden in a 1924 Resolution of the International Law Association (ILA) in Stockholm.[55] The freedom of the state to enact and administer laws regarding nationality, however, was retained. In 1928, as a further example, an inter-American treaty required that each state party 'shall apply its own law' concerning nationality (Article 14).[56]

[49] See, eg, International Law Commission (ILC), 'State Succession and its Impact on the Nationality of Natural and Legal Persons' (A/CN.4/472/Add.1) sect B, A/CN.4/474, reproduced in *ILC Yearbook 1996*, vol II(2), ch 4, para 88. See also ILC, 'Third Report on Nationality in Relation to the Succession of States' (UN Doc A/CN.4/480), *ILC Yearbook 1997*, vol II(1), 7–69.

[50] L van Waas, *Nationality Matters: Statelessness under International Law* (Antwerp, Intersentia, 2008); Somers (above n 43); and Edwards and Ferstman (eds) (above n 21).

[51] UN General Assembly, 'Commentary to the Draft Articles on Diplomatic Protection', UN GAOR 61st sess, Supp No 10, UN Doc A/61/10, ch IV, adopted on 2nd reading (2006). See also the 'Draft Articles on Diplomatic Protection', UN GAOR 59th sess, Supp No 10, UN Doc A/59/10 (2004) ch IV.

[52] Convention Relating to the Status of Refugees (1951), 189 UNTS 137 (entered into force 22 April 1954) (19 signatories, 145 parties).

[53] See, eg, E Lauterpacht and D Bethlehem, 'The Scope and Content of the Principle of Non-refoulement: Opinion', prepared for UNHCR Global Consultations on Refugee Protection Expert Roundtable (Cambridge, 9–10 July 2001), reprinted in E Feller, V Türk and F Nicholson (eds), *Refugee Protection in International Law: UNHCR's Global Consultations on International Protection* (Cambridge, Cambridge University Press, 2003).

[54] Convention Establishing the Status of Naturalized Citizens Who Again Take Up their Residence in the Country of their Origin (Rio de Janeiro,13 August 1906), reprinted in (1913) 7 *American Journal for International Law (Supplement)* 226–29, also reprinted in JB Scott (ed), *International Conferences of American States 1889–1928* (Oxford, Oxford University Press, 1931) 131.

[55] The Resolution prohibited denaturalization by a court or administrative order; no national should be denaturalized as a criminal sentence; a stateless person should not be expelled from a state's territory; and one should lose a nationality upon the acquisition of another nationality. International Law Association (ILA), *Report of the Thirty-Third Conference (Stockholm, 8–13 September 1924)* (London, Sweet & Maxwell, 1925).

[56] Code of Private International Law (Code Bustamante) (Havana, 20 February 1928), 86 LNTS 111, Bk 1, title 1, ch 1.

This freedom included the withdrawal of nationality. The ILC has more recently codified the customary norm to the effect that in the succession of states, a successor state has a duty not to withdraw nationality if the consequence is that an individual becomes stateless.[57] In addition, a state is said to have an obligation not to withdraw nationality if the person concerned is habitually resident in the state's territory or if the person has 'an appropriate connection with a constituent unit of the predecessor state that has remained part of the predecessor state' (Article 25(2)(a) and (b)).

2. Presumption of Nationality in the Succession of States

In the past, the stateless condition has arisen when one state conquers or annexes the territory of another. As a consequence, the ILC has proposed a set of rules that presumes nationality in a succeeding state for anyone whose habitual residence existed in the previous state's territory.[58] As an aside, however, the stateless condition also transpires if one's state of nationality or of habitual residence physically dissolves due to environmental conditions. The thrust of the presumption of nationality has been to recognize the social circumstances of an individual rather than the formal conferral or lack of conferral of nationality by the succeeding state. The Commission quotes approvingly from JF Rezek in this regard: 'the juridical relationship of nationality should not be based on formality or artifice, but on a real connection between the individual and the state.'[59] James Crawford has especially focused upon the need for identifiable international law rules concerning the succession of states, particularly in circumstances of cession and conquest.[60]

The stateless condition seems to disappear on a reading of the ILC's further proposed codification of customary norms. To take an example, the state succession articles assert that states have a duty to 'take all appropriate measures to prevent persons who, on the date of the succession of states, had the nationality of the predecessor State' but who would become stateless on succession (Article 4), 'irrespective of the mode of acquisition of that nationality' (Article 1). A state has a legal duty to 'enact legislation on nationality and other connected issues arising in relation to the succession of states' consistent with the presumption and other provi-

---

[57] ILC, *Nationality of Natural Persons in relation to the Succession of States 1999*, Off Records of Gen Ass, 54th sess, Supp No 10 (A/54/10), reprinted in Gen Ass Resolution 55/153, Annex, 12 December 2000, Art 25.

[58] Ibid, Art 5.

[59] JF Rezek, 'Le droit international de la nationalité' in Hague Academy of International Law, *Recueil Des Cours: Collected Courses of the Hague Academy of International Law, 1986-lll* (Dordrecht, Martinus Nijhoff, 1987) vol 198, 357, as discussed in ILC, *Nationality of Natural Persons* (above n 57) Art 19 (Comm 2).

[60] J Crawford, *The Creation of States in International Law*, 2nd edn (Oxford, Oxford University Press, 2006).

sions of the codification (Article 6). The presumption includes a duty on the part of the state to 'apprise' persons concerned 'of the effect of its legislation on their nationality' (Article 6). Although a successor state might attribute nationality by requiring an individual to renounce her/his nationality in the former state, this requirement might not be applied if the person were rendered stateless (Article 9). Each state has a duty to 'grant a right to opt for its nationality' if a person has an 'appropriate connection with that state' (Article 11). If one lacks an 'effective link with a state', the state is not required to confer nationality unless the person would be stateless as a consequence of such a refusal (Article 19). If one lacks a nationality in a third state, a successor state has a duty to attribute nationality to an individual if the predecessor state had dissolved and if the individual had habitual residence, 'an appropriate connection with a constituent unit of the predecessor state' or was born in a third state but had her/his 'last habitual residence' in the territory of the predecessor state (Article 22). Conversely, if an individual lacks an 'effective link' with the predecessor state or its territory, the successor state need not attribute its own nationality to the individual unless the consequence were to render her/him stateless (Article 19).

3. *Conflicts between Domestic Laws*

During the early efforts to codify rules regarding statelessness, a great deal of attention was devoted to the clarification of conflicts of law rules. One of Paul Weis' studies considered statelessness as primarily caused by such conflicts of domestic laws.[61] Codified rules could guide the interpretation of conflicts situations, if not render a domestic law inoperative in a particular case. The proscription of discrimination or the arbitrary deprivation of nationality would exemplify such transcending coded rules.[62] Laura van Waas has followed this stream of thought by attributing statelessness to textual gaps and contradictions in conflicts of nationality laws.[63] Carol Batchelor's several studies of statelessness have also concentrated upon the need to codify shared domestic rules.[64]

---

[61] Weis, 'Legal Aspects of the Convention of 25 July 1951' (above n 42); and P Weis, *Nationality and Statelessness in International Law* (London, Stevens, 1956).

[62] See, eg, JA Goldston, 'Epilogue' in Blitz and Lynch (eds) (above n 21).

[63] L van Waas, 'Nationality and Rights' in Blitz and Lynch (eds) (above n 21). See also van Waas, *Nationality Matters* (above n 50); and M Manly and L van Waas, 'The Value of the Human Security Framework in Addressing Statelessness' in Edwards and Ferstman (eds) (above n 21).

[64] For examples of Carol Batchelor's work, see C Batchelor, 'Statelessness and the Problem of Resolving Nationality Status' (1998) 10 *International Journal of Refugee Law* 156; C Batchelor, 'Stateless Persons: Some Gaps in International Protection' (1995) 7 *International Journal of Refugee Law* 232; and C Batchelor, 'UNHCR and Issues related to Nationality' (1995) 14 *Refugee Survey Quarterly* 91.

Conflicts of domestic laws have led to the stateless condition, for example, when an individual migrates to another's territory and when the two states possess differing criteria of nationality, the one *sanguinis* ('bloodline', or today described as 'parentage') and the other *soli* (birth). If one state has conferred nationality based upon *sanguinis* and if the individual migrates to another state's territory where birth has been legislated as basis of nationality, s/he would lose her/his nationality. The new state of residence could only recognize the place of birth (*soli*) as the criterion of nationality. The early response to the conflicts of domestic laws was to close this gap by clarifying the scope of preferred rules based upon *soli* and by institutionalizing enforcement mechanisms to that end on behalf of stateless persons.[65]

The codification of conflicts of domestic laws has especially assumed that an international rule could prevent a conflict of laws in the case of a woman who marries someone from another jurisdiction differing in the criterion of nationality.[66] Such a rule has also been thought to resolve a woman's stateless condition upon divorce. A similar attitude may be incumbent for a divorce of persons of the same sex. The International Law Association has explained in detail how the different criteria of domestic laws have caused women to be denaturalized or to remain stateless.[67] As the UNHCR has also explained, 'Women who *have* citizenship may end up living as stateless persons because the statelessness of their spouse or of their children imposes upon them all the attributes of statelessness itself.'[68]

The general approach in this context has been to urge states to adopt the

---

[65] See, eg, ILC, 'Summary Records of the Meetings of 47th Session: State Succession and its Impact on the Nationality of Natural and Legal Persons', UN Doc A/CN.4/SER.A/1995, *ILC Yearbook 1995*, vol I, para 15; and the article reproduced in *ILC Yearbook 1996* (above n 49) para 88. See also DP O'Connell and R Lillich, 'The Current Status of the Law of State Responsibility for Injuries to Aliens' in R Lillich (ed), *International Law of State Responsibility for Injuries to Aliens* (Charlottesville, University of Virginia Press, 1983); and ILC, 'Third Report on Nationality in relation to the Succession of States' (above n 49).

[66] A Edwards, 'Displacement, Statelessness, and Questions of Gender Equality and the Convention on the Elimination of All Forms of Discrimination against Women', background paper for a joint UNHCR and UN Committee on the Elimination of Discrimination against Women seminar (New York, 16–17 July 2009) 57–58, www2.ohchr.org/english/bodies/cedaw/docs/UNHCR_CEDAW_Background_Paper4.pdf; S Chung, C Lee, HT Lee and JH Park, 'The Treatment of Stateless Persons and the Reduction of Statelessness: Policy Suggestions for the Republic of Korea' (2010) 13 *Korea Review of International Studies* 7, 8–9; C McIlwaine, 'The Gendered Exclusions of International Migration: Perspectives from Latin American Migrants in London' in S Chant (ed), *The International Handbook of Gender and Poverty* (Cheltenham, Edward Elgar, 2010) 260–65; ILA Committee on Feminism and International Law, 'Women's Equality and Nationality: Final Report' (London, International Law Association, 2000); MS McDougal, HD Lasswell and LC Chen, 'Nationality and Human Rights: The Protection of the Individual in External Arenas' (1974) 83 *Yale Law Journal* 901, 901–3, 939–40 and 973–74.

[67] ILA Committee on Feminism and International Law (ibid).

[68] Executive Committee of UNHCR, 'UNHCR's Activities in the Field of Statelessness: Progress Report', 21st meeting of the Standing Committee (30 May 2001), UN Doc EC/51/SC/CRP.13.

same legislated criterion of nationality. The preferred criterion has been *soli* (place of birth). This codification effort seems to have been first initiated by a Committee of Experts established by the General Assembly of the League of Nations in 1924. The Committee proposed several treaties in order to require states to adopt a common criterion for the conferral of nationality. It was expected that this codification would eradicate statelessness to the extent at least that it arose from the conflicts of domestic laws.[69] In a similar spirit, the Women's Suffrage Association addressed statelessness in its 1923 and 1926 meetings.[70] In 1926, the Kosusaiko Association (the Japanese branch of the International Law Association) passed a Resolution that aimed to prevent statelessness by adopting a common criterion of nationality. By 1930, an inter-American Committee of Experts proposed three treaties aiming to clarify the rules that override or at least guide states regarding nationality: the Montevideo Convention on the Nationality of Women (1933),[71] the Montevideo Convention on the Rights and Duties of States (1933)[72] and the Montevideo Convention on Nationality (1933).[73] Article 6 of the last required that marriage not alter the nationality of a child, mother or husband. By the late 1930s, six more treaties were ready for signing and ratification.[74] By the early 1950s three

[69] See Research Group in International Law (Harvard University Law School), 'Nationality, Responsibility of States for Injuries to Aliens, and Territorial Waters' [Harvard Draft Convention on Nationality], printed in (1929) 23 *American Journal for International Law (Supplement)* 63. The Draft Conventions and Comments have focused upon the clash between the criterion of nationality by operation of law in one state and a different one in another state.

[70] See AP Mutharika, *The Regulation of Statelessness under International and National Law* (New York, Oceana, 1977) 26–27.

[71] Montevideo Convention on the Nationality of Women (26 December 1933), reprinted in M Hudson (ed), *International Legislation: A Collection of Texts of Multipartite International Instruments of General Interest* (Washington, DC, Carnegie Endowment for International Peace, 1931–50) vol 6, no 356, 589.

[72] Montevideo Convention on the Rights and Duties of States (26 December 1933), entered into force 26 December 1934, reprinted in Hudson (ed) (ibid) vol 6, no 361, 620.

[73] Montevideo Convention on Nationality (26 December 1933), reprinted in Hudson (ed) (above n 71) vol 6, No 356, 593.

[74] Covenant on Certain Questions relating to the Conflict of Nationality Laws (1930), 179 LNTS 89 (entered into force 1 July 1937) (27 states signed but did not ratify). See also Protocol Relating to Military Obligations in Certain Cases of Double Nationality (1937), 178 LNTS 227; Protocol Relating to a Certain Case of Statelessness (1930), 179 LNTS 115 (entered into force 1 July 1937). Art 1 provided that a child shall have the nationality of the mother if the father lacked a nationality and if the child was born in a state that did not confer nationality by the fact of birth. See also Special Protocol Concerning Statelessness (1930), LN Doc C.227.M.114.1930.V, (1973) UKTS 112, Cmnd 5447 (entered into force 15 March 2004), reprinted in (1974) 13 *International Legal Materials* 1–4. According to Art 1, the state of origin has an obligation to readmit someone in two circumstances: first, if the person is 'permanently indigent because of an incurable disease or other reason'; second, if the person has been convicted and served a sentence of more than one month. If the person has entered the territory of the state and thereby lost her/his nationality without acquiring another nationality, the former state of nationality is obligated to readmit the person if so requested by the state of refuge. See also Geneva Covenant on the Status of Refugees (1933), 159 LNTS 199 (entered into force 13 June 1935); and Convention regarding the Status of Refugees from

treaties, which will be examined further below in chapter four, section I, explicitly set out to reduce the stateless condition: the Convention Relating to the Status of Refugees (1954), the Convention Relating to the Status of Stateless Persons (1954) and the Convention on the Reduction of Statelessness (1961).[75] According to the last of these, a signatory state party accepted the duty to confer nationality upon any person born in its territory if the person would otherwise be stateless.

4. Stateless Condition as a Legal Status

Codification has also posited a legal status for 'stateless person'. Some states, such as Russia, have expressly enacted such a status in legislation. In 1936, the Institute of International Law at Brussels proposed that stateless persons be granted a legal status.[76] During the 1950s a major effort was made to address the stateless condition, and to that end, the Convention Relating to the Status of Stateless Persons, which came into force in 1960, recognized the legal status of a stateless person.[77]

5. Nationality on Birth

A further example of the codification effort has been to require all state parties to a treaty to register infants born on their territories as nationals. This effort was institutionalized in the Convention on the Reduction of Statelessness, noted above (and examined further in chapter four below).[78] Article 7 of the Convention on the Rights of the Child (1990) recognized the right of a child to nationality upon being registered after birth.[79] If only states were required to adopt the same rules regarding nationality and, in particular, nationality by birth, statelessness would be a thing of the past – or so jurists have often assumed.

6. Enforcement

Aside from textual gaps and contradictions in nationality laws between two or more states, jurists have taken for granted that the creation of an international institution or the widening of its jurisdiction might well raise the possibility of the enforcement of an international standard. Laura

---

Germany (1938), 192 LNTS 59.

[75] Convention Relating to the Status of Refugees (above n 52); Convention Relating to the Status of Stateless Persons (above n 19); and Convention on the Reduction of Statelessness (1961), 989 UNTS 175 (entered into force 13 December 1975) (5 signatories, 54 parties).

[76] Institut de Droit International (1936) 11 *Annuaire* 292–99.

[77] Convention Relating to the Status of Stateless Persons (above n 19) Art 12.

[78] Convention on the Reduction of Statelessness (above n 75) Arts 1(1) and 2.

[79] Convention on the Rights of the Child (1989), 1577 UNTS 3 (entered into force 2 September 1990) (140 signatories, 193 parties).

van Waas has considered the cause of statelessness to rest with just such a failure of states to enforce codified international rules.[80] As long as no international tribunal possesses the legal authority to investigate and enforce existing codified standards, it has been believed, statelessness will remain. In addition, 'new causes' of statelessness have emerged, including the failure of states to register infants on birth. Rules proscribing widespread migration, irregular migration, human trafficking and refugee conditions have been considered an integral feature of enforcement.[81]

'Technical failings' have been added to the enforcement mechanism of international standards.[82] Statelessness would be less problematic, some have considered, if the conditions of statelessness were publicized, international institutions amended, more international legal rules codified, the identity of rules clarified and the rules more rigorously enforced by international tribunals. So, for example, a recent study has addressed what it considers several 'critical issues': the role of domestic courts in interpreting and applying international refugee law, the standard of proof, the limitation procedures after 9/11, the response of internal and international human rights tribunals, and economic harm.[83]

7. The Problematic of the Codification Approach

The codification efforts have had one major weakness. The enigma of statelessness persists because of the sense of an international community which has reserved the freedom of a state to confer, withdraw and withhold nationality notwithstanding international standards and international institutions. Treaty amendments, new treaties and international enforcement mechanisms of discrete rules are offered to displace the enigma of statelessness. And so legal issues have followed a special line of thought. Does a wife have a nationality independent of her husband? In order to eradicate statelessness, let us require all states to confer nationality to all persons born on the state's territory. Let us justify a domestic nationality law or a 'right to nationality' with reference to Article 38 sources of the Statute of the International Court of Justice (ICJ).[84] Or if the right to nationality is an international customary norm, then perhaps it is also a peremptory norm. The jurists' role is complete, we might assume, if

---

[80] van Waas, 'Nationality and Rights' (above n 63) 31–40. See also van Waas, *Nationality Matters* (above n 50); and Manly and van Waas (above n 63).

[81] van Waas, *Nationality Matters* (above n 50) 151–92.

[82] BK Blitz and M Lynch, 'Statelessness and the Deprivation of Nationality' in Blitz and Lynch (eds) (above n 21).

[83] JC Simeon, 'Introduction: The Research Workshop on Critical Issues in International Refugee Law and Strategies towards Interpretative Harmony' in JC Simeon (ed), *Critical Issues in International Refugee Law: Strategies Toward Interpretative Harmony* (Cambridge, Cambridge University Press, 2010).

[84] Statute of International Court of Justice (1945), appended to UN Charter.

only we could be satisfied of a discrete criterion (rule or test), such as the place of birth of a natural person or the gender equality of domestic nationality laws, were expressly adopted by a treaty or a judicial test.

But the enigma of statelessness remains. In the background there hovers an international community that recognizes and protects the concept of nationality as an essential element of the reserved jurisdiction for each state member of the community. The problem is that as long as nationality is considered an incident in such a residuary, the enforcement outcomes will manifest the sum of the wills of state members of the international community. If a member of the international community has chosen to exclude a natural person from its membership, such a choice is immune from external intervention. An international enforcement mechanism is just such an external source. Statelessness therefore remains an enigma of the international community. Codified rights have left the 'disease' unexplained. The issue remains: why is any written rule or right, justified in terms of the express or implied source in the state's reserved domain, obligatory for a state to protect a stateless person?

V. LEGAL OBLIGATION AND AN INTERNATIONAL COMMUNITY

Paul Weis hit the nail on the head when he asserted that codified rules would not eradicate statelessness: an internationally legislated nationality rule, he suggested, merely identifies 'symptoms of the disease' rather than 'the disease'.[85] It is one thing to identify a right or the absence thereof. To this end, jurists have looked to statutes and judicial precedents of states and to treaties and international customary norms. It is another thing to ask why such an identifiable right is obligatory for states to respect and to enforce an internal or international standard. Does the state possess the authority to claim the boundary of its own freedom, for example? Is a state obligated to withdraw its autonomy in choosing its own members when membership is so important to the identity of a state? Can international standards protect stateless persons if the state-centric protected residuary of the international community includes law-making regarding the conferral, withdrawal or withholding of nationality from natural persons? If international standards dissolve the boundary of the reserved domain, what are the implications for the role of the executive arm of the state, the scope of judicial scrutiny, the sorts of admissible evidence, and the ultimate basis of legal obligation towards the standards of the international community?

These questions raise a further question: what is the nature of a state's

---

[85] P Weis, 'Review of *A Study of Statelessness* (UN Dept of Social Affairs 1949)' (1950) 27 *British Yearbook of International Law* 510, 512; Weis, 'Legal Aspects of the Convention of 25 July 1951' (above n 42); and Weis, *Nationality and Statelessness* (above n 61).

legal obligation in the international community? The justification of a domestically enacted or administered law with reference to the ICJ Article 38 sources cannot ensure the protection of a stateless person. The sources, to be sure, assume that legal obligation rests in the express consent (by a treaty) or implied consent (by a customary norm) of a state. But why would a state be legally obligated to protect a stateless person if nationality laws were protected from external interference by being an incident of the residuary? Why would a state be obligated to protect a stateless person if the state has determined the person stateless? Why would domestic laws be binding upon nationals of a state if there were a risk that, for any one of a variety of circumstances examined in these chapters, her/his nationality might be withheld or withdrawn? Without addressing the issue of legal obligation in the face of statelessness 'by operation of [state] law', one will take for granted that the international community, as an aggregate of the wills of states, is a hard fact. The community will be 'fragmented'.[86]

If one understands legal obligation in terms of overriding international standards, the standards have been frequently justified in terms of 'humanity' or the conscience of humankind. As one commentator recently described, the ultimate source of the international community is constituted from 'moral commandments . . . considered by the conscience of mankind'.[87] Aside from conscience and humanity, jurists have justified the international standards in terms of 'the civilized world',[88] 'the whole of mankind'[89] and 'morality and public policy'.[90] Another jurist has recently

[86] Although the nature of legal obligation is missed, a concern with fragmentation is raised in Simeon (above n 83). Also see ILC, 'Report of the Study Group on Fragmentation of International Law at the Fifty-Eight Session of the International Law Commission 2006' ('Koskenniemi Report'), UN doc A/CN.4/L.682, *ILC Yearbook 2006*, vol II(2), para 62.

[87] See generally B Schlütter, *Developments in Customary Law: Theory and the Practice of the International Court of Justice and the International ad hoc Criminal Tribunals for Rwanda and Yugoslavia* (The Hague, Martinus Nijhoff, 2010) 74–79. See also AA Cançado Trindade, *International Law for Humankind: Towards a New* Jus Gentium (Leiden, Martinus Nijhoff, 2010) 291.

[88] *Sosa v Alvarez-Machain* (2004) 542 US 692. For other American cases, see K Randall, 'Universal Jurisdiction under International Law' (1988) 66 *Texas Law Review* 785, 789–90. McNair takes the condition of civilized states for granted. See AD McNair, *The Law of Treaties* (Oxford, Oxford University Press, 1986) 213–14: 'In every civilized community there are some rules of law and some principles of morality which individuals are not permitted by law to ignore or to modify by their agreements.' For examples from other jurisdictions, see, eg, *Catholic Commission for Justice and Peace in Zimbabwe v Attorney-General of Zimbabwe and Others* (Judgment No SC 73/93), (1993) 14 *Human Rights Law Journal* 323, (2001) AHRLR 248 (Zimb Sup Ct 1993); *Filartiga v Pena-Irala*, 630 F.2d 876, 885–88 (2nd Circ 1980) (Kaufman J); *Riley and Others v Attorney-General of Jamaica* [1982] 3 All ER 469 (PC); and *Attorney General of Israel v Adolf Eichmann*, District Court of Jerusalem, 36 ILR 18 at 25, 26 and 50 (Israel Dist Ct 1961), on appeal in 36 ILR 277, 299 and 304 (Israel Sup Ct 1962).

[89] *Attorney General of Israel v Eichmann* (ibid). See also judgment of the Supreme Court sitting as Court of Criminal Appeals at 36 ILR 277, 299 and 304 (Israel Sup Ct 1962).

[90] See J Dunoff et al, *International Law: Norms: Actors, Process*, 3rd edn (New York, Aspen, 2010) 59.

claimed that international human rights law appeals to an even vaguer referent for its content – namely, 'a philosophical theory'.[91] Which philosophical theory and how there is a connection is left in the air. Such open-ended concepts hardly explain why a domestic nationality law is obligatory. The ICJ has gone so far as to assert in the *Wall Case* that the right of self-determination of a state, along with other rights of a state during armed conflict, are grounded in 'elementary considerations of humanity'.[92] After all, the enquiry as to why an identifiable international right or rule is obligatory has been considered 'too logical and reasonable to be challenged'[93] and 'a matter of faith'.[94]

Such justificatory concepts are vague and opaque if left empty of content. What does humanity, conscience or the whole of humankind signify? How do we know when humanity trumps domestic laws? Why are universal human rights equally shared? Whose conscience matters, what is an uncivilized society, which group's 'faith' is at issue, and is 'public policy' merely a cloak of the jurist's speculative impression? Must we just leave conscience or humanity to the executive of a state? How can jurists take humanity for granted when so many diverse and conflicting justifications have been offered for an understanding of the concept of humanity itself? Are we left with the view that 'the less said the better'[95] or with Peter Fitzpatrick's extensive arguments that the ultimate source (in his view, the state) is a mere empty form?[96]

Powerful justifications for the equality underlying human rights have been offered. Each has very different assumptions and ramifications for the interpretation of treaty provisions and customary norms: membership in a species,[97] the greatest good (JS Mill),[98] an *a priori* concept of respect for

---

[91] RKM Smith, *Textbook on International Human Rights*, 4th edn (Oxford, Oxford University Press, 2010) 176–77.

[92] *Legality of the Threat or Use of Nuclear Weapons*, ICJ Rep 1996, 226, at 257 (para 79), 110 ILR 163, at 207 (para 79), as cited in the *Wall* case, ICJ Rep 2004, 136, at 199 (para 157), 129 ILR 37, at 119 (para 157).

[93] P Malanczuk, *Akehurst's Modern Introduction to International Law*, 7th edn (New York, Routledge, 1997).

[94] H Thirlway, 'Injured and Non-injured States before the International Court of Justice' in M Ragazzi (ed), *International Responsibility Today: Essays in Memory of Oscar Schacter* (Dorrecht, Martinus Nijhoff, 2005).

[95] See, eg, E Wyler and A Papaux, 'The Search for Universal Justice' in RSJ Macdonald and DM Johnson (eds), *The Structure and Process of International Law: Essays in Legal Philosophy Doctrine and Theory* (Dordrecht, Martinus Nijhoff, 1986).

[96] P Fitzpatrick, 'Latin Roots: Imperialism and the Making of Modern Law' in P Fitzpatrick, *Law as Resistance: Modernism, Imperialism, Legalism* (Aldershot, Ashgate, 2008); P Fitzpatrick, 'Justice as Access' (2005) 23 *Windsor Yearbook Access Justice* 1, 9–13; P Fitzpatrick, 'Gods Would Be Needed: American Empire and the Rule of (International) Law' (2003) 16 *Leiden Journal of International Law* 429, 436; and P Fitzpatrick, '"No Higher Duty": *Mabo* and the Failure of Legal Foundation' (2002)13 *Law and Critique* 233, 242.

[97] K Marx, 'On the Jewish Question' in RC Tucker (ed), *The Marx–Engels Reader*, 2nd edn (New York, WW Norton, 1978) 33–34.

[98] JS Mill, 'On Liberty' in M Warnock (ed), *Utilitarianism* (Glasgow, William Collins, 1962).

persons (Kant),[99] equal consideration (Bernard Williams),[100] dignity (Kant),[101] equal respect and concern (Dworkin),[102] recognition respect as opposed to appraisal respect (Vlastos and Darwell)[103] and ethicality (Hegel)?[104] How can the international community reserve and protect the freedom of the state over nationality issues when the treaties and other instruments of the international community claim universality to the contrary? Even more problematic, how can states possess a universal jurisdiction if universal concepts, such as security of the person or the right to legal personhood, are said to be rationally 'applied' to context-specific circumstances? Can the a priori concepts be applied without examining the content of the incorporation of the state's reserved domain into the international community?

The enigma of statelessness can best be appreciated by juxtaposing the traditional quest for discrete rights, such as a right to nationality or a right to being recognized as a legal person, with the ethos of an international community in which such rights are nested. With the one sense of an international community, a right to nationality is read against the fundamental condition of the community: namely, the reserved domain of the community. As such, natural persons will be excluded as well as included into a membership. De jure and effective statelessness will remain despite treaty assertions that the right to nationality applies to 'everyone'. The quest to identify an international legal rule from the traditional Article 38 sources reinforces such an exclusionary international legal norm. A state must expressly (by a treaty) or impliedly (by a customary norm) consent to the discrete international rule or right. Why is any international rule or right binding against a state's authority if the state's authority trumps any such international right or rule in matters of nationality?

To take an example, Article 15 of the Universal Declaration of Human Rights (UDHR) guarantees a right to nationality. But such a right, we shall find of the classic sense of an international community, is contextualized in an international community protective of the legal authority of a state to confer, withhold or withdraw nationality. The right to nationality is institutionalized by virtue of the state's freedom to decide its own (and

---

[99] I Kant, *Metaphysical Elements of Justice*, 2nd edn, J Ladd (trans) (Indianapolis, Hackett, 1999).

[100] B Williams, 'The Idea of Equality' in P Laslett and WG Runciman (eds), *Philosophy, Politics and Society*, 2nd Series (Oxford, Oxford University Press, 1972); and C Cranor, 'Toward a Theory of Respect for Persons' (1975) 12 *American Philosophical Quarterly* 309.

[101] I Kant, *Metaphysics of Morals*, M Gregor (ed) (Cambridge, Cambridge University Press, 1996) 1: 435–36.

[102] R Dworkin, 'What is Equality? Part 1: Equality of Welfare' (1981) 10(3) *Philosophy and Public Affairs* 185; R Dworkin, 'What is Equality? Part 2: Equality of Resources' 10(4) *Philosophy and Public Affairs* 283; and R Dworkin, 'Equality, Luck and Hierarchy' (2003) 31(2) *Philosophy and Public Affairs* 190.

[103] G Vlastos, 'Justice and Equality' in RB Brandt (ed), *Social Justice* (New Jersey, Prentice-Hall, 1962); and S Darwell, 'Two Kinds of Respect' (1977) 86 *Ethics* 36.

[104] See WE Conklin, *Hegel's Laws* (Stanford University Press, Stanford, 2008) esp 162–87.

the international community's) membership. More to the point, it is unlikely that a member of the international community would undermine its own existence by deferring to an obligation of the state to protect some other legal person, such as a stateless person, in comparison with the state's own freedom over its own membership. The enigma of the international community remains.

To take another example, by Article 7 of the Convention on the Rights of the Child, states parties must undertake to have all infants registered when born on their territory. Such a registration process, however, requires a state bureaucracy, including medical institutions to which all have access. Without registration, infants will lack de jure nationality. Why would Article 7 be obligatory of a state if the state lacks an administrative or economic capacity to fulfil the registration requirement? Why would the domestic law of nationality be obligatory upon all natural persons if an infant were excluded, for whatever reason, from the registration process or if the parent, having the onus of completing the registration, is killed, has abandoned the child, or if parentage is uncertain? If legal analysis terminates with the ICJ Article 38 sources, the issue of legal obligation risks being extra-legal. The Article 38 sources take the residuary of the international community for granted. The role of the judiciary is to delineate the residuary's boundary, not the content of the residuary, in an international community constituted from the aggregated wills of state members. Why the sources possess an obligatory character rests in the express or implied state consent taken for granted in each source. But if the state has consented to the right and yet lacked the capacity to effectively administer the right, is the enigma overcome?

The incident of nationality in a protected residuary of laws raises a series of important issues which require an enquiry into the nature of the legal obligation of a state. Is there an international legal tort to address harm against a stateless person? Is there a state obligation to confer nationality on anyone whose social bonding with others on its territory is clear and present? Is the state's obligation to protect a stateless person a general rule, or is it merely a presumption? If a state fails to protect a stateless person, are damages warranted independently of compensation for the state's confiscation of assets or independently of loss of life? If so, how are the damages determined without loss of property? How can there be damages if the person is not 'lawfully' on a state's territory due to her/his lack of any nationality? Does legal liability extend to a state whose territory has become submerged due to climate change? Does legal liability extend to a state that has ceded its territory or had it conquered? Must there be an international armed conflict before a court addresses wrongdoing caused to a stateless person? Is denaturalization a war crime or crime against humanity during intra-state or inter-state armed conflict? Is it a war crime or crime against humanity if denaturalization is accompanied with forcible expulsion or internal displacement? Is mass expulsion necessary before a war crime or crime against humanity has been caused to stateless members of a group?

The above issues beg an enquiry into the nature of the state's obligation to protect stateless persons. Can that issue be adequately addressed without relating the international community, independent of state members, to the context-specific experiences of stateless persons? Does a state's legal obligation to stateless persons displace nationality as an element 'solely' or 'essentially' within a state's internal jurisdiction as the League's Covenant and the UN Charter describe? Does the international community or the state possess the authority to decide the locus of the boundary of the reserved domain? Is the boundary of the reserved domain a product of the state's own determination, or is it the product of the international community's? These issues cannot be adequately addressed without an understanding as to why a law – internal or international – is obligatory for a state as well as for a natural person.

In short, the wrong question is asked about law when one searches for a discrete domestic nationality rule or a general right to nationality in terms of the well-known sources of a law. The appeal to such sources puts to the side the social relationships of stateless persons inside or outside the boundary of the residuary of law-making in the international community. If a state possesses such a protected domain, it may exercise the freedom to withdraw, withhold or deny a nationality from yourself rather than myself. And a state or group of states may systematically detain, forcibly move or remain silent about employment and housing conditions of stateless persons. I shall argue in these pages that there is an international community independent of such a boundary, however. The question is whether such a community is so abstract as to render the 'international community as a whole' inaccessible by virtue of its mere emptiness of necessary social content.

VI. MY APPROACH

There is an important feature of my approach that a jurist may not initially appreciate. As a lawyer, I was trained to intellectually grasp a legal rule or test – the stuff of an identifiable law – as if the rule or test were a concept that I could access through a transparent language. Such a concept is represented or signified by a sign, however. A chain of signs constitutes a discourse. My claim is that there is not one international law discourse but two such discourses. Here, I am mindful of the insights of Michel Foucault about the nature and study of a discourse.[105] The 'international community

[105] M Foucault, 'The Discourse on Language' in *The Archaeology of Knowledge*, AM Sheridan Smith (trans) (New York, Pantheon, 1972), reprinted in R Young (ed), *Untying the Text: A Post-Structuralist Reader* (Boston, Routledge and Kegan Paul, 1981). (Another translation is

as a whole' is concealed *inside* the international law discourse about an international community. The discourse is not a system of concepts 'out there' represented by transparent signs. Rather, the discourse is embodied (that is, given content) by the ethos or culture of an international community.

My approach, in brief, seeks to understand the very ethos or character of two international communities, each embodied in chains of relations between signs and represented rules in the two international law discourses. The ethos of the one international community is constituted from an aggregate of the wills of states. The community accepts the law-making residuary, assigned to each state member, as a hard fact. International standards as to a state's legal obligations to protect stateless persons are 'oughts' in an idealized international community. By incorporating the protected internal jurisdiction into the international community, international legal discourse raises the prospect of stateless persons excluded from a state's legal protection. As an incident of the jurisdiction, each state alone possesses the legal authority to enact and administer laws defining which natural persons are members of the international community.

Turning to the international community as an aggregate of the wills of state members, such a challenge has required that, in addition to the judgements of domestic and international courts and arbitration tribunals, I examine domestic refugee and human rights judicial and quasi-judicial decisions. A radical discontinuity separates the residuary of the international community from the stateless persons inside and outside the boundary of the residuary. My discursive enquiry asks how the boundary of the reserved domain is being displaced in favour of the protection of natural persons otherwise categorized as stateless.

Accordingly, the quest for the identity of a discrete rule or right is misdirected if in isolation of the relation of its content to the ethos of an 'international community as a whole'. I shall also argue, especially in my later chapters, that the boundary of the residuary is dissolving where de jure and effectively stateless persons are concerned. The effect of this dissolution is that the international community exists independent of the freedom of state members. The community exists 'as a whole' rather than as the aggregated wills of state members over nationality. The boundary is displaced in favour of the reciprocal social relationships of natural

under the title 'The Order of Discourse' in M Shapiro (ed), *Language and Politics* (London, Basil Blackwell, 1984).) See also M Foucault, 'Governmentality' in G Burchell, C Gordon and P Miller (eds), *The Foucault Effect: Studies in Governmentality* (Chicago, University of Chicago Press, 1991); and M Foucault, 'What Is an Author?' in P Rabinow (ed), *The Foucault Reader* (New York, Pantheon, 1984). For discourse theory as an alternative to the quest for the identity of a right, see WE Conklin, *The Phenomenology of Modern Legal Discourse: The Juridicial Production and the Disclosure of Suffering* (Aldershot, Dartmouth, 1998). I draw from Bernhard Waldenfels' *Topographie des Fremden* (Frankfurt am Main, Suhrkamp Verlag, 1997) v 1 for the possibility of one discourse being inside the other.

persons *inter se*. The legal bond to the international community as a whole is immanent in the social relationships of natural persons. Such a social immanence inside the international law discourse contrasts with the state's positing of a natural person's allegiance from above the natural person. The 'international community as a whole' is not an 'ought'. The community emerges from the social life in the content of the residuary heretofore immunized from judicial scrutiny.

The clue to the enigma of an international community is that a community cannot exist unless certain social conditions are met. Much like a physical structure supported by pillars, a community dissolves when its existence conditions are absent. As the existence condition of the traditional state-centric shape of an international community, each state member of the community must remain free to enact and administer laws inside the protected residuary of the community. Nationality, again, is an incident of that residuary. There might be international standards that the jurist can find in the Article 38 sources of the International Court statute. But such standards, out of deference to the international community's residuary of law-making, would be obligatory to state members only *after* a state has exercised its freedom by choosing or excluding natural persons from its own (and the international community's) membership. As long as an existence condition is the residuary of the international community and nationality is an incident of such a residuary, natural persons will be excluded from membership in the international community. This will be so, a belief in universal human rights notwithstanding.

Statelessness will only dissolve as a necessity of the ethos if the international community is independent of the state members. The key to this possibility is the legal bond as social relationships rather than as the allegiance of a natural person as determined by a state. Rather than accepting a discrete right or rule or series of rights/rules as conclusive of 'law' and rather than decomposing any such right/rule into analytic micro-parts which enclose social 'facts', my method is generated from social life. I try to understand the forest rather than to focus analytically upon each tree. Put differently, I situate any discrete right, such as the 'right to nationality' or the 'right to be recognized as a person', in the ethos of the international community presupposed in the international law discourses. In contrast with the traditional sources thesis, I unconceal the assumptions and expectations about the ethos of the international communities in which we find ourselves.

VII. OVERVIEW OF THE BOOK

Keeping in mind the approach outlined above, I will begin the following chapters with a brief overview of the two senses of international community. The one, protecting the freedom of states to enact and administer laws defining who are nationals, likens a state's freedom to that of the more familiar freedom of a natural person vis-à-vis a state. Such a freedom is manifested by the usual quest for the identity of domestic laws about nationality in the Article 38 sources. Such an enquiry is nested in an ethos excluding an examination of the content of the bounded residuary from legal enquiry. By virtue of the non-interference into the reserved domain, the enigma of an international community holds steadfast.

The consequences of de jure statelessness are briefly addressed in chapter three. Chapters four and five address whether a right to nationality exists on the part of stateless persons. Such an enquiry is found wanting. The terms of the treaties and the required implied consent of customary norms incorporate an international community's law-making residuary productive of statelessness. Customary norms fall short, I argue, because of an absence of a sense of a state obligation to protect de jure and effectively stateless persons. Chapter five ends by hypothesizing a situation in which the whole of the globe is divided into states, all such states ratify a treaty recognizing the right of nationality and reservations are disallowed. Notably, statelessness would remain with such a treaty. Instead of leading to clarity of analysis, the effort to identify a discrete rule, test or right concerning nationality in human rights treaties and customary norms leads to a legal quagmire. This is so because each state possesses freedom to choose its members, nationality being a matter 'essentially within the internal jurisdiction', as Article 2(7) of the UN Charter has described.

Because of the sustained enigma of treaties and customary norms, I reassess the nature of the legal bond in international legal discourse in chapter six. The bounded reserved freedom of a member of the community presupposes that allegiance bonds the natural person to the state and indirectly with the international community. Effective nationality, however, bonds natural persons to the place where they experience their social relationships. I distinguish the experience of a 'place' from a situs on a state's territory. Social relationships in a place are independent of a state, let alone its bounded reserved domain. Contrary to what one might initially surmise, effective nationality has been deeply ingrained in international legal discourse since the early nineteenth century, and it continues into recent domestic and international judicial and quasi-judicial decisions in the international law discourses.

The retrieval of social bonding as the legal bond of an international community brings into question five principles of general international law. First, as argued in chapter seven, stateless persons are increasingly being recognized as possessing country by virtue of the place where their social relationships have been experienced. The place may not necessarily exist by virtue of one's birth or habitual residence but by virtue of one's social relations with family, friends, school mates, fellow worshippers and detainees, and other 'places' of life-experiences. Second, as argued in chapter eight, the international legal discourse is increasingly rendering the boundary of internal jurisdiction transparent. Third, the consequence of the dissolution of the boundary of internal jurisdiction incorporates international standards into 'the operation of [a state's] law'.[106] Fourth, as documented and examined in chapters six to eight, the judiciary has increasingly scrutinized the content of nationality laws and their administration by the executive arm of the state. Finally, as argued in chapter nine, the jurist is guided by a knowledge which brings the sources thesis into question because statelessness begs that the jurist ask questions about why a state's domestic laws are obligatory and why a state is obligated to protect a stateless person as a third party to the legal bond of the international community as a whole.

---

[106] Convention Relating to the Status of Stateless Persons (above n 19) Art 1.

1

Two International Communities

NATIONALITY, I INDICATED in the Introduction, signifies one's membership in the international community. In this regard, nationality is not synonymous with the citizenship conferred by a state. One may lack a state's citizenship and yet have nationality in the state. Conversely, one may have a state's citizenship and yet lack protection in the international community (such as when an individual is indefinitely detained by another state and yet diplomatically unprotected by her/his state of citizenship). Nationality represents a natural person as a legal person of the international legal structure. The act of recognition, though, is reserved for a state member of the international community. When a state confers nationality onto a natural person, s/he gains recognition as a legal person in the international community. The state is the primary legal person of the international community. Harm caused by one state to a national of another state has been transformed into a harm caused by one state to another state. The international community in this regard is constituted from the aggregate of the wills of states. In sum, a natural person lacks recognition in the international community if s/he lacks a nationality 'by operation of [a state's domestic] law', according to the Convention Relating to the Status of Stateless Persons (1954), as noted in the Introduction chapter.[1]

The main project of the jurist in this regard is to identify a state's domestic law protected by the boundary of the international community's residuary. This project plays itself out because multilateral treaties have provided for limitations of human rights if the limitations are 'by law', 'in accordance with law' or 'lawful'. Limitations have been considered legally permissible

---

[1] Convention Relating to the Status of Stateless Persons (1954), 360 UNTS 117 (entered into force 6 June 1960) Art 1 (emphasis added). See also the American Declaration of the Rights and Duties of Man ('Pact of San José, Costa Rica') (Bogota, 2 May 1948), Novena Conferencia Internacional Americana, OAS Off Rec OEA/Ser.L.V/ll.82 doc.6 rev.1 at 17 (1992), (1953) 6 *Actas y Documentos* 297–302, Art 19. The *Dictionary of International Law and Diplomacy* defines a 'stateless' person as one whose state of nationality no longer protects or assists the national by operation of law: MJ Gamboa, *A Dictionary of International Law and Diplomacy* (New York, Oceana, 1973) 246. Contemporary commentators also accept this formal definition. See, eg, BK Blitz and C Sawyer, 'Statelessness in the European Union' in BK Blitz and C Sawyer (eds), *Statelessness in the European Union: Displaced, Undocumented, Unwanted* (Cambridge, Cambridge University Press, 2011).

if, by virtue of the laws within internal jurisdictions, the domestically enacted and administered laws authorize the limitations. The international community exists and is reinforced by the judicial acceptance of such a sense of legality. The enigma of the international community is played out when a natural person finds her/himself on the territory claimed by a state but lacking nationality in any state. Does that person possess a right to leave or to return to the place where s/he experienced deep social relationships? If nationality has not been conferred onto someone, then does that individual possess the rights attributed to 'everyone'? Is there a sense of 'law' protective of a stateless person, other than the domestically enacted and administered laws of the internal jurisdiction of a state?

International legal discourse has struggled to clarify the boundary of the international community's residuary, restated as the internal jurisdiction of a state, in a series of contexts: conflicts of domestic laws, succession of states, state responsibility, diplomatic protection, indefinite detention, torture, and discrimination against women, children and ethnic groups. I shall continually draw from such contexts as I proceed with my argument. The examples are taken in order to support my points of analysis and clarification. I aim to highlight how the laws enacted, administered and adjudicated inside internal jurisdiction are assumed and justified in terms of a special image of an international community. This image holds out a community protective of internal jurisdiction as the residuary of law-making and law enforcement of the international community. Internal jurisdiction represents the residuary of laws concerning membership of natural persons in the international community. The enigma of statelessness in an international community claiming universality of jurisdiction requires an enquiry as to how statelessness exists by virtue of this sense of an international community. As outlined in the Introduction, this point is often missed by contemporary jurists.[2]

The problem is that the two international law discourses privilege two very different understandings of an international community. The one represents a community constituted from the aggregate of the wills of the state members of the community. The other is greater than the sum of such aggregated wills. More recently, the latter has been signified as 'the international community as a whole'. The prospect of a natural person becoming stateless differs in the one community from the other community.

---

[2] See also, eg, I Shearer and B Opeskin, 'Nationality and Statelessness' in B Opeskin, R Perruchoud and J Redpath-Cross (eds), *Foundations of International Migration Law* (Cambridge, Cambridge University Press, 2012); Blitz and Sawyer (ibid); BK Blitz and M Lynch, 'Statelessness and the Deprivation of Nationality' in BK Blitz and M Lynch (eds), *Statelessness and Citizenship: A Comparative Study on the Benefits of Nationality* (Cheltenham, Edward Elgar, 2011); RD Sloane, 'Breaking the Genuine Link: The Contemporary International Legal Regulation of Nationality' (2009) 50 *Harvard International Law Journal* 1, 1–4 and 15–16; and R Donner, *The Regulation of Nationality in International Law*, 2nd edn (Irvington-on-Hudson, Transnational Publishers, 1994).

So too, the rights and limitations of the rights differ in the two. In the first, each state member possesses an inner freedom within whose boundary nationality is an incident. The key to the relationship between a national and a state is the legal bond of allegiance of the individual towards the state. In the second, nationality is attributed to a natural person by virtue of her/his social relationships with others. Such a social bonding, constituting a very different legal bond, is independent of the state members of the international community. Nationality is attributed to a natural person rather than conferred onto the person by a state. The attribution of nationality as a social bonding represents the members of the international community as a whole. Such an international community radically differs from an international community as the aggregated wills of states.

A note of caution is needed. I am not suggesting that the aggregated international community represents legal reality or that the international community as a whole represents an ideal world toward which jurists and political leaders ought to be aspiring. To the contrary, both international communities constitute a legal reality. The international community as a whole is signified inside the discourse that takes the aggregated community for granted. Any one treaty, judicial decision or legal commentary may manifest both senses of an international community. In the linear quest for a rationally coherent system of discrete international rules and doctrines, what is often missed is the presence and sometimes the conflict of the two analytically very different senses of an international community. The two senses differ substantially with respect to such issues as the nature of the legal bond, the role of judicial scrutiny of the executive and legislative institutions, and the nature of law.

The residuary of the aggregated community encourages jurists to search for the identity of a law in terms of the state's institutional sources protected by the boundary of the residuary. The international community as a whole addresses a very different question than the identity of a law: namely, why is an identifiable law binding? The enigma of statelessness in an international community begs that we ask why the residuary immunizes the internal jurisdiction from external intervention in matters of nationality. Why would a natural person be bound to international standards if the protected residuary may leave one without the nationality to be protected? Indeed, why would a state be obligated to fulfil state obligations to recognize and protect a stateless person if law-making authority in matters of nationality were reserved for the residuary of the international community?

Let us reread the oft-cited judgment of the Permanent Court of International Justice in the *Lotus* case (1927).[3] *Lotus* is usually cited for the

---

[3] *The Steamship Lotus (France v Turkey)* (1927) PCIJ Ser A, no 10, 1.

inviolable freedom of states. It states that international legal rules 'binding upon States . . . emanate from their own free will as expressed in conventions or by usages generally accepted as expressing principles of law'.[4] Despite the stated inviolable freedom of a state, *Lotus* also reminds us that a state's freedom is 'dictated by the very nature and existing conditions of international law';[5] and again, the state's freedom exists 'under international law as it stands at present'.[6] The key to the state's freedom is the boundary of the residuary of the international community. That boundary, though, is an intellectual construction of the international community, not of a state: 'all that can be required of a State is that it should not overstep the limits which international law places upon its jurisdiction; within these limits, its title to exercise jurisdiction rests in its sovereignty'.[7]

Similarly, Article 1 of the Montevideo Convention on the Rights and Duties of States (1936) is often cited as listing the requisites defining a state: a permanent population, a defined territory and a government. Even the Convention did not consider the state as an atomistic legal entity. The state also had to have a capacity to enter foreign relations with other states.[8] Even the judicial decisions of the 1920s and 1930s, including *Lotus*, situated the state in an international community.

The discursive contingency of such a community was acknowledged in subsequent judgements of international tribunals.[9] Symbols of control over territory have varied in importance through time. Ian Brownlie highlighted this point in his classic essay about nationality.[10] To this end, he noted how the first (1905) and later editions of *Oppenheim's International Law* seriously shifted with regard to a state's jurisdiction over nationality.[11] What explained the shift, though? Was it enough just to suggest that the editors' values had changed?

The clue to an explanation rests in the very different juristic assumptions as to what constitutes an international community in legal consciousness. Although the historical context might well suggest that the one sense of an international community began to emerge during the mid-eighteenth

---

[4] Ibid, 18.
[5] Ibid.
[6] Ibid, 19.
[7] Ibid.
[8] Montevideo Convention on the Rights and Duties of States (1936) 165 LNTS 19, 28 AJIL Supp 75.
[9] One historical contingency was the effectiveness of a state's control over territory. See *Compania Naviera Vascongado v Steamship Christine* [1938] AC 485, 496 per Lord Macmillan; *Island of Palmas Case (Netherlands v United States)* (1928) 2 RIAA 829, 4 ILR 3; *Clipperton Island Case (Mexico v France)* (1931) 2 RIAA 1105; *Legal Status of Eastern Greenland Case (Denmark v Norway)* (1933) PCIJ (Ser A/B) No 53; *Lotus* (above n 3) 18–19; and J Crawford, *Creation of States in International Law*, 2nd edn (Oxford, Oxford University Press, 2006) 97.
[10] I Brownlie, 'The Relations of Nationality in Public International Law' (1963) 39 *British Yearbook of International Law* 284, 289.
[11] Brownlie was referring to earlier editions, as well as to L Oppenheim, *International Law*, H Lauterpacht (ed), 8th edn, vol 1 (New York, David McKay, 1955).

century, reaching its full crystallization by the 1930s, and although the international community as a whole has been emerging during recent decades, my point is an analytical one. The assumptions that jurists make about the basis of legal obligation have coloured how one analyses a social problem from the legal point of view. Again, the reasons behind any one judicial decision or one argument in a Memorial or legal commentary may assume two very different senses of an international community. I aim to analytically differentiate the two such senses and how the two senses relate in different ways to the enigma of statelessness.

With this discursive and analytical ambiguity in mind, this chapter begins by highlighting an interest in the international community as a whole as the ultimate referent of legal analysis about nationality. Section II proceeds to outline the international community as an aggregate of the wills of states. Such an international community recognizes and protects a residuary in which each state member of the community has the jurisdiction to confer, withhold or withdraw nationality vis-à-vis a natural person. Stateless persons, as lacking nationality conferred by a state, fall inside and outside the boundary of each state's reserved jurisdiction. Section III of the chapter connects such a residuary to the sources thesis outlined in Article 38(1) of the Statute of the International Court of Justice (ICJ).[12] Statelessness, I suggest, begs that one ask this question: why does an international standard, identified by its justification in terms of an institutional source (such as a treaty or customary norm) of the state, obligate a state to protect a stateless person? Section IV addresses the nature of a state's legal obligation and how such an obligation is lacking within an international community that reserves a residuary.

I. WHAT IS AN INTERNATIONAL COMMUNITY?

Although the classical understanding of an international community is associated with Grotius and the early seventeenth century, the freedom of the state to confer, withhold or withdraw nationality is of an even more recent and European genesis.[13] The next chapter argues that such a free-

---

[12] The sources thesis, as taken for granted domestically, is best elaborated in J Raz, 'Authority, Law and Morality' in *Ethics in the Public Domain: Essays in the Morality of Law and Politics* (Oxford, Clarendon Press, 1994) 215–20 and 230–35; and J Raz, *Between Authority and Interpretation* (Oxford, Oxford University Press, 2009).

[13] For the emergence of the early modern international legal order, see M Koskenniemi, *From Apology to Utopia: The Structure of International Legal Argument (Reissue with a new Epilogue)* (Cambridge, Cambridge University Press, 2005); M Koskenniemi, *The Gentle Civilizer of Nations: The Rise and Fall of International Law, 1870–1960* (Cambridge, Cambridge University Press, 2001) 4, 17 and 406–11; H Lauterpacht, 'The Grotian Tradition in International Law' in E Lauterpacht (ed), *International Law: Collected Papers of Hersch Lauterpacht*, vol 2 (Cambridge, Cambridge University Press, 1975); and H Lauterpacht, 'Private Law Sources and Analogies of International Law' in E Lauterpact (ed) (ibid) 189.

dom has been discursively contingent. Philip Jessup described such an international community as early as 1948 as representing a broad 'principle of community interest in the prevention of breaches of international law'.[14] The 'whole' of the international community possesses what Alfred Verdross once described as a 'higher interest' than the self-interest of a state.[15] The inference is, as suggested by the 'General Comments' of the International Covenant on Civil and Political Rights (ICCPR) Committee, that an international community is greater than the sum of the wills of its members.[16] The ICCPR situates 'the general principles of law' in a '*community* of nations'.[17] But do we just accept on faith that such an international community exists? Does such a community exist separate from states if its standards are the consequence of the aggregated wills of states? And what is the nature of a law of the community as a whole in contrast with such a community as an aggregate of the wills of its distinct and assignable members?

The temptation is to idealize such a sense of an international community. By this, I mean that one is tempted to consider the community as if in an 'ought' world divorced from legal 'reality'. As an ideal, though, it would lack an obligatory character. The best that the international community could do is to guide a state in its conferral, withholding or withdrawing of nationality. I shall offer a very different sense of an international community, independent of the wills of state members and yet nested in legal reality, not in 'oughts'. This 'other' reality is nested *inside* the international legal discourse and yet independent of state members.

For there to be legal objectivity, there must be subjects to the objectivity, a point I shall elaborate in my final chapter. A state is only one subject in this international community. Although the state of an aggregated community may alone represent a harm committed against a corporation,[18]

However, see M Koskenniemi, 'Empire and International Law: The Real Spanish Contribution' (2011) 61 *University of Toronto Law Journal* 1. For the emergence during the late nineteenth century of the association of the freedom of the state with the conferral, withholding and withdrawal of nationality, see below ch 2, s IV (79–88).

[14] See PC Jessup, *A Modern Law of Nations: An Introduction* (New York, Macmillan, 1948) 53. Jessup is preoccupied with the international community separate from states and yet directly related to natural persons throughout the whole book.

[15] A Verdross, 'Jus Dispositivum and Jus Cogens in International Law' (1966) 60 *American Journal of International Law* 55, 58.

[16] See, eg, HRC, 'CCPR General Comment 31: The Nature of the General Legal Obligation Imposed on States Parties to the Covenant' (29 March 2004) in UN, *Human Rights Instruments, Volume I: Compilation of General Comments and General Recommendations Adopted by Human Rights Treaty Bodies*, HRI/GEN/1/Rev.9 (27 May 2008), www.un.org/en/ga/search/view_doc.asp?symbol=HRI/GEN/1/Rev.9(Vol.I), para 2.

[17] International Covenant on Civil and Political Rights (ICCPR) (1966), 999 UNTS 171, Can TS 1976 No 47, in force 23 March 1976, Art 15 (emphasis added).

[18] V Lowe, 'Injuries to Corporations' in J Crawford, A Pellet and S Olleson (eds), *The Law of International Responsibility* (Oxford, Oxford University Press, 2010) 1006–7.

peoples and minorities,[19] the legal subject of the international community as a whole has been extended to include such member-subjects as the United Nations, the International Committee of the Red Cross, regional communities such as the European Union and, most importantly for our purposes, natural persons.[20] Brownlie added sui generis entities legally proximate to states, indigenous peoples, non-self-governing peoples, and belligerents.[21] I am concerned with natural persons as stateless. And with the advent of human rights, humanitarian protection of civilians not involved in armed conflict, and peremptory norms, natural persons are increasingly gaining access to internal and international courts, special tribunals, commissions and committees independent of the wills of states. Such access lends legal status to the natural persons.[22] When 'some sort of existence on the international legal plane' must be attributed to social entities, the international community exists *for* such entities. Such entities are members of the international community (albeit not recognisable as legal persons by the ICJ, to which only states have access).

How is it possible that the objectivity of the international community, independent of its subjects, exists *for* such subjects even though the community is independent of the subjects (except by the consent of the primary subject, the state)? The objectivity of an international community as a whole exists 'out there', separate from natural persons and states as subjects. And yet the legal objectivity exists *for* such members. The stateless condition is brought into serious question once one appreciates the existence of the international community as a whole. How does an international community remain a legal reality (not an 'ought') and yet exist for natural persons independent of state members?

Little effort has been expended in understanding what constitutes the inner 'international community as a whole'. Is it a system of international rules as the 'Fragmentation Report' of the International Law Commission (ILC) suggests?[23] Is the system of rules of a secondary or 'authority-conferring' character? Do the secondary rules authorize various institutions

---

[19] A-L Vaurs-Chaumette, 'Peoples and Minorities' in Crawford, Pellet and Olleson (eds) (ibid) 996–97.

[20] *Reparations for Injuries Suffered in the Service of the United Nations*, ICJ Rep 1949, p 174. I use the term 'composite legal status' rather than 'legal person', drawing from A-K Lindblom, 'The Responsibility of Other Entities: Non-Governmental Organizations' in Crawford, Pellet and Olleson (eds) (above n 18).

[21] J Crawford, *Brownlie's Principles of Public International Law*, 8th edn (Oxford, Oxford University Press, 2012).

[22] C Tomuschat, 'Individuals' in Crawford, Pellet and Olleson (eds) (above n 18) 986.

[23] ILC, 'Fragmentation of International Law: Difficulties Arising from the Diversification and Expansion of International Law' ('Koskenniemi Report'), UN Doc A/CN.4/L.682 and Corr.1 (13 April 2006), daccess-dds-ny.un.org/doc/UNDOC/LTD/G06/610/77/PDF/G0661077. pdf?OpenElement, paras 33 and 251. As the ILC stated in the Study, 'There is seldom disagreement that it is one of the tasks of legal reasoning to establish [the systematic relationships between the various decisions, rules and principles]' (para 33). See also paras 128 and 220.

to enact, adjudicate and administer primary rules?[24] If the community is a system of rules, particularly secondary rules, what justifies the legal authority of the act of instituting a discrete rule? That is, what is the nature of the legal authority of an international community's discrete rules? Why are the rules binding? Does the idea of 'conferral' suggest that the legal basis dwells in a metaphysical objectivity above the natural person? Do we take the objectivity as an 'ought' emptied then of social content? Can we respond to that question without examining the character or ethos of an international community? Does the categorization of a community as a system of authority-conferring or secondary rules, principles and the like finalize the quest for the identity of a law if we do not ask why a discrete law in the system is obligatory or binding? The international community is discursively contingent and not a product of nature, despite the viewpoint of early jurists that the reserved domain is 'natural' – or a 'hard fact', as contemporary jurists are prone to say.[25] We are left with the question: why are identifiable laws of the community binding in this shape of a community rather than in that one? That issue is triggered by the legal condition of statelessness. For the quest for the identity of a law in the usual state-centric sources leaves one with the stateless condition without understanding why the condition exists.

The general descriptions of the 'international community as a whole' leave us with vague concepts that beg rather than settle the question about a state's legal obligation to protect stateless persons. The preamble of the Universal Declaration of Human Rights (UDHR) (1948), for example, asserts that freedom, justice and peace are founded in the rights 'of all members of the human family'. To be sure, one might consider the international community as a family,[26] but what does the international community share with a family? Aside from 'the general principles of law' in a 'community of nations' signified in Article 15 of the ICCPR, other multilateral and regional treaties continue such a relationship between law and

---

[24] ILC, 'Koskenniemi Report' (ibid) para 128; ILC, 'Draft Articles on Responsibility of States for Internationally Wrongful Acts, with Commentaries' in *Report of the International Law Commission on the Work of Its Fifty-third Session*, UN Doc A/56/10 (2001), Introductory Comms 1–3 and Pt 1 (ch III, Comm 4). See also J Crawford, 'Introduction' in J Crawford, *The International Law Commission's Articles on State Responsibility: Introduction, Text and Commentaries* (Cambridge, Cambridge University Press, 2002) 2, 14–17. See also E David, 'Primary and Secondary Rules' in Crawford, Pellet and Olleson (eds) (above n 18) 28.

[25] H Grotius, *The Rights of War and Peace, Including the Law of Nature and of Nations*, AC Campbell (trans) (Washington, M Walter Dunn, 1901 [1609]) Book 1, paras 10 and 12; E de Vattel, *The Law of Nations or the Principles of Natural Law*, G Fenwick (trans) (New York, Klaus, 1916 [1758]) Prolegomena, paras 7–8 and 18; S Pufendorf, *De Jure Naturae et Gentium Libri Octo* (Oxford, Clarendon Press, 1934 [1688]); and J Locke, *Second Treatise of Government* (Indianapolis, Hackett, 1980 [1690]) 8–14.

[26] Hegel went some distance in so understanding the European family of states. See WE Conklin, *Hegel's Laws: The Legitimacy of a Modern Legal Order* (Stanford, Stanford University Press, 2008) 203–4.

a community of states.[27] The mere assertion about an international community as a whole does not respond to the pressing issue as to why a state's law is obligatory in such a community. Perhaps the most often quoted dictum about the two international communities is that expressed in the ICJ case *Barcelona Traction*, according to which an obligation to the international community as a whole differs from an obligation between one state and another.[28] Again, the stated difference does not explain why a norm can be obligatory to the international community as a whole.

Similarly, peremptory norms have been considered obligatory by virtue of their justification in terms of the international community as a whole. As early as the 1940s, jurists justified peremptory norms in terms of the international community.[29] State officials are not immune from prosecution for violating peremptory norms against the international community, according to the House of Lords in *Pinochet* (1999).[30] The dissenting judgment of the European Court of Human Rights (ECtHR) in *Al-Adsani* (2002) recognized 'the international sphere' in which jus cogens has emerged.[31] And jurists have increasingly taken for granted that there is an international community in a legal objectivity separate from the wills of state members.[32] It is this sense of an international community which has been

[27] International Convention for the Suppression of the Financing of Terrorism, GA Res 54/109, para 9, UN Doc A/RES/54/109 (9 December 1999). See also Convention on the Safety of United Nations and Associated Personnel, GA Res 49/59, preamble para 3, UN Doc A/RES/49/59 (15 February 1995); International Convention for the Suppression of Terrorist Bombings, GA Res 52/164, preamble para 10, UN Doc A/RES/52/164 (9 January 1998); and the Rome Statute of the International Criminal Court (17 July 1998), 2187 UNTS 90 (RS), preamble para 9, UN Doc A/CONF.183/9. For other treaties, see International Convention against the taking of Hostages, preamble para 4, 1316 UNTS 205 (17 December 1979); Convention on the Prevention and Punishment of Crimes against Internationally Protected Persons, including Diplomatic Agents (14 December 1973), 1035 UNTS 167, preamble para 3; and the African [Banjul] Charter on Human and Peoples' Rights (adopted 27 June 1981, entered into force 21 October 1987), OAU Doc CAB/LEG/67/3 Rev 5, reprinted in (1982) 21 *International Legal Materials* 58, (1986) 7 *Human Rights Law Journal* 403, Art 27.

[28] *Barcelona Traction, Light and Power Company, Limited (New Application 1962) (Belgium v Spain)*, (1970) 3 ICJ Rep 47, para 91, also in 46 ILR 178.

[29] Green Haywood Hackworth expressed in 1943, for example, that an alien was warranted a standard of protection that was 'essential to the community of nations': GH Hackworth, *Digest of International Law* (Washington, DC, Government Printing Office, 1940–44), reprinted (Buffalo, WS Hein, 1975) vol 5, 471–72. Jessup asserted in 1948 that there is a broad 'principle of community interest in the prevention of breaches of international law': Jessup (above n 14).

[30] *R v Bartle, ex parte Pinochet* [1999] 2 All ER 97, [1999] 2 WLR 827 (HL).

[31] *Al-Adsani v United Kingdom* (2002) 34 EHRR 11, 21 November 2001, Application no 35763/97, Epn Ct Human Rts, 273, per Rozakis and Caflisch joined by Wildhaber, Costa, Cabral Barreto and Vajić.

[32] See, eg, Crawford, *Creation of States* (above n 9) 148–50 and 158–60; B Simma and P Alston, 'The Sources of Human Rights Law: Custom, Jus Cogens, and General Principles' (1988–89) 12 *Australian Yearbook of International Law* 82, 103; J Frowein, 'Obligations Erga Omnes' in R Bernhardt (ed), *Encyclopaedia of Public International Law* (Amsterdam, Elsevier, 1997–2003) vol 3, 757, quoting AG Heffter, *Le Droit international public de l'Europe* (1866) 211; U Linderfalk, 'The Effect of Jus Cogens Norms: Whoever Opened Pandora's Box, Did you Ever Think about the Consequences?' (2008) 18 *European Journal of International Law* 853; RStJ Macdonald, 'International Community' in RStJ Macdonald and DM Johnston (eds),

signified as 'the international community as a whole'. The separation of the international community from state members is especially prominent in the ILC's justification of peremptory norms.[33] Norms establishing the international community have been described as 'substantive', 'of a fundamental character', 'basic', 'intolerable', 'intransgressible', 'the most basic human values' and of 'vital interest' to the international community as a whole.[34] Certain norms, identifying the very existence conditions to the community, have trumped state laws related to nationality.

Why are such norms so basic to the international community? Once again, we return to the enigma of statelessness in an international community. With the community as an aggregate of equal sovereign wills, states have had discretion to choose whether to protect their nationals. Harm, though, is attributed to the state, not to the person actually harmed.[35] If a person lacks a nationality conferred by a state, every state lacks an obligation to diplomatically protect her/him in the international community of aggregated wills of states. With the international community as a whole, however, the natural person can be considered harmed by a state. This is manifested by non-derogatory human rights, peremptory norms and proscriptions against 'grave breaches' as set out in the Geneva Convention IV and Protocol 1 (Article 73).[36] The community possesses a universal jurisdiction with universal standards to which every state is obligated to comply. The obligation does not arise because of a state's consent to the universal standards but because, without the enforcement of the standards, the international community as a whole would not exist. The standards are existence conditions, few in number, of the community. I shall make this point as I proceed in my later chapters. At this point, I wish to clarify the nature of the two international communities.

II. THE INTERNATIONAL COMMUNITY AS THE AGGREGATE OF THE WILLS OF STATES

A state's freedom has been the object of juristic and political commentary since the emergence of the early modern European state in the sixteenth

Towards World Constitutionalism: Issues in the Legal Ordering of the World Community (Leiden, Martinus Nijhoff, 2005) 273 and 296–99; and J Barboza, 'Legal Injury: The Tip of the Iceberg in the Law of State Responsibility' in M Ragazzi (ed), *International Responsibility Today: Essays in Memory of Oscar Schachter* (Leiden, Martinus Nijhoff, 2005) 20–21.

[33] See ILC, 'Draft Articles on State Responsibility' (above n 24) 148–50 and 158–60.

[34] Ibid, Pt 2 (ch III Comm 4), Art 12 (Comm 7) and Art 40 (Comms 3 and 5).

[35] *Island of Palmas Case* (*Netherlands v United States*) (1928) 2 RIAA 829, 839, 4 ILR 3 (sole arbitrator Huber).

[36] Convention (IV) relative to the Protection of Civilian Persons in Time of War (Geneva, 12 August 1949); and Protocol Additional to the Geneva Conventions of 12 August 1949 and relating to the Protection of Victims of International Armed Conflicts (Protocol 1) (8 June 1977), Art 73.

and seventeenth centuries. A natural person, jurists asserted, voluntarily expressed a freedom of choice of which state would be hers/his, and in exchange, the international community, through its state members, would protect the person. My point, noted in my Introduction above, is that just as a natural person was considered free vis-à-vis the state, the state was considered free vis-à-vis the international community. In that respect, the residuary of the international community protected the self-regarding action of the state; the state's other-regarding action brought international standards into issue. The state's domestic laws expressed its will in the community. A state trespassed the boundary between self- and other-regarding state action once the state interfered with the self-regarding action of another state. Like the free individuals inside a state's jurisdiction, the state was free to express itself though its laws and actions so long as its laws did not cause harm to other states. The most important incident of a state's self-regarding domain was its freedom to confer, withdraw or withhold its own membership – and by inference, the membership of the international community.

Now, the enigma of the international community exists by virtue of such a freedom of a state on the one hand against a claim of universal jurisdiction of the international community on the other. The boundary of this freedom, this also being institutionalized by the boundary of the residuary of the international community, has blocked international norms and institutions from interfering with a state's choice of its nationals. The state's choices may be the object of external remonstration, but the condemnation of the state's choices is not legally binding. From the standpoint of the international community as an aggregate of wills of states, international standards represent an external intervention into the protected freedom of state members. The only exception to such a non-intervention principle concerns international standards to which a state has expressly or implicitly consented. A reservation of a treaty is void if it conflicts with the treaty's objective. Why? Because the state has expressly consented to the treaty. The state's consent renders the international standard binding of future state acts. And so, great weight has been placed upon treaties, customary norms, judicial decisions and general principles representing the wills of states. Indeed, some states, such as the United Kingdom, Australia, the United States and Canada, have required the express incorporation of international standards into the content of domestic laws.

In sum, buried in this sense of legal obligation, then, are matters 'essentially within the internal jurisdiction of any state', as Article 2(7) of the United Nations Charter suggests. A state's choice of whether to confer, withhold or withdraw its nationality has been considered one such essential element of the state's freedom. If the state is the sole subject of the international community, then an international standard must be justified in terms of the will of the state as represented by a treaty or customary norm. The international community is constituted from the sum of such wills.

A. The Source of a Discrete Content-Independent Law

The essence to a state's jurisdiction suggests a finality to legal analysis. The state's institutions, such as the legislature, executive and courts, constitute the sources finalizing the justification of a legal rule. The relation of the rule to such sources, not the social relationships presupposed in the content of the rule, identify a legal rule. Article 38 of the Statute of the ICJ manifests just such a finality of legal analysis in the quest for the identity of a law.[37] The next chapter will explain how the sources are framed by the boundary of the international community's residuary. The boundary of such a residuary protects its content from external interference in a state's choices of nationals. The boundary affects how an institution interprets 'law'. When treaties, judgments and commentaries address such terms as 'lawfully admitted', 'lawfully within the territory of a state', 'by law', 'lawfulness' and 'justified by law',[38] it is often taken for granted that 'law' is the rules, principles, doctrines and other standards identified inside the international community's reserved domain, as represented by state institutions.[39] As will be seen in chapter eight, however, the content of such a reserved domain – and therefore what is signified by 'law' – is brought into question by the inner discourse of the international community as a whole.[40]

But does the identity of a law foreclose legal analysis in advance? The enigma of statelessness begs this issue: is a state legally obligated to follow an international standard if the residuary of the international community protects the state's choices of the international community's

---

[37] Statute of the International Court of Justice, Annex to UN Charter, United Nations Conference on International Organization (UNCIO) 355, signed 26 June 1945, in force 24 October 1945.

[38] See *Maroufidou v Sweden*, HRC Communication No 58/1979, UN Doc CCPR/C/12/D/58/1979, (1981) 62 ILR 278, para 9.3; Human Rights Committee (CCPR), 'General Comment 15: The Position of Aliens under the Covenant' (11 April 1986) in UN, *Human Rights Instruments, Volume I* (above n 16) 190 (para 9); and Economic and Social Council Ad Hoc Committee on Statelessness and Related Problems, 'Summary Record of 40th Meeting' (22 August 1950), UN Doc E/AC.32/SR.40.

[39] *Case concerning Ahmadou Sadio Diallo (Republic of Guinea v Democratic Republic of the Congo)* (Merits, Judgment), (2010) ICJ Reports 639, ISSN 0074, Judgment of 30 November 2010, No 103, para 70. In exceptional circumstances, an international tribunal may interpret a domestic law when domestic courts are patently in error.

[40] See *Diallo* (ibid) para 65. See also *Suarez de Guerrero v Colombia*, HRC Communication No 45/1979, 70 ILR 267; *A v Australia*, HRC Communication No 560/1993, UN Doc CCPR/C/59/D/560/1993 (1997), paras 4 and 9.5 (per Bhagwati); and J-M Henckaerts, *Mass Expulsion in Modern International Law and Practice* (The Hague, Martinus Nijhoff, 1995) 29.

members? Why is the state's consent, grounded as it is in an inviolable freedom of the state, so crucial to the binding character of a nationality law if a stateless person may claim harm against the international community as a whole for reason of a state's withdrawal or withholding of nationality, prolonged detention, forced displacement, expulsion or other examples of the failure of a state to protect stateless persons? To be sure, as argued in chapter two below, Emer de Vattel reasoned that the relation of a natural person was immediate with the state. The individual's freedom was thereby assimilated by the state into the law of nations. But does that remain so today?

The sources thesis, nested as it is in the quest for the identity of an international (or domestic) legal rule, concentrates upon consent as the criterion of legal obligation. And the consent needed is that of a state, not the natural person. Does lawfulness exist only if one can justify a rule in terms of such consent? The sources thesis leaves the jurist in a quagmire. Is an affidavit to the effect that one has been habitually resident on a territory adequate for the recognition of that person's nationality? If so, is the requisite of an affidavit or supporting witnesses a reasonable expectation if one is fleeing from an insurgency, armed struggle or natural disaster? [41] Is a travel document, as required by Article 28 of the Convention Relating to the Status of Stateless Persons (1954),[42] sufficient evidence to legally remain on the territory of a state? Or is the jurist not required to examine the social relationships of a natural person experienced at a place over a period of time and in diverse circumstances? If the place of one's experienced social relationships are required of one's nationality, does not such an expectation bring the boundary of the reserved domain into question? And does not such questioning open the legal enquiry to a very different shape of the international community than one that holds the reserved domain the residuary of the community? Does this not require that the jurist turn to the ethos or character of the international community rather than to the sources representing the consent of its state members?

B. International Standards as Supplementary of the Internal Domain

The residuary of an international community and its accompanying state freedom to confer, withdraw or withhold nationality lead to an important issue: what is the role of international standards, whether of treaties or customary norms? On the one hand, international standards often hold out guarantees to everyone. Article 15 of the UDHR, for example, guarantees that 'everyone has the right to a nationality.' Article 8 of the Convention on

---

[41] CA Batchelor, 'UNHCR and Issues related to Nationality' (1995) 14 *Refugee Survey Quarterly* 91, fn 18.

[42] Convention Relating to the Status of Stateless Persons (above n 1).

the Rights of the Child guarantees that 'States Parties undertake to respect the right of the child to preserve his or her identity, including nationality'. Despite such universality, the standards may not necessarily protect stateless persons. Why is that so? When universal norms are contextualized in an international community constituted from the aggregate of the wills of state members, membership in the community is left to the choice of the state members of the community. The latter choice is protected by the boundary of the residuary. The international community's residuary and the internal jurisdiction of a state are synonymous for nationality purposes. Serious legal and social consequences follow, including the freedom of a state to admit or expel a natural person lacking the state's authority. International standards play a role after the state has rendered its choice of the conferral, withdrawal or withholding of its nationality.

Ambiguity, however, colours the boundary of the residuary in nationality matters.[43] Article 13 of the ICCPR raises the issue, for example, whether '[a]n alien lawfully in the territory of a state party to the present Covenant may be expelled therefrom only in pursuance of a decision reached in accordance with law'. The text does not necessitate judicial scrutiny of the executive arm of the state.[44] The boundary of the residuary lies inside the usual judicial discourse about the role of judiciary and of the executive.[45] The ILC memorandum 'Expulsion of Aliens' (2006), for example, recognizes the supplementarity of international standards to the freedom of the state to expel a natural person.[46] The supplementarity of international standards comes into play when a state's exercise of its choice to expel someone impacts upon the self-regarding residuary represented by another state. A state is said to have a duty to receive a national expelled by another state.[47] A state lacks such a duty to receive a stateless person if the jurist works within the image of an international community as an aggregate of the wills of states. The exercise of the state's discretion over the conferral, withholding or withdrawing of nationality is left to internal jurisdiction.

So, too, the ILC 'Draft Articles on Nationality in Relation to the Succession of States' (1999) recognize that a right to nationality is attributed to a natural person if the individual had a nationality in the ceded or ceding state (Article 1).[48] The Commentary to Article 2 suggests that the Draft Articles

[43] ILC, 'Expulsion of Aliens: Memorandum by the Secretariat', 58th sess, A/CN.4/ 565 (10 July 2006), daccess-dds-ny.un.org/doc/UNDOC/GEN/N06/260/29/PDF/N0626029. pdf? OpenElement, para 240.

[44] See below ch 2, s V-A (88–92).

[45] R Plender, 'The Ugandan Crisis and the Right of Expulsion under International Law' (1972) 9 *The Review: International Commission of Jurists* 19, 23–24.

[46] ILC, 'Expulsion of Aliens' (above n 43).

[47] GS Goodwin-Gill, *International Law and the Movement of Persons Between States* (Oxford, Clarendon Press, 1978) 201, as quoted in ILC, 'Expulsion of Aliens' (above n 43) para 23.

[48] ILC, 'Draft Articles on Nationality of Natural Persons in Relation to the Succession of States, with Commentaries' in *Report of the ILC on the Work of its Fifty-First Session*, UN Doc A/54/10, *ILC Yearbook 1999*, vol II (2), 37. See also Art 16 (Comm 1).

include duties of the state to 'every individual', including stateless persons.[49] An earlier draft (1997) of the Articles required that states possess a duty to prevent statelessness that arises when one state succeeds another because of the 'effective nationality' of an individual.[50] Article 5 of the latter Draft Articles provided that persons with 'habitual residence' on a territory are presumed to have the nationality of the state that claims title to the territory of habitual residence. The presumption is considered rebuttable.[51]

Once again, given the incorporation of the reserved domain into the international community, international standards enter the legal discourse *after* the state has exercised its discretion concerning nationality. In 1997, the ILC Special Rapporteur summarized one member's comments in deliberations about nationality and the succession of states:

> Nationality was, of course, *a matter for internal law*, albeit within the limits imposed by international law. Moreover, the paramount principle of equality between states had to be borne in mind. Accordingly, he did not see how one State, acting unilaterally, could judge another, condemn it and immediately impose sanctions, by not recognizing the nationality given to certain persons. Such a provision could only pave the way for pressure tactics or even disputes, which would be undesirable.[52]

At that moment, the state may refuse to give effect to another state's nationality laws or decisions. The state may refuse to do so, for example, if denaturalization is not authorized by a state's domestic law or if such a domestic law is administered arbitrarily.

International standards hold out guarantees to 'everyone'. Such standards have little efficacy, however, if the international community reserves a bounded domain for the state over the conferral, withdrawal and withholding of nationality. Such a reserved jurisdiction may be compromised only if a state explicitly or implicitly consents to a constraint. The international standard is self-determined by the state. Vaclav Mikulka, Special ILC Rapporteur for the 'Third Report on Nationality and the Succession of States', has explained that international standards function negatively in that the standards 'delimit the competence of the predecessor state' to determine one's nationality.[53] That is, the standards delimit the boundary

[49]   Ibid, Art 2(f) (Comm 5).

[50]   ILC, 'Report of the ILC on the Work of its Forty-Ninth Session', UN Doc A/52/10, *ILC Yearbook 1997*, vol II(2), 14, Art 3 (Comms 1 and 8). For the principle of effective nationality as the basis of the presumption, see Art 3 (Comm 4). For state duty, see V Mikulka (Special Rapporteur), 'Third Report on Nationality in Relation to the Succession of States', UN Doc A/CN.4/480 & Corr.1 and Add.1 & Corr.1–2, *ILC Yearbook 1997*, vol II(1), 7, Art 2 (Comms 1–18).

[51]   ILC, 'Report of the Work of its Forty-Ninth Session' (ibid) Art 3 (Comm 2).

[52]   ILC, 'Summary Records of the 2486th meeting (30 May 1997)', *ILC Yearbook 1997*, vol I, 86 (para 75) (Mr Economides), emphasis added.

[53]   Mikulka, 'Third Report on Nationality in Relation to the Succession of States' (above n 50) Preamble (Comm 6).

of the internal jurisdiction. Again, the international standards also come into operation *after* a state has determined one's nationality. At best, without a state's express or implicit consent, international standards supplement the protected domain. The condition of supplementarity forecloses internal or international scrutiny of the content of the state's reserved domain. By 'content', I signify the content of the discrete legal rules and doctrines about nationality and the naturalization process, as posited by the state's legislatures, courts and administrative tribunals, including all such rules and tests authorized inside the bounded reserved domain.[54] By the content of the discrete legal rules and doctrines, I mean the reciprocal social relationships presupposed inside the boundaries of the rules and doctrines.[55] Aside from an absence of judicial review, the supplemental character of international standards relieves state officials of self-blame for the consequential statelessness of natural persons. Let us address several examples.

Immunity from self-blame tainted the expulsion of denaturalized members of the Jewish ethnicity from Nazi-occupied territories during the 1930s and wartime. Immunity from self-blame characterized other European states as well. As a French Minister described the situation in 1934:

> Our frontiers are open for the expulsion of undesirable aliens, but the frontiers of foreign countries are closed to them. In most cases aliens are not admitted or are sent back to our territory under cover of night. They come back, are arrested by the police, convicted again, and the whole procedure starts all over again.[56]

Neither Belgium (the state of habitation) nor France (the state of refuge) recognized stateless persons as possessing a legal status. The immunity from self-blame for the production of stateless persons was represented by the relations between Poland and Nazi Germany. Both states claimed legal authority over nationality as a matter of internal jurisdiction. On 1 April 1938 and 25 February 1939, the Polish state enacted laws denaturalizing all Polish nationals of the Jewish People residing outside the territorial border of Poland. Poland also withdrew nationality from those nationals who had allegedly 'lost contact with the Polish state' or had

---

[54] See below ch 6; Conklin, *Hegel's Laws* (above n 26) 162–87, 279–83 and 317–18; WE Conklin, 'Statelessness and Bernhard Waldenfels' Phenomenology of the Alien' (2007) 38 *Journal of British Society for Phenomenology* 280.

[55] For further on this point, see WE Conklin, *Le savoir oublié de l'expérience des lois*, B Kingstone (trans) (Québec, Laval University Press, 2011) 145–72 and 241–45; WE Conklin, 'The Ghosts of Cemetery Road: Two Forgotten Indigenous Women and the Crisis of Analytical Jurisprudence' (2011) *Australian Feminist Law Journal* 3; WE Conklin, 'Lon Fuller's Phenomenology of Language' (2006) 19 *International Journal for the Semiotics of Law* 93; and WE Conklin, *The Phenomenology of Modern Legal Discourse* (Aldershot, Dartmouth, 1998) 51–101 and 213–48.

[56] As quoted by M Vishniak, *The Legal Status of Stateless Persons* (New York, American Jewish Committee, 1945) 31.

acted against the interests of the Polish Government.[57] Children and spouses were also denaturalized. Any such denaturalized person could not return to Poland's territory without formal Polish authorization.[58] The claim of internal jurisdiction trumped international legal obligations that may have existed. For its part, the Third Reich could harm the denaturalized Polish citizens without fear of their diplomatic protection by Poland. As a consequence, one group of 16,000 Polish-speaking Jewish people were returned to the intolerable conditions of a village (Sbonszyn) located on the border between Poland and Germany.[59]

Of course, one might respond to such historical experiences by saying that the world has changed, what with human rights treaties and customary norms: we now have universal human rights. I shall address human rights in chapters four and five below. Unfortunately, state officials still remain immune from self-blame for the production of statelessness. To take one example from the case of *Harabi v The Netherlands*, after Algeria became independent of France, Mr Harabi left France's territory (in 1958) for a series of other states (Germany, back to Algeria, Portugal [as a stowaway], Venezuela, Spain, Uruguay, Trinidad, Belgium and finally, the Netherlands).[60] At this point, 16 years after he had begun his effort to find a territory on the globe where he could live, he was expelled to Belgium from the Netherlands. The Dutch government justified the expulsion as the 'logical consequence' of an identifiable domestic legal rule regarding the expulsion of aliens. This rule, according to the Dutch government, was 'the law' of the Netherlands.[61] Harabi had been a national of Algeria, according to the Dutch government, because he had been born on the territory now owned by Algeria. To be sure, France had owned the territory at the time of his birth, but Algeria had succeeded France's authority by the time of the litigation.

The European Court of Human Rights (ECtHR) agreed with the Netherlands position. According to the Court, Algerian law provided that one did not lose the nationality of the state of origin by a long absence from Algeria's territory. Algerian domestic law would have accepted Harabi if he had chosen to return there, according to the Dutch Government. In addition, the Court stated that Harabi should have initially considered another state besides the Netherlands. Finally, the Court stated that Harabi was not a refugee within the meaning of the Refugee Convention because he was not fleeing from fear of persecution. Given that the international standard

---

[57] For a general study of Polish laws and the problematic of mass statelessness, see generally G Kaeckenbeeck, *The International Experiment of Upper Silesia: A Study in the Working of the Upper Silesian Settlement, 1922–1937* (London, Oxford University Press, 1942).

[58] As described by Vishniak (above n 56) 25.

[59] Ibid, 25.

[60] *Harabi v Netherlands*, Application No 10798/84 (1986), 46 *Decisions and Reports* 112.

[61] Ibid, 6.

of 'lawfulness' collapses here into the discrete domestic rules of states in nationality matters, the Dutch state considered it 'unnreasonable' for someone to complain about the state's expulsion decision. Harabi himself was considered responsible for his own 'suffering' for continually returning to the Netherlands in contravention of the Netherlands Aliens Act, knowing that he would not be allowed to remain there as a declared persona non grata. The Netherlands, Belgium and Algeria refused to accept any legal or moral responsibility for Harabi. Each state accepted that it was free to exclude him by virtue of its bounded residuary protected by the international community. Harabi was therefore expelled from Dutch and Belgian territories a total of 28 times.

To take another example, after some Palestinians departed from Gaza for Kuwait due to the war of 1948 and after they subsequently left Kuwait due to the 1990–91 and 2000 Gulf Wars, they could not return to Gaza because they lacked identity papers from Israel and Kuwait.[62] Israel had claimed title to the territory where they had been habitual residents prior to 1948. Although the Palestinian Authority has issued passports since April 1995 (which states seem to recognize as travel documents, if not as proof of Palestinian citizenship), the exiles from Gaza and then Kuwait lacked such identity papers.[63] The exiles also lacked Kuwaiti nationality because Kuwait rarely conferred nationality to Palestinian refugees, despite their having lived on Kuwait soil for up to a half century. Because they lacked Kuwaiti nationality, Kuwait refused to allow them to return. As one witness described her situation with regard to other states,

> I'm a Palestinian born and lived in Libya (most of my life) for 19 years. I came to Ireland to study with my sister (Ebtesam AM). Now I've finished my study and I can't go back to Libya. My residency in Ireland is finished, and I can't obtain a visa to my country of origin (Palestine) or any other country. I have an Egyptian travel document (not a passport) which also doesn't entitle me to go to reside in Egypt. The Libyan government refused to issue me a visa to go back to Libya [because in 1993 the Libyan Government ordered all Palestinians to leave]. I can't go back to Palestine, according to the Israeli law and Oslo Agreement, I'm not entitled to go back to Palestine. After I got married, I feel that I lost my freedom of independence.[64]

Because the international community protected the (state-centric) residuary regarding nationality, no state official from anywhere needed to accept blame for this witness's stateless condition.

[62] This is best elaborated in *Case No 0808284* [2009] RRTA 454, paras 3–5.

[63] See for example, United States Bureau of Citizenship and Immigration Services, 'Palestine/Occupied Territories: Information on Passports Issued by the Palestine National Authority' (17 December 1998), PAL99001.ZCH, www.refworld.org/docid/3df0b9914.html. The exiles lacked legal documents because the Palestinian Authority took form after they had left Gaza, and the Authority even then was not recognized as a state.

[64] *SHM v Refugees Appeals Tribunal and Minister for Justice, Equality and Law Reform* (2009) IECH 128, para 10.

In another case involving Palestinians, a family of 50 years on Kuwaiti territory lacked a legal right to enter Israel, Egypt, Gaza and the West Bank.[65] The Australian Refugee Review Tribunal refused to recognize them as stateless refugees.[66] Even though they lacked a right to live anywhere on the globe, according to the Tribunal, 'These are not matters that the Tribunal can take into account in making a decision.'[67] Nor could the Tribunal be concerned that the applicant would suffer serious harm if returned to Kuwait. Indeed, the Tribunal insisted that refugee status could not be accorded to persons merely because they were stateless and unable to return to their countries of former habitual residence.[68]

As a further example, after withdrawing nationality from inhabitants who were of Tartar ethnicity, Stalin deported over 400,000 Crimean Tartars in 1944 to Azerbaijan.[69] After Azerbaijan became independent of the USSR in 1988, Azerbaijan would not recognize the Tartars as possessing legal status. In a 1996 report to the UN Economic and Social Council, Azerbaijan claimed that one million displaced persons and refugees (including Russian-speaking and Kurdish inhabitants) were living on its territory.[70] Although the Ukraine admitted 13,358,[71] large numbers of Tartars lacked legal documentation of any legal status. Still more were stateless in transit between Azerbaijan and the Ukraine.[72] To be sure, a 13 November 1991 Azerbaijan law conferred nationality on 56 per cent of the returnees. However, those who tried to return subsequent to the law were left in 'a no-man's land'.

Similarly, Estonia, Latvia and Lithuania, upon independence from the USSR in 1991, categorized a citizen as any former national prior to Stalin's invasion of their territories in 1938. Russian-speaking inhabitants of several generations therefore lacked nationality in the new states. Latvia and Estonia considered such inhabitants Russian nationals. Russia for its part considered them foreigners. With the similar break-up of Czechoslovakia, the newly independent Slovak and Czech Republics initially recognized

---

[65] *Case No 0808284* (above n 62).

[66] Ibid, para 68.

[67] Ibid, para 114.

[68] *Case No 0805551* (2009) RRTA 24, para 56. That said, the refusal to allow a former inhabitant to return is one of several features that may establish a fear of persecution if one were to return.

[69] UNHCR, 'UNHCR Urges 35,000 Crimean Tartars to Apply for Citizenship before Year End', press release (22 June 1999). See also B Bowring, 'The Tartars of the Russian Federation and National–Cultural Autonomy: A Contradiction in Terms?' (2007) 6 *Ethnopolitics* 417, 425–26.

[70] UNHCR, 'Initial States Parties Report to the Economic and Social Council: Azerbaijan' (17 June 1996) UN Doc E/1990/5/Add.30 (State Party Report), para 185.

[71] UNHCR, *Global Report 2000* (Geneva, UNHCR, 2000) 372.

[72] UNHCR Evaluation and Policy Analysis Unit, 'Evaluation of UNHCR's Role and Activities in Relation to Statelessness' (July 2001) RPAU/2001/09, 20; and UNHCR Regional Bureau for Europe, 'The Czech and Slovak Citizenship Laws and the Problem of Statelessness' (1996) 2(4) *European Series: Citizenship in the Context of the Dissolution of Czechoslovakia* 10.

persons born on their territories as their nationals. Inhabitants of the Czech Republic were considered foreign Slovaks if born on Slovakia's territory. And inhabitants of the Slovak Republic were deemed Czech foreigners if born on the Czech territory. Many habitual residents then became foreigners on territory where they and their families had lived for generations. Again, the enigma of the international community made 'sense'. Each state, in reserving the freedom to confer, withhold and withdraw nationality, simply fulfilled the state's authority recognized by the international community.

C. The Circularity of International Standards

The structure of an international community that reserves a domain of law-making and law administration for state members reinforces a circularity of international standards. Although the standards at first sight seem to extend to everyone universally, the network of standards takes the freedom of the state over nationality for granted. The European Framework Convention for the Protection of National Minorities (1994) exemplifies such circularity.[73] Article 1 defines a 'national minority' as a group of persons who 'a) reside on the territory of that state *and are citizens thereof*; b) maintain longstanding, firm and lasting ties *with that state* . . .'. Although states consented to the incorporation of 'the fundamental principles' of international law into the Convention's legal standards (Article 21), the treaty leaves the term 'national minority' undefined. This textual silence leaves it to the internal jurisdiction of each state to define who is a member of a national minority and how to enforce domestic laws (Article 5(2)).[74] Because nationality is presupposed to be an incident of the residuary, who is a member of the national minority is left to internal jurisdiction. The 'Explanatory Memorandum' concerning the Framework Convention affirms the deference to member state prerogative over nationality in the matter.[75] As a consequence, international legal standards are excluded from consideration of the content of protected residuary of the international community. Human rights principles must be implemented 'through national legislation and appropriate governmental policies'. 'Territorial integrity and national sovereignty of states', not national minorities, emerge as the dominant features that the treaty

---

[73] Framework Convention for the Protection of National Minorities (Strasbourg, 1 February 1995), in force 1 February 1998, ETS No157.

[74] P Keller, 'Re-thinking Ethnic and Cultural Rights in Europe' (1998) 18 *Oxford Journal of Legal Studies* 29.

[75] Council of Europe, 'Explanatory Memorandum on the Framework Convention for the Protection of National Minorities', ETS No 166, (1995) 16 *Human Rights Law Journal* 101, para 29.

protects. The opinion of the draftsperson confirms this.[76] Along the same lines, the Parliamentary Assembly of the Council of Europe in 1993 stated in its Protocol to the European Convention of Human Rights that a national minority must be a citizen.[77] In sum, despite the apparent universality of human rights attributed to all ethnic minorities in Europe, the silence of the Framework Treaty as to who is a member of a 'national minority' has incorporated the protected residuary of the international community, thereby inviting state parties to exclude stateless persons from their national minorities.[78]

The European Court of Human Rights continued to take the reserved domain for granted in *Makuc* (2000): 'as a matter of well-established international law', the state is said to have the authority to decide whether to admit or expel a foreigner.[79] International law obligations do come into play, one is advised, but again they do so *after* a state has determined whether a natural person has its nationality.[80] To take an example, although Germany has ratified both multilateral and regional human rights treaties and, further, has domestically enacted wide-ranging protections of persons seeking asylum in the Basic Law (1949),[81] the Framework Treaty has invited a reading against the incident of nationality in the international community's reserved domain.[82] As of June 2013, over 10 million of the over 80 million inhabitants of the Federal German Republic are of 'international migrant stock'.[83] About 100,000 alien children and 1.63

---

[76] H Klebes, 'The Council of Europe's Framework Convention for the Protection of National Minorities' (1995) 16 *Human Rights Law Journal* 92, 93.

[77] Council of Europe, 'Recommendation 1255 (1995) on the Protection of National Minorities' (Strasbourg, 31 January 1995), reprinted in (1995) 14 *Human Rights Law Journal* 113, para 2.

[78] Council of Europe, 'Explanatory Memorandum' (above n 75) para 30. The Memo is concerned with non-nationals more generally.

[79] See, eg, *Makuc and Others v Slovenia* [2007] ECtHR 523, para 209. See also, eg, *Mamatkulov and Abdurasulovic v Turkey* (2005) 41 EHRR 25, Application Nos 46827/99 & 46951/99 (6 February 2003), para 65; and *Ahmed v Austria* (1996) 24 EHRR 278, para 38.

[80] *Ahmed v Austria* (ibid) para 39.

[81] The Basic Law (1949) had two types of rights: general rights, which applied to all inhabitants (such as freedom of expression), and reserved rights, which applied to German nationals. Article 16(2) of the Basic Law provided that 'the politically persecuted shall enjoy asylum'. In addition to such political refugees and the refugees as defined in the Convention Relating to the Status of Refugees (1951), 606 UNTS 267 (entered into force 4 October 1967), Germany initially accepted refugees who lacked evidentiary proof of well-founded causal relation to a fear of persecution once they had entered the German territory. See P Weil, 'The Transformation of Immigration Policies: Immigration Control and Nationality Laws in Europe – A Comparative Approach' (1999) 7(2) *Collective Courses of the Academy of European Law* 87, 110. The German Constitutional Court had held in 1978 that 'an alien acquires a constitutionally protected reliance interest to remain in Germany as a result of prior routine renewals of his residence permit and his integration into German Society'. See Weil (above) 113.

[82] Keller (above n 74) 44 (fn 61).

[83] The migrant stock totals 10,758,000 of the 83,302,000 inhabitants: UN Department of Economic and Social Affairs (Population Division), 'International Migration Policies 2013' (based on 2010 data), www.un.org/en/development/desa/population/publications/policy/international-migration-policies-2013.shtml.

million stateless persons are annually born in Germany with 7.74 per cent of the inhabitants in 2012 being foreign-born – this being surprisingly below the total foreign-born of 30 per cent for countries within the Organisation for Economic Co-operation and Development (OECD).[84]

The residuary's boundary impacts upon how one understands the identity and nature of an international community. The boundary separates the internal freedom of one state from the internal freedom of another state. Two conditions limit such a freedom: first, the state's explicit and implicit consent to the condition; secondly, the harm caused by one state to the internal freedom of another state. The state's freedom of choice represented by the bounded residuary manifests how each state member has a self-determining character. The stateless condition has accompanied such a self-determining character of each member state. This protected residuary is a familiar background principle of the ethos of one sense of an international community. As the Permanent Court stated in *Lotus*, 'International law governs relations between independent States.'[85] The principle can be retrieved from human rights and the statelessness treaties as well as from customary international norms, as we shall see in chapters three and four.

The legal obligations accepted in the international community of aggregated states conflate into obligations owed to other states. Again, those international norms are obligatory only if they have received from state members either explicit consent (as will be discussed below in chapter four) or implicit consent (as will be discussed below in chapter five). Without such consent, the obligations are merely 'oughts' or hortatory. Such hortatory character of duties reinforces the sense of the international legal objectivity as an idealized heaven of rules and rights. And so, on the one hand, the states parties are called upon to 'promote' 'higher standards of living, full employment, conditions of economic and social progress and development', 'solutions to economic, health and related problems, and international cultural and educational co-operation' (UN Charter, Article 55). According to Article 2(2) of the ICCPR, each state party 'undertakes to

---

[84] For the figure of 30%, see OECD, 'Chapter 1: Recent Developments in International Migration Movements and Policies' in OECD, *International Migration Outlook 2013* (2013), dx.doi.org/10.1787/migr_outlook-2013-en, 36. See also Annex Table A.5 of *International Migration Outlook*: 'Stocks of Foreign Population by Nationality in OECD Countries and the Russian Federation'. By 1999, Germany, with population of 80 million nationals, had 7.3 million non-nationals, of which 50% had been living on German territory for over 10 years and another 30% for over 20 years. C Sonntag-Wolgast,'Trends and Developments in National and International Law on Nationality', opening speech as Secretary of State in the German Ministry of the Interior at 1st European Conference on Nationality (Strasbourg, 18 and 19 October 1999) in Council of Europe, *Proceedings of the First European Conference on Nationality: Trends and Developments in National and International Law on Nationality* (3 February 2000), www.refworld.org/docid/43f202412.html. Admittedly, migrant workers and other non-nationals may well possess nationality from other states.

[85] *Lotus* (above n 3) 18 (emphasis added).

take the necessary steps . . . to adopt such legislative or other measures as may be necessary to give effect to the rights recognized in the present Covenant'. On the other hand, given the hard fact of the residuary, any such obligations are 'oughts'. As a Special Rapporteur of the ILC has put it, international standards regulate the consequences of statelessness as a 'state-to-state erga omnes obligation . . . having no direct legal consequences in the relationship between States and individuals'.[86] The 'oughts' are 'out of bounds' for judicial scrutiny of the content of the internal jurisdiction. For the aggregated community, the 'oughts' are juxtaposed with the internal jurisdiction as legal reality.

III. DESTABILIZATION OF THE INTERNATIONAL COMMUNITY AS THE AGGREGATED WILLS OF STATE MEMBERS

In addressing the enigma of an international community in the international law discourse, one finds a discursive undercurrent that destabilizes the bounded residuary within which nationality has been considered an incident. In this subtext, the international community has been thought to be boundless as a political and legal entity.[87] Legal norms have radically changed with the displacement of a protected internal jurisdiction with an international community as the ultimate referent of legal analysis.[88] Most importantly, the boundary of the reserved internal jurisdiction is increasingly being rendered transparent by universal claims in human rights law, peremptory norms and humanitarian law.

This discursive shift hints that the international community, as constituted from separate and independent of the wills of states, can be harmed. An early modern example, taken from Roman law, has been the harm caused to the community by pirates.[89] So too torture has been described as *hostis humani generis* ['an enemy of all humankind'].[90] More generally, an argument could be made that the international community is harmed by genocide, slavery, the slave trade, the widespread disappearances of natural persons, cruel, inhuman or degrading treatment or punishment, prolonged arbitrary detention and systematic racial or ethnic discrimination.[91]

[86] V Mikulka (Special Rapporteur), 'Second Report on State Succession and Its Impact on the Nationality of Natural and Legal Persons', A/CN.4/474 & Corr.1 & 2 (Chinese only), *ILC Yearbook 1996*, vol II(1), ch 1, para 22. See also ILC, 'Draft Articles on Nationality' (above n 48) ch 1, para 22.

[87] J Bartelson, *Visions of World Community* (Cambridge, Cambridge University Press, 2009).

[88] E Keene, *Beyond the Anarchical Society: Grotius, Colonialism and Order in World Politics* (Cambridge, Cambridge University Press, 2002) 141–43 and 147–48; and E Keane, *Global Civil Society?* (Cambridge, Cambridge University Press, 2003) 200–9.

[89] *Filartiga v Pena-Irala* (1980) 630 F.2d 876, 890 (2nd Circ 1980) (Kaufman J), 77 ILR 169.

[90] Ibid.

[91] UNHCR Evaluation and Policy Analysis Unit, 'Evaluation of UNHCR's Role and Activities' (above n 69) 20. See also UNHCR Regional Bureau for Europe, 'The Czech and

Such labels as 'jus cogens', 'erga omnes' and 'human rights' do not justify the universality of such norms. Rather, the universality of certain norms is obligatory of states because without the norms, the international community does not exist as a legal order.

A. Human Rights

The universal character of the international community has been so separate from the wills of states that David Weissbrodt, a leading jurist, has claimed that the 'architecture of human rights' has rendered nationality passé.[92] Commentaries often take for granted without explanation or justification that human rights are peremptory.[93] Most important in this context, the ICJ stated in its oft-quoted decision in *Barcelona Traction*, one year after the signing of the Vienna Convention on Treaties (which recognized peremptory norms), that if an obligation is owed to the international community as a whole rather than to states inter se, each member of the community possesses a legal interest in the protection of the international community itself.[94] The ILC 'Draft Articles on State Responsibility' makes sustained affirmative references to *Barcelona Traction*.[95] According to *Barcelona Traction*, harm to human rights constitutes harm against the international community as a whole.

Why such harm is caused to the international community as a whole, however, remains rarely addressed in international law discourse. In 1951, the ICJ issued an advisory opinion on *Reservations to the Genocide Convention* in which it distinguished human rights treaties from ordinary treaties: the parties to a human rights treaty 'do not have any interests of their own; they merely have, one and all, a common interest, namely, the accomplishment

---

Slovak Citizenship Laws' (above n 68) 10; and UNHCR, 'Stateless: Prevention and Reduction of Statelessness and Protection of Stateless Persons' (14 February 2006) UN Doc EC/57/SC/CRP.6, reprinted in (2006) 25 *Refugee Survey Quarterly* 72–76.

[92] D Weissbrodt, *Human Rights of Non-citizens* (Oxford, Oxford University Press, 2008). Caroline Sawyer claims that the 'greatest hope must be rooted in the modern human rights system': C Sawyer, 'Legal Frameworks of Statelessness in Europe' in Blitz and Sawyer (eds) (above n 1) 82.

[93] American Law Institute, *Restatement of the Law, Third: Foreign Relations Law of the United States* (Philadelphia, American Law Institute, 1987) para 702 (Comm N). The right to a fair trial is expressly excepted as a peremptory norm.

[94] *Barcelona Traction* (above n 28) paras 33–34, 36 and 91. See also the Independent Opinion of Judge Fitzmaurice, paras 33, 38; *United States Diplomatic and Consular Staff in Tehran (United States of America v Iran)* (1979) ICJ Reports 7, 19 (Order of December 15) and Judgment, 1980 ICJ Reports 3, para 92, 43 (24 May 1980); and *Arrest Warrant of 11 April 2000 (Democratic Republic of the Congo v Belgium)*, Provisional Measures, 2000 ICJ Reports 182 (Order of December 8).

[95] ILC, 'Draft Articles on State Responsibility' (above n 24), Art 1 (Comm 4), Art 12 (Comm 6), Art 26 (Comms 3 and 5), Pt 2 (ch III Comms), Art 40 (Comms 2–5), Art 42 (Comms 11 and 12) and Art 48 (Comms 1 and 6).

of those high purposes which are the raison d'être of the Convention'.[96] Commentators have increasingly relied upon the *Barcelona Traction* distinction between a particular interest of a member of the community and the general interest of the community independent of its members.[97] When the UN Human Rights Committee published 'General Comment 31' on the ICCPR, it had the international community as a whole in mind, stating that the 'basic rights of the human person' are erga omnes, and therefore each state member has 'a legal interest in the performance *by every other State party* of its obligations'.[98] Such a sense of an international community explains why the Committee held in 'General Comment 24' that some human rights norms may not be the subject of reservations in treaties.[99] The international community as a whole has been considered the referent of analysis in a surprising number of domestic judicial decisions involving human rights.[100]

B. Jus Cogens

A second and related context manifesting the referent, the international community as a whole, has concerned the emergence of peremptory or jus cogens norms. Peremptory norms have been considered binding since the late eighteenth century.[101] Indeed, universally shared norms were accepted in the late Roman Republic.[102] The text most often cited for this second context of the international community as a whole is the Vienna Treaty on Treaties.[103] Article 53 provides that a peremptory norm is 'accepted and recognized by the international community of States as a whole'. No state may derogate from the norm. Article 53 continues that the norm may be 'modified only by a subsequent norm of general international law having the same character'. The ICJ has consistently held that peremptory norms

---

[96] *Reservations to the Convention on the Prevention and Punishment of the Crime of Genocide* (advisory opinion), ICJ Rep 1951, 15, at 23, also reported in 18 ILR 364.

[97] Crawford, *Creation of States* (above n 9) 102, 148–50 and 158–60; Simma and Alston (above n 32) 103; H Mosler, 'The International Society as a Legal Community' (1974) 140 *Recueil des Cours* 11, 19; and Frowein (above n 32) 757.

[98] HRC, 'General Comment 31' (above n 16) 243, para 2 (emphasis added).

[99] UN Human Rights Committee (HRC), 'General Comment 24: Issues Relating to Reservations Made upon Ratification or Accession to the Covenant or the Optional Protocols Thereto, or in Relation to Declarations under Article 41 of the Covenant' (4 November 1994), UN Doc CCPR/C/21/Rev.1/Add.6, www.refworld.org/docid/453883fc11.html, para 8.

[100] A list of domestic judicial decisions is listed in *Prosecutor v Anto Furundzija*, Case No IT-95-17/1-A, Appeals Chamber, (2002) ILR 213, para 151 (21 July 2000), 58 n 170.

[101] *Filartiga* (above n 89) 885–88.

[102] See Cicero, *On Duties*, MT Griffin and EM Atkins (eds) (Cambridge, Cambridge University Press, 1991) 3.23 and 3.69; Cicero, *Partitiones Oratoriae*, H Rackam (trans) (Cambridge, MA, Harvard University Press, 1942) 37.129–37.130; and Cicero, 'Commonwealth' in JEG Zetzel (ed), *On the Commonwealth and On the Laws*, (Cambridge, Cambridge University Press, 1999) 3.33.

[103] Vienna Convention on the Law of Treaties (1969) 1155 UNTS 331.

exist by virtue of their relation to the international community as an end in itself.[104]

The Vienna Treaty recognizes peremptory norms as of 'the international community *of States* as a whole'. And yet a close reading of the various references to the community in international law discourse suggests that the community is much wider than a state-centric international community. The *Barcelona Traction* Court excised 'of states' from the reference in Article 53 of the Vienna Treaty. The ILC has never limited the international community as a whole' to a community of states, according to James Crawford.[105] Indeed, most treaty references and judicial decisions do not restrict the community to that of states members only. Although Crawford suggests that the formulation 'the international community as a whole' does not signify a single legal person,[106] various textual contexts of the ILC State Responsibility Articles suggest that 'the international community as a whole' represents a single discrete legal entity. Whether it is considered a social or a legal entity will be left for discussion in later chapters. Of course, the 'international community as a whole' would not likely be considered a discrete legal entity so long as jurists presuppose that the community is constituted from the aggregated wills of states.

There is much to suggest, however, that the international community is a legal entity. Article 64 of the Vienna Treaty, for example, renders void and 'terminates' any treaty norm if the norm contradicts the international community as a whole.[107] A treaty provision may be severed and a treaty considered void if it derogates from a peremptory norm[108] or even if it does so incidentally.[109] A dissenting opinion of the Human Rights Committee has

---

[104] See, eg, *USA v Iran* (above n 94) 19; and *Legal Consequences of the Construction of a Wall in the Occupied Palestinian Territory* (Advisory Opinion) (2004) 136 ICJ 199, para 157. See also *East Timor (Portugal v Australia)* (1995) 90 ICJ Reports 102 (Judgement) and 172–73 and 213–16 (dissenting opinion of Judge Weeramantry); *Military and Paramilitary Activities in and against Nicaragua (Nicaragua v United States of America)* (Merits) (1986) 14 ICJ Rep 100, para 190 (27 June 1986); and *Prosecutor v Anto Furundzija* (ICTY Trial Chamber), Case No IT-95-17/1-T (Judgment of 10 December 1998), reported in 121 ILR 218, 260–62 (paras 151–57). Judge Weeramantry in *East Timor* gave an extensive list of international court decisions in which erga omnes is incorporated into international legal discourse.

[105] ILC, 'Draft Articles on State Responsibility' (above n 24) 40.

[106] Ibid.

[107] This point is developed by Crawford, *Creation of States* (above n 9) 102. See also Vienna Convention on the Law of Treaties (above n 103) Art 45; and ILC, 'Draft Articles on State Responsibility' (above n 24) Art 23 (Comm 5).

[108] Vienna Convention on the Law of Treaties (above n 103).

[109] Ibid, Art 44(5): 'In cases falling under Articles 51, 52, and 53, no separation of the provisions of the treaty is permitted.' See *Kennedy v Trinidad and Tobago*, HRC, Communication No 845/1999 (31 December 1999), UN Doc CCPR/C/67/D/845/1999 (2 November 1999), para 6.7. Even the dissenting opinion expressed in para 8, 'It goes without saying that a State party could not submit a reservation that offends peremptory rules of international law.' Also note HRC, 'General Comment 24' (above n 99) para 8, Art 18: 'Because of the special character of a human rights treaty, the compatibility of a reservation with the object and purpose of the covenant must be established objectively, by reference to legal principles . . . The normal consequence of an unacceptable reservation is not the Covenant will not be in

stated, 'It goes without saying that a State party could not submit a reservation that offends peremptory rules of international law.'[110] Moreover, according to the American Law Institute's *Third Restatement of the Law on Foreign Relations*, 'provisions in the Covenant that represent customary international law (and a fortiori when they have the character of peremptory norms) may not be the subject of reservation'.[111] Peremptory norms may void customary norms and general principles of international law as well as treaty provisions.[112] A series of other treaties expressly hold out how the peremptory norms of 'the international community as a whole' displace the boundary of the residuary of international community.[113] Such a displacement will be examined in more detail in chapter eight.

The ICJ has highlighted the relation of peremptory norms to the international community as a whole.[114] The *Barcelona Traction* judgment offers examples of peremptory norms: 'the outlawing of acts of aggression, and of genocide, as also from the principles and rules concerning the basic rights of the human person, including protection from slavery and racial discrimination'.[115] The ILC 'Draft Articles on State Responsibility' take for granted that a peremptory norm trumps the reserved and protected internal jurisdiction in the content of the reserved domain.[116] The basis of the trumping, indeed, is the consistent appeal to the 'international community as a whole'.[117] The ICJ has asserted that peremptory norms include the outlawing of acts of aggression and of genocide, the basic rights of the human person, including protection from slavery and racial discrimination, and the right of self-determination.[118] The American *Third Restatement* also enumerates the following as peremptory norms: the prohibition

---

effect at all for a reserving party. Rather, such a reservation will generally be severable, in the sense that the Covenant will be operative for the reserving party without benefit of the reservation.'

[110] *Kennedy v Trinidad and Tobago* (ibid).

[111] American Law Institute (above n 93) para 313 (Comm c).

[112] This point is developed by Crawford, *Creation of States* (above n 9) 102.

[113] See above n 27.

[114] See also *Legal Consequences of the Construction of a Wall in the Occupied Palestinian Territory*, Advisory Opinion of 9 July 2004, 2004 ICJ 136, para 157, 199. See also especially *East Timor* (above n 104) 102, 172 and 213–16 (dissenting opinion of Judge Weeramantry); *Military and Paramilitary Activities* (above n 104) 100 (para 190); *Barcelona Traction* (above n 28) para 33; *Legality of the Threat or Use of Nuclear Weapons* (Advisory Opinion) (1996) ICJ Rep 226, 257 (para 79); and *Prosecutor v Anto Furundzija* (ICTY Trial Chamber), Case No IT-95-17/1-T, Judgment of 10 December 1998, 260–62 paras 151–57, also reported in (1998) 121 ILR 218.

[115] *Barcelona Traction* (above n 28) paras 33–34 and 36. See also the Independent Opinion of Judge Fitzmaurice, paras 33 and 38.

[116] ILC, 'Draft Articles on State Responsibility' (above n 24) 148–50 and 158–60. See also the Vienna Convention on the Law of Treaties (above n 103) Arts 55 and 64.

[117] ILC, 'Draft Articles on State Responsibility' (above n 24) 148–50 and 158–60. See also Simma and Alston (above n 32) 103; Mosler (above n 97) 19; and Frowein (above n 32).

[118] *Barcelona Traction* (above n 28) para 33. See also *East Timor* (above n 104) para 29; and *Legality of the Threat or Use of Nuclear Weapons* (above n 114) para 79. See generally ILC, 'Draft Articles on State Responsibility' (above n 24) Art 48 (Comm 9) and Art 40 (Comms 2–6).

against the use of force, torture, enslavement, mass internal displacement, mass disappearances and the right to self-determination.[119] The *Restatement* expresses that several rights in human rights treaties are peremptory.[120] The notion of 'an international community as a whole' has also figured in an increasingly large number of domestic tribunals.[121]

What is crucial in all this is that the traditionally reserved domain of law-making and law administration of the international community is increasingly being destabilized in favour of an international community independent of the state. Given that two senses of an international community are embodied in international legal discourse, the risk is that the adoption of the one against the other will at best be implicit. The mere citation of a norm as jus cogens may well identify a law but hardly explains why the law is obligatory for state members to fulfil and enforce. That explanation, I am offering, depends upon the nexus of the peremptory norm as an existence condition of the international community as a whole. The reserved domain is certainly a fundamental element of the ethos of one international community. But the destabilization of the boundary of that domain suggests the ethos of a very different international community.

C. The Humanitarian Law of Armed Conflict

The enigma of the international community is manifested in a third discursive context: humanitarian law. Certain international criminal law offences are codified in the Geneva Conventions (1949), the Statutes establishing the tribunals relating to the former Yugoslavia and Rwanda, and the Rome Treaty establishing the International Criminal Court.[122]

The commonly ratified Geneva Convention IV particularly provides protection of civilian non-combatants. Although ratified less widely, Protocol 1 includes stateless persons as protected persons (Article 73).

---

[119] American Law Institute (above n 93) para 702. Jean Allain has added the principle of non-refoulement as a peremptory norm: J Allain, 'The Jus Cogens Nature of Non-refoulement' (2001) 13 *International Journal of Refugee Law* 533, 533. Ulf Linderfalk has argued that the logical consequence of peremptory norms is to render the list far wider than has hitherto been considered: U Linderfalk, 'The Effect of Jus Cogens Norms: Whoever Opened Pandora's Box, Did You Ever Think Sbout the Consequences?' (2008) 18 *European Journal of International Law* 853, 853.

[120] American Law Institute (above n 93) para 701 (Rep note 6) and para 702. See also para 331.

[121] *Bartle (Pinochet)* (above n 30); *Al-Adsani* (above n 31) 273; and *Filartiga* (above n 89).

[122] Conventions I–IV (Geneva, 12 August 1949); Protocol Additional to the Geneva Conventions of 12 August 1949, and relating to the Protection of Victims of International Armed Conflicts (Protocol 1) (8 June 1977); Statute of the International Criminal Tribunal for the Former Yugoslavia (25 May 1993), reprinted in (1993) 14 *Human Rights Law Journal* 211; and Statute of the International Criminal Tribunal for Rwanda (8 November 1994), reprinted in (1994) 33 *International Legal Materials* 1590.

State officials may be personally liable for offences, likened to indictable (that is, felony) offences and described in the Convention as 'grave breaches'. Most importantly, common to all four Geneva Conventions, Article 3 addresses harm caused to 'persons taking no active part in the hostilities' 'in the case of armed conflict not of an international character'. Harm includes 'violence to life and person' and 'outrages upon personal dignity, in particular humiliating and degrading treatment'. Article 44 of the Geneva Convention IV states that refugees unprotected by any government may not be treated as 'enemy aliens'. Protocol l adds new principles to the Geneva Convention, not least of which is Article 73, by which stateless persons prior to the beginning of hostilities 'shall be protected persons . . . in all circumstances and without any adverse distinction'. The deportation of natural persons and the forced transfer of civilians are considered war crimes and crimes against humanity during armed conflict. So too the trumping character of the norms of the international community as a whole transcend the discrete rules and rights against the wilful causing of great suffering, serious injury to a natural person's body or health, forced pregnancy, sexual slavery, enforced prostitution and any other form of sexual violence. Such an independence of humanitarian norms vis-à-vis states is also manifested by humanitarian proscriptions against widespread or systematic attacks on national, political, ethnic, racial or religious grounds.

IV. LEGAL OBLIGATION AND STATELESSNESS

The enigma of statelessness in an international community and the destabilization of the boundary of internal jurisdiction cannot be understood nor resolved by the usual quest for the identity of a legal rule, right or test identified in terms of Article 38 sources. The state, as the ultimate source, is represented by treaties and customary norms as well as principles and commentaries about the expression of states. Article 38 of the ICJ Statute has generally been used as an itemized account of the sources.[123] Instead, the enigma of the international community presses jurists to ask the question: why is an identifiable law obligatory or binding upon a state member?

To be sure, the sources thesis assumes an explanation of legal obligation. Each of the Article 38 sources – the express consent in a treaty, the implied consent of a customary norm, the shared domestic general principles of 'civilized societies' and opinio juris – presupposes an international community that is the aggregate of its members states. As noted in section II above, the enigma remains if one adopts or assumes a sense of an international community that privileges and protects a bounded residuary of

---

[123] Statute of the International Court of Justice, 961 UNTS 183, TS No 993 (US), Art 38.

law-making and law administration of nationality by state members. And the boundary of the community's residuary, represented by internal jurisdiction, has been found dissolving in the above three discursive areas of public international law. The enigma begs that one ask the question whether there is a language about an international community that is independent of such a bounded residuary and offers a very different understanding of legal obligation on the part of state members.

The residuary of the international community has had two features related to the production of statelessness. First, the residuary protects the internal jurisdiction to confer, withhold and withdraw nationality from natural persons. Second, any discrete rule is legally identifiable if it can be justified as the exercise of law-making or law administration inside the boundary of the residuary. The institutions (legislatures, administrators, courts, tribunals, governmental agencies, governmental officials) representing and exercising internal jurisdiction constitute the ultimate source to which a rule (or principle or doctrine or social norm) is justified. Third, the executive arm of the state represents the state in the state's relations with other states. Since nationality has signified a natural person's membership or protected legal status in the international community, the executive arm of a state has traditionally been left with the authority to withhold or withdraw nationality in its relations with other states. Bringing these three features together, the legal obligation of a state to recognize or protect a natural person without a nationality has rested with the consent of the state in matters of nationality. An international standard is considered binding upon a state only if the state has expressly or implicitly consented to the standard. Accordingly, the content of the domain is exclusive of external intervention. A state's discrete law, enacted or administered inside the boundary of the international community's residuary, is identified as a law obligated by the sources. The legal obligation depends upon the background ethos of an international community. The residuary is a critical feature of such an ethos.

If the enigma is to be understood, we must review the nature of legal obligation independent of the quest for the identity of a legal rule in an institutional source of the state. A brief retrieval of international legal discourse concerning human rights, jus cogens and humanitarian law suggests a sense of legal obligation that departs from the consent of state members. International law discourse has explicitly addressed the nature of legal obligation in terms of the legal bond between natural person and state. The international community as the aggregated will of states has taken the allegiance of a natural person towards a state as the basis of the legal bond. We shall see in chapter six below that the state alone has been left with the freedom to decide whether someone possesses such an allegiance to a state. The discourse about the international community as a whole, however, suggests a very different sense of a legal bond. In this circumstance, the legal bond rests with the location where a natural person has experienced social relationships with other natural persons. The legal bond is thereby independent of a relation to a state; rather, the state functions as a third party to the social relationship. Legal obligation has shifted with the emergence of the legal bond as a social bond. The natural person is now a subject of the legal objectivity represented by the international community as a whole. And with such shifts, the enigma of statelessness in an international community dissolves.

The challenge is to document how domestic and international judicial and quasi-judicial tribunals are increasingly appealing to social bonding as the legal bond. If this can be documented and argued, the absence of nationality conferred by a state along with the discursive doctrines (reserved domain, universality of human rights, jus cogens, humanitarian rights, the legal bond, sources, and the identity of 'by law', 'lawfulness', 'according to law' and 'by operation of its law') do not finalize legal analysis. To the contrary.

Where is the boundary of the state's internal jurisdiction? And is the state alone free to determine this boundary? Although the international community as the aggregate of state wills does not prohibit actions producing statelessness, a rule also affirms the validity of denaturalization if the natural person possesses nationality in another state.[124] Although international standards are said to limit the consequences of statelessness,[125] consequences of statelessness burden the natural person, as outlined below in chapter three. The enigma does not pose the question 'what is the source of a rule?' but instead requires that one ask, 'Why is such a justified rule only a presumption rather than a state obligation?' That question, the ILC has admitted, is 'another matter'.[126] The response to the enigma is not just 'another matter'.

The 'other matter' lies behind the day-to-day legal issues involving natural persons who lack de jure or effective nationality. Why is an identifiable rule enacted, administered or judicially interpreted as obligatory for a state if natural persons remain unrecognized in the international community? For example, if a natural person lacks a state's conferral of nationality, does s/he lack legal obligations to obey the state's laws or, for that matter, international standards? Is a state legally obligated to extend international standards in order to protect alleged insurgents who are effectively stateless? If so, for example, is prolonged detention without criminal charge

---

[124] See, eg, R Hoffmann, 'Denaturalization and Forced Exile' in R Bernhardt (ed), *Encyclopaedia of Public International Law*, vol 1 (Amsterdam, Elsevier Science Publishers, 1992) 1006.

[125] See, eg, ILC, 'Expulsion of Aliens' (above n 43) paras 894–95.

[126] Crawford, commenting on the Special Rapporteur's Report summary records, 'State Succession and Its Impact on the Nationality of Natural and Legal Persons' (23 May 1995), *ILC Yearbook 1995*, vol I, 60, para 42.

now legally permissible in such cases? Do states or the international community possess obligations to protect de jure stateless persons? Effectively stateless persons? Are the members of alleged terrorist organizations, who often lack nationality or at least lack the protection of a state, obligated to follow international legal standards? Do states possess a duty to admit de jure stateless persons? Or to admit such persons expeditiously and without detention?[127] If a stateless person finds her/himself on a state's territory, may s/he be expelled 'by law' from the state's territory?[128] Does 'by law' infer that a judicial review must precede the expulsion?[129] Do states possess legal obligation to protect their nationals if other states refuse to recognize their conferral of nationality? Does harm caused to stateless persons impact upon harm to the international community as a whole? If so, are the domestic remedies of *delict* or tort now extended to harm caused to de jure or effectively stateless persons? Are there ramifications for the role of the judiciary, doctrines such as state immunity and due process, or the very nature and identity of law?

Even more day-to-day legal issues are being addressed about de jure stateless persons in domestic and international tribunals, issues which beg investigation into the nature of legal obligation by a state towards de jure or effectively stateless persons. As a stateless person, does one possess a 'country of one's own' if one lacks de jure nationality? If not, does such a person possess a right to re-enter the territory where s/he has developed strong social relationships? Can someone lacking de jure nationality still possess the legal capacity to initiate an international or domestic law claim against a state? Does s/he or her/his estate possess the legal capacity to launch a claim if expelled without due process, if assets have been confiscated by the state or if life has been lost?

[127] African [Banjul] Charter (above n 27) Art 12. Art 9(4) of the ICCPR (above n 17) provides, 'Anyone who is deprived of his liberty by arrest or detention shall be entitled to take proceedings before a court, in order that that court may decide without delay on *the lawfulness of his detention* and order his release if the detention is not lawful' (emphasis added). Art 9(5) continues, 'Anyone who has been a victim of unlawful arrest or detention shall have an enforceable right to compensation.' Art 9 of the ICCPR also provides, 'No one shall be deprived of his liberty except on such grounds and in accordance with such procedures [as] are *established by law*' (emphasis added).

[128] Eg, ICCPR (above n 17) Art 13; African [Banjul] Charter (above n 27) Art 12(2) and (4); Convention Relating to the Status of Stateless Persons (above n 1) Art 31; European Convention on Nationality (1997), 2 ETS 166 (entered into force 3 January 2000) 2–12; UN Declaration on the Human Rights of Individuals Who Are Not Nationals of the Country in which They Live, Resolution 40/144 (13 December 1985); Protocol 7 of the European Convention on Human Rights, Art 1; Protocol 7 to the Convention for the Protection of Human Rights and Fundamental Freedoms, as amended by Protocol No 11 (Rome, 4 November 1959), entered into force 3 September 1953, ETS No 5; and the American Convention on Human Rights (1969) 36 OASTS 1, OAS Off Rec OEA/Ser.L./V/11.23 doc. rev.2. (entered into force 18 July 1978) Art 22(6).

[129] ICCPR (above n 17) Art 13 requires 'a review' or 'a decision' involving the expulsion, although the review may take place after the expulsion and it is unclear whether it may be only performed by a government official.

Let us take one right as an example. Article 12(1) of the ICCPR provides: 'Everyone lawfully within the territory of a state shall, within that territory, have the right to liberty of movement and freedom to choose his residence.' Article 12(3) continues that such rights 'shall not be subject to any restrictions except those which are provided *by law* . . . and are consistent with the other rights recognized in the present Covenant'.[130] If we take the requisite of 'by law', do we return to the legislated enactments or administrative acts authored by a statute when we appreciate that such also returns us to an international community as aggregated state wills, of which statelessness is a consequence? In particular, is a de jure stateless person 'lawfully within the territory of a state'? Does s/he possess liberty of movement and freedom to choose her/his residence on a state's territory without jurists examining the nature of legal obligation underlying the international community with a bounded residuary of law-making and law administration? Does the stateless person possess equal legal rights with nationals without such an examination?[131] Can a de jure stateless person be lawfully within the territory of a state if the state's executive has acted arbitrarily or in bad faith in the interpretation of Article 12? Indeed, is bad faith attached to executive or judicial decisions if the decisions contradict or undermine the nature of legal obligation in the international community as a whole?

Is a natural person 'lawfully' on any territory of the globe if s/he has not been recognized as a national by any state on the globe? If not, how can the universality of jurisdiction and of human rights gain effectiveness if such natural persons are not lawfully in any territory on the globe? Does a stateless person possess mobility rights inside the territory of a state? Does a stateless person possess the freedom to choose residence? Can any of these issues be addressed without also asking whether the content of a state's law is obligatory?

One may address the above issues by seeking rules inscribed in the traditional domestic and international law sources. The sources rest in the explicit consent (by a treaty) or the implicit consent (by a customary norm) of a state member of the international community. The social-cultural relationships presupposed in the content of state's internal jurisdiction are immune from legal scrutiny. The content is independent of the justificatory trace of domestic rules to the state-centric sources of a treaty or customary international norm. And yet the historical contingency of the content of the internal jurisdiction becomes crucial. As the Permanent Court of International Justice, itself the source of one particular shape of an international community, stated in 1923, the exclusive internal jurisdiction of a state is 'an essentially relative question; it depends upon the

---

[130] ICCPR (above n 17) Art 12(3).
[131] Ibid, Arts 14(1), 16, 17(2) and 26.

development of international relations'.[132] The exclusionary character of the reserved domain of the state left to the state member may be dissolving in favour of an international community dependent upon the place of experienced social relationships of natural persons. One is hard-pressed to respond competently to these issues without also addressing the nature of legal obligation in the international community as a whole. One also needs to enquire whether the boundary of the residuary of the state-centric international community is dissolving in favour of a very different international community.

V. CONCLUSION

Just as the freedom of the state emerged as the dominant shape of an international community by the end of the nineteenth century and the early twentieth century, so too an international community is now emerging, displacing the boundary of the residuary inside which a state has possessed the legal authority to confer, withdraw or withhold nationality to natural persons. The clue to the emergent international community, for the purpose of understanding the enigma of statelessness, concerns the boundary encircling the residuary. The conferral of nationality has traditionally been considered an incident of the residuary. States have been considered free to choose the members of the international community. That membership for the purposes of inter-state relations has been signified by nationality. The question that needs to be now addressed concerns the boundary of the reserved and protected residuary of which nationality has been an incident in the surface shape of the international community.

The boundary of internal jurisdiction vis-à-vis the international community has increasingly dissolved in such areas as human rights, jus cogens and humanitarian law. Effective nationality has opened legal inquiry into the content of domestic laws hitherto protected as the state's internal jurisdiction. The social content of the residuary has concerned the social relationships and bonding of individuals independent of the state's domestic conferral or withdrawal of formal nationality. The state is not the ultimate referent in these developments. The referent of analysis is a sense of the international community that exists independent of the aggregate will of states.

In sum, the social-cultural content inside the boundary of internal state jurisdiction, otherwise immunized from scrutiny, now constitutes the existence condition of the international community as a whole. Effective nationality represents one such existence condition of the latter community.

---

[132] *Tunis and Morocco Nationality Decrees* (Advisory Opinion) (1923) PCIJ (Ser B) No 4, 7, 24, also reported in (1923) 2 ILR 349.

Effective nationality draws from the very social relationships embodying the ethos of a community. An international community could not exist as a community if its standards were not obligatory. And the exclusionary character of the boundary of the reserved domain undermines the obligatory nature of a law enacted or adjudicated inside the boundary of the domain. Effective nationals are excluded as stateless in the first shape of an international community. Such a 'community' mimics Haemon's exclamation against his father that a 'place for one man alone is not a city'.[133] When the King replied, 'A city belongs to its master. Isn't that the rule?' Haemon quite rightly responded, 'Then go be ruler of a desert, all alone. You'd do it well.' The absence of effective nationality undermines the very obligatory character of domestic laws, let alone international legal standards.

The enigma of the stateless condition in a discourse that claims universal protection to everyone suggests that we put the sources thesis to the side in favour of an enquiry about the nature of legal obligation. We are not quite ready for such an enquiry, however. After all, one might well react to this prospect of legal obligation by suggesting that such a concern is an academic issue with little practical import. I shall address such a reaction by looking to the social consequences of de jure statelessness in chapter three. One might well also react that we have an architecture of human rights treaties and customary international legal norms. I shall address this response in chapters four and five by arguing that de jure statelessness remains, treaties and customary norms notwithstanding. I shall then turn in chapter six to the legal bond as a feature of the nature of legal obligation.

Before I proceed along these lines, one important obstacle stands before us. We are encouraged by pedagogues, judges and state officials to react to my argument with the claim that my line of inquiry involves an idealized international community. However, I emphasized early in this chapter that I am describing legal reality, and the international community as a whole is one such reality. The state-centric international community and the incident of nationality in internal jurisdiction are discursively contingent events. The next chapter renders this latter claim apparent.

---

[133] Sophocles, *Antigone*, P Woodruff (ed and trans) (Indianapolis, Hackett, 2001) line 737.

2

The Discursive Contingency of an International Community

THE CONTEMPORARY STATE-CENTRIC international community is not an uncontrolled and uncontrollable 'given' in public
international law. Indeed, Adda Bozeman in her classic work *Politics
and Culture in International History* identified at least seven fundamentally
different international communities in international history.[1] The residuary
of an international community of equal secular state members historically
emerged from a very different community – Christendom – with its own
universalist pretentions.[2] As Carl Schmitt argued, the universality of the
international community of Christendom was absorbed by and represented by a universality of the territorial jurisdiction of each secular state.[3]
The residuary of the modern international community had been represented by the canons of the Roman Church. No external religious organization could interfere with the content of the Church's canons. With the
rise of secular European states, universalism was transformed into the
state's reserved domain. The reserved domain is more commonly described
today as 'internal' or 'domestic' jurisdiction. The domain represented a
'catch-all' for law-making and law administration in the international
community. The conferral, withdrawal and withholding of nationality
eventually became an incident of such a domain.

This chapter aims to elaborate the discursive contingency of an international community. By doing so, I shall set the stage for the possibility
that de jure statelessness is contingent upon a discursively particular sense
of international community, one that is struggling and being displaced by
the notion of the international community as a whole. Section I of this
chapter describes the emergence of a state-centric international community from the universality of Christendom. Section II highlights the role of
the natural person in the early modern international community. The

---

[1] A Bozeman, *Politics and Culture in International History: From the Ancient Near East to the
Opening of the Modern Age* (New Brunswick, NJ, Transaction Publishers, 1994).
[2] WE Conklin, 'The Exclusionary Character of the Early Modern International Community'
(2012) 81 *Nordic Journal of International Law* 133, 138–54.
[3] C Schmitt, *The Nomos of the Earth: In the International Law of the Jus Publicum Europaeum*,
GL Ulmen (trans) (New York, Telos Press, 2006) 56–59, 62–66, 126–38 and 147–48.

state's authority rested upon the voluntary consent and the sociality of the natural person. Section III retrieves several features of the emergence of the state-centric international community: the state's radical title to all land and objects under its control; the state as an end in itself; the state as a self-creative author; the residuary; and nationality. Section IV examines how domestic UK and American courts institutionalized the residuary as a legal doctrine. Although the doctrine crystallized during the First and Second World Wars, courts continued to adhere to it after World War II. Section V turns to three such doctrines: the role of the executive arm of the state; state immunity; and the content of the residuary as 'fact' rather than as 'law'.

I. THE EMERGENCE OF AN EARLY INTERNATIONAL COMMUNITY OF STATES

It is tempting for contemporary jurists to believe that the state-centric international community is an uncontrollable 'legal fact'. The United Nation Charter takes such a 'legal fact' for granted, with Article 2(7) stating, 'Nothing contained in the present Charter shall authorize the United Nations to intervene in matters which are essentially within the internal jurisdiction of any State . . .' The conferral, withholding and withdrawal of nationality have been incidents of internal jurisdiction and the accompanying prerogative of the executive in nationality matters. Other incidents, such as expulsion of stateless persons or their prolonged detention, are part and parcel of the universal jurisdiction of the state inside its reserved domain. What is missed in the quest for the identity of a nationality law in the sources protected by the reserved domain is that the domain was not an a priori concept but the manifestation of a discursively contingent sense of an international community.

Some jurists have asserted that the present state-centric international community took form only during the early seventeenth century.[4] I argue that there are two present forms of 'international community'. Further, a state-centric international community did not suddenly begin at a specific

---

[4] M Koskenniemi, *From Apology to Utopia: The Structure of International Legal Argument (Reissue with a New Epilogue)* (Cambridge, Cambridge University Press, 2005) 74–85; M Koskenniemi, *The Gentle Civilizer of Nations: The Rise and Fall of International Law, 1870–1960* (Cambridge, Cambridge University Press, 2001) 4, 17 and 406–11; H Lauterpacht, 'The Grotian Tradition in International Law' in E Lauterpacht (ed), *International Law: Collected Papers of Hersch Lauterpacht*, vol 2 (Cambridge, Cambridge University Press, 1975) 307–65; and H Lauterpacht, 'Private Law Sources and Analogies of International Law' in Lauterpacht E (ed), *International Law: The Collected Papers of Hersch Lauterpacht*, vol 2 (Cambridge, Cambridge University Press, 1975), 189. However, see M Koskenniemi, 'Empire and International Law: The Real Spanish Contribution' (2011) 61 *University of Toronto Law Journal* 1.

date (usually posited as the Treaty of Westphalia (1648)).[5] Rather, the state-centric international community was foreshadowed by the city-states of Renaissance Italy during the eleventh to thirteenth centuries.[6] Such a community expanded during the sixteenth and seventeenth centuries to the governmental structures of England, France and Denmark, each of which claimed universality of title over all territory within their borders.[7] A state-centric international community continued to expand to the Lowlands and Portugal, and by the late nineteenth century, it had extended to central Europe.

The key to this emerging international community was the universality inside its residuary of law-making. Such universality characterized Roman Stoicism, as well as the Roman Church.[8] Each form of universality assumed a boundary that excluded non-members from its scope.[9] Otto Gierke described the Christendom as 'a single, universal Community, founded and governed by God himself'.[10] The universalism did not include all natural persons, to be sure, for non-Christians were excluded from the community. The universalism of Christendom eventually dissipated in favour of a

---

[5] Actually, the Westphalia Treaty represented two separate treaties, the Treaties of Münster and Osnabrück. The Treaty of Münster continued to defer to the Empire: 'Such alliances be not against the Emperor, and the Empire, nor against the Publick Peace, and this Treaty, and without prejudice to the Oath by which everyone is bound to the Emperor and the Empire.' The Duke of Saxony, the Margrave of Brandenburg, the Count of Palatine and the Duke of Bavaria chose the Emperor.

[6] Bozeman, *Politics and Culture in International History* (above n 1); FH Hinsley, *Power and the Pursuit of Peace: The Theory and Practice in the History of the Relations between States* (Cambridge, Cambridge University Press, 1963). Joseph Strayer located a system of equal secular states around 1000 CE: J Strayer, *On the Medieval Origins of the Modern State* (Princeton, Princeton University Press, 1970) 10.

[7] AB Bozeman, 'An Introduction to Various Cultural Traditions of International Law: A Preliminary Assessment' in P-M Dupuy (ed), *The Future of International Law in a Multicultural World* (Netherlands, Samson-Sijhoff, 1993); and Bozeman, *Politics and Culture in International History* (above n 1).

[8] For Roman stoicism, for example, see Seneca, 'Letter XC' in R Campbell, *Seneca: Letters from a Stoic* (Hammondsworth, Penguin, 1969) 161–77; Seneca, 'On Leisure' in *Moral Essays*, vol 2, JW Basore (trans) (Cambridge, MA, Harvard University Press, 1932) 2.1–3; Cicero, *On Duties*, MT Griffin and EM Atkins (eds) (Cambridge, Cambridge University Press, 1991) 3.23, 3.26, 3.47 and 3.69; Cicero, *Partitiones Oratoriae*, H Rackam (trans) (Cambridge, MA, Harvard University Press, 1942) 37.129–37.130; and Cicero, 'Commonwealth' in *On the Commonwealth and On the Laws*, JEG Zetzel (ed) (Cambridge, Cambridge University Press, 1999) 3.33. For further texts, see AA Long and DN Sedley, *The Hellenistic Philosophers*, vol (Cambridge, Cambridge University Press, 1987) 179–83 and 429–37.

[9] For discussion of the early modern state, see generally JN Figgis, *Political Thought from Gerson to Grotius: 1414–1625* (New York, Harper, 1960). See also H Bull, *The Anarchical Society: A Study of Order in World Politics* (London, Macmillan, 1977) 27–33; H Bull, 'The Emergence of a Universal International Society' in H Bull and A Watson (eds), *The Expansion of International Society* (New York, Oxford University Press, 1984) 117–20; A Watson, 'European International Society and Its Expansion' in Bull and Watson (eds) (above) 13–17; and O Gierke, *Political Theories of the Middle Ages* (Boston, Beacon Hill, 1958) 18–19. See also Conklin, 'The Exclusionary Character' (above n 2) 138–46; and WE Conklin, 'The Myth of Primordialism in Cicero's Theory of *Jus Gentium*' (2010) 23 *Leiden Journal of International Law* 479.

[10] Gierke (ibid) 10. See also Figgis (ibid) 18–20.

residuary claimed by each state member. By the late eighteenth century, Immanuel Kant (1724–1804) was elaborating a theory of a league of self-creative and self-determining states. By the early nineteenth century, GWF Hegel (1770–1831) was urging the breakup of the dozens of Germanic principalities in central Europe in favour of a single secular state. The United States of America introduced passports to signify membership.[11] The theocratic empires of Europe and the multiplicity of principalities in central Europe collapsed in favour of self-defining and self-reliant states. Anglo-American jurists of the nineteenth century elaborated how the institutional sources of each self-reliant state closed off legal analysis.[12] Soon, the Ottoman and Chinese empires collapsed into secular states. And traditional (namely tribal) societies were assimilated into the legal culture of a state-centric international community. The incident of nationality in the state's universal authority was just one consequence of the residuary of this international community.

The discursively prior universal community of Christendom is important for our purposes for several reasons. For one thing, it contrasts with the emergent state-centric international community: instead of a universal oneness, there emerged a plurality of equal law-enacting entities. Second, the international community of Christendom was of a metaphysical, not territorial, character. Third, universality existed inside the internal jurisdiction of a state's legal authority. There still was an international community, but its members were now autonomous of the community, much as individual citizens were considered free of the state's authority. International standards could only supplement internal laws. Such standards could constrain consequences only after a domestic law had been enacted or enforced. This was especially so with domestic laws regarding nationality. The notion of legal persons who have legal status in the international community devolved into the freedom of a state to choose its own (and the international community's) members.

II. THE ROLE OF THE NATURAL PERSON IN THE EARLY MODERN INTERNATIONAL COMMUNITY

An important feature of the emerging state-centric international community highlighted the role of the natural person. Early modern jurists

[11] See generally J Torpey, *The Invention of the Passport: Surveillance, Citizenship and the State* (Cambridge, Cambridge University Press, 2000); and S Goulbourne, 'Introduction' in S Goulbourne (ed), *Law and Migration*, vol 6 (Cheltanham, Elgar Reference Collection, 1998).

[12] See A Anghie, *Imperialism, Sovereignty and the Making of International Law* (Cambridge, Cambridge University Press, 2004). See also generally P Weil, 'The Transformation of Immigration Policies: Immigration Control and Nationality Laws in Europe – A Comparative Approach' in Academy of European Law (ed), *Collected Courses of the Academy of European Law*, vol 7 (The Hague, Kluwer Law International, 1999) bk 2 (87) 106, 110 and113; and WE Conklin, *Invisible Origins of Legal Positivism* (Dordrecht, Kluwer, 2001) 57–61 and 137–70.

acknowledged that sociality underlay the legal authority of the state. By this, I mean that the state did not exist as a self-creative legal person. Rather, the state's legal authority was considered dependent upon the social relationships of natural persons. Secondly, no doubt as a consequence of such an analytically prior social relation, the natural person possessed the freedom to choose a state's nationality.[13] This freedom continued even when a territory was ceded or conquered by a state other than that of one's nationality. In addition, the relation of a national to the state of nationality was considered reciprocal: in exchange for your allegiance to a state, the state protected you and your family. Although according to the English courts by the end of the eighteenth century, the state possessed the authority to expel natural persons, it could only do so if authorized by statute, and then only from a protective role over natural persons.[14] Conversely, the state was obligated to admit non-nationals seeking refuge from persecution and oppression. An example was the admission of French Protestants into the Netherlands and England.[15]

A. The Protection of Nationals

The social basis of the state's authority translated into the duty of a state to diplomatically protect a national who found her/himself in another state's territory.[16] Interestingly, even though Emerich de Vattel (1714–67) appears to have been the first European jurist to recognize the *domain réservé* as the 'essence' of the emergent state-centric international community, the state of nationality, he maintained, must protect its nationals against other states: the state 'must avenge the deed and, if possible, force the aggressor to give full satisfaction or punish him, since otherwise the citizen will not obtain the chief end of civil society, which is protection'.[17] *Calvin's Case* (1609) was well known for institutionalizing this obligation of the state to diplomatically protect its nationals.[18] The obligation of diplomatic protection, according to Hugo Grotius (1583–1645), also flowed

[13] The International Law Commission (ILC) states that such opting-out and opting-in are legal options in the contemporary context of the succession of states: ILC, 'Draft Articles on Nationality of Natural Persons in Relation to the Succession of States, with Commentaries', UN Doc A/54/10, *ILC Yearbook 1999*, vol II(2), www.refworld.org/pdfid/4512b6dd4.pdf, Art 11 (Comm 7).

[14] *The East India Company v Sandys* (1664) 10 ST 371, 530–31, as discussed in *R v Immigration Officer at Prague Airport and Another, ex parte European Roma Rights Centre and Others* [2005] 2 AC 1, [2005] 2 WLP 1, para 11.

[15] *R v Immigration Officer at Prague Airport* (ibid) para 12.

[16] Grotius, *Prolegomena to the Law of War and Peace*, F Kelsey (trans) (New York, Liberal Library, 1957) Bk 2, ch 2 (ss 23 and 205).

[17] E de Vattel, *The Law of Nations or the Principles of Natural Law*, G Fenwick (trans) (New York, Klaus Reprint, 1916 [1758]) S 17 (14) and S 71 (136).

[18] *Calvin's Case* (1609) 7 Co Rep 1a, 77 ER 377, 2 Brownl 198, 265 Hard 140 (KB).

from the reciprocal relationship of natural person and state.[19] Grotius was explicit about the situations in which the state was so obligated: 'for the sake of the individual's health, a claim of title over "unoccupied and unproductive territory", food, clothing and medicines, and the purchase of goods "at a fair price"'.[20] Claims Commissions, established under the US–UK Jay Treaty (1794), highlighted a special 'letter of reprisal', which allowed a national to directly litigate against a state that had allegedly caused harm to that individual.[21]

B. The Social Basis of the State's Authority

Although Francisco de Vitoria (1492–1546) highlighted sociality as the 'essence' (to use the UN Charter term) of an international community,[22] intermediate legal principles, presupposing the primacy of sociality in the international community, were elaborated by Francisco Suárez (1548–1617), Grotius and Samuel Pufendorf (1632–94). For Suárez, the legal basis of the state rested in historically contingent and shared customary norms amongst natural persons. Suárez asserted:

> The human race, into howsoever different peoples and kingdoms it may be divided, always preserves a certain community, not only as a species, but . . . enjoined by the natural precept of mutual love and mercy [which] applies to all, even to strangers of every nation.[23]

Grotius extended this idea of sociality by highlighting how the international community of states existed by virtue of such a sociality. With the importance of such sociality, the individual possessed the freedom to choose his own state.[24] Quoting from Cicero, Grotius asserted, 'No one is forced to remain in a state against his will', and further, 'each man's power to retain or to abandon his right [is] the foundation of liberty.'[25] Indeed, according to Grotius, the state could not even expel a foreign national

---

[19] Grotius, *De Jure Praedae Commentarius*, GL Williams (trans), Classics of International Law Series (New York, Carnegie, 1950) Bk 2, ch 2 (ss 23 and 205); and Vattel (above n 17) 136. Diplomatic protection was more like a privilege; Vattel describes it as a 'limited right' rather than a right: as cited in EM Borchard, *The Diplomatic Protection of Citizens Abroad; or The Law of International Claims* (New York, Klaus Reprint, 1970 [1915]) 356. The 'limited right' was exercised by the executive rather than by the judiciary in common law countries.

[20] Grotius, *De Jure* (ibid) Bk 2, ch 2, s 15 (201), s 17 (202) and s 18 (203).

[21] See especially *Mavrommatis Palestine Concessions Case*, PCIJ Ser A, No 2 (1924) 12, also in 2 ILR 27.

[22] Conklin, 'The Exclusionary Character' (above n 2) 145–46.

[23] F Suárez, 'A Treatise on Laws and God the Lawgiver' in J B Scott (ed), *Selections from Three Works by Francisco Suarez*, GL Williams, A Brown and J Waldron (trans) (New York, Oceana, 1981) 348–49, para 9.

[24] Grotius, *Prolegomena* (above n 16) s 15, 201 and ch 2, s 22, 204; and Grotius, *De Jure* (above n 19) ch 5, s 25 (253).

[25] Grotius, *De Jure* (above n 19) Bk 2, ch 5, s 25 (253–54).

once the latter had been admitted into its territory.[26] Indeed, if a foreign state excluded or expelled 'a single people', the state had committed a wrong.[27] This was so because Grotius' understood that each state possessed a *telos*. And the *telos*, in turn, was generated from the innate tendency of natural persons to socialize with each other. Accompanying such a *telos*, legal obligation emerged from an historically contingent unwritten custom.[28] The state–natural person relation has varied in time and place with the contingent social relations of natural persons. Accordingly, the obligatory character of a state's law has rested upon the presupposed social content of internal state jurisdiction.

The state itself was a mere 'convenience' to fulfil the sociality of natural persons.[29] In this regard, the state functioned as an intermediary between natural persons and the international community.[30] As such, a domestic law lacked an obligatory character if the content of the law ignored the prior sociality of natural persons. In this regard, as long as a state protected the social relations of natural persons, the state possessed the 'force of natural liberty' over all objects inside its internal jurisdiction.[31]

Without the governmental institutions of a state, Thomas Hobbes (1603–79) argued, natural persons were laid bare without protection.[32] Legal authority therefore rested upon the success of such protection: 'The obligation of subjects to the sovereign is understood to last as long, and no longer, than the power lasteth by which he is able to protect them ... The end of obedience is protection.'[33] Although one state could not legally extinguish 'the right of a sovereign', the natural person's obligation to the state might dissolve if the individual lost protection from the state.[34] The state's authority depended upon the authorship of the authority by natural persons.[35] As Hobbes put it, 'The Consent of a Subject to Soveraign Power, is contained in these words: 'I *authorise, or take upon me, all his actions*; in which there is no restriction at all, of his own former natural Liberty.'[36] The legal bond between state and natural person, in sum, hinged upon social relationships, manifested by language, when natural persons communicate and collectively author the authority of the state.

---

[26] Ibid, ch 2, s 19 (203).
[27] Ibid, s 22 (204).
[28] Ibid, Bk 1, ch 1, s 14(2) (44).
[29] Ibid, Bk 2, ch 5, s 23 (253).
[30] See CS Edwards, *Hugo Grotius: The Miracle of Holland – A Study in Political and Legal Thought* (Chicago, Nelson-Hall, 1981) 101–2.
[31] Grotius, *De Jure* (above n 19) Bk 2, ch 2 (ss 23 and 204).
[32] T Hobbes, *Leviathan, with Selected Variants from the Latin Edition of 1668*, E Curley (ed) (Indianapolis, Hackett, 1994) ch 13 (para 9).
[33] Hobbes (ibid) ch 21 (para 21).
[34] Ibid, ch 29 (para 21).
[35] Ibid, ch 21 (paras 10–15).
[36] Ibid, para 14 (original emphasis).

Pufendorf again emphasized that the sociality of natural persons underlies a state's authority to enact and administer laws. Put differently, a state lacks any independent claim of its own authority over its members. Instead, legal authority rests in the extent to which domestic laws protect 'the safety of the people'.[37] Most importantly, a social bond exists amongst natural persons before a state takes form.[38] Accordingly, the natural person must voluntarily consent to becoming a member of the state. The state, for its part, has a legal obligation to protect those who choose to be members of a state. As Pufendorf explained, 'This is the general rule for all sovereigns: the safety of the people is the supreme law. For, authority has been given them [state officials] to achieve the end for which states were instituted.'[39] And again, 'The overriding purpose of states is that, by mutual cooperation and assistance, men may be safe from the losses and injuries which they may and often do inflict on each other.'[40] With this understanding, one would be hard-pressed to recognize the state as actually owning its territory. If the state no longer protects natural persons, legal authority dissipates: 'a people, can defend itself against the extreme and unjust violence of the Prince'.[41]

The prior social relationships of natural persons continued as the basis of a state's legal authority in the work of John Locke (1632–1704). Any natural subjection of a natural person under colour of allegiance never existed historically, Locke advised.[42] This was so because a natural person is tied to the legal structure of a state only by her/his own consent. Indeed, according to Locke, the inhabitant has a right of rebellion against the state if the natural person withdraws her/his consent.[43] With the loss of an individual's consent to the state's authority, 'all former ties are cancelled.'[44] The reciprocal relationship between natural persons marks why the state owes a duty to protect its members. This point was reinforced by Jean Jacques Rousseau (1712–78),[45] David Hume (1711–76)[46] and Adam Smith (1723–90).[47]

---

[37] S Pufendorf, *On the Duty of Man and Citizen*, J Tully (ed), M Silverthorne (trans) (Cambridge, Cambridge University Press, 1991) Bk 2, ch 11 (para 3).

[38] Ibid, ch 1 (para 5).

[39] Ibid, ch 11 (para 3).

[40] Ibid, ch 7 (para 3).

[41] S Pufendorf, *De Jure Naturae et Gentium Libri Octo: On the Law of Nature and Nations in Eight Books*, CH Oldfather and WA Oldfather (eds) (Oxford, Clarendon Press, 1934) vol 7, 8.4.

[42] J Locke, *Second Treatise of Government*, TP Peardon (ed) (New York, Liberal Arts Press, 1952) para 114.

[43] Locke (ibid) paras 119, 121, 122 and 135.

[44] Ibid, para 232.

[45] 'The essence of the body politic consists in the union of obedience and liberty, and these words, *subject* and *sovereign*, are correlatives, the notion underlying them being expressed in the one word citizen': J-J Rousseau, 'The Social Contract' in LG Crocker (ed), *The Social Contract and Discourse on Inequality* (New York, Signet, 1967) book 3.13.

[46] 'A man living under an absolute government would owe it no allegiance; since by its very nature, it depends not on consent': D Hume, *A Treatise of Human Nature*, PH Nidditch (ed), 2nd edn (Oxford, Oxford University Press, 1978) 549.

[47] A Smith, *Report Dated 1766: Lectures on Jurisprudence*, RL Meek, DD Raphael and PG Stein (eds) (Indianapolis, Oxford University Press with Liberty Fund, 1978) 403, para 18.

III. THE BOUNDED RESIDUARY

During the late nineteenth century and early twentieth century, the obligation of state protection and the sociality justifying legal protection were displaced by the state's claim to its own legal authority. This claim has accompanied another – namely, the state's claim to own or have absolute title to the land that its officials physically control. With the jurists of the early modern state, however, one is hard-pressed to find the state claiming title to its possession of land. The notion of property is a claim of the natural person, not of the state. Although acknowledging how money is introduced prior to the establishment of civil authority, Locke left the title of possessed objects to private persons, not to the state.[48] For Pufendorf, although the state possessed an admitted 'eminent domain', the state could use the private property of citizens only during emergencies.[49] The state could collect taxes or obligate private citizens to use their property to the state's advantage. A prince could moreover personally own property. Once one became a citizen of the state, the state gained 'an authority whose powers include the right of life and death'[50] – but the natural person, not the state, possessed title to objects in the eminent domain.

A. Title to Land

The legal obligation associated with the residuary of authority for an international community (or at least this surface sense of an international community) rests upon the assumption that the state is a self-creative author of a written language, a statute or judicial decision signifying such a written language. The legal obligation in such a community also sets upon a second assumption: namely, a state's radical title to all territory under its control. Both factors work to explain why internal jurisdiction exists as a universality inside state boundaries.[51] The conferral, withholding and withdrawing of nationality is an incident of such a claim to title by a state. The state's claim to title over territory took form, as with the state as author of the reserved domain, during the late nineteenth century and early twentieth century. States are not acknowledged as owning territory until we come to Vattel's *The Law of Nations* (1758). Here, Vattel

---

[48] Locke (above n 42) paras 175–96. Interestingly, CB Macpherson misses this point as an important, if not the most important, factor making for the individual's unlimited right to private property. See CB Macpherson, 'Introduction' in J Locke, *Second Treatise of Government* (Indianapolis, Hackett, 1980) xvi–xix; and CB Macpherson, *The Political Theory of Possessive Individualism: Hobbes to Locke* (Oxford, Clarendon Press, 1962).

[49] Pufendorf, *On the Duty of Man and Citizen* (above n 37) Bk 2, ch 15 (para 4).

[50] Ibid, 5.4(1).

[51] Schmitt (above n 3) 56–59, 62–66, 126–38 and 147–48.

asserted that the state has 'an indiscriminate right to the property' once the state possesses physical control of its territory.[52] A state's right to property followed from the universality represented by Vattel's doctrine of the *domain réservé*.[53] By the early nineteenth century, American and British courts were describing the state's title to its possessed territory as 'radical', 'ultimate' or 'final', as we shall see below. The state did not just physically control territory and dominate the inhabitants: the state possessed legal title or property over the controlled land.

The claim to title, initially elaborated in the UK case *Campbell v Hall* (1774), authorized a state to appropriate and colonize all *terra nullius* land ('the land of no one').[54] Chief Justice John Marshall of the US Supreme Court extended this opinion in a series of judgments concerning the relation of the land occupied by indigenous inhabitants.[55] With 'absolute title', the state's freedom was 'necessarily exclusive and absolute', Marshall explained.[56] This exclusive and absolute authority did not rest on a fact of physical possession, since indigenous inhabitants had occupied the same land for centuries, albeit as nomadic societies (at least east of the Rockies). The exclusivity was of an intelligible character. It was important for a state to claim title. Once a state claimed title, Marshall asserted in 1823, rightful possession followed: 'discovery gave title to the government by whose subjects, or by whose authority, it was made, against all other European governments, which title might be consummated by possession.'[57] The claim of the state's title over all territory justified the reserved domain.[58] The American Constitution manifested such a consequence in that title led to 'all needful rules and regulations respecting the territory' (Article 4, §3, cl 2).

Kant best described this character as a 'juridical possession' or an 'external intelligible possession'.[59] By 'external', Kant meant 'objective' or 'distinct from me'.[60] The reserved domain, being such an intelligible possession, transcended a physical spot on the earth.[61] Kant clarified the state's claim to title. For one thing, the state resembled a moral or legal person: 'Under the law of nations, a state is regarded as a moral Person living with and in opposition to another state in a condition of natural freedom, which itself is

[52] Vattel (above n 17) Bk 1, Prelim s 18; ch 19, s 231; Bk 2, s 82 (165); s 125.

[53] Ibid, esp s 82, but see also ss 79–97, 116–30 and ch 10, ss 131–39.

[54] *Campbell v Hall* (1774) 1 Cowp 204, 98 ER 1045.

[55] *Johnson and Graham's Lease v M'Intosh* (1823), 8 Wheaton 543, 588, 21 US 240. See also his judgment in *Worcester v State of Georgia* (1832), 6 Peters 515, 31 US 530.

[56] *The Exchange v McFaddon* (1812) 11 US 116, 136.

[57] *Johnson* (above n 55) 573.

[58] *McFaddon* (above n 56) 136.

[59] I Kant, *Metaphysical Elements of Justice*, J Ladd (trans) (Indianapolis, Hackett, 1985) lines 245 and 246R.

[60] Ibid, line 253.

[61] Ibid, line 254.

a condition of continual war.'[62] Second, the state, like the moral person, was free in the sense of being an end in itself.[63] Third, because each state and its laws were a priori abstractions or concepts, each state was considered equal and free vis-à-vis any other state. The state was a mere form emptied of social-cultural content from the standpoint of law. International legal obligations drew from such an equality and freedom of each state. As such, the best that one could expect of an international community was a 'league' or confederation of states.

The Permanent Court of Arbitration followed up in the *Palmas* case (1923), stating that international law functions as 'the guardian' of the title to a state's property.[64] The legal bond, for Arbitrator Huber in *Palmas*, was constituted from the 'legal tie' of title to the internal jurisdiction. Title extended to the state's freedom over 'cession, conquest, occupation'.[65] Huber added that the claim of title leads to an immunity of one state from another.[66] Such non-intervention derived from a freedom and equality of each state in its own law-making inside its internal jurisdiction.

The non-intervention principle derived from another factor than that of the freedom and equality shared with the individual vis-à-vis the state: the internal jurisdiction manifested a spatial character. In this regard, Huber explained, 'Territorial sovereignty is, in general, a situation recognized and delimited in space. . .'[67] I shall privilege this spatial character of international jurisdiction in the concluding chapter. Suffice at this point to observe that in *Palmas* title was described as a legal claim over 'space',[68] 'places' or a 'given zone'.[69] This claim over space begins when the state claims title. The courts have described this time as 'a critical date'.[70] The claim of title overrides physical possession of a territory.[71] In this regard, Kant described title as 'juridical possession'.[72] Both legal space and time are a priori concepts, reified vis-à-vis social life.

The Supreme Court of Canada has affirmed that the state's radical title to land explains the universal legal authority of the state over aboriginal lands.[73] Ian Brownlie pointed out in a similar vein that the totality and

---

[62] Ibid, line 343. See also I Kant, 'Perpetual Peace: A Philosophical Sketch' in H Reiss (trans), *Kant's Political Writings*, 2nd edn (Cambridge, Cambridge University Press, 1991) 103.

[63] See generally Kant, 'Perpetual Peace' (ibid) 96.

[64] *Island of Palmas Case* (*Netherlands v United States*) (1928) 4 ILR 3, 2 RIAA 829, 839.

[65] Ibid, 838–39.

[66] Ibid.

[67] Ibid.

[68] Ibid, 839.

[69] Ibid, 848.

[70] *Frontier Dispute* (*Burkino Faso v Mali*) (1986) ICJ 554, 568; and *Territorial Dispute* (*Libya v Chad*) 1994 ICJ 6, 88.

[71] See also *St Catharine's Milling and Lumber Co v The Queen* (1888) 14 App Cas 46, 56 and 58–59.

[72] Kant, *Metaphysical Elements of Justice* (above n 59) lines 245 and 246R.

[73] *Guerin v The Queen* [1984] 2 SCR 335, 13 DLR (4th) 321, para 88; and *R v Sparrow* [1990] 1 SCR 1075, 1103.

exclusivity of internal jurisdiction rested in the state's title over land.[74] One can also read the conflict between Israel and the Palestinian Authority, as interpreted by the International Court of Justice (ICJ) in the *Wall* judgment (2004), in terms of the claims of each entity to space, or what the Court called a 'territorial sphere'.[75] Recent judgments pertaining to stateless persons have affirmed this relation of title to internal jurisdiction.[76] With the claim of title, a state possesses legal authority over all objects and persons within its internal jurisdiction. The state's freedom to confer, withdraw or withhold nationality has traditionally been believed to flow from the claim of title. Other incidents have also flowed from the claim of title: refusal to admit a stateless person, prolonged detention, forced displacement, expulsion and refoulement follow from the state's claim of title and of its own legal authority. The content of the internal jurisdiction leaves state institutions and state officials free to admit or exclude natural persons without nationality.[77]

B. The State as an End in Itself

The late eighteenth and nineteenth-century articulation of a doctrine about the reserved domain did more than justify a state's radical title to its controlled territory. JS Mill (1806–73) offered a deeper 'legal' basis for the doctrine – namely, the freedom and equality of legal personhood of the state as a member in a special shape of the international community.[78] The reserved domain represented the state's 'inner sphere of life'. For Kant, the state was ironically an end in itself, and as such, it could not be ques-

---

[74] J Crawford (ed), *Brownlie's Principles of Public International Law*, 8th edn (Oxford, Oxford University Press, 2012) 211–12 and 216; I Brownlie, *Principles of Public International Law* (Oxford, Oxford University Press, 2003) 119.

[75] *Legal Consequences of the Construction of the Wall in Occupied Palestinian Territory* (2004) ICJ Rep 135. See also 'Summary Legal Position of the Palestine Liberation Organization', Annex II of 'Report of the UN Secretary-General Pursuant to General Assembly Resolution ES-10/13' (24 November 2003), as discussed in *Legal Consequences of the Construction of the Wall* (above) 181, para 115; and *Beit Sourik Village Council v Government of Israel*, HCJ 2056/04 (2004), www.refworld.org/docid/4374ac594.html.

[76] See, eg, *Banković and Others v Belgium and Others* , Application 52207/99, [2001] ECHR 890, Grand Chamber, ECtHR (12 December 2001) paras 59, 66, 71, 78 and 80; *Issa and Others v Turkey*, Application 31821/96, [2004] ECHR 629, (2005) 41 EHRR 27, 17 BHRC 473, ECtHR (16 November 2004); and *R (Al-skeini) v Secretary of State for Defence* [2005] EWCA 1609, paras 124–92, 196 and 205–6.

[77] This has historically included the Canadian state's subordination to the state's laws (and residential schools) of the social and spiritual bonding of indigenous inhabitants to the land. See Royal Commission on Aboriginal Peoples, *Report: Looking Forward, Looking Back*, vol 1 (Ottawa, Minister of Supply and Services, 1996) 126.

[78] JS Mill, 'A Few Words on non-intervention' [1859] in G Himmelfarb (ed), *John Stewart Mill: Essays on Politics and Culture* (Garden City, NY, Anchor Books, 1963) 368, 383; D Winch (ed), *Principles of Political Economy*, (London: Penguin, 1970) 306. Also see I Kant, 'On the Common Saying "This May Be True in Theory, But It Does Not Apply in Practice"' in Reiss (trans), *Kant's Political Writings* (above n 62) 73–81.

tioned as the ultimate source of law.[79] And so, according to Kant, a state could legally turn a stranger away as long as this did not cause her/his death.[80] A state could also charge and convict a natural person of rebellion, treason or sedition if the person questioned the authorizing origin of the state's legal authority.[81] And yet all this was so despite the historically contingent context in which the inviolability of the state's domain had emerged.

C. The State as a Self-Creative Author

In contrast with the analytically prior sociability of natural persons, the state was now projected as analytically prior to sociality. The state was also projected as prior to sociality in chronological time.[82] This was so because the state was considered an author, a self-creative author much as an author is still considered today. The state/author expresses its will in its statutes. As a consequence, the state/author exists externally and analytically prior to its writing. As such, the state/author must be the source of all laws. The sources thesis – the identity of any discrete rule or right in terms of the Article 38 sources of the Statute of the ICJ – suggests that international rules and rights are willed by the author/state. Being prior to the signification of its will, the author/state transcends all writing.[83] As such, the author/state intends and owns the cognitive objects, called rules, that are signified by the state's writing.

The priority of a state/author's laws over the sociality of natural persons implies that natural persons are obligated to obey the will of the author/state. Like the Roman Church of the medieval world, the state began to possess a universal authority to express its will through statutes, the ratification of treaties or state practice. A boundary of a domain represented the will of a state to choose, exclude or restrict rightful membership to the state's territory. Accordingly, in order to identify a law, jurists had to refer backwards to the intent of the author/state. This backwards reasoning was an analytical, not necessarily an historical, enterprise. That is, it was not necessarily the actual intent of state officials (such as legislators) but a rationally and retrospectively constructed intent. The boundary limited the state's intent. If the nationality rule extended outside the boundary, it interfered with the reserved domain of another state/author.

---

[79] Kant, *Metaphysical Elements of Justice* (above n 59) 123–25, lines 318–20; and I Kant, *Metaphysics of Morals*, M Gregor (trans) (Cambridge, Cambridge University Press, 1996) 95.

[80] Kant, 'Perpetual Peace' (above n 62) 106–7.

[81] Ibid, 126; and Kant, *Metaphysical Elements of Justice* (above n 59) 318, 320 and 323.

[82] See generally M Foucault, 'What Is an Author?' in P Rabinow (ed), *The Foucault Reader* (New York, Random House, 1984); and WE Conklin, 'The Invisible Author of Legal Authority' (1996) 7 *Law and Critique* 173.

[83] M Foucault, 'Governmentality' in G Burchell, C Gordon and P Miller (eds), *The Foucault Effect: Studies in Governmentality* (Chicago, University of Chicago Press, 1991) 95.

The author here was an artificial person, not a natural being. Not unlike a novelist or a poet (at least as accepted during the European Enlightenment and post-Enlightenment), the state created itself.

D. The Residuary

The residuary of an international community was the consequence of the emergence of the state as a self-creative author. From the standpoint of the emergent international community, the content of the state's reserved domain had to be empty or content-independent of social-cultural assumptions, expectations, beliefs and social relationships. After all, an identifiable law existed by virtue of the will of its author, the state, not by virtue of the social life of natural persons. Indeed, such an emptiness of the domain, from the standpoint of the quest of the identity of a law, rendered an equality amongst each member of the international community. The international community could, at best, be only a confederation of equal states bound by treaties to which they had contracted. As such, no other state and certainly no international institution possessed the legal authority to constrain the will of the author/state who acted inside its domain.

E. Nationality

Nationality was a critical sign of the author's will. As such, the obligatory character of the state's conferral, withdrawal and withholding of nationality was independent the content of the state's exclusion of members. The state no longer had an obligation to protect its nationals who had been harmed in another state's territory: such diplomatic protection became discretionary. Indeed, the state was not obligated to confer nationality on all natural persons within its territorial boundary. In sum, the situs of nationality in the state's reserved domain shifted from a state's legal obligations resting in the analytically prior voluntary choice and sociality of natural persons, emphasized by Hobbes, Grotius, Pufendorf and Locke, to the state's own determination of whether the individual possessed allegiance to the state.

The incidents of the author's reserved domain addressed more than nationality. For one thing, the state was reserved the freedom to physically control territory signified by a territorial border. For another, the state was reserved the freedom to claim title to territory. Passports, border control cards, work visas and other documentary *indicia* signified membership in this or that state.[84] The boundary of one state's reserved domain

---

[84] See generally Goulbourne (above n 11).

differentiated one state from another. A state might avoid judicial review of a decision to expel a non-national. Treaties were obligatory because state parties had expressly consented to their provisions. A treaty might constrain state acts negatively.[85] As a further incident, a state's freedom to confer, withdraw or withhold nationality became immune from external interference. An international community existed at this stage, but it existed only as an aggregate of the wills of state members.

IV. THE EMERGENCE OF THE JUDICIAL DOCTRINE OF RESERVED DOMAIN

The present-day association of statelessness with 'the operation of its laws' must be understood against the background of such an aggregated international community. Although Vattel had introduced the notion of a *domain réservé*, the judicial doctrine was not fully elaborated in all its rigour until the period between the late nineteenth century and the 1930s. Inside the 'necessarily exclusive and absolute' freedom of the state, a state alone could consent to limitations of its own actions.[86] In 1834, a British Court held, for example, that the state alone had the freedom to decide which inhabitants of a ceded territory were its nationals.[87] Also in 1834, the UK government refused to evaluate the 'particular harshness' of the content of an 'extraordinary and illiberal' American statute.[88] Interestingly, certain important principles of statutory interpretation emerged by the mid-nineteenth century.[89] By the last decade of the nineteenth century, the American Supreme Court affirmed the uncontrolled freedom of the state over nationality.[90]

---

[85] This point is elaborated by the ILC in V Mikulka (Special Rapporteur), 'Second Report on State Succession and Its Impact on Nationality of Natural and Legal Persons', A/CN.4/474, also available in *ILC Yearbook 1996*, vol II(1), Preamble (Comm 6).

[86] See generally, C Rousseau, 'L'indépendance de l'état dans l'ordre international' (1948) 2 *Recueil des Cours* 167, 237–49.

[87] When territory is ceded to a state, the latter possesses the freedom to determine who is a national: *Donegani v Donegani* (1835) 3 Knapp 63, 12 ER 571. The UK Naturalisation Act (1870) affirmed this authority.

[88] Lord McNair (ed), *International Law Opinions* (Cambridge, Cambridge University Press, 1956) vol 2, 105. UK Foreign Affairs legal opinion stated, 'It cannot be denied that every independent state or nation is *entitled* to admit or exclude from its territories the subjects and citizens of foreign states' unless the state had expressly consented to a treaty which allowed such interference: J Dobson (Queen's Advocate), 'Report to the Foreign Secretary on Admission to Louisiana' (4 August 1843).

[89] As an example, a state could not bind itself into the future. Specifically worded statutes rendered generally worded statutes inoperative, and later statutes rendered earlier ones inoperative. See J Willis, 'Statute Interpretation in a Nutshell (1938) 16 *Canadian Bar Review* 1.

[90] See, eg, *Chae Chan Ping v United States* (1889) 130 US 581, 604 (Field CJ); *Nishimura Ekiu v United States* (1892) 142 US 651, 659; *Fong Yue Ting v United States* (1893) 149 US 698, 711; and *Hollander Case* (1895) US For Rel 775, as cited in *Boffolo Case* (1903) 10 RIAA 528. Ian Brownlie suggested that literature first recognized the incident of nationality in a state's freedom by the late nineteenth century: I Brownlie, 'The Relations of Nationality in Public International Law' (1963) 39 *British Yearbook of International Law* 284, 286 (fn 2).

The incident of nationality in the reserved domain led to conditions of mass denaturalization during the nineteenth century. Emperor Francis Joseph of the Austro-Hungarian Empire threatened denaturalization in 1850 if alleged revolutionaries in Lombardy and Venice did not return to the Empire.[91] In 1863, Bismarck instituted a mass denaturalization of Danish-speaking inhabitants upon his annexation of Schlesweig-Holstein.[92] With the practice of mass denaturalization, there evolved a further incident of the reserved domain: expulsion. Bismarck threatened to expel the Danish-speaking inhabitants en masse unless they became Prussian nationals. An 1870 UK Parliament indicated that naturalization could be withheld 'without assigning any reason . . . as most conducive to the public good'.[93] No appeal from the Secretary's decision was permitted. UK courts continued to accept nationality matters as incidents of the reserved domain during the early twentieth century.[94] By 1915, the Great Powers had withdrawn French nationality from the inhabitants of the Saar region, despite this having been their homeland for several generations.[95] The inhabitants became 'foreigners' in their own 'country' (the Saar region).[96] The judicial doctrine of the reserved domain had by all accounts reached full acceptance during the 1920s and 1930s. Assumptions about freedom, equality and property had been institutionalized as hard facts of the international law discourse.

A. Post-World War 1 Legal Discourse

Despite Woodrow Wilson's effort to divide Europe into ethnic nation-states at Versailles (1919) and then to guarantee the protection of linguistic, religious and ethnic minorities, the freedom of the state to confer, withhold or withdraw nationality figured deeply in the legal consciousness of state and municipal leaders.[97] The Covenant of the League of Nations enter-

[91] M Vishniak, *The Legal Status of Stateless Persons*, AG Duker (ed), Jews and the Post-War World Series, No 6 (New York, American Jewish Committee, 1945) 10. See also AP Mutharika, *The Regulation of Statelessness under International and National Law* (New York, Oceana, 1977) 201 (fn 5).

[92] Vishniak (ibid) 10. See also Mutharika (ibid) 201 (fn 5).

[93] UK Naturalisation Act (1870) 33 Vict Ch 14, Art 7.

[94] *Attorney General for Canada v Cain* [1906] AC 542, 546 (JCPC), quoting Vattel (above n 17) Bk 1, ch 19, s 231. For a more recent survey of precedents, see RL Cove, 'State Responsibility for Constructive Wrongful Expulsion of Foreign Nationals' (1988) 11 *Fordham International Law Journal* 802, 815–16 (fn 107).

[95] *In re Alkan, Ann Dig* (1919–42 Supp Vol) Case No 48, 83.

[96] All 'natives or foreigners' who found themselves inhabiting territory of a successor state were given six years to dispose of their property and 'to retire to whatever country they may choose' 'if they should think fit to do'. See Art 7 of the Treaty of Paris (1815) *Cobbett's Political Register*, vol 29, 277–82.

[97] See especially P Alston and R Goodman, *International Human Rights* (Oxford, Oxford University Press, 2013) 102–5 and 111–12. See also *Minority Schools in Albania*, Advisory

tained that some matters were 'solely' within internal jurisdiction and that even the League's Council could not address such matters (Article 15(8)).[98] A state's conferral, withdrawal or withholding of nationality was one such matter. The Permanent Court explained in *Tunis and Morocco* (1923) that without Article 15(8) of the Covenant, international law would have opened the content of the state's reserved domain to scrutiny from sources outside the domain: 'Thus, in the present state of international law, questions of nationality were, in the opinion of the Court, in principle *within this reserved domain*.'[99] Aside from the 'sole' matters in the domain, 'advanced nations' possessed 'tutelage' over colonies and mandated territories that were 'not yet able to stand by themselves under the strenuous conditions of the modern world' (Article 22(1) of the Covenant). In other words, colonies and mandated territories lacked the reserved domain because they were not yet considered self-creative authors.[100] Nor could the League be considered a legal entity worthy of being a party to a legal dispute. Only states could be parties to any legal dispute. Harm during armed conflict was understood with reference to the reserved domain of the other state in military conflict.[101] The international community existed as a league of interdependent yet self-created authors.

The weight of the reserved domain in international and US and UK domestic adjudication was heavy and pervasive in matters of nationality during the post-World War I period. In the United States, Holmes CJ stated in *Schwimmer* (1928) that natural persons lack any 'natural right to become citizens, but only that which is conferred upon them' by the executive arm of the state.[102] The doctrine was justified by the League of Nations Rapporteur in the *Aaland Islands Report* (1921) as necessary for the 'order and stability' of the international community.[103] The reserved

---

Opinion of the Permanent Court of International Justice (1935) Ser A/B, No 64. For a study of how the European states bypassed the Versailles treaty requirements, see especially Vishniak (above n 91).

[98] League of Nations Covenant (Part I of the Treaty of Versailles), in force 10 January 1920. See also British Foreign Service Cases (BFPS) 112: B, 316 (28 June 1919). The Council, however, could refer the dispute to the Assembly.

[99] *Tunis and Morocco Nationality Decrees*, Advisory Opinion, (1923) PCIJ (Ser B) No 4, 7, 24, also reported in (1923) 2 ILR 349 (emphasis added).

[100] *League of Nations Official Journal* (23 April 1923) 604. See also DP O'Connell, 'Nationality in "C" Class Mandates' (1954) 31 *British Yearbook of International Law* 458.

[101] Pursuant to Art 11(1) of the League of Nations Covenant, 'Any war or threat of war, whether immediately affecting any of the members of the League or not, is hereby declared a matter of concern to the whole League. . .' Although not considered a grave harm to another state, mass denaturalization, if accompanied with expulsion, arguably caused harm to 'the whole League'.

[102] *US v Schwimmer* (1928) 279 US 644, 649 (Butler), Holmes dissenting, also reported in (1928) 5 ILR 226.

[103] League of Nations, 'The Aaland Islands Question: Report Submitted to the Council of the League of Nations by the Commission of Rapporteurs', Document of Council B.7.21/68/106 (Geneva, 16 April 1921), (1921) *League of Nations Official Journal Special Supplement No 3*, 22–23.

domain was essential for the very idea of a state as a territorial entity.[104] The Permanent Court of Arbitration confirmed in the *Island of Palmas Case* (1928) that 'the *exclusive* competence of the State in regard to its own territory' represented the 'point of departure in settling most questions that concern international relations. . .'.[105] The Permanent Court reiterated the doctrine in the *Austro–German Customs Union Case* (1931).[106] Nationality was considered an indispensable incident to such a domain.[107] As such, in contradiction to Grotius, Pufendorf and other jurists of the early modern state, the opinion of a state's executive possessed an 'absolute', 'exclusive' and 'untrammelled' discretion to choose whether to diplomatically protect a national.[108] This emergence of a distinct legal doctrine marked a fundamental shift in an international community from sociality, a natural person's voluntary choice of nationality, the protective freedom of the state and the reciprocal relations of persons on the one hand to, on the other hand, an international community in which, as the *Mavrommatis Palestine Concessions Case* asserts, 'a State is in reality asserting its own rights – its right to ensure, in the person of its subjects, respect for the rules of international law'.[109]

By the 1920s and 1930s, the day-to-day nationality decisions of US and UK courts could take for granted that the state claimed its own authority over natural persons. Hence the UK Chancery Court decided in *Stoeck* (1921) that an executive decision regarding nationality, being a matter of the reserve domain, could exclude an inhabitant of 20 years from naturalization.[110] After citing the second edition of *Oppenheim* for the doctrine,[111] the *Stoeck* judgment exclaimed, 'How could it be otherwise?'[112] Perhaps because the frequency of travel and the means of communication that are

---

[104] The point has recently been affirmed by the Inter-American Court of Human Rights, *Proposed Amendments to the Naturalization Provisions of Constitution of Costa Rica* (advisory opinion), OC-4/84, Ser A, No 4 (decision of 19 January 1984), (1984) 5 HRLJ 161, (1984) 79 ILR 28.

[105] *Palmas* (above n 64) emphasis added.

[106] *Austro-German Customs Union Case* (advisory opinion), PCIJ Ser A/B, No 41 (1931) 36, 57–58, also reported in (1931) 6 ILR 26.

[107] *Dickenson Car Wheel Co (US v Mexico)* (1931) 4 RIAA 669, 678, (1931–31) Annual Digest No 115.

[108] *Mavrommatis* (above n 21); *North American Dredging Company* (US–Mexico Claims Commission) (1926) 4 RIAA 26, (1926) 3 ILR 4; and *Panevezys-Saldutiskis Railway Case (Estonia v Lithuania)*, PCIJ Rep Ser A/B, No 76 (1939) 1, 16, also reported in (1939) 9 ILR 308. The discretionary character of diplomatic protection has been recounted in Read's dissenting opinion in the International Court judgment in *Nottebohm (Liechtenstein v Guatemala)* (second phase), (1955) ICJ Rep 4, 23, also reported in (1955) 22 ILR 349.

[109] *Mavrommatis* (above n 21); *US v Germany* (US–Germany Claims Commission) (1924) 7 RIAA 73, 75; *Panevezys-Saldutiskis* (ibid) 16; and *Nottebohm* (ibid) 349 (per Read).

[110] The state interned, expelled and then confiscated the assets of the inhabitant of over 20 years: *Stoeck v Public Trustee* [1921] 2 Ch 67, 78. German law alone could decide whether someone was a German national. See *In re Chamberlain's Settlement* [1921] 2 Ch 533.

[111] LFL Oppenheim, *International Law*, vol 1, 2nd edn (London, Longmans Green, 1912) 387–89, as quoted in *Stoeck* (ibid) 77–78.

[112] *Stoeck* (above n 110) 77–78.

taken for granted today were absent during the case, the Court could state, 'In truth the question of statelessness can have seldom arisen as an important or practical question.'[113] It could be neither important nor practical, needless to say, so long as jurists accepted an image of the international community as the aggregate of the wills of state members.

The reserve domain highlighted the Weimar Republic's approach to nationality in 1921.[114] In 1929, the United Kingdom appealed to customary law as its basis for refusing to admit Leon Trotsky to British territory: 'No alien has the right to claim admission to this country if it would be contrary to the interests of the country to receive him.'[115] UK and American commentators subsequently confirmed the sanctity of the state's jurisdiction over nationality.[116]

A series of treaties during the 1920s and 1930s also recognized the conferral, withdrawal or withholding of nationality as a matter solely within the reserved domain. Article 1 of the Rome Convention (1922) provided, 'The ways of acquiring or losing nationality are regulated by the law of each state.'[117] Article 1 of the American Convention on the Status of Aliens (1928) recognized the freedom of a state 'to establish by means of laws the conditions under which foreigners may enter and reside in their territory'.[118] In addition, state parties had the freedom to expel or internally displace their inhabitants '[f]or reasons of public order or safety'. In addition, any new or succeeding state could retain the freedom to control who were its nationals (Article 11).[119] The Hague Convention on Certain Questions Relating to the Conflict of Nationality Laws (1930) set out in Article 1, 'It is for each State to determine under its own law who are its nationals.'[120] Conversely, each state had an obligation with respect to the legal space of another state in

---

[113] Ibid, 80.

[114] League of Nations, *Conference for the Codification of International Law: Bases of Discussion (Volume 1: Nationality Laws)* (Geneva, 15 May 1929), Doc No C.73.M.38.1929.V, reprinted in S Rosenne (ed), *League of Nations Conference for the Codification of International Law 1930*, vol 1 (Dobbs Ferry, Oceana Publications, 1975) 13.

[115] *Hansard*, HC Deb 18 July 1929, vol 230, col 603.

[116] H Lauterpacht, *The Function of Law in the International Community* (Hamden, CT, Archon, 1966) 300; Borchard (above n 19) 49, 59 and 462–63; and HW Briggs, *Law of Nations: Cases, Documents, and Notes*, 2nd edn (New York, Appleton-Century-Crofts, 1952) 535–37.

[117] Rome Convention, signed by Austria, Czechoslovakia, Hungary, Italy, Poland, Rumnania, the Serb-Croat-Slovene State (6 April 1922). See RW Flournoy and MO Hudson, *A Collection of Nationality Laws of Various Countries as Contained in Constitutions, Statutes and Treaties* (New York, Oxford University Press, 1929) 650, reprinted in MO Hudson, *International Legislation: A Collection of Nationality Laws of Various Countries as Contained in Constitutions, Statutes and Treaties* (Washington, DC, Carnegie Endowment, 1931) vol 2, Treaty no 72 (866).

[118] Art 6 of the Inter-American Convention on the Status of Aliens (1928) 46 Stat 2753 (entered into force 3 September 1929); and Code of Private International Law ('Code Bustamante') (1928) 86 LNTS 111, reprinted in Hudson, *International Legislation: A Collection of Nationality Laws* (ibid) vol 4, Treaty No 189 (2374).

[119] Inter-American Convention on the Status of Aliens (ibid) Art 2.

[120] Hague Convention on Certain Questions Relating to the Conflict of Nationality Law (signed 12 April 1930, entered into force 1 July 1937) 179 LNTS 89, www.refworld.org/docid/3ae6b3b00.html; and Hudson (ibid) vol 5, 359.

matters of nationality: 'Any question as to whether a person possesses the nationality of a particular State shall be determined in accordance with the law of that State' (Article 2). By a Protocol to the Treaty, the domain relieved the state of legal obligations towards a colony, protectorate, overseas territory, mandated territory or parts of the territories of foreign suzerainty.[121] The domain justified a state's 'liberty' to denunciate or to add reservations to its understanding of any treaty.[122] The Hague Convention and subsequent Protocols were followed by the Montevideo Convention on the Rights and Duties of States (1933).[123] This treaty, well known and oft cited for its definition of a state, described the rights of a state as so 'fundamental' that they could not be affected in any way (Article 5).

In sum, an international community had indeed emerged in the international law discourse by the 1930s. Very different from the international community of the early jurists and certainly of the community of Christendom, however, the state members were now the self-creative authors of laws (Article 3 of the Covenant of the League of Nations). Each state possessed a bounded freedom protected from external intervention (Article 8). This freedom pre-existed the natural person in any social-cultural context. There was an international community – but the community protected each state's freedom to enact and enforce nationality laws. States now claimed their own authority in matters of nationality.

B. Post-Second World War Legal Discourse

The weight of the reserved domain in contemporary international law discourse is formidable. I shall argue below in chapters six through nine that a very different international community has emerged from the remnants of the last one. This community, named 'the international community as a whole', is at odds with the continuation of the reserved domain doctrine during the early post-World War II period. The coexistence of two international communities, each rationally coherent with its postu-

---

[121] League of Nations Protocol Relating to Military Obligations in Certain Cases of Dual Nationality (1930) 178 LNTS 227, www.refworld.org/docid/3ae6b38c10.html, Art 15. See also Protocol Relating to a Certain Case of Statelessness, (1930) 179 LNTS 115, www.refworld.org/docid/3ae6b39520.html, Art 13(1); and League of Nations Special Protocol Concerning Statelessness (12 April 1930) C.27.M.16.1931V, www.refworld.org/docid/3ae6b36f1f.html, Art 13(1). The freedom of a state conferred a mandate by the League retained the freedom to choose its own laws regarding nationality for a mandated territory. In addition to the Protocols, see the *League of Nations Official Journal* (23 April 1923) 604. This point is discussed in O'Connell (above n 100).

[122] Hague Convention on Certain Questions Relating to the Conflict of Nationality Law (above n 120); Hudson, *International Legislation: A Collection of Nationality Laws* (above n 117); and Protocol Relating to Military Obligations in Certain Cases of Dual Nationality (ibid) 227 (Art 6). See also Protocol Relating to a Certain Case of Statelessness (ibid) Art 13(1).

[123] Montevideo Convention on the Rights and Duties of States (signed 26 December 1933, entered into force 26 December 1934) 165 LNTS 19, 49 Stat 3097, 3 Bevan 145, 137 BFSR 282.

lates, has left an ambiguity about the applicability of international standards to de jure stateless persons. With this in mind, let us focus upon the two most often cited sources about the universality of international standards and of universal human rights: the UN Charter and the UN Declaration of Human Rights.

i. The UN Charter

Sometimes described as a constitution,[124] the UN Charter again institutionalized the reserved domain by recognizing certain matters as 'essentially within the internal jurisdiction of any State' (Article 2(7)).[125] This internal jurisdiction was described by the Charter as 'inherent', 'inviolable' and 'fundamental'. Notwithstanding a 'faith in fundamental human rights, in the dignity and worth of the human person, in the equal rights of men and women', the Charter considered the state as the sole legal person in the international community (Articles 18(1) and 27(1)). According to Article 2(1), each state was considered equal with the next. The international community was constituted from 'the principle of equal rights and self-determination' (Article 55). Further, each state had the right of 'self-government'. A state's right of self-government extended to territories that lacked self-governing authority (Article 73). When one state militarily interfered in the reserved domain of another state, harm was caused to the reserved domain of the latter state. The latter possessed 'the inherent right of individual or collective self-defence'. According to Article 1(2), the purpose of the United Nations was 'to develop friendly relations *among nations*'. The United Nations, in this context, was 'a center for harmonizing' such relations between states (Article 1(4)). 'Peace and security' would be challenged if the reserved domain of a state were the object of external interference (Chapter VII). 'Universal peace' involved the relations between states; and a 'people' was not a legal entity unless recognized as a state with a defined territorial border. Once that moment of recognition arose, the 'people' could defend themselves as a state. Until that moment, the members of 'the people' were stateless, unless they possessed nationality from some state.

ii. The Universal Declaration of Human Rights

The Universal Declaration of Human Rights (UDHR) has been held out more than any other international instrument as guaranteeing the

---

[124] RStJ MacDonald, 'The International Community as a Legal Community' in RStJ Macdonald and D Johnston (eds), *Towards World Constitutionalism: Issues in the Legal Ordering of the World Community* (Leiden, Martinus Nijhoff, 2005).

[125] UN Charter (signed 26 June 1945, entered into force 24 October 1945), Treaty Series No 993, 59 Stat 1031, 3 Bevans 1153.

universality of the international community. To be sure, the Declaration does not constitute a legal obligation, since the Declaration is a UN General Assembly Resolution, not a treaty. That said, according to Article 6 of the UDHR, 'everyone' is said to possess 'the right to recognition as a person before the law'.[126] Article 15(1) guarantees, 'Everyone has a right to a nationality.'[127] This right to nationality has been recognized in a series of multilateral and regional human rights treaties, which will be examined below in chapter four.[128]

iii. The Reports of the International Law Commission

The International Law Commission (ILC) 'Draft Articles on Diplomatic Protection' (2006) highlight the freedom of the state to decide whether to diplomatically protect a natural or legal person: 'should the natural or legal person on whose behalf it is acting consider that their rights are not adequately protected, they have no remedy in international law.'[129] The Commentary to the ILC Draft Articles adopts the definition of stateless-ness pronounced in the Convention Relating to the Status of Stateless Persons (1954) (which will be examined further in chapter four) and does not examine why the stateless condition exists.[130] According to the Draft Articles, a state has the discretion to protect any of its nationals who are harmed on the territory of another state, but it has no legal obligation to do so.[131] In other words, it is the state, not an injured national, that pos-sesses a right in such a circumstance, and that right relates only to other states. Moreover, 'it is for the state of nationality to determine, in accord-ance with municipal law, who is to qualify for its nationality.'[132] Although international standards may guide states, the Draft Articles do not trump

---

[126] 'Everyone' is said to possess 'the right to seek and to enjoy in other countries' asylum from persecution' (UDHR Art 14), 'the freedom to leave the state of habitation when perse-cuted' (Arts 13(2), 14(1) and (2)), to return to the territory (Art 13(2)), the right to protection against 'arbitrary arrest, detention or exile' (Art 9), as well as a series of rights that address the social context examined below ch 9: 'right to life, liberty and the security of the person' (Art 3), 'freedom of movement and residence within the borders of each State', a proscrip-tion against 'cruel, inhuman or degrading treatment or punishment' (Art 5), the disruption of 'the family home' (Art 12) and the arbitrary state possession of property (Art 17(1)).

[127] Universal Declaration of Human Rights (UDHR) (adopted and proclaimed 10 December 1948), UN GA Res 217 A (III) (emphasis added).

[128] This priority is also represented in Art 1 of the UDHR (ibid).

[129] *Case Concerning the Barcelona Traction Light and Power Company Ltd (New Application: 1962) (Belgium v Spain) Second Phase,* Judgment, (1970) ICJ Rep 3, 44, para 78, as quoted in International Law Commission (ILC), 'Draft Articles on Diplomatic Protection, with Commentaries', UN Doc A/61/10, 58th sess, *ILC Yearbook 2006,* vol II(2), legal.un.org/ilc/texts/instruments/eng-lish/commentaries/9_8_2006.pdf, Art 2 (Comm 2).

[130] See especially ILC, 'Draft Articles on Diplomatic Protection, with Commentaries' (ibid) Art 8 (Comm 2).

[131] Ibid, Art 3 (Comm 1).

[132] Ibid, Art 4 (Comm 1).

state action regarding nationality.[133] Several provisions frame state duties in a permissive way.[134]

In their 'Draft Articles on the Succession of States' (1999),[135] the ILC had previously taken for granted that the international community is an aggregate of the wills of states. Article 5, for example, recognizes a rebuttable presumption of nationality for anyone habitually resident in a state's territory. Echoing the early modern jurists, the natural person has a freedom to opt for a nationality (Article 11(2)).[136] A successor state must not require a person to renounce her/his nationality if such would render the person stateless (Article 9).[137] The Commentary to the Draft Articles continues, however: 'International law cannot correct the deficiencies of internal acts of a State concerned, even if they result in Statelessness.'[138] The thrust of the Draft Articles is that states are left to address nationality issues, including dual nationality, the separation of families, military obligations, social security benefits, the right of residence and the like.[139]

The problematic of the reserved domain remains in the recent study *Responsibility to Protect* by the International Commission on Intervention and State Sovereignty (2001).[140] The study aimed to displace the state's right to non-intervention by an affirmative obligation to protect civilians inside the jurisdiction of the state. At the same moment that the Commission claimed such an obligation, however, it maintained 'the traditional notion of state sovereignty'.[141] The crucial feature of the traditional notion, according to the Commission, is the 'bedrock non-intervention principle' to the effect that each state must respect the 'exclusive and total jurisdiction' of all other states.[142] The Commission was silent as to the relationship between

---

[133] Ibid, Art 16 (Comm 1). See also Arts 2(3), 8, 19 and 19(5). See also comments by Economides at the 2486th meeting of the ILC (30 May 1997), *ILC Yearbook 1997*, vol I, 86, para 75. One might argue that this is manifested in the ILC comments regarding state responsibility: ILC, *Report of the International Law Commission: Fifty-Third Session* (2001), UN Doc A/56/10, 43. Citations and quotations are from J Crawford (ed), *The International Law Commission's Articles on State Responsibility: Introduction, Text and Commentaries* (Cambridge, Cambridge University Press, 2002) Commentaries 74–75. As the International Law Commission states in Art 44(a) of its Articles on State Responsibility, 'The responsibility of a State may not be invoked if: (a) the claim is not brought in accordance with any applicable rule relating to the nationality of claims.' However, the gist of the State Responsibility Articles highlights the objectivity of international law and of the international community independent of the reserved domain. See, eg, Arts 3, 33, 48 and Commentaries, esp Comm 10. See also Crawford, 'Introduction' in Crawford (ed) (above) 40.

[134] See, eg, ILC, 'Draft Articles on Nationality of Natural Persons in Relation to the Succession of States' (above n 13) Arts 6, 10 and 12.

[135] Ibid.

[136] Ibid, Art 11 (Comm 7).

[137] Ibid.

[138] Ibid, Art 19 (Comm 6).

[139] Ibid, Art 18 (Comm 2).

[140] International Commission on Intervention and State Sovereignty (ICISS), *The Responsibility to Protect* (Ottawa, International Development Research Centre, 2001).

[141] Ibid, 2.13 and 2.14.

[142] Ibid, 2.8 and 6.2.

the intra-state violence (this being its initial concern) and statelessness, as well as to the social consequences of statelessness.[143] The latter will be addressed below in chapter three. The issue of what is 'essentially within the internal jurisdiction of any state', as set out in Article 2(7) of the UN Charter, remains admittedly 'undefined' and 'indeed much contested', according to the Commission's study.[144] Despite this caution, the *Responsibility to Protect* report claims that the effective authority of the international community must be displaced in favour of the willingness of states 'to use force on behalf of, as directed by, and for the goals of the United Nations', since the UN lacks 'operational capacity'.[145]

V. THE CONTENT OF THE RESERVED DOMAIN

The reserved domain for a state member of the international community has a protected social-cultural content. That content has been 'out of bounds' from external scrutiny, whether the scrutiny be by a court, another state or an international institution such as the League of Nations or the United Nations. I now wish to highlight three examples of such immunized content. Each feature bears upon the conferral, withdrawal and withholding of nationality and therefore of de jure statelessness.

A. The Role of the Executive Arm of the State

The first example of the social-cultural content concerns the role of the executive arm of the state. Although the executive has been thought to administer the legislative will of a liberal society,[146] the executive represents a unity that would be hard to identify in a legislature.[147] The role of the executive plays in several contexts. For one thing, the executive often plays the determinative role in matters of nationality: the executive has authority to expel stateless persons. To be sure, it may be statutes that authorize such a role for the executive, but executive discretion has especially impacted the production of the stateless condition. Although the legislative branch deliberates and enacts criminal laws and punishment

---

[143] Ibid, 3.21–3.24.
[144] Ibid, 6.2.
[145] Ibid, 6.12.
[146] *Al-Kateb v Godwin and Others* [2004] HCA 37, (2004) 219 CLR 562, (2004) ILDC 33, Australian HC (6 August 2004), para 301 (per Callinan). See also *Chu Kheng Lim v Minister for Immigration* (1992) 176 CLR 1; and *Sosa v Alvarez-Machain* (2004) 542 US 692, 750, US S1245 C (2004) 2739 (per Scalia).
[147] See, eg, *Chief Executive of the Department of Labour v Hossein Yadegary and District Court at Auckland* (13 August 2008), [2008] NZCA 295, para 5.

for contravention of such laws, nationality issues fall under the authority of the executive arm of the state.[148]

Consistent with a state's radical title over all land and objects inside its reserved domain, passports are the property of the state, and the United Kingdom's confiscation of a passport, as described below, was merely part of its prerogative according to the ancient doctrine of *ne exeat regno*. In 1976, the UK government withdrew the passports of mercenaries returning from Angola.[149] The government determined that passports would be collected and not be returned to future mercenaries to Angola unless they signed a declaration that they would not work as mercenaries in Angola and had no intent of doing so.

Even before *ne exeat regno* was invoked by the United Kingdom, the role of the executive arm of a state had already been exemplified in Sri Lanka in the 1952 case *Sudali and Asary*, in which the executive dropped a criminal charge due to insufficient evidence and thereupon arrested the applicant under a deportation order.[150] There is also a series of similar cases involving the role of the executive arm of the Vietnam state towards the well-known boat people from Vietnam.[151] More recently, Filipino judicial decisions have deferred to the executive's authority to detain stateless persons for several years.[152]

Such executive discretion has also pertained to the conferral and withdrawal of nationality.[153] The freedom of a state's executive to act without external scrutiny of the content of its decisions and actions has exemplified

[148] *Behrooz v Secretary of the Department of Immigration and Multicultural and Indigenous Affairs and Others* (16 November 2004) [2004] HCA 36, (2004) 208 ALR 271, para 21. See also Callinan J at para 218 and Gleeson CJ and para 18. See also *Zin Mon Aye v Minister for Immigration and Citizenship et al* (11 June 2010) [2010] FCAFC 69, Fed CA Australia, para 66, 71 (per Lander); and *East India Company v Sandys* (1684) 10 ST 371, 530–1 as quoted in *R v Immigration Officer at Prague Airport and Another, ex parte European Roma Rights Centre and Others* [2005] 1 All ER 527, [2005] 2 AC 1, [2005] 2 WLR 1, para 11.

[149] 'Foreign Office Threat to Mercenaries', *The Times* (20 February 1976) 6; and *The Times* Editorial Staff, '*Ne exeat Regno*' Back Again', *The Times* (20 February 1976) 15.

[150] *Sudali Andy Asary et al v Van den Dreesen (Inspector of Police)* (1952) 54 *New Law Reports* 66, Habeas Corpos Applications Nos 1566–70 (Hatton) (1952), 91.

[151] *Nguyen Tuan Cuong, Long Quoc Tuong and Others v Director of Immigration, the Secretary for Security and the Chairman of the Refugee Status Review Board of the Court of Appeal of Hong Kong* (21 November 1996), Privy Council (Judicial Committee), www.unhcr.org/refworld/docid/3ae6b65910.html. See also *Chu Kheng Lim* (above n 146); and *Tan Te Lam v Superintendent of Tai A Chau Detention Centre* [1997] AC 97.

[152] See *Tan Seng Pao v Commissioner of Immigration*, Republic of Philippines Supreme Court (27 April 1960), GR No L-14246, www.chanrobles.com/scdecisions/jurisprudence1960/apr1960/gr_l-14246_1960.php; *Lam Yin (Alias Lim Yin) v Commissioner of Immigration*, Republic of Philippines Supreme Court (31 March 1966), GR No L-22744, www.chanrobles.com/scdecisions/jurisprudence1966/mar1966/gr_l-22744_1966.php; *Borovsky v Commissioner of Immigration and Director of Prisons*, Republic of Philippines Supreme Court (30 June 1949), GR No L-2852, [1949] PHSC 209; and *Andreu v Commissioner of Immigration and Director of Prisons*, Republic of Philippines Supreme Court (31 October 1951) GR No L-4253, [1951] PHSC 305.

[153] C Lewa, 'Issues to be Raised Concerning the Situation of Rohingya Children in Myanmar (Burma)', submission to the Committee on the Rights of the Child (November 2003), www.burmalibrary.org/docs11/TB-NGO-FA-Rohingyas-CRC2004.pdf, para 2.

the hold of the reserved domain of the international community. [154] The social, economic and psychological consequences for stateless natural persons have been profound, as elaborated below in chapter three. Internment during alleged emergencies of stateless persons from ethnic groups can be for several years. [155] The Philippines, [156] Myanmar [157] and Sri Lanka [158] are examples. The Myanmar Citizenship Law (1982) has explicitly posited that the granting or denaturalizing of nationals lies within the uncontrolled discretion of the executive. As the ILC has emphasized, expulsion of a nonnational is undertaken in order to protect a state rather than to punish the individual. [159]

Another aspect of the privileged role of the executive concerns judicial hesitancy to intervene into the content of the reserved domain. [160] The boundary of the reserved domain separates political matters (which are inside the domain) from legal matters. [161] The content of the domain has been described as a 'policy matter'. [162] One's nationality or lack thereof has

---

[154] That said, there have been periods when domestic UK and US judiciaries have scrutinized the content of executive decisions and actions. The opinions of Edward Coke during the early seventeenth century and some early nineteenth-century US judicial decisions are cases in point.

[155] See, eg, *Tan Seng Pao* (above n 152); *Borovsky* (above n 152); and *Andreu* (above 152).

[156] *Juan Gallanosa Frivaldo v Commission on Elections et al*, Republic of Philippines Supreme Court (23 June 1989), GR No 87193. See also *Ramon L Labo v Commission on Elections (Comelec) en Banc and Luis L Lardizabal*, Republic of Philippines Supreme Court (1 August 1989), GR No 86564. However, see *Juan Gallanosa Frivaldo v Commission of Elections and Raul R Lee*, Republic of Philippines Supreme Court (28 June 1996), GR No 120295; and *Raul R Lee v Commission of Elections*, Republic of Philippines Supreme Court (28 June 1996) GR No 123755 (per Panganiban).

[157] As an example, see the Burma Citizenship Law (Myanmar) (1982), www.unhcr.org/refworld/docid/3ae6b4f71b.html, Art 3. It includes certain ethnic groups that have 'settled in any of the territories included within the State as their permanent home from a period anterior to 1823 CE'. Although there are 135 'national races', the Rohongya are unrecognized as an ethnic group meriting nationality: Lewa (above n 153). In addition, the Council of State alone 'may decide whether any ethnic group is national or not (Art 4)'. This authority includes the decision to denaturalize an ethnic group (Art 8(a)), to decide whether an inhabitant is an 'associate citizen' or 'naturalized citizen' (Art 23) and to revoke a child's associate citizenship if one of the parents who is an associate citizen marries a foreigner (Art 29(b)). One can be naturalized by the Council of State only if one is 'able to speak well one of the natural languages' (Art 44(c)). The Council is composed of three Government Ministers: Home Affairs, Defence and Foreign Affairs.

[158] *Sudali Andy Asary et al v Van den Dreesen (Inspector of Police)* (1952) 54 *New L Rep* 66, Habeas Corpos Applications Nos 1566-1570 (Hatton) (1952), 91.

[159] ILC, 'Expulsion of Aliens: Memorandum by the Secretariat', 58th sess, A/CN.4/ 565 (10 July 2006), daccess-dds-ny.un.org/doc/UNDOC/GEN/N06/260/29/PDF/N0626029. pdf?OpenElement, para 381.

[160] *Saudi Arabia v Nelson*, 507 US 349 (1993).

[161] *Al-Kateb* (above n 146) para 4 (per Gleeson). See also *Zin Mon Aye* (above n 148). In *Case of A and Others v UK* [GC] 26 BHRC 1, [2009] ECHR 301, (2009) 49 EHRR 29, para 15, the European Court of Human Rights expressed that the legality concerned the 'rational connection' between the means (expulsion of non-nationals) and the legislative intent (preventing terrorism in the United Kingdom).

[162] *Zin Mon Aye* (above n 148) para 51 (per Lander).

been an 'ineluctable' feature of the protected domain.[163] The ICJ expressed such a viewpoint in *South West Africa Case* (1966): the protection of non-nationals involved 'a non-judicial character, social humanitarian and other' cause.[164] Even the categorization of a stateless person as an 'alien' would be considered a 'political rather than legal' matter, according to the Court. As one Australian judge put the point, an intervention into the reserved domain of the state (and of the international community) would require a court to address 'political, social and economic developments'.[165]

In this context, courts have taken issue with decisions and actions of a state *after* the executive and legislative arms of the state have determined that a natural person is de jure stateless.[166] Put differently, if a natural person's rights are recognized at all, it is only after the executive or legislative arms of the state have found her/him to be *de jure* stateless. Such prior acts of state executives and legislatures are manifested by the doctrine of marginal appreciation in European human rights discourse.[167] A series of recent domestic judicial decisions suggest that harsh conditions experienced in detention by stateless detainees are justified by virtue of the incident of nationality in the protected reserved domain of the state.[168] Judicial constraint has especially characterized Filipino courts when alleged stateless persons aspire to be politicians.[169] That said, the non-intervention of courts into the reserved domain has constrained the Australian *Ah Hin Teoh* court from adjudicating the content of the domain as represented by the executive's signing of treaties.[170] As a consequence, the Australian

---

[163] Ibid, para 71 (per Lander).

[164] *South West Africa Cases (Ethiopia v South Africa; Liberia v South Africa)*, Preliminary Objections, (1962) ICJ Rep 319, 466, (1962) 37 ILR 3.

[165] *Al-Kateb* (above n 146) para 71 (per McHugh) emphasis added.

[166] *Ahmed v Austria* (1996) 24 EHRR 278, para 39.

[167] See, eg, *Handyside v United Kingdom* (1976), Application No 5493/72, ECHR (Ser A) No 24, (1979–80) 1 EHRR 737, 58 ILR 150; and *Lustig-Prean and Beckett v United Kingdom*, Application No 31417/96, [1999] ECHR 71, (2000) 29 EHRR 548. The familiar doctrine of marginal appreciation of the sovereign authority of the state was reinforced by *Proposed Amendments to the Naturalization Provisions of the Constitution of Costa Rica* (Advisory Opinion), Inter-Am Ct HR, No OC-4/84 (19 January 1984) para 32, reported in (1984) 5 *HRLJ* 161–75 and (1984) 79 ILR 282, paras 32–33. See Chan, 'The Right to a Nationality as a Human Right: The Current Trend towards Recognition' (1991) 12 *Human Rights Law Journal* 1, 6.

[168] *Behrooz* (above n 148) para 153 (per Hayne). Costs were allotted to the detainee. See also *Vo v Minister for Immigration and Multicultural Affairs* (2000) 98 FCR 371, as quoted and discussed in *NAKG of 2002 v Minister for Immigration and Multicultural & Indigenous Affairs*, Fed Ct Australia [2002] FCA 1600, paras 38 and 42. See also *Thompson v Minister for Immigration and Multicultural Affairs* [2004] FCA 139.

[169] *Frivaldo* (1989) (above n 156). See also *Labo* (above n 156). However, see *Frivaldo* (1996) (above n 156); and *Raul R Lee v Commissioner* (above n 156) per Panganiban.

[170] *Minister for Immigration and Ethnic Affairs v Ah Hin Teoh*, High Ct Australia (1995) 183 CLR 273, para 37, 38 (per McHugh); and *Re Minister for Immigration and Multicultural Affairs v Ex parte Lam* (2003) 213 CLR 1, 76 and 147. See also Joint Statement of the Australian Minister for Foreign Affairs and the Australian Attorney-General and Minister for Justice, 'The Effect of Treaties in Administrative Decision-Making' (25 February 1997) in B Horrigan (ed), *Government Law and Policy: Commercial Aspects* (Sydney, Federation Press, 1998) Appendix 1, 52–53.

Court concluded that over 900 treaties signed by the executive of the state had not been legislated into 'law'.

B. State Immunity

The doctrine of state immunity is another example of the importance of the reserved domain. A procedural or jurisdictional bar has characterized state immunity,[171] with the 'bar' representing the boundary of the reserved domain. The European Court of Human Rights held in *Al-Adsani* (2001) that although the proscription against torture is jus cogens, the doctrine of state immunity trumps jus cogens when a state is civilly sued for damages as a consequence of the torture committed within the state's jurisdiction.[172] In a concurring judgment, Judge Pellonpää (joined by Sir Nicolas Bratza) described the jus cogens character of the prohibition against torture as a 'pyrrhic victory':

> International cooperation, including cooperation with a view to eradicating the vice of torture, presupposes the continuing existence of certain elements of *the basic framework for the conduct of international relations*. Principles concerning state immunity belong to that regulatory framework, and I believe *it is more conducive to orderly international cooperation to leave this framework intact* than to follow another course.[173]

More recently, the ICJ has justified state immunity in terms of 'the sovereign equality of states' which, drawing from Article 2(1) of the UN Charter, the Court affirms as 'one of the fundamental principles of the international legal order'.[174] Interestingly, as elaborated in chapter eight below, this principle is said to hinge upon the further premise that jurisdiction is synonymous with the territorial control of a state over all events and persons within its territory.

The boundary of the reserved domain has been described as a matter of 'procedure', while jus cogens is a substantive matter, according to the Court.[175] The Special Court for Sierra Leone has similarly 'derive[d]' state

---

[171] *Jurisdictional Immunities of the State (Germany v Italy: Greece Intervening)*, ICJ judgment of 3 February 2012, para 93; *Al-Adsani v UK*, ECtHR judgment of 21 November 2001, Application No 35763/97; *Al-Adsani v United Kingdom* (2002) 34 EHRR 11, para 48; *Arrest Warrant of 11 April 2000 (Democratic Republic of the Congo v Belgium)*, Provisional Measures by order of 8 December 2000, (2000) ICJ Rep 182, para 60 (exceptions are set out in para 61); and *Presbyterian Church of Sudan v Talisman Energy*, No 01 Civ 9882 (DLC), 2005 WL 2082846, 374 F Supp 2d 331 (SDNY 2005).

[172] *Al-Adsani v UK*, ECtHR judgment of 21 November 2001, App No 35763/97, 34 ECHR (Grand Chamber) 273, para 61.

[173] *Al-Adsani* (ibid) Annex B. See also *Doe v Exxon Mobil*, 473 F.3d 345 (District Columbia 2007), affirming the caution of *Sosa* (above n 146) 733, fn 21. See also *Sarei v Rio Tinto*, 456 F.3d 1069 (9th Circuit 2006); and *Samantar v Yousef*, 130 SCt 2278 (2010).

[174] *Jurisdictional Immunities of the State* (above n 171) para 57.

[175] Ibid, para 93.

immunity from an international community of equal sovereign states, none of which may interfere with the internal jurisdiction of another.[176] In sum, a court's scrutiny of action over the content of the reserved domain of another state is immune from judicial intervention.

C. The Content of the Reserved Domain as 'Fact' Rather Than as 'Law'

The third social-cultural feature of the incident of nationality in the reserved domain arises from the perception of the reserved domain as fact. By labelling the content of the reserved domain as 'fact', jurists ensure that judicial scrutiny of nationality matters will be 'out of bounds' for adjudication,[177] for the very term 'fact' suggests a natural rather than judicially constructed phenomenon and therefore an absence of judicial control. As an example of how the 'fact' of the reserved domain works to foreclose judicial scrutiny, the English Chancery Court in the 1920s recognized the jurisdiction of the German Nazi government to choose its nationals as it pleased and therefore maintained that Nazi nationality decisions could not be the object of judicial scrutiny in Britain.[178] As the Australian Government more recently stated, the 'factual' character of nationality in the reserved domain 'does not give rise to legitimate expectations in administrative law'.[179] In sum, the attribution of 'factuality' rather than legality to matters of nationality forecloses the judicial scrutiny of executive acts.

This point has been extended in cases concerning refugees. When a person's return to her/his state of habitual residence has led to actual fear of persecution, the fear has been categorized as a matter of objective fact rather than of law, thereby leaving the individual's subjective fear as 'out of bounds' as material.[180] The categorization of a stateless person's actual fears as 'fact' hinges to a great extent upon the 'objectivity' of the given

---

[176] *Prosecutor v Charles Taylor*, Case No SCSL-2003-01-1, Special Court for Sierra Leone (Appeals Decision on Immunity from Jurisdiction), 31 May 2004, (2004) ILR 239, para 51.

[177] *Case No 0908370* [2010] RRTA 33, paras 133 and 136.

[178] *Stoeck* (above n 110); and *In re Chamberlain's Settlement* (above n 110).

[179] Joint Statement of the Australian Ministers (above n 170).

[180] *SB v Denis Linehan (Sitting as the Refugee Appeals Tribunal) and the Minister for Justice, Equality and Law Reform* (2007) 1034 JR (High Ct Ireland), [2009] IEHC 270, para 11; and *SHM v Refugee Appeals Tribunal and Minister for Justice, Equality and Law Reform* [2009] IEHR 128, paras 54 and 56. See also *Refugee Appeal No 74540* (New Zealand: Refugee Status Appeals Authority) 1 August 2003, para 413; *SA and IA (Undocumented Kurds) v Secretary of State of the Home Department*, CG [2009] UKAIT 00006, paras 40, 93 and 95; *Refugee Appeal Nos 75960, 75961 & 75993* (New Zealand Refugee Status Appeals Authority, 10 January 2008) [2008] NZRSAA 2, para 125; *MA (Ethiopia) v Secretary of State for the Home Department* [2009] EWCA Civ 289, para 68 (per J Stanley Burton); and *SH (Palestinian Territories) v Secretary of State for the Home Department* [2008] EWCA Civ 1150, paras 22 and 49.

inter-state relations privileged in the international community.[181] The dissenting opinions of the leading ICJ precedent, *Nottebohm* (1955), describe just such judicial scrutiny of the social relationships inside the content of the domain as 'fact' rather than as law.[182] Judge Read, dissenting, cautioned that 'municipal laws are merely facts which express the will and constitute the activities of states, and . . . the Court does not interpret the national law as such.'[183] Ad hoc Judge Guggenheim, also dissenting, insisted as well that domestic law must be regarded as fact.[184] As Judge Klaestad, also dissenting, stated, the 'fact' is that the naturalization of aliens rests within the exclusive competence of the state, and therefore the manner and conditions of a state's regulation of nationality is beyond interference by another state or a court (except as a matter of domestic authority).[185] The attribution of the reserved domain as fact has continued into recent judicial decisions.[186]

VI. CONCLUSION

The reserved domain, with nationality as its primary incident, has been described as 'well-established', 'classical',[187] 'orthodox',[188] 'traditional'[189] and 'nearly unlimited'.[190] Such a standpoint emerged from the Roman Church's claim of universal jurisdiction in Christendom. In the juristic opinions of the early state-centric international community, inhabitants were said to possess a voluntary choice of nationality, a reciprocal relationship vis-à-vis a state and social bonding in the region of their habitation, or what jurists of the early modern state described as 'sociality', which justified the legal authority of states. By the late nineteenth century, however, the doctrine of the reserved domain had displaced such a social basis for the international community.

The key to this displacement has been the residuary of the international community. The residuary has been considered content-independent from the standpoint of the international community. The explanatory

---

[181] *SKM v Secretary of State for the Home Department* [2010] CSOH 172, para 34; *MA (Ethiopia)* (ibid) para 47; and *Case No 0908370* (above n 177).

[182] *Nottebohm* (above n 108)

[183] Ibid, 36.

[184] Ibid, 51–52 (s 1, para 2).

[185] Ibid, 28 (para 1).

[186] *Taiem v Minister for Immigration & Multicultural Affairs* [2001] FCA 611, para 17 (Federal Court of Australia).

[187] RY Jennings, 'General Course on Principles of International Law', in (1967) 121(2) *Recueil des cours* 503.

[188] Brownlie, 'The Relations of Nationality in Public International Law' (above n 90).

[189] ICISS (above n 140) 2.13 and 2.14.

[190] K Doerhring, 'Aliens, Expulsion and Deportation' in R Bernhardt (ed), *Encyclopaedia of Public International Law*, vol 1 (Amsterdam, Elsevier Science Publishers, 1992) 110–11.

basis of this 'given fact' is the idea of the state as a self-creative author. As an author, the content of a state's laws and administrative choices should be free from intervention by other states. Therefore, for matters inside the domain, the state has had uncontrolled discretion to legislate or administer refusal to admit, expulsion, detention and the like. This discretion has especially encumbered the conferral, withdrawal and withholding of nationality by a state legislature or executive.

At best, then, international standards have reinforced and supplemented internal jurisdiction relating to nationality. The supplemental and circularity of international standards have been protected by treaties, internal and international decisions, and opinio juris. Even the UN Charter and the UDHR, contemporary public conceptions notwithstanding, privilege the reserved domain and the concomitant incident of nationality. The reserved domain is of an international community constituted from the aggregate of the wills of states. The consequence of such a shape of the international community has been an enigma: namely, that some natural persons have remained unprotected, leaving a human toll, to which I shall now turn.

3

The Consequences of Statelessness

T
HE LEGAL AND social consequences of de jure statelessness are profound. De jure statelessness, as discussed in the previous chapters, depends upon the content and administration of domestic nationality laws. Section I of this chapter identifies a series of administrative consequences of domestic nationality law: the administrative acts of state officials, admission to the state's territory, withdrawal of nationality, expulsion and prolonged detention. Section II outlines how de jure statelessness leaves a stateless person without legal protection. Section III turns to the consequences of de jure statelessness for three particularly vulnerable groups: women and children, members of nomadic and travelling groups, and indigenous inhabitants. Section IV identifies a series of economic, social and psychological consequences for stateless persons.

I. CONSEQUENCES OF THE 'OPERATION' OF NATIONALITY LAW

The requisite of 'its law' in the treaty-based definition of a stateless person has heretofore been taken as a state's domestic law.[1] The definition has two aspects to it: first, a state law itself; and second, 'the operation' of that law. Commentators have focused upon the first condition. I shall address the second because of its apparent role in effective nationality, aside what any statute formally provides.

The important assumption in the phrase 'the operation under its law' is the presupposed sense of an international community. Such a sense of an international community protects the state's expression of its will inside the boundary of the international community's residuary. Such a residuary of the international community incorporates the reserved domain of a state. Accordingly, when I examine the residuary of such an aggregated international community, I consider the residuary and the reserved domain of a state synonymously. Inside the boundary of such a domain, the state claims a universal authority of law-making and law administra-

---

[1] UN High Commissioner for Refugees (UNHCR), 'Guidelines on Statelessness No 1: The Definition of "Stateless Person" in Article 1(1) of the 1954 Convention Relating to the Status of Stateless Persons' (20 February 2012) HCR/GS/12/01, www.refworld.org/docid/4f4371b82.html.

tion over all territory and objects.[2] *Quid-quid est in territorio, est etiam de territorio*. Malcolm Shaw has signified the universality inside the boundary of the reserved domain as follows: 'The scope of a state to extend its nationality to whomsoever it wishes is unlimited, except perhaps in so far as it affects other states.'[3] As pointed out in the previous chapter, Carl Schmitt documented the close relation of such universality to the territoriality controlled by a state.[4]

The universal jurisdiction of the residuary is manifested in various ways. For one thing, a state's domestic universal authority is protected if the very survival of the state is threatened (which survival, until recently, was posited by the executive arm of the state).[5] Aside from its connection with collective and self-defence, the absence of such universal law-making authority inside the protected reserved domain has been believed to undermine statehood. For our purposes, the state defines its own identity by setting conditions for the conferral, withdrawal and withholding of nationality and naturalization. Such conditions impact upon whether a state can legally refuse to admit, expel or forcibly displace a stateless person. The lack of a state's freedom to choose its own members would negatively impact the self-identity of a state. The state's freedom, as represented by the domain, has protected the content (that is, the state's choices) inside the boundary of the domain.

States have enacted laws according to two criteria of nationality: *sanguinis* (bloodline or parentage) and *soli* (birth). Napoleon extended *sanguinis* throughout central Europe. The colonies of France, Spain, Portugal, Italy and Germany adopted *sanguinis* as the legislated criterion of nationality. The Third Reich, I documented in chapter one, also adopted *sanguinis* in its nationality laws. After the collapse of the Soviet Union, Hungary's citizenship law likewise gave preference to refugees with Hungarian ethnicity.[6] The adoption of *sanguinis* by post-World War, newly independent states, has often had a discriminatory impact in favour of the

---

[2] See, eg, *R v Immigration Officer at Prague Airport and Another, ex parte European Roma Rights Centre and Others* (2005) 1 All ER 527, [2005] 2 AC 1, [2005] 2 WLR 1, para 12; and *Al-Kateb v Godwin* (6 August 2004) Australian High Court, (2004) HCA 37, 219 CLR 562, 208 ALR 124, 78 ALJR 1099, para 62, 65.

[3] MN Shaw, *International Law*, 5th edn (Cambridge, Cambridge University Press, 2003) 724.

[4] C Schmitt, *The Nomos of the Earth: In the International Law of the* Jus Publicum Europaeum, GL Ulmen (trans) (New York, Telos Press, 2006).

[5] *Case Concerning Military and Paramilitary Activities in and against Nicaragua (Nicaragua v United States): Merits* (27 June 1986), (1986) ICJ Rep 14, 76 ILR 349, paras 30, 41, 48 and 96; Legality of the Threat or Use of Nuclear Weapons (Advisory Opinion of 8 July 1996), (1996) 110 ILR 163, (1996) ICJ Rep 226, para 105 E, p 290 para 8 (separate opinion of Judge Guillaume) and cf p 417–27 (dissenting opinion of Judge Shahbuddeen).

[6] Military service excluded stateless persons. Non-ethnic inhabitants had problems accessing employment. Over 90% were classified as refugees. Housing, privacy and the freedom to leave were impacted. See M Fullerton, 'Hungary, Refugees, and the Law of Return' (1996) 8 *International Journal of Refugee Law* 499, 526.

dominant ethnic group on the states' territories.[7] In addition, in its post-colonial role, the United Kingdom gave preference to British subjects of diverse national origins when they sought admittance to UK territory. British nationality law has also negatively affected stateless applicants.

Sanguinis as a criterion of nationality can negatively impact social groups in two ways. For one, a natural person may find her/himself on a state's territory where s/he was not born or where s/he lacks the parentage required by the state of origin. By virtue of China's nationality law, for example, anyone born abroad is a Chinese national if both or one parent is a Chinese national. As a consequence, the state where one finds oneself may withhold conferring nationality out of deference to China's domestic jurisdiction.[8]

Sanguinis may impact statelessness in a second manner: a state may administer the *sanguinis* criterion in a manner that excludes unwanted 'strangers'. As an example, upon gaining independence in 1949, the Parliament of the former British colony of Ceylon enacted two citizenship statutes, the Ceylon Citizenship Act (1948) and the Indian and Pakistani Residents (Citizenship) Amendment Act (No 3) (1949).[9] The first allowed for citizenship either by descent (Sinhalese) or by registration (naturalization). The registration process could not be the object of judicial review. An applicant could be registered as a national only if the applicant had proof of a certain amount of capital and either seven or ten years of 'uninterrupted residence' on the territory.[10] Since it had been the custom for estate Tamil workers to regularly return to India to visit relatives and family (including spouses), the majority of estate Tamils were disqualified from gaining Sri Lankan nationality. Although almost all estate Tamils

---

[7] As Mahalic and Mahalic have expressed it, a legal category is discriminatory if it is based upon a biological sense of national origin or descent rather than upon the conferment of nationality per se: D Mahalic and G Mahalic, 'The Limitation Provisions of the International Convention on the Elimination of All Forms of Racial Discrimination' (1987) 9 *Human Rights Quarterly* 74, 76 (n 11) and 82. For the Nazi adoption, see DB Klusmeyer, 'Aliens, Immigrants, and Citizens: The Politics of Inclusion in the Federal Republic of Germany' (1993) 122 *Daedalus* 81, 85. For UK impact upon Roma, see Mahalic and Mahalic (above) 78.

[8] *Case No 0905355* (Australia Refugee Review Tribunal, 31 January 2010) [2010] RRTA 42. The Chinese nationality statute provides that the children of parents with Chinese nationality also have Chinese nationality: Nationality Law of the People's Republic of China (1980) Art 4, www.npc.gov.cn/englishnpc/Law/2007-12/13/content_1384056.htm. This is so even if the children are born outside China's territory (Art 5). One has Chinese nationality if habitually resident, born on Chinese territory and parents are stateless or 'of uncertain nationality' (Art 6).

[9] The Ceylon Citizenship Act (1948) cap 248; and the Indian and Pakistani Residents (Citizenship) Amendment Act (No 3) (1949). There have been three Constitutions of Sri Lanka: the 1947–48 Soulbury Constitution ('Ceylon Constitution and Independence Orders in Council, 15 May 1947', Gazette No 9554 (17 May 1946) (see also Ceylon Independence Act 1947, UK St ch 7 [1947]); the 1972 First Republican Constitution ([Cap 1] No 1 of 1972, 22 May 1972); and the Second Republican Constitution ([Cap 1] No 1 of 1978, I/3, 7 September 1978).

[10] See generally P Sahadevan, *India and the Overseas Indians: The Case of Sri Lanka* (New Delhi, Kalinga Publishers, 1995) 128.

applied for registration as citizens, the two statutes together, as applied, had the consequence of excluding 975,000, or 95 per cent, of estate Tamils from citizenship.[11] Sinhalese leaders expressed anxiety that the admission of the Tamils as nationals would dissolve the identity of the Sinhalese ethnicity, which in turn was considered synonymous with the state of Sri Lanka. Estate Tamils remained stateless until 1971, when India agreed to accept over a half million Tamils.[12] 150, 000 remained stateless for another 10 years, although the Minister possessed 'absolute discretion' to grant or refuse citizenship to any Tamils who lost a nationality in 1949.[13]

The above example is not an aberration from some norm of hospitality. As another example, successive Myanmar (Burma) governments have refused to give identity papers to an estimated 800,000 Rohingya.[14] The consequence has been that the Rohingyas have had difficulties in gaining employment, access to medical treatment and public education, the right to marry, permission to travel inside and across the state's borders, and the right to own property.[15] In 1982, the Burma Nationality Law also had the effect of denaturalizing inhabitants of Chinese and Indian descent.[16]

Aside from Myanmar, Bangladesh, Thailand, Philippines and Malaysia have excluded the Rohingyas from nationality.[17] During recent years, the Czech and Slovak Republics, Sri Lanka, the Philippines, Japan and the

[11] See G Khan, 'Citizenship and Statelessness in Southern Asia' New Issues in Refugee Research Working Paper No 47 (UNHCR, 2001), www.unhcr.org/cgi-bin/texis/vtx/home/opendocPDFViewer.html?docid=3bf0ff124&query=citizenship%20and%20statelessness%20in%20south%20asia. See also M Weiner, 'Rejected Peoples and Unwanted Migrants in South Asia' in M Weiner (ed), *International Migration and Security* (Boulder, Westview, 1993) 154.

[12] India agreed to repatriate 525,000 Tamils and to confer Indian nationality to them over a 15-year period. Sri Lanka agreed to confer nationality to 300,000 Tamils over the same period. See Khan (ibid). See also 'Ceylon–India Agreement on the Status and Future of Persons of Indian Origin in Ceylon (Citizenship and Nationality)' (1965) 4(1) *International Legal Materials* 103–8.

[13] The Minister's discretion, by virtue of s 8(3), had to be exercised so as to maintain the ratio of 4:7 for those 'repatriated' to India. Furthermore, the Ministerial discretion had to be exercised so that no more than 300,000 stateless persons born before 30 October 1964 should be granted citizenship. Thus, in addition to the 150,000 who remained stateless, no more than the ratio of 4:7 could be eventually granted Sri Lankan nationality over the 15-year period. See generally 'India-Sri Lanka: Agreement to Establish Peace and Normalcy in Sri Lanka' (1987) 26 *International Legal Materials* 1175.

[14] UNHCR, *Global Report 2012*, www.unhcr.org/gr12/index.xml, 148.

[15] D Weissbrodt, *The Human Rights of Non-Citizens* (Oxford, Oxford University Press, 2008) 97–99.

[16] Equal Rights Trust, 'Trapped in a Cycle of Flight: Stateless Rohingya in Malaysia' (January 2010) paras 11–22; and C Lewa, 'North Arakan: An Open Prison for the Rohingya in Burma' (2009) 32 *Forced Migration* 11, 11.

[17] The Muslim Rohingya historically lived in a territory bordering on Bangladesh and Myanmar. After Burma annexed the region following the 1824–26 armed struggle, Indian residents migrated to the area. Upon independence in 1948, successive Myanmar governments considered the migration illegal and the Rohingya as 'Bengalis'. The stateless condition of those in this group (about 80,000 at present) led the Rohingya to try to migrate to Bangladesh, Malaysia, Thailand and the Philippines. See Equal Rights Trust, 'Trapped in a Cycle of Flight' (ibid).

Côte d'Ivoire have deferred to the absence of blood relations as the basis for refusing to confer nationality upon inhabitants.[18] Undocumented persons often work as domestic servants, such as in Kuwait, with serious consequences, such as passport deprivation, debt bondage, rape, illegal confinement and other physical assault.[19] Studies also suggest a serious loss of social benefits for Roma who lack identity papers in Romania, for example.[20]

A. The Administrative Process of Naturalization

Notwithstanding the outward appearance of a nationality statute, which may very well formally respect due process and legal equality on its face, the statute may be applied in a manner that excludes members of an unwanted group. A common facility to speak and write in the dominant language of a state may be required for naturalization, for example: an applicant for naturalization to Thailand must possess 'a regular occupation' and must have 'knowledge of the Thai language'.[21] Indigenous 'hill tribe residents', who have lived on Thai territory for centuries, often do not know the Thai language.[22] The Philippines requires that nationals 'must be able to speak and write English or Spanish and any one of the principal Philippine languages'.[23] The Citizenship Law (1985) of Bhutan requires proficiency in speaking, reading and writing Dzongkha, in addition to residence within the territory for twenty years if one's parents were not born on the territory.[24] Large numbers of migrants and non Dzonghkan-speaking inhabitants have faced statelessness.

There are also unintended consequences of statelessness. For example, a state may lack the financial resources and administrative support to register

[18] See, eg, *Tennekoon v Panjan* (1958) 59 NLR 512; and *MMA Pasangna v Register-General* (1965) 67 NLR 33.

[19] Committee on the Elimination of Racial Discrimination (CERD), 'Report of the Committee (42nd session), UN Doc A/48/18 (15 September 1993), daccess-dds-ny.un.org/doc/UNDOC/GEN/N94/032/66/PDF/N9403266.pdf?OpenElement, para 362.

[20] See the Joint UN/Romanian Government Seminar on the Improvement of the Situation of the Roma in Romania (Bucharest, 2–3 November 2001), www.refworld.org/pdfid/3dbf-cc3f4.pdf, 97–98.

[21] Nationality Act (No 4) (2008) (Thailand) BE 2551, s 10. For the complexity of the process, see Vital Voices Global Partnership, 'Stateless and Vulnerable to Human Trafficking in Thailand' (June 2007), www.humantrafficking.org/uploads/publications/Vital_Voices_Stateless_and_Vulnerable_to_Human_Trafficking_in_Thailand.pdf, text associated with nn 137–42.

[22] Vital Voices Global Partnership (ibid) text associated with nn 48–63.

[23] Commonwealth Act No 473 (revised Naturalization Law) to Provide for the Acquisition of Philippine Citizenship by Naturalization and to Repeal Acts Numbered Twenty-Nine Hundred Twenty-Seven and Thirty-Four Hundred and Forty-Eight (as amended) (17 June 1939), www.refworld.org/docid/3ae6b5007.html, Art 5.

[24] BK Blitz, 'Statelessness, Protection and Equality', Forced Migration Policy Briefing 3 (Refugee Studies Centre, 2009) 12.

all infants born on its territory, as required by the UN Convention on the Rights of the Child (UNCRC) (1989) and by various treaties (which will be examined in the next chapter). The World Health Organization (WHO) has estimated that only one third of the global population lives in territories where 90 per cent or more of births and deaths are registered.[25] A major reason for the stateless condition of 220,626 inhabitants of Thailand in 2010 was the lack of registration at birth.[26] This in turn is often caused by a lack of awareness or by parental fear that registering the date of a child's birth may cause them later administrative harm. In addition to the absence of birth certificates, application and appeals processes are often complex with not infrequent changes in regulation.[27] Kuwait, Myanmar and the Democratic Republic of Congo have effectively excluded the Bedoon, Rohingya and Banyamulenge respectively from nationality through their birth registration processes.[28] Article 122(4) of Singapore's Constitution authorizes nationality if an individual has the blood relations ('by descent') of Singapore citizens; however, if within 12 months of attaining the age of 21, an individual has not applied for 'the Oath of Renunciation, Allegiance and Loyalty', as precisely worded, s/he ceases to be a citizen. Similarly, anyone who leaves North Korean territory and tries to claim asylum in South Korea risks statelessness if lacking documentation of birth registration.[29] If one has a *huaqiao* background (that is 'Chinese blood' but living outside China), one's citizenship in both North and South Korean is precarious.

B. Admission to a State's Territory

The absence of legal protection characterizes the freedom of the state to refuse admission of a de jure stateless person to its territory. Ambiguity colours the treaty-setting standards to guide and obligate state parties to protect stateless persons. As an example, Article 33(1) of the UN Convention Relating to the Status of Refugees (1951) provides that 'no state shall expel or return (*refouler*) in any manner whatsoever to the frontier of territories where his life or freedom would be threatened on account of his race,

[25] World Health Organization, 'Country Health Information Systems: A Review of the Current Situation and Trends' (2011) 21.

[26] Nationality Act (Thailand) (above n 21) s 23. D Paisanpanichkul, P Unkeao and K Wattanabhoom, '2009 Annual Report: A Situation of Personality Status and the Rights of Stateless Persons/Persons without Nationality' (Stateless Watch for Research and Development Institute of Thailand, January 2010), www.burmalibrary.org/docs08/SWITAnnualReport2009 (en).pdf, paras 2.3–2.6.

[27] Vital Voices Global Partnership (above n 21).

[28] See Equal Rights Trust, 'Trapped in a Cycle of Flight' (above n 16) paras 11–22.

[29] This and other problems in the nationality laws of the Republic of Korea are examined in S Chung, C Lee, HT Lee and JH Park, 'The Treatment of Stateless Persons and the Reduction of Statelessness: Policy Suggestions for the Republic of Korea' (2010) 13 *Korea Review of International Studies* 7, 26.

religion, nationality, membership of a particular social group or political opinion'.[30] That said, the *Handbook on Procedures and Criteria for Determining Refugee Status* asserts unequivocally that not all stateless persons crossing the state border of habitual residence are categorized as refugees.[31]

Recent domestic tribunals have set high thresholds for legally overriding a state's executive decision not to admit a stateless refugee.[32] The Human Rights Committee (HRC), in its 'General Comment 15' to the International Covenant on Civil and Political Rights (ICCPR) (1966), defers to domestic law for standards of admission: 'The Covenant does not recognize the right of aliens to enter or reside in the territory of the State party. It is in principle a matter for the State to decide who it will admit to its territory' except if non-discrimination, inhuman treatment or family life are negatively impacted.[33]

The Supreme Court of Canada recently connected the state's prerogative over the admission of non-nationals to the state's reserved domain in this way:

> People do not expect to be able to cross international borders free from scrutiny. It is commonly accepted that *sovereign states have the right to control both who and what enters their boundaries*. For the general welfare of the nation, the state is expected to perform this role. Without the ability to establish that all persons who seek to cross its borders and their goods are legally entitled to enter the country, *the state would be precluded from performing this crucially important function*.[34]

Citing dicta concerning the state's freedom of choice over the admission and expulsion of stateless persons,[35] the Canadian Federal Court decision

[30] Convention Relating to the Status of Refugees (signed 28 July 1951, entered into force 22 April 1954), 189 UNTS 150.

[31] UNHCR, *Handbook on Procedures and Criteria for Determining Refugee Status under the 1951 Convention and the 1967 Protocol Relating to the Status of Refugees*, HCR/IP/4/Eng/REV.1 (1979), re-edited, Geneva, January 1992, www.unhcr.org/3d58e13b4.html, para 102 (emphasis added). Art 101 incorporates Art 87 into its procedures regarding stateless persons: 'It is a general requirement for refugee status that an applicant who has a nationality be outside the country of his nationality. There are no exceptions to this rule.'

[32] *HS v Secretary of State for the Home Department* [2011] UKUT 124 (IAC), paras 179–80 and 185; *Johnstone v Pedlar* [1921] 2 AC 262, 283 (per Lord Atkinson); and *T v Secretary of State for the Home Department* [1996] AC 742, 754 (per Lord Mustill). See also J Hathaway, *The Law of Refugee Status* (Toronto, Butterworths, 1991) 62, 63 and 125. Cf GS Goodwin-Gill, *The Refugee in International Law*, 2nd edn (Oxford, Clarendon Press, 1996) 69–70.

[33] Human Rights Committee (HRC), 'General Comment 15' in UN, *Human Rights Instruments, Volume I: Compilation of General Comments and General Recommendations Adopted by Human Rights Treaty Bodies*, HRI/GEN/1/Rev.9 (27 May 2008), www.un.org/en/ga/search/view_doc.asp?symbol=HRI/GEN/1/Rev.9(Vol.I), Arts 5 and 9. The HRC General Comment does continue that 'in certain circumstances an alien may enjoy the protection of the Covenant even in relation to entry or residence, for example, when considerations of non-discrimination, prohibition of inhuman treatment and respect for family life arise'. See also S Joseph, J Schultz and M Castan, *International Covenant on Civil and Political Rights: Cases, Materials and Commentary* (Oxford, Oxford University Press, 2000) 105 and 383 (para 13.16).

[34] *R v Simmons* [1988] 2 SCR 495, para 49 (emphasis added).

[35] Ibid, para 24.

in *Chesters* has further widened the boundary of Canada's reserved domain so as to exclude the admission of a spouse of a Canadian citizen because she had multiple sclerosis.[36]

National security can also be a critical factor in conferring or withholding nationality, according to the HRC.[37] Once again, a very particular sense of an international community is presupposed in the above judgments and dicta, one which takes for granted that state officials may decide the boundary of the state's reserved domain.

C. Withdrawal of Nationality

The incident of nationality in the reserved domain of the aggregated international community justifies a state's withdrawal of its nationality from a natural person. Opinio juris continues to support such a freedom of the state to denaturalize its nationals in certain circumstances.[38] The problem is that with rare exceptions, stateless persons lack documentation to be legally admitted onto a state's territory.[39] This is not surprising, since even if some individuals have such documentation, they often must leave their homes on short notice due to emergencies such as armed conflict, a sudden climate event or other environmental change. Because one cannot leave the territory of a state without travel documents, departure may be occasioned contrary to the domestic law of both the state of origin and of refuge.[40] The stateless person's situation is even more complicated if s/he, lacking documentation or legal status, desires to return to the territory of origin. In order to appreciate the extraordinary consequence of the reserved domain, let us return to the post-World War I and post-World War II international law discourses concerning a state's withdrawal or withholding of nationality.

---

[36] *Chesters v Canada (Minister of Citizenship and Immigration)* [2002] FCJ No 992, (2002) FCT 727, Court No IMM-1316-97, para 127. Multiple sclerosis would likely be a hardship on the public health system of Canada, the Court contended. The self-preservation of the state overrode the protection and unity of the family as a competing social entity.

[37] *Tsarjov v Estonia*, HRC Communication No 1223/2003, CCPR/C/D/1223/2003, para 7.3 affirming *Borzov v Estonia*, HRC Communication No 1136/2002, HRC Communication No 1136/2002, CCPR/C/81/D/1136/2002.

[38] For such dicta, see International Law Commission (ILC), 'Expulsion of Aliens: Memorandum by the Secretariat', 58th sess., A/CN.4/565 (10 July 2006), daccess-dds-ny.un.org/doc/UNDOC/GEN/N06/260/29/PDF/N0626029.pdf?OpenElement, paras 894–96. See also Joseph, Schultz and Castan (above n 33) 105 and 383 (para 13.16).

[39] Russia's legislation does recognize the legal category of a stateless person.

[40] A stateless person is not entitled to de jure nationality, as evidenced by a passport, and therefore s/he cannot obtain a proper exit visa. See *SA/IA v Secretary of State of the Home Department* [2009] UKAIT 00006, paras 46 and 77.

i. Post-World War I

The most well-known expulsions of ethnic and religious groups occurred in Europe during the inter-war period.[41] When the Ottoman Empire was dissolving in 1917, domestic law denaturalized nationals if they crossed the territorial border of the Empire.[42] One and three quarters million Armenians were deported to Syria and Palestine. One million of the populace were either executed or starved upon being expelled to the desert.[43] The absence of state protection for the denaturalized inhabitants had become 'a new method of massacre', as Leo Kuper put it.[44] The expulsion and killing of 1917 followed massacres of the Armenians during 1894–96 and 1909. When Turkey succeeded a territorial part of the Ottoman Empire in 1921, Turkey refused to recognize the Nansen passport as evidence of one's nationality.[45] By the Treaty of Lausanne (1923), state parties forced the migration of 1.9 million Turkish-speaking Greeks and Greek-speaking inhabitants of Turkey in what Bernard Lewis has described as 'a brutal but effective method of exchange of populations'.[46] State denaturalization followed the migration of large numbers of persons of Armenian ethnicity to Europe, Syria and Palestine.[47] The newly created state of Turkey denaturalized all persons of Armenian ethnicity in Syria once Turkey occupied Syria in 1922. Nationality was withdrawn from persons of Armenian

[41] The mass expulsion and migration of 10–12 million German-speaking inhabitants of central and eastern Europe to German territory was resolved at the Potsdam meeting of Roosevelt, Churchill and Stalin. See Protocol of the Proceedings (1 August 1945), available at www.pbs.org/wgbh/americanexperience/features/primary-resources/truman-potsdam/.

[42] See L Kuper, 'The Turkish Genocide of Armenians, 1915–1917' in RG Hovannisian (ed), *The Armenian Genocide in Perspective* (New Brunswick, Transaction Books, 1986). See also RW Smith, 'The Armenian Genocide: Memory, Politics, and the Future' in Hovannisian (ed) (above). Bernard Lewis is of the opinion that 1.5 million perished: B Lewis, *The Emergence of Modern Turkey*, 2nd edn (London, Oxford University Press, 1968) 356.

[43] The United States Ambassador Henry Morgenthau described the massacres in vivid detail: H Morgenthau, 'Ambassador Morgenthau's Story', 308–9, as quoted in Kuper (ibid) 46–47. For other descriptive accounts, see Hovannisian (ed) (ibid) 138. Although paramilitary groups may have played an important role in the expulsion, it would be naïve to consider state officials as lacking responsibility.

[44] Kuper (above n 42) 48.

[45] See AG Duker (ed), *The Legal Status of Stateless Persons* (New York, American Jewish Committee, 1945) 22 and 44. The holder of a 'Nansen passport' could travel through Europe during the inter-war period. It was honoured by 52 governments. Stateless inhabitants of Russia especially used the passport to escape from Stalin's regime.

[46] Lewis (above n 42) 255. The statistics are drawn from JJ Preece, 'Ethnic Cleansing as an Instrument of Nation-State Creation: Changing State Practices and Evolving Legal Norms' (1998) 20 *Human Rights Quarterly* 820, 824. Lewis estimates that between 1923 and 1930 about 1.25 million Greek Orthodox Turks were exiled from Turkey to Greece, and a smaller number of Muslim Greeks from Greece to Turkey. See Treaty of Lausanne (Treaty of Peace of the British Empire, France, Italy, Japan, Greece, Romania and the Serb-Croat-Slovene State with Turkey) (1923) 28 LNTS 12, reprinted in L Martin (ed), *The Treaties of Peace, 1919–1923*, vol 2 (New York, Carnegie Endowment for International Peace, 1924) 959.

[47] See Kuper (above n 42) 43–59. See also Smith (above n 42); R Cohen, 'Diasporas and the Nation-State: From Victims to Challengers' (1996) 72 *International Affairs* 507.

ancestry if they had not participated in Turkey's War of Independence and if they had not returned to Turkey during the period between 24 July 1923 and 23 May 1927. The latter date was the effect start date for Turkey's domestic jurisdiction.[48]

Despite the effort of the Great Powers to protect linguistic and ethnic minorities in the new states configured at Versailles,[49] the Permanent Court of International Justice assured states members of the international community that they possessed the freedom to confer, withhold or withdraw nationality.[50] The old and newly recognized states following Versailles frequently refused to recognize stateless refugees as possessing legal status worthy of nationality.[51] Article 1 of the Rome Convention (1922), for example, stated, 'The ways of acquiring or losing nationality are regulated by the law of each State.'[52] The Permanent Court opinions in *Exchange of Greek and Turkish Populations* (1923) and *Administrative Decision No V* (1924) reaffirmed nationality as an incident of the reserved domain.[53]

Shortly after the Treaty of Versailles, some state practices, such as those of Poland, Romania, Latvia and Lithuania, recognized conditions of nationality in manners that excluded members of specific ethnic, linguistic and religious groups.[54] Other state practices, such as those of Slovakia, Hungary, Romania and the Protectorate of Bohemia-Moravia, required that 'evidence' be provided by members of linguistic, religious and ethnic minorities of a cultural linkage with the *Heimat* – the local village or city which had traditionally determined whom was entitled to social security. Ethnic minorities were not given a role in the monitoring or

[48] M Vishniak, *The Legal Status of Stateless Persons*, AG Duker (ed) (New York, American Jewish Committee, 1945) 22 and 44.

[49] Treaty of Peace and Minorities between Poland and Principal Allied and Associated Powers (Versailles, 28 June 1919) 225 CTS 412, Art 64; Treaty of St Germain-en-Laye (10 September 1919) 8 LNTS 25, Art 56; and Treaty of Trianon (4 June 1920) 6 LNTS 188. Hungary lost two thirds of its territory and its population: its territory was reduced from 125,000 to 36,000 square miles. Thus, large numbers of Hungarian-speaking persons inhabited Czechoslovakia, Romania and Yugoslavia. Over two million former Hungarians lived in Romania alone as a consequence of the treaty. See Fullerton (above n 6) 503 and 506.

[50] *Acquisition of Polish Nationality*, PCIJ Ser B, No 7, Advisory Opinions, vol 1 (1922–25), 6–26, 16, 2 ILR 292.

[51] See generally Vishniak (above n 48) 154. See also 28.

[52] Rome Convention (6 April 1922), reprinted in RW Flournoy and MO Hudson, *A Collection of Nationality Laws of Various Countries as Contained in Constitutions, Statutes and Treaties* (New York, Oxford University Press, 1929) 650.

[53] *Exchange of Greek and Turkish Populations*, PCIJ Ser B, No 10 (1923), 3 ILR 362, 19; and *Administrative Decision No V (US v Germany)*, Administrative Decision & Opinions, vol 1, 189, 193, (1923–24) Ann Dig Case No 10, (1924) 7 RIAA 119, 119, 2 ILR 185.

[54] Marc Visniak has documented how Hungary and Czechoslovakia went beyond the treaties so as to grant nationality to anyone born within their territories: Vishniak (above n 48) 9–20. The same was the case with Finland: 'when it is in the interest of the State, the president of the Republic may declare a Finnish national deprived of his nationality.' See Vishniak (above n 48) 20.

enforcement of protections: that was left to the bureaucrats of the League of Nations.[55]

Hannah Arendt powerfully described how the Third Reich similarly denaturalized persons of the alleged Jewish bloodline upon their forcible transport, which occurred according to domestic law.[56] On 21 January 1938, for example, Romania enacted a law that required a rigorous bureaucratic procedure to validate 'evidence' of one's right to Romanian nationality.[57] Mark Vishniak documented that Romanian officials during the pre-World War II period assumed that if one were a member of the Jewish People and claimed Romanian nationality, then the nationality must have been obtained by fraud.[58] Non-nationals carried the onus of proof to establish non-fraud. Such an onus required evidence that one lacked nationality in any other state, even if one had fought on behalf of Romania during World War I. A government report of 15 September 1939 stated that 225,222 applications for nationality (36 per cent) had been denied.[59] Fifty per cent of these were denied because of the reverse onus, 33 per cent for failure to apply within the time limit and 11.49 per cent due to 'mistake' or 'fraud'. By the end of 1940, over 350,000 Romanian nationals of the Jewish religion had become stateless under this procedure. Since former nationals, categorized legally and administratively as 'Jews', were no longer allowed to participate in Romania's political process, Romania found it legally possible to impose a new tax law upon them as foreigners on 3 December 1938.[60]

Sanguinis was followed in Nazi-annexed territories as the basis of categorizing nationals and non-nationals. Nazi Germany and its annexed countries, such as Poland, denaturalized millions of persons identified with the Jewish People, homosexuality, the Roma, liberalism and physical disabilities ('life unworthy of life'). Once denaturalized (assuming the coercion did not render void the application of the domestic laws), they

---

[55] See esp Vishniak (above n 48) 19 and 154. The Minorities Treaties were negotiated and signed between states without the consultation or involvement of the minorities. See MC Lâm, *At the Edge of the State: Indigenous Peoples and Self-Determination* (Ardsley, NY, Transnational, 2000) 94. Few complaints were scrutinized; and possible complainants became discouraged from alleging treaty violations as a consequence: Lâm (above) 9.

[56] H Arendt, *The Origins of Totalitarianism* (New York, World Publishers, 1951) 289–90.

[57] Norman Bentwich, in a close examination of how the Minorities Treaties depended upon the conferral of nationality by the states' posited law, concluded that Romania's departure from the Minorities Treaties was intentional. See N Bentwich, 'Statelessness through the Peace Treaties after the First World War' (1944) 21 *British Yearbook of International Law* 171, 174.

[58] Vishniak (above n 48) 26.

[59] These statistics are from Vishniak (above n 48) 26.

[60] For further economic laws against persons of alleged Jewish bloodline, described in some decrees as 'foreigners', see the Nizkor Project, 'The Persecution of the Jews' in Office of the US Chief of Counsel for the Prosecution of Axis Criminality, *Nazi Conspiracy and Aggression, vol 1* (Washington, DC, US Government Printing Office, 1946), www.nizkor.org/ hweb/imt/nca/nca-01/nca-01-12-jews-02.html, ch 12. See also Vishniak (above n 48) 27.

could be expelled and exterminated without external intervention into the state's domestic policies and practices.[61]

Although treaties of the 1920s and 1930s did address statelessness, the treaties also manifested the protected reserved domain of state parties. The domestic laws authoring the withdrawal of nationality were not limited only to Turkey, the Soviet Union and Nazi Germany. Many European states authorized denaturalization on the grounds of the national security of the state.[62] In particular, denaturalization was justified by European and Middle Eastern states in a series of circumstances: fraud, serious crime or disloyalty (Egypt, the United Kingdom, Canada);[63] residence abroad (Austria, Germany, Poland, France); acts contrary to the interest of the state (Austria);[64] or by being someone who had 'shown himself by act or speech to be disaffected or disloyal to His Majesty' (United Kingdom),[65] had chosen a nationality under the Minorities Treaties but who had 'shown themselves unworthy thereof by their political conduct' (Italy),[66] had been deemed to have caused a disturbance by virtue of living abroad (Italy), had committed 'any act against the public order', any act 'detrimental to the interests of Italy or to her reputation and prestige' or had disseminated 'false, exaggerated or biased' information about the politics of the state (Italy),[67] had been born in a territory now controlled by an enemy and had been found disloyal (Romania),[68] or was living abroad and 'betray[ed] by deed, word of mouth or writing, the duties which every member of the national community is bound' (France).[69] Moreover,

---

[61] For the Nazi laws, see OD Kulka and E Jäckel (eds), *The Jews in the Secret Nazi Reports on Popular Opinion in Germany, 1933–1945* (New Haven, Yale University Press, 2010) 756, 782–83 and 817–18; LS Dawidowicz (ed), *The Holocaust Reader* (New York, Behrman, 1976) 37; H Friedlander, 'German Law and German Crimes in the Nazi Era' in FC DeCoste and B Schwartz (eds), *The Holocaust Ghost: Writings on Art, Politics, Law and Education* (Edmonton, University of Alberta Press, 2000) 283–89; M Lippman, 'Law, Lawyers and Legality in the Third Reich: The Perversion of Principle and Professionalism' (1997) 14 *Temple International and Comparative Law Journal* 199; and G Kaeckenbeeck, *The International Experiment of Upper Silesia: A Study in the Working of the Upper Silesian Settlement, 1922–1937* (London, Oxford University Press, 1942).

[62] See Flournoy and Hudson (above n 52) 489.

[63] See British Nationality and Status of Aliens Acts (1914), 4 & 5 Geo 5, c 17, s 7; and JF Williams, 'Denaturalization' (1927) 8 *British Yearbook of International Law* 45. Shortly after WWII the Canadian government considered it 'mandatory' to indefinitely detain, regulate and deport racial minorities as well as minorities defined as disabled. See Canada's Minister, Ross M Winter, in Economic and Social Council (Ad Hoc Committee on Statelessness and Related Problems), 'Summary Record of 40th Meeting', UN Doc E/AC.32/SR.40 (22 August 1950). Winter was responding to the Proposed Draft Convention Relating to the Status of Refugees, Art 26 (Refugees not lawfully admitted) 2.

[64] Arendt (above n 56) 279, fn 25.

[65] British Nationality and Status of Aliens Acts (1914) (ibid) Art 7(1), as amended by 8–9 Geo V, c 38 (8 August 1918) and 12 & 13 Geo V, c 44 (4 August 1922).

[66] See Williams (above n 63) 47.

[67] As quoted in Vishniak (above n 48) 21 and 154.

[68] Williams (above n 63) 49, fn 3.

[69] As cited by Vishniak (above n 48) 32 and 154.

France denaturalized citizens born on enemy territory, persons born in Portugal from fathers who spoke German, and Belgian nationals who committed anti-German acts in the previous war.[70] The loss of legal protection under this wide range of circumstances is apparent.

ii. Post-World War II

Mindful of the reservations, limitations and derogation clauses to several human rights treaties and the three statelessness treaties (which will be examined further in the next chapter),[71] mass expulsion of stateless persons continued into the post-World War II period. Although the detention of persons 'of Japanese ancestry' (the US category) and 'of the Japanese race' (the Canadian category) ended with the termination of World War II, Canadian nationals of the latter category had to have their movements approved (even between cities) by a state official (likened to a probation officer) until 1952.[72]

As another example, in 1971, Adi Amin of Uganda revoked entry permits and certificates of residence formerly granted to 'any person who is of Asian origin, extraction or descent and who is a subject or citizen of' the United Kingdom, India, Pakistan or Bangladesh'.[73] The confiscation of assets, rape, plunder and forcible removal followed.[74] Between 80,000 and 90,000 denaturalized inhabitants were killed within two years.[75] UK offi-

[70] Arendt (above n 56) 164 and 279 (fn 25).

[71] International Covenant on Civil and Political Rights (ICCPR) (1966), 999 UNTS 171 (entered into force 23 March 1976); International Covenant on Economic, Social and Cultural Rights (ICESCR) (1966), 993 UNTS 3 (entered into force 3 January 1976); International Convention on the Elimination of All Forms of Racial Discrimination (ICERD) (1965), 660 UNTS 195 (entered into force 4 January 1969); Convention on the Rights of the Child (1989), 1577 UNTS 2 (entered into force 2 September 1990); African [Banjul] Charter on Human and Peoples' Rights (1981), OAU Doc CAB/LEG/67/3 rev 3, (1982) 21 ILM 58 (entered into force 21 October 1986); African Charter on the Rights and Welfare of the Child (1990), OAU Doc CAB/LEG/24.9/49 (1990) (entered into force 29 November 1999), reprinted in (1994) *African Yearbook of International Law* 295; Inter-American Convention on Human Rights (1969), OAS Off Rec OEA/Ser.L./V/11.23 doc.rev.2, 36 OASTS 1 (entered into force 19 July 1978); and Convention on the Rights of Persons with Disabilities (2006), 2515 UNTS 3 (entered into force 3 May 2008). The three statelessness treaties are the Convention Relating to the Status of Stateless Persons (1954), 360 UNTS 117 (entered into force 6 June 1960); Convention on the Reduction of Statelessness (1961), 989 UNTS 175, UN Doc A/CONF. 9/15(1961) (entered into force 13 December 1975); and Convention Relating to the Status of Refugees (1951), 189 UNTS 150 (entered into force 22 April 1954).

[72] For the consequences in the USA, see WE Conklin, *Phenomenology of Modern Legal Discourse* (Aldershot, Dartmouth, 1998) 83–92. For the Canadian experience, see WE Conklin, 'The Transformation of Meaning: Legal Discourse and Canadian Internment Camps' (1996) 9 *International Journal for the Semiotics of Law* 227.

[73] A Amin, 'Speech' (6 December 1971), meeting of Asian leaders in Uganda, reprinted in J-M Henckaerts, *Mass Expulsion in Modern International Law and Practice* (The Hague, Martinus Nijhoff, 1995) 210–15.

[74] See International Commission of Jurists, *Uganda and Human Rights: Reports to the UN Commission on Human Rights* (Geneva, International Commission of Jurists, 1977) 7–14.

[75] Ibid, 27–63.

cials stated that although 'in international law a state is under a duty as between other states to accept in its territories those of its nationals who have nowhere else to go', refugees from Uganda were detained upon admission and required to satisfy special administrative procedures.[76] Aside from concerns of unemployment (stated to be a million at the time) and housing in the United Kingdom, the United Kingdom's main concern was the lack of proper notice (90 days) from the Ugandan government for expelling the denaturalized individuals.[77] In other words, out of respect for the incidence of nationality in Uganda's reserved domain, the UK government did not ask for an explanation for the denaturalization and expulsion.

The withdrawal or withholding of nationality has also occurred in the context of the physical disappearance of territory due to climate change, as well as the annexation or cession of territory as a consequence of armed conflict.[78] It has also taken place as punishment for disclosing embarrassing government documents (as in the recent US case of Edward Snowden).[79] A state may refuse to recognize denaturalization by another state. A case in point was the UK practice concerning stateless Jewish refugees who had been denaturalized by Nazi Germany. Once a state dissolves or a state's territory disappears, a national of the state risks becoming stateless as long as jurists and officials assume the international community is the aggregate of the wills of states. Chapters four and five will show that standards of behaviour within the aggregated international community enter the international law discourse only after a state's act of denaturalization or after a state has dissolved.

D. Expulsion

Expulsion is frequently a further legal consequence of the stateless condition. Nonetheless, the International Law Commission (ILC) has displayed

---

[76] HL Deb 14 September 1972, vol 335, col 497.

[77] UK Foreign Minister Douglas-Home, as recorded in 27 UN GAOR (2042nd plenary meeting) 12, UN Doc A/PV.2042 (1972).

[78] For the loss of nationality as a consequence of annexation or secession of states, see ILC, 'Draft Articles on Nationality of Natural Persons in Relation to the Succession of States (with Commentaries)' in UN Doc A/54/10, *ILC Yearbook 1999*, vol II(2).For denaturalization as a consequence of climate change, see J McAdam, 'Disappearing States, Statelessness and the Boundaries of International Law' in J McAdam (ed), *Climate Change and Displacement: Multidisciplinary Perspectives* (Oxford, Hart Publishing, 2010); J McAdam, *Climate Change, Forced Migration, and International Law* (Oxford, Oxford University Press, 2012); and E Crawford and R Rayfuse, 'Climate Change and Statehood' in R Rayfuse and SV Scott (eds), *International Law in the Era of Climate Change* (Cheltenham, Edward Elgar, 2012) 243–53.

[79] In the former case, the US withdrew Edward Snowden's passport, thereby leaving him without documentation to leave the Moscow airport or to be admitted as an American national in any other state. See *The Guardian* (2 July 2013).

ambiguity towards the expulsion of stateless persons. Jurists went to great lengths during the 1920s and 1930s to emphasize how acts of expulsion were protected by the boundary of the reserved domain.[80] The Constitutional Bench of Calcutta went so far in 1955 as to hold that such a state freedom was absolute and 'unrestricted' despite a written constitution.[81] More recently, the India Supreme Court held that due process extends to expulsion only if one is legally on the state's territory.[82] Furthermore, 'reasons of national security' impact any required 'review'.[83] The Inter-American Court of Human Rights has been concerned with the expulsion of undocumented non-nationals who have inhabited a territory for a substantial time.[84]

E. Prolonged Detention

The state's reserved domain has had an added consequence: namely, the prolonged detention of stateless persons. Such has arisen generally in two sets of circumstances. First, a stateless refugee may find her/himself on a state's territory where the state withholds the conferral or recognition of her/his nationality. Although the state has an international obligation to find a third-party state that will admit the individual to its territory, the state may detain the individual until such is possible. The second circumstance arises when a state claims that it may detain a de jure stateless person, a person whose nationality is unknown, or a national who is left diplomatically unprotected by the state of nationality because of their threat to the security of the state. Let us address each circumstance in turn.

---

[80] See ILC, 'Third Report of Special Rapporteur, Nationality in Relation to the Succession of States' (2478th Meeting, GA 49th sess), UN Doc A/CN.4/479, para 54 (per J Crawford). The ambiguity continues as to whether a national standard or a minimum international standard guides a state. See ILC, 'Expulsion of Aliens: Memorandum by the Secretariat', 58th sess, A/CN.4/565 (10 July 2006), daccess-dds-ny.un.org/doc/UNDOC/GEN/N06/260/29/PDF/N0626029.pdf?OpenElement, paras 240–55. For the state's freedom to expel during the inter-war period, see GH Hackworth, *Digest of International Law*, vol 3 (Washington, DC, Government Printing Office, 1940–44) 717–18.

[81] *Hans Muller of Nuremburg v Superintendent, Presidency Jail, Calcutta*, AIR 1955 SC 554, as cited in *Anand Swaroop Verma v Union of India & Anon* (8 August 2002), 2002 VI AD (Delhi) 1025 CRLW No 746/2002, para 11.

[82] *Sarbananda Sonowal v Union of India (UOI) and Another*, India Supreme Court, Decision of 7 December 2005, Writ Petition No 131 of 2000, para 49, www.unhcr.org/refworld/docid/46b1c2eb2.html.

[83] Joseph, Schultz and Castan (above n 33) 105 and 383 (para 13.16).

[84] *Juridical Condition and the Rights of Undocumented Migrants*, advisory opinion (17 September 2003) Inter-American Court of Human Rights, OC-18/03, para 47.

i. Prolonged Detention until State of Refuge Found

The prolonged detention of stateless persons is not unfamiliar today.[85] Perhaps surprisingly, in a world with human rights treaties, prolonged detention is not uncommon, even in the case of stateless persons within territories where states claim respect for the universality of human rights.[86] As one senior Australian judge has posited, a stateless person can be mandatorily detained for life if such a person is 'unlawfully' on the state's territory.[87] Indefinite detention of a stateless person by the executive of the state does not 'impinge upon the separation of powers required by the Constitution'.[88] As such, according to Justice Gleeson of the Australian High Court, a stateless person 'lacks permission to enter or remain on Australian territory'.[89] Stateless persons are not considered criminally punished if indefinitely detained.[90]

ii. Prolonged Detention for the State's Self-Protection

Habeas corpus proceedings have not always been successful in protecting detained stateless persons.[91] 33 per cent of the prison population of Estonia is composed of stateless persons.[92] Statistics document remarkable numbers of stateless persons detained in Mexico, the United Kingdom, the Ukraine, Turkey and Bangladesh.[93] North Korea indefinitely detains

[85] See, eg, *A v Australia*, HRC, Communication No 560/1993, UN Doc CCPR/C/59/D/560/1993 (1997); *Minister for Immigration and Multicultural and Indigenous Affairs v Al Khafi* [2004] HCA 38, 208 ALR 201; and *Al-Kateb* (above n 2). See generally F Morgenstern, 'The Right of Asylum' (1949) 26 *British Yearbook of International Law* 327.

[86] *Al-Kateb* (above n 2) para 55.

[87] Ibid, paras 16 and 18.

[88] Ibid, para 268 (emphasis added). See also *Behrooz v Secretary of the Department of Immigration and Multicultural and Indigenous Affairs and Others* (16 November 2004) [2004] HCA 36, (2004) 208 ALR 271; *Vo v Minister for Immigration and Multicultural Affairs* (2000) 98 FCR 371, as quoted and discussed in *NAKG of 2002 v Minister for Immigration & Multicultural & Indigenous Affairs* (Australia) [2002] FCA 1600, paras 38 and 42. See also *Thompson v Minister for Immigration and Multicultural Affairs* [2004] FCA 139.

[89] *Al-Kateb* (above n 2) para 18. Callihan adds, 'Nor should the appellant [stateless person] be accorded any special advantages because he has managed illegally to penetrate the borders of this country over those who have sought to, but have been stopped before they could do so' (para 301).

[90] Ibid, para 266.

[91] *Sudali Andy Asary et al v Van den Dreesen (Inspector of Police)*, Habeas Corpos Applications Nos 1566–70 (Hatton), (1952) 54 NLR 66, 91; *Tan Seng Pao v Commissioner of Immigration*, GR No L-14246 (PHSC, 27 April 1960); *Lam Yin, alias Lim Yin v Commissioner of Immigration*, GR No L-22744 (PHSC, 31 March 1966); *Borovsky v Commissioner of Immigration and Director of Prisons*, GR No L-2852 [1949] PHSC 209 (30 June 1949), *Borovsky v Commissioner of Immigration*, GR No L-4352, 47 Off Gaz 136 (PHSC, 28 September 1951); *Andreu v Commissioner of Immigration and Director of Prisons*, GR No L-4253 [1951] PHSC 305 (31 October 1951); and Lewa, 'North Arakan' (above n 16) para 2.

[92] Equal Rights Trust, 'The Protection of Stateless Persons in Detention', Research Working Paper (January 2009) para 17.

[93] Ibid, paras 35–40 and 48.

political prisoners and often their family members of the past three generations as well.[94]

The best known example of prolonged detention for the self-protection
of a state is the American detention of natural persons at Guantánamo for
over twelve years without charge or civil proceedings. Many such detainees are de jure nationals, though left diplomatically unprotected by their
states of nationality. Without such diplomatic protection of their states of
nationality, their states of origin, their states of habitual residence or the
state of their detention, such persons have been effectively stateless. Two
issues have been central to the prolonged detention.

First, non-nationals have been distinguished from US nationals in terms
of due process rights. As of 22 July 2011, only one non-national at
Guantánamo had been civilly tried in American courts.[95] American legislation considers prolonged if not indefinite detention of non-nationals justifiable during 'the war on terror'.[96] Indeed, a legal opinion of the United
States has particularly isolated non-nationals for the US justification of
killing of persons by drones.[97]

Second, the self-protection of the state has traditionally been left to the
executive arm of governments. As explained in chapter one, nationality, at
least in the aggregated image of an international community, has been considered a matter of the inter-relation between states. Consistent with this
principle, the US executive has stated that the detention of non-nationals is
subject to review by the executive arm and not by the courts.[98] Although the
US Supreme Court held in *Rasul v Bush* (2004) that the Guantánamo detainees possessed a statutory right to habeas corpus because the lease with
Cuba rendered effective control over the territory to the United States,[99] the
US Detainee Treatment Act (2005) subsequently eliminated the judicial

[94] D Hawk, 'North Korea's Hidden Gulag: Interpreting Reports of Changes in the Prison
Camps' (Committee for Human Rights in North Korea, 2013).

[95] *Hamden v Rumsfeld*, 126 S Ct 2749 (2006).

[96] D Hawk, *The Hidden Gulag: The Lives and Voices of 'Those Who are Sent to the Mountains'*,
2nd edn (Washington, DC, Committee for Human Rights in North Korea, 2012) 9.

[97] US Department of Justice, 'Lawfulness of a Lethal Operation against a US Citizen Who
Is a Senior Operational Leader or Al-Qa'ida or an Associated Force', white paper (undated),
copy released by NBC news, now available at users.polisci.wisc.edu/kmayer/408/020413_
DOJ_White_Paper.pdf (last accessed 15 November 2013). Aside from Anwar-al-Awlaki, the
American religious leader suspected of being a member of a terrorist group, and the information agent of a political movement, Anwar-al-Awlaki's child was killed by a drone and
justifiably so according to US Governmental officials. Although they possessed American
citizenship, the father and son were effectively stateless, lacking any due process rights entitled of someone alleged to have committed a crime punishable by death. See *The Guardian*
from 30 September 2011, 1 October 2011 and 18 July 2012.

[98] Shortly after 9/11, the US Congress enacted the Military Commission Act, which
authorized the Secretary of Defence to create Commissions that could try Guantánamo
detainees: Military Commission Act (2006) 120 Stat 2600, USC ss 948–49.

[99] *Rasul v Bush*, 124 SCt 2686 (2004), 542 US 466, 159 L.Ed.2d 548 (per Stevens, joined by
O'Connor, Souter, Ginsburg and Breyer).

authority to review habeas corpus over Guantánamo detainees.[100] American officials have justified indefinite (not prolonged) detention of non-nationals by appealing to the executive arm of the state in matters inside the reserved domain.[101] The executive has the prerogative to determine the allegiance or security threat to the United States.[102] In March 2011, the executive arm of the state determined that of 240 detainees at Guantánamo, 48 could be detained indefinitely without criminal charge due to an alleged threat to US national security. The executive also determined that 30 Yemen nationals could be indefinitely detained based on the legislature's category of 'conditional detention'.[103] More recently, mandatory detention has been extended only to non-nationals.[104]

II. THE ABSENCE OF LEGAL PROTECTION

The above examples bring to the fore how an individual may possess nationality according to 'the operation of a state's law' and yet lack legal protection by the state. Such a condition is best described as 'effective statelessness'. Several other examples, including that of inter-family blood feuds in Albania, provide a sense of the significance of effective statelessness.[105]

A study in 2000 established that six per cent (2750 families) of the total populace of Albania regularly locked themselves in their homes for fear of

---

[100] Detainee Treatment Act (2005) 42 USC s 2000dd. The Court then held the exclusion of habeas corpus proceedings to be constitutionally invalid: *Boumediene v Bush*, 553 US 723, 476 F.3d 981, 69–70 (per Kennedy).

[101] USA, 'Response of the United States to Request for Precautionary Measures: Detainees in Guantánamo Bay, Cuba' (15 April 2002), (2002) 41 ILM 1015; Detainee Treatment Act (2005) (ibid) ss 1005 (e)(1) and (2); and Organization of American States (Inter-American Commission on Human Rights), Resolution No 2/11 regarding the Situation of the Detainees at Guantánamo United States, MC 259-02 (22 July 2011) 1 and 36.

[102] US Executive Order 13567: Periodic Review of Individuals Detained at Guantánamo Bay Naval Station Pursuant to the Authorization for Use of Military Force (10 March 2011), Federal Register 76(47) s 2.

[103] Inter-American Commission on Human Rights (above n 101) 1.

[104] The US 'National Defense Authorization Act for Fiscal Year 2012' provided that mandatory detention excluded US citizens and applied to members of Al Qaeda, 'associated groups' and 'lawful resident aliens', although the latter term was left undefined. If detention of lawful resident aliens was based on conduct occurring on US territory, detention was mandated only to the extent permitted by the Constitution of the United States." See JK Elsea and MJ Garcia, 'National Defense Authorization Act for Fiscal Year 2012: Detainee Matters', Congressional Research Service 7-5700 (28 August 2013), R42143, www.fas.org/sgp/crs/natsec/R42143.pdf.

[105] *STCB v Minister for Immigration and Multicultural and Indigenous Affairs and Another* [2006] HCA 61, paras 63–67. The Majority held that such was not a particular social group because blood reprisals were revenge for a criminal act rather than a customary law (paras 38–39). Empirical evidence about the subjective experiences of Albanians was considered necessary in order to establish discrimination towards a social group.

blood reprisal.[106] 29 persons were killed from blood feuds in 2000.[107] Moreover, at least 1000 families were prevented from voting in the 2009 election due to the fear of blood feuds.[108] The Federal Court of Canada has held that, despite a refugee tribunal's claim that a blood feud is a 'private vendetta', a blood feud triggers a Convention reason proscribing discrimination.[109] The UK Immigration Appeal Tribunal in 2004 held that Albania did not have an institutional system of protection of subjects who feared violent reprisal.[110]

The New Zealand Refugee Tribunal has accepted the empirical evidence of failures of several states to protect stateless members of ethnic groups. Eritrea, for example, has been recognized as failing to protect stateless Pentecostal Christians.[111] Syria has been found to fail to protect stateless Kurds.[112] Turkey has failed to protect women from intra-family violence and killing.[113] In 1997, Israel reportedly denaturalized persons of the Jewish religion who converted to Christianity.[114] During the American and British occupation of Iraq's territory, harm was also caused to 'nationals' on the basis of religious affiliation.[115] Subsequent to the occupation, the UK Immigration Appeal Board described how the Shia majority in Iraq failed to protect the small Palestinian population.[116] Kuwait has seri-

[106] Organization for Security and Co-operation (OSCE), 'Republic of Albania Parliamentary Elections 2009: OSCE/Office for Democratic Institutions and Human Rights (ODIHR) Election Observation Mission Final Report' (Warsaw, 14 September 2009), www.osce.org/odihr/elections/albania/38597, 11 and 18.

[107] The Kanun, a code of customary law, required that a male member be killed by a male member of the victim's family. The Kanun (signifying 'rule') supplemented sharia (Islamic law) and the Sultan's discretion in the Ottoman Empire.

[108] OSCE (above n 106).

[109] *Pepa v Canada (Minister of Immigration and Immigration)* [2002] Fed Ct Rep 834.

[110] *Brozi* [2003] UKIAT 06978, 14, as quoted in *TB (Blood Feuds: Relevant Risk Factors) Albania CG* (Immigration Appeal Tribunal, 8 June 2004) [2004] UKIAT 00158, para 34; and *Koci v Secretary of State for Home Department* [2003] EWCA Civ 1507.

[111] *Refugee Appeal No 74911* (New Zealand Refugee Status Appeals Authority, 1 September 2004), www.refworld.org/docid/477cfbb5d.html.

[112] *Refugee Appeal No 75779* (New Zealand Refugee Status Appeals Authority, 10 May 2006), www.refworld.org/docid/477cfbc4e.html.

[113] *Refugee Appeal No 76044* (New Zealand Refugee Status Appeals Authority, 11 September 2008), www.refworld.org/docid/48d8a5832.html, paras 44–56.

[114] *Refugee Appeal No 76077* (New Zealand Refugee Status Appeals Authority, 19 May 2009) [2009] NZRSAA 37, www.refworld.org/docid/4a2e24702.html. The tribunal took the claim at face value. Cf *Refugee Appeal No 76168* (NZ Refugee Status Appeals Authority, 30 June 2008), www.refworld.org/docid/487c98b72.html, paras 62–67.

[115] *Refugee Appeal No 76163* (NZ Refugee Status Appeals Authority, 18 February 2008), www.refworld.org/docid/47c57dd22.html.

[116] *NA (Palestinians: Risk) Iraq v Secretary of State for the Home Department* (UK Asylum and Immigration Tribunal), CG [2008] UKAIT 00046, www.unhcr.org/refworld/docid/48316e902.html. France authorized denaturalization as a criminal sentence if a national were convicted of a felony or if s/he were absent from French territory for more than five years. Spanish nationality can be withdrawn as a sentence for the commission of a crime against the external security of the State. Also note that the withdrawal of Edward Snowden's US passport in June 2013 upon suspicion of having committed a crime rendered him effectively stateless, if not de jure stateless. See above n 79.

ously discriminated against the 120,000 stateless Bedoons, including historical disenfranchisement, physical persecution and generally a 'twilight existence'.[117]

To take another example of formal denaturalization, the inhabitants of the West Bank were nationals of Jordan prior to the Israeli occupation from 1967. In 1988, the state of Jordan renounced its claim of title to the West Bank and then withdrew its nationality from West Bank inhabitants. Jordan also claimed legal authority to deport anyone with a Jordanian passport to the West Bank.[118] Serious suffering has been caused to stateless Palestinians in Gaza (which Jordan controlled at the time) because family members were alleged to have played a role in the Palestinian uprising in Jordan in 1970.[119]

Other recent examples of effective statelessness arise from refugee tribunals. Documentation has been accepted by tribunals that members of the Roma ethnic group have been subject to harassment by police, discrimination in the workplace, restricted access to public education, and hate violence.[120] China has been found to turn a blind eye to the extraordinary and widespread ethnic discrimination of the Uyghur people.[121] Cambodia has ignored the rape, violence, economic vulnerability to public officials and police abuse suffered by 'Cambodian women who are second wives'.[122] The harm has included social rejection, a lack of the means of survival, absence of freedom of movement and years of quasi-detention in abusive families. Afghanistan has also considered Assyrian Christians as threatening the life of the state.[123] The state of Zimbabwe has allowed state officials and paramilitary groups to harass, intimidate and physically harm members of particular political parties.[124] Egyptian officials

---

[117] *Refugee Appeal No 76506* (NZ Refugee Status Appeals Authority, 29 July 2010), www.refworld.org/docid/4c6a51ea2.html, paras 77 and 81.

[118] See *Al-Kour v Governor of the Department of Inspection, Minister of Interior* (1990–91) 6 *Palestine Yearbook of International Law* 68, as discussed in *MA (Palestinian Territories) v Secretary of State for the Home Department* [2008] EWCA Civ 304 UK CA (Civ Div), para 49.

[119] *Refugee Appeal Nos 73952–58* (NZ Refugee Status Appeals Authority, 26 May 2005), www.refworld.org/docid/477cfbc00.html.

[120] *Case No 1002353* [2010] RRTA 589 (Australia Refugee Review Tribunal, 18 July 2010), www.refworld.org/docid/4c879cf52.html, paras 24–37.

[121] *Case No 1002472* [2010] RRTA 591 (Australia Refugee Review Tribunal, 12 July 2010), www.refworld.org/docid/4c879f712.html.

[122] *Case No 1002606* [2010] RRTA 484 (Australia Refugee Review Tribunal, 16 June 2010). However, the Australian Refugee Review tribunal has recently held that the proscription against discrimination under a human rights treaty is not constituted from the threat, assault, abuse or physical attack upon a woman by her husband: *Case No 1004365* [2010] RRTA 740 (2 September 2010), www.refworld.org/docid/4ce2bfd32.html, para 78. The particular social group must have some common element which unites them. The group must not be defined by the persecution (para 72). Women are not such a group, according to the Tribunal (para 78).

[123] *Case No 1005628* [2010] RRTA 822 (Australia Refugee Review Tribunal, 21 September 2010), www.refworld.org/docid/4cbf28c12.html.

[124] *Case No 1002650* [2010] RRTA 595 (Australia Refugee Review Tribunal, 14 July 2010), www.refworld.org/docid/4c87a1742.html.

have been allowed to be 'intolerant' toward those whose religious practices appear to 'deviate from mainstream Islamic beliefs and whose activities are alleged to jeopardize communal harmony'.[125] Complex Russian legislation requiring strict residence in naturalization applications has led to members of ethnic groups in central Asia and the Caucasus remaining stateless or with undetermined nationality.[126] Turkey's officials have been stated to have arbitrarily detained, interrogated upon arrival and categorized a substantial number of Turkish citizens of Kurdish ethnicity.[127] An unsubstantiated claim has been made that the state of Bangladesh would condone the stoning to death of homosexuals.[128] During 2012, a global total of 8,395,000 individuals fled their homes, meaning that on any given day, an average of 23,000 persons had fled their homes.[129]

Internal displacement represents a further example of effective statelessness. During 2012, 17.7 million internally displaced persons benefitted from protection and assistance from the UN High Commissioner for Refugees (UNHCR), an increase of 2.2 million over 12 months. 45.2 million persons were forcibly removed from their homes.[130] Internal displacement in the Soviet Union during the 1990s involved substantial numbers.[131] In 2010, an estimated 2.5 million people were displaced in eastern and central Asia, of which 2.19 million were displaced directly because of the collapse of the USSR.[132]

When India became independent in 1947, the Bihari people, who are Muslim in religion and largely Urdu-speaking, found themselves effectively stateless. This in turn left them without legal protection against atrocities.[133] The surviving members (one million) thereupon migrated to East

---

[125] *Case No 1003232* [2010] RRTA 561 (Australia Refugee Review Tribunal, 1 July 2010), www.refworld.org/docid/4c878aa52.html.

[126] UN HRC, 'Report of the Human Rights Committee', vol I, GA, A/65/40, para 68(9).

[127] *Case No 1003878* [2010] RRTA 746 (Australia Refugee Review Tribunal, 9 August 2010), www.refworld.org/docid/4cbf23442.html.

[128] *Case No 1003995* [2010] RRTA 580 (Australia Refugee Review Tribunal, 7 July 2010), www.refworld.org/docid/4c879a0c2.html.

[129] UNHCR, *Global Trends 2012: Displacement, the New 21st Century Challenge*, available at unhcr.org/globaltrendsjune2013/, 21.

[130] Ibid.

[131] For examples, see *Sisojeva v Latvia* GC [2005] ECHR Application No 60654/00, (2007) 45 EHRR 33, paras 58–61; *Tatishvili v Russia*, Application No 1509/02, (2007) 45 EHRR 52, 91; and *Kaftailova v Latvia*, European Court of Human Rights Application No 59643/00 (22 June 2006), www.refworld.org/docid/44e5c05e4.html.

[132] JP DeBarry and B Petrini, 'Forced Displacement in Europe and Central Asia: Social Development' (World Bank, 2011) 2–3.

[133] When India was divided into India and Pakistan, 30,000 Muslim Biharis in India were massacred in October–November of 1947. This historical experience is summarized in S Sen, 'Stateless Refugees and the Right to Return: The Bihari Refugees of South Asia, Part 1' (1999) 11 *International Journal of Refugee Law* 625; and S Sen, 'Stateless Refugees and the Right to Return: The Bihari Refugees of South Asia, Part 2' (2000) 12 *International Journal of Refugee Law* 41. See generally Associated Press, 'Tikka Khan: Pakistan's "Butcher of Bengal"', *Toronto Globe and Mail* (2 April 2002) R7. More recently, the Supreme Court of Bangledesh has held that the Biharis are citizens of Bangledesh and therefore entitled to vote: *Abid Khan and*

Pakistan. Sharing the same language as the Pakistani, the Biharis benefited from Urdu-speaking Pakistani governments. But when Bangladesh became independent of Pakistan in 1971, the 750,000 Biharis were displaced to refugee camps, where they were subject to mob attacks, kidnappings and killings (over 1000 civilians). It appears that 250,000 to 300,000 remain de jure stateless because Bangladesh state officials consider them nationals of Pakistan. This is so despite their social bonding on Bangladesh territory for many years.

III. THE CONSEQUENCES FOR THREE GROUPS

De jure statelessness raises several social consequences that need highlighting. Stateless persons are too frequently considered to be unlawfully inhabiting a state's territory by virtue of an absence of nationality 'by operation of the state's law'. Since, we shall see in the next chapter, various rights require that one be lawfully on a state's territory for their enforcement, international legal protection of de jure stateless persons is suspect. This in turn affects the economic insecurity and psychological well-being of inhabitants who are expelled or displaced to refugee camps.[134]

A. Women and Children

Statelessness impacts especially negatively upon women and children. 48 per cent of the refugee population and 51–78 per cent of the stateless population have involved women and girls during recent years.[135] It bears repeating that during 2012, children under 18 years of age constituted 46 per cent of refugees, 34 per cent of asylum-seekers and roughly 50 per cent of all persons of concern to the UNHCR.[136] 21,300 unaccompanied children launched asylum applications in 2012.[137] The UNHCR recently

---

Others v Government of Bangladesh and Others, Writ Petition No 3831 of 2001 (Bangladesh Supreme Court, 5 March 2003), www.refworld.org/docid/4a54bbcf0.html.

[134] 'There are inevitable tensions between international obligations and national responsibilities when countries called upon to host large refugee populations, even on a temporary basis, are suffering their own severe economic difficulties, high unemployment, declining living standards, shortages in housing and land and (or) continuing manmade and natural disasters': High Commissioner for Refugees Programme Sub-Committee of the Whole on International Protection, 'Implementation of the 1951 Convention and the 1967 Protocol Relating to the Status of Refugees', UN Doc EC/SPC/54 (7 July 1989), paras 8–22.

[135] UNHCR, *Global Trends 2012* (above n 129) 3.

[136] UNHCR, 'Statistical Yearbook 2011: Trends in Displacement, Protection and Solutions' (Geneva, 8 April 2013), www.unhcr.org/516282cf5.html, 46–47. See generally UNHCR, 'Revised Background Note on Gender Equality, Nationality Laws and Statelessness' (8 March 2013), www.refworld.org/docid/4f59bdd92.html.

[137] UNHCR, *Global Trends 2012* (above n 129) 3 and 28.

outlined a series of states that do not allow mothers to confer their nationality to their children, including Qatar, Kuwait, Lebanon, Somalia, Swaziland, Madagascar, Senegal, Brunei Darussalam and Iran.[138] These states moreover do not allow for administrative discretion in favour of women. Other states allow children to adopt the nationality of their mothers if the father is stateless or unknown, including Jordan, Libya, Saudi Arabia, the United Arab Emirates, Syria, Bahrain, Mauritania and Yemen. Some states possess gender equality in constitutional texts but lack nationality laws that reflect such equality (Burundi, Liberia, Sudan and Togo). Another group of states, including the Bahamas, Barbados and Suriname, excludes children from having the nationality of their mothers if the mother is born outside the country's territory. In Suriname, children born out of wedlock take on the father's nationality.

With little or no legal protection, the 'ordinary' circumstances of stateless children and women mean that they are even more vulnerable to kidnapping, trafficking and smuggling for sexual slavery or enforced military service.[139] Because the Myanmar Citizenship Act does not recognize members of the Rohingya group as Myanmar citizens, Rohingya children in the past have been subject to forced labour.[140] A surprisingly large number of children are abandoned or their parents killed or disappeared.

Sanguinis as the criterion of nationality has had especially negative consequences for women. Alice Edwards has recently surveyed these consequences.[141] *Sanguinis* has left women without nationality especially where states turn to the bloodline of husbands. Married women may not transfer their Jordanian citizenship to their children or husbands, for example.[142] Similarly, a married Filipino woman may not extend her application for nationality to include her husband (although her children may petition to

---

[138] UNHCR, 'Revised Background Note' (above n 136).

[139] See Refugees International, 'Statelessness: International Blind Spot Linked to Global Concerns' (2 September 2009), www.refintl.org/sites/default/files/090209_stateless_0.pdf; and A Lansink (Rapporteur), 'Women and Migration' in International Law Association, *2006 Conference Report*, www.ila-hq.org/download.cfm/docid/F62AC486-97F2-4197-978A1DB72E152795. The Final Report of the UNHCR's Questionnaire concerning statelessness concludes that women and children are 'disproportionately' affected by being stateless in regard to human trafficking: UNHCR Department of International Protection, 'Preliminary Report Concerning the Questionnaire on Statelessness Pursuant to the Agenda for Protection' (September 2003), para 69. See A Conklin and BM Meir, 'A "Vector of Rights" Approach for Public Health: Towards an Intersectional Human Rights Framework for Considering the Prevention and Treatment of Harms to Girl Child Soldiers' (2008) 13 *Australian Journal of Human Rights* 65.

[140] Lewa, 'North Arakan' (above n 16) para 2. This information is dated 2009.

[141] UNHCR, 'Sex Breakdown for Stateless Populations in Selected Countries, end-2008', as cited in A Edwards, 'Displacement, Statelessness and Questions of Gender Equality and the Convention on the Elimination of All Forms of Discrimination against Women', background paper prepared for a joint UN High Commissioner for Refugees and UN Committee on the Elimination of Discrimination against Women seminar (August 2009), www.refworld.org/docid/4a8aa8bd2.html, 57–58.

[142] Blitz, 'Statelessness, Protection and Equality' (above n 24) 14.

have their alien certificates cancelled).[143] A similar problem applies to a woman whose child is born in South Korea but the father is from another state.[144] Not infrequently, efforts are made by states to make it difficult for nationals to marry stateless inhabitants.[145] One indirect way of doing so is to shift the nationality of the woman to that of the husband upon marriage.[146] If the husband is stateless, so too does the wife become stateless. The common language testing of the European states negatively impacts upon the capacity of stateless women to gain nationality if they are culturally excluded from obtaining education.[147]

In other contexts, women may be unable to pass their citizenship to their children even if the result is that the children will lack nationality. This may be the case if, for example, a child is born in a state where nationality is only passed on through fathers yet the child's father is de jure stateless. This is also the case if the mother has the nationality of the state of the child's birth and yet the child finds her/himself without a father in a state where the *sanguinis* of the father determines the child's nationality. Under Jordanian law, if the father is of Palestinian ethnicity, his children are thereby rendered stateless.[148] Children are prone to become stateless when they have not been registered at birth, especially during military/political strife or natural disaster.[149] In 2012, 40 million or one third of all births on the globe were unregistered, largely due to the lack of resources or state bureaucracy.[150] The United Nations Children's Fund (UNICEF) has estimated that 80 states lack 'well-functioning civil registrations systems' to document births.[151] The lack of judicial intervention into these matters has been justified in terms of the executive's authority, as an incident of the

[143] An Act Making the Citizenship of Philippine Citizens Who Acquire Foreign Citizenship Permanent, Republic Act No 9225 (23 August 2003) s 12.

[144] Chung, Lee and Park (above n 29) 8–9.

[145] See generally C McIlwaine, 'The Gendered Exclusions of International Migration: Perspectives from Latin American Migrants in London' in S Chant (ed), *The International Handbook of Gender and Poverty* (Cheltenham, Edward Elgar, 2010) 260–65; and International Law Association, 'Final Report of the Committee on Feminism and International Law, Women's Equality and Nationality' (London, 2000).

[146] MS McDougal, HD Lasswell and LC Chen, 'Nationality and Human Rights: The Protection of the Individual in External Arenas' (1974) 83 *Yale Law Journal* 901, 901–3, 939–40 and 973–74.

[147] See generally, Edwards (above n 141).

[148] Blitz, 'Statelessness, Protection and Equality' (above n 24) 14.

[149] Council of Europe Committee of Ministers, 'On the Nationality of Children', Recommendation CM/Rec (2009) 13, wcd.coe.int/ViewDoc.jsp?id=1563529.

[150] World Health Organization, 'Country Health Information Systems: A Review of the Current Situation and Trends' (Geneva, 2011), www.who.int/healthmetrics/news/chis_report.pdf, 1. According to Plan International in the context of Universal Birth Registration, 51 million children go unregistered every year. See the Universal Birth Registration website at plan-international.org/birthregistration/the-campaign/faq/ #what-is-the-problem.

[151] United Nations Children's Fund (UNICEF), 'Strengthening Birth and Death Registration', press release (19 April 2013), www.unicef.org/media/media_68810.html. See also UNICEF, 'Innocenti Insight: Birth Registration and Armed Conflict' (Innocenti Research Centre, 2007) 7.

reserved domain of the state, to mandatorily detain children.[152] The onus to prove legal status before applying for entry to a state has been imposed even on stateless children.[153]

Statistics about de jure statelessness understate the social consequences for women and children. The UNHCR explained in 2001, 'Women who *have* citizenship may end up living as stateless persons because the statelessness of their spouses or of their children imposes upon them all the attributes of statelessness itself.'[154] The internal displacement and forced migration of de jure and effectively stateless women and children may lead to psychological confusion or trauma, sexual assault, disrupted and broken families or abandonment or death of parents. Effectively stateless girls and women experience special health problems when conscripted as soldiers.[155] So too, girls and women are effectively or 'essentially stateless', according to the UNHCR, when they becomes objects of sex trafficking.[156]

Afghanistan has been found to ignore the harm widely suffered by 'elderly Afghan women without male protection'.[157] This includes women who are divorced, unmarried non-virgins or have broken marriage engagements. Pakistani officials have also tolerated familial violence towards women.[158] Sexual slavery of women and girls may be the consequence of an absence of documented legal identity.[159] A UK tribunal, although deciding the refugee status of a male applicant, made clear that one's effective statelessness is definitively a matter of a state's reserved domain, even if – or perhaps especially if – the circumstances causing statelessness have 'nothing to do with persecution for Convention reasons'.[160]

De jure and effective statelessness has significant effects on the access of children to public education. The Permanent Court recognized this in 1935.[161] Expected future social costs have often deterred states of refuge from accepting parentless children in particular. As an example, the UK government and public were hesitant to support the entry of 'refugees' from Reich-controlled territories until after Kristallnacht (10 November

---

[152] *Minister for Immigration and Multicultural and Indigenous Affairs v B & Another* [2004] HCA 20; and *Odhiambo v Minister for Immigration & Multicultural Affairs* [2002] FCAFC 194, para 130.

[153] See, eg, *B & Another* (ibid).

[154] UNHCR, 'UNHCR's Activities in the Field of Statelessness: Progress Report' (30 May 2001), UN Doc EC/51/SC/CRP.13.

[155] See Conklin and Meir (above n 139).

[156] UNHCR, 'Statelessness: Prevention and Reduction of Statelessness and Protection of Stateless Persons' (14 February 2006), UN Doc EC/57/SC/CRP6, 4. Although a woman or girl may well possess a passport or other identity card, such documents are often confiscated by pimps, with the consequence that the woman or girl is left effectively stateless.

[157] *Case No 1005628* (above n 123).

[158] *Minister for Immigration & Multicultural Affairs v Khawar* (2002) 1 CLR 1, 11–12.

[159] See Conklin and Meir (above n 139).

[160] *Odhiambo* (above n 152) para 130. The applicant was apparently expected 'to fend for himself on the streets of Mombasa' during the Rwandan genocide.

[161] *Albania Minorities Schools Case*, PCIJ Ser A/B, No 3 (1935) 1, 8 ILR 386, para 128.

1938).[162] Moreover, during the war, stateless children in the United Kingdom were threatened with expulsion to their states of origin as a form of adolescent discipline.[163] Children (as well as adults) were categorized as 'enemy aliens' rather than refugees.[164] In Romania, children born from stateless parents have been found to lack access to child benefits and to other forms of social and medical protection.[165] There have been cases reported of Roma parents renouncing what de jure nationality they may have and changing their names in order to gain entrance to another state's territory, sometimes using forged documents.[166] If refused admission to the new state, they are returned to the state of 'habitual residence' – but now without legal status. Their children who retain their unregistered family names and documentation have had difficulty in gaining access to public education. Elena Rozzi has recently documented the subtle social, educational and economic consequences of statelessness for undocumented children in Italy.[167]

B. Nomadic and Travelling Groups

De jure and effective statelessness often affect members of nomadic groups and travelling groups. The European Court of Human Rights has described nomadic groups in the modern international legal order as paradoxical, in that from the standpoint of the state, there is no solution to them.[168] The absence of citizenship documentation for nomads or travellers has led to 'a sub-category of humanity', as the *New York Times* recently

---

[162] In the nine months after Kristallnacht, 9,354 unaccompanied (and very vulnerable) children (of a total of 20,000 Jewish children) entered Great Britain. See G Dubrovsky, *Six from Leipzig* (London, Frank Cass, 2002) 8–21 and 25–34.

[163] Dubrovsky (ibid) 34. See also a Home Office memo dated 13 July 1939, HO 45/20226 – tc 3727 (London), copy in possession of the author. Charles Stead, the overseer for refugees, appreciated that the children in question would likely be killed if expelled from Britain; but with the threat, the children 'would be likely to fall into line', he stated. In addition, 'the general understanding is that these boys are to be emigrated on reaching 18.'

[164] In a memorandum dated 2 April 1941, a volunteer organization called the Friendly Aliens Protection Committee of London urged a re-categorization of the refugees from 'enemy aliens' to a more hospitable legal category. The Committee believed that the refugees, as 'enemy aliens, risked being considered loyal supporters of the Nazis and, indeed, risked being interned under the royal prerogative. Friendly Aliens Protection Committee, 'Memorandum on the Legal Position of Refugees from Germany, Austria and Italy' dated 2 April 1941 from 'Friendly Aliens Protective Committee' HO 45/23514–tc 3727 (on file with author).

[165] For the above facts, see the Joint UN/Romanian Government Seminar (above n 20).

[166] Ibid, 98.

[167] E Rozzi, 'Undocumented Migrant and Roma Children in Italy: Between Rights Protection and Control' in J Bhabha (ed), *Children without a State: A Global Human Rights Challenge* (Cambridge, MA, Massachusetts Institute of Technology Press, 2011) 181–84.

[168] *Kalderas Gipsies v Federal Republic of Germany*, European Commission of Human Rights, Applications No 7823/77 and 7824/77, 11 D & R 221 (6 July 1977). There is no legal solution if one presupposes the international community as an aggregate of the wills of states, as argued below in ch 9.

put it.[169] Nomadic and travelling groups are important because their occupational and social relationships lack the fixed territorial situs pre-supposed in treaty and customary doctrinal norms. We shall note in chapter six that two criteria trigger de jure protection of a natural person: allegiance to a state and habitual residence. Nomadic and travelling groups certainly lack habitual residence on a territory. And continual movement contradicts the requisite of a fixed address, which is usually needed for access to medical services, public education and employment, not to mention de jure nationality or other legal status even in states of the northern hemisphere (which are generally associated with 'developed economies'). Members of nomadic and travelling groups may often be effectively stateless even if states provide them with documented evidence signifying de jure nationality.

Nomadic groups comprise two types: pastoralists/agro-pastoralists; and hunter-gatherers. Estimates for the latter are difficult to estimate, but their numbers seem relatively small, except for traditional societies, which are identified below. Pastoralism is understood as 'strategic mobility'. Estimates of such pastoralism vary, but a study published by the African Union in 2010 estimated there to be 268 million pastoralists on the globe.[170] 43 per cent of Africa's land mass is occupied by such pastoral groups.[171] Another study, published in 2006 and based upon 2002 data, estimated 120 million pastoralists on the globe, with 50 million in sub-Saharan Africa, 31 million in west and north Africa and 40 million elsewhere.[172] An Indian government study in 2009 put the members of 'denotified, nomadic and semi-nomadic' tribes at 60 million members in India alone.[173] In another 2001 study, Bangladesh was said to have 1–5 million Bede (occupational travellers, also called 'river gypsies').[174] The study estimated Pakistan has having 'millions' of nomads (mainly pastoral).

[169] M Carr, 'Europe's War against Immigrants', *New York Times* (7 November 2010) 2.
[170] African Union (Department of Rural Economy and Agriculture), 'Policy Framework for Pastoralism in Africa: Securing, Protecting and Improving the Lives, Livelihoods and Rights of Pastoralists Communities', (October 2010), rea.au.int/en/sites/default/files/Policy%20Framework%20for%20Pastoralism.pdf?q=dp/rea/sites/default/files/Policy%20Framework%20for%20Pastoralism.pdf.
[171] See European Commission in Partnership with the African Union Commission, 'Brussels Policy Briefing No 26: New Challenges and Opportunities for Pastoralism in ACP countries' (22 February 2012), brusselsbriefings.files.wordpress.com/2012/02/br26_pastoralism_note.pdf.
[172] N Rass, 'Policies and Strategies to Address the Vulnerability of Pastoralists in Sub-Saharan Africa', PPLPI Working Paper No 37 (14 September 2006), www.fao.org/Ag/AGAInfo/programmes/en/pplpi/docarc/wp37.pdf, 10. See also the Dom Research Centre studies website at www.domresearchcenter.com/population/index.html.
[173] A Dandekar, 'The Issue of Denotified Tribes in Independent India', Working Paper 214 (Institute of Rural Management Anand, May 2009), www.irma.ac.in/pdf/randp/731_77836.pdf. A denotified tribe is defined as a tribe that the earlier colonial regime created.
[174] A Sharma, 'South Asian Nomads: A Literature Review', Create Pathways to Access Research Monograph No 58 (University of Sussex Centre for International Education, January 2011), www.create-rpc.org/pdf_documents/PTA58.pdf.

When we turn to empirical studies about travelling groups, the European Union alone has addressed a variety of such groups: bargee families, circus/fairground/carnival travellers, seasonal workers, Roma, Sinti, Irish Travellers (and other travellers), as well as Sami.[175] The number of school-age children in the European Union (other than Roma) is estimated at just under 10,000 of a total of 2,168,256 members of travelling groups.[176]

Empirical research suggests a correlation for nomadic and travelling groups between the condition of de jure statelessness on the one hand and negative social and economic consequences on the other. Difficulties in the context of education have been well documented.[177] In particular, as noted above, access to public education for children is difficult when parents have changed their names in order to gain access to the territory of another state and then, upon deportation from the latter, the children's last name differs from the parents'. Aside from the prejudice and racism against Roma children in the schools of France, Italy, Portugal and Spain, the restrictions placed upon the length of time permitted to camp more generally affects regular attendance at school.[178] Frequent interruptions in learning and parental absence cause deep social harm for the children of nomadic and travelling groups.[179] Access to public health initiatives and health services is problematic, as evidenced by the surprisingly short life-expectancy of members of Irish traveller groups.[180]

Diverse and complex movements of nomadic groups characterize the Middle-East,[181] and there is a similar absence of legal and social protection. In Kuwait, 120,000 nomadic Bedoons have suffered from unequal and inadequate social and economic conditions (such as lack of legal capacity to register marriages or to access state health services and welfare) in comparison with Kuwaiti nationals.[182] The New Zealand Refugee

---

[175] Ecorys UK (formerly ECOTEC Research and Consulting), 'Study on the School Education of Children of Occupational Travellers in the EU: A Final Report to the Directorate General for Education and Culture of the European Commission' (January 2008), ec.europa.eu/education/more-information/doc/travel_en.pdf, 11–34.

[176] Ibid, 15, 18–19, 21, 27 and 33.

[177] Ibid.

[178] Ibid, 30.

[179] Rozzi (above n 167). See also Ecorys (above n 175) 38–42.

[180] All Ireland Traveller Health Study Team, 'Summary of Findings' (School of Public Health, Physiotherapy and Population Science, University College Dublin, September 2010) 86–95.

[181] N Dyson-Hudson, 'The Study of Nomads' in W Irons and N Dyson-Hudson (eds), *Perspectives on Nomadism* (Leiden, Brill, 1972); R Dyson-Hudson, 'Pastoralism: Self Image and Behavioral Reality' in Irons and Dyson-Hudson (eds) (above); and DG Bates, 'Differential Access to Pasture in a Nomadic Society: The Yörük of Southeastern Turkey' in Irons and Dyson-Hudson (eds) (above).

[182] *Refugee Appeal No 74467* (New Zealand Refugee Status Appeals Authority, 1 September 2004), www.refworld.org/docid/477cfbb50.html, paras 63–71. Roma have remained stateless on Spanish territory for over 10 years. See *Refugee Appeal No 76506* (above n 117) paras 77 and 81. See also R Zaretsky, 'France and the Gypsies, Then and Now', *International Herald Tribune* (7 September 2010); S Erlanger, 'In France, Roma Are Wedge Issue', *International*

Tribunal has found that from 1986 onwards, the Kuwaiti state has denied travel documents to the Bedoons, rendered them unemployed, denied them driver's licenses, denied public education to their children and denied their eligibility to professional organizations. Gender discrimination has reinforced the exclusionary character of Kuwaiti economic and social practices against the Bedoons: only children born from Kuwaiti fathers are recognized as nationals. If they were allowed to return to Kuwait at all after the second Iraq War, many Bedoons feared further persecution.

Members of nomadic and travelling groups generally lack fixed addresses, which are needed to qualify for nationality documentation. The reserved domain of the state means state officials are free to leave members of such groups without legal documentation. As an example, nationality has been withheld from Roma by several European states.[183] This is so globally for 51 million children in 65 states according to a 2007 UNICEF study.[184] Asylum applicants, if successful, may well receive social benefits, which they share with inhabitants to whom the state has conferred nationality. Roma migrant workers from Romania, Poland and Slovakia are legally distinguished from asylum applicants.[185] Once Romania, Poland and Slovakia were admitted to the European Union, the Roma from such states could no longer claim refugee status in applications for residency to other EU member states: they were categorized as 'habitual residents' inside the Union. Indeed, the European Commission of Human Rights held that no state has an obligation towards nomadic groups because of their temporary situation on a state's territory at any given moment.[186] Various international tribunals have documented the social marginalization and discrimination in employment, housing and public education experienced by members of the Roma, the largest ethnic minority in Europe (10–12 million).[187] The Human Rights Committee, for example, has recently reported racial profiling and 'virulent and widespread anti-Roma statements' by public figures, the media and the dis-

---

Herald Tribune (20 August 2010) 1; L Davies, 'Nicolas Sarkozy Gets Tough on France's Itinerant Groups', *The Guardian* (27 July 2010); R Kushen, 'Scapegoating Will Not Solve "Roma Problem"', *The Guardian* (3 August 2010); and E Brooks, 'Stop This State Persecution of Roma', *The Guardian* (18 August 2010).

[183] Some Roma have remained stateless in Spain even after 10 years: see the Joint UN/Romanian Government Seminar (above n 20) 37. See also Zaretsky (ibid); Erlanger (ibid); Davies (ibid); Kushen (ibid); and Brooks (ibid).

[184] UNICEF, 'Progress for Children: A World Fit For Children Statistical Review No 6' (December 2007), www.unicef.org/progressforchildren/2007n6/files/Progress_for_Children_-_No._6.pdf, 42.

[185] 'Land of Hope?' *The Independent* (26 February 2004) 14.

[186] *Kalderas Gipsies v Germany* (above n 168) para 37.

[187] See UN Human Rights Committee (HRC), 'Report to General Assembly', 66th session (2011), Supplement No 40, A/66/40, vol 1, para 84(7) (Poland), para 87(18)(20) (Hungary) and para 89(8)(13) (Slovakia), 29. Roma populations in France, Italy, Portugal and Spain represent between one million and 1,300,000.

banded Magyar Gàrda in Hungary.[188] The Committee has reported racist attacks in Slovakia by police, with inadequate compensation for the victims.[189] Forced sterilization and 'widespread discrimination' in education (eg, de facto segregation of Roma children), housing, health and political participation has xalso been reported in the context of Roma people in Slovakia.[190] In Serbia, stereotypes of Roma women and an absence of legal documentation for them persist.[191] The list of such examples goes on.

As of 2002, 20–90 per cent of the Roma in the Czech Republic were unemployed, and Roma children were segregated from children of nationals by being required to attend special schools.[192] Once Roma families arrive from the Czech Republic to the territorial space of another state, it has been found that there is a real, as opposed to a remote or speculative, chance of persecution if they return to the Czech Republic.[193] The Senate of Romania has recently documented alarming social problems as a consequence of the statelessness of the Roma: obstacles to legal employment, lack of access to medical assistance, difficulties in having children accepted in schools, lack of child support otherwise available to de jure nationals, lack of social benefits otherwise available to de jure nationals and the 'impossibility of exercising civil and administrative rights'.[194] A recent study has further documented that UK immigration officers at the Prague airport refused UK entry to 90 per cent of Czech applicants because the officers knew that they were mostly Roma; only 0.2 per cent of non-Roma applicants were refused permission.[195] In other words, Roma applicants had a 400 per cent less chance of receiving permission to enter Britain.

C. Indigenous Inhabitants

The consequences of de jure and effective statelessness are of particular concern in the context of indigenous peoples throughout the globe. A surprising number of states claim territory where traditional (tribal) societies have habitually resided for centuries. States have been unable or unwilling to modify the jurisdictional boundary of their reserved domain in order to adjust to inhabitants who are indigenous to their territories. The

---

[188] Ibid, para 87(18).

[189] Ibid, para 89(8).

[190] Ibid, para 89(13) and (17).

[191] Ibid, para 90(8).

[192] UN Committee on Economic, Social and Cultural Rights, 'Summary Record of the 3rd Meeting: Czech Republic' (Summary Record, 30 April 2002), UD Doc E/C.12/2002/SR.3, para13.

[193] See, eg, *Refugee Appeals Nos 76468–73* (New Zealand Refugee Status Appeals Authority, 25 June 2010) paras 65–81.

[194] See generally the Joint UN/Romanian Government Seminar (above n 20) 35–36.

[195] *R v Immigration Officer at Prague Airport and Another, ex parte European Roma Rights Centre and Others* [2005] 1 All ER 527, [2005] 2 AC 1, [2005] 2 WLR 1 (HL), para 34.

reasons are complex. Each state and group of indigenous inhabitants (of which there may be many inside the territorial border of a state) possesses its own context-specific social problems. De jure statelessness often slips into effective statelessness due to the ethnic hierarchies taken for granted on any particular territory.[196] Several of the social consequences outlined in this chapter (especially the impact upon children and women) are also experienced by indigenous inhabitants.[197] The financial cost of registering infants born on a state's territory, for example, may leave many indigenous inhabitants without documentation of nationality.

IV. SOCIAL, ECONOMIC AND PSYCHOLOGICAL CONSEQUENCES

Statelessness may be effective as well as de jure. By effective statelessness, I mean more than the absence of diplomatic protection for nationals. I also mean more than persons with uncertain nationality. One may be a national and yet lack legal protection in the administration of a nationality law. Effective statelessness especially characterizes members of the three groups just documented: women and children, nomadic and travelling groups, and members of traditional societies. I shall now document three forms of consequences making for effective statelessness.

A. Economic Harm

Statelessness may well be the most important factor making for economic harm. As is well known, contracts with denaturalized Jewish inhabitants of the central European states during the inter-war and wartime periods were held void.[198] The impact of statelessness for financial ownership and employment continued during the early post-World War period.[199] Although a recent study by the Organisation for Economic Co-operation and Development (OECD) does not isolate stateless persons, the incidence of negative employment opportunities and discrimination in the

[196] The state may well offer de jure nationality to members of a group, but the group refuses to legitimize the nationality and refuses to accept the benefits in order not to compromise treaty claims.

[197] See, eg, Asian Indigenous and Tribal Peoples Network, 'The State of India's Indigenous and Tribal Peoples' (2009), www.aitpn.org/Reports/Tribal_Peoples_2009.pdf. Royal Commission on Aboriginal Peoples (Canada), 'Report: Restructuring the Relationship', vols 1 and 2 (Ottawa, 1996); and Department of Indian Affairs and Northern Development (Canada), 'First Nations in Canada' (Ottawa, 1997).

[198] *Eric Charell Case* as discussed in I Müller, *Hitler's Justice: The Courts of the Third Reich* (London, IB Taurus, 1991) 116. See also Arendt's discussion of the case: Arendt (above n 56) 179.

[199] Stateless individuals have usually found it impossible to earn livelihoods even in the private sector during post-war periods: Vishniak (above n 48) 8.

housing and labour market is compelling.[200] The executive committee of the UNHCR recently stated that economic insecurity is part and parcel of the internal and external displacement of stateless persons.[201] The social and economic conditions of Palestinian refugee camps in Lebanon are well documented.[202] During 1995–96, the Iraqi government confiscated properties and would not employ non-Shia Iraqi nationals.[203] As of 2001 (and after 30 years), serious economic and health consequences have followed the stateless conditions of the 250,000–300,000 Biharis in refugee camps in Bangladesh.[204] In Sri Lanka, an early statute required that one register one's nationality or any change of nationality before one could own a business.[205] As the Overseas Chinese experience in Vietnam has shown, employment and ownership of property have periodically been seized and economic opportunities denied (at least since the 1950s). This occurred in 1995 for example.[206] From the 1950s to the 1970s, Vietnam taxed overseas Chinese inhabitants as 'a foreign group' (at a higher rate) and restricted their ownership of property and employment.[207] This was in addition to the accompanying absence of social security benefits.[208] As a less subtle form of ethnic discrimination, Rohingya children in Myanmar have been subject to forced labour, the Rohingya being excluded as an ethnic group worthy of nationality, despite the fact that 135 other 'national

[200] OECD, *International Migration Outlook 2013* (Paris, OECD Publishing, 2013) ch 4 'Discrimination against Immigrants: Measurement, Incidence and Policy Instruments', dx. doi.org/10.1787/migr_outlook-2013-7-en, 203–4 and 209. See also *Odhiambo* (above n 152) para 128.

[201] 'There are inevitable tensions between international obligations and national responsibilities where countries called upon to host large refugee populations, even on a temporary basis, are suffering their own severe economic difficulties, high unemployment, declining living standards, shortages in housing and land and (or) continuing man-made and natural disasters': High Commissioner for Refugees Programme Sub-Committee (above n 134) paras 8–22.

[202] See, eg, *Case No 1113683* (Australia Refugee Review Tribunal, 9 August 2012) [2012] RRTA 611 (per A Rozdilsky, Tribunal Member).

[203] See M van der Stoel (Special Rapporteur), 'Human Rights Situations and Reports of Special Rapporteurs and Representatives: Situation of Human Rights in Iraq' (15 October 1997), UN Doc A/52/476, para 30. UN Economic and Social Council, 'Report of the High Commissioner for Human Rights on Human Rights and Mass Exoduses' (30 January 1998), UN Doc E/CN.4/1998/51.

[204] Minority Rights Group International, 'World Directory of Minorities and Indigenous Peoples: Bangladesh Biharis' (2008), www.refworld.org/docid/49749d58c.html; Khan (above n 11) 14; and UN Economic and Social Council, 'Report on Human Rights and Mass Exoduses' (ibid) 4.

[205] *David De Silva v Ramanathan Chettiar* (1960) SC 150-DG (Inty) Kandy, 1602/MB, 65 NLR 409.

[206] Vietnam excluded non-Vietnamese from 11 occupations during 1955–65. See TL Lee, 'Chinese Nationality and the Republic of China (Taiwan)' (1995) 7 *International Journal of Refugee Law* 201, 209–11; and R Mushkat, 'Hong Kong as an International Legal Person' (1992) 6 *Emory International Law Review* 105.

[207] Lee (ibid) 209–11.

[208] See especially I Goris, J Harrington and S Köhn, 'Statelessness: What It Is and Why It Matters' (2009) 32 *Forced Migration* 4, 4–5.

races' have been recognized.[209] Having no legal status and being socially categorized as 'foreigners', the Rohingya have been subject to xenophobia, lack the right to own property or land, and even a right to marry or travel without state permission.[210]

Financial institutions have been known to require denaturalized individuals to sell their assets for a nominal price under penalty of total confiscation.[211] Denaturalized South African inhabitants of colour during the 1950s lost any right to sign the usual 30-year lease to live in the Black South African townships. South Africa also threatened to withdraw any right to commence or to expand a business.[212] The Bantu Administration Minister also threatened to expel the indigenous inhabitants from all territory that the South African state effectively controlled and claimed as its own. Applications for travel or work papers by 'black' and 'coloured' inhabitants met with administrative harassment.

Amongst other factors, documentation of nationality is invariably needed in many states in order to establish prospective employability. In order to gain employment, about 400,000 Palestinians fled Gaza to Kuwait after 1948.[213] Kuwait, however, did not automatically naturalize the newcomers. A stateless person with this background could gain legal residency by being sponsored by a 'genuine' Kuwaiti employer or by paying a bribe to an employer who would register the person under false pretences.[214]

The ability to obtain work, however, is not necessarily synonymous with the 'right to work'.[215] When the US–UK invasion of Iraq in the first Gulf War resulted in Palestinians migrating to various Middle Eastern states, they often did not find hospitable receptions. Jordan authorized Palestinian refugees to hold two-year temporary passports, and this prevented them from having 'the right to work, obtain driver's licenses, own

---

[209] Burma Citizenship Law (1982), www.unhcr.org/cgi-bin/texis/vtx/refworld/rwmain?d ocid=3ae6b4f71b. See Lewa, 'North Arakan' (above n 16) para 2; C Lewa, 'Issues to be Raised Concerning the Situation of Stateless Rohingya Women in Myanmar (Burma)', Arakan Project Submission to the Committee on the Elimination of Discrimination against Women (CEDAW), CEDAW/C/MMR/3 (October 2008); and CEDAW, 'Concluding Observations of the Committee on the Elimination of Discrimination against Women: Myanmar', CEDAW/C/ MMR/CO/3 (7 November 2008).

[210] *Refugee Appeal No 76254* (New Zealand Refugee Status Appeals Authority, 16 September 2008), www.refworld.org/docid/48e342ca2.html, paras 30–34.

[211] *Flegenheimer Case*, Decision No 182 (1958) 25 ILR 91, 14 Rep Int'l Arbitral Awards 327, 332–33 (paras 12 and 15) and 385 (para 69).

[212] The South African state created a new 'state', Transkei, and then declared all members of the Xhosa tribe to have lost South African citizenship. Transkei offered the nationality of the Transkei state to the denaturalized South African nationals. See L Roth, 'Transkei: A Tale of Two Citizenships' (1976) 9 *New York University Journal of International Law and Politics* 205, 220.

[213] *Case No 0808284* (Australian Refugee Review Tribunal, 21 May 2009) [2009] RRTA 454, www.refworld.org/docid/4a55d2bd2.html, para 3.4.

[214] Ibid, para 1.2; and *Refugee Appeal No 76254* (above n 210) paras 30–38.

[215] *Case No 0808284* (above n 213) para 54.

property or access free medical care'.[216] They were barred from practising several professions, were denied membership in co-operative associations, had difficulty in obtaining employment in private banks due to the failure to obtain security clearance, and were excluded from training and employment programmes established by the state.[217] Except for the wealthy, few Palestinian refugees in Egypt have gained access to citizenship.[218] This denial has impacted upon their employment opportunities and social benefits. In the same 'spirit', Kuwait's laws have created a two-tiered employment structure that ensures high wages for Kuwaiti citizen employees, with substantially lower wages for non-citizen workers.[219] Working conditions between Kuwaiti citizens and Palestinian refugees also differ significantly.[220] Indeed, upon the American invasion of Iraq in the second Gulf War, approximately 360,000–370,000 of the 400,000 former stateless habitual residents in Kuwait departed from Kuwait only to find it difficult to return to Kuwait, especially without employer sponsorship.[221] They were both de jure and effectively stateless.[222]

During the 1955–65 period, the Iraqi government forcibly dispersed nationals with Kurdish, Turkish or Assyrian ethnicity.[223] Kurdish refugees in Iraq were assaulted by persons working for the Iranian government.[224] In 1980, the Iraqi state denaturalized 220,000 Feyli Kurds.[225] Although the Iraqi state repealed the denaturalization law in 2006, 100,000 remained stateless as of 2009. In April and May 1969, Iraq brutally expelled large numbers of persons who had Iranian nationality at a moment's notice.[226] Palestinians had played important roles in the Ba'athist regime of Saddam. The UNHCR has documented the absence of effective legal protection for

---

[216] *Case No 0805551* (Australia Refugee Review Tribunal, 15 January 2009) [2009] RRTA 24, www.refworld.org/docid/49e702dc2.html, para 43.

[217] Ibid, para 59.

[218] *Case No 0808284* (above n 213) para 78.

[219] Ibid, para 69.

[220] Ibid.

[221] Ibid, para 60. For those who remained, aside from restrictions to access to employment, Kuwait restricted access of non-Kuwaiti students to 25%.

[222] The Palestinians had sought employment in Kuwait after the Middle East War of 1948. By 1990, 400,000 Palestinians were living in Kuwait. The Kuwaiti state's discriminatory actions against Palestinians before and after the invasion by Saddam Hussein and then by the American forces in the Gulf War of 1990–91 worked to encourage the Palestinians to leave Kuwait.

[223] See MD Copithorne (Special Representative of the Commission on Human Rights), 'Human Rights Situations and Reports of Special Rapporteurs and Representatives: Situation of Human Rights in Iraq', interim report to the UN General Assembly (15 October 1997), UN Doc A/52/472, as discussed in *Case No 0808284* (above n 213) para 30. See also UN Economic and Social Council, 'Report on Human Rights and Mass Exoduses' (above n 203).

[224] UN Economic and Social Council, 'Report on Human Rights and Mass Exoduses' (above n 203) para 20.

[225] BK Blitz, 'Advocacy Campaigns and Policy Development' (2009) 32 *Forced Migration* 25, 27.

[226] See GS Goodwin-Gill, *International Law and the Movement of Persons between States* (Oxford, Clarendon Press, 1978) 217–18.

the Palestinians who remained in Iraq subsequent to the American invasion.[227] A UK refugee judgment has also recently documented the loss of legal protection.[228]

Unemployment as a result of statelessness continues through the present day, not least because of the increasingly large-scale migration of peoples. Although there are treaties, particularly the Convention Relating to the Status of Stateless Persons (1954) and the Convention on the Rights of the Child, that require states parties to register all births on their territories and to enact legislation recognizing the nationality of all registered births, estimates of 215 to 232 million inhabitants of the globe no longer inhabit the territory of their birth.[229] 30 per cent of the total population of the 46 OECD countries is foreign-born.[230] To take one group of migrants alone, one half (six million) of those born on Mexican territory have migrated to other countries; two and a half million of those have migrated to the United States alone.[231] It is commonly accepted that there are around 11 million undocumented inhabitants in the United States (although it is unclear whether they are all undocumented in their states of origin as well). The absence of nationality documentation also affects migrants in South America.[232] The trend of increasing migration across the globe brings into question the expectations and suitability of the old criteria of *soli* (birth) and *sanguinis* (bloodline).

---

[227] UNHCR, COIR Report on Iraq (April 2007), as quoted in *NA (Palestinians, Risk) v Secretary of State for the Home Department CG* [2008] UKAIT 00046, para 40.

[228] *NA v Home Department* (ibid).

[229] For references and documentation regarding these figures, see above Introduction chapter, n 36 (10).

[230] OECD, *International Migration Outlook 2013* (above n 200) ch 1, Table A.5 'Stocks of Foreign Population by Nationality in OECD Countries and the Russian Federation', www.keepeek.com/Digital-Asset-Management/oecd/social-issues-migration-health/international-migration-outlook-2013/stocks-of-foreign-population-by-nationality-in-oecd-countries-and-the-russian-federation_migr_outlook-2013-table127-en. For the figure of 30%, see also *International Migration Outlook 2013* (above n 200) ch 1, 36. By 1999, for example, Germany, with a population of 80 million nationals, had 7.3 million non-nationals, of which 50% had been living on German territory for over 10 years and another 30% for over 20 years: C Sonntag-Wolgast, 'Opening Speech as Secretary of State in the German Ministry of the Interior', First European Conference on Nationality 'Trends and Developments in National and International Law on Nationality' (Strasbourg, 18 and 19 October 1999), www.refworld.org/docid/43f202412.html, 15. Admittedly, migrant workers and other non-nationals may possess nationality from another state.

[231] As quoted and affirmed by AA Burelli in *Case of the Yean and Bosico Children v The Dominican Republic* (Inter-American Court of Human Rights, 8 September 2005), Ser C, No 130, www.refworld.org/docid/44e497d94.html, para 2.

[232] See especially *Yean and Bosico* (ibid) paras 132–33.

B. Social Security and Public Education

Insecurity and inequity (vis-à-vis nationals) in the context of social benefits, such as pensions and health facilities, complicates the social experiences of stateless persons.[233] The UNHCR recently noted, 'Statelessness
often limits access to birth registration, identity documentation, education,
health care, legal employment, property ownership, political participation
and freedom of movement.'[234] The lack of access to education and health
care for nomadic and travelling group members was outlined above.
Refugee camps for stateless Palestinians in Lebanon are plagued by over-
crowding, poor sanitation and poor heating in winter.[235] Kuwait's refusal
to recognize the nationality of Palestinian inhabitants has led to a lack
of public education for Palestinian children there.[236] Bangladesh has
warehoused the stateless Biharis, with a serious impact upon access to
nutrition and medical facilities, public education, housing and security of
employment.[237] Syria has refused to confer nationality upon 200,000–
360,000 Kurds, with the consequence that they have severe barriers to public health services, employment, participation in public life and enjoyment
of property rights, as well as lacking the ability to leave the country.[238]

C. Social Ostracism and Trauma

De jure statelessness, like effective statelessness, is widely accompanied
by social ostracism and psychological harm. Stateless individuals, families or groups may be socially ostracized in their territory of habitation,

[233] *Odhiambo* (above n 152) para 128. An ironic example of the social impact of statelessness is that under French law during 1989, stateless inhabitants (along with nationals) would
have been entitled to a 'top-up' of their pensions. Mr Zaoui was held to lack French nationality. He was thereby disqualified from a 'top-up' to his pension: *Saada Zaoui v Caisse Regionale
D'Assurance Maladie de l'ile de France* [1987] ECR 5511, [1989] 2 CMLR 646, Court of Justice of
the European Communities (4th Chamber). Mr Zaoui's wife was of French nationality, while
Mr Zaoui lacked nationality in any other state. If he had been held stateless, he would have
qualified for the 'top-up'.
[234] UNHCR Division of International Protection, 'UNHCR Action to Address Statelessness:
A Strategy Note' (March 2010) 4. For the standard of health care of Palestinian 'foreigners' in
the Gulf states, see UNHCR, 'Regional Operations Plan 2008: Saudi Arabia, Kuwait, UAE,
Qatar, Bahrain, Oman' (September 2007) 12, as quoted in *Case No 0808284* (above n 213) para
68.
[235] *MM and FH (Stateless Palestinians – KK, IH, HE reaffirmed) Lebanon* [2008] UKAIT 00014,
para 111.
[236] In particular, Kuwait considered the stateless Palestinians as 'foreigners', and the education system had set quotas with no more than 25% of the students being 'non-Kuwaiti':
Case No 0808284 (above n 213) paras 65–69.
[237] Sen, 'Stateless Refugees and the Right to Return, Part I' (above n 133) 640–45.
[238] *Refugee Appeal No 75779* (above n 112). For consequences of the stateless condition for
children in Australia, see *Odhiambo* (above n 152) para 130.

even amongst other groups in a refugee camp.[239] This social hierarchy may persist despite the formal legal claims of international organizations that food and shelter are being distributed equally.[240] The hierarchy may differentiate between old and new refugees, or between one ethnic group and another.[241] Differences in language and religious practices may add to the experience of exclusion. Officials of the state of refuge may also make distinctions based upon the ethnicity and race of stateless persons.[242]

Scepticism and suspicion may colour the treatment of refugees and stateless persons.[243] Against a social and political background of xenophobia and anti-Semitism, the use of the legal term 'enemy alien' added fuel to public reaction to the influx of Jewish refugees. Gertrude Dubrovsky, who wrote an account of *kindertransport* activities during the lead-up to World War II, described the UK position towards stateless children during this time as being 'torn between the urge to help and the worry about how they were going to "get rid of [Jews]" in the future'.[244] Even the chief rabbi of London is reported as being critical of the influx of refugees, whom he feared would take jobs from British Jews.[245] During the 1930s and early 1940s both British immigration policy and the protected reserved domain for states raised obstacles for refugees. Jewish inhabitants of Austria, for example, were caught in a trap of international law. On the one hand, when the Third Reich annexed Austria, the Nazis sometimes refused to allow Austrians to exchange their Austrian passports for German ones, and without German passports, such Austrians were owed no legal obligation from the German government to diplomatically protect them, for

---

[239] As to the former, although the UK tribunal did not find the testimony helpful in this regard, see *MM and FH* (above n 235) paras 133–39. The differential treatment between stateless Palestinians and refugees who are nationals of other states continues into education, real estate ownership, employment, housing, the maintenance of housing within camps, and health care, at least in Lebanon.

[240] *Taiem v Minister for Immigration & Multicultural Affairs* [2001] FCA 611, para 9; appealing *Rishmawi v Minister for Immigration and Multicultural Affairs* (1997) 77 FCR 421, 427.

[241] A social hierarchy characterized the camps of refugees from the European states prior to and during World War II. During the 1930s and early 1940s, both the public and the UK Government considered refugees from Germany, Austria and Italy as 'enemy aliens'. See Friendly Aliens Protection Committee (above n 164). See also Dubrovsky (above n 162) 96–100.

[242] Thus, according to the Friendly Aliens Protection Committee, the Home Office counselled that stateless persons from Austria or Germany should not be admitted to the UK 'save in exceptional circumstances of aliens who are not clearly in a position to maintain themselves'. See 'Memorandum on the Legal Position of Refugees' (above n 164). The practicality, access or reliability of proving one's financial position would be unlikely.

[243] For example, Whitehall assured the British public that Jewish refugees would not be 'stayers' and would not displace non-Jewish employees from their jobs: Dubrovsky (above n 162) 17–18. See also Dubrovsky's sources indicating the resistance of the general public to the influx of 20 million Jewish children from Germany, Austria and Poland. See also a letter from the Home Office to Sir Neville Bland (dated 14 March 1938), copy on file with author.

[244] Letter dated 16 February 2004 from Dubrovsky to the author. Dubrovsky described the general xenophobic anti-foreigner attitude at the time in Dubrovsky (above n 162) 75–78.

[245] Ibid, 96–98, 100 and 107.

example when they applied for refugee entry into UK territory. On the other hand, when the Nazi government did grant passports to Austrian nationals, their German nationality was withdrawn once they left German-controlled territory. Their German nationality was also withdrawn if they did not register with the German consulate in Austria (per the Nazi decree of 3 February 1938). Without nationality, such persons were at the mercy of any state of refuge; they were considered to be owed no legal obligation.

Following the dissolution of the Soviet Union, Hungary enacted a citizenship law that gave preference to refugees with Hungarian ethnicity and furthermore preference to refugees over stateless persons ('temporarily protected persons').[246] Differential social hierarchy inside refugee and displacement camps may become pronounced in terms of living conditions, privacy, freedom to leave and employment opportunities.[247]

The loss of self-respect and profound trauma often experienced by stateless persons is well documented.[248] The HRC has required compensation to particular stateless refugees who have experienced psychological trauma during detention pending refugee status.[249] It is psychologically difficult for stateless persons to protest about working conditions or differential wages to employers.[250] When Ethiopia announced in 1998 that all 'Eritreans' on Ethiopian territory were no longer nationals of Ethiopia, the impact was personally devastating because many had developed deep social ties, which had led them to believe that Ethiopia was their homeland.[251] After being tortured and detained without trial, one national

---

[246] Employment was restricted to ethnic Hungarians in some occupations. Over 90% of displaced persons who lacked Hungarian ethnicity were classified as refugees. As such, they could not gain employment, were offered a poorer standard of housing, lacked privacy and had their freedom to leave the territory restricted; stateless peoples were also excluded from military service. See Fullerton (above n 6) 526.

[247] The influx of displaced persons into camps from Bosnia during the early and mid-1990's exemplified such differential treatment: Fullerton (above n 6) 531.

[248] UN Ad Hoc Committee on Refugees and Stateless Persons, 'A Study on Statelessness' (1 August 1949), UN Doc E/1112/Add.1, s 3; and McDougal, Lasswell and Chen (above n 146) 901–3.

[249] *Kalenga v Zambia* (27 July 1993), Communication No 326/1988, CCPR/C/48?D/326/1988, para 8.8; *Natalia Schedko v Belarus*, Communciation No 886/1999, UN Doc CCPR/C/77?D/886/1999 (1999), paras 9.3 and 10.2; and *C v Australia* (13 November 2002), CCPR/C/76/D/900/1999, paras 8.4 and 10.

[250] See, eg, D Weissbrodt, 'Prevention of Discrimination: The Rights of Non-Citizens', Final Report of the Special Rapporteur, Addendum' (26 May 2003), UN Doc E/CN.4/Sub.2/2003/23/Add.3, para 3.

[251] They were stigmatized as 'aliens'; furthermore, their property was auctioned and the profits confiscated by the state. See generally UN Security Council, 'Progress Report of the Secretary-General on Ethiopia and Eritrea' (19 June 2001), UN Doc S/2001/608; UN Security Council, 'Progress Report of the Secretary-General on Ethiopia and Eritrea' (4 September 2003), UN Doc S/2003/ 858; Eritrea–Ethiopia Claims Commission (Permanent Court of Arbitration), 'Partial Award Central Front: Eritrea's Claims 2, 4, 6, 7, 8 & 22' (28 April 2004); and Eritrea–Ethiopia Claims Commission, 'Partial Award Central Front: Ethiopia's Claim 2' (28 April 2004), both available at www.pca-cpa.org/showpage.asp?pag_id=1151.

of Iraq, aged 29, decided to work for M15 when told by a government official, 'No one really wants you. You are a stateless person.'[252] The Inter-American Court of Human Rights has highlighted the negative impact upon collective memory, self-esteem, self-perception, trust and personal safety, in particular with regard to stateless Haitians in the Dominican Republic.[253] A similar psychological condition has been described of stateless inhabitants in Slovenia.[254] According to the European Advisory Committee, the loss of de jure nationality means 'loss of access to fundamental rights attached to residence, including the right to work and access to healthcare and other social rights, along with the annulation of personal documents and exposure to a risk of deportation'.[255] UN studies have in addition described the impact of racism and xenophobia on stateless inhabitants in the context of vote-getting by local legislators.[256]

V. CONCLUSION

The enigma of the international community is not merely an academic matter. The consequences of statelessness have been deep and profound for tens of millions of people. Ironically, the incident of nationality in the reserved domain of the state has led to arbitrariness as well as suffering. I say 'ironically' because from the standpoint of the international community with a state-centric residuary, clarity and precision are believed to be the priority, in contrast to any 'extra-legal' focus upon the social consequences of domestic law. Instead, opaqueness has accompanied such domestic laws in matters of nationality. Inside the boundary of the reserved domain, states have claimed universal or plenary legal authority. This authority has extended to the choice of members, admission to a

---

[252] As recounted and quoted in R Verkaik, 'A Man Called David and an Irresistible Offer', *The Independent* (23 July 2010) 4–5; and R Verkaik, 'Moroccan Man Illegally Taken from Belgium to Work for MI5', *The Independent* (23 July 2010) 4.

[253] Although the Dominican-Haitians are 'culturally Dominican', are 'loyal to the Dominican Republic' and seek 'to obtain legal citizenship of the country in which they were born and the only one they know', the 'leaders of opinion' in the Dominican Republic speak of Haitians 'as an undifferentiated mass' who are Haitian even as second-generation inhabitants on the territory of the Republic: *Yean and Bosico* (above n 231) 28 (paras 60–61).

[254] Upon independence, the names of citizens of the former Yugoslavia were erased by the new state of Slovenia unless they had applied for Slovenian citizenship within a short time. Those not registered were listed on the register of foreigners. Of the 18,305 inhabitants initially erased, 6000 inhabitants were left without legal status, some were deported and 12,000 gained permanent residency status from 1999 rather than from the date when they were erased as citizens (26 February 1992). This was so even though many had lived in Slovenian territory for 'a long time'. See European Commission against Racism and Intolerance (ECRI), 'Third Report on Slovenia', CRI(2007)5 (adopted 30 June 2006), hudoc.ecri.coe.int/XMLEcri/ENGLISH/Cycle_03/03_CbC_eng/SVN-CbC-III-2007-5-ENG.pdf, paras 109–16. See also *Makuc and Others v Slovenia* [2007] ECHR 523, para 140.

[255] ECRI (ibid) para 109.

[256] *Makuc* (above n 254) paras 141–44.

state's territory, expulsion, forced internal displacement, prolonged and even indefinite detention, and difficulty leaving or returning to the state of habitual residence. No state, including Canada, the United States and the United Kingdom, has been excepted from choices leading to such consequences. The consequences of de jure statelessness have moreover been accompanied by effective statelessness. The negative impact upon women and children, employment, social security, access to public education and other matters are common examples of effective statelessness.

The usual response to consequences of the stateless condition has been that human rights treaties and customary norms need to be better enforced, particularly by international tribunals. This response has a particular underlying supposition: namely, that the juristic method ought to find an identifiable discrete and self-standing right, such as the right to nationality, the right to personhood or the right to non-refoulement for stateless persons. But is there any such right for stateless persons as long as nationality remains an incident of the reserved domain and as long as the domain itself is accepted as the protected residuary of an international community? The problem arises from two very different issues. The one issue concerns the justification of a law in terms of its source – a statute, a precedent, a treaty or an international customary norm. Article 38 of the Statute of the International Court of Justice (ICJ) highlights such sources. From this perspective, a stateless person is someone who lacks the nationality conferred by domestic laws and protected by the boundary of the reserved domain. The second issue, however, concerns whether an identifiable domestic law is obligatory or binding. The following two chapters outline how the second issue has been forgotten in the widespread preoccupation with a discrete and self-standing right to nationality.

4

The Reserved Domain for the Treaty Right to Nationality

I. INTRODUCTION

T HE CONSEQUENCES OF statelessness, which were briefly outlined in the previous chapter, have led jurists to rely upon human rights norms as the solution to statelessness. Rather than institutionalizing the forms of a domestic civic state and rather than codifying clear and precise international rules, the apparent universality of human rights has been thought to intellectually transcend any stateless condition.[1] A leading international human rights jurist, David Weissbrodt, has insisted that human rights law is exclusive of the traditional freedom of a state over nationality: 'Because being human is the sole requirement entitling us to human rights, whether or not one possesses a nationality should have no bearing on whether we enjoy all of our human rights.'[2] Weissbrodt is not alone in this faith in universal human rights; it can be traced through a series of post-World War II studies about statelessness. When statelessness was an object of UN study early on, for example, it was often accepted that Article 15 of the Universal Declaration of Human Rights (UNDHR) (1948) recognizes the entrenchment of the right of nationality.[3] Peter Mutharika, in an exhaustive study of statelessness in 1977, concluded that with the UNDHR, the international community was 'now committed to the total elimination of statelessness and to an attack on the principle of exclusive

---

[1] See, eg, CF Doebbler, 'A Human Rights Approach to Statelessness in the Middle East' (2002) 15 *Leiden Journal of International Law*; and S Benhabib, *The Rights of Others: Aliens, Residents and Citizens* (Cambridge, Cambridge University Press, 2004) 140 and 142.

[2] D Weissbrodt, *The Human Rights of Non-Citizens* (Oxford, Oxford University Press, 2008) 82. See also D Weissbrodt, 'Final Report on the Rights of Non-Citizens' (2003), UN Doc E/CN.4/Sub.2/2003/23, Executive Summary, 1: 'Based on a review of international human rights law the Special Rapporteur has concluded that all persons should by virtue of their essential humanity enjoy all human rights unless exceptional distinctions, for example, between citizens and non-citizens, serve a legitimate State objective and are proportional to the achievement of that objective.'

[3] Economic and Social Council, 'Ad Hoc Committee on Statelessness and Related Problems: Summary Record', 1st sess, 29th Meeting (14 February 1950), UN Doc E/AC.32/SR.2923, para 50.

competence by states in nationality matters'.[4] Michel Autem, former Head of the Legal Department of the French Naturalization Directorate, expressed at the First European Conference on Nationality (1999):

The recognition of individual rights in the field of nationality, and thus of the expression of the individual will, necessarily implies that in the field of exclusive sovereignty, states should, if not abandon their sometimes old-age prerogatives, at least limit their effects.[5]

The International Law Commission (ILC) confirmed in its 1999 Report on nationality that Article 15 of the UNDHR had institutionalized the right of nationality.[6] Such a right to nationality has often been taken to represent a universal human right.[7] If only states 'signed' up, the enigma of statelessness, it seems, would be erased from the international community.

We shall see in a moment that as Catherine Dauvergne has pointed out, 'Despite the "human" in human rights, being merely human is not enough to ensure legal standing in many instances.'[8] Hannah Arendt also pointed to this aspect of international law:

No paradox of contemporary politics is filled with a more poignant irony than the discrepancy between the efforts of well-meaning idealists who stubbornly insist on regarding as 'inalienable' those human rights, which are enjoyed only by citizens of the most prosperous and civilized countries, and the situation of the rightless themselves. Their situation has deteriorated just as stubbornly, until the internment camp . . . has become the routine solution for the problem of domicile of the 'displaced persons'. Even the terminology applied to the stateless has deteriorated.[9]

But why do the international community's universalist claims about humanity leave stateless inhabitants unprotected as legal persons? Are simple appeals to treaty provisions or repeated citations of a right to nationality adequate in addressing whether states are obligated to protect stateless persons?

[4] P Mutharika, *The Regulation of Statelessness under International and National Law* (New York, Oceana, 1977) 32.
[5] Council of Europe, 'First European Conference on Nationality: "Trends and Developments in National and International Law on Nationality" (Strasbourg, 18–19 October 1999) – Proceedings' (3 February 2000), www.coe.int/t/dghl/standardsetting/nationality/Conference%201%20(1999)Proceedings.pdf.
[6] 'Report of the ILC on the Work of its Fifty-First Session' (9 July 1999), UN Doc A/54/10, *ILC Yearbook 1999*, vol II(2), 37, commentary to Art 16, para 1.
[7] See, eg, C Forcese, 'A Distinction with a Legal Difference: The Consequences of Non-Citizenship in the "War on Terror"' in A Edwards and C Ferstman (eds), *Human Security and Non-Citizens* (Cambridge, Cambridge University Press, 2010) 422–29 and 432–33; and L van Waas, *Nationality Matters: Statelessness under International Law* (Antwerp, Intersentia, 2008) 339–88.
[8] C Dauvergne, *Making People Illegal: What Globalization Means for Migration and Law* (Cambridge, Cambridge University Press, 2008) 21.
[9] H Arendt, *The Origins of Totalitarianism* (New York, Harcourt Brace Jovanovich, 1979 [1951]) 279.

I shall argue in this chapter that a 'right to nationality', as inscribed in treaties, has been situated in an international community that protects the freedom of the state in those circumstances most productive of stateless-ness and its negative consequences. Why would a state legislature or state administration, as agents of the self-creative state/author, allow a norm, such as the right to nationality or right to legal personhood, to trump the state's traditional freedom to choose its own members? And if the inter-national community is assumed to be an aggregate of the wills of states, why would a domestic judiciary actively scrutinize legislative and execu-tive deliberation about the content of the reserved domain of the state? If the domain's content is judicially scrutinized, are international stand-ards merely supplementary and circular vis-à-vis the exercise of internal jurisdiction? Are domestic and international tribunals limited to only particular legal remedies – say, declarations? Or may a stateless person's representative seek an injunction against expulsion or compensatory and punitive damages for forced displacement, indefinite detention or any of the other consequences identified in the previous chapter?

These issues lie in the background of the right to nationality and to legal personhood as recognized in the three statelessness treaties and the six human rights treaties. In section II below I address whether the terms of the three statelessness treaties would end the enigma if only all states 'signed up' to them. I shall outline several common problems with such a viewpoint. Section III offers an overview of the human rights treaties and their understating of effective rights to nationality and to legal person-hood. In section IV, I identify a series of provisions that reinforce the sense of an international community as the aggregated will of state members. Section V turns to the limitations clauses of the human rights treaties in order to emphasize how the state retains the freedom to confer, withdraw and withhold nationality – the rights to nationality and legal personhood notwithstanding. Section VI addresses the non-derogation clauses in the context of alleged emergencies.

II. THE STATELESSNESS TREATIES

Against a background of Europe's inter-war and wartime periods, which saw the emergence of the stateless condition on a large scale (described in brief in the previous chapter), three multinational treaties were drafted and ratified: the Convention Relating to the Status of Refugees (1951),[10] the Convention Relating to the Status of Stateless Persons (1954)[11] and the

---

[10] Convention Relating to the Status of Refugees (1951), 189 UNTS 137 (entered into force 22 April 1954) (19 signatories, 145 parties).
[11] Convention Relating to the Status of Stateless Persons (1954), 360 UNTS 117 (entered into force 6 June 1960) (23 signatories, 79 parties).

Convention on the Reduction of Statelessness (1961) (hereafter the 'Reduction Treaty').[12] The thrust of the treaties was threefold. For one thing, a new legal status was recognized. Statelessness would be reduced, it was believed, if all states were to recognize the legal status of 'stateless persons' and if all births were registered on the territories of all signatories. The intent was to protect stateless persons even if they were not categorized as refugees. Despite the prima facie effect of the treaties, the drafting committee for the Convention Relating to the Status of Stateless Persons and the Convention on the Reduction of Statelessness was predisposed to retain and protect the bounded reserved domain of states over nationality issues. After all, why would a community member intentionally agree to dilute the traditional authority of a state member (including itself)? In particular, although the General Assembly requested the Secretary General in December 1954 to establish a new conference on statelessness,[13] the Secretary General did not do so until five years later because a quorum was lacking. Only 23 states initially signed the Convention Relating to the Status of Stateless Persons. It took another six years for the required number of ratifications. The required number of ratifications for the Reduction Treaty took 14 years.[14] As even the ILC admitted at the time, its work met with 'great difficulties of a non-legal nature which beset the problem of present statelessness'.[15] The historian of the ILC explained:

> The Commission's attempts to deal with the topic of nationality, including statelessness, can therefore be seen not to have been resoundingly successful. Its work on the nationality part of the topic made little headway, while its work on statelessness was only hesitantly received, and resulted in only partial treatment of the subject.[16]

State resistance to efforts to address statelessness worked its way into the very terms and scope of the three statelessness treaties. The explanation for state resistance rests in the power of the ethos or character of an international community protecting the residuary of law-making for state members.

---

[12] Convention on the Reduction of Statelessness (1961), 989 UNTS 175 (entered into force 13 December 1975) (5 signatories, 54 parties).

[13] UNGA Resolution 896 on the Elimination or Reduction of Future Statelessness, 9th sess, (4 December 1954),www.refworld.org/docid/3b00f1de3c.html.

[14] Convention on the Reduction of Statelessness (above n 12).

[15] As quoted in A Watts, *International Law Commission, 1949–1998*, vol 3 (New York, Oxford University Press, 2000) 1768.

[16] Ibid, vol 1, 140.

A. The Convention Relating to the Status of Stateless Persons (1954)

The Convention Relating to the Status of Stateless Persons (1954), signed on 28 September 1954 and entered into force on 6 June 1960, posited the international norm that all inhabitants of the state parties should possess the nationality of the territory of birth.[17] The states parties undertook to naturalize and assimilate any stateless person 'as far as possible' (Article 32). It became incumbent upon states parties not to withhold or withdraw nationality on the basis of race, religion or country of origin (Article 3). The state must protect a stateless person's right of religion and religious education to the extent and 'as favourable as that accorded to their nationals' (Article 4). In exceptional circumstances ordinarily allowing a state to restrict derogated rights, stateless persons may not be the object of such measures 'solely on account of his having previously possessed the nationality of the foreign state in question' (Article 8). This state obligation is modified if the state needs to take 'provisional measures' 'in the interests of national security' (Article 9). The treaty continues with other rights (contracts, property, artistic rights, industrial property, association, access to courts, employment and welfare, including housing and public education, public relief, labour rights and social security) (Articles 17–24). As of March 2013, however, only 77 states are parties to the treaty.

By the simple agreement of states to a treaty that so recognized a new category of legal person and by extending state duties regarding nationals to the newly categorized persons, statelessness might seem to have been eradicated as an enigma of the international community. By conferring legal status upon all children born on the territories of states parties, it seemed that all inhabitants of the globe would eventually have nationality. The problem, however, is that birth registration as the basis of the new category of legal person has remained in the externally uncontrolled reserved domain of the state. In 2012, one third of all births on the globe failed to be registered.[18] To add to this, each state has retained the freedom to decide whether a person is really stateless. The de jure definition of a stateless person, discussed above in the Introduction chapter, is phrased

---

[17] Convention Relating to the Status of Stateless Persons (above n 11). The main working document was a memorandum of the Secretary General, E/CONF. 17/3, reproduced in UNHCR, *Collection of International Instruments and Legal Texts Concerning Refugees and Others of Concern to UNHCR* (Geneva, June 2007) vol 1, 84. See also P Weis, 'The Convention Relating to the Status of Stateless Persons' (1961) 10 *International and Comparative Law Quarterly* 255, 255–57.

[18] World Health Organization, 'Country Health Information Systems: A Review of the Current Situation and Trends' (Geneva, 2011), www.who.int/healthmetrics/news/chis_report.pdf, 1. In 2007, over 51 million children remain unregistered: UNICEF, *Progress for Children: A World Fit for Children (Statistical Review)* (No 6) (December 2007), www.unicef.org/progressforchildren/2007n6/files/Progress_for_Children_-_No._6.pdf, 42. The number is also cited on the website of Plan International: plan-international.org/birthregistration.

as 'under the operation of *its* laws'. The reserved domain of the state has thereby been incorporated into the international community as the latter's residuary of law-making and law administration. 'The operation of its laws' has been considered the domestic laws of a state, in other words, 'the operation of the state's laws'.

The incorporation of the state's reserved domain into the universality of international community leads to several consequences. For one thing, the state of origin may deem that a stateless person is a habitual resident of the state of origin even though the individual has fled the latter's territory for fear of persecution. Secondly, the state of origin might not recognize nationality claims by a state of refuge. We observed in chapter two that a serious problem arises when a state of origin withdraws someone's nationality yet the state of refuge refuses to accept the withdrawal of nationality. Thirdly, the state of refuge might refuse to recognize the plight of a stateless person. In this way, the Final Act of the Convention precludes any scrutiny of the social-political conditions leading to forced migration.

Aside from birth, the Convention Relating to the Status of Stateless Persons recognizes habitual residence as the criterion of nationality. Habitual residence is met if one inhabits a territory for five years. One problem, however, is that during the five-year period, the state of refuge might expel a stateless person to the state of origin or to the state of birth. If the state of origin or of refuge has enacted laws incorporating *sanguinis*, a stateless person could gain nationality through her/his parent. This would be so even if the applicant never inhabited the territory of the parent's nationality [Article 4(1)]. The state, however, might ascribe *sanguinis* to the parent of its choice. Furthermore, nationality does not attach to a stateless person who has habitually resided in the state's territory if the person has been convicted of 'an offence of national security' or '*has always been stateless*'. Registration of a child is unlikely if the state lacks the financial or bureaucratic resources to administer the registration process. Another problem arises, we saw in chapter three, when parentage or even birth does not settle someone's nationality because s/he is born out of wedlock, lacks parents or inhabits a territory not owned by the state of the parent's nationality. The reliance upon the good will of the executive arm of the state also bears upon the equal application of domestic law. Socially contingent factors enter into national origin, and yet they are a very different legal phenomenon from nationality.

The Convention Relating to the Status of Stateless Persons continues that a state's freedom to expel a stateless person on grounds of 'national security or public order' must be 'in accordance with due process of law' and with 'reasonable time' for the stateless person to be admitted to another state (Article 31). That said, if a state determines that someone is stateless and that s/he threatens national security, 'nothing in this Convention shall prevent ... [a state] ... from taking provisionally measures which [the state] considers to be essential to national security in the case of the particular person' (Article 9). In addition, since a de jure stateless person is not 'lawfully on the state territory', s/he may be expelled by negative implication (Article 31(1)). This would seem to extend to an applicant for admission as well as a stateless person or a national whose nationality is withdrawn or withheld from recognition. Such may include 'exceptional measures against the person, property or interests of a stateless person' unless the measures are enforced because the person was a former national of a foreign state (Article 8). Furthermore, although the state of habitation must make a 'determination as to whether an individual is stateless', the Convention on its face does not require a judicial or quasi-judicial hearing, nor does it require a reason or evidence for such a determination. Furthermore, it is left to the executive arm of the state to determine whether a stateless person poses a threat to the state's security.

B. The Convention on the Reduction of Statelessness (1961)

When, in 1950, the Economic and Social Council requested the ILC to draft a treaty concerning the nationality of married women,[19] the ILC expanded the scope of the project to include 'nationality, including statelessness'. After the UN Geneva Conference from 28 March to 18 April 1959 failed to agree to adopt the treaty, a further conference was held two years later (15–28 August 1961). According to the new treaty, the Convention on the Reduction of Statelessness, a state cannot withdraw nationality unless the individual in question is conferred nationality from another state (Article 7(1)).[20] If territory has been ceded to another state, the latter must give 'an assurance' that the inhabitants of the ceded territory will obtain their nationality (Article 7(2)). One's nationality can be retained if one crosses a territorial border, resides abroad or for 'any similar ground' (Article 7(3)). Moreover, a person can lose nationality for residing abroad only if s/he has lived abroad for seven consecutive years (Article 7(4)) or has committed deception upon applying for nationality.[21]

---

[19] Economic and Social Council, 'Official Records of the Economic and Social Council: 5th Year, 11th Sess', Supp No 6 (E/1712). See also ILC, 'Report of the Commission on the Status of Women (Fourth Session)', resolutions of 14 and 17 July 1950, ECOSOC Res 304D (X1), A/CN.4/33, *ILC Yearbook 1950*, vol II, 363. For historical background, see generally P Weis, 'The United Nations Convention on the Reduction of Statelessness, 1961' (1962) 11 *International Comparative Law Quarterly* 1072, 1073–80.

[20] Convention on the Reduction of Statelessness (above note 12).

[21] *Final Judgment on Individual Constitutional Complaint*, (Germany) 2 BvbR 669/04, Oxford Reports on International Law in Domestic Courts 441 (DE 2006), BVerfGE 116, 34.

C. The Convention Relating to the Status of Refugees (1951)

The last treaty that is relevant to our discussion was drafted first. The Convention Relating to the Status of Refugees (1951) again defers to the freedom of the state to confer, withhold or withdraw nationality.[22] In contrast to the definition of 'refugee' in the first Covenant on the Status of Refugees (in force in 1935), the Refugee Convention applies only to persons who have crossed a territorial border. However, we have already observed in chapter three that the legal, economic, social and psychological consequences of statelessness can exist *inside* a state's territorial borders. Moreover, the state of refuge need not accept a stateless refugee, although once s/he is admitted, the state of refuge is obligated not to return him to the state of origin if 'his life or freedom would be threatened on account of his . . . nationality' (Article 33). However, once recognized as a stateless refugee, one is obligated to accept the legal authority of the state of refuge (Article 31). If unrecognized as a refugee or if a stateless person does not 'show good cause' to authorities for her/his 'illegal' entrance into the state's territory, s/he is illegally on the territory (Article 31). By negative implication, again, a stateless person without refugee status may be expelled (Article 32(1)). Also by negative implication, the rights in human rights treaties, such as non-refoulement, are problematic.

D. The Common Problems

The stateless condition generally remains a prospect with all three treaties. Most importantly, the Convention Relating to the Status of Stateless Persons and the Reduction Treaty ironically protect the very reserved domain that has been so pivotal to the production of the stateless condition. The two treaties have especially been protective of the reserved domain when alleged emergencies are declared by the executive arms of states. Does a stateless person possess access to the evidence wielded by the executive that declares supposed emergencies? Do stateless persons have a right to representation when denaturalized, expelled, detained at a border or withheld entry to the territory where they have had deep social relationships? Indeed, does a stateless person possess a right of judicial

---

[22] Convention Relating to the Status of Refugees (above note 10). The first Refugee Treaty was signed on 28 October 1933 and in force 13 June 1935: Geneva Covenant on the Status of Refugees (1933), 159 LTS 199. The earlier treaty responded to the denaturalization of large numbers of Armenians in the Ottoman Empire, the Tartars and White Russians from the Soviet Union, and persons of the alleged Jewish bloodline from Austria, Romania, Poland and Germany. The obligations of the 1951 Convention include minimum standards of movement, rationing, housing, public education, public relief, labour standards and social security once a person has entered its territory.

scrutiny of the executive's exercise of the state's internal jurisdiction during an alleged emergency?

These issues are raised by the Convention Relating to the Status of Stateless Persons itself. Article 8 provides:

> Nothing in this Convention shall prevent a Contracting State, in time of war or other grave and exceptional circumstances, from taking provisionally measures which [the state] considers *essential to the national security* in the case of a particular person, pending a determination by the Contracting State that the person is in fact a stateless person and that the continuance of such measures is *necessary in his case in the interests of national security.*[23]

Although Article 8(1) of the Reduction Treaty provides that 'a contracting state shall not deprive a person of its nationality if such deprivation would render him stateless', Article 8(2) recognizes the state's authority to denaturalize or withhold recognition of a person's nationality from another state.[24] Article 8(3) continues:

> Notwithstanding the provisions of paragraph 1 of this article, a contracting state may retain *the right to deprive a person of his nationality*, if at the time of signature, ratification or accession it specifies its retention of such right on one or more of the following grounds, being grounds existing *in its national law* at that time:
>
> a) that, inconsistently with his *duty of loyalty* to the contracting state, the person,
>
> > i) has, in disregard of *an express prohibition by the contracting state* rendered or continued to render services to, received or continued to receive emoluments from, another state, or
> > ii) has conducted himself in a manner seriously *prejudicial* to *the vital interests* of the state.

In addition, nationality matters are domestically administered such that they lie within the prerogative of the executive. State officials are also left to determine whether the state's 'vital interests' are offended. The legal obligation of the state to act in a manner that does not leave persons stateless is lifted during an alleged emergence. In sum, the executive arm of the state is left with the freedom to determine crucial issues leading to the consequences outlined above in chapter three: the 'vital interest' of the state, 'national interest and public order', statelessness itself, 'disloyalty', justified expulsion and the right to remain on a state's territory.

So long as officials of a state of origin act within the protected residuary, they may claim that a natural person has a nationality of another state. In such a circumstance, state responsibility is unclear. The guarantee in the International Covenant on Civil and Political Rights (ICCPR) (1966) that everyone has 'the right to recognition everywhere as a person before the

---

[23] Convention Relating to the Status of Stateless Persons (above n 11) emphasis added.
[24] Convention on the Reduction of Statelessness (above note 12).

law' is institutionalized as a matter of domestic law to the extent that the international community protects the reserved domain of state members.[25] This perspective is reinforced by the definition of a stateless person in the Convention Relating to the Status of Stateless Persons to the effect that it is left to the state to confer nationality. Accordingly, the opinion of the state of refuge may determine that a natural person is not a national 'under the operation of its laws'. The generating Final Act of the two Status Treaties confirms the deference to the freedom of a state of refugee to decide whether a natural person is a legal person.[26] Similarly, the state of origin is unlikely to protect a national diplomatically if the state executive does not believe the individual is in fact its national. The state of refuge, its paramilitary groups or its inhabitants may at the same time refuse to civilly or humanely receive stateless persons. In such a context, such a state or other states parties may 'consider sympathetically the possibility of according to that person the treatment which the Convention accords to stateless persons'. The Final Act continues that if a state has decided to treat an individual as if stateless, other states must comply with this recognition. The latter duty, though, is hortatory. A judicial scrutiny of the social-cultural context leading to an exodus from the state of origin is unlikely to follow on from the terms of the treaties.

More generally, the right to nationality hinges upon a state's internal jurisdiction. With the international community understood as the aggregated will of states, legal obligation is based upon the inter-relations of states. The three statelessness treaties reinforce a sense of the international community as the aggregate of states' wills. James Hathaway has extended this focus more generally:

> The general principles that emerged from the network of interstate arrangements on the protection of aliens do not, however, endow aliens themselves with rights and duties. International aliens law was conceived very much within the traditional contours of international law: the rights created are the rights of national states, enforced at their discretion under the rules of diplomatic protection and international arbitration.[27]

A consequence of this understanding of the aggregated international community of states, as a New Zealand refugee tribunal has recently pointed out, is the sustained or systematic violation of human rights.[28] Richard Lillich concluded in this regard, 'The fate of the individual is worse than

---

[25] International Covenant on Civil and Political Rights (1966) (ICCPR), UNGA Resolution 2200A (XXI), 999 UNTS 171 (entered into force 23 March 1976) Art 16.

[26] Final Act, UN Conference of Plenipotentiaries on the Status of Refugees and Stateless Persons (Geneva, 25 July 1951), www.unhcr.org/40a8a7394.html.

[27] J Hathaway, *The Rights of Refugees under International Law* (Cambridge, Cambridge University Press, 2005) 78. See also J Hathaway, *The Law of Refugee Status* (Markham, Butterworths, 1999) 57: 'It is an underlying assumption of refugee law that wherever available, national protection takes precedence over international protection.'

[28] *Refugee Appeal No 76467* (29 June 2010), [2010] NZRSAA 83, para 103.

secondary in this scheme: it is doctrinally non-existent [and he] in the eyes of traditional international law, like the alien of the Greek city-state regime, is a non-person'.[29]

The internal jurisdiction has been protected even when states have been under a legal obligation to register all births on their territories. The Reduction Treaty, the Convention on the Rights of the Child (1989)[30] and the ICCPR all indicate that naturalization and nationality by law are matters of internal jurisdiction. The Convention on the Rights of the Child defers to its state parties to recognize 'the right of a child to acquire a nationality', 'in particular where the child would *otherwise be stateless*' (Article 7). In addition, the state shall not conduct 'unlawful interference' with respect to a child's 'identity', name, family relations or nationality (Article 8). Likewise, according to Article 4(1) of the Reduction Treaty, state parties agree that the recognition of nationality is left to the enforcement of the states themselves: the enforcement must be 'in the manner prescribed by national law'.[31]

Article 24(3) of the ICCPR does require that states parties undertake to ensure that 'every child has the right to acquire a nationality'.[32] However, the UN Human Rights Committee (UNHRC) has pointed out in 'General Comment 17' that this undertaking 'does not necessarily make it an obligation for states to give their nationality to every child born in their territory'.[33] A state is obligated only to 'adopt every appropriate measure, both internally and in cooperation with other states, to ensure that every child has a nationality when he is born'. Hence the state is again left with the bounded freedom to decide whether an inhabitant is a national or is stateless.

The administrative discretion on the part of state officials is especially problematic in that the treaties place the onus of registration for a child's nationality on the part of parents or guardians.[34] Once a child has reached the age of majority, the onus of registration shifts to the child. An application for nationality does not ensure that the nationality will be granted. Until such occurs, the infant or child remains stateless. As documented in the Introduction chapter, 51 million children remain unregistered, not

[29] R Lillich, *The Human Rights of Aliens in Contemporary International Law* (Manchester, Manchester University Press, 1984) 12.

[30] Convention on the Rights of the Child (1989), 1577 UNTS 2 (entered into force 2 September 1990) (140 signatories, 193 parties).

[31] Convention on the Reduction of Statelessness (above note 12) Art 4(1).

[32] ICCPR (above n 25).

[33] UN Human Rights Committee (HRC), 'General Comment 17: Article 24 (Rights of the Child)', reprinted in UN, *Human Rights Instruments, Volume I: Compilation of General Comments and General Recommendations Adopted by Human Rights Treaty Bodies*, HRI/GEN/1/Rev.9, www.un.org/en/ga/search/view_doc.asp?symbol=HRI/GEN/1/Rev.9(Vol.I), para 8.

[34] Convention on the Reduction of Statelessness (above n 12) Art 1(b); Convention on the Rights of the Child (above n 30) Art 7; and Convention Relating to the Status of Stateless Persons (above n 11) Art 25(2).

least because of the lack of financial or administrative resources on the part of states. In addition, we have observed how domestic laws are administered in a manner to keep members of ethnic, religious or ethnic groups stateless.

The domestic sources of the legal conditions for conferring nationality remain protected by the reserved domain, independent of child registration processes. Article 7(2) of the Convention on the Rights of the Child provides, 'States Parties shall ensure the implementation of these rights in accordance with their national law and their obligations under the relevant international instruments in this field.' Against the background of the reserved domain of the state, the standards of this treaty are circular because the reserved internal jurisdiction is incorporated for matters of nationality. In addition, the treaty holds out that a stateless person would be obligated to conform to the laws of the state on whose territory s/he finds her/himself.[35] Again, a state may denaturalize a stateless person if, in the opinion of state officials, the person is deemed disloyal to the state.[36]

The Reduction Treaty offers four circumstances when the officials might so determine: first, if the stateless person has rendered or continues to render services or to receive emoluments from another state; second, if the stateless person 'has conducted himself in a manner *seriously prejudicial to the vital interests of the state*'; third, if the stateless person has made an oath of allegiance to another state; or fourth, if evidence is disclosed showing that the stateless person has repudiated or is likely to repudiate her/his allegiance to the state.[37] In the latter circumstance, the individual may be expelled on grounds of national security or public order.

It is therefore difficult not to conclude that the statelessness treaties assume an international community aggregated from the wills of its state members.

III. THE HUMAN RIGHTS TREATIES

While the statelessness treaties discussed above have been shown to fail at preventing statelessness, many jurists hold out hope that the stateless condition may otherwise be reduced by 'the architecture of the human rights regime'.[38] Human rights are said to be universally shared. In particular, the

---

[35] Convention Relating to the Status of Stateless Persons (above n 11) Art 2.
[36] Ibid, Art 31(2).
[37] Convention on the Reduction of Statelessness (above note 12) Art 8(3)(a)(b).
[38] Caroline Sawyer has claimed that the 'greatest hope must be rooted in the modern human rights system': C Sawyer, 'Legal Frameworks of Statelessness in Europe' in C Sawyer and B Blitz (eds), *Statelessness in the European Union: Displaced, Undocumented, Unwanted* (Cambridge, Cambridge University Press, 2011) 82. See also Weissbrodt, *The Human Rights of Non-Citizens* (above n 2) 82; Weissbrodt, 'Final Report' (above n 2). The International Court of Justice certainly shared such a viewpoint in the *Wall Case* when it stated (affirming

right of nationality has been declared inviolable, all natural persons have been coded as legal persons, and everyone has been assured of being equal before the law. Human rights treaties have also recognized a state obligation to institutionalize remedies for the protection of 'everyone'. The treaties proscribe discrimination on grounds that include national origin and birth. The inference in all this has been that treaty rights trump any state law or state action causing harm to stateless persons.

A. The Right to Nationality

The UN Charter itself states in Article 1(3) that one of the purposes of the United Nations is to promote and encourage 'respect for human rights and for fundamental freedoms for all without discrimination as to race, sex, language or religion'. The scope of the non-discrimination clauses of the UNDHR is also left open by Article 2 so as to possibly include nationality: 'without discrimination *of any kind*'. A UN General Assembly Resolution on the Succession of States (2000) and the Brasilia Declaration (2010) follow the spirit of the UNDHR.[39] The Inter-American Court of Human Rights has further described nationality as an 'inherent right of all human beings'.[40]

In a call-back to eighteenth-century natural rights theory generally,[41] several other multilateral human rights treaties have recognized a right to nationality for everyone: the Convention on the Rights of Persons with

the *Nuclear Weapons Case*) that a state's right of self-determination, along with other rules during armed conflict, is grounded in 'elementary considerations of humanity'. See *Construction of a Wall*, 2004 ICJ Rep 199, para 157 (also in 129 ILR 37, 119, para 157); and *Legality of the Threat or Use of Nuclear Weapons*, 1996 ICJ Rep 257, para 79 (also in 110 ILR 163, 207, para 79).

[39] UN General Assembly Resolution on Nationality of Natural Persons in Relation to the Succession of States, UN GA Res 55/153, UN doc A/55/610 (12 December 2000), reprinted in (2000) 13 *International Journal of Refugee Law* 463. Art 19 recognizes a duty of the state to prevent statelessness. The Resolution frames the withholding of nationality as an offence of a legal obligation rather than of a hortatory duty. See also the Brasilia Declaration on the Protection of Refugees and Stateless Persons in the Americas (Brasilia, 11 November 2010), adopted by the countries present at the International Meeting on Refugee Protection, Statelessness and Mixed Migration Movements in the Americas, www.unhcr.org/refworld/docid/4cdd44582.html.

[40] *Proposed Amendments to the Naturalization Provisions of the Constitution of Costa Rica*, Advisory Opinion (19 January 1984), OC-4/84, Inter-American Court of Human Rights, Ser A, No 4, para 32, reported in (1984) 5 *HRLJ* 161 and 79 ILR 282.

[41] See generally R Tuck, *The Rights of War and Peace: Political Thought and the International Order from Grotius to Kant* (Oxford, Oxford University Press, 1999); J Bartelson, *A Geneology of Sovereignty* (Cambridge, Cambridge University Press, 1995); J Bartelson, *Visions of World Community* (Cambridge, Cambridge University Press, 2009); and E Keene, *Beyond the Anarchical Society: Grotius, Colonialism and Order in World Politics* (Cambridge, Cambridge University Press, 2002).

Disabilities (2006),[42] Convention on the Rights of the Child,[43] International Convention on the Protection of the Rights of Migrant Workers (1990),[44] the Reduction Treaty,[45] the ICCPR[46] and the International Convention on the Elimination of All Forms of Racial Discrimination (ICERD) (1965).[47] Article 5(d)(iii) of ICERD in particular provides that

> States Parties undertake to prohibit and eliminate racial discrimination *in all its forms* and to guarantee the right of everyone, *without distinction* as to race, colour,

---

[42] Convention on the Rights of Persons with Disabilities (2006), 2515 UNTS 3 (entered into force 3 May 2008), www.un.org/disabilities/convention/conventionfull.shtml. According to Art 18(1):

> States Parties shall recognize the rights of persons with disabilities to liberty of movement, to freedom to choose their residence and to a nationality, on an equal basis with others, including by ensuring that persons with disabilities:
>
> > Have the right to *acquire and change a nationality and are not deprived of their nationality arbitrarily or on the basis of disability;*
> >
> > Are not deprived, on the basis of disability, of their ability to obtain, possess and utilize documentation of their nationality or other documentation of identification, or to utilize relevant processes such as immigration proceedings, that may be needed to facilitate exercise of the right to liberty of movement;
> >
> > Are free to leave any country, including their own;
> >
> > Are not deprived, arbitrarily or on the basis of disability, of the right to enter their own country. Children with disabilities shall be registered immediately after birth and shall have the right from birth to a name, *the right to acquire a nationality* and, as far as possible, the right to know and be cared for by their parents.

According to Art 18(2), 'Children with disabilities shall be registered immediately after birth and shall have the right from birth to a name, *the right to acquire a nationality* and, as far as possible, the right to know and be cared for by their parents' (emphasis added).

[43] Convention on the Rights of the Child (above n 30) Arts 7 and 8.

[44] International Convention on the Protection of the Rights of All Migrant Workers and Members of Their Families (1990), 2220 UNTS 3 (entered into force 1 July 2003).

> Art 1(1) The present Convention is applicable, except as otherwise provided hereafter, to all migrant workers and members of their families without distinction of any kind such as . . . nationality . . . birth or other status.
>
> Art 1(2) The present Convention shall apply during the entire migration process of migrant workers and members of their families . . .
>
> . . .
>
> Art 7 States Parties undertake . . . to respect and to ensure to all migrant workers and members of their families within their territory or subject to their jurisdiction the rights provided for in the present Convention without distinction of any kind such as . . . nationality, . . . birth or other status.
>
> . . .
>
> Art 29 Each child of a migrant worker shall have the right to a name, to registration of birth and to a nationality.

[45] Convention on the Reduction of Statelessness (above note 12) Art 8(4).

[46] ICCPR (above n 25) Art 24(3).

[47] International Convention on the Elimination of All Forms of Racial Discrimination (ICERD) (1965), 660 UNTS 195 (entered into force 4 January 1969).

or national or ethnic origin, to equality before the law, notably in the enjoyment of the following rights: d) Other civil rights, in particular: iii) *the right to nationality*.[48]

Regional treaties have also affirmed a right to nationality for everyone, including the African Charter on the Rights and Welfare of the Child (1990),[49] the European Convention on Nationality (1997)[50] and the Inter-American Convention on Human Rights (1969).[51]

B. The Right to Legal Personhood

Aside from the explicit recognition of a right to nationality, a second right implicitly supports a right to nationality for everyone: the right to legal personhood. Here, one needs to distinguish between a natural person (who is entitled to all human rights) and a legal person (who is recognized as possessing rights if s/he possesses de jure nationality). The famous *Persons Case* of the British Privy Council explained why women had to be considered legal persons.[52] In a similar vein, the International Covenant on Economic, Social and Cultural Rights (ICESCR) (1966) sets out social and economic rights that protect 'everyone', including presumably stateless persons.[53] Article 16 of the ICCPR states that 'Everyone shall have the right to recognition everywhere as a person before the law.'[54] This universality is reaffirmed in Article 2:

> Each State Party to the present Covenant undertakes to respect and to ensure *to all individuals* within its territory and subject to its jurisdiction the rights recognized in the present Covenant, without distinction of any kind, such as race, colour, sex, language, religion, political or other opinion, *national or social origin,* property, *birth or other status*.[55]

---

[48] Ibid, emphasis added.

[49] African Charter on the Rights and Welfare of the Child (1990), OAU Doc CAB/LEG/ 24.9/49 (1990) (entered into force 29 November 1999), reprinted in (1994) *African Yearbook of International Law* 295, Art 6(3).

[50] European Convention on Nationality (1997), ETS No166 (entered into force 1 March 2000), Arts 4(a), 4(b), 18 and 29.

[51] American Convention on Human Rights (1969), OAS Off Rec OEA/Ser.L./V/11.23 doc. rev.2, 36 OASTS 1 (entered into force 19 July 1978), Arts 3 and 20(1).

[52] *Edwards v Canada (Attorney-General)* ('Persons Case') [1930] AC 124, 1 DLR 98.

[53] International Covenant on Economic, Social and Cultural Rights (ICESCR) (1966), 993 UNTS 3 (entered into force 3 January 1976).

[54] ICCPR (above n 25). An initial draft of Art 16 provided: 'No person shall be deprived of his juridical personality.' This draft limited the scope of the Covenant, as a consequence, to human subjects who already had been recognized as possessing legal status. In addition, the discussion surrounding the drafting of the provision suggested that the reference to the 'drive of his juridical personality' lacked a well-defined signification: N Jayawickrama, *The Judicial Application of Human Rights Law: National Regional and International Jurisprudence* (Cambridge, Cambridge University Press, 2002) 595–96.

[55] ICCPR (above n 25) emphasis added.

Aside from Article 24(3), which explicitly guarantees that 'every child has the right to acquire a nationality', the ICCPR implies that 'everyone', presumably including stateless persons, and 'all members of the human family' are deserving of 'inherent dignity' and 'equal and inalienable rights'. The Optional Protocol (1966) of the ICCPR went so far as to institutionalize a procedure to hear complaints by 'everyone' against states for violations of ICCPR norms.[56]

Regional human rights treaties also recognize that every natural person is a legal person before domestic and international tribunals. Article 17 of the American Declaration of the Rights and Duties of Man (1948), for example, provides, 'Every person has the right to be recognized everywhere as a person having rights and obligations, and to enjoy the basic civil rights.'[57] Article 3 of the Inter-American Convention on Human Rights (1969) guarantees that 'every person has the right of recognition as a person before the law'.[58] Article 5 of the African Charter on Human and Peoples' Rights (1981) affirms, 'Every individual shall have the right . . . to the recognition of his legal status.'[59]

IV. THE PRIORITY OF THE RESERVED DOMAIN OVER THE RIGHT TO NATIONALITY

The question we need to face is whether jurists are correct in their hope and expectation that 'the architecture of human rights' protects de jure and effectively stateless persons. This section argues that given the sense of the international community as an aggregate of the wills of states, such hope and expectation is naive. I shall discuss three aspects of such naivety.

A. Reservations

For one thing, the human rights and statelessness treaties outlined briefly above were signed and ratified by states that continued to reserve their freedom to confer, withdraw or withhold nationality from natural persons. To

---

[56] Optional Protocol to the ICCPR (1966), 999 UNTS 302 (entered into force 23 March 1976). The Committee has over time evolved to become much like a quasi-judicial tribunal: HJ Steiner, 'Individual Claims in a World of Massive Violations: What Role for the Human Rights Committee?' in P Alston and J Crawford (eds), *The Future of UN Human Rights Treaty Monitoring* (Cambridge, Cambridge University Press, 2000).

[57] American Declaration of the Rights and Duties of Man ('Pact of San José, Costa Rica'), Bogota, 2 May 1948, Novena Conferencia Internacional Americana, OAS Off Rec OEA/Ser.L.V/ll.82 doc.6 rev.1 at 17 (1992), (1953) 6 *Actas y Documentos* 297.

[58] American Convention on Human Rights (above n 51).

[59] African [Banjul] Charter on Human and Peoples' Rights (1981), OAU Doc CAB/LEG/67/3 rev 3, (1982) 21 ILM 58 (entered into force 21 October 1986).

be sure, the Vienna Convention on the Law of Treaties (1969) provides that a reservation must not be 'incompatible with the object and purpose of the treaty' (Article 19(c)).[60] The Human Rights Committee of the ICCPR has emphasized the importance of the rational coherency of any reservation and the objectivity of treaties.[61] More generally, Article 18 of the Vienna Convention on the Law of Treaties states that a state is obligated 'to refrain from acts which would defeat the object and purpose of a treaty'. According to Articles 53 and 64 of the Vienna Convention, state parties have undertaken to consider void any treaty provision that conflicts with a peremptory norm or with jus cogens. Human rights treaties are generally accepted as representing jus cogens norms.[62] An ILC submission to the UN General Assembly has confirmed that a reservation is void if it contradicts 'the essential element' of a treaty 'in such a way that the reservation impairs the raison d'être of the treaty'.[63] The ILC has added that if a treaty provision trumps the exercise of internal jurisdiction, a reservation 'does not affect the binding nature of that norm'.[64] The Human Rights Committee of the ICCPR has reiterated this opinion.[65]

Such an approach to treaty reservations is usually accompanied by a list of peremptory norms that by their very nature exclude the right to nationality and the right to legal personhood. The usual list of peremptory norms, however, excludes a right to nationality or a right to legal personhood.[66] The latter rights possess a character similar to a peremptory norm but require an understanding of a very different sense of an international community than that of the aggregated wills of states. As the UNHRC stated in 'General Comment 24', human rights treaties 'are not a web of

---

[60] Vienna Convention on the Law of Treaties (1969), 1155 UNTS 331 (entered into force 27 January 1980) (45 signatories, 113 parties).

[61] HRC, 'General Comment 24: Issues Relating to Reservations Made upon Ratification or Accession to the Covenant or the Optional Protocols Thereto, or in Relation to Declarations under Article 41 of the Covenant', in UN, *Human Rights Instruments, Volume I* (above n 33).

[62] HRC, 'General Comment 24' (ibid) para 8.

[63] UN General Assembly, 'Reservations to Treaties: Conclusions on the Reservations Dialogue Provisionally Adopted by the Working Group on Reservations to Treaties on 6, 12 and 14 July 2011', ILC 63rd sess (15 July 2011), UN Doc A/CN.4/L.793, Art 3.1.4. If a state's domestic laws 'exclude or modify the legal effect of certain provisions of a treaty or of the treaty as a whole . . . [a reservation] may be formulated only insofar as it does not affect an essential element of the treaty or its general tenor': Art 3.1.5.5.

[64] Ibid, Art 4.4.3.1. And again, a reservation 'cannot exclude or modify the legal effect of a treaty in a manner contrary to a peremptory norm of general international law': Art 4.4.3.2.

[65] HRC, 'General Comment 24' (above n 61) para 8.

[66] ILC, 'Text to the Draft Articles on Responsibility of States for Internationally Wrongful Acts' in *Report of the ILC on the Work of Its Fifty-third Session*, UN GAOR, 56th Sess, UN Doc A/56/10 (Supp No 10) (2001), www.un.org/documents/ga/docs/56/a5610.pdf, 43, reprinted in J Crawford (ed), *International Law Commission's Articles on State Responsibility: Introduction, Text and Commentaries* (Cambridge, Cambridge University Press, 2002) Comm 1 (74–75), Art 40, Comms 2–6 (245–46) and Art 48, Comm 9. See also American Law Institute, *Restatement of the Law, Third: Foreign Relations Law of the United States* (Philadelphia, American Law Institute, 1987) 161.

inter-state exchanges of mutual obligations. . . The principle of inter-state reciprocity has no place.'[67]

The priority of an image of an international community that is independent of state members, addressed in more detail in later chapters below, is evidenced by reservations, declarations and the right of states to denunciate treaties.[68] The United States, for example, has maintained that any ratified treaty is effectively revoked if its objective contradicts a reservation.[69] More specifically, on signing the ICESCR, Belgium added a reservation to the effect that the non-discrimination clause does not prevent the state from protecting non-nationals differently than nationals.[70] Argentina's reservation excludes any other state from expressing an opinion about its nationality policy concerning state succession if 'sovereignty is the subject of discussion'. Jurisdiction over the conferral of nationality, as well as the related procedures and enforcement policies, has been reserved by Netherlands and Ireland. Some states parties (eg, the Philippines, United Kingdom, Austria and Tunisia) have reserved the discretion to denaturalize inhabitants, to expel denaturalized inhabitants (eg, Ireland and the United Kingdom), to refuse to provide equitable social security, employment standards and/or property ownership to stateless inhabitants (eg, Demark, Sweden, Honduras, Ireland, Finland, Germany, Guatamala, the Philippines and the United Kingdom), not to treat stateless persons according to domestic standards applicable to nationals (eg, Spain, various Latin American states and all members of the Organization of American States), to categorize 'undesirable aliens' as 'unskilled workers' and declare when public order or national security justify action against stateless inhabitants (eg, the Philippines, United Kingdom, Kiribati and Zambia) and to preclude judicial review of decisions regarding nationality (eg, France). My point is that, despite the Vienna Treaty's object and purpose test for reservations, state parties to human rights treaties continuously fall back upon

[67] HRC, 'General Comment 24' (above n 61) para 17. Even here, however, the Comment deferred to the possible internal jurisdiction under Art 41.

[68] Denunciation is the object of examination by the Human Rights Committee in 'CCPR General Comment 26: Continuity of Obligations', CCPR/C/21/Rev.1/Add.8/Rev.1, also in UN, *Human Rights Instruments, Volume I* (above n 33). For reservations, see HRC, 'General Comment 24' (above n 61) paras 8 and 18. In 'General Comments' such as these, the Committee has entertained a very different sense of an international community than that which I am presently elaborating.

[69] See HJ Steiner, P Alston and R Goodman, 'Comment on Severability' in HJ Steiner, P Alston and R Goodman (eds), *International Human Rights in Context: Law, Politics and Morals*, 3rd edn (Oxford, Oxford University Press, 2008) 1147. See also *Kennedy v Trinidad and Tobago*, HRC, CCPR/C/67/D/845/1999 (2 November 1999) Communication No 845/1999; and R Goodman, 'Human Rights Treaties, Invalid Reservations, and State Consent' (2002) 96 *American Journal of International Law* 531.

[70] UN, 'Multilateral Treaties Deposited with the Secretary-General: Status as at 31 December 1991', UN Doc St/LEG/SER.E/10, 123, as quoted in MCR Craven, *International Covenant on Economic, Social and Cultural Rights: A Perspective of its Development* (Oxford, Clarendon Press, 1995) 172.

their own internal jurisdiction as the source of legality. Such reservations indicate a background acceptance of a view of the international community as the aggregate of the wills of states – the objective or terms of human rights treaties come what may.

B. Enforcement

In the Introduction chapter above, I suggested that statelessness would continue even if an international institution is created for the sole purpose of eliminating statelessness or if the jurisdiction of a human rights tribunals is widened. I also raised the prospect of continued statelessness for some persons even if international standards are codified or if conflicts between domestic laws and technical failings are resolved. Let us look at a second example of the relation of enforcement problems and the residuary of the international community: the hortatory character of the enforcement provisions of human rights treaties. For example, although Article 8(1) of the Convention on the Rights of the Child recognizes a child's legal identity in terms of her/his nationality, Article 8(2) of the treaty phrases enforcement in hortatory terms: when a child has been deprived of nationality, the state must 'provide appropriate assistance and protection *with a view* to re-establishing speedily his or her identity'.[71] Similarly, Article 2(3) of the ICCPR frames the enforcement of rights in terms of aspirations: 'Each state party to the present Convention *undertakes to take the necessary steps . . . as may be necessary* to give effect to the rights recognized in the present Covenant.' Article 2(1) of ICESCR similarly states, 'Each state party to the present Convention undertakes to take steps . . . to the maximum of its available resources, with a view to achieving progressively the full realization of the rights recognized in the present Covenant. . .' As a further example, Article 2(1) of ICERD provides that all states parties to the treaty 'undertake' '*to pursue by all appropriate means* and without delay a *policy* of eliminating racial discrimination in all its forms and promoting understanding among all races'.[72] By Article 2(2), the state parties undertake 'when the circumstances so warrant, take, in the social, economic, cultural and other fields, special and concrete measures to ensure the adequate development and protection of certain racial groups or individuals belonging to them'. So too, the Convention Governing the Specific Aspects of Refugee Problems in Africa (1969) requires that states parties 'use their

[71] Convention on the Rights of the Child (above n 30) Art 8(2), emphasis added.
[72] ICERD (above n 47). See Committee on the Elimination of Racial Discrimination, 'Record of the 8th Session (148th mtg)', UN Doc CERD/C/SR.148 (1973), 37, as cited in D Mahalic and G Mahalic, 'The Limitation Provisions of the International Convention on the Elimination of All Forms of Racial Discrimination' (1987) 9 *Human Rights Quarterly* 74, 76 (n 11) and 82.

best endeavours consistent with their respective legislations to receive refugees and to secure [their] settlement'.[73]

C. The Exclusion of Nationality from Non-discrimination Clauses

The non-discrimination clauses of the human rights treaties are invariably phrased in strong terms. The usual categories of non-discrimination are race, colour, sex, language, religion, national origin and social origin. Birth is sometimes added. But nationality as such is invariably excluded from the list of proscribed categories. Indeed, although the ICERD offers very wide proscriptions against discrimination, the treaty adds the caveat in Article 1(2) that the non-discrimination norm 'shall not apply to distinctions, exclusions, restriction or references made by a state party to this Convention between citizens and non-citizens'.[74] Article 1(3) continues: 'Nothing in this Convention may be interpreted as affecting in any way the legal provisions of states parties concerning *nationality, citizenship or naturalization,* provided that such provisions do not discriminate against any particular nationality.'[75] The treaty also excludes protection of stateless persons from forced displacement, departure and return (Article 5(d) (i) and (ii)).[76]

It is sometimes argued that nationality can be read into the proscribed category 'national origin'. As an example, a version of the Sierra Leone Constitution limited citizenship to persons of 'Negro African descent'.[77] There is a crucial analytic difference, however, between national origin and nationality. National origin exists by virtue of historical contingency.[78] Although language and dress may well suggest one's national origin,[79] they are socially contingent matters. Indeed, language and dress may well be contingent upon one's dialect or custom from a particular geographic area or class inside a state's territorial border. Nationality, on the other hand, exists by virtue of a juridical construction: 'by operation of [a state's]

---

[73] OAU Convention Governing the Specific Aspects of Refugee Problems in Africa (Addis Ababa, 10 September 1969), in force 20 June 1974, 1001 UNTS 45, Art 11 (1) and V.

[74] ICERD (above n 47).

[75] Emphasis added. The *travaux préparatoires* suggest that the intent of the draftspersons of the Convention was to proscribe discrimination on grounds of race with respect to laws related to nationals and non-nationals. See generally Mahalic and Mahalic (above n 72) 76.

[76] HRC, 'General Comment 23: The Rights of Minorities (Art 27)', CCPR/C/21/Rev.1/Add.5, also in UN, *Human Rights Instruments, Volume I* (above n 33).

[77] See Committee on the Elimination of Racial Discrimination, *Sierra Leone Case,* UN Doc CERD/C/SR.204 (1974), 10th sess (204th mtg), 43–48.

[78] The HRC understands the contingent factors as culture, religion and language: HRC, 'General Comment 23' (above n 76).

[79] K Boyle and A Baldaccini, 'A Critical Evaluation of International Human Rights Approaches to Racism' in S Fredman (ed), *Discrimination and Human Rights* (Oxford, Oxford University Press, 2001) 155.

law'. If a person finds her/himself on state territory that withholds or withdraws her/his nationality, the person's national origin is immaterial.

Undifferentiated nationals of an ethnic group may be the object of discrimination.[80] So too may undifferentiated stateless persons. A Sri Lankan Court has held that the state possesses the freedom to categorize inhabitants as 'Tamil Ceylonese nationals'.[81] As a further point of distinction between national origin and nationality, national origin is associated with members of a group, but it is individuals who possess nationality.[82] As Sarah Joseph, Jenny Schultz and Melissa Castan have suggested, nationality, as a legal status, is 'intrinsically more important to guard against discrimination' than is economic status.[83] One's national origin may positively impact a person's personality, and yet the same person may lack nationality.[84]

It does not help stateless persons that the ICCPR non-discrimination proscription in the context of alleged public emergencies is silent with respect to discrimination on the basis of 'national origin' (Article 4(1)). In addition, the general non-discrimination clause (Article 2(1)) only extends to individuals 'within [a state's] territory and *subject to its jurisdiction*'. To take an example, a Cambodian statute proscribed discrimination on grounds of 'political, racial or religious bases' but was silent with respect to nationality.[85] Cambodian government officials had detained non-nationals on suspicion of spying for foreign states. Most such detentions, however, involved de jure stateless persons.[86] The silence regarding nationality in the non-discrimination clauses of the human rights treaties has rendered it difficult to establish a discriminatory intent on the part of state officials against stateless persons. Once again, the international standard related to non-discrimination reinforces the understanding of an international community as the aggregated wills of state members.

---

[80] I Ziemele and GG Schram, 'Article 15' in G Alfredsson and A Eide (eds), *The Universal Declaration of Human Rights: A Common Standard of Achievement* (The Hague, Martinus Nijhoff, 1999) 311.

[81] *SZMFL v Minister for Immigration and Citizenship and Refugee Review Tribunal* [2009] FCA 146, para 21.

[82] See ICCPR (above n 25) Art 27. See also HRC, 'General Comment 23' (above n 76) para 1.

[83] See S Joseph, J Schultz and M Castan, *The International Covenant on Civil and Political Rights: Cases, Materials and Commentary* (Oxford, Oxford University Press, 2000) para 23.27.

[84] *London Borough of Ealing v Race Relations Board* [1972] AC 342; and *SZMFL v Minister for Immigration and Citizenship and Refugee Review Tribunal* (Federal Court of Canada), [2009] FCA 146, para 21.

[85] *LIM Suy-Hong et al*, Extraordinary Chambers in the Courts of Cambodia (ECCC), Case File/ Dossier No 001/18-07-2007/ECCC/TC (26 July 2010), paras 313, 326 and 379. The ECCC Law established the 'Extraordinary Chambers in the Courts of Cambodia for the Prosecution of Crimes Committed during the Period of Democratic Kampuchea', NS/RKM/ 1004/006 (10 August 2001 with amendments on 27 October 2004). See *Kaing Guek Eav, alias Duch*, Case File/Dossier No 001/18-07-2007/ECCC/TC (26 July 2010).

[86] *LIM Suy-Hong* (ibid) para 325.

V. THE LIMITATIONS CLAUSES

The rights to nationality and to legal personhood are subject to limitations clauses in the human rights treaties. It does not help a stateless person that the referents of the limitations are vague: 'the life of the nation' (ICCPR); 'the rights and freedoms of others', 'the just requirements', 'morality', 'public order', 'general welfare', 'democratic society' or 'the community' (UNDHR, Article 29); 'war or other grave and exceptional circumstances' or 'national security' (Convention Relating to the Status of Stateless Persons, Article 9); 'the general welfare in a democratic society' (ICESCR, Article 4); 'the security of all', 'the just demands of the general welfare' and 'the advancement of democracy' (American Declaration of the Rights and Duties of Man, Articles 19 and 28);[87] 'armed conflict not of an international character' and 'hostilities' (Rome Statute, Article 8(2));[88] or even more generally, 'matters which are essentially within the domestic jurisdiction of any state' (UN Charter, Article 2(7)). Article 25 of the African Charter includes the protection of the right to nationality during armed conflict, natural disaster, civil strife or the breakdown of the social and economic order 'however caused'. Since a declaration of emergency is required only if human rights are at issue, the right to nationality and the right to legal personhood are exempted from non-derogation because they are not considered human rights. A legal obligation is owed by a natural person to another natural person, thereby leaving the state's domain intact (see, eg, Article 29(3) of the UNDHR).

Let us return to two limitations clauses in the ICCPR. First, Article 12(1) of the ICCPR provides, 'Everyone *lawfully* within the territory of a state shall, within that territory, have the right to liberty of movement and freedom to choose his residence.' Article 12(2) adds, 'Everyone shall be free to leave any country, including his own.' The above rights of movement, the choice of one's state and of return to the state of habitual residence are limited, however, by Article 12(3) of the ICCPR:

> The above-mentioned rights shall not be subject to any restrictions except those which are provided by law, are necessary to protect national security, public order (ordre public), public health or morals or the rights and freedoms of others, and are consistent with the other rights recognized in the present Covenant.

---

[87] American Declaration of the Rights and Duties of Man (above n 57) Arts 19 and 28. Similarly, Art 31 of the Convention Relating to the Status of Refugees (above n 10) affirms the authority of the state to expel a refugee on grounds of national security or public order, leaving it to the state of refuge to decide whether the condition of statelessness threatens its own national security or public order.

[88] Rome Statute of the International Criminal Court (1998, last amended 2010), 2187 UNTS 38544 (entered into force 1 July 2002) (139 signatories, 122 parties).

To be sure, such limitations must be 'consistent with the other rights recognized in the present Covenant', and Article 24(3) does recognize a right to nationality for 'every child', as noted above. However, nationality is excluded from the non-discrimination clauses of the human rights treaties. In addition, a de jure stateless person has the onus of establishing why compelling national security does not justify an expulsion order.[89] Indeed, in deference to the principle of non-intervention into state jurisdiction, the HRC has frequently refrained from reviewing decisions protected by the reserved domain of the state: 'It is not for the Committee to test a sovereign state's evaluation of an alien's security rating.'[90] Added to this, as the HRC has stated, 'neither the Covenant nor international law in general spells out specific criteria for the granting of citizenship through naturalization. . .'[91]

The ground for such denaturalization is an individual's loyalty to the state, as determined by the state (Article 8(3) of the Convention on the Reduction of Statelessness). And it is generally left to the executive of a state to determine whether the individual has conducted her/himself 'in a manner seriously prejudicial to the vital interests of the state' ((Article 8(2)(a)(ii)). This takes us to the all-important limitations clause of the Convention on the Reduction of Statelessness. As noted above, the limitation clause of that treaty provides, 'A contracting state shall not deprive a person of his nationality if such deprivation would render him stateless.' The right against denaturalization, however, is subject to the state's freedom to denaturalize its nationals, '[n]otwithstanding the provisions of paragraph 1 of this article'.[92]

The ramification of the limitation clauses is threefold. For one thing, a state's internal jurisdiction, not international standards, determine the 'vital interests' of the state. Second, it is domestic institutions that get to ascertain whether a stateless person has contradicted the state's vital interests. Third, executive action inside the reserved domain is not justiciable regarding nationality matters. Once again, the right to nationality and to legal personhood are conflated into internal state jurisdiction as representative of the international community's residuary.

---

[89] The same holds for Art 13 of the ICCPR (above n 25), which provides that an 'alien' may be expelled if the expulsion is 'in accordance with law' and if 'compelling reasons of national security otherwise require'.

[90] *JRC v Costa Rica*, HRC, Communication No 296/1988, UN Doc CCPR/C/35/D/296/1988 (1989), para 8.4.

[91] *Vjatseslav Borzov v Estonia*, HRC Communication No 1136/2002 (24 August 2004), UN Doc CCPR/81/D/1136/2002, www.refworld.org/docid/4162a5a40.html, para 7.4. See also *Šipin v Estonia*, HRC Communication No 1423/2005 (4 August 2008), UN Doc CCPR/C/93/D/1423/2005, para 7.4.

[92] The grounds for denaturalization include living abroad for seven years (Art 7(4)), being born outside the state's territory, failing to reside in the state for one year after the age of majority (Art 7(5)) or misrepresenting facts in one's application for nationality (Art 8(2)).

In brief, the international community incorporates internal state juris-diction to locate the conditions and limitation of any right to nationality. The state is left to determine in effect how to enforce the rights of national-ity and legal personhood (Reduction Treaty, Article 17). According to Article 19 of the American Declaration of the Rights and Duties of Man, the right to nationality exists, and yet it is left to the internal jurisdiction to entitle a natural person to possess or change it: 'Every person has the right to the nationality to which he is entitled by law and to change it, if he so wishes, for the nationality of any other country that is willing to grant it to him.'[93] Once again, the right may be limited by the state in the exercise of such overbroad referents as 'the security of all, and by the just demands of the general welfare and the advancement of democracy' (Article 28).

VI. THE NON-DEROGATION CLAUSES

The most common examples of de jure and effective statelessness emerge from alleged state emergencies. I shall examine such circumstances more closely in later chapters. For now, taking Article 4 of the ICCPR as an example, several features of the non-derogation clauses of the human rights treaties render the rights to nationality and to legal personhood suspect. According to Article 4(1),

> In time of public emergency which threatens the life of the nation and the exist-ence of which is officially proclaimed, the states parties to the present Covenant may take measures derogating from their obligations under the present Covenant to the extent strictly required by the exigencies of the situation, pro-vided that such measures are not inconsistent with their other obligations under international law and do not involve discrimination solely on the ground of race, colour, sex, language, religion or social origin.

To be sure, the state must declare an emergency and, in the case of the European human rights regime, submit its declaration to a tribunal. The 'life of the nation' must be threatened. The derogation of state obligations, including the obligation to refrain from acting in a manner that renders someone stateless, must be 'required by the exigencies of the situation'. And the derogation must treat everyone equally without discrimination solely on the usual grounds.

Let us look more closely at these provisions of the ICCPR. The 'life of the nation' is hardly a precise term, especially when used to justify the withdrawal or withholding of a person's nationality. The overly broad

---

[93] American Declaration of the Rights and Duties of Man (above n 57) emphasis added. Chan has remarked that the deprivation of nationality during a state of siege constitutes an unjustifiable penalty and, as such, violates Art 19: JMM Chan, 'The Right to a Nationality as a Human Right: The Current Trend towards Recognition' (1991) 12 *Human Rights Law Journal* 1, 5.

nature of the referent is shared by the non-derogation clauses of other human rights treaties.[94] The apparent incorporation of other international standards ('not inconsistent with their other obligations under international law') invites a very supplemental and circulatory role for such standards. We have seen that these standards themselves implicitly accept internal jurisdiction as the residuary of the international community in nationality matters. And when we turn to the non-discrimination clause of Article 4 of the ICCPR, nationality is once again omitted as a proscribed discriminatory ground during any state emergency. Indeed, even here, the clause is silent as to the inclusion of 'national origin' as a ground. More generally, because inter-state relations have been represented by the executive arms of states and because nationality signifies one's membership in a state (and in the international community) vis-à-vis other states, judicial scrutiny of the exigencies of the situation and the extent to which a stateless person threatens the state's life is unlikely.

The problematic cause of statelessness is further apparent when one looks closely too at the rights protected by the usual non-derogation clause regarding state emergencies. Article 4(2) of the ICCPR itemizes those rights that are non-derogable:

> No derogation from Articles 6 ['inherent right to life'], 7 ['shall not be subject to torture or to cruel, inhuman or degrading treatment or punishment'], 8 (paragraphs 1 ['held in slavery; slavery and the slave trade in all their forms'] and 2 ['held in servitude']), 11 ['imprisoned merely on the ground of inability to fulfil a contractual obligation'], 15 [double jeopardy], 16 ['the right of recognition everywhere as a person before the law'] and 18 ['right to thought, conscience and religion'] may be made under this provision.

This list of rights leaves other rights open to derogation by negative implication. And yet such rights (namely to nationality and to legal personhood) address precisely the circumstances when a natural person is at risk of de jure or effective statelessness.

VII. CONCLUSION

Is there a right to nationality? Does the right to nationality trump domestic law and 'the operation' of such law? I have outlined how the human rights treaties have been signed and ratified with reservations that immunize internal state jurisdiction from international standards about the conferral, withdrawing and withholding of nationality. The texts of the treaties

---

[94] Art 27(1) of the American Convention on Human Rights (above n 51) Art 19, to take another example, authorizes the state to derogate from its legal obligations in the Convention 'to the extent and for the period of time strictly required by the exigencies of the situation'. The 'situation' encompasses 'war, public danger, or other emergency that threatens the independence or security of a State Party', all of which are very broad terms.

exclude nationality as a prohibited discriminatory ground. Limitations and non-derogatory clauses reinforce the internal jurisdiction. Such limitations have also characterized the statelessness treaties despite the texts' claims to ensure the nationality of all natural persons and to reduce the circumstances of the stateless condition. Against this background, the obligations to recognize and protect the human rights of stateless persons have been framed in hortatory language. The human rights treaties claim a universality of scope for everyone. And yet such a freedom of the natural person is subject to the state's freedom to confer, withhold and withdraw nationality. This freedom is especially apparent from the limitations clauses of the two statelessness treaties. As a consequence, treaty provisions intended to protect everyone are subsumed into the reserved domain of a state-centric international community. The universal international standard is thereby separated from the hard fact of the bounded residuary. What is now an issue then is whether, independent of the wording of the statelessness and human rights treaties, a customary international norm trumps a state's freedom – and if so, whether such a norm trumps the production of de jure and effective statelessness. I shall now turn to this possibility.

5

Customary Norms and a Right to Nationality

T HE RESERVED DOMAIN of the international community, synonymous with the reserved domain of state members, has manifested a sense of an international community as the aggregate of the
wills of states. Inside the boundary of such a domain, the state has been
'free to adopt the principles which it regards as best and most suitable', as
the Permanent Court of International Justice stated in *Lotus* (1927).[1]
Statelessness and human rights treaties have been drafted in a manner
that protects such a domain. Do customary international norms succeed
in dissolving the enigma, although treaties do not? If so, how?

Human rights law is for the most part customary international law
rather than treaty law.[2] Sections I and II of this chapter address the two
requisites of an international customary norm: a state's sense of obligation
and state practices.[3] In section III, I contextualize such customary norms
in an effort to establish how an international community as an aggregated
will of state members fails to institutionalize a customary norm that protects the right to nationality. Section IV continues this line of argument by
returning to the notion of an 'international community as a whole' as outlined in chapter one. I shall conclude that the customary character of an
international legal norm fails to support a right to nationality for all natural persons.

---

[1] *Case of the SS Lotus (France v Turkey)*, PCIJ Ser A, No 10 (1927) 18, at 35 and 44, also reported
in (1927) 4 ILR 5.
[2] See generally JC Simeon, 'Introduction: The Research Workshop on Critical Issues in
International Refugee Law and Strategies towards Interpretative Harmony' in JC Simeon
(ed), *Critical Issues in International Refugee Law: Strategies toward Interpretative Harmony*
(Cambridge, Cambridge University Press, 2010).
[3] For the sense of obligation, see O Schachter, *International Law in Theory and Practice* (The
Hague, Martinus Nijhoff, 1991). For state practices, see M Byers, *Custom, Power and the Power
of Rules: International Relations and Customary International Law* (Cambridge, Cambridge
University Press, 1999) 193. For a close application of this requirement for customary norms,
see J-M Henckaerts, 'Study on Customary International Humanitarian Law: A Contribution
to the Understanding and Respect for the Rule of Law in Armed Conflict' (2005) 87
International Review of the Red Cross 175.

I. A SENSE OF OBLIGATION

The required 'sense of obligation' toward a customary norm is manifested by indicia of the norm. If treaties were the main source of such a sense of obligation, one could hardly claim the right to nationality as a customary norm in the light of the previous chapter. Other indicia of obligation, however, include the UN Charter, the various acts preceding the ratification of treaties, UN General Assembly Resolutions, persistent objections, the silence of states to other state actions, domestic and international judicial decisions, and opinio juris. A 'sense of obligation' is an opaque notion. One school of thought has framed the sense of obligation in terms of 'state beliefs' and shared 'ethical principles'.[4] How can a state, as opposed to a natural person, possess an intentionality associated with a belief? More importantly as a practical matter, what is an 'ethical' principle? Are 'ethical' principles mere 'oughts'? If ethicality concerns 'oughts', does this not just return us to the 'hard fact' of the reserved domain in the international community? Why would the choices made by state institutions and officials be legally obligatory if they are protected against international standards as 'oughts'? And are the beliefs and values posited as starting points of analysis, or must jurists retrieve the acts of meaning constituting the beliefs and values?

The latter issue is especially important because a particular customary norm has recently been described as a 'sliding scale' of customary norms.[5] A peremptory norm is said to be the pinnacle of the sliding-scale. But what referent of analysis justifies the locus of a right to nationality on such a scale? Is the right to nationality, as a customary norm, at the top or at the bottom of the hierarchy? Can the referent be identified without a study of the nature of a state's legal obligation to enforce the customary norm?

The right to nationality, as a customary norm, is problematic for another reason. The weight of time is a relevant factor in the constitution of a sense of obligation. Indicia of a sense of obligation suggest an obligation to protect the reserved domain, not a discrete right to nationality or to legal personhood. How many years or months must transpire before a sense of obligation exists? A right may take time before it emerges as a legally

---

[4] BD Lepard, *Customary International Law: A New Theory with Practical Applications* (Cambridge, Cambridge University Press, 2010) 127, 173, 245–69 and 312; and Byers (above n 3). For a close application of this requirement for customary norms, see Henckaerts (above n 3).

[5] F Kirgis, 'Custom as a Sliding Scale' (1987) 81 *American Journal of International Law* 146; and *Prosecutor v Furundzija*, (ICTY) Case No IT-95-17/1-T (Trial Judgment), 10 December 1998, 121 ILR 218, 260–61, paras 153–54.

identifiable rule.[6] It may also lapse through time.[7] Any one of the historical examples of state action in earlier chapters renders the right of nationality less weighty into the future.[8] Indeed, if anything, the examples manifest a sense of obligation towards protection of the reserved domain of a state in nationality matters. According to the American Law Institute's *Third Restatement on Foreign Relations*, 'Traditional international law did not question the authority of a state to terminate the nationality of any of its nationals.'[9] Why is a norm that protects stateless peoples obligatory of all states if the international community is constituted from the wills of states themselves? To make matters worse, we shall soon see that deference to the reserved domain has dissolved in a discursive struggle with a radically different sense of a legal bond in an international community.

II. STATE PRACTICES

The problematic character of a customary norm, at least as it has been understood, is reinforced when we turn to the second requisite of the norm: state practices by 'most or nearly all states' behaving and accepting the norm.[10] Even peremptory norms have been understood as existing, as the *Third Restatement* puts it, if 'a very large majority of states, even if over dissent by "a very small number" of states' consent to the norm.[11] State practices are important as elements of legal obligation because the practices are said to represent actual social practice.[12] But the stateless condition is a social practice. And is not such a social practice of a more interpersonal social relation than the interrelations of states? Is this not so if the social content of the reserved domain is immune from scrutiny? Indeed, is not state practice precisely the phenomenon that produces the enigma of statelessness?

[6] *Island of Palmas Case* (1928) 2 RIAA 829, 839.

[7] *Forti v Suarez-Mason*, 694 F Supp 707 (ND Cal 1988) (J Jensen); and Vienna Convention on the Law of Treaties (1969) 1155 UNTS 331 (entered into enforce 27 January 1980) Art 55. See also Lepard (above n 4) 258: 'even jus cogens norms, like all customary norms, can indeed evolve and should be allowed to evolve.'

[8] D'Amato, 'Is International Law Really "Law"?' (1985) 79 *Northwestern University Law Review* 1293, 1297 (fn 7). Bin Cheng has denied a circularity in this subjectivity sense, however: B Cheng, 'Custom: The Future of General State Practice in a Divided World' in RStJ Macdonald and DM Johnston (eds), *Towards World Constitutionalism: Issues in the Legal Ordering of the World Community* (Leiden, Martinus Nijhoff, 2005) 513 and 530–32. I use the terms 'norm' and 'rule' interchangeably.

[9] American Law Institute, *Restatement of the Law, Third: Foreign Relations Law of the United States* (St Paul, American Law Institute, 1987) para 211 (Comm e).

[10] Byers (above n 3) 94; and Schachter (above n 3).

[11] American Law Institute (above n 9) para 102 (Rep note 6). See also paras 102(2) and 702 (Comm n). Cf L Henkin, 'Human Rights and State "Sovereignty"' (1995/96) *Georgia Journal of International and Comparative Law* 31, 37.

[12] JC Hathaway, *Rights of Refugees under International Law* (Cambridge, Cambridge University Press, 2005) 18.

I have documented in this and earlier chapters how state practices have accepted the customary international norm of the reserved domain as the foundation stone of a state-centric international community. European states especially institutionalized such a sense of an international community between the First and Second World Wars. Mass denaturalization is a clear manifestation of such a sense of an international community. The key to 'the operation' of 'its laws', the defined criteria of statelessness in the Convention Relating to the Status of Stateless Persons (1954),[13] determines whether stateless persons possess allegiance to the state, as we shall see in the next chapter.

In brief, any claim of a customary international right to nationality works against the current of international legislative practices, which reinforce nationality as an incident of internal domestic jurisdiction. Several UN General Assembly Resolutions have reinforced the reserved domain in this manner.[14] The Human Rights Committee (HRC) 'General Comment 15' to the International Covenant on Civil and Political Rights (1954) (ICCPR) defers to domestic jurisdiction in the admission and expulsion of non-nationals.[15] The HRC has also adjudicated claims of stateless persons to that effect.[16] Domestic tribunals have continued to read the right to nationality as an incident of the reserved domain.[17] A stateless person is not infrequently considered unlawfully on a state's territory.[18] International standards have sometimes been put to the side in favour of

[13] Convention Relating to the Status of Stateless Persons (1954), 360 UNTS 117 (entered into force 6 June 1960) Art 1. See discussion above in the Introduction and ch 2; and below ch 6 (ss III and VI), ch 7 (s I), ch 8 (s IV) and ch 9 (s IV).

[14] Declaration on the Granting of Independence to Colonial Countries and Peoples (1960), UNGA Res 1514, 15 UN GAOR Supp No 16, UN Doc A/4684, 66 and 67; Declaration on the Inadmissibility of Intervention in the Internal Affairs of States and the Protection of their Independence and Sovereignty (1965), UNGA Res 2131, UN GAOR 1st Comm, 20th Sess, Agenda Item 107, at 11, Arts 1 and 2; Declaration on Principles of International Law Concerning Friendly Relations and Co-operation among States in Accordance with the Charter of the United Nations (1970), UNGA Res 2625 (XXV), UN GAOR 6th Comm, UN Doc A18028 (1971), 25th Sess, Supp No 28 (Agenda Item No 85), Art 5.

[15] Human Rights Committee (HRC), 'General Comment 15: The Position of Aliens under the Covenant' (1994), UN Doc HRI/GEN/1/Rev.1, 18, paras 5 and 9, also in UN, *Human Rights Instruments, Volume I: Compilation of General Comments and General Recommendations Adopted by Human Rights Treaty Bodies*, HRI/GEN/1/Rev.9 (27 May 2008), www.un.org/en/ga/search/view_doc.asp?symbol=HRI/GEN/1/Rev.9(Vol.I). The Comment does continue, 'In certain circumstances an alien may enjoy the protection of the Covenant even in relation to entry or residence, for example, when considerations of non-discrimination, prohibition of inhuman treatment and respect for family life arise.'

[16] *Šipin v Estonia*, HRC, Communication No 1423/2005, UN Doc CCPR/C/93/D/1423/2005, para 7.4; *Borzov v Estonia*, HRC, Communication No 1136/2002, UN Doc CCPR/C/81/D/1136/2002 (2004), para 7.4.

[17] *Sarbananda Sonowal v Union of India (UOI) and Another*, Writ Petition No 131 of 2000, India Supreme Court (7 December 2005), www.unhcr.org/refworld/docid/46b1c2eb2.html, paras 22, 36, 49 and 56; *Canepa v Canada*, HRC, Communication No 558/1993, UN Doc CCPR/C/59/D/558/1993; and *Maroufidou v Sweden*, HRC, Communication No 58/1979, UN Doc CCPR/C/12/D/58/1979.

[18] *Canepa* (ibid); and *Maroufidou* (ibid).

the state's freedom over nationality issues.[19] International legal standards in this context have also been said to lack identifiable criteria of law.[20] The Australian High Court in particular has explicitly justified the incident of nationality in the reserved domain as hinging upon a state-centric international community.[21] The state's unconstrained freedom to choose whether to diplomatically protect a stateless person is hence widely accepted,[22] Including by European states, which accept the sole and absolute freedom of the state in matters of diplomatic protection.[23] In other words, treaties and domestic adjudication have left the enigma of statelessness unresolved.

The International Law Commission (ILC) has also recognized state practices that support a protective reserved domain in matters relating to de jure and effective statelessness. This has especially been so in its 'Draft Articles on Diplomatic Protection', the 'Draft Articles on Nationality' and the report on 'Expulsion of Aliens'.[24] Early ILC rapporteurs left little room to question such state practices.[25] Although the leading International

---

[19] See, eg, *Šipin* (above n 16) para 7.4. See also *VMRB v Canada*, HRC, Communication No 236/1987, UN Doc CCPR/C/33/D/236/1987 (1988), para 6.3. This opinion was reinforced in *JRC v Costa Rica*, HRC, Communication No 296/1988, UN Doc CCPR/C/35/D/296/1988 (1989), para 8.4; *Hammel v Madagascar*, HRC, Communication No 155/1983, UN Doc CCPR/C/OP/2, 179, (1990) 94 ILR 415; *Tsarjov v Estonia*, HRC, Communication No 1223/2003, UN Doc CCPR/C/D/1223/2003, para 7.3, affirming *Borzov v Estonia* (above n 16); and *Maroufidou* (above n 17) para 10.1.

[20] *Šipin* (above n 16) para 7.4; and *Borzov v Estonia* (above n 16) para 7.4.

[21] *Nagv and Nagw of 2002 v Minister for Immigration and Multicultural and Indigenous Affairs & Another* [2005] HCA 6, paras 14, 15, 16 and 17; and *Minister for Immigration and Multicultural Affairs v Thiyagarajah* (1997) 80 FCR 543 (Australia).

[22] See, eg, *Lay Kon Tji v Minister for Immigration and Ethnic Affairs* (1998) 158 ALR 681 (Fed Ct Australia), 693 (per Finkelstein J); and *Reparations Case* (1949) ICJ Rep 174, 177–78 (also reported in 16 ILR 318). See also *Banco Nacional de Cuba v Sabbatino* (1964) 374 US 398 (428–29), 84 S Ct 923 (940–41) (per Harlan J), also reported in (1964) 35 ILR 2. If the individual is detained or the object of criminal prosecution in another state, the latter state has an obligation to inform the state of nationality of the detention or prosecution without undue delay as well as any communication by a detainee to the state of nationality. The state also has an obligation to inform the national of a right to consular notification: Vienna Convention of Consular Relations (1963) 596 UNTS 261, Can TS 1974 No 25, Art 36(1).

[23] JMM Chan, 'The Right to a Nationality as a Human Right' (1991) 12 *Human Rights Law Journal* 1, 7–10.

[24] ILC, 'Draft Articles on Diplomatic Protection, with Commentaries', UN Doc A/61/10, *ILC Yearbook 2006*, vol II(2), legal.un.org/ilc/texts/instruments/english/commentaries/9_8_2006.pdf, Art 2 (Comm 3), Art 8 (Comms 4, 7 and 11) and Art 19 (Comms 1, 2, 4 and 5); ILC, 'Draft Articles on Nationality of Natural Persons in Relation to the Succession of States, with Commentaries' in *Report of the ILC on the Work of its Fifty-First Session*, UN Doc A/54/10, *ILC Yearbook 1999*, vol II(2), www.refworld.org/pdfid/4512b6dd4.pdf, Art 19 (Comm 6); and ILC, 'Expulsion of Aliens: Memorandum by the Secretariat', Doc A/CN.4/565 (10 July 2006), paras 23 and 41–120.

[25] See, for example, MO Hudson (Special Rapporteur), 'Nationality, Including Statelessness', A/CN.4/50 (21 February 1952), *ILC Yearbook 1952*, vol II, 4, 7–12; M Bennouna, 'Preliminary Report on Diplomatic Protection', UN doc A/CN.4/484, *ILC Yearbook 1998*, vol II(1), 313 (para 19); and V Mikulka, 'First Report on State Succession and its Impact on the Nationality of Natural and Legal Persons', UN Doc A/CN.4/467, *ILC Yearbook 1995*, vol II(1), 161 (para 16).

Court judgement of *Barcelona*[26] is affirmatively and frequently cited in the ILC commentary to the 'Draft Articles on State Responsibility',[27] the *Barcelona* Court also insisted that some matters, such as diplomatic protection, fall 'in a domain essentially within their domestic jurisdiction'.[28] Leading jurists also frequently focus on the state's freedom in matters of diplomatic protection.[29] More generally, jurists have begun their legal analyses of statelessness with the 'given' that states have internal jurisdiction over the conferral, withdrawal, withholding of nationality and over the admittance and expulsion of non-nationals.[30] Hence the effectively stateless character of nationals, documented in chapter three, remains with us on a daily basis.[31]

See also R Rosenstock, 'The Forty-Ninth Session of the International Law Commission' (1998) 92 *American Journal of International Law* 107.

[26] *Barcelona Traction, Light and Power Co Case (Belgium v Spain)* (1970) ICJ Rep 3, 46 ILR 178, 206 (para 33).

[27] ILC, 'Draft Articles on Responsibility of States for Internationally Wrongful Acts, with Commentaries', *ILC Yearbook 2001*, vol II(2), also in *Report of the ILC on the Work of Its Fifty-third Session*, UN Doc A/56/10 (2001), www.un.org/documents/ga/docs/56/a5610.pdf, 43.

[28] *Barcelona Traction* (above n 26) 207 (paras 35 and 38). See also T Gill, '*Elettronica Sicula SpA (ELSI) (United States v Italy)*, 1989 ICJ Rep 15, 28 ILM 1109' (1990) 84 *American Journal of International Law* 249; and FA Mann, 'The Effect of Changes of Sovereignty upon Nationality' (1942) 5 *Modern Law Review* 218.

[29] See, eg, D Weissbrodt, *The Human Rights of Non-citizens* (Oxford, Oxford University Press, 2008) 84; Hathaway (above n 12) 211 (fn 267) and 626–27; A Vermeer-Künzli, 'As If: The Legal Fiction in Diplomatic Protection' (2007) 18 *European Journal of International Law* 37; P Weis, *Nationality and Statelessness in International Law* (London, Stevens, 1956) 35; and H Lauterpacht, 'Allegiance, Diplomatic Protection and Criminal Jurisdiction over Aliens' (1947) 9 *Cambridge Law Journal* 330.

[30] J Crawford, *Brownlie's Principles of Public International Law*, 8th edn (Oxford, Oxford University Press, 2012) 510–11 and 518–25; GS Goodwin-Gill, *The Refugee in International Law*, 2nd edn (Oxford, Clarendon, 1996) 242; and R Jennings and A Watts (eds), *Oppenheim's International Law: Peace*, 9th edn, vol 1 (London, Longman Publishing, 1992) 852. For the 8th edition, edited by Hersch Lauterpacht, see a similar view at vol 1, 643. See also JL Brierly, *The Law of Nations: An Introduction to the International Law of Peace* (Oxford, Clarendon Press, 1963) 357; H von Mangoldt, 'Stateless Persons' in R Bernhardt (ed), *Encyclopaedia of Public International Law* (Amsterdam, North Holland, 1992) vol 4, 656–60; Hathaway (above n 12) 177 and 173–86; and S Joseph, J Schultz and M Castan, *The International Covenant on Civil and Political Rights: Cases, Materials and Commentary* (Oxford, Oxford University Press, 2000) 270, para 13.07.

[31] See, eg, *Re Democratic People's Republic of Korea v Republic of Korea* (Refugee Review Tribunal of Australia, 21 September 2010), Refugee Appeal No 1001549, [2010] RRTA 843. For the effective statelessness of a Canadian citizen, see F Iacobucci, 'Internal Inquiry into the Actions of Canadian Officials in Relation to Abdullah Almalki, Ahmad Abou-Elmaati and Muayyed Nureddin', final report, Public Works and Government Services (2008), epe.lac-bac.gc.ca/100/206/301/pco-bcp/commissions/internal_inquiry/2010-03-09/www.iacobucciinquiry.ca/pdfs/documents/final-report-copy-en.pdf. The archived proceedings are at epe.lac-bac.gc.ca/100/206/301/pco-bcp/commissions/internal_inquiry/2010-03-09/www.iacobucciinquiry.ca/en/terms-of-reference/index.htm. See also S Sen, 'Stateless Refugees and the Right to Return: The Bihari Refugees of South Asia – Part 1' (1999) 11 *International Journal of Refugee Law* 625; S Sen, 'Stateless Refugees and the Right to Return: The Bihari Refugees of South Asia – Part 2' (2000) 12 *International Journal of Refugee Law* 41; Associated Press, 'Tikka Khan: Pakistan's "Butcher of Bengal"', *Toronto Globe and Mail* (2 April 2002) R7; *Abid Khan v Government of Bangladesh et al*, Writ Petition No 3831 (5 May 2003), Sup Ct

The Human Rights Council stated in 2009 that the 'acquisition and loss of nationality are essentially governed by internal legislation'.[32] The *Third Restatement* has confirmed more generally that a state 'is free to establish nationality law and confer nationality as it sees fit'.[33] In a similar vein, nationality, reserved as an incident of the state's bounded domain, 'provide[s] no protection for persons who have no nationality'.[34] In other words, while international juristic recognition of state practices does manifest an international community, such a community is an aggregate of the wills of state members, each with uncontrolled freedom to determine whether to protect or cease to protect any particular national.[35] In sum, state practices have led to 'the most tragic phenomena of the contemporary world', in the words of a UN organization: expulsion and forced internal displacement.[36]

III. THE PROBLEM OF AN EMPTY INTERNATIONAL COMMUNITY

In order to better appreciate whether a right to nationality could emerge as a hierarchically weighty customary norm, let us assume that all states on the globe possess both a sense of obligation and state practice recognizing an obligation to protect stateless persons. Rather than requiring all states to register all infants as nationals (and thereby missing the 51 million who are not registered), let us imagine a norm that requires all states to recognize all their inhabitants as nationals even if some individuals were admitted or remained on their territories contrary to domestic law. Let us assume that this agreement is institutionalized in a treaty and that no reservations, declarations or denunciations to the treaty are allowed. The ILC has raised this as a possible solution to the 'problem of statelessness'.[37] And the Convention on the Reduction of Statelessness (1961) arguably aims to reduce statelessness by holding out the opportunity for all states of the globe to agree to confer nationality through discrete domestic

Bangladesh; *Borzov v Estonia* (above n 16) para 3.3; CJ Levy, 'Soviet Legacy Lingers as Estonia Defines Its People', *New York Times* (15 August 2010); and CJ Levy, 'Estonia Raises Its Pencils to Erase Russian', *New York Times* (7 June 2010).

[32] Human Rights Council, 'Human Rights and Arbitrary Deprivation of Nationality: Report of the Secretary-General', UN Doc A/HRC/13/34, Agenda item 3 (14 December 2009), para 19. And again, the deprivation of nationality is allowed, but 'it must be in conformity with domestic law' (para 25).

[33] American Law Institute (above n 9) para 211 (Comm c). Para 210 of the *Third Restatement* states, 'Traditional international law did not question the authority of a State to terminate the nationality of any of its nationals.'

[34] Ibid, para 713 (Comm D).

[35] *Barcelona Traction* (above n 26) paras 35, 38, 78, 79, 88 and 379.

[36] UN Secretary-General, 'A Study on Statelessness', UN Doc E/1112/Add.1 (August 1949), s 3.

[37] ILC, 'Draft Articles on Nationality in Relation to the Succession of States' (above n 24) Art 4, comm 5.

laws or through naturalization of all inhabitants on those states' territories. Article 10 of the Convention, for example, provides that the transfer of territory 'shall include provisions designed to secure that no person shall become stateless as a result of the transfer'. The state to which territory is transferred 'shall confer its nationality on such persons as would otherwise become stateless as a result of the transfer or acquisition'. Again, let us now assume that all states on the globe have agreed to confer nationality on all inhabitants who find themselves on a territorial authority claimed by states.

This hypothetical situation highlights the problems encumbered by the international customary human rights norms as the hope to reduce statelessness. For one thing, there may be territories where states do not effectively control or claim to own the territories. The territories, for example, may be occupied and controlled by nomadic groups without fixed location. So too, other non-state entities, such as traditional societies, may effectively control a territory. Or the states may not diplomatically protect their nationals when those nationals find themselves on another state's territory.

Putting aside such problems (although they are all too common today), let us assume that all territory of the globe is effectively controlled and claimed by secular states. To begin with, the state parties may in the future agree to repeal the treaty that requires them to recognize the right of nationality. Or they may agree to a new treaty that clarifies or re-institutionalizes the freedom of states to confer, posit conditions on and withdraw nationality. So long as a customary norm protects nationality as an incident of the reserved domain of the state, the state – not a natural person – will remain the subject of the international legal order. As a subject, the state will retain the jurisdiction to choose its nationals and non-nationals. This jurisdiction of the state will trump any moral or legal claim of a natural person even when a treaty may seem to grant the person recognition as a national.

There is another hypothetical possibility. Let us assume that a customary norm might emerge that implicitly obligates states to recognize and protect all stateless inhabitants as nationals of the states. Might such a customary norm prevent statelessness? At first sight, the answer may seem to be yes. First, a treaty might be declaratory of the customary norm, and in such a context, a state would be bound to the norm even if the state repudiated the treaty. Second, the right to nationality, as a customary norm, might take on the character of a peremptory norm. In such a case, any treaty provision, customary norm or general principle of law that contradicted the right of nationality would be void.[38] However,

---

[38] Vienna Convention on the Law of Treaties (1969) (above n 7) Arts 53 and 64. Crawford has opined that a peremptory norm extends to conflicting treaty provisions, customary legal norms and general principles of law. J Crawford, *Creation of States in International Law* (Oxford, Oxford University Press, 2006) 102.

statelessness would inevitably remain in such a scenario. Assuming there is even agreement on how to establish a customary right to nationality for all inhabitants within a state's territory,[39] the customary character of the norm may change through time. Could a sense of obligation and state practices not return legal analysis to the internal jurisdiction of states and displace the customary norm concerning the right to nationality? Indeed, how could an international tribunal or court possess jurisdiction to entertain such a customary norm unless another customary norm had authorized the tribunal or court's own legal authority? Put differently, would one not have to ask the question: why is a customary norm obligatory?

The problem is, once again, that the referent for the existence of a right to nationality as a customary norm is the bounded reserved domain of the state: this state or that state. Even customary norms are said to exist by reference to the consent (albeit implied consent) and practices of states.[40] Elihu Lauterpacht and Daniel Bethlehem have taken for granted in an important study, for example, that the norms against torture, cruel and unusual punishment, and non-refoulement are based upon customary norms.[41] Customary practices can generate a 'fundamentally norm-creating character', according to Lauterpacht and Bethlehem.[42] What renders a norm 'fundamental'? Which norm-creating norms are more or less fundamental? Is a norm 'fundamental' if it is the object of the implied consent of a substantial number of states? Lauterpacht and Bethlehem have suggested that such implied consent exists if accepted and practised by a 'widespread and representative' group of states 'whose interests are socially affected' and which have exhibited a 'consistent practice and general recognition of the rule'.[43] Inaction or the absence of diplomatic objection on the part of a state evidences acquiescence to the norm. The norm needs to have 'wide acceptance among the states particularly involved in the relevant activity'. The enigma of the international legal order remains, however, for a state's practices may evolve through time to the point that an obligatory norm of a right to nationality dissipates.

A customary norm presupposes that before there is any analytically discrete legal rule or principle, there must be an ethos of an international community. The nature of legal obligation is nested in such an ethos, as will be seen below in chapters seven through nine. It is apparent from earlier chapters above that the ethos of a state-centric international community assumes that each state member possesses an essence. Article 2(4)

[39] M Koskenniemi, 'The Pull of the Mainstream' (1990) 88 *Michigan Law Review* 1946, 1948.
[40] As exemplified by *The Paquete Habana* (1900) 175 US 677, 20 SC 290, per Justice Gray.
[41] E Lauterpacht and D Bethlehem, 'The Scope and Content of the Principle of Non-refoulement: Opinion' in E Feller, V Türk and F Nicholson (eds), *Refugee Protection in International Law: UNCHR's Global Consultations on International Protection* (Cambridge, Cambridge University Press, 2003) 149–58 and 163–64.
[42] Ibid, 143–46.
[43] Ibid, 146-49.

of the UN Charter, for example, holds out some matters as 'within the internal jurisdiction of any state of the essence of a state'. Accordingly, any right to nationality would have to be adopted by the domestic legal order before it obligates a state.

Two issues have resulted from this customary norm of the reserved domain. First, why would a state recognize a right to nationality if the right is read against the background of such a content-independent reserved domain? After all, the UN Charter itself expresses that a state possesses an essence. And the conferral, withdrawal and withholding of nationality has been considered an incident of such an essence. As long as the state claims its own authority to determine the essence of its jurisdiction and as long as membership in the international community is left to such an essence, inhabitants lacking such recognition will remain stateless. Second, as long as a state must adopt an internationally recognized right to nationality for it to be obligatory, the domestic and international legal structures will be considered exclusive of each other. The consequence is that stateless persons will remain outside the protection of the international community because of the exclusivity of domestic legal orders. Any right to nationality will remain unenforceable by the international legal structure. The opaque lacunae of statelessness remain.

There is another problem. Let us assume again that a customary norm has emerged recognizing a legal obligation for all states of the globe to confer nationality on all inhabitants of the states. But a legal/political entity may remain unrecognized as a state. Such has sometimes occurred, for example, as a result of climate change or with cession or conquest of territory. Social and political chaos may result. So too a territorial entity may secede and yet, as in the case of the Palestinian Authority, the entity may lack recognition as a state by its neighbour. As such, the inhabitants will presumably lack nationality: they will lack a state of which they can be members.

The appeal to a customary norm leaves jurists in a conundrum. The very nature of international legal obligation as a customary international norm raises the possibility that some inhabitants will lack a state. A state obligation will be owed to insiders recognized by the state; but some people may be unrecognized if the state does not exist. The germ of the problem is that the legal obligation associated with an international customary norm depends upon a sense of the international community constituted from the aggregate of the wills of states. Even the human rights obligations, drawing as they do from customary norms, may well withdraw into one state's respect of the other's protected reserved domain. All states need not impliedly consent to a customary international norm since the norm need only be 'widely accepted' by 'a substantial number of states'.[44]

---

[44] American Law Institute (above n 9). See especially Byers (above n 3).

But if some states need not expressly or impliedly consent to a treaty or customary international norm, has not the very basis of the obligatory character of an international norm dissolved? Is this especially not so concerning peremptory norms?

Let us take a different turn. Let us again hypothesize that an international customary norm recognizes a state obligation to confer nationality upon all inhabitants within its territory. Of course, the right to nationality has not been itemized on the usual list of peremptory norms that proscribe state conduct: norms against genocide, slavery, murder or the disappearance of people, torture or other cruel, inhuman or degrading treatment, prolonged arbitrary detention, systematic racial discrimination and a consistent pattern of gross violations of internationally recognized human rights.[45] The point I wish to emphasize here is that commentaries about peremptory norms have worked within a structure of argument that presupposes that the international legal order is constituted from the aggregate of the particular wills of states. Why is the consent of the majority of states necessary for the existence of a discrete peremptory norm without examining the ethos in which the discrete norm is contextualized? Can the consent eventually be withdrawn by the majority of states? Can such an international community, which protects a bounded reserved domain, even entertain the possibility that customary international norms exist independent of the domain? If so, how could the right to nationality be a peremptory norm? My point is that something very different from customary norms is needed in order to explain why an international legal norm, such as a state duty to confer and retain nationality, is binding upon all states.

IV. THE INTERNATIONAL COMMUNITY AS A WHOLE

This enigma continues upon examination of various efforts that refer to 'the international community as a whole'. The ILC commentary regarding the 'Draft Articles on State Responsibility' consistently appeals to the 'the international community as a whole' as the referent of state obligations.[46] Treaties increasingly also refer to the international community 'as a whole'.[47] The international community as a whole is moreover increasingly

---

[45] See UNHCR, 'Statelessness: Prevention and Reduction of Statelessness and Protection of Stateless Persons' (14 February 2006), UN Doc EC/57/SC/CRP6, www.unhcr.org/43f1f6682.pdf, reprinted in (2006) 25 *Refugee Survey Quarterly* 72–76.

[46] ILC, 'Draft Articles on State Responsibility' (above n 27) Art 1 (Comm 4), Art 12 (Comm 6), Art 26 (Comms 3 and 5), Art 33 (Comms 1 and 4), Chap III (gen comms 1–7), Art 40 (Comms 2–5), Art 42 (Comms 11 and 12) and Art 48 (Comms 1 and 6).

[47] See, eg, Vienna Convention on the Law of Treaties (above n 7), Art 53. For other treaties, see above ch 1, n 27 (38).

the object of analysis by international and domestic judicial tribunals.[48] So too, is the international community as a whole the object of study in juristic commentaries.[49] More often than not, jurists have taken for granted that there is an international community 'out there', independent of the state members. But what is the character of legal obligation in such a community? For example, what is the relation of members of the community to the objectivity represented by the community's legal structure?

One suggestion is that the international community as a whole is constituted from what 'shocks the conscience of mankind'.[50] This takes for granted that we shall know the dictates of such 'a conscience' when we observe something abhorrent done by a state. Does not 'shock to one's conscience' hinge upon the subject's social-cultural ethos? But whose conscience? Similarly, another suggestion is that the community is composed of 'basic human values'.[51] But whose values are the basic ones? Who is the 'we' – the voice of an alleged rational will of state members of the community? Is it the voice of the dominant ethnic or cultural group in a state? And if the recognition of stateless peoples is left to the determination of 'the peoples' values' or 'jurists' values', will we not be returned to the state as the ultimate author, the final decision-maker as to who is a national?

The independence of legal norms vis-à-vis the bounded reserved domain of state members begs this question: what is the character or ethos of an international community independent of its members? Hedley Bull had such a community in mind when he described its members as 'conscious of certain common interests and common values, for a society in the sense that they conceive themselves to be bound by a common set of rules in their relations with one another, and share in the working of common institutions'.[52] Presumably, the universal right to nationality could well be such a common rule of which members would be conscious. A treaty could represent such a common rule as could a customary norm.

[48] The most often cited judgment in this regard is *Barcelona Traction* (above n 26) para 91. For other examples, see above ch 1, nn 94 (53) and 100 (54).

[49] PC Jessup, *A Modern Law of Nations: An Introduction* (New York, Macmillan, 1948) 53; and A Verdross, 'Jus Dispositivum and Jus Cogens in International Law' (1966) 60 *American Journal of International Law* 55, 58. For other sources, see above ch 1, n 32 (38).

[50] Crawford was satisfied with this criterion at one point: Crawford, 'Introduction' in J Crawford (ed), *The International Law Commission's Articles on State Responsibility: Introduction, Text and Commentaries* (Cambridge, Cambridge University Press, 2002) 38, quoting *Reservations to the Convention on the Prevention and Punishment of the Crime of Genocide* (Advisory Opinion) (1951) ICJ Rep 15, 18 ILR 364. Dan Dubois has cited a series of scholars who are satisfied with the conscience of the international community as the root of peremptory norms: D Dubois, 'The Authority of Peremptory Norms in International Law: State Consent or Natural Law' (2009) 78 *Nordic Journal of International Law* 133, 154 (fn 72) and 155 (fn 77).

[51] Dubois (ibid) 161–66.

[52] H Bull, *The Anarchical Society: A Study of Order in World Politics* (London, Macmillan, 1977) 13. See also CAW Manning, *The Nature of International Society* (London, Macmillan, 1975).

Once again, however, we are left with the possibility of statelessness, even despite the shock to the jurist's conscience or the common interests and values of state practices. The international community once again is presupposed to be the aggregate of the wills of the state members. Something more than a mere referent – 'the international community as a whole' – is needed. This is so because a customary norm is identified with reference to the boundary of the residuary incorporating the domain of a state. The consequences of such a residuary, identified above in chapter three, have included the expulsion of stateless persons, indefinite detention, discrimination on the basis of statelessness, barriers to employment, lack of access to public education and public health, harm to women and children, the exclusion of nomadic, travelling and indigenous groups and so on.

One commentator has asserted that 'the international community as a whole' is 'too logical and reasonable to be challenged'.[53] Another has stated that, like a belief in God, the existence of the international community is 'a matter of faith'.[54] Given the vacuity of the referent, two other commentators have suggested that 'the less said the better' about the content of 'the international community as a whole'.[55] James Crawford and the ILC certainly take the international community as a whole for granted without examining the nature of the community nor how the community differs from some other sense of an international community, let alone why the community is justified.[56] And still another commentator offers that we just cannot get beyond the fact that the international community as a whole is constituted from shared domestic rules of states.[57] The referent, the international community as a whole, is said to be a mere metaphor.[58]

The problem with such unhelpful assertions and assumptions is that any norm that might transcend the particular wills of state members ultimately rests, like the reserved domain, upon a content-independent shell or form called 'the international community as a whole'.[59] Because of its

---

[53] P Malanczuk, *Akehurst's Modern Introduction to International Law*, 7th revised edn (London, Routledge, 1997) 58.

[54] H Thirlway, 'Injured and Non-injured States before the International Court of Justice' in M Ragazzi (ed), *International Responsibility Today: Essays in Memory of Oscar Schachter* (Leiden, Martinus Nijhoff, 2005).

[55] See, eg, E Wyler and A Papaux, 'The Search for Universal Justice' in Macdonald and Johnston (eds) (above n 8) 296–99.

[56] Crawford, 'Introduction' (above n 50).

[57] J Barboza, 'Legal Injury: The Tip of the Iceberg in the Law of State Responsibility' in Ragazzi (ed) (above n 54) 20–21.

[58] JP Kelly, 'The Twilight of Customary International Law' (1999–2000) 40 *Virginia Journal of International Law* 449, 465–69.

[59] Peter Fitzpatrick has framed this issue in terms of sovereignty: P Fitzpatrick, 'Latin Roots: Imperialism and the Making of Modern Law' in *Law as Resistance: Modernism, Imperialism, Legalism* (Aldershot, Ashgate, 2008); P Fitzpatrick, 'Justice as Access' (2005) 23 *Windsor Yearbook of Access Justice* 1, 9–13; P Fitzpatrick, '"Gods Would Be Needed . . .": American Empire and the

lack of determinate content, 'sometimes', the ILC records, 'things must be done for people's well-being, be it against their wishes'.[60] Although the ILC has stated that 'the preponderance of the interests of states over the interests of individuals has subsided' (notwithstanding my claim otherwise in chapter three),[61] the empty shell of the international community leaves nationality to the state's reserved domain.

The vacuity of 'the international community as a whole' leads to the circularity of the claim of universality and the reserved domain. According to Martti Koskenniemi, customary norm is likely to be identified with reference to its binary – that is, another customary norm.[62] More generally, the vacuity of the referent 'the international community as a whole' leads jurists to differentiate between domestic laws of one state and another. And yet state practices themselves are relevant to the identity of a norm only if the practices manifest a sense of obligation by state officials. The consequence of Koskenniemi's analysis is that statelessness can be addressed only in terms of the identity of a discrete right or norm. Koskenniemi's focus upon discrete rules (as opposed to the ethos manifested by the content of the rules) is evident in the study that he conducted for the ILC, 'The Fragmentation of International Law'.[63] The circularity of the identity of a discrete right/norm assumes that the identity of a right, if ever established, would clarify why a right to nationality differs from an ordinary international norm, however one understands the latter. But too many puzzles remain. Indeed, it is tempting to write such a conclusion and be done with an effort to understand why the enigma remains in an international community.

That said, we must examine whether an international community is more than a shell filled by interests, values and common interests of states. Such a sense of the international community would be the embodiment of the social relationships of natural persons, independent of states. The ILC has certainly constructed its complex schemata of norms as if there were

---

Rule of (International) Law' (2003) 16 *Leiden Journal of International Law* 429, 436; and P Fitzpatrick, '"No Higher Duty": *Mabo* and the Failure of Legal Foundation' (2002) 13 *Law and Critique* 233, 242. Chusei Yamada has expressed frustration in the endeavour to justify peremptory norms in terms of the ultimate referent of the international community: C Yamada, 'Revisiting the International Law Commission's Draft Articles on State Responsibility' in Ragazzi (ed) (above n 54) 120–21.

[60] The cited words were spoken by Mr Pellet, Chair of the meeting (ILC 2490th meeting, 10 June 1997) and recorded in *ILC Yearbook 1997*, vol I, 110 (para 17).

[61] ILC, 'Draft Articles on Nationality' (above n 24) Art 1 (Comm 5).

[62] M Koskenniemi, 'The Politics of International Law' (1990) 1 *European Journal of International Law* 4, 26–27. See also M Koskenniemi, *From Apology to Utopia: The Structure of International Legal Argument*, reissue (Cambridge, Cambridge University Press, 2005) 324.

[63] ILC, 'Conclusions of the Work of the Study Group on the Fragmentation of International Law: Difficulties Arising from the Diversification and Expansion of International Law', *ILC Yearbook 2006*, vol II (2).

something exterior to state-centric laws that justified norms.[64] Can a state be obligated to protect stateless inhabitants so long as officials presuppose an international community that privileges the customary legal norm of non-intervention into the internal jurisdiction of a state? To respond to this question, we had better reconsider the legal bond that has explained and justified such as a jurisdiction. Such a legal bond, which will be examined in the next chapter, highlights the allegiance of a natural person to the state. Is there a sense of legal bond in international law discourse that raises the prospect of nationality independent of the state? If there is such a criterion, then does the enigma of statelessness in an international community thereby dissolve?

V. CONCLUSION

This chapter has looked closely to the two requisites of customary international law. In the end, a right to nationality for everyone remains suspect, and there appears to be no way out of the production of statelessness. Why would state officials agree to dilute attributes of the core of its negative freedom, as protected by the UN Charter,[65] if the state were not legally obligated to do so? But why is a state obligated to respect and protect a stateless person? What is the nature of such legal obligation? The appeal to customary international norms, like that to the statelessness and human rights treaties discussed in the previous chapter, incorporates the bounded reserved domain of state members into the international community. Treaties and international customary law identify rights, to be sure. But neither treaties nor customary norms explain why a state is legally obligated to recognize, protect and enforce an identifiable right that protects stateless persons. A law or a right such as the right of nationality may be identifiable in a constitutional text, a treaty or the indicia of a customary norm, and yet such a law or right may not be legally obligatory. The phenomenon of statelessness begs an inquiry into the issue: why is an identifiable right obligatory for a state to protect? Such an issue concerns the nature of a legal bond. Such a legal bond, we shall now appreciate, began as a matter of allegiance or loyalty in a state–natural person relation. I shall argue in the next chapter, however, that an international legal discourse has highlighted a second sense of a legal bond, one based upon a factor that is independent of internal jurisdiction.

---

[64] See, eg, ILC, 'Draft Articles on State Responsibility' (above n 27) Art 40 (Comm 10). However, I Brownlie suggested that the State Responsibility Articles only contemplate non-derogation of peremptory norms when states have already consented to such norms. See Crawford, *Brownlie's Principles* (above n 30) 489.

[65] Art 2(7) of the UN Charter (1945).

6

The Legal Bond

THE ENIGMA OF an international community remains. Both human rights treaties and customary international legal norms recognize and protect the freedom of states to confer, withdraw and withhold nationality. So long as nationality is an incident of the state's reserved domain, statelessness will remain the enigma of an international community. What is often forgotten is that the reserved domain represents an international community as well as the state. So long as state officials presuppose the boundary of the domain, international standards will reinforce internal domestic jurisdiction as if the latter is content-independent or empty of social relationships. This is so because any nationality rule or right to nationality exists by virtue of its justificatory relation to the sources signifying the boundary of the reserved domain. Against such a background, the judiciary's role is to clarify the locus of the boundary in legal consciousness.

Statelessness begs that one enquire into the nature of legal obligation in such an empty residuary. The International Law Commission (ILC) has addressed the issue by considering the legal obligation of the international community as a matter of secondary as opposed to primary rules.[1] Although a secondary rule may well finalize the quest for the identity of a legal rule, why a secondary rule, such as the reserved domain, is obligatory remains unaddressed. Why a rule or right is obligatory for state laws or state actions attends to the legal bond presupposed in an international community. Nationality signifies such a legal bond. Statelessness represents the absence of such a legal bond and the absence of a correspondingly justified legal obligation.

International legal discourse offers two very different senses of a legal bond. The one highlights allegiance or loyalty toward a particular state. The second centres on the social bonding of natural persons inter se.

---

[1] International Law Commission (ILC), 'Text to the Draft Articles on Responsibility of States for Internationally Wrongful Acts' in *Report of the ILC on the Work of Its Fifty-Third Session*, UN GAOR, 56th Sess, UN Doc A/56/10 (Supp No 10) (2001), www.un.org/documents/ga/docs/56/a5610.pdf. The Draft Articles with ILC Commentary are also in J Crawford (ed), *The International Law Commission's Articles on State Responsibility: Introduction, Text and Commentaries* (Cambridge, Cambridge University Press, 2002). See in particular Crawford's 'Introduction' (14–17).

Jurists have described the latter as 'the effective link',[2] 'un rattachement réel' [real connection or 'an appropriate legal connection'],[3] 'a substantial connection',[4] 'a sufficient link',[5] 'a genuine connection'[6] and 'a bond of a legal nature'.[7] This effective or genuine bond concerns the social relationships experienced in a place rather than on a specific territory.[8]

Section I of this chapter examines how legal obligation concerns an effort to understand and address the enigma of statelessness. Section II outlines the discursive struggle between a state's claim for its own authority and the undercurrent discourse that focuses upon a radically different sense of legal bond. Section III retrieves the sense of legal bond as social bonding from the leading International Court of Justice (ICJ) judgment in *Nottebohm (Liechtenstein v Guatemala)* (1955). Section IV then retrieves the discursive tradition of effective nationality from the early nineteenth century, and section V identifies a series of factors making for effective nationality. Finally, section VI identifies how courts, refugee tribunals and arbitrators have extended effective nationality in diverse circumstances involving de jure stateless persons.

I. LEGAL OBLIGATION

Chapter four explained how the surface sense of an international community means that nationality is an issue for the internal jurisdiction of states. This is so because the domain of law-making and law administration, of which nationality is an incident, is reserved for the state. Such an association of nationality with the reserved domain helps to explain why jurists are preoccupied with legality as a matter of the justified source of a rule in

---

[2] ILC, 'Draft Articles on Nationality of Natural Persons in Relation to the Succession of States, with Commentaries' in 'Report of the ILC on the Work of its 51st Session', UN Doc A/54/10, *ILC Yearbook 1999*, vol II(2), 20–47, Art 19 (Comm 3).

[3] JF Rezek, 'Le droit international de la nationalité' (1986) 198 *Recueil des cours* 333, 357. See also ILC, 'Draft Articles on Nationality' (ibid) Art 4 (Comm 4).

[4] UNHCR Regional Bureau for Europe, 'The Czech and Slovak Citizenship Laws and the Problem of Statelessness' (1996) 2(4) *European Series: Citizenship in the Context of the Dissolution of Czechoslovakia* 10. See also ILC, 'Draft Articles on Nationality in Relation to the Succession of States' (above n 2) Art 4 (Comm 4).

[5] DP O'Connell, *State Succession in Municipal Law*, vol 1 (Cambridge, Cambridge University Press, 1967) 499, as quoted in ILC, 'Draft Articles on Nationality in Relation to the Succession of States' (above n 2) Art 19 (Comm 2).

[6] *Nottebohm (Liechtenstein v Guatemala)* (second phase) (1955) ICJ Rep 4, 23 (also reported in (1955) 22 ILR 349), www.refworld.org/docid/3ae6b7248.html, quoted in ILC, 'Draft Articles on Nationality in Relation to the Succession of States' (above n 2) Art 19 (Comm 4, fn 104). The Commentary notes the 'equivalent' expression in French: *rattachement effectif*.

[7] ILC, 'Draft Articles on Nationality in Relation to the Succession of States' (above n 2) Art 23 (Comm 8).

[8] ES Casey, *Getting Back into Place: Toward a Renewed Understanding of the Place-World*, 2nd edn (Bloomington, Indiana University Press, 2009); and M Merleau-Ponty, *Phenomenology of Perception*, C Smith (trans) (London, Routledge & Kegan Paul, 1962).

an institutional source such as a state legislature or a treaty or customary norm (which is subject to a state's consent). However, the quest for an identifiable source for every legal rule reinforces the enigma of such an international community when stateless persons are concerned. The crucial issue is why any state nationality law, justified as an incident of the reserved domain, is binding upon other states and upon international tribunals and courts? For that matter, why is any such nationality law binding upon natural persons who are stateless or, as in the case of all of us, may one day be stateless? Is a person's social life an unknown and unknowable world to jurists, external to legal knowledge? After all, if nationality is an incident of the state's inner reserved domain, it would seem to matter little whether a natural person is really bonded in her/his social life. Indeed, quoting affirmatively from an earlier case, Judge John Read, dissenting, insisted in *Nottebohm* that an enquiry into the actual social relationships of natural persons takes 'international law as it might be' – an 'ought' rather than an 'is'.[9] The 'is', of course, is assumed to be the reserved domain of a state.

The ironic twist, though, is that the 'is' of the reserved domain, being content-independent for the purposes of identifying a discrete domestic legal rule or right, is reified vis-à-vis the social relationships presupposed in the content of the reserved domain. In other words, the legal 'is' ironically becomes an idealized picture of a domain the content of which is immaterial from the standpoint of the quest for an identifiable domestic law. A legal bond as effective nationality, in contrast, turns the attention of jurists to the singular and shared social relationships of natural persons before the reserved domain is constructed in an international law discourse. Effective nationality rests inside the international law discourse about the reserved domain and allegiance. In this vein, evidence about an applicant's or a litigant's social relationships addresses an analytically and experientially prior legal phenomenon than the reserved domain. Effective nationality as legal bond thereby displaces what is otherwise often assumed to be hard fact.

The importance of the legal bond as the criterion of citizenship is not of recent times. Roman Stoic writings and Roman law privileged the legal bond of allegiance.[10] To be sure, Cicero wrote of 'right reason', which he claims binds all human beings in the cosmos.[11] Such a bond, Cicero explained, is very different from the state as the source of lawfulness: 'The most stupid thing of all, moreover, is to consider all things just which have been ratified by a people's institutions or laws.'[12] More generally, one is

---

[9] *Nottebohm* (above n 6) ICJ Rep 4.
[10] See, eg, Cicero, *On the Commonwealth and on The Laws*, JEG Zetzel (trans) (Cambridge, Cambridge University Press, 1999) 1.18, 1.22, 1.28 and 1.42.
[11] Ibid, 1.18, 1.42 and 2.11.
[12] Ibid, 1.40.

born into this or that family or social group; one's family of birth is not chosen. The legal bond between inhabitant and state is likewise not to be determined by the state but by the social bonding of natural persons in the cosmos. Cicero framed the legal bond represented by such sociability as the *jus gentium*.[13] In this context, Cicero recognized two senses of a legal bond. The one is the family/clan; the second is the commonwealth, a notion that, though quite different from a state today, we can take as a state-like entity.[14] A natural person's bloodline or *sanguinis* represented a person's loyalty to the one 'fatherland' of the family/clan. The commonwealth, the second 'fatherland', marked a very different sense of allegiance. Although both senses of allegiance may have manifested social bonding in Cicero's day, such can hardly be said of our contemporary state-centric international community today. This is so because legal analysis justifies any nationality rule or right to nationality in terms of an institutional source independent of the presupposed social content of the rule/right.

To be sure, during the early modern state, Grotius took for granted that each natural person possessed the freedom to choose her/his state of nationality.[15] Even Thomas Hobbes described the leap of natural persons from the state of nature to civil society as taking place once natural persons were social (this occurring once they acquired language).[16] With language, he emphasized, one could enter into promises with others, and what could indicate sociability more than a promise?[17] As explained further below, John Locke and Jean-Jacques Rousseau also shared the view that sociability is the critical element of the bond of allegiance.[18] In exchange for a natural person's choice of her/his own nationality, state officials undertook to protect the individual from threats and from harm caused by other states. Hints of this understanding of a natural person's voluntary choice in nationality continue to be detectable even in contemporary commentaries.[19] By the late nineteenth century and certainly by the 1920s and 1930s, however, the determination of a natural person's nationality became a right of the state vis-à-vis other states rather than the right of a natural person vis-à-vis a state. In theory, 'an injury to the

[13] Cicero, *On Duties*, MT Griffin and ET Atkins (trans) (Cambridge, Cambridge University Press, 1991) 3.23 and 3.69; Cicero, 'Partitiones Oratoriae' in *De Fato; Paradoxa Stoicorum; De Partitione Oratoria*, H Rackham (trans) (Cambridge, MA, Harvard University Press, 1942) 37.129–37.130; and Cicero, *On the Commonwealth* (above n 10) 3.33.

[14] Cicero, *On the Commonwealth and on The Laws* (above n 10) 2.5.

[15] H Grotius, 'De Jure Praedae Commentarius' in *Classics of International Law Series*, GL Williams (trans) (New York, Carnegie, 1950) Book 2, ch 5, ss 25, 253 and 254.

[16] See generally WE Conklin, *The Invisible Origins of Legal Positivism: A Rereading of a Tradition* (Dordrecht, Kluwer, 1979) 78–90.

[17] T Hobbes, *Leviathan*, CB Macpherson (ed) (London, Penguin, 1968) 264–65 and 268–69.

[18] J Locke, *Second Treatise of Government*, TP Peardon (ed) (New York, Liberal Arts Press, 1952) paras 114, 119, 121, 122, 135 and 232; J-J Rousseau, 'The Social Contract' in LG Crocker (ed), *The Social Contract and Discourse on Inequality* (New York, Signet, 1967) 3.13.

[19] See, eg, *ILC Yearbook 1999*, vol 2(2), Art 11, A/CN.4/SER.A/1999/Add.1 (Part 2) (2003).

national [was] an injury to the state itself', although even the ILC has admitted that this has always been a 'fiction'.[20]

II. THE DISCURSIVE STRUGGLE

The two discourse about an international community are not each identifiable with one stream of judicial decisions or another. One judgment, treaty or commentary may well express both images of an international community. The two images of an international community are nested in two analytically separate international law discourses. This discursive struggle is readily apparent when we isolate and examine two contradictory themes that emerge from the legal literature and judicial opinions; each undermines the community's sense of a legal bond.

A. The State's Claim to Its Own Authority

One theme involves the state's claim to its own authority. The voluntary consent of a natural person, associated with sociality in the juristic writings of the early European state as documented in chapter two, discursively clashed with the state's claim to its own authority. The latter, especially as articulated in the works of Emmanuel Vattel, highlighted the reserved domain of the state. To be sure, Vattel acknowledged the freedom of natural persons to renounce allegiance to a state.[21] That said, if the reciprocal bond of allegiance had dissolved because the state had failed to protect the individual, the state could expel the individual (or the individual could leave voluntarily).[22] Vattel went some distance in elaborating the state's claim to its own authority.[23] This claim rested upon the property interest of the state over the territory it controlled.[24] Rousseau represented just such a claim as the problematic of modernity: 'Man is born free; and everywhere he is in chains.'[25] Rousseau explained, 'The essence of the body politic consists in the union of obedience and liberty, and these words, *subject* and *sovereign*, are correlatives, the notion underlying them being expressed in the one word *citizen*.'[26] That is, one could not be a

---

[20] ILC, 'Draft Articles on Diplomatic Protection, with Commentaries' *ILC Yearbook 2006*, vol II(2), UN Doc A/61/10, Art 1 (Comm 4).

[21] E de Vattel, *The Law of Nations or the Principles of Natural Law*, G Fenwick (trans) (New York, Klaus Reprint, 1916) Bk l, c 19, para 223.

[22] Ibid, para 223(3).

[23] Ibid, Bk 3, c 3, paras 26, 36–37 and 69.

[24] Ibid, Bk 2, c 7, para 82. See also paras 81, 86 and 88. Note Vattel's description of internal jurisdiction as territorial knowledge (paras 79–97).

[25] Rousseau (above n 18) Bk 1, 7.

[26] Ibid, Bk 3, 13.

subject (in other words, a citizen or a national) without the state. Although they struggled with the idea, both David Hume and Adam Smith also left it to the state to decide whether a natural person had allegiance to the state.[27] With Kant, the state's claim to legal authority was lifted from social life into an intelligible world of a priori concepts.

The reserved domain crystallized as a legal doctrine by the late nineteenth century. The legal bond of allegiance was moreover being articulated at this time.[28] 'By allegiance', Field asserted in *Carlisle v USA* (1872), 'is meant the obligation of fidelity and obedience which the individual owes to the government under which he lives, or to his sovereign in return for the protection he receives'.[29] The state's claim to authority depends upon the categorization by state officials of inhabitants who possess allegiance to the state.[30] Such categorization is administered by the executive arm of the state because allegiance is an issue in interstate relations.[31] By the 1950s, an executive determination of disloyalty could justify the withdrawal of nationality.[32] With the state's claim to authority over nationality came the idea that the will of the state is the final referent for the identity of a law pertaining to stateless persons.[33] Shortly after World War II, a Filipino court stated that the categorization of a stateless person by the state overrides any dream that one might have of being a member of a state, the state's will constituting 'the stark reality' of allegiance 'independent of the will of the inhabitants concerned'.[34] According to some domestic laws, in fact, if a natural person holds nationality in two states at the same time, disloyalty on her/his part is the appropriate

[27] D Hume, *A Treatise of Human Nature*, PH Nidditch (ed), 2nd edn (Oxford, Oxford University Press, 1978) 549; and A Smith, *Report Dated 1766: Lectures on Jurisprudence*, RL Meek, DD Raphael and PG Stein (eds) (Indianapolis, Oxford University Press I Liberty Fund, 1978) 403, para 18.

[28] See, eg, *Chae Chan Ping v United States* (1889) 130 US 581, 604 (per Field C J); *Nishimura Ekiu v United States* (1892) 142 US 651, 659; *Fong Yue Ting v United States* (1893) 149 US 698, 711; and *Hollander Case* (1895) US For Rel, 775 as cited in *Boffolo Case* (1903) 10 RIAA 528.

[29] *Carlisle v US* (1872) 83 US 147 154.

[30] *Ping v US* (above n 28) 604; *Ekiu v US* (above n 28) 659; and *Hollander* (above n 28) 775. See also *Case No 0901642* (Refugee Review Tribunal of Australia), [2009] RRTA 502, www.refworld.org/docid/4a76ddbf2.html, para 60; and *Refugee Appeal No 76077* (NZ Refugee Status Appeals Authority, 19 May 2009), [2009] NZRSAA 37, www.unhcr.org/refworld/docid/4a2e24702.html, para 92.

[31] *North American Dredging Company* (US–Mexico Claims Commission) (1926) 4 RIAA 26, 3 ILR 4.

[32] Convention on the Reduction of Statelessness (1961), UN Doc A/CONF. 9/15 (in force 13 December 1975), 989 UNTS 175, Art 8(3).

[33] *Case No 0901642* (above n 30) para 60; and *Appeal No 76077* (above n 30) para 92. International standards lack the specificity and intellectual rigour, we are advised, to justify overriding internal jurisdiction: *Borozov v Estonia*, HRC, Communication No 1136/2002, UN Doc CCPR/C/81/D/1136/2002 (2004), para 7.4.

[34] *Palanca v Republic of the Philippines*, GR No L-301 (Supreme Court of the Philippines, 7 April 1948).

conclusion.[35] Disloyalty and allegiance are two sides of the same coin, after all.[36] Moreover, allegiance is not restricted to those who habitually reside on a state's territory.[37] In 1999, France declared that 95 per cent of all its inhabitants were of French nationality, although the state had never offered inhabitants the opportunity to choose if they wished to be French nationals.[38] More generally, judicial review of an executive's determination of disloyalty would constitute an external intervention into the reserved domain.[39]

In sum, for one international legal discourse, the legal bond of allegiance is characterized by one-way evaluation and determination – of the inhabitant by the state . As a Canadian judge has put it,

> The [non-]status of statelessness is not one that is optional for an applicant. The condition of not having a country of nationality must be one that is beyond the power of the applicant to control. Otherwise, a person could claim statelessness merely by renouncing his or her former citizenship.[40]

This state prerogative over who exhibits loyalty exemplifies what Giorgio Agamben called 'the state of exception'.[41] Even the two traditional criteria of nationality, *soli* and *sanguinis*, represent the legal bond of allegiance in international law.[42] The one, the 'law of the soil' (*jus soli*), presumes loyalty to a state if one is born on the territory owned by that state. The other, 'place of birth' (sometimes understood as 'parentage' or 'bloodline'), assumes that natural persons will be loyal to a state if they share the dominant bloodline or ethnicity of that state. One's personal desire to self-identify with or *not* with a state falls by the wayside.

[35] This is discussed at length in *Ernesto S Mercado v Eduardo Barrios Manzano and Commission on Elections*, GR No 135083 (Supreme Court of the Philippines, 26 May 1999), sc.judiciary.gov. ph/jurisprudence/1999/may99/135083.htm.

[36] Convention on the Reduction of Statelessness (above n 32) Art 8(3)(b).

[37] *Nottebohm* (above n 6) ICJ Rep 44.

[38] P Weil, 'The Transformation of Immigration Policies: Immigration Control and Nationality Laws in Europe – A Comparative Approach' (1999) 7(2) *Collected Courses of the Academy of European Law* 87, 134.

[39] See, eg, *Chief Executive of the Department of Labour v Hossein Yadegary and District Court at Auckland* [2008] NZCA 295, para 5.

[40] *Bouianova v Canada (Minister of Employment and Immigration)* (1993) 67 FTR 74, para 12.

[41] G Agamben, *Homo Sacer: Sovereign Power and Bare Life*, D Heller-Roazen (trans) (Stanford, Stanford University Press, 1998); and G Agamben, *State of Exception*, K Attell (trans) (Chicago, University of Chicago Press, 2005).

[42] P Weil, 'Access to Citizenship: A Comparison of Twenty-Five Nationality Laws' in A Aleinikoff and D Klusmeyer (eds), *Citizenship Today: Global Perspectives and Practices* (Washington, Carnegie Endowment for International Peace, 2001) 20; J Crawford (ed), *Brownlie's Principles of Public International Law*, 8th edn (Oxford, Oxford University Press, 2012) 511–13; and I Brownlie, 'The Relations of Nationality in Public International Law' (1963) 39 *British Yearbook of International Law* 284, 302 and 314.

184 The Legal Bond

B. The Undercurrent

The discursive acceptance of the state as the determining source of a person's allegiance hides a countervailing subtext. At the same moment that the international legal discourse incorporates the reserved domain as the community's residuary, the discourse insists that nationality must be the outcome of voluntary choice on the part of natural persons. This voluntary choice of nationality sits in opposition to a state's determination of a person's allegiance. In its Commentary to the 'Draft Articles on State Responsibility' in 2001, the ILC stated:

> In the view of the Commission, the respect for the will of the individual is a consideration which, with the development of human rights law, has become paramount. However, this does not mean that every acquisition of nationality upon a succession of states must have a consensual basis.[43]

Although Article 12 of the International Covenant on Civil and Political Rights (ICCPR) (1966) guarantees that 'everyone lawfully within the territory of the state [has the] freedom to choose his residence', the right is subject to state limitations and derogations regarding nationality, as was discussed in chapter four.

The United States undertook to respect the voluntary consent of natural persons in 1868 when a federal statute declared that an individual could renounce her/his citizenship – this freedom of renunciation being 'a natural and inherent right of all people indispensable to the enjoyment of the rights of life, liberty, and the pursuit of happiness'.[44] The freedom was said to constitute one of 'the fundamental principles of the Republic'. Following World War I, various other states also acknowledged a duty to respect the freedom of individuals to choose nationality. In 1919, the Harvard International Law Group proposed a formal right to adopt or refuse to adopt the nationality of a successor state, commenting, 'This article is believed to express a rule of international law which is generally recognized.'[45] In 1930, the US Supreme Court in *Perkins v Elg* reiterated

[43] ILC, 'Draft Articles on State Responsibility' (above n 1) Art 11 (Comm 6). The ILC expressed a similar view in its 'Report of the 47th Session', UN Doc A/CN.4/SER.A/1995/Add.1(Part 2), *ILC Yearbook 1995*, vol II(2), paras 186–87. Para 192 states, 'While the view was expressed that the Commission should, on the basis of state practice, endeavour to strengthen the right of option, it was also said that there could be no unrestricted free choice of nationality and that the factors which would indicate that a choice was bone fide should be identified and the State must respect and give effect to them by granting its nationality.' See also ILC, 'Draft Articles on Nationality in Relation to the Succession of States' (above n 2) Art 11 (Comms 1–3).

[44] Expatriation Act (27 July 1868), 15 Stat 223, 8 USC, ss 223, 800.

[45] Research in International Law of Harvard Law School, 'Harvard Draft Convention on Nationality' (1929) 23 *AJIL Supplement* 1, 60 (Art 18(2)). The individual's freedom to refuse or renounce nationality also applied to the partition and division of territory.

that the right to voluntarily choose nationality is 'constantly admitted and sanctioned'.[46] In 1934, the US Department of State expressed that the United States 'greatly regretted' that Turkey had withdrawn the freedom of Turkish nationals to renounce their nationality.[47]

In 1958, the ICJ in *Flegenheimer* affirmed the freedom of an individual voluntarily to choose a state.[48] The ILC has also highlighted that allegiance is subject to an individual's freedom to consent to membership in a state.[49] Again, this freedom is said to include the right to opt out of membership as well as to opt in.[50] The *Third Restatement* was explicit: 'For a state to impose its nationality on a person against his will, or to insist on a nationality that the individual has renounced, may violate international law'.[51] It adds, 'It is a violation of international law for a state to impose its nationality upon a person after birth without the person's consent.'[52] If an individual renounces the bond, s/he need not substitute it for another,[53] and even if a state claims that a particular person has a legal bond with a prior state, that person may choose allegiance with a third state.[54] In like spirit, according to Article 18 of the Disabilities Treaty, state parties undertake to recognize disabled persons' 'freedom to choose their residence and to a nationality, on an equal basis with others'.[55]

Despite the sustained view that natural persons possess the freedom to choose their nationality, this question is inescapable: how can the freedom of natural persons to choose the state of their nationality be maintained alongside the state's reserved domain, a primary incident of which is the right of the state to choose its own nationals? It is just not good enough to posit dicta and treaty provisions. One has to reconsider the nature of the legal bond in an international community in order to understand the discursive struggle and in order to understand how one sense of an international community, nested in one discourse, attempts to trump the voluntary choice of natural persons through the state's claim to authority in matters of nationality.

---

[46] *Perkins v Elg* (1939) 307 US 325, as discussed in *Flegenheimer Claim: Decision No 182* (1958) 16 RIAA 327, 367 (para 53), 25 ILR 91 (Italian–US Conciliation Commission).

[47] GH Hackworth, *Digest of International Law*, vol 5 (Washington, US Government Print Office, 1943) 821–22.

[48] *Flegenheimer* (above n 46) 357–63, paras 44–49.

[49] ILC, 'Draft Articles on Nationality in Relation to the Succession of States' (above n 2) Art 11(1) and Art 23.

[50] Ibid, Art 11 (Comm 7).

[51] American Law Institute, *Restatement of the Law, Third: Foreign Relations Law of the United States* (St Paul, American Law Institute, 1987) para 211 (Comm d).

[52] Ibid, Art 211 (Rep Note 2 and Comm d).

[53] Ibid, Art 211 (Comm d).

[54] Ibid, Art 211 (Rep Note 2).

[55] Convention on the Rights of Persons with Disabilities (2006), UNGA Res 61/106, Annex 1, UN GAOR, 61st Sess, Supp No 49, UN Doc A/61/49 (entered into force 3 May 2008), 65.

III. THE LEGAL BOND AS A SOCIAL BOND: *NOTTEBOHM*

The crux of the struggle between the two discourses about international community concerns the nature of a legal bond. The surface discourse, as I have just outlined, focuses upon allegiance. The second shifts away from the relation between a natural person and the state to the social relations between natural persons.[56] This second sense of legal bond analytically and experientially precedes the state's claim of authority over the conferral, withholding and withdrawal of nationality. The Majority in the ICJ case *Nottebohm* (1955) explained that in contrast with a state's determination of allegiance, 'Nationality is *a* legal bond having as its basis *a social fact* of attachment, a genuine connection of existence, interests and sentiments, together with the existence of reciprocal rights and duties.'[57] This type of bond is constituted from social-cultural relationships between natural persons.

The contrast between the formal conferral of nationality by a state and the generation of social-cultural relationships between persons needs noting. The former involves a one-way decision made by a state regarding a natural person. The latter emanates from collective memories (which will be discussed below in section IV) and instances of experiences with others. The ILC had this contrast in mind when it stated that nationality is not actually 'conferred' onto an individual so much as it is an 'attribute' of an individual's social life.[58] A person is effectively a member of a state by virtue of her/his experiences with others, who may also be members of the state. This experiential sense of legal bond harks back to the juristic opinions of the early modern state examined in chapter two. Grotius, Pufendorf, Locke and Rousseau highlighted the same sense of social bonding, which they called 'sociality'. A focus upon such sociality affects the role of the judiciary.

I am not suggesting that there is an alternative sense of legal bond in some idealized world 'out there', independent of the 'is' of the reserved domain. The legal bond as social bond is nested inside the very discourse about international law. Hence, we find the ICJ in *Nottebohm* insisting that social bonding is just as legally 'real' as allegiance. The ILC has moreover described effective nationality as 'personal' 'emotional attachment to a particular country'.[59] On another occasion, James Crawford stated during

---

[56] This is noted in *Refugee Appeal No 75028* (New Zealand Status Appeals Authority,13 May 2004) para 44. Although JC Hathaway does not recognize the importance of effective nationality for stateless persons (and indeed, has little to say about stateless condition), one might consult his earlier *The Law of Refugee Status* (Toronto, Butterworths, 1991) 59.

[57] *Nottebohm* (above n 6) ICJ Rep 23, emphasis added.

[58] See, eg, ILC, 'Draft Articles on Nationality in Relation to the Succession of States' (above n 2) Art 11 (Comm 7).

[59] ILC, 'Report of the 47th Session' (above n 43) 37, para 186.

ILC proceedings that the relation of a natural person to a territory constitutes 'a social reality in the link between people and territory'.[60]

The *Nottebohm* facts need to be reviewed in order to appreciate the competing senses of legal bond. Friedrich Nottebohm was born in Germany. As a young man, he moved in 1905 to Guatemala, where he carried on a business for 38 years. In spring of 1939 he left Guatemala for Germany. One month after World War II began, Nottebohm applied for naturalization by Liechtenstein. Liechtenstein waived its three-year residency requirement and conferred nationality upon Nottebohm. Shortly after, Nottebohm returned to the territory of his habitual residence, Guatemala. At the request of the US government, Nottebohm was arrested in October 1943 and three days later deported from Guatemala to the United States, where he was interned for two years. He was not offered legal proceedings in Guatemala or the United States. Guatemala commenced 54 proceedings against Nottebohm in 1944, with a view to expropriating his assets without compensation. Nottebohm was also charged with treason against Guatemala.[61] Nottebohm returned to Liechtenstein to live there permanently in 1946. His assets in Guatemala were expropriated in 1949. The issue before the ICJ was whether Nottebohm had indeed gained nationality from Liechtenstein and was thereby eligible to be diplomatically protected by Liechtenstein against Guatemala. On the other hand, if he could be considered a national of Liechtenstein, could he also be considered a national of Guatemala (in which case, Liechtenstein would not be able to diplomatically protect Nottebohm from Guatemala's confiscation of his assets)? The issue before the Court ultimately depended upon the nature and locus of Nottebohm's legal bond with the international community.

A. The Three Choices

The territories of three states were potentially at issue in *Nottebohm*.[62] The nationality issue, according to the ICJ Majority, could not be resolved by referring to the reserved domain of the state of Liechtenstein to formally grant nationality to Nottebohm. The boundary of that domain was

---

[60] ILC, 'Nationality in Relation to Succession of States', record of the 2481st meeting, A/CN.4/SER.A/1997, *ILC Yearbook 1997*, vol II(1), 52, para 9. See also V Mikulka (ILC Special Rapporteur), 'Third Report on Nationality in Relation to the Succession of States', UN Doc A/CN.4/480 & Corr 1 and Add 1 & Corr 1–2, 12 (para 9), *ILC Yearbook 1997*, vol II(1).

[61] The proceedings involved more than 170 appeals, which required Nottebohm's presence in Guatemala.

[62] A fourth state, the United States, was not a serious contender for Nottebohm's nationality. Although after some years, he realised that his father had been conferred American nationality, the Court rejected this fact as authority for Nottebohm's possible American nationality.

challenged in this case. Scrutiny of the content of Liechtenstein's reserved domain, of which the conferral of nationality was an incident, was waived in favour of maintaining a very different sense of legal bond.

Germany was one candidate for Nottebohm's state of nationality. For this to be the case, he would have been a national of Germany by virtue of *jus soli*. However, Germany followed the criterion of *sanguinis* as the basis of nationality. As a result, Nottebohm, being of the 'Jewish bloodline' according to domestic German law,[63] lacked German nationality. In addition, if he had once had German nationality (his father and grandfather had been German nationals), this would have been lost because Nazi law automatically withdrew German nationality if one departed from Germany and lived abroad. The Law for the Protection of German Blood and German Honour (1935) was prefaced by Hitler's speech introducing the legislation: the legislation, according to Hitler, aimed 'to regulate by law a problem which, in the event of repeated failure, would have to be transferred by law to the National Socialist party for the final solution'.[64] Consistent with the nationality criterion of *sanguinis*, nationality was conferred only upon those with 'German and kindred blood' and 'persons of German or cognate blood'.[65] The Law recognized 'the inflexible will to ensure the existence of the German nation at all times'. In addition to being the cause of criminal proceedings, the race defilement law anchored the social ostracism of Jews, homosexuals and all others, including the disabled, liberals and aliens, who were categorized as not 'full-blooded' German. Ironically, *sanguinis* worked doubly against Nottebohm. First, the Nazi regime had denied his German nationality because he lacked the pure bloodline required of *sanguinis* as the criterion of nationality by the Nazi state. Second, it was determined in 1947 that he did not have American nationality.[66]

A second candidate for the state of Nottebohm's nationality was Liechtenstein. After all, with due deference to the incident of nationality in internal jurisdiction, Liechtenstein had expressly conferred nationality upon Nottebohm. The problem was that the legal bond, according to the

---

[63] This being the Nazi view of 'race'.

[64] As quoted by LS Dawidowicz (ed), *The Holocaust Reader* (New York, Behrman, 1976) 37. Hitler's speech indicates that the 'final solution' was Nazi policy some years earlier than has traditionally been assumed.

[65] Reich Citizenship Law (15 September 1935), translated in Dawidowicz (ed) (ibid) 44–45; First Decree to the Reich Citizenship Law (14 November 1935), translated in Dawidowicz (ed) (ibid) 45–47; and the Law for the Protection of German Blood and German Honor (15 September 1935), translated in Dawidowicz (ed) (ibid) 47–48. The Blood Protection Law proscribed 'race defilement', which was characterized by marriages and extramarital intercourse between 'full-blooded Germans' with Jews and *Artfremde* ('aliens'). See OD Kulka and E Jäckel (eds), *The Jews in the Secret Nazi Reports on Popular Opinion in Germany, 1933–1945* (New Haven, Yale University Press, 2010) 828–29. 'Full-blooded German' women were also prohibited from working as domestics in Jewish homes.

[66] See above n 62.

Nottebohm Majority, was not determined by states. Rather, the bond depended upon the context-specific social relationships of the applicant/ claimant. Such a social bond between Nottebohm and others with respect to Liechtenstein's territory was 'extremely tenuous'.[67] Indeed, according to the Court, Nottebohm's naturalization by Liechtenstein

> ... was not based on any real prior connection with Liechtenstein, nor did it in any way alter the way of life of the person upon whom it was conferred in exceptional circumstances of speed and accommodation. In both respects, it was lacking in the genuineness requisite to an act of such importance, if it is to be entitled to be respected by a State in the position of Guatemala. It was granted without regard to the concept of nationality adopted in international relations.[68]

If Nottebohm had not had genuine social relations with others on Guatemalan territory, the Court would have had to examine the place of his social experiences even more closely. *Soli* and *sanguinis*, the usual criteria of domestic laws in the context of nationality, would both have left Nottebohm without nationality – and therefore, domestic laws would have left him in a stateless condition.

A third candidate for Nottebohm's state of nationality was Guatemala, and it was this conclusion that the Court settled on. In doing so, the Court put both *jus soli* and *jus sanguinis* to the side, directing its attention instead to the reciprocal social relationships experienced by Nottebohm. Although Nottebohm had lived on Guatemalan territory for 38 years and had immediately returned there upon receiving nationality from Liechtenstein, it was not habitual residence that constituted the basis of the Court's attribution of nationality to Guatemala. His habitual residence on Guatemalan territory was only evidence of a deeper complex of social relationships experienced there.

In effect, the Court unhesitatingly pierced the boundary of the internal jurisdiction of the states of Germany, Liechtenstein and Guatemala in a quest to understand the complex of Nottebohm's social-cultural relationships. The Court's conclusion regarding Nottebohm's effective nationality radically differed from the traditional legal bond of allegiance accepted by European states leading up to World War II.[69] If this traditional legal bond

---

[67] *Nottebohm* (above n 6) ICJ Rep 25.

[68] Ibid, 26.

[69] The denaturalization of citizens because of their potential lack of loyalty was authorized in many European states at the time: Portugal, Belgium, Egypt, Austria, Italy, the Netherlands, the Soviet Union ('constructive renunciation' of citizenship due to a citizen's living abroad and 'against the interests of the People' or due to the citizen's commission of 'acts against the People'), the United Kingdom, Poland, Slovakia, Hungary, Rumania, the Protectorate of Bohemia-Moravia, and France. A UK court refused to 'interfere' with the operation of Germany's domestic law regarding nationality in *Stoeck v The King* [1921] 2 Ch 67, 78. See also *In re Chamberlain's Settlement* [1921] 2 Ch 533. Subsequently, on 25 November 1941, Order No 11 denaturalized all persons alleged to have the *sanguinis* ('bloodline') of

had been maintained in *Nottebohm*, Germany would have refrained from questioning or challenging Liechtenstein's conferral of nationality upon Nottebohm. As a consequence, Liechtenstein would have been recognized as having the freedom to diplomatically protect Nottebohm's assets in Guatemala (and Germany, if he had still had assets on the latter's territory). In other words, the reserved domain was displaced by the social bond.

B. The Legal Bond as a Social Bond

What has been considered the nature of a social bond, according to jurists? The Majority of the *Nottebohm* Court considered nationality as 'a legal bond having as its basis a social fact'.[70] In other words, nationality is a legal sign translating the social bond into a legal bond:

> According to the practice of states, to arbitral decisions and judicial decisions and to the opinion of writers, nationality is *the legal bond* having as its basis *a social fact of attachment, a genuine connection of existence, interests and sentiments, together with the existence of reciprocal rights and duties.* . . [It] constitutes a translation into juridical terms of the individual's connection which has made him its national.[71]

Social relationships (family, religious, linguistic, educational, professional and others) are 'translated' into the legal conception of nationality. The Court indicated that several factors other than habitual residence implicate the legal bond: family ties, participation in public life and the state's recognition of a person as possessing legal status, legal rights and legal duties. The ILC has especially emphasized social relationships as synonymous with effective nationality.[72] For example, in its 'Third Report on Nationality', the ILC Rapporteur added such social factors as an individual's place of residence, the unity of a family, military obligations and the entitlement to pensions.[73] According to the ILC, a 'personal' and 'genuine link' involve an individual's 'emotional attachment to a particular country'.[74] Such a complex of social factors embodied Nottebohm's own

---

Jews residing outside the physical territorial borders of the *Reich*. This was examined more closely above ch 2.

[70] *Nottebohm* (above n 6) ICJ Rep 23, emphasis added.

[71] Ibid, emphasis added.

[72] See, eg, ILC, 'Report of the ILC on the Work of its Forty-Ninth Session', UN Doc A/52/10, *ILC Yearbook 1997*, vol II(2), 14, Art 3 (Comms 1 and 8). For the effective nationality principle as the basis of the presumption, see Art 3 (Comm 4). For the state duty, see also Mikulka, 'Third Report on Nationality' (above n 60) Art 2 (Comms 1–18).

[73] Mikulka, 'Third Report on Nationality' (above n 60) Art 5 (Comm 4). See also the discussion of the 'Third Report' by ILC members in *ILC Yearbook 1997*, vol II(1), 3–141.

[74] ILC, 'Report of the 47th Session' (above n 43) 37 (para 186).

life-world, not the judiciary's: effective nationality concerns the '*social reality* in the link between people and territory'.[75]

The ILC 'Draft Articles on Diplomatic Protection' (2006) has added a further series of indicia of a social bond:

> The authorities indicate that such factors include habitual residence, the amount of time spent in each country of nationality, date of naturalization (ie, the length of the period spent as a national of the protecting state before the claim arose); place, curricula and language of education; employment and financial interests; place of family life; family ties in each country; participation in social and public life; use of language; taxation, bank account, social security insurance; visits to the other state of nationality; possession and use of passport of the other state; and military service.[76]

Along these lines, effective nationality has the effect of piercing the boundary of the internal jurisdiction of states.[77]

Put simply, with the legal bond of effective nationality, what now mattered for Nottebohm was his personal biography, his place of habitation, his friendships and family, his personal and collective memories, the place of his business and the like. We shall see in sections IV and V below that domestic refugee tribunals and international arbitrations have added further factors contributing to the social bond. Note that the legal bond is not between a natural person and the state; rather, the link rests in social relationships inter se.[78] It just happens that this rather than that state claims to own the place where social experiences have transpired.

C. Allegiance Versus Effective Nationality

A social bond as a legal bond contrasts with allegiance as a legal bond. With allegiance, the state is a party to the relationship with a natural person. With a social bond, the state is but a third party to experienced reciprocal relationships between natural persons.[79] This contrasts with the one-way evaluation and determination by state officials of an inhabitant's

---

[75] J Crawford in ILC, 'Nationality in Relation to Succession of States', record of the 2481st meeting (above n 60); and Mikulka, 'Third Report on Nationality' (above n 60) 12 (para 9).

[76] ILC, 'Draft Articles on Diplomatic Protection' (above n 20) Art 8 (Comm 5).

[77] See, eg, International Law Association (ILA) Committee on Diplomatic Protection of Persons and Property, 'Second Report', New Delhi Conference (2002), www.ila-hq.org/download.cfm/docid/BEBDE60D-0E28-473E-BDBC7C956CAD51B9, 13.

[78] This point is not addressed by commentators, to my knowledge. More often than not, jurists have read into *Nottebohm* that the genuine relationship addresses the direct relation of a natural person to the state. See, eg, JR Dugard (ILC Special Rapporteur), 'First Report on Diplomatic Protection', A/CN.4/506 (7 March 2000), paras 110–15.

[79] For a discussion of the third party and nationality, see WE Conklin, 'Statelessness and Bernhard Waldenfels' Phenomenology of the Alien' (2007) 38(3) *Journal of the British Society of Phenomenology* 289.

allegiance or loyalty. As a third party to the social relationships between natural persons that so crucially make for effective nationality, the state has a fiduciary duty to protect such relationships.

In effect, the legal bond as allegiance between Nottebohm and a state was recognized analytically *after* his social relationships had been experienced. Social relationships experientially precede any legal category of nationality. Put differently, the legal bond *post facto* translates into 'reciprocal rights and duties' experienced as social relations with others.[80] One's social relationships embody (that is, give body to) one's social identity. The place of one's social experiences is not some territorial space; one experiences a place through one's relations with others.[81]

In this respect, one might well reread *soli* and *sanguinis* as indicia of such social bonding. *Soli* and *sanguinis*, however, are only the tip of the iceberg: so many inhabitants of the globe now live on territories where they were not born; moreover, *sanguinis* has been used perniciously by state officials to cause legal and social exclusion.[82] Once an individual's social bonding is identified, her/his effective nationality rests with social relations that are independent of the state that happens to own the territory where her/his effective social relationships are manifested. Again, although reciprocal legal rights and duties may characterize the relation of a state to a natural person, the legal bond of effective nationality has shifted to 'a social fact of attachment, a genuine connection of existence, interests and sentiments', as the Majority stated in *Nottebohm*.[83]

As mentioned above, one might speculate that the core issue in *Nottebohm* is the association of legal bond with habitual residence. More recently, the Australian refugee tribunal has held that an applicant for refugee status must have actually lived in the state of origin for some time.[84] Ironically, however, habitual residence has been considered absent even when someone has resided on a territory for twenty years.[85] Indeed, Justice Read, dissenting in *Nottebohm*, pointed out that habitual residence is not synonymous with legal bond.[86] To be sure, it did not help Nottebohm's argument that he had departed from Liechtenstein for Guatemala immediately upon conferral of naturalization by Liechtenstein. Nor could it have aided his case to have Liechtenstein waive the domestic three-year requirement of residency before nationality was granted. To be sure, habitual residence is important, but we need to seek another explan-

---

[80] *Nottebohm* (above n 6) ICJ Rep 23.

[81] The difference between territorial space and a place is examined in Casey, *Getting Back into Place* (above n 8); and Merleau-Ponty (above n 8).

[82] For more on the topic of *soli* and *sanguinis*, see the Introduction to this book and above ch 3.

[83] *Nottebohm* (above n 6) ICJ Rep 24.

[84] *Case No 0901642* (above n 30) para 59.

[85] *Case No 0908370* [2010] RRTA 33.

[86] *Nottebohm* (above n 6) ICJ Rep 43.

ation for legal bond, for habitual residence is only one indicia of social bonding amongst several.

D. Legal Obligation

From a legal standpoint, there is a crucial difference between allegiance and social bonding. When one justifies a nationality rule because it is 'under the operation of its law', whether it be a statute on its face or as applied (administered), citing the criterion of nationality such as *soli* or *sanguinis*, 'its law' has been taken as synonymous with the institutional sources inside internal jurisdiction. This approach incorporates the reserved domain into the international community's residuary of law-making and law administration. The project of justifying such a nationality rule takes for granted that the rule is obligatory because of a state institution's explicit or implicit consent. A legal bond thereby exists between the state and the person conferred nationality by the state. The conferral, withholding or withdrawal of nationality by a state institution hinges upon the state's determination of the individual's loyalty or likely loyalty to the state. This determination likewise takes for granted that the state claims its own authority. Accordingly, the conclusion that a law is obligatory follows on from the state laws and decisions regarding the allegiance of natural persons to the state as determined by the state.

A state's implied consent, represented by the justification of the rule or right to an Article 38 source of the Statute of the International Court, nests in the state's claim to authority. The process of tracing the nexus of a rule or right to the Article 38 sources assumes that the state thereby expressly or impliedly defines its own authority over nationality matters. Because the international community has protected the reserved domain, the state's determination of nationality will thereby be recognized by other states. And the state will have discretion whether to diplomatically protect nationals against other states. In sum, the allegiance of a natural person to the state, as determined by state institutions, ultimately rests upon the universalism over all persons and objects within the internal jurisdiction.

The problem is, however, that allegiance does not resolve the obligatory character of an identifiable rule. This is so because a state claims its own authority over the content-independent reserved domain. What could be more arbitrary than such a claim, particularly in the light of the consequences of the production and consequences of the stateless condition elaborated in chapter three?

This takes us to a crucial difference between allegiance and social bonding as the basis of legal obligation. Something other than the self-positing by and for a state's own claim to authority is needed in order to understand why a right to nationality – or for that matter, a nationality rule enacted, administered or adjudicated inside internal jurisdiction – is obligatory. The Majority in *Nottebohm* was concerned with just such a 'something other'.[87] Judge Klaestad was especially concerned with the issue of the obligatory character of nationality rules traditionally protected by the reserved domain.[88] Contrary to Klaedstad's opinion, however, the obligatory character of social bonding addresses the social content presupposed in the reserved domain. In addition, the pleadings leading to the ICJ judgment were preoccupied with the relation of nationality law with the legal bond as context-specific social bonding.[89] Accordingly, a state's claim to authority over nationality issues, as an incident of the internal jurisdiction, is suspect if one's social life has happened to take place on another state's territory or even in a detention centre for a prolonged stay. A state's claim to authority is suspect even though the state claims authority to legislate or administer law regarding nationality as an incident of its reserved domain heretofore often incorporated in the international community.

In the case of Nottebohm, the obligatory character of nationality law brought into question the exclusivity of the reserved domain of Liechtenstein, Nazi Germany and Guatemala. As the Court held, Nottebohm's 'actual connections' with Liechtenstein were extremely tenuous, and Liechtenstein's hurried procedures leading to the conferral of Nottebohm's nationality were occasion for judicial scrutiny. Nottebohm lacked 'any bond of attachment', let alone a 'genuineness', in his social relationships with others on the territory controlled and claimed by Liechtenstein. The obligatory character of any identifiable law in internal jurisdiction was nested in Nottebohm's 'long-standing and close connection' with others. And such relationships just happened to have been experienced on Guatemalan territory. *Nottebohm* begs an inquiry into the obligatory character of a law independent of the 'operation of a [state's domestic] law'.

E. The Discursive Struggle over a Legal Bond

How one understands the legal bond between a natural person and the international community is pivotal to how one understands the nature and identity of an international community. The one sense of international

---

[87] Ibid, 21.

[88] Ibid, 29. See also the Majority at ICJ Rep 20–21.

[89] See especially *Nottebohm (Liechtenstein v Guatemala)* (1955), ICJ Pleadings, vol 1, www.icj-cij.org/docket/files/18/9009.pdf. See the other documents of the *Nottebohm* case (available at www.icj-cij.org/docket/index.php?sum=215&p1=3&p2=3&case=18&p3=5), including: *Contre-Mémoire du Guatemala* (20 IV 54) 188–98; Reply of Government of Guatemala, 383 (para 21); Reply of Government of Liechtenstein (14 VII 54), 382–83 (paras 18–21); *Replique du Guatemala* (2 XI 54) 510–17; and *Plaidoire de M Rolin* (Guatemala – 19 II 55) 301.

community, best represented by the dissenting opinion of Judge Read in *Nottebohm*, upholds the state's reserved domain, of which nationality is an incident. The second sense, represented by the Majority opinion in *Nottebohm*, takes for granted that legal bond draws from social relationships which are independent of the state's claim to its own authority. Such a claim to authority has had a deep discursive tradition presupposing states as self-creative and self-determining authors of law. The social bond, however, displaces the state's traditional freedom concerning the conferral, withholding or withdrawal of nationality.

In issuing its seminal judgment in *Nottebohm*, the ICJ was certainly cognizant of the negative social consequences (discussed above in chapter three) of maintaining nationality as an incident of the reserved domain: 'Nationality has its most immediate, its most far-reaching and, for most people, its only effects within the legal system of the state conferring it.'[90]

That said, *Nottebohm* itself exemplifies an unresolved discursive struggle over competing senses of legal bond. While the social bonding of natural persons went some way to displace the traditional discursive hold of the legal bond as allegiance, the Majority judgment nonetheless accepted that states remain free to confer, withhold and withdraw nationality: 'It is for every sovereign state, to settle by its own legislation the rules relating to the acquisition of its nationality, and to confer that nationality by naturalization granted by its own organs in accordance with that legislation.'[91] Indeed, the Majority continued that within a state's bounded jurisdiction, state institutions possess complete legal authority. Such a totality of legal authority, aside from the enactment of laws, includes governmental legislative, judicial and administrative functions, the deliberative content and enforcement of any law, taxation, matters of self-defence of the state and all other governmental functions. Accordingly, international standards, given the legal bond as allegiance, at best supplement the content of deliberative acts once again, hitherto immunized from external interference: 'It is not necessary to determine whether international law imposes any limitations on its freedom of decision in this domain.'[92] The domestic and international legal orders are considered exclusive of each other, and 'ne'er the two shall meet'. The Majority wanted it both ways: an international community grounded in social bonds and a community with a residuary that has nationality as its incident.

There is a common thread in the majority and dissenting judgments of *Nottebohm*. This concerns how the two doctrines of legal bond – allegiance and social bonding – exist by virtue of international law, not domestic law. The lawyer for Nottebohm (Hersch Lauterpacht), claiming that

---

[90] *Nottebohm* (above n 6) ICJ Rep 20.
[91] Ibid.
[92] Ibid.

Liechtenstein was the appropriate state of Nottebohm's nationality, conditioned his argument upon international law:

> It is an accepted rule of international law that the conferment of nationality is a matter within the exclusive competence of the State concerned, subject to such limitations as may follow from customary international law, from treaties, and from general principles of law.[93]

After recognizing that states possess a freedom to determine nationality, the Majority concurred on this point: 'To exercise protection, to apply to this Court, is to place oneself on the plane of international law. It is international law which determines whether a state is entitled to exercise protection and to seise the Court.'[94] Even the *Flagenheimer* arbitration, which is often cited as directly opposed to *Nottebohm*, shares with the *Nottebohm* Majority the assumption that the reserved domain exists by virtue of and is incorporated into the international community. As stated in *Flagenheimer*, 'every state is sovereign in establishing the legal conditions' of nationality because of 'an unquestioned principle of international law'.[95]

IV. THE DISCURSIVE TRADITION OF EFFECTIVE NATIONALITY

The doctrine of effective nationality as the explanatory and justificatory grounding of legal bond did not suddenly emerge in *Nottebohm*. Nor did the doctrine end with *Nottebohm*. I shall now retrieve the pre- and post-*Nottebohm* discursive tradition.

A. The Early Modern Tradition

The association of the legal bond with effective nationality appears to have been first made in the 1834 Privy Council judgment of *Drummond*.[96] John Drummond had accompanied James II to France upon James' abdication in 1707. Drummond remained in France for the remainder of his

---

[93] H Lauterpacht, 'In re Friedrich Nottebohm' in Hersch Lauterpcht (ed), *International Law: Collected Works*, vol 4 (Cambridge, Cambridge University Press, 1978) 9. See also V Mikulka (ILC Special Rapporteur), 'First Report on State Succession and Its Impact on the Nationality of Natural and Legal Persons', UN Doc A/CN.4/467, *ILC Yearbook 1995*, vol II(1), 161 (para 16); ILC, 'Report on the Work of its Fifty-First Session' (above n 2) ch 4, 27; and R Rosenstock, 'The Forty-Ninth Session of International Law Commission' (1998) 92 *American Journal of International Law* 107.

[94] *Nottebohm* (above n 6) ICJ Rep 21. The international law context is especially highlighted in JM Jones, 'The *Nottebohm* Case' (1956) 5 *International and Comparative Law Quarterly* 230.

[95] *Flegenheimer* (above n 46) 337 (para 24).

[96] *James Louis Drummond* (1834) Case 2 Knapp, PC Rep 295, 12 Eng Rep 492. Indeed, *Drummond* cites several earlier judgements of the late eighteenth century, as well as *Doe v Acklam* (1824) 2 Bar and Cress 779; *Auchmuty v Mulcaster*, 5 Bar and Cress 771; and *Indian Chief*, 3 Rob 4.

life, marrying a French woman and establishing social relationships there. He was never naturalized by the French state. Though he was born in Britain (as was his son), the British government considered him a French subject. As such, although diplomatic protection was considered non-discretionary in international law at the time, he was not owed such protection, according to the English courts. But France considered him British because of his birth on British soil. Accordingly, his assets were confiscated, sold and placed in the coffers of the French government. Drummond was 'in the unfortunate state of having no country at all', as his lawyer put it.[97] On appeal, the Privy Council acknowledged that he was a national of Britain ('though formally and literally, by the law of Great Britain, he was a British subject'). That said, the Privy Council declared him effectively a French national and therefore ineligible for British diplomatic protection.[98] Drummond's conduct indicated that he and his son intended 'to accept the character of French subjects'.[99]

By the early twentieth century, the doctrine of effective nationality was regularly accepted in international arbitrations[100] and domestic tribunals.[101] For example, the arbitration award of the *Canevaro Claim* (1912) made extensive reference to the phenomenon of effective nationality.[102] Raphael Canevaro was considered a national of both Peru and Italy. Peru considered Canevaro a national because he had been born on Peruvian soil. Italy considered him a national because, following the principle of *jus sanguinis*, Canevaro's bloodline could be traced through his father to Italy. The problem was that the Peruvian government owed him substantial monies and was in the process of paying its debt by issuing cheques to Canevaro when a military coup in Peru stopped payment. In the circumstances, Canevaro needed Italy to diplomatically protect his financial claim against Peru. The Permanent Court of Arbitration held that even if Italy had conferred de jure nationality upon Canevaro, he had effective nationality with Peru and as such could not seek diplomatic

---

[97] *James Louis Drummond* (ibid) 496.

[98] Ibid, 499.

[99] Ibid, 507.

[100] See the arbitrations of the British–Venezuelan Mixed Claim Commission: *Brignone Case*, reported in JH Ralston, *Venezuelan Arbitrations of 1903* (Washington, Government Printing Office, 1904) 754–61; *Stevenson*, reported in Ralston (above) 710–204; *Milliani*, reported in Ralston (above) 754–62; and *Mathison Case*, reported in Ralston (above) 429–38. The *Milliani* decision, for example, highlights such social factors making for nationality as family relationships and the equities of a decision. The Umpire Plumley in *Mathison* rejected the idea, held out by the dissent of Grisanti, that nationality is based upon allegiance. As the dissent stated, a national is 'born out of the king's obedience'.

[101] See, eg, *Hein v Hildersheimer Bank* (1919–22) 1 Ann Dig Case No 148 (26 April 1922 and 10 May 1922), 216, Anglo–German Arbitral Award. The ILC Report on Diplomatic Protection cites other early arbitral awards that adopted the effective nationality principle: ILC, 'Draft Articles on Diplomatic Protection' (above n 20) fn 77.

[102] *Canevaro Case (Italy v Peru)* (Permanent Court of Arbitration) (1912) 11 RIAA 397, translation in (1912) 6 AJIL 746.

protection from Italy. In other words, effective nationality trumped the incident of nationality inside the reserved domain of a state. Evidence of effective nationality included Canevaro's candidacy for the Peruvian Senate, which required that one be a Peruvian citizen. In addition, Canevaro had represented the Peruvian government as Consul General to the Netherlands, this post being authorized by both the Peruvian government and the representatives in the Peruvian Congress. Canevaro's political and social life had manifested social bonds with others on territory that happened to be owned by Peru.

A decade later, the *de Montfort* case (1926) framed social bonding as 'the principle of active nationality, ie, the determination of nationality by a combination of fact and law'.[103] The complainant had been born on French territory and had lived there throughout her life, although she had also gained German nationality through the naturalization process.[104] The French–German Mixed Arbitral Tribunal concluded that her effective nationality, described as 'active nationality', was French. Active nationality concerned evidentiary 'facts' as well as identifiable legal rules. The complainant was effectively a national of France by virtue of her social relationships through time there.

A domestic Appeal Court in Portugal also affirmed the principle of social bonding in the same year.[105] In *Oliveira Machado v Neri Pinto*, the defendant was a Brazilian national who did not lose her Brazilian nationality by marrying a foreigner. She had acquired Portuguese nationality through a Portuguese law that extended nationality to spouses of Portuguese nationals. However, the Court concluded that she remained effectively a national of Brazil as well. As such, she was subject to Brazilian law and could not consent to divorce there, the law of Brazil not recognizing divorce.

In like vein, the arbitrator in *Georges Pinson* (1928) declared that the effective nationality principle applied to a situation in which two states 'effectively consider . . . and treat . . . the person in question as its national'.[106] In this case, Pinson had been naturalized by France, but he was recognized as an effective national of Mexico. Effective nationality represented 'the common sense of the tribunal, independently of the national rules of evidence'.[107] *Soli*, as evidenced by a birth certificate, was not conclusive of nationality. Pinson had sought diplomatic representation from France against Mexico. However, a national could not be diplo-

---

[103] *Barthez de Montfort v Treuhaner Hauptverwaltung* (1925–26) 3 Ann Dig Case No 206 (10 July 1926) 279, Anglo–German Mixed Arbitral Award.

[104] Ibid, 279.

[105] *Oliveira Machado v Neri Pinto* (1925–26) 3 Ann Dig Case No 207 (9 February 1926), 279. The French jurist Basdevant characterized nationality in 1909 as 'the real nationality': *Mergé Claim* (1955) 14 RIAA 236, 22 ILR 443, 453–54.

[106] *Georges Pinson Case* (1927–28) 4 Ann Dig Case No 194 (19 October 1928), 297.

[107] Ibid, 298.

matically protected if he had dual nationality and was claiming diplomatic protection by one state of nationality against another.[108] In this case, Pinson was ineligible for diplomatic protection by France against Mexico. This was so even though Mexico 'had always considered him, officially and exclusively, as a French subject'.[109] *Pinson* thus recognized effective nationality as a principle of international law: 'International tribunals, however, as organs of the law of nations, must neglect even the Constitution of a State in favour of international law.'[110] A statement of a government official 'could not be accepted as authoritative'.[111]

The Hague Convention on Certain Questions Relating to the Conflict of Nationality Laws (1930) also hints at effective nationality as a concept to be turned to in conflict situations.[112] According to Article 5, nationality rests in the territory owned by a state where one is habitually and principally resident. Article 5 of the treaty was followed as the basis of effective nationality in the Filipino case *Juan Gallanosa Frivaldo* (1989).[113] Effective nationality has also been the object of detailed pre- and post-World War II English and French scholarship.[114] In addition, the Italian–US Conciliation Commission, established after World War II, adopted the effective nationality principle in over 50 cases.[115]

B. Post-*Nottebohm*

The internal jurisdiction of states, protected by and incorporated into the international community as the community's residuary in nationality matters, has also been brought into question by a series of international and domestic tribunals since *Nottebohm*. Several post-war judgements of the Supreme Court of the Philippines, for example, followed the doctrine

---

[108] Ibid, as discussed in ILR 1955, 451 per Verzil. This principle was subsequently affirmed in *Reparation for Injuries Suffered in the Service of the United* Nations (1949) ILJ Rep 186, also reported in (1949) ILR 112.

[109] *Georges Pinson* (above n 106) 300.

[110] *Pinson Case* (1927–28) 4 Ann Dig Case No 4 (19 October 1928) 9 and 11.

[111] *Pinson Case* (1927–28) 4 Ann Dig Case No 324 (19 October 1928) 474–75.

[112] Hague Convention on Certain Questions Relating to the Conflict of Nationality Laws (1930), 179 LNTS 89 (in force 1 July 1937), reprinted in M Hudson (ed), *International Legislation: A Collection of Texts of Multipartite International Instruments of General Interest* (Washington, DC, Carnegie Endowment for International Peace, 1931–50) vol 5, 359. According to Art 5, nationality rests in the territory owned by a state where one is habitually and principally resident. Art 5 of the Convention has been followed as the basis of effective nationality in *Juan Gallanosa Frivaldo v Commission on Elections et al*, GR No 87193 (Supreme Court of the Philippines, 23 June 1989).

[113] *Frivaldo* (ibid).

[114] As documented in the *Mergé Claim* (above n 105) ILR 452–53. See also Dugard (above n 78) Art 5, paras 112–17.

[115] ILC, 'Draft Articles on Diplomatic Protection' (above n 20) Art 5 (Comm 8). See examples in fn 80.

of effective nationality when the persons in question had two nationalities.[116] More generally, jurists have evaluated and determined the effective nationality lying behind the formal conferral of nationality by states.

In the *Mergé Claim* (1955), decided in the same year as *Nottebohm*, two states, the United States and Italy, formally registered the complainant's nationality as their own.[117] A dispute arose from the compensation provisions set out in the Peace Treaty (1947) between the United States and Italy. The Treaty was silent as to whether someone who was a national of two states at the same time had a legal claim. The Claims Commission thereupon fell back upon two general, competing principles of international law. The one recognizes the formal equality of states, and by virtue of this principle, the Commission stated that each state was free to determine who its nationals were. The second principle, however, identifies nationality in terms of the personally experienced social relationships of the community.

Interestingly, the Claims Commission decided that the effective nationality principle reinforced the equality of states inter se.[118] The Hague Convention on the Conflict of Nationality Laws aided in this regard.[119] The content of the residuary of the international community was not taken for granted. Instead, the Commission examined empirical evidence which documented the depth and longevity of Mergé's social relationships. As the Commission put it, effective nationality seriously differed from a state's reserved authority over formal nationality. The crucial issue concerned 'the facts' of the individual's situation:

> Habitual residence can be one of the criteria of evaluation, but not the only one. The conduct of the individual in his economic, social, political, civic and family life, as well as the closer and more effective bond with one of the two states must also be considered.[120]

The freedom of the state to enact, administer or adjudicate nationality inside its internal jurisdiction '*must yield before the principle of effective nationality* whenever that nationality is that of the claiming state'.[121] In cases in which 'the predominance' of social bonding is absent and effective nationality cannot be claimed, the authority of state enacted nationality laws eliminates uncertainty.[122]

---

[116] See, eg, *Eremes Kookooritchen v Solicitor General*, GR No L-1812 (Sup Ct Philippines, 27 August 1948).

[117] *Mergé Claim* (above n 105).

[118] A state could not diplomatically protect a national if the individual was effectively a national of a second state: *Frivaldo* (above n 112).

[119] Hague Convention on the Conflict of Nationality Laws (above n 112).

[120] *Mergé Claim* (above n 105) ILR 455.

[121] Ibid.

[122] Ibid, ILR 443 and 455.

In sum, *Nottebohm* and its discursive tradition suggest that the reserved domain of the state can be displaced in efforts to identify the legal bond of an applicant. Returning to *Nottebohm*:

> A state cannot claim that the rules it has thus laid down are entitled to recognition by another state unless it has acted in conformity with this general aim of making the legal bond of nationality accord with the individual's genuine connexion with the state which assumes the defence of its citizens by means of protection as against other states.[123]

The key issue in interstate relations concerns whether evidence of social bonding points to a 'closer and more effective bond' between natural persons. That a person happens to find her/himself on the territory of this state or that state is immaterial except as an indication of that social bonding.

By the mid-1980s, many individual US citizens had brought claims before the Iran–US Arbitration Commission. One claim arose from the confiscation of American assets following the overthrow of the government of the Shah of Iran.[124] The issue was whether the Commission had jurisdiction to hear complaints from persons lacking de jure American nationality according to American domestic law. Relying upon *Nottebohm* and *Mergé Claim*, the Arbitration Commission held that a complainant could have effective nationality even though neither the United States nor Iran had expressly conferred nationality upon the complainant. The crucial inquiry was whether a claimant had 'real and effective' social relationships on the territory of this or that state. Once again, the issue concerned the social relationships of complainants as natural persons. Such social relationships, according to the Commission, were manifested by such factors as 'habitual residence, centre of interests, family ties, participation in public life and other evidence of attachment'.[125] The Commission did not in the least find that examining such factors would 'open up the floodgates'. Nor did the Commission find the issue of effective nationality opaque.

The continued focus upon social bonding, framed as active, effective, genuine or actual nationality, has brought the boundary of the reserved domain into question. For example, procedural protections of stateless persons must be effective and not pro forma.[126] Although women and girls, for example, have frequently been conferred nationality by virtue of

---

[123] *Nottebohm* (above n 6) ICJ Rep 23.
[124] *Iran–United States Case No A/18* (Iran–United States Claims Tribunal) (1984) 5 Iran–USCTR251, (1984) 23 ILM 489, 75 ILR 175.
[125] Ibid, ILR 194.
[126] Human Rights Committee (HRC), 'General Comment 15: The Position of Aliens under the Covenant', A/41/40 (11 April 1986), Annex VI (117–19), para 10. See also *Giry v Dominican Republic*, HRC Communication No 193/1985, UN Doc CCPR/C/39/D/193/1985 (1990), 95 ILR 321. Cf *Maroufidou v Sweden*, HRC Communication No 58/1979, UN Doc CCPR/C/12/D/58/1979 (1981), 62 ILR 278.

the operation of domestic laws,[127] they have also been considered 'essentially stateless' in social circumstances, as shown above in chapter three. Even setting aside the social consequences of statelessness documented in chapter three, the focus upon social relationships opens the door for domestic and international tribunals to scrutinize the content of domestic laws and state actions. Such a focus leads to the reconsideration of state freedom over prolonged detention, expulsion, forced displacement, the enactment and administration of nationality laws, the totality of legal authority inside the boundary of the reserved domain of the state, the exclusionary character of the national/alien binary, discrimination on the grounds of statelessness, as well as the discretion of states to determine when national security is threatened. In short, effective nationality opens the door for the judiciary to scrutinize the content of the residuary of the international community.[128]

V. EVIDENCE OF SOCIAL BONDS AS LEGAL BOND

Mindful of the weight of the legal bond of allegiance in an international community constituted from the aggregate of the wills of states, commentators have frequently interpreted *Nottebohm* as if it reinforces such an international community.[129] For example, in *Flegenheimer*, three years after *Nottebohm*, *Nottebohm* was reread as establishing that the legal bond is merely 'a nominal link between a state and an individual'.[130] The *Flegenheimer* arbitration went so far as to deny that *Nottebohm* concerned social relationships.[131] The doctrine of effective nationality, according to the *Flegenheimer* decision, constitutes a 'sociological' inquiry. Despite the contradictory, uncertain and discretionary exercise of internal jurisdiction in nationality matters, a grounding of legal bond in social relationships, according to *Flegenheimer*, would render nationality obscure and discriminatory.[132] Such an immunity from external scrutiny, however, risks a reification of social life.[133] As with Nottebohm, both *jus soli* and *jus sanguinis* left Flegenheimer stateless.

---

[127] UNHCR, 'Statelessness: Prevention and Reduction of Statelessness and Protection of Stateless Persons', UN Doc EC/57/SC/CRP.6 (14 February 2006), www.refworld.org/docid/4a54bbdbd.html, 4.

[128] HRC, 'General Comment 15' (above n 126) Annex VI (117–19), para 10. See also *Giry* (above n 126); and cf *Maroufidou* (above n 126).

[129] Eg, ILA Committee on Diplomatic Protection (above n 77) 8.

[130] *Flegenheimer* (above n 46) 147.

[131] Ibid, 150.

[132] Ibid. See also *KA v Secretary of State for the Home Department* [2008] UKAIT 00042 (UK Asylum and Immigration Tribunal).

[133] *Flegenheimer* (above n 46) 385 (para 69, conclusion 5).

If one accepts the reserved domain and nationality as an incident thereof as hard facts, it is a short step to exclude social bonding as too subjective or 'sociological', as the Arbitration Commission did in *Flegenheimer*.[134] An early ILC Rapporteur on state succession and the ILC Reports on Diplomatic Protection have also expressed concern about *Nottebohm* along these lines.[135] Social relationships, reified into the a priori character of rules and rights protected by internal jurisdiction, might direct jurists to extra-legal subjectivity. Once so categorized, a focus on social bonds would invite arbitrariness.[136] Indeed, Václav Mikulka, the ILC Rapporteur for the 'First Report on State Succession and Nationality', commented that *Nottebohm* focused 'more on the sociological aspect than the strictly legal aspect of the concept [of nationality]. Clearly, it would not be easy to pro-vide an entirely satisfactory definition of nationality.'[137] Jurists need to be prudent, we are advised.[138] And prudence had traditionally assumed that 'the operation of law' is synonymous with rules or tests enacted and administered by states. Before jurists cross the boundary of legal knowl-edge, they must flesh out what is meant by effective nationality.[139]

Effective nationality concerns the tacitly accepted norms drawn from social relationships. As a legal bond, unwritten norms embody the ethos of an international community as a whole. Personally experienced rela-tionships are important in this respect. There are other factors, though. Legal obligation, when social relationships are accepted as the legal bond, rests in an ethos where social relations and the assumptions and expecta-tions manifested by such relations explain why a state is obligated to pro-tect a stateless person. The ethos phenomenologically and analytically pre-exists the state and the state's reserved domain.

Allegiance, in contrast, hangs upon the presupposed explicit or implicit consent of the state. But the legal bond of effective nationality does not rest with the state's consent. The obligatory character of a discrete domes-tic nationality rule hinges upon the reciprocal social relations heretofore excluded as subjective or extra-legal to the sources thesis. Without social bonding amongst natural persons, an international community would not exist as a community. The ethos is not the product of self-conscious reflection about discrete written rules in legal objectivity. The ethos does have a language. The language of the ethos is nested in the pre-analytic expectations and memories presupposed of a stateless person as well as of a jurist.

---

[134] Ibid, 150.
[135] Mikulka, 'First Report' (above n 93); and Dugard (above n 78).
[136] Mikulka, 'First Report' (above n 93) 41.
[137] V Mikulka (Special Rapporteur), 'Summary Record of the 2475th Meeting (13 May 1997)', A/CN.4/SER.A/1997, *ILC Yearbook* 1997, vol I, 8 (para 19).
[138] Ibid.
[139] ILC, 'Report of the 47th Session' (above n 43) 37 (para 186).

One might be helped in this regard by revisiting Oscar Schachter's analysis of customary international legal norms.[140] Schachter associated customary international legal norms with two requisites: a sense of obligation toward a norm and state practices manifesting the norm. Schachter and others have assumed that state practices represent social practice.[141] In this light, the reserved internal jurisdiction is believed to constitute social practice. As with interrelations amongst states, effective nationality now brings such a claim into question. The 'beliefs' and 'social life' of the juridically constructed 'rules of the 'state' are not displaced in favour of the unwritten assumptions and expectations of natural persons finding themselves de jure and effectively stateless. Such assumptions and expectations analytically and experientially take form *prior* to a state's recognition of nationality as a legal category.

The challenge for jurists is to enquire whether any one stateless person possesses effective nationality despite an absence of the formal conferral of nationality by any state on the globe. As an analytic issue, the place where the stateless person has had experiences can be considered 'subjective' or 'extra-legal' by virtue of the privileged reserved domain within which state institutions are free to confer nationality laws. Such a reserved domain is a hard fact from the standpoint of an international community as the aggregated wills of state members. The boundary of the reserved domain demarcates the boundary of legal knowledge. It is just such 'extra-legal' social phenomena, however, that determine the legal bond of effective nationality, as we have seen. With the concerns of *Flegenheimer* in mind, let us identify factors that domestic tribunals have highlighted in understanding the social relationships determinative of the effective nationality of stateless persons.

---

[140] O Schachter, *International Law in Theory and Practice* (The Hague, Martinus Nijhoff, 1991) 336. Schachter directs one, for example, to domestic constitutions and statutes; he frequently references UN Resolutions and Declarations as to state duties, the condemnations of human rights violations by other international bodies, public statements by officials of one state who criticize the actions of officials of another state, dicta of the International Court of Justice to the effect that certain norms are *erga omnes*, and decisions of domestic courts that refer to treaties and customary international standards.

[141] JC Hathaway, *The Rights of Refugees under International Law* (Cambridge, Cambridge University Press, 2005) 18; BD Lepard, *Customary International Law: A New Theory with Practical Applications* (Cambridge, Cambridge University Press, 2010) 127, 173, 245–69 and 312; M Byers, *Custom, Power and the Power of Rules: International Relations and Customary International Law* (Cambridge, Cambridge University Press, 1999) 193.

A. Personal and Collective Memories

An important part of effective nationality is personal and collective memories.[142] Such memories impact upon the identity of an individual as well as how s/he is socially bonded to members of a group.[143] Collective memory incorporates the memories of a group, independent of the personal experiences on a single member. A personal memory, arising as it does from a personal experience, can be retrieved through therapy or flashbacks; collective memory cannot be retrieved in this way.[144] Collective memories, which precede the birth of an individual and endure after her/his death, are subtly transferred through bodily rituals, myths, formal and informal education, social relationships, religious practices and day-to-day experiences. Both jurists and stateless persons possess collective memories. Indeed, professional legal education is largely the inculcation of such collective memories.

The most important collective memory in the international community understood as the aggregated wills of states is the belief in the reserved domain of law-making and law administration. The very belief that the globe is organized according to territorial borders protecting the reserved domains represents an important assumption in the collective memory of jurists. We share such elements of a collective memory with other jurists from other states. As jurists, we are a group with our own assumptions and discourse embodying our collective memories before we become professional lawyers and judges. The legal bond in an international community as aggregated wills of states exists by virtue of such a collective memory. A state's claim to its own authority in nationality matters merely manifests this deeper sense of collective memory. The problem is that there is a competing collective memory that assumes an international community as a whole, independent of the reserved domain.

That said, rarely, if ever, has there been a perfect fit of the collective memories of an ethnic nation with the territorial border of a state. After all, territorial borders in Europe, for example, have often been determined

---

[142] See generally ES Casey, *Remembering: A Phenomenological Study*, 2nd edn (Bloomington, Indiana University Press, 2000); and P Ricoeur, *Memory, History, Forgetting*, K Blamey and D Pellauer (trans) (Chicago, University of Chicago Press, 2004) 93–132. See also K Jung, 'The Concept of the Collective Unconscious' in WK Gordon (ed), *Literature in Critical Perspective* (New York, Appleton-Crofts, 1968) 504–8; M Halbwachs, *The Collective Memory*, FJ Ditter Jr and VY Ditter (trans) (New York, Harper Colophon Books, 1980) 78–84; P Nora and LD Kritzman (eds), *Realms of Memory: Rethinking the French Past*, A Goldhammer (trans) (New York, Columbia University Press, 1996); and P Nora, 'Between Memory and History: *Les Lieux de Mémorie*', M Roudebush (trans) (1989) 26 *Representations* 7.

[143] A concurring opinion by Higgins in *TK v France* continues this point of view with the assertion that the existence of persons belonging to a minority is 'a factual matter': *T K v France*, HRC Communication No 220/1987, UN Doc CCPR/C/37/D/220/1987 (1989).

[144] See the sources listed above n 142.

arbitrarily by states, nature, military conquest or even the Pope in medieval times. Stateless nomadic groups, migrant workers, visitors and detainees may experience social bonding through singular events rather than to a territorial state or its border.[145] What binds individuals together are, in the words of the ICCPR, 'their own culture . . . religion or . . . language' (Article 27). The Human Rights Committee, in its 'General Comment 23' to the ICCPR, has described social bonding as a sharing of a community with others who 'belong' in a common culture with collectively shared memories.[146] This 'belonging' is said to address one's 'enjoyment of a particular culture', 'a way of life'.[147] Such belonging draws from one's collective memories and personally experienced memories. Recent Supreme Court of Canada decisions have attempted to articulate the collective memories shared by contemporary indigenous groups in terms of the pre-contact, orally expressed experiential knowledge of their ancestors, which are otherwise inadmissible in civil proceedings.[148] With this understanding, time no longer begins at some founding moment of the state but in terms of social relationships making for effective nationality. In this context, collective memories have been material even though an individual has not experienced discrimination.[149]

B. Statistical Evidence

A second source of evidence for effective nationality concerns statistical evidence supporting the cultural bonding and fears of members of groups. For example, statistical evidence by nongovernmental organizations (NGOs) monitoring the Rohingyas of Myanmar has been held sufficient to establish an applicant's fear of persecution if forced to return to Myanmar.[150] Tribunals have complained of the absence of statistical evidence and have been known to return applications back to trial because of the failure of counsel to provide statistical or anthropological evidence.[151]

---

[145] HRC, 'General Comment 15' (above n 126) para 5.2.
[146] HRC, 'General Comment 23: Article 27 (Rights of Minorities)', CCPR/C/21/Rev.1/Add.5 (8 April 1994), www.refworld.org/docid/453883fc0.html.
[147] HRC, 'General Comment 15' (above n 126) para 3.2.
[148] See, eg, *R v Marshall* [1993] 3 SCR 456, paras 15–17, 22–35 and 41–44. There are many recent examples of this. By way of example, see *Delgamuukw v Province of British Columbia* [1997] 3 SCR 1010, 115 ILR 446, paras 85–87.
[149] *Case No 0903639* [2009] RRTA 971, para 186; *MA (Ethiopia) v Secretary of State for the Home Department* [2009] EWCA Civ 289, paras 78–83 (per Stanley Burnton J); and *KK and Others (Korea) v Secretary of State for the Home Department* [2011] UKUT 92 (IAC), para 67.
[150] *Case No 0802146* [2008] RRTA 274, paras 69–73 and 84.
[151] *Refugee Appeal No 75971* (NZ Refugee Status Appeals Authority, 15 May 2007), www.refworld.org/docid/46a485451a.html, paras 67–68; *R Pamajewon* [1996] 2 SCR 821, 138 DLR (4th) 204; F Houle, 'Pitfalls for Administrative Tribunals in Relying on Formal Common Law Rules of Evidence' in R Creyke (ed), *Tribunals in the Common Law World* (Sydney, Federation Press, 2008) 107, cited favourably in *A-G v Ahmed Zaoui* (2004) SC Civ 19, [2005] NZSC 38, para 37.

Although the 'facts' of a case may seem straightforward for the application of domestic law, tribunals sometimes draw heavily from economic statistical evidence about a refugee's state of origin in order to evaluate the authenticity of the person's fear of returning to the state of her/his habitual residence.[152]

C. The Social Biographies of Applicants

Aside from statistical evidence, the social biographies of stateless persons have been considered material in refugee cases.[153] Inquiries along these lines have been made in refugee cases involving the legal and social harm being caused inside the territorial borders of Israel, Somalia[154] and Sudan;[155] clan warfare in various territories of the globe; and blood feuds in Albania.[156] In such cases, tribunals seek 'any credible information as to the appellant's true identity, background and experiences'.[157] A tribunal in the United Kingdom, for example, relied on a refugee's absence of access to public health care and public education in Kuwait in determining that the applicant was Bedoon; it was not the woman's lack of documentation from the Kuwaiti state that was determinative of her stateless condition.[158] Similarly, an Australian refugee tribunal deemed a Palestinian applicant stateless based on the fact that he was beaten and regularly persecuted in a Lebanese refugee camp.[159] A conclusion of statelessness was similarly reached in New Zealand regarding an applicant who had been convicted of forging passports.[160] Such cases illustrate how some tribunals and courts prioritize context-specific social-cultural phenomena rather than relying on formal nationality documentation or the lack thereof in determining the stateless status of applicants. Such social phenomena, not formal statutes

---

[152] *Ad v Refugee Status Branch of Department of Labour* [2011] NZIPT 800042, paras 30–34.

[153] See, eg, *KK and Others* (above n 149) paras 70–73; and *Refugee Appeal No 76077* (above n 30) paras 93, 101 and 103.

[154] *Refugee Appeal No 76376* (NZ Refugee Status Appeals Authority, 11 May 2010), www.refworld.org/docid/4c174eb22.html, para 99, as documented in Refugee Appeals No 76062 (NZRSAA, 15 October 2007) paras 55 and 84, as well as in *Refugee Appeal Nos 76335 and 76364* (NZRSAA, 29 September 2009) paras 47–49. Documentation was also cited from the International Crisis Group (2007), the Human Rights Watch (2007), the United Nations Children's Fund (2009) and the UN High Commissioner for Refugees (2009). See *Refugee Appeal No 76376* (above) paras 93–97.

[155] *Refugee Appeal No 73378* (NZ Refugee Status Appeals Authority, 11 December 2003), www.refworld.org/docid/477cfba5d.html.

[156] *Brozi* [2003] UKIAT 06978, 14, as quoted in *TB (Blood Feuds – Relevant Risk Factors) Albania CG* [2004] UKIAT 00158, para 34; and *Koci v Secretary of State for Home Department* [2003] EWCA Civ 1507.

[157] See, eg, *Refugee Appeal No 75971* (above n 151) paras 67–68.

[158] *SA (Kuwait) v Secretary of State for the Home Department* [2009] EWCA Civ 1157, para 1.

[159] *Case No 1001150* [2010] RRTA 404 (19 May 2010), para 77.

[160] *Ajeil v Minister of Immigration*, DRT 043/05 (NZ Deportation Review Tribunal, 29 November 2007).

or decisions by state administrative officials, can be the basis of determining whether someone is effectively stateless.

D. Context-Specific Experiences of Group Members

Collective and personal memories, statistics and context-specific experiences of particular stateless persons have been highlighted as material evidence in judicial and quasi-judicial decisions about stateless persons, as noted above. A context-specific tribunal's association of a stateless person with a group has often satisfied any evidentiary requirement to establish particular harm to the individual. This has been so of the Bedoons in the Middle East, the Roma in Europe,[161] applicants in Algeria over a 15-year period[162] and applicants for refugee status due to fear of persecution from a clan.[163] Tribunals have conducted close readings of empirical evidence showing the attitudes towards different ethnic groups in specific states.[164] For example, Bedoon refugees have been considered stateless even when they lack evidence that they have been direct victims of discrimination.[165] In this regard, judicial scrutiny has been directed towards groups (rather than individuals) that have been harmed on the basis of race, religion, nationality, political affiliation or membership in a particular social group.[166]

A person's 'true identity' includes being part of an ethnic group, and credible evidence to this effect can be shown.[167] Tribunals have admitted as evidence and given great weight to analytically and empirically rigorous studies by prominent social scientists, NGOs such as Amnesty International, and the media.[168] The diplomatic and military relationship between France and Algeria, the life of insurgents and acts of denaturali-

---

[161] *KK and Others* (above n 149) para 83; ILC, 'Report on the Work of Its 51st Session' (above n 2) 37, Article 15.

[162] *Refugee Appeal No 74540* (NZ Refugee Status Appeals Authority, 1 August 2003), paras 33–58.

[163] *Refugee Appeal No 76376* (above n 154) para 100.

[164] See eg, *Case No 0903639* (above n 149) paras 96 and 105. See also *Case No 0908370* (above n 85) para 46.

[165] *AAAAD v Refugee Appeals Tribunal and the Ministry for Justice, Equality and Law Reform* [2009] IEHC 326 (Ireland High Court), para 86.

[166] In *Case No 0903639* (above n 149) paras 96 and 105, for example, the Australian Refugee Tribunal concluded that there was evidence of racist violence in Latvia against Roma, Egyptians and Armenians. However, no such evidence supported a similar claim against ethnic Russians or Ukrainians (para 115). Conversely, language and religious restrictions against ethnic Russians and Ukrainians had been abolished. Of the 630,380 ethnic Russians in Latvia, 367,662 are Latvian citizens, 22,000 hold Russian passports, and the rest are de jure stateless (para 113).

[167] See, eg, *Refugee Appeal No 75971* (above n 151) paras 67–68; and *Refugee Appeal No 76376* (above n 154) para 100.

[168] *Refugee Appeal No 74540* (above n 162) paras 54–57, 59–62 and 70–82.

zation have all variously been documented and examined as material to a stateless person's social group.[169]

E. Expectations

One final evidentiary matter has been the expectations of stateless persons. Such expectations have followed on from the signing of human rights treaties or from having lived on a territory for some time.[170] As an Australian judge has expressed it, a treaty's ratification provides 'an adequate foundation for a legitimate expectation, absent statutory or executive indications to the contrary, that administrative decision-makers will act in conformity with the Convention'.[171] Such an expectation is 'tantamount to treating [the treaty] as the rule of law'.[172] Habitual residence, for example, signified an expectation interest in the well-known case of *Olga Tellis* (1986), in which the state of India planned to uproot hundreds of thousands of inhabitants of the slums in Calcutta.[173] The Indian Supreme Court held that the effectively stateless inhabitants who had registered 'addresses' could not be evicted without proper notice and without access to nearby alternative places of living. (However, those without a registered address were still excluded from legal protection.) In other words, the 'right to life' incorporates social-economic 'livelihood'. The UN Special Rapporteur on the Right to Food has moreover extended the principle of effective nationality to cover circumstances leading to the eviction of small farmers, members of castes and 'scheduled tribes' deprived of 'productive resources'.[174]

---

[169] Ibid, paras 63–69; and *Refugee Appeal No 76078* [2009] NZRSAA 38 (19 May 2009), para 95. See also *EB (Ethiopia) v Secretary of State for the Home Department* [2007] EWCA Civ 809, [2008] 3 WLR 1188.

[170] *Minister for Immigration and Ethnic Affairs v Ah Hin Teoh* (1995) 183 CLR 273 (High Court of Australia), para 34. In *Minister for Immigration v Teoh*, a Malaysian citizen was deported from Australia because he had committed a serious offence. On his brother's death, he had married the brother's spouse. His deportation would cause him to be separated from his six children, who were all under ten years of age, three of whom had been fathered by his deceased brother.

[171] Ibid, para 34.

[172] *Minister v Ah Hin Teoh* (above n 170) para 36. Independent of the expectation principle, a treaty is incorporated into domestic law if the statute or subordinate legislation is ambiguous (para 26).

[173] *Olga Tellis v Bombay Municipal Corporation* (1986) AIR 180, (1985) 2 Supp SCR 51.

[174] J Zeigler (Special Rapporteur), 'Report on the Right to Food', UN Doc E/CN.4/2006/44/Add.2 (16 March 2006), daccess-dds-ny.un.org/doc/UNDOC/GEN/G06/118/82/PDF/G0611882.pdf?OpenElement, para 26.

VI. THE JUDICIAL SCRUTINY OF SOCIAL RELATIONSHIPS

What is the scope of judicial scrutiny into the content of the international community's reserved domain in matters of de jure and effective nationality? As pointed out in chapter two, the 'operation' of domestic law has traditionally been left to state executives. Executive state action has sometimes been considered free from criticism and legal action by other states.[175] The question now posed is whether effective nationality opens up the reserved domain to the extent that domestic executive decisions inside the domain can be judicially reviewed.

A. Judicial Scrutiny of Executive Action during Alleged Emergencies

Persons lacking de jure nationality from any state by 'operation of its law' have faced severe social, legal and economic consequences during alleged state emergencies. A declared state of emergency triggers the applicability of non-derogation clauses of human rights treaties, which means that a state can derogate from their usual human rights obligations. The clauses expressly incorporate 'other obligations under international law'.

Article 4 of the ICCPR requires that any declared state emergency must 'threaten the life of the nation and the existence of which is officially proclaimed'. The specific wording of this and other treaties, however, raises serious problems for de jure and effectively stateless persons. For example, under Article 4(1) of the ICCPR, discrimination is allowed during a declared emergency so long as it is not 'solely' on the ground of 'race, colour, sex, language, religion or social origin'. The consequence is that a state executive, representing the state in foreign relations as explained in chapter two, may claim that any discrimination that occurs during a declared emergency is a mere tertiary consequence of the object of protecting the 'life of the nation'.

In addition, Article 4(2) itemizes a series of treaty rights that states may not infringe during declared emergencies. By inference, rights not listed as non-derogable may be restricted when 'the life of the nation' is threatened. Such derogable rights are precisely the rights that stateless persons most commonly rely on during alleged emergencies. For example, Article 9 guarantees a set of rights that are derogable by virtue of their absence from the list of non-derogable rights in Article 4(2): the right to liberty and security of the person, freedom from arbitrary arrest and detention, the right to court 'proceedings' within 'a reasonable time' upon arrest and 'the enforceable right to compensation'. Because such rights constitute the

---

[175] *Saudi Arabia v Nelson* (1993) 507 US 349.

core principles of due process of law, de jure and effectively stateless persons are especially at the mercy of the executive arm of the state during alleged state emergencies.

According to Article 10, stateless detainees during 'exceptional circumstances' should be separated from criminals and treated with the respect 'appropriate to their status as unconvicted persons'. However, Article 12 contains another set of rights that are subject to state jurisdiction when 'national security' or 'public order' are threatened, including freedom of movement and the freedom to choose one's residence, leave one's own country and return to one's own country. Moreover, while Article 13 appears to provide the right for detainees to submit reasons to a 'competent authority' against her/his own expulsion, 'the operation of its laws' – the criterion by which de jure statelessness is defined in Article 1 of the Convention Relating to the Status of Stateless Persons (1954) – may leave a stateless person illegally on a state's territory. As a result, s/he may be considered ineligible for protection by this right.

Article 14 provides for legal equality, but it is likewise omitted from the list of non-derogable rights in Article 4(2). And once again, a stateless person may not be protected by this right during a declared emergency. Such a person may also not be protected from 'arbitrary or unlawful interference' into her/his privacy, family, home, honour and reputation, which are otherwise guaranteed by Article 17.

With the legal bond of allegiance, the state is a party to any legal bond. As we have seen, the state's officials thereby claim authority to decide whether a natural person has allegiance to the state. On the other hand, the legal bond of social bonding, as we have also seen, is independent of the state. The state is a third party to such a legal bond, and the role of the judiciary shifts from passive to active in the scrutiny of the social conditions of stateless persons. As the New Zealand Supreme Court has recently expressed, 'Security cannot provide a basis for a blanket exclusion of such cases [in which stateless persons seek bail].'[176] In like vein, the European Court of Human Rights in *Al-Nashif v Bulgaria* (2002) overturned Bulgaria's decision to expel a stateless non-national.[177] The Court found that the very evidence used by Bulgaria to determine that the detainee was a threat to national security was also crucial to establish his effective nationality.[178] Aside from having a Muslim marriage in Bulgaria as well as friendships there, Al-Nashif had helped construct a Muslim community centre and had then given religious lessons at the Centre. Bulgaria owed a legal obligation directly to the international community in this context and indirectly to Al-Nashif. The state had to give compelling reasons why it

[176] *A-G v Ahmed Zaoui* (2004) SC Civ 19, [2005] NZSC 38, para 44.
[177] *Al-Nashif v Bulgaria* [2002] ECHR 497, Application No 50963/99 (20 June 2002), para 119.
[178] Ibid, paras 112 and 114.

desired to expel the alien.[179] The legal bond was generated from the inter-relations of natural persons, which were independent of the Bulgarian state executive and of even the European Court.[180]

The House of Lords exemplified a similar intervention into the social content of the reserved domain in *A and Others v UK* (2009).[181] Contrary to a statute that authorized Ministers to state a 'belief' that a 'non-national' was 'a risk to national security' or suspected of being 'an international terrorist', the state was held to have a legal obligation to protect a stateless person as if a national of the United Kingdom. The Minister's certificate of belief lacked an obligatory character because the Court had authority to examine the content of the reserved domain. The judicial duty, according to the Joint Parliamentary Committee, was to ascertain 'objective, rational and proportionate justification' of detention or expulsion of non-nationals with reference to the de facto circumstances independent of the executive's opinion.[182] Such justification was amiss when only non-national alleged terrorists were the object of expulsion. Both the European Court and the House of Lords found that the exercise of internal jurisdiction disproportionately impacted upon non-nationals.[183]

B. Prolonged Detention

The principle of effective nationality has brought with it judicial scrutiny of prolonged detention of stateless persons. Four circumstances have tended to make possible such prolonged detention. These circumstances are the consequence of nationality being an incident of the state's reserved domain. They include: the stateless person as a threat to the state; refugee status; the withholding of recognition; and the social conditions making for effective statelessness. The latter include a lack of access to healthcare and poor treatment of detainees.[184] Although the Majority in the Australian High Court decision of *Behrooz* (2004) stated that harsh and inhumane conditions of internment were justifiable,[185] Kirby J (dissenting) stated that prolonged detention undermines the very reason for such detention

---

[179] Ibid, paras 94, 114, 119, 133 and 137.

[180] Ibid, para 137. See also *Z and Others v UK* [2001] ECHR 333.

[181] *Case of A and Others v UK* [GC], Application No 3455/05 (19 February 2009), (2009) 49 EHRR 29, esp paras 126–28 and 173–74. At least one victim (the first applicant) was stateless. The record is unclear whether the third, fifth, sixth, seventh and ninth applicants had de jure nationality from some state. Almost 30% of terrorism suspects were said to be of British nationality (para 98).

[182] Ibid, para 100.

[183] Ibid, para 190.

[184] *Marinich v Belarus*, HRC Communication No 1502/2006 (16 July 2010).

[185] *Behrooz v Secretary of the Department of Immigration and Multicultural and Indigenous Affairs and Others* [2004] HCA 36, (2004) 208 ALR 271.

– namely, the distinction between 'immigration detention' and criminal detention.[186] Even persons detained for criminal wrongdoing are guaranteed some semblance of judicial hearing or trial; stateless persons have no such guarantee. Moreover, the fact that decisions authorizing such prolonged detention are usually rendered by the executive arm of a state means that such actions are often non-reviewable by a court. This again contrasts with criminal proceedings.[187]

In 1984, the Privy Council held in *Hardial Singh* that the length of detention by the executive arm of a state is subject to judicially determined limitations.[188] First, an executive may not use detention for any purpose other than removal from the state's territory to a state of effective nationality. Second, detention is 'impliedly limited' for a period only 'reasonably necessary for that purpose'. In the case of *Hardial Singh*, Browne-Wilkinson held that further detention was not possible within a reasonable time.[189] Third, an executive should take expeditious steps to remove the detainee. Courts should construe such authority on the part of the executive 'strictly', even if the legislature has extended the time for the detention of a stateless person.

The Privy Council restated the authority of the courts to review and override the executive's indefinite detention of effectively stateless persons in *Tan Te Lam* (1997).[190] In addition, the New Zealand High Court decided in *Mohebbi* (2007) that indefinite detention of a stateless person (over three years and nine months in this case) constitutes cruel and degrading treatment on account of harm to the detainee's family, the detainee's right to liberty, and the rule of law.[191] Interestingly, the Philippine Supreme Court has even held that the executive's prolonged detention of a stateless person is *functus officio* even if the detainee is disloyal to the state.[192] This is especially so if the stateless person legally entered the state's territory.[193] The Philippine Supreme Court has also been known to take into account

---

[186] Ibid, para 62. See also Kirby's judgment in *Al-Kateb v Godwin and Others* [2004] HCA 37, (2004) 219 CLR 562, (2004) ILDC 33 (Australian High Court, 6 August 2004), paras 152 and 160–68.

[187] *Behrooz* (above n 185) para 114.

[188] *R v Governor of Durham Prison, ex parte Hardial Singh* [1984] 1 All ER 983, [1984] 1 WLR 704 (QBD), 706 (per Woolf J).

[189] Ibid, 111.

[190] *Tan Te Lam v Superintendent of Tai A Chau Detention Centre* [1997] AC 97, 111. See also *NAKG of 2002 v Minister for Immigration & Multicultural & Indigenous Affairs* [2002] FCA 1600, para 41.

[191] *Mohebbi v Department of Labour* (High Court of Auckland, 23 August and 5 November 2007), CIV 2007-404-3710, paras 56, 66, 70, 71 and 84(d); *Cisinski v Minister for Immigration & Multicultural & Indigenous Affairs* [2004] FCA 507 (Fed Ct Australia), paras 32–42 and 54.

[192] *Vadim N Chirskoff v Commissioner of Immigration and Director of Prisons*, GR No L-3802 (Supreme Court of the Philippines, 26 October 1951), following *Borovsky v Commissioner of Immigration*, GR No L-4352, 47 Off Gaz 136 (28 September 1951); and *Boris Mejoff v Director of Prisons*, GR No L-4254, 47 Off Gaz 177 (26 September 1951).

[193] *Boris Mejoff* (ibid).

the stateless condition of a spouse and consequently render a legislated nationality law inoperative.[194]

C. Expulsion

Expulsion, as we saw in chapter three, is another consequence of de jure statelessness. Enquiry into expulsion directives by state executives has also accompanied the emergence of the concept of effective nationality.[195]

D. Denial of Entry and Restriction of Internal Movement

As another consequence of de jure statelessness, states have claimed authority to deny re-entry to stateless persons. Chapter three raised the importance of this consequence regarding Palestinian stateless persons in Kuwait. However, as the UK Court of Appeal stated in *MA (Ethiopia)* (2009), if a natural person is 'arbitrarily refused' the right of return for a Convention reason, 'one of the most fundamental rights attached to nationality, namely the right to live in the home country and all that goes with that, is denied'.[196] And as a New Zealand tribunal has affirmed, when stateless persons have been tortured in their state of habitation, 'no exceptions are permitted to the prohibition against refoulement'.[197] Although the mere crossing of a territorial border does not necessarily signify that a stateless person is a refugee,[198] the conditions attached to the refugee status of a stateless person may hinge upon the extent to which the individual's social relationships with a spouse, social groups, employers, government officials and others constitute a basis for the applicant's fear of persecution.[199] A lack of documentation of a legal departure from the territory of habitual residence may cause an applicant to fear persecution if s/he were to return to the territory. Such persecution may involve

---

[194] *Commonwealth of the Philippines v Gloria Baldello* (Sup Ct Philippines, 12 April 1939), GR No L-45375.

[195] *Zl v Prosecutor-General, Final Judgment*, Case No C.07.0385.Fs, ILDC 1113 (Belgium, 6 June 2008). See also *Tijdschrift voor Vreemdelingrnrecht*, Nr C.06.0390.N (Court of Cassation, 27 September 2007), 2 and 134, as discussed by Michèle Morel in *Zl* (A7).

[196] *MA (Ethiopia)* (above n 149) para 60.

[197] *Ahmed Zaoui A-G v Ahmed Zaoui*, SC Civ 19/2004, [2005] NZSC 38, para 33, following UNHCR, 'Summary Conclusions: The Principle of *Non-Refoulement*' in E Feller, V Türk and F Nicholson (eds), *Refugee Protection in International Law: Global Consultations on International Protection* (Cambridge, Cambridge University Press, 2003) 179.

[198] *Case No 0805551* [2009] RRTA 24, para 56. See also *SHM v Refugee Appeals Tribunal and Ministry for Justice, Equality and Law Reform* [2009] IEHR 128, paras 41, 45 (High Ct Ireland); and *Revenko v Secretary of State for the Home Department* [2001] QB 601.

[199] *Case No 0908370* (above n 85); *Case No 1001150* (above n 159); *Case No 0905729* [2009] RRTA 981 (28 September 2009); and *Case No 071814262* [2008] RRTA 12. See also *SHM* (ibid) para 45.

severely diminished employment opportunities and lack of access to public education for one's children as a result of not having proper documentation, as well as detention and expulsion. Such factors contribute to the categorization of refugees in states of refuge. It is a 'coincidence', to use Grotius' term, that any one internment or refugee camp happens to be on territory owned by this or that state.

Social relations as legal bond have been applied to issues of security throughout a state's borders, including the right to move freely within its territorial borders.[200] As such, a stateless refugee applicant should not be expected to move to the territory of another state. Conversely, a state is obligated to move a stateless person to a part of its territory where the fear of persecution does not exist for that person.[201] Moreover, a succeeding state is obligated to recognize as its own national anyone who would otherwise become stateless.[202]

In like vein, the shift in discourse from an international community composed of the aggregated wills of state to the international community as a whole has meant that unlimited state discretion over diplomatic protection is no longer an 'accurate position', according to the ILC.[203] The crucial issue is whether a state has offered effective protection to its nationals.[204] More generally, state discretion is limited.[205] Diplomatic protection must extend to any stateless person 'who, at the date of injury and at the date of the official presentation of the claim, is lawfully and habitually resident in that state'.[206] Further, just because there is some limit to a state's discretion to diplomatically protect stateless persons, this 'is *not* concerned with the conferment of nationality upon such persons'.[207] The state's obligation to diplomatically protect a stateless person is owed 'regardless of how he or she became stateless'.[208]

---

[200] *SZATV v Minister for Immigration and Citizenship & Anor* [2007] HCA 40, para 64 (per Kirby).

[201] Ibid, para 65. However, see Kirby's response to this condition at para 78. Callihan of the Australian High Court has gone so far as to assert in *SZATV* that a person might reasonably be expected to refrain from voicing her/his political opinions wherever she/he might live on a state's territory (para 106).

[202] *Tatishvili v Russia*, Application No 1509/02, (2007) 45 EHRR 52. See also *Yean and Bosico v Dominican Republic*, Preliminary Objections, Merits, Reparations and Costs, Ser C No 130 (Inter-Am Ct HR, 8 September 2005); and EJ Féliz De Jesús, 'Analysis: *Servicio Jesuita a refugiados y Migrantes and Others v Dominican Republic*', Direct Constitutional Complaint Procedure, BJ 1141.77, ILDC 1075 (DO 2005), Oxford Reports on International Law in Domestic Courts.

[203] ILC, 'Draft Articles on Diplomatic Protection' (above n 20) Art 8 (Comms 1 and 2).

[204] *Al-Anezi v Minister for Immigration & Multicultural Affairs* [1999] FCA 355, paras 12–15.

[205] See *SRPP v Minister for Immigration and Multicultural Affairs* [2000] AATA 878, para 110.

[206] ILC, 'Draft Articles on Diplomatic Protection' (above n 20) Art 8(1) and Art 8 (Comm 11). See also *Al Rawi et al v Secretary of State for Foreign and Commonwealth Affairs and Another* [2006] EWCA Civ 1279, para 31 (G Goodwin-Gill's opinion quoted affirmatively).

[207] ILC, 'Draft Articles on Diplomatic Protection' (above n 20) Art 8 (Comm 12).

[208] Ibid, Art 8 (Comm 3).

E. Restrictions on Political Participation

There is one final set of circumstances that has led courts and tribunals to pierce the veil of the reserved domain in an effort to ascertain the effective nationality of de jure stateless persons. The issue is whether de jure stateless persons are entitled to voting rights and the right of political participation. If a natural person lacks a state's de jure nationality, it is a short step to conclude that s/he also lacks allegiance to the state as determined by the state. It is not surprising that de jure stateless persons would not risk being known to participate politically in the territory of habitual residence.

In an international community that is understood as the aggregated wills of states, the right to vote and to political participation has been left to the discretion of domestic law and state officials.[209] However, the turn to social bonding as determinative of a de jure stateless person's legal bond has refocused attention on the voting rights and political participation of de jure stateless persons. The Indian Supreme Court, for example, has stated that the discretion of the state in such matters is suspect with regard to effective nationals who have been denied political participation for a substantial period of time.[210] To that end, the Philippine Supreme Court has required that de jure stateless persons be put on voters' rolls.[211]

VII. CONCLUSION

The condition of de jure statelessness hinges upon the absence of nationality 'under the operation of [a state's] law'. Two very different international law discourses have privileged two very different senses of legal bond.

---

[209] For an example of such rights being interpreted as within the purview of the reserved domain, see *Mercado* (above n 35); *Frivaldo* (above n 112); *Valles v Commission on Elections & Lopez*, GR No 137000, [2000] PHSC 870 (9 August 2000); and *Md Sadaqat Khan (Fakku) and Others v Chief Election Commissioner, Bangladesh Election Commission*, Writ Petition No 10129 of 2007 (Bangladesh Sup Ct, 18 May 2008), www.unhcr.org/refworld/docid/4a7c0c352.html. See also *Abid Khan and Others v Government of Bangladesh and Others*, Writ Petition No 3831 of 2001 (Bangladesh Sup Ct, 5 May 2003), www.unhcr.org/refworld/docid/4a54bbcf0.html; US Bureau of Citizenship and Immigration Services, 'India: Information on Tibetan Refugees and Settlements' (30 May 2003), www.refworld.org/docid/3f51f90821.html; *National Human Rights Commission v State of Arunchal Pradesh* (1996) SCC (1) 742; Equal Rights Trust, 'Trapped in a Cycle of Flight: Stateless Rohingya in Malaysia' (January 2010), www.equalrightstrust.org/ertdocumentbank/ERTMalaysiaReportFinal.pdf.

[210] *People's Union for Civil Liberties & Committee for Citizenship Rights of the Chakmas of Arunachal Pradesh through its President v Sh GyaliTaji et al*, 'Civil Contempt Petition No 537' (High Ct of Delhi, 2001). See also *Gangadhar Yeshwant Bhandare v Erasmo de Jesus Sequiria* (1975) AIR SC 972; and *The Rights of the Chakmas of Arunachal Pradesh through its President v Sh GyaliTaji et al*, 'Civil Contempt Petition No 537' (High Ct of Delhi, 2001).

[211] *Frivaldo* (above n 112). The Court concluded that the applicant should be put on the voter roll even though he lacked Philippine nationality. See also *Raul R Lee v Commission of Elections*, GR No 123755 (Sup Ct of the Philippines, 28 June 1996) per Panganiban.

The one entails allegiance. Each state has taken upon itself to decide whether a natural person possesses or is likely to possess loyalty to the state. But nationality, we can now appreciate, signifies the legal bond that took form with the development of the modern state. Jurists of the early modern state highlighted sociality as the generating and justifying referent of a legal bond: in exchange for allegiance, a state undertook to protect its nationals. Such sociality has been signified in the discourse as 'effective', 'vital' or 'genuine' nationality. Nationality has been posited by domestically enacted and administered laws, and yet such laws have lacked compelling character when stateless persons are involved.

Effective nationality addresses a different question than the traditional project of identifying a discrete right associated with allegiance. Most importantly, why is a state obligated to protect a person if the person lacks de jure nationality? Similarly, is a state obligated to protect a person who has de jure nationality but is effectively stateless? The answer revolves around our understanding of 'law'. One can identify a law by turning to the institutional sources of the state's reserved domain.[212] Such a sources approach is content-independent.[213] On the other hand, the legal bond as social bonding addresses the social relationships heretofore immunized from external scrutiny.

In the classical theory of international law – in which nationality is an incident of the reserved domain of the state – jurists are satisfied by identifying the rules enacted and administered inside the boundary of the reserved domain. There is a sense of legal obligation underlying such a view of 'law'. Legal obligation here exists by virtue of a state's implied consent. The reserved domain of the state represents such implied consent. Such a view of legal obligation, however, is misdirected once one attends to social relationships as inside the content of the internal jurisdiction. Something different is required than a quest for the identity of a law in the reserved domain.[214] Put differently, jurists are compelled to ask why the inner freedom of the state to determine nationality, which is justified and protected by the legal bond of allegiance in the international community, must be accepted as an exclusionary rule when the enigma of the international community remains.

In particular, the second inquiry – why is an identifiable law of the state obligatory of states? – has been addressed in terms of two possibilities. The one concerns the allegiance of natural persons to states. Mindful of

---

[212] This distinction is emphasized and elaborated in J Raz, 'Authority, Law, and Morality' in J Raz, *Ethics in the Public Domain: Essays in the Morality of Law and Politics* (Oxford, Oxford University Press, 1994).

[213] See HLA Hart, 'Commands and Authoritative Legal Reasons' in J Raz (ed), *Authority* (New York, New York University Press, 1990) 101–2.

[214] M Nowak, *UN Covenant on Civil and Political Rights: Commentary* (Strasbourg, NP Engel, 1993) 171. A concern is exemplified in ILC, 'Draft Articles on State Responsibility' (above n 1) Art 26 (Comm 6) and Art 33 (Comm 3).

Socrates' 'Speech of the Laws' in the *Crito* and the social contract jurists of the seventeenth and eighteenth centuries, we can see that a natural person's voluntary choice of her/his state of nationality functions to explain why the state's laws are binding. And mindful of Jeremy Bentham and John Austin of the nineteenth century, we can see that legal obligation follows on merely from the populace's habit of obedience.[215] The habit of obedience hardly offers a concrete and clear basis of guidance in nationality concerns.

That said, prioritizing allegiance means taking the state for granted as the referent for the binding character of identifiable laws. And the state is presupposed to be a self-generating and self-determining author. As such, the state claims its own authority. Once allegiance is established, a national is recognized as a legal person in a state-centric international legal order. The national's interest may be represented against another state that has caused harm to the national. So long as an identifiable right is obligatory by virtue of allegiance, there will be natural persons whose choice of nationality lacks a reciprocal recognition by the state of choice. Alternatively, there will be natural persons whose habits are not included in the obedience to the state's institutions. The absence of blood relations or of birth records on the state's territory risks the exclusion of some inhabitants as to whether allegiance exists in this rather than that state.

In contrast, the legal bond as social bonding exists independent of states. 'Effective nationality', the term coined for such social bonding, concerns the relation of one natural person with other natural persons. One may possess an identifiable right to nationality according to some treaty or customary international legal norm, and yet the right may not possess a corresponding obligation on the part of a state because the state possesses internal jurisdiction, incorporated into the international community as its residuary, to decide over all objects and persons inside its territorial border. Conversely, a natural person may lack an identifiable right, and yet the state is bound to recognize the person as a legal person. Indeed, the state's domestic laws are binding only by virtue of social relationships independent of both domestic and international laws. This question of the obligatory character of an identifiable law requires an examination of the social relationships presupposed in the otherwise content-independent reserved domain.

Effective nationality as the second sense of legal bond emerged alongside the sense of legal bond as allegiance. Indeed, allegiance really took form as determinative of nationality during the late nineteenth century, in contrast to the focus on social bonding in the juristic studies of the early modern state. This second sense of legal bond opens an enquiry into the

---

[215] This is documented and explained in Conklin, *Invisible Origins* (above n 16) 145–51 and 158–59.

assumptions and expectations of each stateless person. Collective and personal memories, expectations about the state of habitation, statistical evidence and other indicia factor into the scrutiny of a stateless person's social bonding. The factors concern the content of 'the operation of [a state'] law', which has hitherto been protected as an incident of the reserved domain.

What is critical is that the enquiry into the obligatory character of particular laws no longer hinges upon the incident of nationality in the reserved domain of a state. A radically different sense of 'lawfulness' goes hand in hand with social bonding. The obvious problem, addressed in the next chapter, is this: if a natural person lacks nationality conferred by a state, is it possible for such a person to have a country? Conversely, if a natural person experiences social bonding which happens to take place on this territory rather than that territory, does a state that 'by coincidence' owns that territory also owe a legal obligation to protect the social relationships of such a person?

7

Does a Stateless Person have a Country?

T HE PREVIOUS CHAPTER introduced the prospect of two very different senses of a legal bond between a natural person and the international community. One sense of a legal bond hinges upon the allegiance of a person to a state. Against the background of an international community that protects a bounded reserved domain of law-making and law administration for states, it is left to a state to determine whether a natural person owes allegiance toward that state. If so determined affirmatively, the state's institutions constitute the source of law in an international community. The second sense of a legal bond depends upon the place where a natural person has experienced social relationships. This idea of 'place' is not synonymous with territory. A place itself is experienced rather than measured as if a spot on a map. One may possess personal and collective memories as well as present experiences through friendships, schools and religious organizations, as well as through relationships with family members, fellow workers and the like. Such experiences are usually associated with a *place* rather than a physical territorial space.[1] Accordingly, one may experience several different places as an effective national, in contrast with de jure nationality, which presupposes one's allegiance to a single fixed territory with a defined border – namely, a state. With the second sense of a legal bond, the bond exists independent of states.

Given the two very different senses of a legal bond and the two corresponding senses of an international community, the traditional approach to analysing international law adjudication and arbitration decisions is misdirected. Traditionally, such analysis has justified a decision by following or distinguishing the rationale of one source from earlier rationales of

[1] See generally, ES Casey, *Getting Back into Place: Toward a Renewed Understanding of the Place-World*, 2nd edn (Bloomington, Indiana University Press, 2009); M Merleau-Ponty, *Phenomenology of Perception*, C Smith (trans) (London, Routledge & Kegan Paul, 1962); and HL Lefebvre, 'Space and the State' in HL Lefebrve, *State Space World: Selected Essays*, N Brenner and S Elden (eds), G Moore, N Brenner and S Elden (trans) (Minneapolis, University of Minnesota Press, 2009) 223–53. The notion of legal space is briefly elaborated in WE Conklin, 'A Phenomenological Theory of the Human Rights of the Alien' (2006) 13 *Ethical Perspectives* 245, 261–72.

such a source or some higher-ordered source.[2] The source functions as the referent of justification. At some point the analysis may lead to a recognition that the linear direction of analysis has taken a turn in any particular ratiocination process. What I wish to emphasize is that when we concentrate upon the nature of legal obligation rather than the identity of a source justifying this or that ratio, or this or that material category of facts, what is really at stake are two very different international law discourses. The one discourse is not 'real' and the other an 'ought'. Both are real. Both presuppose a particular sense of a legal bond between a natural person and the laws of an international community. The legal bond, however, radically differs in the two discourses. The two discourses, the one inside the other, struggle to be the determinative context for the recognition and enforceability of human rights. The inner discourse, which was examined above in chapters one and six, can be traced to the early nineteenth century.

The reality of two very different senses of international law discourse characterizes how statelessness has been addressed in various contexts. This chapter highlights one such discursive context: namely, the discourse about the identity of 'one's own country'. This term, 'one's own country', is raised in several bilateral and multilateral treaties.[3] Several rights flow from having a country. The UN Human Rights Committee (HRC) in its 'General Comment 27' on the International Covenant on Civil and Political Rights (ICCPR) (1966) has identified several such rights: the entry of a non-national into a state's territory (paragraph 4); the right to move from place to place within the territorial border of a state (paragraph 5); protection against forms of internal displacement (paragraph 7); the right to enter or remain in a defined territorial part of a state's territory (para-

---

[2] Of course, the analytic method is far more complex than that. See, eg, HLA Hart, *The Concept of Law*, 3rd edn (Oxford, Oxford University Press, 2012) vi–vii, 239–44; R Dworkin, *Law's Empire* (Cambridge, MA, Harvard University Press, 1986) 65–73, 87–94; Dworkin, *Justice for Hedgehogs* (Cambridge: Harvard University Press, 2011) 6–11, 23–28; S Perry, 'Hart's Methodological Positivism' in J Coleman (ed), *Hart's Postscript: Essays on the Postscript of Hart's Concept of Law* (Oxford, Oxford University Press, 2001) 311–54; J Raz, *Practical Reason and Norms*, 2nd edn (Princeton, Princeton University Press, 1990); L Alexander and E Sherwin, *Demystifying Legal Reasoning* (Cambridge, Cambridge University Press, 2008); J Derrida, 'The Force of Law: The "Mystical Foundation of Authority"' in J Derrida, *Acts of Religion* (New York, Routledge, 2002) 228–98.

[3] Universal Declaration of Human Rights (UDHR) (1948), GAQ Res 217 (lll), UN Doc A/Res/217(lll) (entered into force 10 December 1948), Art 13(2); International Covenant on Civil and Political Rights (ICCPR) (1966), 999 UNTS 171 (entered into force 23 March 1976), Art 12(4); International Convention on the Rights of Persons with Disabilities (2006), 2515 UNTS 3 (entered into force 3 May 2008), Art 18(1)(c)(d); Protocol No 4 to the European Convention for the Protection of Human Rights and Fundamental Freedoms, ETS 46, (entered into force 2 May 1968), Art 2(2); and the American Convention on Human Rights (1969), OAS Off Rec OEA/Ser.L./V/11.23 doc.rev.2, 36 OASTS 1 (entered into force 19 July 1978), Art 22(2). Art 6(4) of the African Charter on the Rights and Welfare of the Child (1990), OAU Doc CAB/LEG/24.9/49 (entered into force 29 November 1999), reprinted in (1994) *African Yearbook of International Law* 295, associates a child's country as the state of birth.

graph 7); the right of women from private interference with a woman's right to move and choose freely her place of residence independent of the decision of another person, including her relative (paragraph 6); and the right to acquire de jure nationality (paragraph 20).[4]

Such treaties and doctrinal analyses make one of two possible assumptions: 'one's own country' is the state to which one owes allegiance; one's own country is the territory where one is habitually resident. In chapters three and six, I discussed the legal and social consequences of both such assumptions. Such consequences encumber such contexts as the withdrawal or withholding of nationality, state succession (the cession of territory, conquest and annexation), state responsibility and the discrimination enveloping the administrative registration of nationals. Rather than relating the legal bond to a state institution that identifies whether a natural person possesses allegiance to the state, the issue of the nature of legal obligation asks very different issues. Various approaches have been taken towards the nature of legal obligation.[5]

What I am suggesting is that in interpreting 'one's own country' and in resolving whether a de jure or effectively stateless person has such a country, there have emerged two discourses, each struggling to displace the other. The association of the right to remain in 'one's own country' identified by Article 12(4) of the ICCPR has exemplified such a struggle. In the one discourse, 'one's own country' has been determined as the state where one has been conferred nationality.[6] In the other, 'one's own country' has been determined by the place where one has experienced social bonding with other natural persons. The latter attitude towards the identity of 'one's own country' is independent of the state. It is also separate from the issue of whether any state has conferred nationality on the individual. Here, the legal obligation of a state to protect a de jure or effectively state-

---

[4] Human Rights Committee (HRC), ('CCPR General Comment 27: Article 12 (Freedom of Movement)' (2 November 1999), www.refworld.org/docid/45139c394.html, reprinted in UN, *Human Rights Instruments, Volume 1: Compilation of General Comments and General Recommendations Adopted by Human Rights Treaty Bodies*, HRI/GEN/1/Rev.9 (27 May 2008), www.un.org/en/ga/search/view_doc.asp?symbol=HRI/GEN/1/Rev.9.

[5] I examine how legal obligation plays into the identity of an international community below ch 9 and Conclusion. For different views of legal obligation, see, eg, J Tasioulas, 'The Legitimacy of International Law' in S Besson and J Tasioulas (eds), *Philosophy of International Law* (Oxford, Oxford University Press, 2010) 97–116; D Luban, 'Fairness to Rightness: Jurisdiction, Legality, and the Legitimacy of International Criminal Law' in Besson and Tasioulas (eds) (above) 569–88; A Duff, 'Authority and Responsibility in International Criminal Law' in Besson and Tasioulas (eds) (above) 589–604; and F Mégret, 'From "Savages" to "Unlawful Combatants": A Postcolonial Look at International Humanitarian Law's "Other"' in A Orford (ed), *International Law and its Others* (Cambridge, Cambridge University Press, 2012) 265–317.

[6] See, eg, *Canepa v Canada*, HRC Communication No 558/1993, UN Doc CCPR/C/59/D/558/1993 (1997), para 11.3. Canada cautioned against considering 'one's own country' as other than one's state of nationality as such would 'seriously erode' its sovereignty: para 9.2. See also *Madafferi v Australia*, HRC Communication No 1011/2001, UN Doc CCPR/C/81/D/1011/2001 (2004), para 9.6.

less person pursuant to Article 12(4) of the ICCPR depends upon the social bonding of an applicant vis-à-vis others, independent of the state. The issue is not one of searching for the latest or 'highest' 'source' of law in a linearly directed analysis of rules and tests. Rather, the issue links legal obligation to the very nature of an international community. Such an international community is not pronounced because of the community's reserved domain for law-making and law administration. Nationality is considered an incident of such a community. As a prelude to chapter nine and to my Conclusion chapter, let me point out now that such an international community exists independent of states, and it does so because the basis of legal obligation is the social bonding of natural persons. 'One's own country', as a requisite for an entitlement to legal protection for de jure and effectively stateless persons, invites a retrieval of the inner discourse about the legal character of such social relationships.

I. HABITUAL RESIDENCE

It is apparent from the previous chapters that the enigma of an international community remains if 'the operation of its law' – the criterion for de jure nationality in Article 1 of the Convention Relating to the Status of Stateless Persons (1954) – is associated with a bounded reserved domain for the state. The enigma also remains, however, if habitual residence is taken as the criterion of 'one's own country'.[7] Recent demographic changes due to migration and internal displacement, documented above in the Introduction to this book and in chapter three, undermine the expectation that habitual residence is a realistic basis for determining the experienced place of 'one's own country'. And so, for example, the UK Court of Appeal has read the judgment of the International Court of Justice in *Wall* as categorizing stateless Palestinians as 'somewhere in between persons who have rights of citizenship at one end of the spectrum and stateless habitual residents of a territory who have no rights at the other'.[8] In addition, a stateless person's right to de jure nationality has sometimes been considered an aspiration, if habitual residence is considered the 'hard reality' of legal identity.[9] More generally, the question of

---

[7] See, eg, *HS v Secretary of State for the Home Department* [2011] UKUT 124 (IAC), para 178, affirming *Expatriate Civil Servants of Hong Kong v Secretary for the Civil Service* [1995] 5 HKPLR 490. See also *D Mansouri-Rad v Minister of Labour* (NZ Refugee Status Appeals Authority, 19 May 2009) Refugee Appeal No 76077, para 92, affirming *Refugee Appeal No 72635* (6 September 2002); and I Sipkov, 'Introduction Note' (1987) 26 *International Legal Materials* 422, 424. However, see I Sipkov, 'Introductory Note' (1990) 29 *International Legal Materials* 538, 539.

[8] *MT (Palestinian Territories) v Secretary of State for the Home Department* [2008] EWCA Civ 1149 (22 December 2008) para 20, citing para 78 of *Legal Consequences of the Construction of a Wall in the Occupied Palestinian Territory* (Advisory Opinion), (2004) ICJ Reports 136, 199.

[9] See, eg, *Mansouri-Rad v Minister of Labour* (above n 7).

habitual residence has also left legal analysis opaque. How long, for example, does it take for residence to become habitual? How do we account for the exclusion of nomadic and traveller groups or the continued risk of the withdrawal of nationality? What if there is not a perfect fit between a state's border and the habitual residents of its territory, and what if a person is unable to return to her/his state of habitual residence?

Despite such problems, habitual residence can be understood as one *indicium* for something other than a state's recognition of a natural person's allegiance to the state: namely, the likelihood of a social bond with others. As long as a state's institutions or officials are free to determine who owes allegiance, any internationally recognized 'right' to nationality merely supplements the prior freedom of a state's officials to choose its nationals. The consequences of statelessness, however, raise a very different issue: namely, why is a state's choice obligatory in an international community? And that issue brings the obligatory character of the reserved domain and the laws of that domain into question. The basis of legal obligation in an international community's laws may well be the social relationships amongst natural persons. Such a social bonding exists independent of a state's determination of its de jure nationals. An individual's habitual residence may not adequately cover the place where one has experienced her/his social relationships.

II. ONE'S OWN COUNTRY AS THE PLACE OF ONE'S SOCIAL BONDING

Let us take an example of how the place of a person's social relationships has factored into a tribunal's understanding of the individual's country. In the HCR case *Stewart v Canada* (1993), the applicant had been born in the United Kingdom.[10] Stewart's claim, however, was that his country was Canada, not the United Kingdom. The issue was important, according to Stewart, because Article 12(4) of the ICCPR provides that 'no one shall be arbitrarily deprived of the right to enter his own country'. Stewart's country, according to the Committee, was Canada because of his having experienced 'special ties to or claims': he had lived in Canada for thirty years (since the age of seven), although he had never become a Canadian citizen. His familial and social relationships had been experienced on Canadian territory, not on UK territory. He had been raised in Canada, married in Canada, had two children in Canada, and had a mother and disabled brother who lived in Canada.

The Canadian Government perceived Stewart's social attachments in a

---

[10] *Stewart v Canada*, HRC Communication No 538/1993, UN Doc CCPR/C/58/D/538/1993 (1996), 115 ILR 318, www1.umn.edu/humanrts/undocs/538-1993.html.

different light. He had been convicted of 42 crimes in Canada, largely for petty and traffic offences, although he was also convicted for assaulting his girlfriend. The Canadian government proceeded to deport the complainant to the United Kingdom. From the standpoint of the Canadian government, Stewart's nationality was attached to the United Kingdom, where he was born. The UK government had conferred nationality on Stewart. The *soli* ('birth') criterion governed UK nationality policy, and Stewart's 'own country' was therefore the United Kingdom, according to the Canadian government. Accordingly, he was considered an alien on Canadian territory (with all the legal, social and economic consequences of effective statelessness). This was so even though he was socially bonded with others on Canadian territory (paragraph 5.1).

A majority of eight Committee members held that there was no a priori reason why Stewart's country could not be considered his adopted Canada. Although Canadian state officials considered that the extent of Stewart's family bond with others in Canada over a period of years was material, they believed they possessed the legal authority to deport him to Scotland, as they considered that Canada could not be his country. However, the Majority of the Committee opined that 'one's own country' is wider in scope than 'the country of nationality' (paragraph 12.3). Taking a cue from the wording of Article 13 ('an alien lawfully in the territory of a state party'), the Committee determined that 'his own country' was not limited to the state where the applicant had de jure nationality; nor was it limited to 'aliens' within the signification of Article 13. Someone who has 'special ties or claims in relation to a given country' is not a 'mere alien' (paragraph 12.4). The Committee especially highlighted someone as having 'his own country' if he has been denaturalized against international standards or if a succeeding state has denied nationality to the individual. In sum, the notion of 'one's own country' permits a 'broader interpretation' to include a stateless person 'arbitrarily deprived of the right to acquire a nationality' (paragraph 12.4). A state's bad faith, unreasonable action and arbitrariness are said to factor into the resolution of such an issue (paragraph 12.5). Despite the broad interpretation of 'one's own country', the Majority nonetheless fell back upon the blameworthiness of Stewart, which was of 'his own making': namely, his failure to apply for naturalization from Canada (paras 12.7 and 12.8).

Both majority and dissenting opinions in *Stewart* suggest a departure from a strict association of one's country with the state of de jure nationality. In his separate but concurring opinion, Laurel Francis suggested that non-nationals are protected even if they have been illegally resident on a territory (paragraph 2). It is not a treaty provision such as Article 12(4)) that justifies the protection of a natural person but rather the social relationships the person has experienced independent of whether this or that state claims that s/he has been on its territory contrary to the state's domestic laws. This point was extended by the dissenting opinion of Elizabeth Evatt, Cecilia Medina Quiroga and Francisco José Aguilar Urbina into a full theory of effective nationality. As the three dissenting Members pointed out, instead of 'a formal link to the state', a person has a country because of 'the web of relationships that form his or her social environment' (paragraph 5). Such a web of social relationships involves 'the strong personal and emotional links an individual may have with the territory where he lives and with the social circumstances obtaining it' (paragraph 5). The determination of nationality by a state mattered little. It was just happenstance that the Canadian state was involved. Quiroga and José were explicit:

> The words 'his own country' on the face of it invite consideration of such matters as longstanding residence, close personal and family ties and intentions to remain (as well as to the absence of such ties elsewhere). Where a person is not a citizen of the country in question, the connections would need to be strong to support a finding that it is his 'own country'. Nevertheless, our view is that it is open to an alien to show that there are such well-established links with a state that he or she is entitled to claim the protection of Article 12, paragraph 4 [of the ICCPR].[11]

Indeed, as the three dissenting Committee Members stated, one may possess nationality from two or more states 'and yet have only the slightest or no actual connections of home and family with one or more of the States in question' (paragraph 5). Accordingly, Stewart was arbitrarily prevented from being admitted to his country, which was Canada. Stewart's social life had been experienced on Canadian soil.

The *Stewart* case makes clear that social attachment to others temporally and spatially precedes de jure nationality, whether it is conferred, withheld or withdrawn by a state. It is precisely because of this temporal and spatial existence condition of a domestic or international legal order that the HRC concluded 'General Comment 27' by stating:

> The scope of 'his own country' is broader than the concept 'country of his nationality'. It is not limited to nationality in a formal sense, that is, nationality acquired at birth or by conferral; it embraces, at the very least, an individual who, *because of his or her special ties to or claims in relation to a given country*, cannot be considered to be a mere alien.[12]

The 'special ties', I suggest, are to other social beings and only indirectly to the state as a third party to such social relationships. 'General Comment 27' continues that such special ties generate the recognition of denaturalized persons as well as persons rendered de jure stateless as a consequence of the succession of states. The 'special ties' extend the recognition of

---

[11] Ibid, Appendix III, para 6.
[12] HRC, 'General Comment 27' (above n 4) para 20, emphasis added.

'one's own country' to 'other categories of long-term residents, including but not limited to stateless persons arbitrarily deprived of the right to acquire the nationality of the country of such residence' (paragraph 20). Significantly, the General Comment distinguishes the special social ties between natural persons from the relationship of a natural person to a state. In particular, the special ties are prior in time and space and prior analytically to a person's relationship with a state: the special social ties may as a matter of course eventually also result in 'the establishment of close and enduring connections between a person and a county'. The social bonding amongst natural persons hence constitutes an existence condition of the legal order. And unless jurists address such social bonding, one may conclude as Rudolf Dolzer did in the *Encyclopaedia of Public International Law* (1987) that the focus upon the rights of a state to the exclusion of the rights of a natural person then the very foundation of the legal order is undermined.[13]

The sorts of factors embodying the social connection between an applicant and other persons on this or that territory have been reaffirmed and analytically examined in two recent decisions of the Human Rights Committee. Both decisions relied heavily upon the displacement of the state's authority to confer nationality in favour of social bonding as the basis of an effectively stateless person having a country. The Committee explicitly followed 'General Comment 27' with regard to social bonding and the identity of 'one's own country'.[14] In the *Warsame* case (2011), the Canadian state had expelled the applicant to the state of his birth (Somalia), despite the fact that the applicant had left the latter state at the age of four and had never returned, could not speak the language of the state nor the local language, lacked an extended family there and lacked any support of friendships there.[15] In contrast and with respect to the applicant's 'own country' of Canada, his social bonding was embodied by his close ties with his sisters and mother, his Canadian education and his felt identity with Canada. Along the same lines, in the *Nystrom* decision (2011), the Committee focused on similar indicia of the applicant's social bonding in Australia and the lack of such bonds in the state to which he was deported (Sweden).[16] The applicant believed Australia to be his own country, he had lived there throughout his life, his mother even believed that he was an Australian citizen, and his departure 'caused great emotional distress to the family which [was] irreparably and indefinitely disrupted'. Upon arrival in Sweden, he lacked Swedish language skills,

---

[13] R Dolzer, 'Diplomatic Protection and Foreign Nationals' in R Bernhardt (ed), *Encyclopaedia of Public International Law*, vol 2 (Amsterdam, Elsevier, 1992–2000) 1067–70.

[14] *Jama Warsame v Canada*, HRC Communication No 1959/2010, UN Doc CCPR/C/102/D/1959/2010 (2011), para 8.4; and *Nystrom, Nystrom & Turner v Australia*, HRC Communication No 1557/2007, UN Doc CCPR/C/102/D/1557/2007 (2011), para 3.2.

[15] *Warsame v Canada* (ibid).

[16] *Nystrom v Australia* (above n 14).

social assistance and governmental support.

Let us look more closely at the relationship between social bonding and the determination by a state as to the identity of one's own country. The point I wish to emphasize is that the HRC has been recognizing the priority of social bonding vis-à-vis the state's formal determination of one's nationality (or lack thereof). Such has been an analytic priority as well as an experiential phenomenon. For example, the Committee's decision in *Canepa v Canada* (1993) reaffirmed such priority as crucial for identifying one's own country.[17] With such a priority, a stateless person may suddenly appear to have a country after all. Such a 'country' exists independent of any claim of title to a state's territory or to territorial jurisdiction. And the bounded reserved domain of an international community is no longer taken for granted as the condition of the international community.

Although the majority opinion in *Canepa* raised the issue as to whether one's own country is synonymous with a state's conferral of formal nationality, Martin Sheinin, dissenting, added that a state's expulsion of an individual, authorized by domestic law, does not determine the legality of the expulsion. Rather, again, the individual's social bonding with others analytically and anthropologically precedes a state's or international tribunal's categorization of the legality or illegality of an individual's actions. As such, effective nationality as social bonding determines lawfulness. So too, such social bonding might well justify an individual's right to return to the territory. The sharing of a language manifests such social bonding. One's friendships similarly exist independent of a state's will and independent of one's territory of habitual residence. In sum, according to Sheinin, 'It would be impossible or clearly unreasonable for him or her to integrate into the society corresponding to his or her *de jure* nationality.'[18] Elizabeth Evatt and Cecilia Medina Quiroga, again dissenting in *Canepa*, added that 'there are factors other than nationality which must establish *close and enduring connections* between a person and a country'.[19] Christine Chanet, also dissenting, continued that 'one's own country' is hardly synonymous with a state's de jure conferral of nationality onto an individual; the best that one can say is that one's country is a 'geographical place *whose content and boundaries are less precise*'.[20]

Notably, the connection between social bonding and the identity of one's own country helps to explain why de jure stateless persons are entitled to human rights. I have argued in earlier chapters that human rights have been co-opted into the legal prerogative of states because of the special domain reserved by an international community. Because nationality

[17] *Canepa v Canada* (above n 6).
[18] Ibid.
[19] Ibid, emphasis added.
[20] Ibid, emphasis added.

has been considered an incident of such a reserved domain, one's own country and human rights more generally have often been thought to rest in the legal authority of the state where one has nationality. Since it is possible to lack such nationality, the universality of human rights has been suspect. Now, however, in the same way that effective nationality and effective statelessness can be seen to emerge from an inner discourse whereby the legal bond is nested in one's social relationships, so too such social relationships can be seen to determine the identity of a de jure or effectively stateless person's country. As noted above, a chain of rights has accompanied such identification.

To take an example, *Celepli v Sweden* (1994) has made clear that when a person's country can be determined by his/her social bonding with others, then that person possesses freedom of movement on the territory.[21] One's effective nationality, that is, determines the identity of one's own country and the freedom to move inside the country's borders.

López Burgos v Uruguay (1981) had earlier developed this point. In that case, the state of Uruguay had arrested Burgos and detained him without charge for four months in 1974 due to his trade union activities. Upon release, Burgos moved to Argentina. Aided by Argentine paramilitary groups, the secret service of Uruguay kidnapped Burgos at the Buenos Aires airport and clandestinely transported him to Uruguay, where he was detained incommunicado, tortured and subject to cruel treatment by Uruguayan security forces at a secret prison for three months. The issue concerned whether the HRC had jurisdiction to ensure ICCPR rights for Burgos. Uruguay claimed the HRC had no jurisdiction because Burgos had been on territory controlled by Argentina, while the complaint involved alleged harm done by Uruguay. The issue arose because Article 2(1) of the ICCPR and Article 1 of the Optional Protocol appeared to bar Burgos' spouse from making a complaint to the HRC: 'Each State Party to the present Covenant undertakes to respect and to ensure to all individuals within its territory and subject to its jurisdiction, the rights recognized in the present Covenant . . .' (Article 2(1)). Article 1 of the Optional Protocol to the ICCPR states, 'A State Party to the Covenant that becomes a party to the present Protocol recognizes the competence of the Committee to receive and consider communications from *individuals subject to its jurisdiction* who claim to be victims of a violation by that State Party of any rights set forth in the Covenant'.[22]

The HRC stated that what determined its jurisdiction over Uruguay was 'not the place where the violation occurred [Argentina], but rather the relationship between the individual and the state [Uruguay] in relation to a violation of any of the rights set forth in the Covenant, wherever

---

[21] *Celepli v Sweden*, HRC Communication No 456/1991, UN Doc CCPR/C/51/D/456/1991 (1994).
[22] Emphasis added.

they occurred'.[23] In other words, the human rights protected by the ICCPR exist independent of territorial control by Uruguay. Therefore, Uruguay had a legal obligation to protect Burgos that was independent of Burgos' legal status as a political refugee and independent of any of Uruguay's domestic laws that might have authorized his arrest and detention.

A further example of the association of one's own country with effective nationality can be seen in the HRC decision *El-Megreisi* (1994).[24] The applicant, residing in the United Kingdom, addressed the HRC on behalf of his brother, a stateless person of Libyan origin who had been kidnapped by the Libyan secret police, detained without charge, held incommunicado in a location unknown to his family and allegedly tortured. After three years, his wife was finally allowed to visit him. He was informed that there were no charges against him, since his detention was described by Libyan authorities as mere 'routine'. The HRC claimed authority to consider his complaint, holding that El-Megreisi had been subjected to arbitrary arrest and detention, contrary to Article 9 of the ICCPR.[25] Furthermore, because he had been detained for three years, incommunicado and in a secret location, with only one visit from his wife, the Committee held that Libya had contravened the ICCPR provisions against torture and cruel and unusual treatment (Articles 7 and 10(1)).[26] This was so despite the fact that El-Megreisi had been on territory (the United Kingdom) where he had not been born and for which he had no formal travel papers.

Perhaps the most pertinent and recent example of the association of one's country with the place experienced through one's social experiences arises from *Winata and Li v Australia* (2001). Winata and Li had independently entered Australian territory with student and visitor visas.[27] The Australian state, immersed in surface discourse about the state's freedom to confer nationality as a matter inside the reserved domain of the inter-

---

[23] *López Burgos v Uruguay*, HRC Communication No 52/1979, UN Doc CCPR/C/13/D/52/1979 (1981), paras 12.2.

[24] *El-Megreisi v Libyan Arab Jamahiriya*, HRC Communication No 440/1990, UN Doc CCPR/C/50/D/44-/1990 (1994).

[25] *International Covenant on Civil and Political Rights*, adopted by General Assembly Resolution 2200A (XXI), 16 December 1966, entry into force 23 March 1976, 999 UNTS 171, Art 9(1), 'No one shall be subjected to arbitrary arrest or detention. No one shall be deprived of his liberty except on such grounds and in accordance with such procedures as are established by law' . . . (4) Anyone who is deprived of his liberty by arrest or detention shall be entitled to take proceedings before a court, in order that that court may decide without delay on the lawfulness of his detention and order his release if the detention is not lawful'. (5) Anyone who has been a victim of unlawful arrest and detention shall have an enforceable right to compensation'.

[26] Ibid, Art 7: 'No one shall be subjected to torture or to cruel, inhuman or degrading treatment or punishment . . .'. Art 10(1):'All persons deprived of their liberty shall be treated with humanity and with respect for the inherent dignity of the human person'.

[27] *Winata and Li v Australia*, HRC Communication No 930/2000, UN Doc CCPR/C/72/D/930/2000 (2001).

national community, took the surface international law discourse about formal nationality for granted. Although Winata and Li remained in Australia, married and had a child, Australia ordered the couple deported to Indonesia, where they held de jure nationality. Although their student visas to Australia had long expired, their son had been conferred Australian citizenship because he had been born in Australia and had lived there for ten years. The consequence of the parents' deportation, however, was that the family would be separated. The son, being 10 years of age, was given the choice of living in Australia alone, with periodical visits with his parents, or moving to Indonesia and losing all his social relationships with friends, teachers, religious attachments and the like. The son had never visited Indonesia; he knew no one in Indonesia and had no relatives there.[28] Relying upon Articles 17, 23 and 24(1) of the ICCPR,[29] Winata and Li held that Australia had a duty to protect the integrity of the family. Australia claimed instead that the three could still live as a family through periodic visits. Such a view, we have seen in the previous chapter, is the consequence of the traditional association of nationality with the jurisdiction of a state.

The HRC reasoned in *Winata and Li* that 'one's own country', with respect to the child, was Australia because all the child's social and cultural relationships had been experienced on Australian territory. So too, the parents' country was held to be Australia. Although the parents had remained illegally on Australian territory, they were nonetheless entitled to all the rights of freedom of movement within the territory in which they had taken up residence.

Clearly, the issue in *Winata and Li* concerned whether a person could be deported to her/his state of origin if the person had failed to comply with a residency requirement. The message of *Celepli* and 'General Comment 27', addressed above, suggests that if a person has been admitted legally into a state's territory, a change in legal status does not nullify or negate the individual's fundamental freedom of movement inside the state's territorial border.[30] Rather, the onus would appear to rest upon the state to establish why the individual lacks the protection of a human right recognized by the ICCPR. In particular, the state needs to justify why an individual's internal movement should be restricted in context-specific circumstances. Although Winata and Li, as aliens, did not possess the right to remain on the territory of a sovereign state, they could not be arbitrarily expelled from the territory.[31] And if 'substantial changes to long-settled family life

---

[28] Ibid.
[29] Articles 17 and 23 identify proscriptions against intervention into one's family as 'the natural and fundamental unit of society'. Article 24(1) proscribes forms of discrimination, including place of birth.
[30] *Celepli v Sweden* (above n 21). See also HRC, 'General Comment 27' (above n 4).
[31] HRC, 'General Comment 27' (above n 4) para 6.3.

would follow' from a deportation order, then doing so would constitute an arbitrary expulsion.[32] The parents in this case were entitled to freedom of movement within their country – this being the state that owned the territory they had inhabited as a family. If, in contrast, the Human Rights Committee had taken the territorial boundary of the state for granted, the social life of the family would have been put to the side.

In *Winata and Li* and the other HRC cases outlined above, the formal lack of de jure nationality required an enquiry into the inner, and underlying, discourse about the international community as a whole. The determinative factors of one's social relationships include one's personal memories. Winata and Li had lived their adult lives on Australian territory; and they had a 'strong and effective family life' with deep experiences of social bonding with others. Their understanding of space was not measureable by territorial borders. Nor did their understanding of time refer to entry and exit dates or the years spent on this or that territory owned by this or that state.[33] Space was an unquantifiable experiential; and time too was experiential rather than being measureable by a clock or monthly calendar. Deeply experienced social relationships, drawn from such experiential time and space, analytically precede any determination by state officials that a de jure or effective stateless person is not a member of the state.

III. CONCLUSION

De jure and effective stateless persons do have a country, contrary to the traditional association of one's country with allegiance to a state or as signified by habitual residence. The enigma of an international community remains if we take for granted that the community incorporates a reserved domain within which states are free to determine their members. In such a context, there are admittedly international standards that guide states or attempt to hold them accountable for treatment of de jure and effectively stateless persons in ways that are contrary to the standards to which the states have expressly or implicitly consented. Such standards, however, enter the discourse after a state has acted through its laws or the administration of such laws. The standards therefore supplement or at best guide the domestic laws and acts of states. One can hardly expect that a state member of an international community would act against its own self-interest in a manner undermining its freedom to choose its own members.

Immersed in a state-centric international community, analytic distinctions have refined 'the operation of law', with the referent of analysis being

---

[32] Ibid, para 7.2.
[33] See, eg, *Stewart v Canada* (above n 10) para 12.3.

the boundary of the reserved domain. We accept such a view of an international community as if it were a 'given'. This 'givenness' constrains jurists from asking why such a sense of law is obligatory. Why is a domestic law concerning nationality binding for a natural person to accept and obey? Why is a domestic law concerning nationality binding upon a state to protect its choice of members? The obligatory character of a law opens up a very different series of issues than a quest for the identity of a law in a reserved domain of the law-making and law-administering authority of the international community. Justice Fujita Tokiyasu of the Japanese Supreme Court recently expressed the point thus:

> Due to various distinctions made to distinguish people like him/her from others, irrespective of what he/she wishes or how hard he/she tries to avoid – distinctions made under the existing law to determine whether or not to grant nationality (distinction on the basis of the time of birth and distinction based on whether or not the parents are married), as well as distinction based on the factual cause, distinction based on which of his/her parents (father or mother) is a Japanese citizen, and he/she was caught in a web of these distinctions.[34]

While Justice Fujita noted that jurists traditionally avoid the web of distinctions described above by examining each criteria 'one by one', he advocated a different approach: courts possess an obligation to broadly construe legislative policy.

The notion of legal bond as social relationships offers a sense of 'one's own country' that breaks from the web of analytic methodology with which jurists are most familiar. Such a methodology identifies 'one's own country' with reference to the reserved domain of the international community of the surface international law discourse. An alternate international law discourse opens up the identity of a second sense of an international community. Inside the discourse about the reserved domain, there exists another discourse that takes for granted a radically different sense of legal bond. Domestic tribunals and courts have manifested a focus on the social bonding of individuals in relation to other natural persons. A stateless person does have a 'country' – a country based upon the place where s/he has experienced reciprocal social relationships. Such a country is not necessarily synonymous with a state's determination of the person's allegiance or the territory of the person's habitual residence. The social bonding, which just happens to occur on the territory of this or that state, impacts very directly upon what we mean by 'one's own country'. At best, the state is a third party to the social relationships that generate the legal bond. With this understanding, the international community

---

[34] *Case to seek revocation of the disposition of issuance of a written deportation order*, 2006 (Gyo-Tsu) No 135 (4 June 2008), 62(6) *Minshu* 657, www.courts.go.jp/english/judgments/text/2008.06.04-2006.-Gyo-Tsu-.No..135-111255.html, para 3 (per Justice Fujita Tokiyasu).

exists independent of states, and radically different issues now take form. A de jure or effectively stateless person does have a country, after all. Such a country is identifiable as a place experienced through one's social relationships with others.

8

The State Obligation to Protect Stateless Persons

T HE LEGAL OBLIGATION of a state to protect a de jure or effectively stateless person has been discursively tied to the boundary of the state's internal jurisdiction. This has been so for both senses of an international community in the international law discourse. With the international community understood as an aggregate of the wills of states, the boundary protects the freedom of the state to confer, withhold and withdraw the nationality of natural persons. Such a boundary took legal form as the reserved domain during the nineteenth century and reached its full discursive dominance during the 1920s and 1930s. With an understanding of the international community as a whole, the boundary dissolves in favour of the social relations of stateless persons, independent of the state's determination of those persons' allegiance to the state. By virtue of the boundary of internal jurisdiction and the incident of nationality that resides therein, the stateless condition is produced.

This chapter outlines the factors that play a role in dissolving the boundary of internal state jurisdiction. With such dissipation of the boundary, a state obligation to protect stateless persons emerges. Section I takes up the issue of legal obligation as outlined in my earlier chapters. The notion of an international community constituted from the aggregate of the wills of the state relies on two features of such a sense of legal obligation. The one is the sources thesis, which jurists have taken for granted when identifying a discrete or self-standing right or rule. The second is the state's claim to title over the territory it controls. Both features, against the background of states as self-creative authors (outlined above in chapter two), reinforce the boundary of internal jurisdiction over nationality. Section II of this chapter addresses the displacement of the territorial and territorial-like boundary of internal state jurisdiction. Here, the territoriality of the boundary of jurisdiction is being displaced in matters of international criminal law. A series of legal doctrines also render incoherent the bounded protection of a state over the conferral, withdrawal and withholding of nationality. Section III then turns to the recent role of the courts in scrutinizing the content of internal state jurisdiction as it relates to de jure and effective stateless persons.

Section IV reassesses what is signified by 'the law' or 'lawfulness', the requisite of treaty rights as well as the limitations and derogation of treaty rights in order to protect stateless persons. Section V outlines the nature of the legal obligation to protect stateless persons by drawing from the nature of a legal bond when the international community is understood as a whole.

I. LEGAL OBLIGATION AND THE AGGREGATED INTERNATIONAL COMMUNITY

The residuary of the international community as aggregated from the wills of states has taken the sources thesis as the ultimate referent of legal analysis. It is often supposed that the sources, generally identified in Article 38 of the Statute of the International Court of Justice, found international legal analysis. The consequence has been that the juridical aim has been to identify any right to nationality or any rule conferring, withdrawing or withholding nationality as if it were a self-standing and discrete unit of the legal order. Internal state jurisdiction has meant that any discrete right, rule or test must be identified in terms of a statute, regulation or judicial decision, each of which is intellectually situated in its own vertical hierarchy of similarly functioning institutions. With the quest for identifiable international standards, a similar hierarchy has been assimilated into international law reasoning. Such a hierarchy is represented by Article 38: treaties, international custom, general principles of law recognized by civilized states, and opinio juris 'of the most highly qualified publicists of the various nations'.[1] The crux of the identity of a law is its justification in terms of a higher-ordered institutional source, signified in writing by the source. De jure and effective statelessness has been the product of the quest for the identity of law as if a right/rule/test is a self-standing and discrete unit of legal knowledge. This has especially been so of the contemporary studies of de jure and effective nationality.

This juristic quest for the identity of law in a 'source' has missed an important issue regarding statelessness: namely, is a state legally obligated to protect de jure and effectively stateless natural persons? Domestic sources and the international law sources represented by Article 38 of the Statute of the International Court of Justice (ICJ) presuppose that the sources render a nationality right, rule or test obligatory. Express or implied state consent justifies such legal obligation.

Chapter three identified how each day, de jure and effectively stateless persons face economic, social and psychological consequences, which beg the question as to whether any state is obligated to protect such stateless persons. For example, is a state on whose territory a stateless person finds

---

[1] Statute of the International Court of Justice (1945) 961 UNTS 183, TS No 993 (US), Art 38.

her/himself legally obligated to recognize oral testimony of the person's previous social bonding? Is such evidence weighty for the admission of a stateless person, her/his return, the choice of where s/he lives on the state's territory or the decision to leave the territory if s/he lacks documentation, even a 'travel document'? Is the state obligated to accept the collective or personal memories, orally retold, or collective memories, documented by non-governmental and scholarly studies, in lieu of an affidavit about a person's social bonding in circumstances where the person has had to flee from insurgency, armed struggle or natural disaster?[2] Are state officials obligated to protect the mobility of a stateless person or the choice of place where to live inside the state's territorial border? Is the state, through its administration and judiciary, obligated to ensure that a stateless person possesses the same social entitlement (access to public education, medical services, unemployment insurance, property rights, for example) as nationals do?[3] When de jure or effectively stateless persons are impacted by domestic law, is the judiciary obligated to read into 'by law' unwritten standards, such as non-arbitrariness, good faith, proportionality of the means to fulfil a statutory objective, the legitimacy of a statutory objective or self-executory clauses of a treaty? Does the state possess an obligation to release a stateless person from detention if the state is unable to find a third-party state that will accept the person? After all, most states on the globe have undertaken to adjudicate immediately the detention and release of anyone unlawfully detained.[4] In addition, they have agreed to compensate anyone so detained without adjudication or, if adjudicated, unlawfully detained.[5] Most states have undertaken to protect stateless persons after they are admitted to their territory.[6] After

[2] CA Batchelor raises this problem without addressing that it raises the issue of legal obligation. See CA Batchelor, 'UNHCR and Issues Related to Nationality' (1995) 14 *Refugee Survey Quarterly* 91, fn 18.

[3] Arts 14(1), 16, 17(2) and 26 of the International Covenant on Civil and Political Rights (ICCPR) (1966) 999 UNTS 171, Can TS 1976 No 47, GA Res 2200A (XX1), 21 UNGA OR Supp (No 16) 52, UN Doc A/6316 (1966).

[4] According to Art 9(4) of the ICCPR (ibid), 'Anyone who is deprived of his liberty by arrest or detention shall be entitled to take proceedings before a court, in order that that court may decide without delay on the lawfulness of his detention and order his release if the detention is not lawful.' See also Art 12 of the African [Banjul] Charter on Human and Peoples' Rights (1981), (1984) 21 ILM 58, OAU Doc CAB/LEG/67/3 rev 5. Art 9 of the ICCPR provides, 'No one shall be deprived of his liberty except on such grounds and in accordance with such procedures [as] are established by law.'

[5] Art 9(5) of the ICCPR (above n 3) continues, 'Anyone who has been a victim of unlawful arrest or detention shall have an enforceable right to compensation.'

[6] Eg, ICCPR (above n 3) Art 13; Banjul Charter (above n 4) Art 12(2)(4); Convention Relating to the Status of Stateless Persons (1954) 360 UNTS 117, Art 31; European Convention on Nationality (1997) 2 ETS 166, 2-12; Protocol 7 to the Convention for the Protection of Human Rights and Fundamental Freedoms, as amended by Protocol No 11, ETS No 5; American Convention on Human Rights (1969) 36 OASTS 1, OAS Off Rec OEA/Ser.L./V/11.23 doc.rev 2, Art 22(6); and UN Declaration on the Human Rights of Individuals Who Are Not Nationals of the Country in which They Live, Resolution 40/144 (13 December 1985).

admission, stateless persons have been said to be entitled to judicial review of any expulsion order or proposed expulsion.[7] By Article 13 of the International Covenant on Civil and Political Rights (ICCPR) (1966), state parties undertake to provide 'a review' and 'a decision' with 'compelling reasons' and evidence as to why an expulsion relates to the exigencies of the situation if a person is 'lawfully on the territory'.

If one responds to the above issues by taking a state-centric sense of an international community for granted, two consequences follow. For one thing, any right to nationality or any rule that confers, withholds or withdraws nationality (or the administration of any such rule during the naturalization process) may be considered 'legal' and yet lack an obligatory character. Secondly, such a right to nationality or any state nationality rule or state administration acts regarding nationality may lack a source, such as a statute or treaty or customary norm – and yet a state may be obligated to enforce an international norm protecting stateless persons. The de jure and effectively stateless condition begs that we ask whether there is a sense of legal obligation independent of the identity of a distinct rule or right by the Article 38 sources.

The familiar search for the identity of a law has implicitly accepted a particular sense of legal obligation: namely, a state's claim to its own legal authority. Such a claim is most certainly implicit in the acceptance of a domestic statute or regulation even if it expressly incorporates international standards. So too, the Article 38 sources of the ICJ Statute implicitly take states as the ultimate source of identifiable law. A treaty represents a contract-like undertaking by states. A customary international norm exists by virtue of the sense of obligation of state officials as well as of state practices. A general principle of a civilized society has generally been taken as a shared principle of the internal jurisdictions of states. And contemporary opinio juris is preoccupied with outlining identifiable rules justified by treaties and international customary norms. This sources thesis reinforces the very residuary within which law-making and law administration is deferred to the state. I have argued and documented how such a residuary has been institutionalized in treaties and international customary norms. More importantly, the very sources inscribed in Article 38 of the ICJ Statute institutionalize the freedom of the state as the justified grounding of legal obligation.

In addition, it is not just that the state represents the final referent of justificatory reasoning of the Article 38 sources. Absent a distinct and self-standing domestic right, rule or test, there is a residuary or 'leftover' in the international community of law-making, lawadministration and legal standards for adjudication. If a state has not expressly or implicitly consented to an international standard that constrains its acts in the context of

---

[7] Batchelor (above n 2) fn 18.

nationality, the source of such internal law-making rests inside the boundary of the residuary of the international community. The residuary of law-making and law administration catches all laws for which states have not implicitly or explicitly consented. The notion of an aggregated international community assumes that such a residuary is a hard fact, as if it were posited by nature. The residuary exists for matters *'essentially* within the domestic jurisdiction of any state', in the terms of Article 2(7) of the UN Charter. The residuary, representing an 'essence', is considered inviolable, much as an individual natural person's autonomy or freedom vis-à-vis a state has been considered inviolable. International law discourse about the identity of distinct and self-standing rights and rules has accepted the conferral, withdrawal and withholding of nationality as one incident of such an essence. The sources take the territorial-like boundary of the residuary for granted. A boundary necessarily includes and excludes; and if no other state recognizes a particular natural person as its member, the boundary of the international community must also exclude such persons. Inside the boundary, the relation of a rule to a source immunizes the content of the rule from judicial scrutiny. The content is embodied, amongst other aspects, by social relationships. The content, assuming the international community as the aggregated wills of states, is 'purely political' or extra-legal.

The enigma of statelessness exists in an international community precisely because nationality is considered an incident of this bounded residuary. Contemporary commentators often take the residuary for granted.[8] The boundary of the internal jurisdiction has been said to represent a 'jurisdictional bar'.[9] For the aggregated international community, social relationships have fallen into the residuary for law-making inside the residuary. This residuary, for the purposes of any identifiable law, has been empty or content-independent. This has been so because legality rests in the justificatory relation of a discrete rule posited inside the residuary vis-à-vis the institutional source in the boundary of internal jurisdiction represented by Article 38 sources. The content of the rule or more generally of the reserved residuary may be the cause of remonstration against the withholding or withdrawal of nationality and the consequences thereto. And remedies of the committees of the six human rights treaties are commonly accepted as mere recommendations, not legally binding obligations.[10] What happens inside the legal space of the jurisdictional bar is immune from external (state, international or judicial) intervention.

[8] See above Introduction chapter, n 21 (6).
[9] *Jurisdictional Immunities of the State (Germany v Italy, Greece Intervening)* (2012) ICJ Rep (3 February 2012) para 93.
[10] For the extent to which UN Human Rights Committee (HRC) 'decisions' are ignored by states because of their conceived 'non-binding' character, see P Alston and R Goodman, 'Comment on Outcome of the Communications Procedures in Interim Measures' in *International Human Rights: Text and Materials* (Oxford, Oxford University Press, 2013) 832–34.

The crux of the enigma of an international community is that without such a boundary, there would not be an internal jurisdiction within which the state is free to exclude and include members of the international community. And without such a protected jurisdiction, the relegation of a law to the reserved domain would be displaced by a very different sense of a legal bond, one's own country, lawfulness and an international community itself. Such a possibility, which I have documented as present even within treaties, as well as in the decisions of domestic and international tribunals, has brought the notion of legal bond as allegiance into question.

Allegiance, we have found, emerged during nineteenth-century international law discourse as a protected incident of the internal jurisdiction of each state. A legal obligation to protect a stateless person is empty if international standards aim to protect the interdependent international community of free and equal internal jurisdictions. The enquiry for the identity of a rule or right misses the nature of legal obligation attaching to the content of internal state jurisdiction. With the notion of effective nationality, however, what jurists take as the 'hard fact' of the residuary is not the boundary of internal jurisdiction but rather the social content of the heretofore immunized space. Effective nationality thereby dissolves the facticity of the boundary precisely because the social content of the bounded residuary represents whether harm has been caused to a de jure or effectively stateless person.[11] The enigma of the international community, now analytically dissolving by virtue of the legal bond understood as social relationships, leads to a very different sense of legal obligation – and therefore to a very different sense of 'its law' and 'the operation of its law'.

II. THE DISPLACEMENT OF THE BOUNDARY

A series of discursive contexts suggest the displacement of the very boundary that has protected the freedom of states to decide who are their members, who may be excluded and the legal rights of those excluded. Although human rights tribunals have most certainly rendered suspect the territoriality of internal state jurisdiction,[12] I shall focus for a moment upon international criminal norms protecting stateless persons. In the other

---

[11] *Chahal and Others v United Kingdom* (1997) 23 EHRR 413, 108 ILR 385; *Al-Nashif v Bulgaria* [2002] ECHR 497, Application No 50963/99 (20 June 2002); and *Case of A and Others v UK* [ECtHR GC], Application No 3455/05, (2009) 49 EHRR 29, para 19.

[12] For examples of the displacement of the territorial border, see, eg, *A v Australia*, HRC Communication No 560/1993, UN Doc CCPR/C/59/D/560/1993 (1997); *Baban v Australia*, HRC Communication No 1014/2001, UN Doc CCPR/C/78/D/1014/2001 (2003); *Bakhtiyari v Australia*, HRC Communication No 1069/2002, UN Doc CCPR/C/79/D/1069/2002 (2003); *D and E v Australia*, HRC Communication No 1050/2002, UN Doc CCPR/87/D/1050/2002 (2006); and *Saed Shams et al v Australia*, HRC Communications Nos 1255, 1256, 1259, 1260, 1268, 1270 and 1288/2004, UN Doc CCPR/C/90/D/1255, 1256, 1259, 1260, 1266, 1268, 1270, 1288 (2007).

discursive context, counsel have successfully advocated a series of legal doctrines that cannot be understood in terms of the privileged boundary of internal state jurisdiction within an aggregated international community.

A. The Displacement of Territorial Jurisdiction in Armed Conflict Law

Two features of humanitarian law render the wall of internal state jurisdiction suspect in matters of statelessness. For one, stateless persons are expressly protected from the criminal acts of state officials during armed conflict between states. For example, Control Council Law Number 10 (1945) of the Allied Powers recognized 'crimes against humanity' 'committed against any civilian population . . . whether or not in violation of the domestic laws of the country where perpetrated'.[13] The whole civilian populace, not just those persons with de jure German nationality, was the object of protection.

The London Agreement (1945),[14] which was the culmination of several conferences of the Allied Powers at the end of World War II and is better described perhaps as a treaty, appended a Charter. The Charter recognized the criminal nature of even those state actions that occur inside the traditional boundary of the reserved domain. Included amongst such state and personal actions were 'forced deportation . . . and other inhumane acts committed against any civilian population' (Article 6(c)). Since the Nazi denaturalization laws of the 1930s and early 1940s had left millions of former citizens without constitutional and legal rights,[15] the Charter explicitly addressed state action against stateless persons through the use of the term 'any civilian population'. Such actions were deemed criminal whether or not they were authorized by domestic laws (Articles 7 and 8). That said, the circumstances of formerly stateless persons were not comprehensively addressed. As a result of the Military Regulations of the Allied Powers, German nationality could be re-conferred onto denaturalized Jewish persons who had lived abroad for 'some years' (the latter being the ground of denaturalization under Nazi laws); however, as Hersch Lauterpacht pointed out, their properties could be confiscated under post-war German internal law.[16]

---

[13] Control Council No 10, Punishment of Persons Guilty of War Crimes, Crimes against Peace and Against Humanity (3 December 1945) 3, Official Gazette Control Council for Germany 50–55 (1946), Art 2(2).

[14] London Agreement for the Prosecution and Punishment of the Major War Criminals of the European Axis ('London Agreement') (1945) 82 UNTS 280, 5 Stat 1544, EAS No 472 (signatories: USA, USSR, Britain and France).

[15] See above ch 3, s III-C (106–7).

[16] H Lauterpacht, 'The Nationality of Denationalized Persons' (1948) *Jewish Yearbook of International Law* 164, reprinted in E Lauterpacht (ed), *International Law: Collected Papers*, vol 3 (Cambridge, Cambridge University Press, 1977) 383–404.

The dissolution of the territorial border as the bar protecting state responsibility has continued with more recent international criminal law treaties. The dissolution has taken two forms. To begin with, the treaties implicitly cover harm that is caused to stateless persons. Aside from the common Article 3 provisions of the four Geneva Conventions (1949), various clauses destabilize nationality as an incident of internal state jurisdiction: prosecution is justified 'regardless of nationality'.[17] Article 4(1) of the Geneva Convention IV, which was intended to protect civilians during armed conflict, defines 'protected persons' as those 'in the hands of a party to the conflict or Occupying Power of which they are not nationals' (although nationals of a state not bound by the treaty remain unprotected). According to Article 44, one's nationality (or presumably absence thereof) cannot be the basis of a detaining state's treatment of an individual as an 'enemy alien'. According to Article 48, every protected person (which includes stateless persons) possesses the right to leave the territory of an Occupying Power. In addition, according to Article 49, a protected person may not be deported to another territory, whether controlled by the Occupying Power or a non-occupying state.

In support of the extension of protection to stateless persons, the Appeal Court of the International Criminal Tribunal for the Former Yugoslavia (ICTFY) has read Article 4 of Geneva Convention IV so as to expressly protect de jure stateless persons.[18] Recalling a theme from chapter six above, the protection extends to refugees who are effectively stateless. This is so, according to the Court, because as refugees, they 'no longer owe allegiance' to the occupying state and therefore lack diplomatic protection from the state.[19] In *Tadic* (1999), the Court stated that 'already in 1949 the legal bond of nationality was not regarded as crucial',[20] and Article 44 protects effectively stateless persons. Furthermore, the Court concluded that 'refugees who do not, in fact, enjoy the protection of any government' shall not be treated 'as enemy aliens exclusively on the basis of their nationality de jure of an enemy state' because the absence of a

---

[17] See Geneva Convention (I) for the Amelioration of the Condition of Wounded and Sick in Armed Forces in the Field (1949) 75 UNTS 31, Art 49; Geneva Convention (II) for the Amelioration of the Wounded, Sick and Shipwrecked Members of the Armed Forces at Sea (1949) 75 UNTS 85, Art 50; Geneva Convention (III) Relative to the Treatment of Prisoners of War (1949) 75 UNTS 135 (entered into force 21 October 1950) Art 129; and Geneva Convention (IV) Relative to the Protection of Civilian Persons in Time of War (1949) 75 UNTS 287 (entered into force 21 October 1950) Art 146. This point is incorporated by reference in the First Additional Protocol to the Geneva Conventions and concerning the Victims of International Armed Conflicts (1977) 1125 UNTS 3 (entered into force 7 December 1978).

[18] *Prosecutor v Tadic*, Appeals Chamber, International Criminal Tribunal for the Former Yugoslavia (ICTFY), Case No IT-94-1-AR72 (15 July 1999), www.icty.org/case/tadic/4, para 164.

[19] Ibid, para 164.

[20] Ibid, para 165.

legal bond of allegiance has been 'regarded as more important than the formal link of nationality'.[21]

The extension of protection to stateless persons has been institutionalized again in more recent humanitarian treaties. The Statute of the ICTFY (1993),[22] for example, incorporates the 'protected persons' clause of the Geneva Convention IV. Article 3 of the Statute of the International Criminal Tribunal for Rwanda (1994) identifies one crime as 'a widespread or systematic attack' on national, political, ethnic, racial or religious grounds 'against any civilian population'.[23] As for the Rome Statute of the International Criminal Court (1998), Article 7(1)(d) includes as crimes against humanity 'state action involving a widespread or systematic attack directed against any civilian population, with knowledge of the attack'.[24] The prolonged detention of stateless persons is now a crime against humanity because such detention is effectively synonymous with 'imprisonment' or 'severe deprivation of physical liberty', both of which are crimes against humanity by virtue of Article 7(1)(e) of the Rome Statute. The inclusion of stateless persons as protected from international law crimes again brings into question the territorial boundary of the residuary of the aggregated international community.

The notion of a territorial boundary for the residuary of an international community is suspect for a second reason. It is not just that stateless persons are expressly or impliedly protected by international criminal law treaties. Rather, the treaties accept that territorial borders dissolve in matters of international law crimes. Such dissolution of territorial borders was manifested, for example, by the London Agreement, as noted above. According to Articles 7 and 8, internal state laws could not exempt or waive heads of state and responsible officials from prosecution.[25] The common Article 3 of the four Geneva Conventions expressly address crimes committed 'in the case of armed conflict not of an international character occurring in the territory of one of the High Contracting Parties.'[26] In addition, states lack the authority to derogate from the Geneva obligations even through agreements with other states (Article 11). The Geneva Convention IV includes as a grave breach the 'unlawful deportation or transfer or

---

[21] Ibid. This point was affirmed in *Prosecutor v Delalic and Others*, Appeals Chamber (ICTFY), Case No IT-96-21-A (2001) paras 28 and 30.

[22] Adopted by SC Res 827 of 25 May 1993, amended by SC Res 1166 of 13 May 1998 and SC Res 1329 of 30 November 2000 (ICTY Statute), Art 2.

[23] Adopted by SC Res 955 of 8 November 1994, amended by SC Res 1165 of 30 April 1998, SC Res 1329 of 30 November 2000, SC Res 1411 of 17 May 2002 and SC Res 1431 of 14 August 2002 (ICTR Statute).

[24] Rome Statute of the International Criminal Court (17 July 1998), UN Doc A/CONF. 183/9, 2187 UNTS 90, as corrected by the *process-verbaux* of 10 November 1998, 12 July 1999 and 8 May 2000.

[25] London Agreement (above n 14).

[26] See above n 17.

unlawful confinement' of any protected person.[27] Moreover, Article 48 provides that domestic laws cannot 'absolve' a state party 'of any liability'. Protocol II to Geneva Convention IV extends the dissolution of the territorial boundary of internal jurisdiction to intra-state conflict.[28]

Although the American *Third Restatement of the Law* omits forcible transfers of the populace from a jus cogens norm, the *Restatement* adds support for territorial transparency with its conclusion that forcible transfer is a crime 'regardless of motive' of a state.[29] In its important report on the freedom of movement, the UN Commission on Human Rights highlighted how effective nationality, based upon the social bonding of individuals, justifies the dissolution of a territorial boundary when the human rights of inhabitants are involved.[30]

The treaties establishing the jurisdiction of international criminal tribunals also expressly or implicitly extend protection to stateless persons by expressly or implicitly recognizing the dissolution of the territorial boundary of jurisdiction. Recent judicial decisions have reinforced such transparency of the territorial boundary of internal state jurisdiction. For example, the Appeals Chamber of the Former Yugoslavia tribunal declared, 'It is now a settled rule of customary international law that crimes against humanity do not require a connection to international armed conflict.'[31] And the ILC has recognized that a state owes a legal obligation to protect stateless persons even if the perpetrators and/or victims are absent from the territory of the state of prosecution.[32] The Inter-American Court of Human Rights has held that even during a condition of siege, the withdrawal of an insurgent's nationality constitutes an unjustifiable penalty that is contrary to Article 19 of the American Convention on Human Rights.[33] According to Article 19 of

---

[27] Geneva Convention IV (above n 17) Art 8(2)(a)(iii).

[28] Protocol Additional to the Geneva Conventions of 12 August 1949 and Relating to the Protection of Victims of Non-international Armed Conflicts (Protocol II) (1977) 1125 UNTS 609 (entered into force 7 December 1978) Art 17. See also Rome Statute (above n 24) Art 8(2).

[29] American Law Institute, *Restatement of the Law, Third: Foreign Relations Law of the United States* (Philadelphia, American Law Institute, 1987) vol 1, para 702 (note m). Para 147 states that 'unlawful deportation or transfer . . . of a protected person' is a 'grave breach'. See also Arts 17 and 85(4) of the First Protocol to the Geneva Conventions (above n 17).

[30] AS Al-Khasawneh (Special Rapporteur), 'Final Report: Human Rights and Population Transfer', UN Doc E/CN.4/Sub.2/1997/23 (27 June 1997), unispal.un.org/UNISPAL.NSF/0 /480844B6EC1F52A905256500004CCF31. See also AS Al-Khasawneh and R Hatano, 'Preliminary Report: The Human Rights Dimensions of Population Transfer, Including the Implantation of Settlers', UN Doc E/CN.4/Sub.2/1993/17 and Corr.1 (6 July 1993). The Sub-Commission endorsed the former Report in Sub-commission Resolution 1997/29. For more on social bonding, see above ch 6.

[31] *Tadic* (above n 18) para 141.

[32] *Case Concerning the Arrest Warrant of 11 April 2000 (Democratic Republic of the Congo v Belgium)*, judgment of 14 February 2002, ICJ Rep 2002, para 59.

[33] *Proposed Amendments to the Naturalization Provisions of the Constitution of Costa Rica* (Advisory Opinion), Inter-Am Ct HR (19 January 1984), No OC-4/84, para 32, reported in (1984) 5 *HRLJ* 161–75 and 79 ILR 282 at paras 32–33. See the American Convention on Human Rights (above n 6). See also JMM Chan, 'The Right to a Nationality as a Human Right' (1991)

the American Declaration of the Rights and Duties of Man, 'Every person has the right to the nationality to which he is entitled by law and to change it, if he so wishes, for the nationality of any other country that is willing to grant it to him.'[34]

In a particular example, the ICJ in *Arrest Warrant (Congo v Belgium)* (2002) addressed how the traditional association of a territorial border with internal jurisdiction dissolves in matters of alleged crimes against humanity.[35] The issue was whether Belgian judicial authorities could prosecute violations of international humanitarian law regardless of where the acts were committed and regardless of the nationality of the victims, the complainants not being the victims. Although the prosecution of offenders of peremptory norms presupposed territorial jurisdiction by a state, the Court held, 'This does not necessarily indicate, however, that such a [non-territorial] exercise would be unlawful.'[36] For the Court, 'No territorial or nationality linkage is envisaged [with a peremptory norm], suggesting a true universality principle.'[37] The transparency of the territorial border is 'based on the heinous nature of the crime rather than on links of territoriality or nationality (whether as perpetrator or victim).'[38] Moreover, to use the Court's term, 'contemporary trends' of legal obligation have been directed towards 'bases of jurisdiction other than territoriality'. Legal obligation is owed moreover in order to prevent the 'effects' or 'impact' of domestic laws.[39]

With the inclusion of stateless persons as protected persons and with the dissolution of the territorial border of internal jurisdiction in matters of harm against stateless persons during inter-state and intra-state armed conflict, an important issue arises: why is a harm to a stateless person 'heinous' or 'grave'? Is the gravity more serious for a stateless person than for a national of a state? Does a state possess a special fiduciary relation to stateless persons during armed conflict and alleged emergency conditions inside a state's internal jurisdiction? How many stateless civilians must be detained for a prolonged time, forcibly displaced, disappeared, tortured or killed before such acts are considered 'grave'? Are 'the fundamental rules of international law' different and more 'fundamental' for stateless persons who are 'transferred' or 'severely' deprived of physical liberty

12 *Human Rights Law Journal* 1, 5; and ILC, 'Report of the ILC Covering its Second Session', UN Doc A/1316, *ILC Yearbook 1950*, vol II, 364–86, 377 (para 120).

[34] American Declaration of the Rights and Duties of Man ('Pact of San José, Costa Rica'), OAS res 30 (Bogata, 1948), Vovena Conferencia Internacional Americana, 6 *Actas y Documentos* 297–302 (1953).

[35] *Case Concerning the Arrest Warrant (Congo v Belgium)* (above n 32) 3.

[36] Ibid, para 45.

[37] Ibid, para 31.

[38] Ibid, para 46.

[39] Ibid, para 47.

than for nationals?[40] And what distinguishes a 'fundamental' rule from a non-fundamental rule of international law when de jure or effectively stateless persons are harmed? If action against stateless persons is proven to have been specifically authorized by a head of state or minister and to have been 'grave', is the head or the minister immune from criminal prosecution until after s/he leaves office? These issues demand self-conscious examination of the nature of legal obligation for an international community that is independent of the internal jurisdictions of state members.

B. The Displacement of Boundary in International Legal Discourse

Territoriality is only one factor in generating the boundary of the protected internal jurisdiction of states. The boundary, particularly manifested by title, is a concept with a territorial-like character. As such, the boundary is subject to intellectual revision and displacement.

i. Non-arbitrariness

Judicial scrutiny of alleged arbitrary state action has rendered such a boundary transparent in three ways. First, a discrete rule has been considered arbitrary if it is so vague in scope as to lack predictability.[41] The content of the rule or of the space must generally be 'formulated with sufficient precision to enable the citizen to regulate his conduct', according to the European Court of Human Rights.[42] A stateless person or a national who faces the threat of denaturalization must be able to foresee such a prospect as authorized by domestic written rules.[43] The domestic enactment of a rule or right may well be identifiable in terms of the sources protected by the bounded internal jurisdiction. Such sources may not be obligatory, though. This may be so because the rules and tests in the content of the reserved internal jurisdiction leave future state action unpredictable, thereby undermining the social bonding needed for legal bond.

Second, a state's domestic laws have not been accepted as obligatory if the content of the laws reflect arbitrariness. Article 9(1) of the ICCPR, for example, states, 'No one shall be subjected to arbitrary arrest or detention.' Article 12(4) similarly provides, 'No one shall be arbitrarily deprived of the

---

[40] See Art 7(d) and (e) of the Rome Statute (above n 24).

[41] *Van Alphen v The Netherlands*, HRC Communication No 305/1988, UN Doc CCPR/C/39/D/305/1988 (1990), para.5.8; and *A v Australia* (above n 12) para 9.2.

[42] The leading case in this respect is *Sunday Times v United Kingdom* (1979–80) 2 EHRR 245, 271.

[43] *Tatishvili v Russia*, Application No 1509/02, (2007) 45 EHRR 52, 91; and *Kaftailova v Latvia*, ECHR Application No 59643/00 (22 June 2006), www.refworld.org/docid/44e5c05e4.html.

right to enter his own country.' In addition, absent such an express condition in a treaty, courts and tribunals have appealed to non-arbitrariness as a condition of the obligatory character of domestic laws. Article 13 of the ICCPR, for example, requires a review of 'compelling reasons' for expulsion except 'by law' and where compelling reasons of national security so require. The reference to 'by law', according to 'General Comment 27' of the UN Human Rights Committee (HRC), means that a state action must not be arbitrary.[44] Even for human rights treaty provisions that are silent regarding the condition of non-arbitrariness for the limitation of a right, courts and tribunals have read the obligation of non-arbitrariness into the texts.[45] The executive arm of a state could hardly be assigned the duty to enquire as to what is an arbitrary act by the executive. This is especially pertinent regarding de jure or effectively stateless persons. How else would one know whether a domestic law is arbitrarily administered other than to scrutinize the very content of the domestic law, which is otherwise barred from external intervention?

Third, judicial scrutiny of the social experiences of stateless persons is required, independent of the boundary of internal state jurisdiction. When a UN committee first proposed a draft treaty regarding the conditions of refugees and stateless persons in 1950, Louis Henkin frequently expressed concern that 'public order' as a justification for denaturalization would allow states to refuse to admit stateless persons or, conversely, to expel them 'for one reason or another, [as] an undesirable person'.[46] 'General Comment 16' of the HRC emphasizes that the content of an internal state law must be consistent with the provisions, aims and objectives of the ICCPR 'and should be, in any event, reasonable in the circumstances'.[47] In contrast with the content-independent quest for a justified source at the cost of actual social relationships, 'General Comment 16' requires an evaluation of the social content of the reserved domain. As one study has recently suggested, 'arbitrariness' emanates from 'above', not 'inside' the content of a state's internal jurisdiction.[48] Legality concerns what is 'real,

---

[44] HRC, 'CCPR General Comment 27: Article 12 (Freedom of Movement)' (2 November 1999) in UN, *Human Rights Instruments, Volume I: Compilation of General Comments and General Recommendations Adopted by Human Rights Treaty Bodies* (27 May 2008), www.un.org/en/ga/search/view_doc.asp?symbol=HRI/GEN/1/Rev.9(Vol.I), paras 14–16.

[45] Ibid, para 8.

[46] Economic and Social Council (Ad Hoc Committee on Refugees and Stateless Persons), 'Proposed Draft Convention Relating to the Status of Refugees (continued), Art 27 (Expulsion of Refugees Lawfully Admitted)' in *Summary Record of 40th Meeting*, UN Doc E/AC.32/SR.40 (22 August 1950).

[47] HRC, 'CCPR General Comment 16: Article 17 (Right to Privacy): The Right to Respect of Privacy, Family, Home and Correspondence, and Protection of Honour and Reputation' (8 April 1988) in UN, *Human Rights Instruments, Volume I* (above n 44) para 4.

[48] See also S Joseph et al, *The International Covenant on Civil and Political Rights: Cases, Materials and Commentary*, 2nd edn (Oxford, Oxford University Press, 2004) 211–12, para 11.10.

not merely formal', according to the HRC.[49] Can one understand anything 'under the law' 'from above' without examining the assumptions and expectations about social relationships presupposed in the content of a discrete rule? Is this not especially compelling if a domestic law authorizes the detention, expulsion, internal displacement or refusal of admittance for stateless persons? International standards of reasonableness and non-arbitrariness hence apply to 'the content of domestic laws'.[50]

A 'law' is more than a concept when stateless persons are at issue. It concerns the presupposed social relations in the content of the concept. So, for example, the HRC held in *Kwok v Australia* (2005) that secured detention of an 'unlawful non-national' in excess of four years without chance of substantive judicial review constitutes arbitrariness within the meaning of Article 9(1) of the ICCPR.[51] Arbitrariness was also read into a stateless person's detention after having been imprisoned for fourteen years by the same government.[52] The state had the onus of justifying such a lengthy detention. A person could not be categorized as dangerous to the community without factual evidence, including that of psychiatric experts, to the effect that rehabilitation could not have been achieved by a less intrusive means.[53]

According to the HRC, arbitrariness is manifested if a state denaturalizes or expels members of a group en masse, even though mass denaturalization is rarely mentioned in human rights treaties.[54] The European Court of Human Rights in *Al-Nashif* (2002) considered that without more, an executive's order of expulsion of a stateless person is not binding, even if the order identifies the stateless person as a member of a group deemed a threat to the state.[55] Why? Again, because the legal obligation of the state rests upon the social relations of the natural person inter se rather than upon allegiance as determined by the state. Mass withdrawal or mass expulsion fails to address the singular context-specific experience making for a stateless person's social bonding with others. Along the same lines, the House of Lords determined in *A and Others* (2004), which was affirmed by the European Court of Human Rights, that the executive arm of a state cannot 'pick and choose' whom to subject to the enforcement of legisla-

---

[49] *A v Australia* (above n 12) para 9.5. See also *A and Others v Secretary of State for the Home Department* (2004) UKHL 56, para 29 (per Bingham).

[50] HRC, 'CCPR General Comment 16: Article 17 (Right to Privacy): The Right to Respect of Privacy, Family, Home and Correspondence, and Protection of Honour and Reputation' (8 April 1988) in UN, *Human Rights Instruments, Volume I* (above n 44) para 4.

[51] *Kwok Yin Fong v Australia*, CCPR/C/97/D/1442/2005 (HRC (ICCPR), 23 November 2009), www.refworld.org/docid/4b1d223d2.html.

[52] *Fardon v Australia*, CCPR/C/98/D/1629/2007 (UN HRC, 10 May 2010), www.refworld.org/docid/4c19e97b2.html.

[53] Ibid.

[54] See HRC, 'CCPR General Comment 15: 'The Position of Aliens under the Covenant' (11 April 1986) in UN, *Human Rights Instruments, Volume I* (above n 44) para 10.

[55] *Al-Nashif* (above n 11).

tion.[56] The detention, expulsion or internal displacement of stateless persons, separate from nationals, exemplifies such arbitrary picking and choosing.[57] The statutory exclusion of de jure nationals from the operation of a statute disproportionately impacts stateless persons, alleged state emergencies notwithstanding. So too, a statute that authorizes the withdrawal of nationality may be so widely phrased that the boundary of the internal jurisdiction is suspect.

ii. Good Faith

This takes us to a second feature of the transparency of the boundary of internal state jurisdiction. Tribunals and courts have read into state action the need for 'good faith'. Bad faith has been attributed to expulsion due to racial intent,[58] the commission of a crime,[59] punishment by exile,[60] a state official's failure to act reasonably or with reasons[61] and disproportionality between the means of expulsion and the offence of the expellee.[62] The obligation of a state to act in good faith 'is an obligation in itself', the European Human Rights Court has stated.[63] This duty extends to situations involving state emergencies as well as to ordinary circumstances.[64]

Good faith was accepted by the House of Lords as a customary international norm in the *European Roman Rights* case (2004).[65] Good faith represents a radically different sense of legal obligation than that associated with the legal bond of allegiance.[66] Allegiance, as discussed elsewhere in this book, has more recently been determined by states. For the protected residual space of internal jurisdiction, legal obligation rests upon a state's

---

[56] *A and Others v Secretary of State* (above n 49) paras 190 and 252; and *Case of A and Others v UK* (above n 11) para 19.

[57] *A and Others v Secretary of State* (above n 49) para 68.

[58] P Weis, *Nationality and Statelessness on International Law* (London, Stevens, 1956) 241–46.

[59] See generally J-M Henckaerts, *Mass Expulsion in Modern International Law and Practice* (The Hague, Martinus Nijhoff, 1995); and E Suy, 'The Concept of Jus Cogens in Public International Law' in *Papers and Proceedings of the Lagonissi Conference on International Law, Volume 2: The Concept of Jus Cogens in International Law* (Geneva, Carnegie Endowment for International Peace, 1967).

[60] HRC, 'Consideration of Reports Submitted by States Parties under Article 40 of the Covenant: Dominican Republic' (5 May 1993), UN Doc CCPR/C/79?Add.18, www.refworld.org/docid/3ae6b0084.html, para 6.

[61] Hersch Lauterpacht, *International Law and Human Rights* (Hamden, CT, Archon Books, 1968) 346–32.

[62] *Stewart v Canada*, HRC Communication No 538/1993, UN Doc CCPR/C/58/D/538/1993, (1996) 115 ILR 318. See also Joseph et al (above n 48) 32 (para 1.68); *Libyan Arab Jamahiriya*, HRC Communication No 440/1990, UN Doc CCPR/C/32/D/440/1990 (1994); and HRC, 'General Comment 15' (above n 54).

[63] *European Roma Rights Case* (2004) UKHL 55, para 34.

[64] Ibid, para 36.

[65] Ibid (per Goodwin-Gil for the intervenor UN High Commissioner for Refugees).

[66] *Merricks v Nott-Bower* (1964) 1 AER 717, [1965] 1 QB 57, [1965] 2 WLR 702, CA UK (per Denning): the purpose of a statute or regulation must not be 'misused or abused by being applied to an ulterior purpose'.

claim to its own authority.[67] The principle of good faith trumps such a claim. The good faith of a state is manifested by the state's accounting for the social relations occurring inside the reserved domain of the state. Why is the will of a state to return a stateless person to her/his country lacking in any obligatory character? If a domestic law authorizes the expulsion or refoulement of a stateless person, such a state action, though authorized by a domestic or even an international source, is not obligatory.[68] Hence, good faith, as a legal obligation, suggests a sense of an international community that contradicts the idea of a community constituted from the aggregated wills of states.[69]

If we take a page from the 'Speech of the Laws' in Plato's *Crito*,[70] we might ask the question: is a domestic law obligatory if a natural person lacks the opportunity to persuade state officials of the wrongdoing of their actions in a particular circumstance? According to Plato, before Socrates' (self-)execution, Socrates stated through his personification of the 'Laws':

> Or are you so wise that it has escaped your notice . . . that you must either persuade [the polis] or else do whatever it commands; that you must mind your behaviour and undergo whatever treatment it prescribes for you, whether a beating or imprisonment; that if it leads you to war to be wounded or killed, that's what you must do, and that's what is just . . . not to give way or retreat or leave where you were stationed but, on the contrary, in war and law courts, and everywhere else, to do whatever your city or fatherland commands *or else persuade it as to what is really just* . . .[71]

Socrates had been given the opportunity to persuade the Laws that they were unjust in his circumstances. Unsuccessful at trial and the Laws having offered two unmet arguments as to why he ought to obey, Socrates had to accept the execution order.[72]

With Socrates' counsel in mind, can executive state officials exempt themselves from liability for causing harm to stateless persons without addressing the context-specific circumstances and consequences of such persons? Lawfulness hardly exists if, as in the case of the former Soviet and East German nationality laws, state officials alone may decide who is

---

[67] *North Atlantic Coast Fisheries Case* (1910) 11 UNRIAA 167, 188, as quoted in *European Roma Rights* (above n 63) para 31.

[68] *European Roma Rights* (above n 63) para 40.

[69] E Lauterpacht and D Bethlehem, 'The Scope and Content of the Principle of Non-refoulement' in E Feller, V Turk and F Nicholson (eds), *Refugee Protection in International Law* (Cambridge, Cambridge University Press, 2003) 87 (para 76), as quoted in *European Roma Rights* (above n 63) para 54.

[70] Plato, *Crito*, CDC Reeve (trans and ed) (Indianapolis, Hackett, 2002).

[71] Ibid, lines 51a7–51b10 (emphasis added).

[72] The editor and translator CDC Reeve (above n 70) has indicated that 'persuasion' would only need to address the execution order (fn 23). He omits whether the defence at trial would constitute sufficient opportunity to justify the obligatory character of the legal authority of a state institution.

'worthy' of citizenship.[73] Although allegiance may prove the legal bond for an international community of aggregated wills of states, such a legal bond is meaningless if the boundary of the reserve domain can be overcome through external scrutiny and intervention from outside the boundary of the domain. Such external scrutiny and intervention is manifested when good faith in the context of state action is at issue.

iii. Proportionality

The third discursive doctrine affecting the otherwise territory-like nature of the boundary of internal state jurisdiction is frequently used by counsel on behalf of stateless persons – namely, proportionality. Proportionality has been accepted as the basis of judicial scrutiny of the content of the reserved domain during alleged emergencies. At its most basic, it asks whether the means chosen by a state legislature or executive fulfils the objective of the domestic law. On its face, the proportional relation of a means to a statutory objective is suggested by the objective of the statute. In such a situation, however, the means and objective may not really be separate from each other: the objective may suggest the means. The judicial scrutiny of the relation may thereby be illusionary. The problem is that the means is likely to be overbroad vis-à-vis the alleged social or political problem that the legislated or administrative rule is intended to address.

It is not enough for a state executive to point to political circumstances to justify the means of overcoming a 'public emergency', 'national security' or 'public health'. The means may well involve withholding or withdrawing the nationality of a person or persons. The means may also involve the various legal and social consequences of the stateless condition, which I identified in chapter three. Such a state decision, without evidence or argument, will not establish that the means is proportionate to the threat to the state posed by a de jure or effectively stateless person.

The proportionality of state action in the context of statelessness requires the consideration of the actions and past conduct of particular natural persons as a question of evidence. Proportionality also concerns the duration, geographical coverage of the state exigency and the material

---

[73] According to Art 18 of the Soviet Law of Citizenship, nationality could be withdrawn if a natural person was found 'damaging to the prestige or state security of the USSR': Law of the Union of Soviet Socialist Republics on Citizenship of the USSR, 1978 (1981) 20 ILM 1207. A 'stateless person', a legal status in the Soviet Union (Arts 9 and 32), was considered a 'foreign citizen' who could be expelled for such open-ended reasons as 'state security, protecting public order' or the 'prestige of the state' (Art 31). Similarly, the citizenship law of the former East Germany authorized state officials to withdraw nationality if 'the citizen proves not worthy of citizenship of the German Democratic Republic through gross disregard of the obligations assumed with the granting of citizenship': Art 12 of the German Democratic Republic Citizenship Law (1967) 6 ILM 466–67.

scope of the state emergency, according to the HRC's 'General Comment 29' to the ICCPR.[74] Although legal reasoning often identifies a one-liner as the objective of a complex and lengthy statute, such oversimplification risks social consequences that the abstraction representing the objective conceals. With the limitation clauses of human rights treaties, the objective of the means institutionalized by a statute or regulation must be consistent with 'the due recognition and respect for the rights and freedoms of others and of meeting the just requirements of morality, public order and the general welfare in a democratic society'[75] and with 'the promotion of *the general welfare of a democratic society'*.[76] Similarly, limitations must not 'involve discrimination solely on the ground of race, colour, sex, language, religion or social origin';[77] they may not maintain 'unequal or separate rights for different racial groups after the objectives for which they were taken have been achieved',[78] 'change the nationality of the wife, render her stateless or force upon her the nationality of her husband',[79] nor directly bring about the other consequences examined above in chapter three.

Once again, this search outside the boundary of internal state jurisdiction for the identity of law destabilizes the legal obligation traditionally associated with the express or implicit consent of states. How can a jurist flesh out what is 'morality', 'a just requirement', the nature of 'the right to nationality', 'the general welfare of a society' or 'justice' without enquiring about the nature of legal obligation in the two senses of an international community that I have outlined in this book? How can a law be considered binding without such an enquiry? The traditional quest for the identity of a self-standing right or rule takes for granted a sense of legal obligation that, we are now appreciating, is dissolving with the incorporation of non-arbitrariness and good faith as requisites for the identity of law. The HRC view in *Suarez de Guerrero v Colombia* (1979) indicates that international standards play a role in the identity of a law drawn from the obligatory character of the legal bond as a social bond.[80] So, for example, the Inter-American Court of Human Rights held in *Sawhoyamaxa Indigenous Community* (2006) that the 'close ties' between an indigenous group and a territory are protected by Article 21 of the American Convention. The 'close

---

[74] HRC, 'CCPR General Comment 29: States of Emergency (Article 4)' (31 August 2001) in UN, *Human Rights Instruments, Volume I* (above n 44).

[75] Universal Declaration of Human Rights (UNDHR) (1948), GA res 217A (III), Art 29(2).

[76] International Covenant on Economic, Social and Cultural Rights (ICESCR) (1966), GA res 2200A (XXI), 21 UN GAOR Supp (No 16) 49, UN Doc A/6316, 993 UNTS 3, Art 4.

[77] ICCPR (above n 3) Art 4.

[78] International Convention on the Elimination of All Forms of Racial Discrimination (ICERD) (1965) 666 UNTS 195 (entered into force 4 January 1969) Art 2(2).

[79] Convention on the Elimination of All Forms of Discrimination against Women (1979) 1249 UNTS 13 (entered into force 3 September 1981) Art 9(1).

[80] *Suarez de Guerrero v Colombia*, HRC Communication No 45/1979, 70 ILR 267. See also *A v Australia* (above n 12) paras 4 and 9.5. See also Henckaerts (above n 59) 29.

ties' were evidenced not only by the fact that the territory was a means of survival but also because it pervaded their 'worldview, . . . their religiousness, and consequently, . . . their cultural identity'.[81]

What is really at stake in the latter enquiry is the 'legitimacy' of the objective of any one domestic law. How can one identify a 'legitimate purpose' as opposed to an illegitimate purpose, without also situating and examining the legal culture of the international community in which the purpose is immersed? When a state lacks the evidence to prosecute a stateless person, for example, the person may not be detained for a prolonged period of time.[82] More generally, as the International Law Commission (ILC) stated in its 'Draft Articles on the Nationality in Relation to the Succession of States' (1999), state succession 'should not entail negative consequences for the status of persons concerned as habitual residents'.[83] Conversely, as the General Assembly resolved in 1996, states should adopt national legislation to reduce statelessness, 'in particular by preventing arbitrary deprivation of nationality'.[84] Negative consequences are just the sorts of factors that I raised in chapter three: indefinite detention, expulsion, lack of access to public education and medical benefits, barriers to employment and the like. Such consequences loosen the social bonds that the international community needs for law to be binding. The boundary of internal state jurisdiction is thus no longer self-standing.

iv. Self-Executory Norms

A fourth doctrine adds to the transparency of the boundary of internal state jurisdiction. A self-executory norm, usually from a multi-lateral treaty, binds a state without the need for domestic legislation that enacts the terms of the treaty.[85] Such a norm has immediate effect. As an example,

---

[81] *Sawhoyamaxa Indigenous Community v Paraguay* (Merits, Reparations and Costs), Inter-Am Ct HR (29 March 2006) para 118. See also *Indigenous Community Yakye Axa v Paraguay* (Merits, Reparations and Costs), Inter-Am Ct HR Series C No 125 (17 June 2005). The *Sawhoyamaxa Indigenous Community* judgment of the Human Right Committee led to an Agreement between the community, the government and two corporations. See Amnesty International, 'Paraguay to Restore Indigenous Community's Ancestral Lands' (29 September 2011), www.amnesty. org/en/news-and-updates/paraguay-restore-indigenous-community%E2%80%99s-ancestral-lands-2011-09-29.

[82] *Sudali Andy Asary et al v Van den Dreesen (Inspector of Police)* (1952) 54 *New Law Reports* 66.

[83] ILC, 'Draft Articles on the Nationality of Natural Persons in Relation to the Succession of States, with Commentaries' in *Report of the ILC on the Work of its Fifty-First Session*, UN Doc A/54/10, www.refworld.org/pdfid/4512b6dd4.pdf, reprinted in *ILC Yearbook 1999*, vol II(2) A/CN.4/SER.A/1999/Add.1, Art 14(1) (Comm 1).

[84] Comprehensive Consideration and Review of the Problems of Refugees, Returnees, Displaced Persons and Related Migratory Movements, UN GA Res 32/151 (9 February 1996), adopted without a vote.

[85] HRC, 'CCPR General Comment 31: The Nature of the General Legal Obligation Imposed on States Parties to the Covenant' (29 March 2004) in UN, *Human Rights Instruments, Volume I* (above n 44).

according to Article 2 of the ICCPR, each state party 'undertake[s] to respect and to ensure to all individuals within its territory and subject to its jurisdiction the rights in the present Covenant without distinction'. Similarly, Article 2 of the International Covenant on Economic, Social and Cultural Rights (ICESCR) (1954) requires that states undertake to 'guarantee' that certain rights 'will be exercised without discrimination'. Although Article 2(1) provides for step-by-step progress in the full realization of the Covenant's rights, 'General Comment 3' of the ICESCR Committee emphasizes the obligation 'to move as expeditiously and effectively as possible toward that goal'.[86] The General Comment continues that 'minimum essential levels of each of the rights is incumbent upon every state party'.[87]

How is it possible for a treaty to recognize a state obligation if the treaty provision is directly enforceable without domestic legislation? Philip Alston and Ryan Goodman have suggested that such a question is immaterial because 'a state is obligated under international law to do whatever may be required under its internal law (such as legislative enactment) to fulfil its treaty commitments'.[88] Such a view, though, is problematic in its isolation of the issue from the legal culture of an international community. For one thing, chapter four above argued and documented how such a culture underlay the drafting and interpretation of the right to nationality in human rights treaties. Furthermore, although a state's reservations to a treaty must nominally be consistent with the objective of the treaty, chapter four enumerated a series of reservations that have conditioned ratification in terms of state jurisdiction over nationality matters. In addition, chapter five argued and documented how a right to nationality as a customary international norm has been trumped by the deeper cultural acceptance of nationality as an incident of the state's reserved domain. Moreover, Article 62 of the Vienna Treaty acknowledges that a treaty provision may be void if fundamental changes have occurred.[89] Is a state still bound to a self-executory treaty provision if a fundamental change has taken place – if, for example, the state has collapsed due to natural disaster or been overrun by paramilitary insurgents? And is a right to nationality a self-executory norm of practical import if a state's executive decides whether the right may be limited on the basis of the 'morality' or 'public order' of the state? In brief, a self-executory norm is not possible if the international community is constituted from the aggregate of the internal jurisdictions of states.

[86] Committee on Economic, Social and Cultural Rights (CESCR), 'General Comment 3: The Nature of States Parties' Obligations (Art 2(1) of the Covenant)' (14 December 1990), UN Doc E/1991/23, in UN, *Human Rights Instruments, Volume I* (above n 44) para 9.

[87] Ibid, para 10.

[88] See especially Alston and Goodman, *International Human Rights: Text and Materials* (above n 10) 1076.

[89] Vienna Convention on the Law of Treaties (1980) 1155 UNTS 331, Art 62.

The point is that one can better understand the existence of self-executory norms in terms of a state's legal obligation in an international community that is independent of the wills of individual states. In this vein, the HRC has stated that some treaty rights may not be suspended even during emergencies.[90] I noted above that such was recently the view of the House of Lords and the European Court of Human Rights.[91] Although a state's duty to protect stateless persons is not enumerated in the usual list of peremptory norms,[92] Jean Allain has added the principle of non-refoulement as a peremptory norm, and Ulf Linderfalk has insisted that the list could be far wider.[93] My point is that the justification of a peremptory norm and an obligation to protect stateless persons share the same sense of an international community as a whole – as does a state's obligation to protect stateless persons.[94] In addition, a self-executory norm exemplifies an obligatory character that is independent of a state's internal jurisdiction. A peremptory or self-executory norm exists independent of treaties or customary norms. The obligation also attaches to non-parties of treaties in the same way that the Rome Treaty may apply to non-state organizations. The obligation exists independent of the limitations and derogation clauses of human rights treaties. This 'pre-legal' obligation to protect stateless persons has emerged because, as argued in chapter six, the legal bond of an international community as a whole rests in the social relationships of natural persons independent of a state's determination of those persons' allegiance.

---

[90] See also HRC, 'CCPR General Comment 24: Issues Relating to Reservations Made upon Ratification or Accession to the Covenant or the Optional Protocols Thereto, or in Relation to Declarations under Article 41 of the Covenant' (4 November 1994) UN Doc CCPR/C/21/Rev.1/Add.6, in UN, *Human Rights Instruments, Volume I* (above n 44) paras 8 and 10; and CESCR, 'General Comment 9: The Domestic Application of the Covenant', UN Doc E/1999/22 Annex IV (1 December 1998), in UN, *Human Rights Instruments, Volume I* (above n 44) paras A.2, B.4 and C.11.

[91] See *A and Others v Secretary of State* (above n 49) para 68; *A and Others v UK* (above n 11) paras 11 and 19; and *Chahal* (above n 11) paras 128 and 132.

[92] Art 702 of the *Third Restatement* lists the following examples: genocide; slavery; the murder or disappearance of people; torture or other cruel, inhuman or degrading treatment or punishment; prolonged arbitrary detention; systematic racial discrimination; and a consistent pattern of gross violations of internationally recognized human rights: American Law Institute (above n 29) vol 2, 161, § 702.

[93] J Allain, 'The Jus Cogens Nature of Non-refoulement' (2001) 13 *International Journal of Refugee Law* 533; and U Linderfalk, 'The Effect of Jus Cogens Norms: Whoever Opened Pandora's Box, Did You Ever Think about the Consequences?' (2008) 18 *European Journal of International Law* 853.

[94] This is expanded regarding peremptory norms in WE Conklin, 'The Peremptory Norms of the International Community' (2012) 23 *European Journal of International Law* 837; and WE Conklin, 'The Peremptory Norms of the International Community: A Rejoinder to Alexander Orakhelashvili' (2012) 23 *European Journal of International Law* 869, 869–72.

III. THE ROLE OF THE COURTS WITH REGARD
TO STATELESS PERSONS

The seemingly hard fact of the bounded internal jurisdiction of states leaves nationality law to the legislative and executive arms of states. However, a different role for the judiciary has been highlighted in recent adjudication about stateless persons.

First, by agreeing to human rights treaty terms, states have taken on an active judicial role that runs counter to the executive prerogative in inter-state relations. The state parties to the ICESCR, for example, have undertaken 'to take steps' to 'progressively and fully realize the rights in the treaty 'by all appropriate means'.[95] State parties to the ICCPR similarly 'undertake to take the necessary steps . . . to adopt . . . measures as may be necessary to give effect to the rights recognized in the present Covenant'.[96] Such undertakings are especially relevant to the fiduciary duty of states to protect stateless persons. Although Article 2(3) of the ICESCR reserves the protected internal jurisdiction of 'developing countries' in the economic consequences of the absence of nationality, by negative implication, the onus is imposed on all states to justify any failure to provide domestic legal remedies for violations of economic, social and cultural rights.[97] In addition, Article 2(2) of the ICCPR does not just require legislative measures to protect natural persons; states parties also undertake to 'adopt legislative *or other measures* as may be necessary to give effect to the rights recognized' in the treaty, 'ensure that any person whose rights and freedoms as herein are recognized are violated shall have *an effective remedy*', 'ensure that any person . . . shall have his right thereto determined by competent judicial, administrative or legislative authorities, or by any other competent authority' and 'ensure that the competent authorities shall enforce such remedies'.

'General Comment 9', which addresses the domestic application of the ICESCR standards, interprets the ICESCR in a manner that 'requires each state party to use all the means at its disposal to give effect' to the treaty rights.[98] Aside from the obligation for states to recognize international norms 'in appropriate ways within the domestic legal order', 'General Comment 9' extends the obligation to redress, remedies and governmental accountability and affirms the obligation of to institutionalize domestic juridical remedies to fulfil international obligations.[99] Moreover, the rem-

---

[95] ICESCR (above n 76) Art 2(1).
[96] ICCPR (above n 3) Art 2(2).
[97] CESCR, 'General Comment 9' (above n 90) para 3. The importance of this obligation arises from the consequences of the absence of de jure protection of stateless persons. These consequences are outlined in detail above ch 3.
[98] CESCR, 'General Comment 9' (above n 90) para 2.
[99] Ibid, paras 2 and 3.

edies, which call the executive arm of a state into account for the with-drawal or withholding of nationality, must 'operate directly and immediately within the domestic legal system of each state party'.[100] With effective nationality as the legal bond of an international community,[101] the identity and nature of the roles of the executive and the judiciary now change. According to 'General Comment 9', any 'self-executing' treaty provision 'in most states . . . will be a matter for the courts, not the executive or the legislature'.[102] The Human Rights Committee of the ICCPR has also emphasized that domestic judicial remedies must extend 'to all individuals' under a state's jurisdiction.[103]

It is not just treaties, as interpreted by the human rights treaty commit-tees, that have entertained an active judicial role in deciding matters that have hitherto been considered inside the state's legal space. More recent judicial and quasi-judicial judgments have described the 'situs' of internal state jurisdiction as an object of judicial determination. For one thing, the simple declaration of an emergency by the executive arm of a state does not foreclose the incorporation of international standards as material to the judicial evaluation of the content of internal jurisdiction pertaining to stateless persons. In particular, a court may evaluate the actual or imma-nent impact of the emergency for individual stateless persons and whether an alleged emergency concerns the whole nation, poses a threat to the continuance of organized life inside the state's borders, or constitutes an exception to ordinary domestic acts regarding public safety, health and order.[104]

Courts have intervened when a state executive could not adequately address or ameliorate the social circumstances in which the state found itself. As the early European human rights judgment of *Ireland v UK* (1978) indicated, 'states do not enjoy an unlimited power' to decide whether they are threatened by 'public emergency'.[105] In particular, courts are 'empowered to rule on whether the states have gone beyond the "extent strictly required by the exigencies" of the crisis'.[106] *Chahal* (1997) in par-ticular indicated that courts have a special role to play in protecting a non-national if s/he has been detained for several years without criminal charge. As noted above, this duty of a court extends even if the detainee

---

[100] Ibid, para 4.
[101] See above ch 6, s II, III, IV (184–202).
[102] CESCR, 'General Comment 9' (above n 90) para 11.
[103] HRC, 'CCPR General Comment 3: Article 2 (Implementation at the National Level)' (29 July 1981) in UN, *Human Rights Instruments, Volume I* (above n 44) para 1.
[104] *Greek Case* (1969) YECHR 12, para 153.
[105] *Ireland v United Kingdom* (13 December 1977) 5310/71, ECHR (Ser A) No 25 (1978), (1979–80) 2 EHRR 25, refworld.org/docid/3ae6b7004.html, quoting *Lawless v Ireland (No 3)* (Merits) (1961) 31 ILR 290 (1 July 1961), Series A no 3, 55 (para 22) and 57–59 (paras 36–38).
[106] *Ireland v United Kingdom* (ibid) para 207. See also *Lawless v Ireland (No 3)* (Merits) (ibid).

poses a threat to the national security of the state.[107] Detention can be justified only if the state intends to deport the detainee to a third state. Even in this context, however, the absence of a willing third-party state would require the release of the stateless person.[108] More generally, the ultimate obligatory character of a law in matters of statelessness rests with the scrutiny of the social relationships presupposed in the content of the legislation.[109] So, for example, the ILC has inferred such when it has asked whether an act carried out under domestic law is null and void if denaturalization is an element of the persecution of an ethnic minority.'[110]

In sum, the boundary of the international community's residuary is now a matter of standards that concern the very existence of the international community as a whole.[111] The House of Lords in the *Case of A v Secretary of State for the Home Office* (2006) stated in no uncertain terms that a state does 'not enjoy an unlimited discretion': 'It is for the Court to rule whether inter alia the states have gone beyond the "extent strictly required by the exigencies" of the crisis.'[112] This may be so even if the 'life of the nation' is in fact threatened according to the belief of the executive officials of the state. The state's counsel has to provide evidence that an immanent attack against the state is transpiring.[113] Lord Hoffman, dissenting in *A v Secretary of State*, stated that the judiciary especially has an obligation to scrutinize the political and cultural evidence as to why state officials have decided to expel a stateless person:[114] 'the real threat to the life of the nation comes not from terrorism but from [domestic] laws such as these.'[115] The House of Lords generally held that singling out non-nationals represented a 'disproportionate' means of addressing a threat to national security.[116] Indefinite detention of non-nationals over many months or years is suspect even on account of a state emergency.[117] In other words, the court, not the executive, has a duty to define the locus of

---

[107] *Chahal* (above n 11) paras 128 and 132. See also *A and Others v Secretary of State* (above n 49) para 11; and *A and Others v UK* (above n 11) para 68.

[108] *Baban* (above n 12) para 7.2. In *Baban*, the non-national had been detained for over two years without justification by state officials and without any chance of substantive judicial review. See also *Chahal* (above n 11) paras 118 and 129.

[109] See, eg, *A v Australia* (above n 12); *Baban* (above n 12); *Bakhtiyari* (above n 12); *D and E* (above n 12); and *Saed Shams* (above n 12).

[110] ILC, 'Report on the Work of the 47th Session', UN Doc A/32/10, *ILC Yearbook 1995*, vol II(2), 37 (paras 183–85).

[111] *Chahal* (above n 11) paras 128 and 132. See also *Case of A and Others v UK* (above n 11) para 19; and *Al-Nashif* (above n 11) para 116.

[112] *A and Others v Secretary of State* (above n 49) para 68, quoting *Ireland v United Kingdom* (above n 106) para 207.

[113] *A and Others v Secretary of State* (above n 49) para 18.

[114] It remains unclear from Lord Hoffman's dissent in *A v Secretary of State* whether his state of origin was Syria or Kuwait. The Court did not rule out the relevance of domestic laws.

[115] *A and Others v Secretary of State* (above n 49) para 97.

[116] Ibid, para 68.

[117] Ibid. See also *Case of A and Others v UK* (above n 11) paras 128 and 190.

the boundary of internal state jurisdiction in a rights-based democracy.[118] On appeal, the European Court of Human Rights privileged the role of the court even when 'the life of the nation' is threatened.[119]

Effective nationality focuses upon a 'place' experienced, not the territory to which a state claims title.[120] The focus upon 'place' rather than territory destabilizes the mental mapping of jurists who have taken the aggregated international community and its Article 38 sources as hard facts since the late nineteenth century.[121] As an example, the Eritreans had lived for many generations on territory claimed by Ethiopia. The Eritreans were expelled to one part of Ethiopia, Eritrea, which declared independence in 1993. The territorial place of birth or habitual residence of Eritreans was considered of secondary importance. What were crucial were the close social contacts and 'clubs' that the expellees had experienced as Eritreans on the territory claimed by Ethiopia. They had celebrated and remembered their Eritrean culture there even though they had inhabited the territory owned by Ethiopia.[122] By virtue of its radical title to the territory, Ethiopia claimed nationality on the basis of allegiance, not the social bonding of the Eritreans. Expulsion of those believed to be lacking allegiance legally followed. If social bonding had been the basis of the legal bond, however, Eritreans would have been entitled to effective nationality on Ethiopian territory, with rights as de jure or effectively stateless persons being the consequence.

To offer another example, in 1996 the Indian Supreme Court conferred voting rights on a migrant group from the former East Pakistan because for over twenty-five years, the members of the group had established businesses, worshipped and developed other social bonds in India.[123] The Court did so despite enormous political pressure by students and local politicians to evict the stateless group from their homes and to expel them from the territory.

To take another example, the European Court of Human Rights held in *Slivenko v Latvia* (2003) that the expulsion of inhabitants, even stateless

---

[118] *A and Others v Secretary of State* (above n 49) para 42, quoting from J Jowell, 'Judicial Deference: Servility, Civility or Institutional Capacity?' (2003) *Public Law* 593, 597. For the role of the judiciary in political and 'legal' matters, see also *A and Others v Secretary of State* (above n 49) para 29.

[119] *A and Others v UK* (above n 11) paras 128 and 190.

[120] By 'place', again I do not signify territory but rather a space where one experiences others. For the difference between territorial space and experienced place, see ES Casey, *Getting Back Into Place: Toward a Renewed Understanding of the Place-World*, 2nd edn (Bloomington, Indiana University Press, 2009); and M Merleau-Ponty, *Phenomenology of Perception*, C Smith (trans) (London, Routledge, 1962) 98–147 and 243–98.

[121] For examples of displacement of territorial borders, see, eg, *A v Australia* (above n 12); *Baban* (above n 12); *Bakhtiyari* (above n 12); *D and E* (above n 12); and *Saed Shams* (above n 12).

[122] Conversely, an applicant was held to experience a fear of persecution as a Pentacostal Christian (a minority comprising 20,000 of the 3.5 million inhabitants of Eritrea) if she were returned to Eritrea as the place of her effective nationality.

[123] *National Human Rights Commission v State of Arunachal Pradesh and Another* (1996) SCC (1) 742.

inhabitants, breached Article 8 of the European Convention for the Protection of Human Rights and Fundamental Freedoms when family relationships were of concern.[124] Article 8 states, 'Everyone has the right to respect for his private and family life, his home and his correspondence.' The *Slivenko* Court declared that habitual residence must therefore manifest a 'degree of social integration'. As such, social integration constitutes a criterion of law.[125] In addition to family relationships, a person's social bonding is manifested by friendships, the sharing of dire circumstances (such as prolonged detention), a common language, shared religious practices and so on – not just habitual residence.[126] After all, as the Australian Federal Court has reminded us, a person can possess more than one state of habitual residence, just as a person can have more than one nationality.[127] The judiciary must examine 'network[s] of personal, social and economic relations that make up the private life of every human being'.[128]

IV. WHAT IS 'THE OPERATION OF ITS LAW'?

Article 1 of the Convention Relating to the Status of Stateless Persons (1954) defines a stateless person as a natural person 'not considered as a national by any state under the operation of its law'.[129] I have documented above and in chapter four how statelessness and human rights treaties entertain rights if one is lawfully on a state's territory. Human rights treaties moreover allow for the limitation and derogation of rights in certain circumstances 'by law'. The South African Constitutional Court has moreover stated, 'The primary duty of the courts is to the Constitution and the law.'[130] But what is 'the law'?

The displacement of the boundary of internal state jurisdiction and the accompanying legal obligation to protect stateless persons bring into question what is signified by 'the operation of its law'. It is one thing for a court or tribunal to 'find' a 'self-standing' right or rule in the texts of the Article 38 sources and another for a court to enquire about the social rela-

---

[124] *Slivenko v Latvia* [2003] ECHR 498, (2004) 39 EHRR 24.

[125] Ibid, para 95.

[126] Ibid. As another example, the European Court of Human Rights found in *Sisojeva v Latvia* that the applicants spoke Russian but identified socially with non-Russians in Latvia: *Sisojeva v Latvia* [2005] EctHR Application No 60654/00, (2007) 45 EHRR 33, paras 58 and 61.

[127] *Taiem v Minister for Immigration & Multicultural Affairs* [2001] FCA 611, para 9.

[128] *Slivenko* (above n 124).

[129] Convention Relating to the Status of Stateless Persons (above n 6). See also the American Declaration of the Rights and Duties of Man (above n 34) Art 19. The *Dictionary of International Law and Diplomacy* defines a 'stateless' person as one whose state of nationality no longer protects or assists the national by operation of law: MJ Gamboa, *A Dictionary of International Law and Diplomacy* (New York, Oceana, 1973) 246.

[130] *Minister of Health and Others v Treatment Action Campaign and Others (No 2)* (CCT8/02) [2002] ZACC 15, (2002) 5 SA 721, (2002) 10 BCLR 1033 (Constitutional Court of South Africa, 5 July 2002).

tionships presupposed inside the content of the international community's residuary of law-making. Not infrequently, what is 'law' is said to exclude extra-legality. What is law inferentially depends upon what jurists signify by 'extra-legal' or 'purely political'. The latter is usually taken as self-evident and sometimes called 'obvious'.[131] But how can a jurist delineate the boundary between law and extra-law without pressing further than the assumption that a judicial enquiry encumbers extra-law? I have suggested that the key to the boundary between what is law and what is extra-law is a particular sense of an international community constituted from the aggregate of the wills of states. However, what jurists have taken as the hard fact of internal state jurisdiction dissolves if the international community is understood as a whole. It is not just treaty provisions that have recognized a radically different sense of 'law' than that assumed by the notion of an aggregated international community. This different sense of 'law' has been manifested in other contexts.

First, the legal obligation drawn from the legal bond as social relations has rendered the content of internal state jurisdiction justiciable in matters of statelessness. By Article 27 of the Vienna Convention of the Law of Treaties, states parties undertake to 'not invoke the provisions of its internal law as justification for its failure to perform a treaty'.[132] This principle, as the HRC has pointed out in 'General Comment 31', is reinforced by Article 2(1) of the ICCPR, which obligates each state party 'to respect and to ensure to all individuals within its territory . . . without distinction of any kind, such as race, . . . language, religion, national or social origin, . . . birth or other status'.[133] 'General Comment 31' specifies that the latter undertaking requires that domestic law institutionalize remedies that enforce the obligation. 'General Comment 31' adds that domestic remedies must recognize all natural persons (presumably including stateless persons) as legal persons, as required by Article 16 of the ICCPR. 'General Comment 31' also refers to Article 24(3) of the ICCPR, which requires that the domestic remedies enforce rights guaranteed to nationals as well as the right of every child to acquire a nationality.[134] Both provinces and the national units in federal constitutional structures are subject to international obligations according to Article 50 of the ICCPR. And notably, by a General Assembly Resolution, states have agreed to adopt domestic legislation that reduces statelessness as part of the wider structure of 'fundamental principles of international law'.[135]

---

[131] This is explained, eg, in *Minister of Health v Treatment Action Campaign* (ibid) paras 37–38 and 96–99; and *A and Others v UK* (above n 11) paras 29, 35 and 37.

[132] Vienna Convention (above n 89).

[133] HRC, 'General Comment 31' (above n 85) paras 4–8.

[134] Ibid, para 4.

[135] UNGA Res 32/152, Office of the UN High Commissioner for Refugees 32nd sess, Agenda Item 109, 97th Plenary Meeting, passed on 21 December 1995 (9 February 1996), para 16.

Aside from the incorporation of international norms into internal jurisdiction, states have undertaken to provide a series of remedies to fulfil
their undertakings. Indeed, Article 9(5) of the ICCPR guarantees a right of
compensation to 'anyone who has been a victim of unlawful arrest or
detention' by a state (or international organization). According to Article
2(2), 'other measures' than legislation may be necessary 'to give effect' to
the Covenant rights. The HRC has institutionalized diverse and effective
remedies: declarations, compensation, restitution, injunctions, refusal to
denunciate a human rights treaty, compulsory repeal of statutory provisions and mandated public investigations.[136] Similar judicial remedies
have been expected for the effective domestic enforcement of international
standards. Once again, the legal obligation of stateless persons brings the
'non-binding' character of human rights committee decisions into question. The lawfulness of a detention order is not confined merely to questions regarding its compliance with domestically posited legal standards
within the boundary of the state's internal jurisdiction.[137] 'Lawfulness'
includes the incorporation of Covenant standards.

Secondly, domestic and international tribunals and courts are increasingly incorporating international standards into such terms as 'by law',
'legally' and 'lawfulness' when stateless persons are of concern.[138] The HRC
held in *Maroufidou v Sweden* (1985) that 'law' in Article 13 of the ICCPR
requires that the relevant domestic laws be 'compatible' with the ICCPR.[139]
In *Hernandez v The Philippines* (2007), the Committee stated that when
remedies have been unreasonably delayed, 'law' incorporates issues and
standards outside the boundary of the internal jurisdiction.[140]

Third, non-discriminatory rights have been increasingly considered to
possess a self-executory character, independent of any domestic law or its
administration. As the HRC has recently stated, 'There are elements of the
right to non-discrimination that cannot be derogated from *in any circumstances*'.[141] The Committee has restated the principle in even more explicit
terms: 'the international protection of the rights of persons belonging to

---

[136] See, eg, *KNLH v Peru*, Communication 1153/2003, UN Doc CCPR/C/85/D/1153/2003/
Rev.1 (14 August 2006) para 8; *Toonan v Australia*, Communication 488/1992, UN Doc CCPR/
C/32/D/488/1992 (31 March 1994) para 11; and *Minister of Health v Treatment Action
Campaign* (above n 130) paras 106 and 112. See also H Steiner, P Alston and R Goodman,
International Human Rights in Context: Law, Politics and Morals, 3rd edn (Oxford, Oxford
University Press, 2008) 'Comment on Remedies and Interim Measures' 895–96.

[137] *A v Australia* (above n 12) para 9.5.

[138] *Case Concerning Ahmadou Sadio Diallo (Republic of Guinea v Democratic Republic of the
Congo)*, Merits, Judgment, (2010) ICJ Reports 639, ISSN 0074, Judgment of 30 November
2010, No 103, para 66. However, an international tribunal does not possess authority to substitute its own opinion for that of a domestic court; it is for each state to interpret its own
domestic law, para 70.

[139] *Maroufidou v Sweden*, HRC Communication No 58/1979, UN Doc CCPR/C/12/D/58/
1979, (1985) 62 ILR 278, para 9.2.

[140] *Hernandez v The Philippines*, CCPR/C/99/D/1559/2007 (20 August 2010).

[141] HRC, 'General Comment 29' (above n 74) para 8 (emphasis added).

minorities includes elements that must be respected *in all circumstances*.[142] Indeed, even more specifically, according to Article 12 of the ICCPR, 'everyone lawfully within the territory of a state' possesses the right to liberty of movement, the freedom to choose her/his residence, the freedom to leave her/his country and the right to enter her/his own country. The HRC has stated with respect to Article 12, 'The legitimate right to derogate from Article 12 of the ICCPR during a state of emergency can never be accepted as justifying such measures' as the 'forced displacement by expulsion or other coercive means from the area in which the persons concerned are lawfully present'.[143] Even a declaration of emergency under Article 4 of the ICCPR cannot be used to justify the incitement 'to national, racial or religious hatred' or 'discrimination, hostility or violence'.[144]

Fourth, the boundary itself of internal state jurisdiction is increasingly considered justiciable. The recent UK High Court decision in *Al Rawi* (2006) suggests the justicability of the boundary of an executive decision does not protect an effectively stateless person, however.[145] Nonetheless, the ultimate authority to decide 'the legal edge' between the executive and the judicial arms of the state was 'the court's duty to decide'.[146] The House of Lords has documented how the boundary of internal jurisdiction has been rendered justiciable in refugee cases as a consequence of interpretations of the European Convention on Human Rights and other texts.[147] In like vein, the Federal Court of Australia has also held that the judiciary may review foreign affairs decisions of the Executive more generally.[148] The judiciary is 'equipped' to clarify the boundary of internal jurisdiction (while leaving the content of the legal space inside the boundary to the state's domestic laws).[149] The Constitutional Court of South Africa has also highlighted the judicial role in determining the boundary of internal state jurisdiction because such is necessary in order to protect inhabitants 'against a gross abuse of international human rights norms'.[150]

In general, the executive arm of states has not been left alone to choose whether to withhold admission from or to expel stateless persons. As the ICJ recently stated in *Diallo*, 'It cannot simply be left in the hands of the

---

[142] Ibid, para 13(c) (emphasis added).

[143] Ibid, para 13(d). See the discussion of judicial decisions above ch 7, sVIA (210–12).

[144] Ibid, para 13(e).

[145] *Al Rawi et al v Secretary of State for Foreign and Commonwealth Affairs and Another* [2006] EWCA Civ 1279.

[146] Ibid, para 148.

[147] Ibid, para 145.

[148] *Zin Mon Aye v Minister for Immigration and Citizenship et al* [2010] FCAFC 69 (Fed CA of Australia, 11 June 2010) paras 103 (per Lander) and 122 (per McKerracher).

[149] Ibid, para 73 (per Lander). See also *FAI Insurances Ltd v Winneke* (1982) 151 CLR 342, 380, as quoted in *Zin Mon Aye* (ibid) para 83 (per Lander).

[150] *Kaunda and Others v President of the Republic of South Africa and Others*, Case CCT 23/04 (South Africa Constitutional Court, 4 August 2004), www.refworld.org/docid/502390682. html, para 69, as quoted in *Al Rawi* (above n 145) para 105.

state in question to determine the circumstances which, exceptionally, allow that guarantee [regarding expulsion procedures in Article 13 of the ICCPR] to be set aside.'[151] The House of Lords has also recently expressed that the proscription against racial discrimination especially trumps domestic laws and their administration by the executive.[152]

V. THE LEGAL OBLIGATION TO PROTECT STATELESS PERSONS

A. Legal Obligation as the Social Bonding of Effective Nationality

I argued in chapter six that with an understanding of the international community as a whole, legal obligation rests in the social relations of natural persons, independent of states. As such, what is especially pertinent is the 'place' experienced by a stateless person in her/his social relationships. Such an experienced place was described in *Nottebohm* as 'effective nationality'.[153] A 'place' is *experienced* rather than being a hard fact. So too, the time of social bonding is experienced rather than measured on a calendar or a clock. In this sense of experienced space and time, one's state is a mere 'convenience', as Grotius once put it.[154] Indeed, one's social bonding may well be experienced in years of living in a slum (as in the *Olga Tellis* case[155]), in a refugee camp (as with the Biharis in Bangledash),[156] in a detention centre such as Guantánamo or on a state's territory, such as that of the United States, which has an estimated eleven million unauthorized migrants today.[157] Such social bonding has been described by jurists as 'effective', 'vital', or 'genuine' nationality. Such reciprocal social relations have been experienced analytically prior to and independent of a state's determination of allegiance. Any domestic laws conferring, withholding or withdrawing nationality enter into the discourse after the legal bond is experienced.

The enigma of the international community dissolves with a sense of legal obligation as social bonding signified by effective nationality. With the notion of state allegiance, there was a direct, one-way relation of the

---

[151] *Diallo* (above n 138) para 74.

[152] *European Roma Rights* (above n 63) para 46 (per Steyne).

[153] *Nottebohm (Liechtenstein v Guatemala)* (second phase) (1955) ICJ Rep 4, 23 (also reported in (1955) 22 ILR 349), www.refworld.org/docid/3ae6b7248.html.

[154] Grotius, *De Jure Praedae Commentarius*, GL Williams (trans), Classics of International Law Series (New York, Carnegie, 1950) Bk 2, ch 5, s 23, 253.

[155] *Olga Tellis v Bombay Municipal Corporation*, AIR 1986 SC 180, [1985] 2 Supp SCR 51. The case is discussed above ch 6, sVE.

[156] Discussed above ch 3 s 11 (116–000).

[157] See Migration Information Source, 'Frequently Requested Statistics on Immigrants and Immigration in the United States' (March 2012); and Rew Research, 'Unauthorized Immigrant Population: National and State Trends: 2010' (1 February 2011), www.pewhispanic.org/2011/02/01/unauthorized-immigrant-population-brnational-and-state-trends-2010/.

state towards natural persons. In contrast to the traditional role of the executive as the voice of the state's will in such a linear legal obligation, the judiciary has taken on a challenging role to protect stateless persons.[158] With the notion of effective nationality, the state is a third party to the relationships between social beings. Much like the Canadian state's fiduciary relation to indigenous inhabitants,[159] the state, as a third party to social relationships between natural persons, has a fiduciary relation to protect stateless persons from harm caused by one or several states, even if the states acted in the belief that the international community protected the state's reserved domain in matters of nationality. Effective nationality, the legal doctrine representing this fiduciary duty, is independent of the will of any one state. As a consequence, the boundary of the residuary has dissolved in the face of the legal bond of effective nationality.

Legal obligation is not owed to a state, as allegiance had presupposed, but to the international community as a whole. The ILC 'Draft Articles on State Responsibility' especially hold out a legal obligation on the part of a state if the obligation is 'of such a character as radically to change the position of all other states to which the obligation is owed with the further performance of the obligation'.[160] Such an obligation is exemplified by disarmament treaties, nuclear-free zone treaties 'or any other treaty where each parties' performance is effectively conditioned upon and requires the performance of each of the others'.[161] The obligation exists because of its relation to 'a group of states' or to 'the international community as a whole'.[162] Although the obligation may 'specially affect' a particular state, it may also harm the international community as a whole without harming a particular state. The important point is that a state's obligation is independent of the aggregated wills of states.

B. An Idealized International Community

To be sure, there might remain a third sense of an international community. This community would be idealized in a heaven of a priori concepts,

---

[158] See, eg, *A v Australia* (above n 12); *Baban* (above n 12); *Bakhtiyari* (above n 12); *D and E* (above n 12); and *Saed Shams* (above n 12).

[159] *Guerin v The Queen* [1984] 2 SCR 335, 13 DLR (4th) 321 (per Dickson CJ and Wilson); *R v Sparrow* [1990] 1 SCR 1075 (per Dickson and La Forest); and *Haida Nation v British Columbia (Minister of Forests)* [2004] 3 SCR 1075 (per McLachlin).

[160] ILC, 'Draft Articles on Responsibility of States for Internationally Wrongful Acts: Adopted by the International Law Commission at its Fifty-Third Session', UN Doc A/56/10 (2001), www.refworld.org/docid/3ddb8f804.html. The Draft Articles with ILC Commentary are also in J Crawford, *The International Law Commission's Articles on State Responsibility: Introduction, Text and Commentaries* (Cambridge, Cambridge University Press, 2002) 74–75, Art 42 (Comm 1).

[161] Ibid, Art 42 (Comm 13).

[162] Ibid, Art 42(b).

much as Kant outlined.[163] But such a legal community would be reified from the legal bond as social bonding. The community would be reified vis-à-vis the social ethos of the international community. The community's legal norms would be superimposed from above onto the internal jurisdiction of states. If natural persons were protected by such norms, this would be a matter of *fortune*. The international community would not exist, or if it existed at some point in time, it either would exist by coercion or would socially collapse. As the International Criminal Tribunal for the former Yugoslavia (ICTY) has stated, '[T]he principle at issue cannot be derogated from by states through international treaties or local or special or even general customary rules not endowed with the same normative force.'[164] The needed sense of social belonging, as highlighted by the 'General Comments' of the HRC, would be absent.

C. The Shift in Focus

It is not surprising, then, that recent judicial decisions related to nationality have placed the onus upon state officials to provide justificatory evidence and 'compelling reasons' why the state has acted towards stateless persons the way it has.[165] The state possesses a positive obligation to protect a stateless person after s/he has developed social relationships through the years.[166] The state's title to territory, itself a social construction, is a matter of happenstance. So too is a person's habitation on this state's territory rather than that state's territory. Legal obligation, according to the ILC, is owed by all states that deny, withhold or withdraw nationality from an injured natural person.[167]

This shift in focus as to the nature of legal obligation is not pie in the sky. Recent refugee judgments, noted in above and in chapters six and seven, have recognized how the standards of the international community have displaced the boundary of the internal jurisdiction of states when officials are charged with crimes against jus cogens. Such standards are

---

[163] I Kant, 'On the Relationships of Theory to Practice in International Right' in H Reiss (ed), *Kant's Political Writings*, 2nd edn (Cambridge, Cambridge University Press, 1977) 87–92; I Kant, 'Perpetual Peace: A Philosophical Sketch' in Reiss (ed) (above) 93–130; and I Kant, *Metaphysical Elements of Justice*, 2nd edn, J Ladd (trans) (Indianapolis, Hackett, 1999) 151–64.

[164] *Prosecutor v Anto Furundzija* (Trial Judgement), IT-95-17/1-T, (ICTY, 10 December 1998), www.refworld.org/docid/40276a8a4.html, para 153, quoted affirmatively in *Al-Adsani v United Kingdom* (2002) 34 EHRR 11 (21 November 2001), Application no 35763/97, Epn Ct Human Rts, para 30.

[165] *Diallo* (above n 138) paras 70, 72 and 74.

[166] *Sisojeva* (above n 126) paras 104, 105 and 110. See also *Gangadhar Teshwant Bhandare v Erasmo de Jesus Sequiria* [1975] INSC 21, AIR 1975 SC 972, (1975) SCR (3) 425, (1975) SCC (1) 544 (4 February 1975).

[167] ILC, 'Draft Articles on Diplomatic Protection, with Commentaries', UN Doc A/61/10, *ILC Yearbook 2006*, vol II(2), www.refworld.org/docid/525e7929d.html, Comm Art 4(7).

not posited in terms of this treaty provision or that treaty provision, as if treaties were a higher-ordered set of secondary rules, the International Law Commission notwithstanding. Rather, the international community as a whole exists immanent in the social world. And its laws emerge inside the very international law discourse that has held out the reserved domain and allegiance as hard legal facts. In brief, the referent of legal analysis now is an international community as a whole, independent of state members.

D. The Break from the Traditional Theory of International Law

This is not an exception to or aberration from the traditional theory of the residuary of the international community.[168] The traditional theory is being displaced through the emergence of an international law discourse that has a 'place' for stateless persons. Indeed, even denaturalization is now subject to international standards.[169] So too are the social benefits of migrant workers.[170] The issue is a matter not for state executives but rather for courts. And the background issue in all this is the nature of legal obligation in context-specific circumstances.

More generally, according to Justice Michael Kirby of the Australian High Court in *Nagv and Nagw* (2005), the 'classical theory of international law', which has heretofore privileged the boundary of the internal jurisdiction, has now dissolved in favour of the obligation of a state to protect stateless persons.[171] Jurists must not forget the mass migrations of persons of alleged Jewish bloodline during the inter-war period, Kirby has advised.[172] Even though in *Nagv and Nagw*, a stateless person would have been received positively by the state of origin, Australian legal protection of a stateless person was required in the light of her/his collective memory of harm in the state of origin. As a consequence, the central 'significant development in international law' over the past fifty years, according to Kirby, has been the transformation of natural persons, including stateless

---

[168] See, eg, *Rottmann v Freistaat Bayern*, C-135/08 (Court of Justice of the European Union, 2 March 2010), www.unhcr.org/refworld/docid/4be130552.html, paras 45 and 46.

[169] Ibid, para 48.

[170] See the Annotation of Regulation (EEC) No 1408/71 of the Council of 14 June 1971 on the Application of Social Security Schemes to Employed Persons and Their Families Moving within the Community. The Regulation has been repealed but remains in force for certain purposes. Details can be found at europa.eu/legislation_summaries/employment_and_social_policy/social_protection/c10516_en.htm.

[171] *Nagv and Nagw of 2002 v Minister for Immigration and Multicultural and Indigenous Affairs & Another* [2005] HCA 6.

[172] Persons of the alleged Jewish bloodline 'were shipped from pillar to post searching often fruitlessly for a place of refuge' without support of the European states. See *Nagv and Nagw* (ibid) paras 68 and 96. It is 'astonishing', Kirby insisted, that the state obligations under the treaty and customary law were withdrawn throughout the globe because of the way one state classified a Jew (para 97).

persons, into subjects of international law.[173] Guy Goodwin-Gill has successfully tested this new-found subjecthood on behalf of stateless persons
before the House of Lords in the recent *European Roma Rights Case*.[174] In
that case, the House of Lords concluded that it is 'incorrect' to say that
Parliament may change international legal obligations.[175]

E. Pre-legality

State obligations are owed to effectively stateless persons as well as to de
jure stateless persons.[176] As a refugee is entitled to protection before an
international organization or state has recognized her/him as having refugee status,[177] so too a stateless person is entitled to protection before s/he
is recognized as stateless. Just as a refugee is qualified for refugee status if
s/he fears persecution from the state of her/his habitual residence,[178]
so too a state owes a duty of protection to effectively stateless persons.
The obligation of protection analytically and experientially precedes the
conferral of legal status because the legal bond of the international
community as a whole is generated from the social relations of natural
persons independent and separate from states. This is analytically as well
as experientially 'pre-legal'.

This pre-legal social phenomenon justifies 'independent and rigorous'
judicial scrutiny of the personal memories and social bonding of effectively stateless persons, as the European Court of Human Rights has
recently affirmed.[179] Such pre-legal legal bonding explains why the content
of internal state jurisdiction is evaluated in terms of international standards. International standards are appropriate even to protect a stateless

---

[173] *Nagv and Nagw* (above n 171) para 68.
[174] *European Roma Rights* (above n 63) para 86.
[175] Ibid, para 88.
[176] See, eg, *Case of de Souza Ribeiro v France*, Application no 22689/07 (ECtHR, 13 December 2012, www.refworld.org/docid/511cf0a22.html; *SRPP v Minister for Immigration and Multicultural Affairs* [2000] AATA 878, paras 106 and 110; and *Lay Kon Tju v Minister for Immigration & Ethnic Affairs* [1998] FCA 1380 (Fed Ct of Australia, 30 October 1998), www.refworld.org/docid/3ae6b76014.html.
[177] JC Hathaway, *Rights of Refugees* (Cambridge, Cambridge University Press, 2005) 159: 'It is one's de facto circumstances, not the official validation of those circumstances, that gives rise to Convention refugee status.' And again at 11: 'As a fundamental principle, the acquisi-tion of refugee rights under international law is not based on formal status by a state or agency, but rather follows simply and automatically from the fact of substantive satisfaction of the refugee definition.' Guy S Goodwin-Gill has also stated, 'In principle, a person becomes a refugee at the moment when he or she satisfies the definition, so that determina-tion is declaratory, rather than constitutive . . .' See GS Goodwin-Gill, *The Refugee in International Law*, 2nd edn (Oxford, Oxford University Press, 1996) 32. See also *MA v Attorney General*, Civ 2006-404-1371 (High Court of Auckland, 21 September 2007) para 103.
[178] ILC, 'Draft Articles on Diplomatic Protection, with Commentaries' (above n 167) para 23.
[179] *Ribeiro v France* (above n 176).

person who has been expelled for committing a criminal act.[180] This state obligation to protect effectively stateless persons is of a legal, not moral, character.[181] However a person is categorized – 'undocumented', 'illegal', 'non-working migrant', 'of unknown nationality', stateless or 'alien' – a state possesses a legal obligation of protection. The Human Rights Committee has required such judicial scrutiny 'even in relation to entry or residence, for example, when considerations of non-discrimination, prohibition of inhuman treatment and respect for family life arise'.[182] In brief, the effective nationality of all undocumented migrants, independent of any domestic immigration status, constitutes an existence condition of the international community. In this respect, effective nationality is on par with the character of peremptory norms.[183] All members of the international community owe an obligation to protect and enforce effective nationality. Effective nationality conditions an international community independent of its members, including states and natural persons, and yet such a community exists *for* the protection of such members.

The critical issue, then, concerns whether the boundary of the reserved domain is dissolving in nationality matters. And that issue depends upon an international community that is very different from one understood as the aggregated wills of states members. This emerging international community, which is nested inside traditional international law discourse, represents a legal bond that is independent of state members. And yet the independent community exists *for* its members, and its members are not just states. Accordingly, the quest for the identity of a rule or test in the traditional sources of Article 38 of the ICJ Statute may not be obligatory for a state official.[184] Put differently, the product of 'the operation of a state's law' – the key criterion for defining a de jure stateless person in the Convention Relating to the Status of Stateless Persons – incorporates binding international legal norms that are protective of an international community independent of the aggregated wills of state members. The international community as a whole raises an issue that the traditional quest for the identity of law in internal state jurisdiction excludes from analysis.

---

[180] Ibid, para 77.

[181] Ibid, per Judges Pinto de Albuquerque and Vučinić.

[182] HRC, 'General Comment 15' (above n 54) para 5. Elsewhere in the Comment, the HRC stated that 'the competent parties of the state party' must be 'observing, however, such requirements under the Covenant as equality before the law' (Art 26). See para 9.

[183] This characterization of peremptory norms is developed in Conklin, 'The Peremptory Norms of the International Community' (above n 94); and Conklin, 'A Rejoinder to Alexander Orakhelashvili' (above n 94). For the list of peremptory norms, see generally ILC, 'Draft Articles on Responsibility of States' (above n 160) Art 48 (Comm 9), Art 40 (Comms 2–6); and American Law Institute (above n 29) vol 1 (161, para 702). Similarly, Art 4 of the ILC's 'Draft Articles on Diplomatic Protection' (above n 167) provides that nationality is acquired 'in accordance with the law of that state [of nationality] . . . not inconsistent with international law'.

[184] *Jurisdictional Immunities of the State (Germany v Italy)* (above n 9) para 93.

VI. CONCLUSION

The enigma of an international community rests in the juridical construction of a boundary that encompasses and protects the essential matters of the state. The conferral, withdrawal and withholding of nationality has been an important incident of such a bounded legal space. The boundary, though, is dissolving. Legal obligation has taken on a very different character than that claimed by and for the reserved domain of the state. Such is so, at least, for the legal obligation to protect stateless persons. Courts are bringing the boundary into question by scrutinizing the social content of the bounded domain when stateless persons are of concern. The territoriality of the boundary is therefore dissolving in matters of both interstate and intrastate conflict. The doctrines of non-arbitrariness, good faith, proportionality and self-executory treaty provisions are not reconcilable with the territorial-like boundary of internal state jurisdiction. The analysis of an identifiable, self-standing right or rule in terms of a source within a state is hence misdirected. Instead, the social bonding represented by effective nationality forces a re-examination of the relationship between natural persons and the state, and we can begin to appreciate the emergence of a very different international community with a very different sense of legal bond.

9

The International Community as a Whole

THE BINDING CHARACTER of a discrete right, rule or test, whether domestic or international, depends upon the extent to which natural persons reciprocally recognize and respect each other as manifested in the heretofore immunized content of the residuary of a state-centric international community. Put differently, what jurists have imagined as the boundary of the residuary has been dissolving, at least for stateless persons. What jurists formerly assumed was 'extra-legal' scrutiny of the content of the residuary has now been justified by an understanding of the legal bond as social relationships, better signified as 'effective nationality'. This book has outlined how the latter sense of legal bond exists independent of states and therefore independent of an international community that protects a residuary of law-making and law administration. On the other hand, when the international community understood as an aggregate of state wills incorporates the bounded domain of a state, the legal bond has assumed a focus on the relation of each natural person to the state. Allegiance, as indicated by Article 8(3)(a) of the Convention on the Reduction of Statelessness (1961), has been considered synonymous with loyalty to a state.

Chapter six documented how each state determines who is loyal to it and, as a consequence, determines who has a legal bond to the international community. The ultimate obligatory character of international standards has rested upon scrutiny of the social content of the residuary. But is the ultimate source of a nationality right or rule obligatory if the state is both the subject and the object of the international legal structure? By this, I mean to suggest that because a state is considered the subject of international legal order and because the legal order, as an objectivity, is constructed from the express or implied consent of a state, legal obligation is self-defined by and for states. This explains why states have claimed their own authority. In this light, a natural person has enforceable international rights only by virtue of a residuary wherein rights and rules are the object of the express or implied consent of states.

The aim of this chapter is to explain why the protection of the social relationships of stateless persons is critical to the notion of an international community as a whole. Section I outlines the identity and character of such a community, and the traditional juristic explanations of its character are found wanting. Section II addresses the nature of a 'community' more broadly. Section III examines the existence conditions of the international community as whole. Section IV then turns to legal objectivity and the problem of such objectivity if the community is the aggregated wills of state members. Section V then turns to stateless persons as subjects of the objectivity. Finally, section VI demonstrates how harm caused to any de jure or effectively stateless person constitutes harm to the international community as a whole.

I. THE CHARACTER OF THE INTERNATIONAL COMMUNITY AS A WHOLE

The notion of international community, independent of its state members, raises the prospect that the international community itself can be harmed. Such harm entails any breach of norms, even in a case in which the state in question has not enacted a domestic law nor implicitly consented to the norm. Two features of this possibility stand out: first, the identity of the community as a source of discrete rights and rules; and second, efforts to explain why the community exists as a legal entity independent of state members.

A. The International Community as the Common Interest of State Members

The issue before us is this: what is the ethos or character of the international community as a whole? This ultimate referent is not an empty form, nor is it a recent sign of modern international legal discourse. The international community as a whole was described as the 'family of nations' as early as 1900 in the US Supreme Court case *The Paquete Habana*.[1] Indeed, in 1980 the US Court of Appeals declared in *Filartiga* that the universality of the international community had trumped the state's freedom as early as the late eighteenth century.[2] In chapter six, I examined how the legal bond of an international community was nested in social relations, or what jurists during the seventeenth and eighteenth centuries called 'sociability'. Such sociability, shared amongst natural persons, analytically and experientially

---

[1] *The Paquete Habana* (1900) 175 US 677, 20 SCt 290.
[2] *Filartiga v Pena-Irala* (1980) 630 F (2d) 876 (2nd Circuit) 885–88 (per Kaufman), also reported in 77 ILR 169.

preceded the emergence of the state. Since the mid-twentieth century, the international community as a whole has again been increasingly privileged in international law discourse.[3]

However, my discussion of international law discourse has revealed how two very different notions of the international community with two very different corresponding senses of a legal bond have emerged. The crucial distinction is this: the one international community has been constituted from the self-interest of the state members of the community. I argued in chapter four that statelessness and human rights treaties, on their face, have taken for granted that an international community is constituted in such a manner. The sources thesis, recognized by deference to Article 36 of the Statute of the ICJ, has taken the aggregated international community for granted.[4] Buried in such a discourse, however, there has emerged what jurists have described as 'the international community as a whole'. Such a community has been constituted from some factor other than the self-interest of states. The often cited dictum of the International Court of Justice (ICJ) in *Barcelona* needs to be repeated in this regard:

> An essential distinction should be drawn between *the obligations of a state towards the international community as a whole*, and those arising vis-à-vis another state in the field of diplomatic protection. By their very nature, *the former are the concern of all states*. In view of the importance of the rights involved, all states can be held to have a legal interest in the protection of obligations *erga omnes*.[5]

The obligations of states towards the international community as a whole raise the prospect of a legal objectivity independent of states.

Opinio juris continues to take for granted that there is something very special about the international community as a whole other than a state-centric character.[6] However, even in the International Law Commission

---

[3] For treaties, international court dicta and domestic dicta, see text above ch 1 between n 24 and 34. Early scholarly studies are exemplified by Green H Hackworth expressed in 1943, for example, that the alien was warranted a standard of protection that was 'essential to the community of nations': GH Hackworth, *Digest of International Law*, vol 5 (Washington, DC, US Government Print Office, 1940–41) 471–72. Jessup asserted in 1948 that there is a broad 'principle of community interest in the prevention of breaches of international law'. Jessup was preoccupied with such a view throughout PC Jessup, *A Modern Law of Nations: An Introduction* (New York, Archon Books, 1968).

[4] See above ch 1, s II (41–42).

[5] *Barcelona Traction, Light and Power Co Case (Belgium v Spain)*, (1970) ICJ Rep 3, 46 ILR 178, 206 (para 33), emphasis added.

[6] See generally above ch 1, s 11A (41–42). See also M Shaw, *International Law*, 5th edn (Cambridge, Cambridge University Press, 2003) 116–19; A de Hoogh, 'The Relationship between Jus Cogens, Obligations Erga Omnes and International Crimes: Peremptory Norms in Perspective' (1991) 42 *Austrian Journal of. Public International Law* 183, 193–96; JP Kelly, 'The Twilight of Customary International Law' (1999–2000) 40 *Virginia Journal of International Law* 449, 465–69; GM Danilenko, 'International Jus Cogens: Issues of Law-Making' (1991) 42 *European Journal of International Law* 42; A Brudner, 'The Domestic Enforcement of International Covenants on Human Rights: A Theoretical Framework' (1985) 35 *University of Toronto Law Journal* 219, 249–50; H Mosler, 'The International Society as a Legal Community' (1980 [1974]) 140 *Recueil des Cours de l'Academie de Droit International de la Haye* 11, 19;

(ILC) 'Draft Articles on State Responsibility', there are at best only references to 'the international community as a whole'; other than the pro-
nouncement in *Barcelona*, there has been little formal insight into the ethos
of the international community as a whole. Unless we can gain a grasp of
what is embodied in the content of this concept, 'the international community as a whole' is a mere empty form, much as Peter Fitzpatrick has
described the state.[7]

One suggested explanation is that the institutional community as a whole
is constituted from principles representing the common interests of the state
members. In the ICJ case *Reservations to the Convention on Genocide* (1951),
common state interest is seen as generating norms that trump any particular
state's individual will.[8] It was noted in chapter one above how, as early as
1948, Philip Jessup associated the international community with a broad
'principle of community interest in the prevention of breaches of international law'.[9] Jessup's dissent in the *South-West African Cases* (1966) moreover
described the 'international regime' as representing 'the common benefit of
the international society'.[10] Such a viewpoint, though, is circular in that the
international law is said to depend upon the community of interest, and
the latter, in turn, is justified by international law. The common benefit is the
lowest common denominator of the wills of each state member.

A further sense of commonality is manifested by the conceptual dependency of any one state upon the good will of other states.[11] We observed in
earlier chapters how key efforts to reduce statelessness have involved
attempts to codify rules that aim to prevent conflicts in domestic nationality
rules. It has been in the self-interest of each state to agree to such codified
rules. More generally, treaties exemplify the interdependency of each state
party on the other state parties. Such interdependency works its way into
the domestic enforcement of agreed norms. So too, customary international
norms have emerged from such interdependency. However, the problem

---

H Mosler, *The International Society as a Legal Community*, revised edn (Alphen aan den Rijn,
Sijthoff & Nordhoff, 1980) 19; and A Verdross, 'Jus Dispositivum and Jus Cogens in
International Law' (1966) 60 *American Journal of International Law* 55.

[7] Fitzpatrick has left the ultimate referent (in his case, the state) an empty form. See
P Fitzpatrick, 'Latin Roots: Imperialism and the Making of Modern Law' in P Fitzpatrick,
Law as Resistance: Modernism, Imperialism, Legalism (Farnham, Ashgate, 2008); P Fitzpatrick,
'Justice as Access' (2005) 23 *Windsor Yearbook of Access to Justice* 1, 9–13; P Fitzpatrick, 'Gods
Would Be Needed . . .: American Empire and the Rule of (International) Law' (2003) 16 *Leiden
Journal of International Law* 429, 436; and P Fitzpatrick, '"No Higher Duty": *Mabo* and the
Failure of Legal Foundation' (2002) 13(3) *Law and Critique* 233, 242.

[8] *Reservations to the Convention on the Prevention and Punishment of the Crime of Genocide*
(Advisory Opinion), (1951) ICJ Rep 15, 23 (also reported in 18 ILR 364).

[9] See Jessup (above n 3) esp 53.

[10] See his dissenting opinion in *South West Africa Cases (Ethiopia v South Africa; Liberia v
South Africa)* (second phase), (1966) ICJ Rep 373, reported at 37 ILR 243.

[11] See also *Legality of the Threat or Use of Nuclear Weapons* (advisory opinion), (1996) ICJ Rep
257 (263), 110 ILR 163 (213, para 96); and *East Timor (Portugal v Australia)*, (1995) ICJ Rep 90,
per Skubiszewski (dissenting), 119–22, also reported in 105 ILR 226.

identified above in chapters four and five is that such interdependency pre-supposes the will of states as its starting point. Such interdependency means that any state party to a treaty or any state that consents to a custom-ary norm must respect the domestic laws and decisions of every other state party, even if those domestic laws and decisions produce statelessness.

This shared dependency once again is generated from a community aggregated from the particular wills of state members. The social content of each state's protected and bounded reserved domain remains immune from external intervention unless a state or a substantial number of states consents to the intervention. The international community is thereby con-stituted from the sum of the wills represented by the reserved domains, without an examination of such domains. Indeed, the domestic and inter-national judiciaries, as external to the prerogative of the executive arms of the states in matters regarding the content of the reserved domain, end up trying to clarify the boundary of each state's domain. With the presumed freedom of states in matters of the content of their reserved domain, such judicial clarification necessarily focuses on preventing one state from causing harm to other states. The international community stands or falls by virtue of such a sum of the particular wills of the state members. International standards, as a consequence, must directly or indirectly respond to particular state wills. Unless international standards do so, the standards are hortatory as to how state members ought to act.

One idea underlying the commonality of shared state interests is that of a common enemy to a system of states. During the nineteenth century, the 'enemy' was considered to be a different category from 'civilized states'.[12] More recently, the House of Lords suggested in the *Pinochet* case that the international community is unified by the 'common enemies of all mankind'.[13] Accordingly, state practice can be considered a practice of an enemy of humankind, as was concluded in *Pinochet*. Such a viewpoint, however, bases the commonality of the international community upon an

---

[12] See generally, A Anghie, 'Finding the Peripheries: Sovereignty and Colonialism in Nineteenth-Century International Law' (1999) 40 *Harvard International Law Journal* 22; *Imperialism, Sovereignty and the Making of International Law* (Cambridge, Cambridge University Press, 2004). For recent studies of injury to the international community, see *Catholic Commission for Justice and Peace in Zimbabwe v Attorney-General*, Supreme Court of Zimbabwe Judgement No SC 73/93, (1993) 14 *Human Rights Law Journal* 323, 100 ILR 622; *Filartiga* (above n 2); and *Riley and Others v Attorney-General of Jamaica* [1982] 3 ALL ER 469 (PC). See also ILC, 'Draft Articles on Responsibility of States for Internationally Wrongful Acts' in *Report of the International Law Commission on the Work of Its Fifty-third Session*, UN Doc. A/56/10 (2001), www.refworld.org/docid/3ddb8f804.html, Art 42 (Comm 1); and J Crawford, 'Introduction' in *International Law Commission's Articles on State Responsibility: Introduction, Text and Commentaries* (Cambridge University Press, Cambridge, 2002) 39–43.

[13] *R v Bartle, ex parte Pinochet Ugarte* [1999] 2 All ER 97, [1999] 2 WLR 827 (HL). In the charge against Eichmann, the Israeli District and Appeal Courts held out the existence of an offence against 'the whole of mankind' and a 'shock[ing]' of the conscience of nations'. See *Attorney General of Israel v Adolf Eichmann*, District Court of Jerusalem (1961) 36 ILR 18, 25, 26, 50. See also the judgment of the Israeli Supreme Court sitting as the Court of Criminal Appeals at (1962) 36 ILR 277, 299 and 304.

externality to the community. Presumably, the common enemies are unrecognisable stateless peoples, such as those outlined in chapter three: nomadic and travelling groups, traditional societies, unregistered inhabitants and members of ethnic, linguistic or religious groups that lack legal status. More importantly, since the reserved domain of states is a hard legal fact against which knowledge outside the domain's boundary is extra-legal according to the aggregated wills of states, the common interest understood in terms of the common enemies of human kind is excluded from legal knowledge. The international community as a whole thereby depends upon an unexaminable and unknowable non-object. Since the international community, as an external 'other,' lacks legal knowability – except as arbitrarily posited by domestic laws – the international community is itself arbitrarily circumscribed, just as the state's claim to its own authority is.

B. The International Community as a Whole

In contrast to the image of an aggregated international community outlined above, the notion of the international community as a whole suggests that the community's character is generated from something other than the particular common wills of state members. Such a possibility is borne out by the ICJ judgments in *South West Africa Cases* (1966), *East Timor* (1995), *Nuclear Weapons* (1996) and *Genocide (Bosnia v Serbia)* (1996), which were examined above in chapter one.[14] To be sure, the international community as a whole shares the same structure of institutions and norms as does the international community as the aggregate of the wills of states. The difference between the two senses of an international community, however, rests in what jurists have taken for granted in each international law discourse in which the community is nested. The aggregated community has assumed a residuary of law-making and law-administration assigned to the state. Nationality has been an accepted incident fo such a residuary. The boundary of such a residuary has been dissolving in the international community as a whole. As a consequence, de jure and effective nationality have become matters of the international community as a whole.

The uncertainty and contradictions relating to recent debates concerning state immunity can be explained by the two very different senses of an international community. I documented in chapter two how the dominant stream of state immunity doctrine presupposes the community as aggre-

---

[14] See *South West Africa Cases* (above n 10) per Jessup; *East Timor (Portugal v Australia)* (above n 11) 172 and 213–16 (per Weeramantry, dissenting), also reported in 105 ILR 226; *Legality of the Threat or Use of Nuclear Weapons* (Advisory Opinion), (1996) ICJ Rep 226, para 83; and *Application of the Convention on the Prevention and Punishment of the Crime of Genocide (Bosnia and Herzegovina v Serbia and Montenegro)* (Preliminary Objections), (1996) ICJ Rep 595, 615–16 (paras 31–32), also reported in 115 ILR 1, 28–29. For a discussion of these cases, see above ch 1, s III (52–58).

gated from self-creative and self-determining states as authors. One can also find a sub-discourse in recent judgements, however. This sub-discourse has taken the international community as a whole as the referent of legal understanding. Christos Rozakis and other judges of the European Court of Human Rights have urged us to understand state immunity, for example, by first addressing the 'framework' or 'international sphere' represented by 'the collective judgment of the international community' as a whole.[15] As the ILC Draft Articles on State Responsibility suggest, the international community can be harmed even though no single state member is directly harmed. In addition, compensation does not necessarily accrue to a state even though a legal obligation is owed to the state.[16] The legal bond of the community is not determined by states or by international institutions. Rather, the bond is generated immanently from the social relationships of natural persons. International institutions, like domestic institutions, possess a fiduciary duty to protect such social relations.

C. What Grounds the International Community as a Whole?

The association of the international community with the common interests of states must lead us to ask: what distinguishes the common interest of states from the self-interest of individual states? Various alternatives to the notion of 'common interests of states' have been offered: the 'conscience of humankind',[17] human rights,[18] public policy,[19] the 'criteria of morality and

---

[15] *Al-Adsani v UK*, App No 35763/97 (ECtHR Grand Chamber, 21 November 2001) (Rozakis and Caflisch dissenting, joined by Wildhaber, Costa, Cabral Barreto and Vajin), www.refworld.org/docid/3fe6c7b54.html. See also *Prosecutor v Charles Taylor* (Appeals Decision on Immunity from Jurisdiction), Case No SCSL-2003-01-1 (Special Court for Sierra Leone, 31 May 2004), (2004) ILR 239, para 51. See also the opinion of the former legal adviser of the US Government, Harold Koh, as quoted in P Alston and R Goodman, *International Human Rights* (Oxford, Oxford University Press, 2013) 1198–99.

[16] 'Draft Articles on State Responsibility' (above n 12) Art 31 (Comm10), Art 33 (Comm 3) and Art 48 (Comms 1, 10 and 12). See also Crawford, 'Introduction' (above n 12) 36.

[17] AA Cançado Trindade, *International Law for Humankind: Towards a New Jus Gentium* (Leiden, Martinus Nijhoff, 2010) 291. Crawford was satisfied with this criterion at one point: J Crawford, 'Introduction' (above n 12) 38, quoting *Reservations regarding Genocide* (above n 8) 23. Dan Dubois has cited a series of scholars who are satisfied with the conscience of the international community as the root of peremptory norms: D Dubois, 'The Authority of Peremptory Norms in International Law: State Consent or Natural Law' (2009) 78 *Nordic Journal of International Law* 133, 154 (fn 72) and 155 (fn 77).

[18] *Reservations regarding Genocide* (above n 8) 23. See also ILC, 'Draft Articles on State Responsibility' (above n 12); Human Rights Committee (HRC), 'CCPR General Comment 26: Continuity of Obligations', para 4. 12/08/1997, CCPR/21/Rev.1/Add.8/Rev.1, www.refworld.org/docid/453883fde.html, in UN, *Human Rights Instruments, Volume 1: Compilation of General Comments and General Recommendations Adopted by Human Rights Treaty Bodies*, UN Doc HRI/GEN/1/Rev.9 (vol 1), (27 May 2008), www.un.org/en/ga/search/view_doc.asp?symbol=HRI/GEN/1/Rev.9.

[19] See RKM Smith, *Text and Materials on International Human Rights* (Oxford, Oxford University Press, 2007) 15; G Schwarzenberger, 'International Jus Cogens?' (1964–65) 43

public policy',[20] 'basic human values',[21] 'all organized entities endowed with the capacity to take part in international legal relations', [22] 'inclusiveness'[23] and mere metaphor.[24] One recent approach has attempted to bring three criteria together (*'opinio juris communis'*, 'conscience' and 'humanization') as if the combination is obvious.[25]

The problem with each of these alternatives to the notion of the common interests of states is that their empty content returns jurists to the more familiar bounded residuary as the source of nationality law. And other critical questions remain: what makes a society 'civilized' – what criteria distinguish a civilized society from an uncivilized one? Does an international community as a whole exist if uncivilized states are excluded from it? What renders a value 'basic' and another not basic? Are the values of jurists determinative? If so, why the values of jurists rather than those of stateless persons? How can a community be 'more inclusive' if de jure and effective statelessness excludes tens of millions of natural persons? If the international community is but a metaphor, what is the second-level referent to which the metaphor refers? Is the community simply an a priori concept, as Kant would have it? How does a human right differ from an ordinary right? Does a human right return us to Kant's empty notion of dignity, that is, an immeasurable a priori concept? Can a deep and longstanding assumption of a legal culture such as the reserved domain be whisked off the charts with a mere assertion that something else trumps it? How can there be legal obligation in the air – that is, dwelling in a world of a priori concepts, reified from the legal bond nested in social-cultural phenomena?

The above crucial questions point to the fact that searching for a common interest amongst states is a circular endeavour.[26] Instead, we can better understand the ethos of the international community in terms of who is excluded from it. Looking at such exclusion requires an investigation into the legal bond of the international community (which was addressed in chapter six) and the dissolution of the very boundary that has excluded

---

Texas Law Review 455, 476; and H Bull, *The Anarchical Society: A Study of Order in World Politics* (London, Macmillan, 1977) 63–67.

[20] This was recognized in the debate concerning the drafting of Arts 53 and 64 of the Vienna Convention on Treaties. See J Dunoff et al, *International Law: Norms: Actors, Process*, 3rd edn (New York, Aspen, 2010) 59–60.

[21] Dubois (above n 17) 161–66.

[22] H Mosler, 'International Legal Community' in R Bernhardt (ed), *Encyclopedia of Public International Law*, vol 2 (Amsterdam, Elsevier, 1997) 1251–52.

[23] See, eg, ILC, 'Draft Articles on State Responsibility' (above n 12) Comments to Art 48. However, Brownlie suggested that the 'Draft Articles on State Responsibility' only contemplate non-derogation of peremptory norms when states have already agreed to such. See J Crawford (ed), *Brownlie's Principles of Public International Law*, 8th edn (Oxford, Oxford University Press, 2012) 115–26.

[24] Kelly (above n 6) 465–69.

[25] Cançado Trindade (above n 17).

[26] See above ch 1, s III (49–52).

de jure and effective stateless persons. The legal bond of social relations between natural persons and the dissolution of the boundary of domestic jurisdictions for the purpose of protecting stateless persons together raise the prospect of harm being committed against the international community as a whole.

II. A COMMUNITY

This international community as a whole exists independent of its state members and, indeed, independent of its other members, such as international organizations, non-governmental organizations, corporations and (most importantly for our purposes) natural persons. The said members are subjects of legal objectivity. Simultaneously, however, the international community exists *for* its members as well as independently of them. How is it possible that a community, independent of its subjects, exists for its subjects? More specifically, how is it possible that a community's laws, independent of an ethno-cultural people, exist for such a people? How is it possible for a community's laws, independent of nomadic and travelling groups lacking fixity on territory, exist for such groups?

The germ of an explanation rests in the character of a discrete obligatory law. The mere quest for the identity of any particular legal rule or test, which has heretofore rested in the residuary of the international community, is necessarily misdirected in matters of statelessness when one addresses the nature of legal obligation. The search for an identifiable right/rule/concept presupposes the reserved domain, which has left millions of natural persons de jure and effectively stateless. Traumatic social consequences have resulted, as identified in chapter three. Since legal obligation in an international community as a whole depends upon a legal bond of social relationships, as argued in chapter six, the residuary is no longer a hard fact. And the conferral, withholding and withdrawal of nationality by states are no longer legally binding elements of the international community. The social phenomenon of statelessness raises this issue: why would a discrete international legal norm be binding if an existence condition of an international legal objectivity were absent, if not intentionally undermined by a state member?

The enigma of an international community must be understood in terms of the community's ethos. Such an ethos is constituted from assumptions and expectations generating the attitudes shared in a community, whether the community is a family, a village, an ethnic-cultural people or even an international community. The contemporary challenge for jurists is to understand the ethos of the particular sense of an international community – an ethos manifested by a legal bond as the social content of treaties and customary norms. The protected residuary or leftover of law-making –

obligatory because of the state's determination of allegiance – manifests the ethos of one international community. But the displacement of such a residuary by a legal bond of social relations manifests a radically different ethos of an international community.

The first point to note is that social bonds, as explained by the Human Rights Committee (HRC) in reference to the International Covenant on Civil and Political Rights (ICCPR), inculcate a community.[27] One can belong to a community and yet inhabit another community's territory. This very sense of a community, I have argued, has dissolved the bounded residuary of the international community, at least regarding de jure and effectively stateless persons.[28] Social bonding is embodied by the reciprocal social relations of natural persons. Such embodiment emanates from common culture with collectively shared memories.[29] As the HRC has indicated, this 'belonging' with others, independent of any state, manifests 'a way of life'.[30] A 'culture', the HRC has added elsewhere, gives body to the form of a community. The embodiment draws from attachment to territorial resources, shared family and group experiences and collective memories signified by ethnic songs, clothes, dance, books, media, family practices and other social and cultural gestures.[31] One might say that the Inter-American Court of Human Rights had an ethos in mind when it described the culture of a traditional society in this way:

> The close ties the members of indigenous communities have with their traditional lands and the natural resources associated with their culture . . . must be secured under Article 21 of the American Convention. ['(1) Everyone has . . . the right to the use and enjoyment of his property. . . (2) No one shall be deprived of his property except upon payment of just compensation. . .] The culture of the members of indigenous communities reflects a particular way of life. Of being, seeing and acting in the world, the starting point of which is their close relation with their traditional lands and natural resources, not only because they are their main means of survival, but also because they form part of their worldview, of their religiousness, and consequently, of their cultural identity.[32]

The Court continued that ownership of such land centres upon group and community, not upon individuals.[33] In addition, the treaty's reference

---

[27] *Sandra Lovelace v Canada*, HRC Communication No R6/24 (1981), UN Doc Supp No 40 (A/36/40), 166, (1981) 68 ILR 17, para 14.

[28] See also, eg, ILC, 'Report of the ILC on the Work of Its Forty-Seventh Session', UN Doc A/50/10, in *ILC Yearbook 1995*, vol II(2), 37 (para 186).

[29] HRC, 'CCPR General Comment 23: Article 27 (Rights of Minorities)' in UN, *Human Rights Instruments, Volume I* (above n 18).

[30] HRC, 'CCPR General Comment 15: The Position of Aliens under the Covenant' in UN, *Human Rights Instruments: Compilation* (above n 18) para 3.2.

[31] Ibid, para 5.2.

[32] *Sawhoyamaxa Indigenous Community v Paraguay*, Inter-Amer Ct Human Rts (29 March 2006), para 118.

[33] Ibid, para 120.

to property addresses 'material' things, not just formal rights.[34] Such material factors, not the rights and rules, embodies one's legal personality.[35] One might add that shared experiences of detained stateless persons may inculcate a shared belonging, and this in turn may constitute effective nationality. The social 'belonging' just happens to have transpired on this or that territory, on territory owned by this or that state. What binds individuals together is 'their own culture . . . religion or . . . language', according to Article 27 of the ICCPR. Effective nationality recognizes just such a sense of culture experienced by de jure and effectively stateless persons.

The second point that must be made is that this social bonding analytically and experientially precedes the juridical construction of the boundary of a reserved domain.[36] Along the same lines, the social bonding analytically and experientially precedes any discrete right to nationality or any domestically posited rule conferring, withholding or withdrawing nationality. In other words, for refugees and stateless persons, social life is experienced before any international or domestic institution has legally recognized it through the conferral, withdrawal or withholding of nationality.[37] That is, a natural person acquires nationality as a right from a state *after* s/he has experienced a 'place' with others.[38]

In the light of the pre-legal condition of any de jure or effectively stateless person, effective nationality is nested in her/his reciprocal social relations. As such, regardless of de jure or effective nationality or statelessness and regardless of the habitual residence or formal documentation of a person's 'state of origin' or 'state of refuge', s/he has effective nationality by virtue of a legal bond very different from that of allegiance. The determination of

---

[34] Ibid, para 121.

[35] Ibid, para 187.

[36] This point is drawn out above ch 6 ss III–IV (186–202).

[37] JC Hathaway, *Rights of Refugees* (Cambridge, Cambridge University Press, 2005) 159: 'It is one's de facto circumstances, not the official validation of those circumstances, that gives rise to Convention refugee status.' And again at 11: 'As a fundamental principle, the acquisition of refugee rights under international law is not based on formal status by a state or agency but rather follows simply and automatically from the fact of substantive satisfaction of the refugee definition.' Guy Goodwin-Gill has also stated, 'In principle, a person becomes a refugee at the moment when he or she satisfies the definition, so that determination is declaratory, rather than constitutive. . .' See GS Goodwin-Gill, *The Refugee in International Law*, 2nd edn (Oxford, Oxford University Press, 1996) 32. See also *MA v Attorney General*, Civ 2006-404-1371 (High Court Auckland, 21 September 2007), para 103; and ILC, 'Draft Articles on Diplomatic Protection, with Commentaries', UN Doc A/61/10, *ILC Yearbook 2006*, vol II(2) n 13 (para 23).

[38] African Charter on the Rights and Welfare of the Child (1990), CAB/LEG/24.9/49, reprinted in (1994) *African Yearbook of International Law* 295–309. By a 'place', again, I do not signify a territory but rather a space where one experiences social relationships with others. For the difference between territorial space and an experienced place, see ES Casey, *Getting Back into Place: Toward a Renewed Understanding of the Place-World*, 2nd edn (Bloomington, Indiana University Press, 2009); and M Merleau-Ponty, *Phenomenology of Perception*, C Smith (trans) (London, Routledge, 1962) 98–147 and 243–98.

allegiance by a state's laws or by state officials and the person's (lack of) habitual residence on a state's territory have now lost priority in the international community as a whole. Although allegiance to a territory or state may well enter into one's social bonding with other natural persons, the state's determination of one's allegiance is mere happenstance. Stateless asylum seekers, refugees and migrant workers are now subjects of the international legal order.[39]

III. THE EXISTENCE CONDITIONS OF THE INTERNATIONAL COMMUNITY AS A WHOLE

Is what is generally taken as legal objectivity – judicial institutions, legal standards, legal sources, legal reasoning and the boundary between law and extra-law – really objective if genocide, torture, slavery and widespread disappearances transpire without state de facto proscription against such activities? Although objectivity may be represented by institutions called 'courts', is there still objectivity if the courts administer domestic laws about stateless persons arbitrarily or in bad faith? Is there still a legal objectivity if de jure and effectively stateless persons are detained for prolonged periods, or if they cannot predict whether they will have their nationality withdrawn or cannot expect administrative or judicial enforcement of treaty rights pertaining to them? Are not the conditions of non-arbitrariness, good faith, proportionality, legitimacy of domestic objectives and self-executory treaty undertakings necessary for the very existence of legal objectivity?

Peremptory norms, I have argued elsewhere, are peremptory not because over time they enjoy widespread acceptance amongst states but because they are conditions for the very existence of legal order.[40] Without state respect and protection of such norms, the international legal structure would not exist as legal objectivity. Too often, jurists end their analyses by repeating what other jurists have listed as peremptory norms. But a peremptory norm represents an assumption without which an international legal order would not effectively exist. As the dissenting judgment of the European Court of Human Rights in *Al-Adsani* (2001) expresses, what renders a norm peremptory is 'the [binding] character of the rule as a peremptory norm and its interaction with a hierarchically lower rule'.[41] The obligatory character of a peremptory norm justifies judicial inter-

---

[39] HRC, 'CCPR General Comment 31: The Nature of the General Legal Obligation Imposed on Parties to the Covenant', UN Doc CCPR/C/21/Rev.1/Add.13 (2004), in UN, *Human Rights Instruments: Compilation* (above n 18) para 10.

[40] WE Conklin, 'The Peremptory Norms of the International Community' (2012) 23 *European Journal of International Law* 837; and WE Conklin, 'The Peremptory Norms of the International Community: A Rejoinder to Alexander Orakhelashvili' (2012) 23 *European Journal of International Law* 869.

[41] *Al-Adsani* (above n 15) per joint dissenting opinion of judges Rozakis and Caflisch.

vention in a domestic jurisdiction, as the House of Lords concluded in *Pinochet* (2000).[42] So too, a peremptory norm may trump state immunity in a civil action in a domestic court if state officials act in a manner that lacks legal obligation.[43] What is at issue in deliberating over peremptory norms is a legal order's dependence upon the norm for the order's own existence – not whether judicial dicta say this or that norm is jus cogens. Ironically, even the term 'jus cogens' is translated from Latin as 'binding law'.

This relation of a peremptory norm to the existence of a legal order also explains why the legal bond of effective nationality is so important. If genocide, systematic torture, the mass displacement of inhabitants or slavery characterize a society, one could hardly say that a legal order exists even though there may be statutes or regulations or judicial precedents authorizing the genocide, torture, mass displacement, etc. If a legal order cannot be said to exist in such a tyranny, one can extend the question to a society with effectively and de jure stateless persons. At what point would the society be said not to possess a legal order? If there is a society of twelve million, eight million of which are effectively stateless, would the society possess a legal order? If the effectively stateless persons were members of a distinct ethno-cultural group, would the society possess a legal order? My point is that effective nationality, grounded as it is in the legal bond of social relationships as elaborated in chapters six to eight, is just as much an existence condition of a legal order – domestic or international – as are the commonly identified jus cogens norms. The problem is that scrutiny of such an existence condition of a legal order – the relation of effective statelessness to the non-existence of a legal order – is precluded by the jurisdictional boundary protecting the reserved domain of a state.

Put differently, the possibility of large-scale numbers of effectively stateless persons in an international community aggregated from the wills of states renders a claim of the universalism of human rights an oxymoron. It is commonly accepted that not all rights in the six human rights treaties are human rights. Dignity, the human species, equal respect and concern, human conscience and other referents have been taken to justify human rights. What renders a human right human from the standpoint of law, however, is the right as an existence condition of legal objectivity.

By an existence condition I do not mean Hans Kelsen's idea that legal reasoning presupposes a hypothetical condition finalizing the justificatory trace of one norm to another.[44] Such a hypothetical condition is neither

---

[42] *R v Bow Street Metropolitan Stipendiary Magistrate and Others, ex parte Pinochet (No 3)*, (HL) [2000] 1 AC 147, [1999] 2 All ER 97, [1999] 2 WLR 827, per Lords Browne-Wilkinson, Hope of Craighead and Millett. See also *Jones v Saudi Arabia* [2006] UKHL 26.

[43] *Al-Adsani* (above n 15) paras 61 and 65.

[44] H Kelsen, *General Theory of Norms*, A Wedberg (trans) (New York, Russell & Russell, 1961) 222; H Kelsen, *Introduction to the Problems of Legal Theory* (Oxford, Clarendon Press, 1992) 13. See generally WE Conklin, *Invisible Origins of Legal Positivism* (Dordrecht, Kluwer, 2001) 182–87.

chosen nor invented but rather a logically necessary condition in a system of norms, according to Kelsen. That said, the logical necessity of a hypothetical condition exists only after the network of norms has taken form in a legal discourse.[45] Effective nationality, even though unrecognized as a peremptory norm or human right, is a very different existence condition. What I mean by an existence condition of a legal order is a condition that anthropologically and experientially precedes any structure of norms. It is a social-cultural condition needed for any institutional or normative structure to exist.[46] In this respect the existence condition of an international community constituted from the aggregate of the wills of states is the bounded, law-making and law-administrating residuary within which state members are free to confer, withhold or withdraw nationality. Allegiance is a further existence condition of such a sense of an international community. In contrast, the existence condition of the international community as a whole concerns the extent to which the social bonding of effective nationals is respected and protected. Such a sense of effective nationality is unrecognizable as the basis of legal obligation in the international community if the community is understood as the aggregate of the wills of state members.[47] Conversely, effective nationality would be recognized as an existence condition of the international community as a whole. There might be institutions such as courts, a legislature, police and an army. The state might be free to determine anyone's allegiance to the state. The bounded reserved domain of the state or what I have called the residuary of the international community constitutes the facticity within which de jure and effective statelessness is produced. Courts and tribunals have used different terms to signify the facticity of the boundary of the residuary: 'jurisdiction fact', 'jurisdictional bar' and 'procedural condition' are examples.[48] As the Australian High Court stated in *Minister v SZMDS*, 'In the English system,

---

[45] See WE Conklin, 'Hans Kelsen on Norm and Language' (2006) 19 *Ratio Juris* 101, 120–24.

[46] See, eg, *United States Diplomatic and Consular Staff in Tehran (USA v Iran)*, (1979) ICJ Rep 19 (Order of 15 December 1979) and (1980) ICJ Rep 3 (Judgment), 43 (para 92), also reported in 61 ILR 502. See also the dissenting opinion of Judge Weeramantry in *East Timor (Portugal v Australia)* (above n 11) 172 and 213–16; *Military and Paramilitary Activities in and against Nicaragua (Nicaragua v United States)* (Merits), (1986) ICJ Rep 14, 100 (para 190), also reported in 76 ILR 349; and *Prosecutor v Anto Furundzija* (ICTY Trial Chamber), Case No IT-95-17/1-T, Judgment of 10 December 1998, 260–62 (paras 151–57), reported in 121 ILR 218. Judge Weeramantry gave an extensive list of international court decisions in which there has been an incorporation of the just cogens principle. See *East Timor (Portugal v Australia)* (above n 11) 214. See also *Legal Consequences of the Construction of a Wall in the Occupied Palestinian Territory* (Advisory Opinion), (2004) ICJ Rep 136, 199 (para 157), also reported in 59 ILR 30.

[47] See, eg, *Al-Adsani* (above n 15) per Rozakis and Caflisch (dissenting), joined by Wildhaber, Costa, Cabral Barreto and Vajić.

[48] *Minister for Immigration and Citizenship v SZMDS* [2010] HCA 16, paras 24–31 (per Gummow and Kiefel JJ). See also *Jurisdictional Immunities of the State (Germany v Italy: Greece Intervening)*, ICJ judgment of 3 February 2012, para 93; *Al-Adsani* (above n 15) para 48; *Arrest Warrant of 11 April 2000 (Democratic Republic of the Congo v Belgium)*, Provisional Measures by order of 8 December 2000, (2000) ICJ Rep 182, para 60; and *Presbyterian Church of Sudan v Talisman Energy*, No 01 Civ 9882 (DLC), 2005 WL 2082846, 374 F Supp 2d 331 (SDNY 2005).

the "jurisdictional fact" was an appropriate marker for the enforcement of legality.'[49] Although the High Court has gone to great lengths to differentiate logical from illogical reasoning,[50] the difference in matters of statelessness, I suggest, is conditional upon the existence condition of there being a bounded residuary.

The problem is that with the displacement of the presupposed jurisdictional fact of a bounded reserved domain as argued in my chapters six to eight, the 'fact' of the boundary is no longer the appropriate marker for the enforcement of legality. A crucial existence condition of the international community has dissolved in favour of a legal bond as reciprocal social relationships of natural persons. The old existence condition, namely the boundary of the reserved domain, is brought into question.[51] The emergence of such an existence condition of the international community impacts what is signified by 'the operation of law' and 'lawfulness'.

This understanding of law as social phenomena may be what Ian Brownlie meant when he wrote that a state's unlimited discretion inside its domestic jurisdiction would allow the state 'to contract out of the very system of legal obligation'.[52] Brownlie also expressed the point in this way: 'A sovereignty in principle unlimited by the existence of other states is ridiculous.'[53] The shift in existence condition also explains why Paul Weis testified as early as 1956 that it is 'erroneous' to believe that statelessness could be reduced if one takes the bounded domestic jurisdiction as a 'given'.[54]

IV. LEGAL OBJECTIVITY

To understand the character of the international community, we must start with the nature of legal objectivity, not with the commonality of self-interested state members. Such legal objectivity is not possible, however, unless there is a subject (or subjects) that is separate and different from the legal objectivity. One might respond to this point by suggesting that I have entertained that a legal objectivity may have many subjects. There might be many subjects in an international community as a whole – natural persons as well as states and international organizations. There may also be many legal objects, such as this desk or this paper or this automobile or us

---

[49] *Minister v SZMDS* (ibid) para 18 (per Gummow and Kiefel).

[50] See esp *Minister v SZMDS* (above n 48) paras 121–36 (per Crennan and Bell).

[51] *SZMDS v Minister of Immigration* (2009) 107 ALD 361, paras 29–30 (Fed Ct Australia), overruled by *Minister v SZMDS* (above n 48).

[52] I Brownlie, 'The Relations of Nationality in Public International Law' (1963) 39 *British Yearbook of International Law* 284, 293.

[53] Crawford (ed), *Brownlie's Principles* (above n 23) 510.

[54] P Weis, *Nationality and Statelessness in International Law* (London, Stevens, 1956) 98 and 101.

legal persons or this land. Such objects are things to be instrumentally used and claimed by legal subjects such as states. Discrete rules represented in judicial decisions, statutes, treaties, international customary norms and opinio juris have often been taken as synonymous with 'the law'. Such a viewpoint shies away from the possibility that there is a very different sense of 'the law' than the aggregate of particular rules or tests. My focus upon legal objectivity addresses such a sense of 'the law'.[55] With such a sense of legal objectivity (or 'the law'), there may be many legal subjects but only one legal objectivity.

Indeed, if there were two or more legal objectivities – such as that of a state and another of an indigenous community – there would presumably be continuous legal (and political) struggle as to which objectivity was authoritative. Indeed, such a discursive struggle, I have argued and documented in earlier chapters, has permeated the judgments of domestic and international tribunals and courts when the international community as the aggregated wills of state members has been taken for granted. In identifying the definition of a stateless person in Article 1 of the Convention Relating to the Status of Stateless Persons (1954) as 'not considered as a national by any state under *the operation of its law*',[56] for example, legal objectivity is often taken for granted as the boundary of the protected reserved domain of a state. The domain mimics a geographical space, except that the space is constituted in legal consciousness. The boundary of the space encloses the reserved domain without having to address whether another sense of legal objectivity exists, for example, by virtue of the legal bond as social bonding, independent of the state. Put differently, an enquiry into the content of the reserved domain is thereby estopped by the boundary of the presupposed legal objectivity.

The consequence is that such a sense of legal objectivity is constituted from and represented by the express or implied self-interested wills of states as subjects. The problem is that there is no separation of such subjects from the legal objectivity as constituted from the sum of the wills of state members. Without such a separation, there cannot be subjects or a legal objectivity.[57] And law becomes the arbitrary posit of 'laws'. The legal

---

[55] It may also be implicit in what Ronald Dworkin was trying to get at in his *Justice for Hedgehogs* (Cambridge, MA, Harvard University Press, 2011).

[56] Convention Relating to the Status of Stateless Persons (1954), 360 UNTS 117 (entered into force 6 June 1960) Art 1.

[57] This point is missed perhaps in recent studies of legal objectivity. See eg R Dworkin, *Justice for Hedgehogs* above n 50, 6–11, 23–28, 172–78; N Stavropulos, 'Objectivity in Law' in *Blackwell Guide to the Philosophy of Law and Legal Theory* , Golding and W Edmundson (eds) (Oxford, Blackwell Press, 2005), 315–22; B Leiter, 'Law and Objectivity' in *The Oxford Handbook of Jurisprudence & Philosophy of Law*, J Coleman & S Shapiro (eds), (Oxford, Oxford University Press, 2004) 969-89; A Marmor, *Positive Law and Objective Values* (Oxford, Clarendon Press, 2001), 112–22; GJ Postema, 'Objectivity Fit for Law' in *Objectivity in Law and Morals* , B Leiter (ed), (Cambridge, Cambridge University Press, 2001); R Dworkin, 'Objectivity: You'd Better Believe It' in (1996) 25(2) *Philosophy and Public Affairs* 87;

objectivity becomes synonymous with the aggregated wills of the subjects, the subjects being the state members. As a consequence, the subject and object are one and the same. They are fused together in this frame of reference. But without a separation of the subject from the objectivity in adjudication and the enforcement of the state's laws, natural persons lacking de jure or effective nationality are excluded from the fused subjects/ objectivity. The basis of the obligatory or compelling character of a rule or right depends entirely upon the express or implicit consent of state members, but the quest for the identity of a discrete rule or right lacks a reference back to the stateless person as a subject. This is so because there is no subjectivity. The supposed hard fact of the reserved domain therefore lacks both a legal objectivity that is independent of stateless persons and therefore a legal objectivity 'out there' and legal subjects constituting a legal subjectivity. The state's will represents both its own will (that is, as a subject) and legal objectivity .

Lawfulness, from the standpoint of a stateless person, is thereby tautological: lawfulness exists by virtue of the express or implied wills of states; law exists for and by the wills of states in the name of the rule of law. And the crux of whether a natural person has a right to nationality depends upon the state, as subject and object, to decide the person's allegiance. There is no separation between the bounded reserved domain and legal objectivity. Such a fused subject/object renders a stateless person a stranger to the international community. States may ratify treaties or implicitly consent to customary norms pertaining to how a stateless person ought to be treated, but such standards do not pierce the boundary of the residuary unless one situates the standards in an ethos of an international community that is independent of the state as a subject/object.

A natural person is a subject who is separate from the ethos of an international legal objectivity as aggregated wills of state. The ethos of this particular shape of an international community is highlighted by a residuary, the laws of nationality and naturalization of which are posited by state members. A legal structure of the international community as a whole again cannot exist if the alleged community lacks a legal bond amongst the social relationships of natural persons. The community may 'exist' in the signifying relations of legal rhetoric; there may be institutional sources, such as executive agencies, legislatures and courts of a state, to which a right can be traced; there may even be legislated texts, such as constitutional bills of rights; and executive agencies may sign and ratify international human rights treaties. But for there to be an objective structure to the community, the community has to be embodied by the social relationships of natural persons, as discussed above in chapter six. Such a content of the community addresses the cultural assumptions and expectations of the natural persons towards the legal objectivity. Effective nationality manifests such a social-cultural context. As such, the laws enacted and administered inside the content of the reserved domain must recognize and protect the effective nationality of natural persons. The objectivity of the legal structure must effectively and reciprocally represent the subjects of the objectivity.

The ICJ outlined a similar theme in the *Reparations* case (1949).[58] As the ICJ stated, the United Nations and its organizations had gained an '*objective* international personality and not merely personality recognized by them alone, together with capacity to bring international claims'.[59] An international organization, the Court maintained, represents 'its own right, the right that the obligations due to it should be respected'.[60] This idea of a legal objectivity in its own right is not something that can be ignored. One state act, if allowed to persist, may undermine the very possibility of such an objectivity. The objectivity may become a legal system for and by private persons. This may be so whether a member state or other legal person (as opposed to natural person) in an aggregated international community is a tyrant, warlord under the colour of law, secret organization or political party claiming to represent the whole.

V. LEGAL SUBJECTIVITY

One important issue remains: why would a stateless person be a subject of the international legal order? Two factors point to an explanation. According to one, for the laws of an international community to be nested in an objectivity, there needs to be but a subject or subjects. As a consequence, the international legal community would have to be separate from its members, such as states, natural persons, international organizations and the like. According to the second factor, the legal bond, as I argued in chapter six, would have to exist independent of the states as both the subjects and the authors of legal objectivity. I have retrieved an inner discourse that has offered social bonding amongst natural persons as the generating instrument of such a legal objectivity. Without the displacement of the boundary of the reserved domain of a state, there could not be a legal objectivity independent of the wills of states. And without such a separation of the legal objectivity from subjects, there would be neither a legal objectivity nor subjects representing subjectivity.

---

[58] *Reparation for Injuries Suffered in the Service of the United Nations* (Advisory Opinion), (1949) ICJ Rep 174.
[59] Ibid, 185 (emphasis added).
[60] Ibid, 184.

A. A Stateless Person as a Subject of a Legal Order

A subject exists only if separate from legal objectivity. There might be other international communities, such as existed in feudal estates, traditional societies, ethno-cultural peoples, empires or, for that matter, self-defining and self-determining monadic states. But for there to be a subject, least of all a stateless person as a subject, there needs to be a legal objectivity that is independent of the subject. The dissolution of the territorial-like boundary of the international community's residuary, argued in chapters seven and eight, has brought with it the emergence of a legal objectivity that is separate from state members. Such the legal objects of such a legal objectivity are obligatory because of the presence of a legal bond as effective nationality. The consequence has been a fiduciary obligation on the part of states to protect stateless persons.

i. The Fusion of Subject and Object

The consequence of the bounded residuary is that states claim their own authority for their own laws. Such a claim is protected by the boundary of the residuary. A state becomes dependent upon other states to recognize and protect its domestic jurisdiction. I have documented how treaties and United Nations resolutions, which along with customary norms represent the express or implied will of states, recognize the principle of non-interference into the inner freedom of states.[61] How can a stateless person be a subject of such an international legal order, existing as s/he does outside the state's bounded domestic jurisdiction?

There is a more serious problem, though. For there to be a subject and a legal objectivity, there has to be a separation of the one from the other. The problem is that the legal framework of the international community, when it is understood as constituted from the aggregate wills of states, takes for granted that the legal objectivity is the consequence of the wills of states. The state is both the subject and the source of legal objectivity in such an international community. There is neither subjectivity nor objectivity. Natural persons do not exist as subjects. Without subjects, there cannot be objectivity 'as a whole'. How can a natural person, in particular, be said to be a subject of an international community whose residuary protects the freedom of a state to deny, withhold or withdraw her/his legal personality? The legal subjects and legal objectivity are one and the same in the aggregated international community. Jurists are thereby locked into such a fusion as if it were a hard fact.

---

[61] See above ch 4, ss II–IV (138–56), ch 3, ss 1–2 (163–68).

The consequence of this fusion is that jurists must accept international standards pertaining to de jure and effectively stateless persons as 'oughts'. The boundary of the residuary defines what is an 'is', or hard fact, from what is an 'ought'. The international standards are 'out there' in a heaven of a priori ideals, distanced from the hard fact of the boundary of domestic jurisdiction. Such a legal heaven, so often assumed in the interstitial 'cut-and-paste' legal analysis of the sources thesis, builds its own irrelevance into legal objectivity and objectivity's need for a subject. The boundary leaves the heaven as aspirational and therefore 'impractical' to jurists. The sources identified in the Statute of the ICJ play into just such an idealization of an international community because the sources take the fusion of subject and object for granted. The state, as subject and object, claims its own legal authority, of which its title to territory is an incident. And the jurisdictional bar remains intact except for the consent of states. Statelessness remains as the enigma of the international community.

ii. *The Stateless Person as a Subject of the International Legal Order*

Effective nationality is so indispensable for legal objectivity because it introduces the possibility of a separation of subject from objectivity. This is so because of the legal bond understood as sociality is separate from the state. A stateless person, as a legal person rather than a natural person, exists because s/he is now a subject separated from the former fused legal subjects/objectivity. Without a legal structure of the international community as a whole, there could not be a legal objectivity. Without an objectivity, there could not be subjects.

When we address the production of statelessness, we appreciate that natural persons are also subjects of the objectivity. What matters are the social relationships amongst natural persons, as shared through the experiences of time and place. Such social relationships make for the ethos or character of the community in which an identifiable rule is situated. Legal analysis in this context requires that jurists turn to the social-cultural presuppositions in the content of the reserved domain. Only in this case, the community is something more than the aggregate of the wills of state members. The nature of an international legal obligation by a state member of the community must be justified by some factor independent of the boundary of the reserved legal space, which is perhaps better signified as domestic or international jurisdiction. Such social relationships are independent of the territorial-like domain. Being independent of the state, effective nationality embodies the socially effective character of an ethos. The stateless condition, a product of the bounded residuary of the international community, can be bypassed altogether in this way. States are but third-party intermediaries between stateless persons and the international legal objectivity. A state owes a fiduciary duty to ensure that the legal objectivity protects de jure and effectively stateless persons. In this frame-work, international standards are elements of the legal objectivity, and the judiciary of both states and international organizations must recognize and enforce international standards.

B. The Protection of Stateless Persons as an Existence Condition of an International Community

International legal discourse has of recent years widened the scope of subjectivity. The ICJ has affirmed that the international community is composed of natural persons as well as of social groups such as indigen-ous peoples.[62] So too the Human Rights Committee has presupposed in many of its 'General Comments' regarding the ICCPR that the inter-national community is composed of individual natural persons as well as of states. James Crawford has added to states, the United Nations, the European Union and the International Committee of the Red Cross.[63] But how does one justify the inclusion of non-state actors as subjects of a state-centric international community if legal analysis presupposes a fusion of subject and object? The point is that without existence condi-tions for an international legal order, a legal order would not exist as a legal order. The community would be either a state-centric aggregate of the wills of states or an idealized heaven of rights and duties. The sub-jects listed above (ie, natural persons, the UN, EU, Red Cross) would be idealized subjects whose rights would be at the discretion of a state's claim to authority. An existence condition of an international legal order offers an entry point for the legal obligation to protect a stateless person as a subject.

There are other existence conditions of the international community as a whole. The proscription against piracy has been acknowledged as one;[64] the proscription against torture is another.[65] Similarly, the international community can hardly be said to exist if prolonged or arbitrary detention, systematic racial discrimination, genocide, slavery, the disappearing of persons, or cruel, inhuman or degrading treatment occur regularly while jurists believe they work inside a legal order.[66] Nor can legal reasoning, consistent with legal order, cut and paste dicta from a discourse as if such

---

[62] See, eg, *The Effect of Reservations on the Entry into Force of the American Convention on Human Rights (Arts 74 and 75)*, Advisory Opinion OC-2/82, Inter-Am Ct HR (1982) Ser A, No 2, (1982) 67 ILR 559, 22 ILM 33.

[63] Crawford, 'Introduction' (above n 12) 41.

[64] *Filartiga* (above n 2) per Kaufman J.

[65] Ibid.

[66] See UNHCR, 'Stateless: Prevention and Reduction of Statelessness and Protection of Stateless Persons,' UN Doc EC/57/SC/CRP.6 (14 February 2006), reprinted in (2006) 25 *Refugee Survey Quarterly* 72–76.

dicta 'establishes' or recognizes a right to nationality or a right to protect stateless persons.

Rather, what is critical for the existence of an international legal order is the ethos or culture of the international community. Such a culture possesses assumptions and expectations that if violated or lapsed, a legal objectivity, separate from subjects, no longer exists. A state could claim authority in order to determine an individual's allegiance. But without the fulfilment of the existence conditions of the ethos of the community, the legal order would again 'exist' in a heaven of a priori concepts.

Effective nationality is an existence condition of an international community as a whole. That is, without the recognition and protection of effectively stateless persons, a contingent condition of the international community as a whole is absent. The legal bond manifesting such effective nationality, I argued in chapter six, is nested in the social relationships of natural persons, including stateless persons. The prospect of effective statelessness and of the absence of a legal bond of social relationships remains as long as a state is still believed to be free to withdraw nationality or to remain silent when nationals and non-nationals are effectively unprotected. Such an absence of protection may be manifested by entitlement or programmes administered in bad faith, arbitrary action by state officials, legislation or state action institutionalizing a disproportionate means to fulfil a state's objective, failure by judges to enforce self-executory treaty provisions, and failure by state officials and judges to administer state objectives. Conversely, as argued above in chapters two and six, by incorporating nationality as an incident of the protected reserved domain of a state, the possibility of a legal bond as social relationships – what Cicero, Grotius, Pufendorf and others called 'sociability' – is analytically displaced by a very different sense of a legal bond (allegiance) and of an international community. The latter sense of an international community has been taken for granted when tens of millions of natural persons have lacked a legal voice because they have been de jure and effectively stateless.

I suggested in chapter one that there are two international law discourses corresponding to two different senses of an international community. Any judicial decision or commentary may well manifest both contradictory discourses. Chapters two to five elaborated how the surface discourse addresses nationality in a manner that produces de jure and effective statelessness. Chapters six to eight identified an inner discourse with a very different sense of legal bond with very different ramifications for the protection of de jure and effectively stateless persons. The Reports of the ILC have exemplified both senses of an international community. On the one hand, as documented in chapter two, the ILC Reports regarding diplomatic protection and the succession of states generally exhibit a sense of the international community as constituted from the wills of states. On the other hand, one can also find in the diplomatic protection studies an acknowledged legal obligation owed by all states to protect de jure and effectively stateless persons.[67] More generally, the state responsibility articles and commentary take for granted that the international community as a whole justifies the incorporation of international standards into the content of the reserved domain.[68] In addition, any conferral, withholding or withdrawal of nationality must be situated 'within a general, flexible framework posed by international law'.[69] Crawford, as an ILC Special Rapporteur, expressed such a framework of legal consciousness when he submitted:

> Nationality was a creation of national law, but international law could not be excluded even though it might not perform the primary role. Consequently, provided that some flexibility was maintained, it [seems] useful to talk about the idea of *nationality for international purposes* – about *a kind of imputed nationality*, as it were, which might have consequences particularly in the framework of a set of presumptions.[70]

That said, Crawford has also adopted the aggregated sense of an international community on another occasion.[71]

In the light of my above arguments, we must ask whether mere presumptions rather than obligatory norms characterize the international community as a whole. That question, the ILC has admitted, is 'another matter'.[72] So too the role of judicial scrutiny of alleged public emergencies is 'another matter', as are all the other conditions of 'lawfulness' raised earlier. HRC 'General Comment 15' suggests that the norms are not mere presumptions: a stateless person is entitled to Covenant rights 'irrespective of his or her nationality or statelessness'.[73] That being so,

---

[67] ILC, 'Draft Articles on Diplomatic Protection' (above n 37) Comments to Art 4(7).

[68] ILC, 'Draft Articles on State Responsibility' (above n 12) 148–50 and 158–60. See also B Simma and P Alston, 'The Sources of Human Rights Law: Custom, Jus Cogens and General Principles' (1988–89)12 *Australian Yearbook of International Law* 82, 103; Mosler, *International Society as a Legal Community* (above n 6) 19; and JA Frowein, 'Obligations Erga Omnes' in R Bernhardt (ed), *Encyclopaedia of Public International Law*, vol 3 (Amsterdam, Elsevier, 1997–2003) 757.

[69] A Pellet, at the 2411th meeting of the ILC (5 July 1995), 'State Succession and Its Impact on the Nationality of Natural and Legal Persons', *ILC Yearbook 1995*, vol I, 215 (para 20).

[70] Crawford, commenting on the Report of the Special Rapporteur, 2388th meeting of the ILC (23 May 1995), 'State Succession and Its Impact on the Nationality of Natural and Legal Persons', *ILC Yearbook 1995*, vol I, 60 (para 42), emphasis added.

[71] J Crawford, 'Sovereignty as a Legal Value' in J Crawford and M Koskenniemi (eds), *Cambridge Companion to International Law* (Cambridge, Cambridge University Press, 2012) 117–133.

[72] Crawford at the 2388th meeting (above n 70) para 43.

[73] HRC, 'General Comment 15' (above n 30) para 7 sets out such rights as 'the inherent right to life, protected by law', protection against torture and cruel and unusual treatment, liberty and security of the person, treatment with humanity if lawfully deprived of liberty, liberty of movement and free choice of residence, freedom to leave a state, equality before the courts and tribunals, a fair and public hearing before a competent court, recognition before the law, and protection against 'arbitrary or unlawful interference with their

which institution – the executive or the judiciary – may determine whether 'the life of the nation' is at stake? Can an administrative or judicial decision be lawful if the evidence of a threat to the state posed by a stateless person remains an official secret of the executive? Are international standards in the human rights treaties relevant to resolving these issues without asking why derogation or limitation of a right to nationality is justified for stateless persons? Such issues rest not in the presumptive character of effective nationality but in the obligatory character of the norms. And effective nationality addresses the (non-)obligatory character of domestic laws relating to stateless persons. The existence condition is rooted in the ethos or culture that the sources thesis of the aggregated community excludes as extra-law. The problem again is that an international legal objectivity could not even exist if torture, genocide, widespread disappearances and sexual slavery persist inside the boundary of a state's domestic jurisdiction. The same may be said of the absence of effective nationality.

The point is not a new one: Sophocles made it 2400 years ago through the voice of Haemon, the son of King Creon, in Sophocles' *Antigone*.[74] After finding that Antigone knowingly contravened his edict, the King sentences her to be buried alive in a cave. When Haemon counsels the King that he is losing public support through this action, Creon takes offence and describes his son as 'breaking ranks' (*l* 730) and 'fighting for the woman's cause' (*l* 740). By interpreting Antigone's disobedience as a treasonous act, the King has effectively withdrawn Antigone's legal bonding of allegiance. Effectively stateless persons can be so constructed by the state, as we regularly observe today. Once her citizenship to the city-state is thus withdrawn, Creon takes for granted that he can authoritatively change her sentence from stoning to starvation in a cave. Haemon objects by pointing out that the polis could not exist if Antigone's legal bond as an effectively social bond can dissolve: 'A place for one man alone is not a city' (*l* 737). The King ridicules Haemon and replies, 'A city belongs to its master. Isn't that the rule?' To which Haemon quite rightly responds, 'Then go be ruler of a desert, all alone. You'd do it well' (*l* 739).

Effective statelessness, the consequence for one natural person, characterizes the enigma of a contemporary international community. A state may claim radical title to a territory, and yet natural persons may well lack the protection of effective nationality by the state represented, despite

---

privacy, family, home or correspondence'. Children are recognized as having special protection. Aliens are entitled 'in community with other members of their group, to enjoy their own culture, to profess and practise their own religion and to use their own language'. See also paras 2 and 5; and HRC, 'CCPR General Comment 29: Article 4 and Derogations during a State of Emergency' in UN, *Human Rights Instruments: Compilation* (above n 18) para 11.

[74] Sophocles, *Antigone*, P Woodruff (trans and ed) (Indianapolis, Hackett, 2001).

deep social relationships of such persons on the state's territory or inside its reserved domain. Such a state lacks legal objectivity except in form and on paper. Effective nationality, as a consequence, is an existence condition of the very legal order of the international community. Effective nationality is the basis of legal obligation. To put it another way, effective nationality, understood as a hard fact, emerges from the existence conditions of an imminent and historically contingent social ethos. This ethos did not come into being through some document, such as the UN Charter, nor is it self-consciously and deliberately authored by the Great Powers or by the majority of state members of some constituent assembly. The unwritten ethos, as Sophocles' Antigone exclaims, lacks a precise origin:

> These laws weren't made now
> Or yesterday. They live for all time,
> And no one knows when they came into the light.[75]

The ethos is unwritten.

Perhaps Sophocles was wrong on one point, however. The unwritten laws exist only so long as they are nested in social relationships. The ethos to which Antigone appeals concerns the culture of an extended family or traditional society. When she goes to sprinkle sand upon the body of her deceased brother, she does not first look for a self-standing intellectualized rule in some text, nor does she ask a lawyer for an opinion as to whether she has a right to nationality. Such would require deliberation about the justification of her act with reference to sources of written laws to which the representatives of the polis (the king and his council) have consented. Antigone appeals to unwritten practice. Without this or other unwritten practices and assumptions, her ethos would not exist even if some self-authored rule were to say it exists.

VI. HARM TO STATELESS PERSONS AS HARM TO THE
INTERNATIONAL COMMUNITY AS A WHOLE

International legal discourse has considered the prospect of harm done to the international community, independent of any harm to an individual state member.[76] I wish to add that harm caused to a de jure or effectively stateless person constitutes harm to the international community as a whole.

---

[75] Ibid *l* 457–58.
[76] See generally above ch 1, ss III and IV (52–63); ch 8, ss II and III (240–60); and ch 8, s V (264–69).

A. Harm to the International Community as a Whole

A series of treaties expressly entertain the notion of harm to international community.[77] The ILC State Responsibility Report specifies that any state, even an uninjured state, may invoke the obligation of any other state to the international community as a whole.[78] Human rights of natural persons are important not because of some a priori concept, such as Kant's notion of dignity, but because of the relation of human rights to the existence conditions of the international community as a whole.

Judicial remedies have increasingly been extended to circumstances in which the international community as a whole has been harmed. The 1971 ICJ Advisory Opinion in *Namibia*, for example, contemplates the idea that harm can be caused to the international legal objectivity legal order as a whole even if there is no identifiable harm for an individual state claimant.[79] A natural person lacking effective nationality (as well as de jure nationality) may possess a civil or criminal remedy even though a state member did not suffer compensatory losses. The *Filartiga* case is well-known in this regard.[80] The US Supreme Court in *Sosa* also awarded a remedy in a case involving torture, concluding that the international community had been harmed by state action.[81] Immunity for heads of states, as raised in chapter two, is increasingly at issue.[82] The HRC has similarly expressed in 'General Comment 31' to the ICCPR that the 'basic rights of the human person' are erga omnes, and therefore every state has 'a legal interest in the performance by every other state party of its obligations'.[83]

---

[77] Rome Statute of the International Criminal Court (1998), 2187 UNTS 90, Preamble (paras 3 and 9); International Convention against the Taking of Hostages (1979), 1316 UNTS 205, Art 4; Convention on the Prevention and Punishment of Crimes against Internationally Protected Persons, including Diplomatic Agents (1973), 1035 UNTS 167, Art 3; International Convention for the Suppression of the Financing of Terrorism (1999), UN Res 54/49, para 9, reprinted in (2000) 39 ILM 270. See also Convention on the Safety of United Nations and Associated Personnel (1994), 2051 UNTS 391, Preamble (para 3); and International Convention for the Suppression of Terrorist Bombings (1997), 2149 UNTS 256, Preamble (para 10). For other treaties, see African [Banjul] Charter on Human and Peoples' Rights (27 June 1981), OAU Doc CAB/LEG/67/3 rev. 5, (1984) 21 ILM 58, Art 27.

[78] ILC, 'Draft Articles on State Responsibility' (above n 12) esp Art 48 (Comm 9). See also Crawford, 'Introduction' (above n 12) 36.

[79] *Legal Consequences for States of the Continued Presence of South Africa in Namibia (South-West Africa) notwithstanding Security Council Resolution 276* (Advisory Opinion), (1971) ICJ Rep 12, 49 ILR 2.

[80] *Filartiga* (above n 2).

[81] *Sosa v Alvarez-Machain* (2004) 542 US 692 (SCUS), 127 ILR 691. For other American cases, see KC Randall, 'Universal Jurisdiction under International Law' (1987–88) 66 *Texas Law Review* 785, 789–90.

[82] See above ch 2, s V-B. See eg, *R v Bartle (Pinochet)* (above n 13). Regarding the prosecution of the former head of state of Egypt, see J Foakes, 'Immunity for International Crimes? Developments in the Law on Prosecuting Heads of State in Foreign Courts', Chatham House Briefing Paper (London, November 2011) 3.

[83] HRC, 'General Comment 31' (above n 39) para 2 (emphasis added).

Since effective nationality shares with peremptory norms the fact that it is an existence condition of the legal order of the international community, the legal order may not be the subject of treaty reservations pertaining to the withdrawal or withholding of nationality.[84] Although obligations are owed to the international community by states, such obligations are also owed to individual natural persons by virtue of the legal bond as social bonding.[85] What we understand as 'law', 'lawfulness' or 'by law' includes treaties, customary norms and other international standards, even though a state may object to them. As Antonio Augusto Cançado Trindade of the ICJ stated with regardto the Australian domestic court judgment in *Diallo* (2010), 'a new *jus gentium*' has emerged that focuses upon 'the framework of the rights of the human person, individually and collectively'.[86]

A legal objectivity now exists.[87] This *ordre public*, better known as the international community as a whole, extends to 'the whole *corpus juris* of the international protection of the human person', including international humanitarian law, human rights law and international refugee law. When it has presupposed the concept of an aggregated international community notwithstanding,[88] the American *Third Restatement of the Law* has also acknowledged that *erga omnes* duties are owed by all states.[89] Crawford moreover has advised that if harm is caused to a foundational pillar of a UN organization, so too the organization itself is harmed.[90]

States, then, are not self-creative and self-determining authors, as presupposed by the notion of the aggregated international community; they are but third parties to the social relations between natural persons that embody the content of the residuary of the international community. States thereby owe duties because of their third-party fiduciary role in protecting the international community. Jochen Frowein has documented several contexts in which third-party states have intervened to claim harm to an injured state and thereby to represent the international community as a whole.[91] In addition, other recent international law judgments have

[84] HRC, 'CCPR General Comment 24: Issues Relating to Reservations made upon Ratification or Accession to the Covenant or the Optional Protocols Thereto, or in relation to Declarations under Article 41 of the Covenant', UN Doc CCPR/C/21/Rev.1/Add.6 (1994), in UN, *Human Rights Instruments: Compilation* (above n 18) para 8.

[85] See HRC, 'General Comment 26' (above n 18) para 4.

[86] *Case concerning Ahmadou Sadio Diallo (Republic of Guinea v Democratic Republic of the Congo)*, ILC Rep (2010) 639, para 22 (per Judge Cançado Trindade).

[87] Ibid, paras 88–90.

[88] See above ch 5, nn 9 (164) and 33 (169). However, the *Third Restatement* also assumes the existence of peremptory norms. See American Law Institute, *Restatement of the Law, Third: Foreign Relations Law of the United States*, vol 2 (St Paul, American Law Institute, 1987). See also above ch 1, nn 111 (57) and 119 and 120 (57); and ch 6, n 57 (187).

[89] American Law Institute (ibid) Art 702 (Comm O).

[90] This point is developed by J Crawford, *The Creation of States in International Law*, 2nd edn (Oxford, Oxford University Press, 2006) 102.

[91] See Frowein (above n 68), quoting AG Heffter, *Le Droit international public de l'Europe* (Berlin, EH Schroeder, 1866) 211.

made clear how the principle of the international community as a whole justifies the prosecution of state officials and heads of state,[92] as well as justifying the jurisdiction of the Special Court for Sierra Leone.[93] And the ILC 'Draft Articles of State Responsibility' consistently specify how the referent, the 'international community as a whole', justifies diverse state obligations, although the ILC itself has not been consistent in adopting this referent.[94] Jean-Marie Henckaerts has gone further by suggesting that the international community extends generally to all aspects of law.[95]

B. Harm to Stateless Persons as Harm to the International Community

A right to nationality, as a discrete and identified norm, is not of itself binding upon natural persons or, for that matter, upon states. What binds members of an international community is the ethos of the international community in which member-subjects are situated. And that requires scrutiny of the domestic jurisdiction of states. A rule or right is binding because the content of the residuary – heretofore immune from external intercession – represents the assumptions, expectations, collective memories, personal memories and other factors making for social relationships. Such assumptions and the like manifest the content of domestic jurisdictions. Like the proscriptions against torture, the mass disappearance of civilians, mass rape, systemic racial and ethnic discrimination and other examples offered of peremptory norms, effective nationality too is a foundational principle of the ethos of an international community as a whole. In particular, prolonged detention, a common consequence of de jure statelessness, undermines the integrity of the international community as a whole: 'States parties may in no circumstances invoke Article 4 of the [ICCPR] as justification for acting in violation of humanitarian law or peremptory norms of international law, for instance . . . by imposing collective punishments, through arbitrary deprivations of liberty. . .'[96] In other

---

[92] See respectively *Arrest Warrant of 11 April 2000* (above n 48) (in which unfortunately, the nature of the international community as a whole is not directly elucidated); and *Charles Taylor* (above n 15) para 52.

[93] *Charles Taylor* (above n 15) para 51. However, see *Al-Adsani* (above n 15) para 66.

[94] See, eg, Crawford, 'Introduction' (above n 12), quoting *Reservations regarding Genocide* (above n 8) 38. See also ILC, 'Draft Articles on State Responsibility' (above n 12) Art 1 (Comm 4), Art 3 (Comms 7 and 8), Art 26 (Comm 5), Art 33 (Comms 1–4), Ch 3 (Comms 1–7), Art 40 (Comm 2) and Art 48 (Comms 5 and 10). That said, the ILC itself is not consistent in its adoption of the international community as a whole as the referent of legal analysis in other studies, including ILC, 'Draft Articles on Diplomatic Protection' (above n 37); and ILC, *Report of the Study Group on Fragmentation of International Law*, UN Doc A/CN.4/L.682 and Corr.1, reprinted in *ILC Yearbook 2006*, vol II(2).

[95] J-M Henckaerts (ed), *Mass Expulsion in Modern International Law and Practice* (The Hague, Martinus Nijhoff, 1995) 29.

[96] HRC, 'General Comment 29' (above n 73) para 11.

words, the consequences of statelessness impact upon the existence conditions of the international community as a legal order.

The dissolution of the reserved domain of the state – and by inference, of the international community – raises the prospect that harm can be caused to the legal objectivity of the international community as a whole. This is important because harm to stateless persons undermines the very legal bond of the legal objectivity of an international community. Effective nationality is an existence condition of the international community and therefore of all state members. De jure and effective statelessness causes harm to the ethos of an international community as a whole. If harm is caused to such an ethos, harm is caused to the international community as a whole. If one individual is allowed to become stateless, the whole legal order is brought into question. Therefore obligations are owed by states to the entity as a whole rather than to the individual members and agents of the community, according to the ICJ.[97]

The distinction between the identity and obligation of a distinct legal rule is not a new one. Plato pointed out the distinction when he described Socrates' traumatic concern in the final hours after Socrates had been convicted and sentenced to death for corrupting the morals of the youth and creating false deities. In order to address whether he should flee to a Greek island after his close friend Crito had organized an escape, Socrates personalized the Laws as if the Laws were a human subject. Was he obligated to follow the verdict and sentence when he believed that the verdict was unjust? Socrates' conclusion of course was that he was obligated to follow the verdict. The standards of the legal structure would be nullified and destroyed by private persons if the Laws were to allow Socrates to avoid the sentence of the court and escape to a Greek island – everyone properly bribed – to live happily ever after.[98]

Socrates's conclusion hinged on the nature of the legal bond between natural persons and the state. To elucidate this, he implied a legal bond between two persons: himself and the Laws as a person. The Laws had provided him with benefits such as marriage, family, education and other social matters. Interestingly, though, legal obligation did not depend upon a one-way relationship that moved from the Laws (the metaphor of a natural person) to Socrates (the actual natural person). Rather, the relationship was reciprocal. The crux of the relationship was the opportunity that Socrates had to persuade the Laws that their content was wrong. But in

---

[97] This principle was affirmed in *Reparation for Injuries Suffered in the Service of the United Nations* (Advisory Opinion), (1949) ICJ Rep 174, also reported in (1949) ILR 318 (Case No 112), 327.

[98] *Crito* 50a5–50b5 in E Hamilton and H Cairns (eds), *Collected Dialogues of Plato, Including the Letters* (Princeton, Princeton University Press, 1961) 27–39. See also above ch 8, text to nn 55–56. See generally WE Conklin, *Hegel's Laws: The Legitimacy of the Modern Legal Order* (Stanford, Stanford University Press, 2008) 139–41, 146 and 238.

the end, the Laws responded that Socrates would effectively undermine the legal order as a whole if he escaped from his sentence:

> Now, Socrates, what are you proposing to do? Can you deny that by this act which you are contemplating, you intend, so far as you have the power, to destroy us, the Laws, and the whole state as well? Do you imagine that a city can continue to exist and not be turned upside down, if the legal judgments which are pronounced in it have no force but are nullified and destroyed by private persons?[99]

The Laws insisted that the only condition necessary for legal objectivity to exist is that there must be opportunity to persuade the Laws that its content is unjust.[100] So long as an individual has had such an opportunity, the legal bond of social reciprocity comes to fruition. All citizens are thereby obligated to obey the content of the laws.

The theme of the 'Speech of the Laws' is not isolated in the history of legal thought. Plato also addressed the issue in the *Gorgias*,[101] as well as in his last work, *The Laws*.[102] Cicero also outlined the harm caused to a legal community as a whole by unjust war[103] and crimes against humanity,[104] as well as by the commonwealth's failure to protect persons,[105] to fulfil duties to domestic *alieni*[106] and to fulfil duties to *alieni juris*.[107] Any such harm caused by state laws or state action to the *ius gentium* rendered the laws no longer obligatory.[108] Hegel addressed the same issue of legal obligation in *Philosophy of Right* and in his lectures on the legitimacy of law:[109] why is a self-conscious or thinking subject obligated to obey the discrete laws of a legal structure if the structure is separate from the subject? In short, the notion of harm to the international legal order has been long recognized, and it has been justiciable since the late eighteenth century.

---

[99] Crito lines 50a5–50b5 (ibid).

[100] Ibid, 51b4, 51b10 and 51e5.

[101] *Gorgias* in Hamilton and Cairns (eds) (above n 98) 471e–d, 484a–c, 486a–c and 493c. See generally Conklin, *Invisible Origins* (above n 44) 13–16 and 302–4.

[102] *The Laws* in Hamilton and Cairns (eds) (above n 98) 3.875a–876.

[103] See Cicero, *On Duties*, MT Griffin and EM Atkins (eds) (Cambridge, Cambridge University Press, 1991) 1.35–38 and 2.26; Cicero, *Partitiones Oratoriae*, H Rackam (trans) (Cambridge, MA, Harvard University Press, 1942) 37.129–130; Cicero, *Commonwealth* in *On the Commonwealth* and *On the Laws*, JEG Zetzel (ed) (Cambridge, Cambridge University Press, 1999) 3.35a; and Cicero, *The Laws* (ibid) 2.34. See generally WE Conklin, 'The Myth of Primordialism in Cicero's Theory of Jus Gentium' (2010) 23 *Leiden Journal of International Law* 479.

[104] *The Laws* (above n 102) 1.32; and *On Duties* (ibid) 1.34.

[105] *Commonwealth* (above n 103) 3.24b; and *On Duties* (above n 103) 1.51, 3.23, 3.47 and 3.70.

[106] *Commonwealth* (above n 103) 3.36.

[107] *On Duties* (above n 103) 1.37, 1.51, 3.23, 3.47 and 3.70.

[108] *The Laws* (above n 102) 1.42; and *Commonwealth* (above n 103) 3.43, 3.45 and 5.1.

[109] For this sense of *Recht*, see Conklin, *Hegel's Laws* (above n 98) 43–48. Julio Barboza had this sense of an international community in mind in J Barboza, 'Legal Injury: The Tip of the Iceberg in the Law of State Responsibility' in M Ragazzi (ed), *International Responsibility Today: Essays in Memory of Oscar Schachter* (Leiden, Martinus Nijhoff, 2005) 20–21.

VII. CONCLUSION

The emergence of the notion of the international community as a whole suggests that we put the boundary of the domestic jurisdiction to the side. The exclusivity of domestic legal orders vis-à-vis the international legal order has increasingly yielded in favour of a legal bond nested in social relationships. Jurists have designated a legal sign for such social relationships: effective nationality. The territorial-like boundary of the residuary, likened to legal space, is dissolving in favour of the place experienced by natural persons through social relationships. The state is not the ultimate referent in these developments. What is critical is a sense of the international community that exists *independent* of the aggregate of the wills of states and yet *for* such members. This is so because of a separation of legal objectivity from subjects. States are no longer immediate with international legal objectivity. The corollary of this is that without effective nationality, the international legal community would not exist as a community.

The international community, resting as it does in an ethos, opens up a set of issues that is entirely different than a quest for the identity of specific laws as the express or implied consent of states. International legal objectivity exists by virtue of the unwritten existence conditions of an ethos in which legal order is independent of natural persons, as members of the international community. And yet the existence conditions are *for* such subjects because without the existence conditions, there would not be a legal objectivity separated from subjects and there would then not be subjects. 'Accidental' states, as third parties to the legal bond, have a fiduciary obligation to protect de jure and effectively stateless persons.

The legally obligatory character of the residuary does not rest in the large number of jurists who have cited it nor in the incorporation of words such as 'human' or 'dignity' into the legal discourse but rather in the social contingency of an international community that exists without certain norms, of which effective nationality is one. Unless jurists examine the unwritten structure of the ethos of an international community as a whole, the boundary of the reserved domain cannot be recognized. Indeed, seemingly identifiable laws risk becoming unlawful. In sum, the pillars of the international community are the very existence conditions of the state. Whether or not effective nationality is described as 'peremptory', its absence undermines the obligatory character of identifiable laws of the residuary.

Conclusion

A N ENIGMA ARISES from the conceived reality of an international community claiming to have universal human rights
and legal standards of humanitarian law despite the exclusion of
tens of millions of de jure and effectively stateless persons. The enigma
exists by virtue of an international community that incorporates the
reserved domain of state members as its own residuary of law-making
and law administration regarding nationality. The residuary exists by and
for each state member of the community. No other state or international
organization may interfere with the content of such a residuary without a
state's express or implicit consent. To this end, international standards
may only supplement a state law or acts of state officials, and then only
with the consent of state parties. Treaties and international customary
norms are representations of such express and implicit consent.

A stateless person is defined by the Convention Relating to the Status of
Stateless Persons (1954) as a natural person lacking nationality 'under the
operation of [a state's] law'.[1] Even rights that claim to protect stateless persons are subject to limitation and derogation 'by law'. But the notion of 'by
law', when read against the background of the international community's
residuary, inevitably rests on the freedom of states to confer, withhold and
withdraw nationality within their own jurisdictions. International standards are hence supplementary as well as circular with reference to domestically enacted laws within the residuary. Accordingly, in spite of international
standards that claim universality, interpretation of the standards has proceeded against the implicit background of the reserved domain of the state.
Such assumptions underlie any state's radical title to all land and all objects
on the land. The state has been a self-creative author of legal language and
of a territorial-like boundary that separates legal knowledge from extra-
law. Given such a boundary around legal knowledge, stateless persons

---

[1] 360 UNTS 117, Art 1 (entered into force 6 June 1960) See also the American Declaration
of the Rights and Duties of Man ('Pact of San José, Costa Rica') (Bogota, 2 May 1948), Novena
Conferencia Internacional Americana, OAS Off Rec OEA/Ser.L.V/ll.82 doc.6 rev.1, 17 (1992),
(1953) 6 *Actas y Documentos* 297–302, Art 19. The *Dictionary of International Law and Diplomacy*
defines a 'stateless' person as one whose state of nationality no longer protects or assists the
national by operation of law: MJ Gamboa, *A Dictionary of International Law and Diplomacy*
(New York, Oceana, 1973) 246.

serve to signify the identity of rules and rights inside the bounded residuary of the international community.

As a consequence of the bounded residuary of the international community, the recognition of a natural person as a legal person – as protected, for example, by Article 16 of the International Covenant on Civil and Political Rights (ICCPR) (1966), which provides that 'everyone shall have the right to recognition everywhere as a person before the law' – is left to the operation of a state's domestic laws. This deference was described by jurists initially as the 'reserved domain' and more recently as the 'internal jurisdiction' of the international community. The internal jurisdiction, I have argued, is not the consequence of a self-creative authorial state but rather of an international law discourse that recognizes its members as self-creative states. This community is a discursively contingent construct, for the most part constructed by the courts of the United States, United Kingdom and European states during the nineteenth century.[2] The community reached its clearest expression during the 1920s and 1930s.[3]

Three main issues have emerged concerning the enigma of the stateless condition. The first addresses the nature of a state member's freedom to choose who is a member of the international community. The latter legal phenomenon accompanies a critical analytic point: the boundary of the residuary is an intellectual construct peculiar to only one sense of an international community. Accordingly, the boundary exists in legal consciousness rather than in the geological fact of nature such as a river or mountain.

The discursive contingency of the boundary of the residuary has coloured the relationship between a state and a natural person. The relationship, though, has not always been a linear, state-to-person, relation. During the early state-centric international community of the seventeenth and eighteenth centuries, jurists privileged the social relationships of natural persons as independent of and prior to the international community. Such social relations, or sociality, generated the legal bond of an international community and, by extension, the legal bond between a natural person and law-making in the reserved domain. The state's legal authority was mere convenience, according to Grotius.[4] By the late nineteenth century and certainly by the 1920s and 1930s, however, the US/European-centred international community left the choice of membership to 'the operation of [a state's] laws'. The consequence was the legalized perception by the executives of states as to the loyalty of natural persons to the state. And 'its law', as required of the legal definition of a stateless person, was considered synonymous with a law posited inside the internal jurisdiction of a state.

---

[2] See above ch 1, ss I and II (79–84) and ch 2, s I (66–68), s III (73–79).
[3] See above ch 2, s IV-A (79–84).
[4] See above ch 2, s IV-A, esp text at n 29 (71).

The second major issue concerns whether the enigma of the international community can by dissipated by human rights treaties or international customary norms. Is it enough, for example, that a treaty or customary norm recognizes a right to nationality for everyone? The point here is that the quest for the identity of a discrete right or a rule, although the traditional project of the professional knowers of rules and rights, has presupposed the validity of the right or rule if it can be justified in terms of Article 38 sources.[5] And the sources have been treaties or customary international norms, statutes or the reasons for particular judgments of courts. Each source expressly or implicitly expresses the will of a state. The referent of the justification has been an institutional source of a state. The bounded residuary of an international community represents just such a consensual referent. It also represents the boundary between law and extra-law in nationality matters.

The crucial point is that in this justificatory linkage of a discrete right to a state-centric institutional source, the actual choice of membership in an international community is immaterial to the legal validity of a rule or right. What is material is the justificatory source. This justificatory trace has characterized the nature of the residuary of the international community. The legality of a natural person's presence in this or that territory has hinged upon the freedom of a state to enact a law or to administratively decide whether the person is a member of the international community. Who is included and who is excluded matter nought. What does matter is the content-independent residuary and the justification of any one nationality law or act of state with reference to the boundary of the residuary.

The third major point is that the enigma has started to dissolve only in those situations when jurists redirect their legal analysis to the nature of legal obligation rather than to the quest for the identity of a legal rule or right. To be sure, the sources thesis assumes that the ultimate referents of the justificatory process, the Article 38 sources, represent state consent. Such state consent in turn takes allegiance as critical to a legal bond. A natural person's allegiance to a state represents the legal bond. Such a bond ensures the obligation of the state to protect its members in exchange for allegiance from them.

Although liberalists have focused upon ways to render the state's institutions accessible, such efforts have been conditional: natural persons who have rights of access are members of the state. And the determination of membership has evolved from the voluntary choice by a natural person to the state's own decision as to a person's loyalty to the state. The relation of loyalty and legal obligation has thereby reinforced the very enigma of statelessness. Statelessness is the outcome of an international community protective of the freedom of each state member to choose

---

[5] Statute of the International Court of Justice (1946), appended to UN Charter.

those members whom the state considers in its self-interest. The territorial-like partition of the residuary has isolated internal jurisdiction from international standards – all consistent with the ethos of an aggregated sense of an international community. Tens of millions of natural persons, mostly in the southern hemisphere, have thereby been left without de jure or effective recognition as members of the international community.

A very different sense of legal obligation is needed if this enigma is to be understood as a contingent phenomenon of the past. To this end, I have unconcealed a sub- or inner discourse that also has existed more quietly since the early nineteenth century. Legal obligation within this alternative framework rests in domestic and international judicial decisions that are grounded in a legal bond independent of the international community's residuary. This legal bond has rested upon the social relationships of natural persons *inter se*. The legal discourse has had a name for such social relationships: effective nationality. Contrary to the usual claim of the a priori universalism that intellectually transcends the state-centric international community, the legal obligation of effective nationality is embodied (that is, given content) from the reciprocal recognition of natural persons in their social relationships. This embodied international community begs a very different set of issues than the quest for the identity of a discrete right or a rule justified with reference to the institutional sources of a state.

The enigma of statelessness raises important questions about the international community. How can a general norm such as the right to nationality be contextualized in an international community that protects the bounded legal space of a state? Do human rights treaties explain such a possibility? Indeed, is a right to nationality, posited in several treaties, also a human right? Do principles of humanitarian law trump the territorial-like boundary of the residuary of the state-centric international community? Are the principles directed towards persons who are de jure stateless? Would the stateless condition disappear if effective nationality were added to the list of peremptory norms? Why is effective nationality peremptory with regard to internal jurisdiction? Or does the residuary of the state-centric international community foreclose such questions?

The clue to answering these questions lies in the realization that there is not one black-and-white network of discrete and self-standing rights and rules. One must contextualize any such discrete right or rule in the ethos of an international community. An international community that privileges a residuary for the choice of the community's members represents only one such ethos. But another community has a very different ethos – what may be referred to as 'the international community as a whole'. This approach focuses on a stateless person's 'country', the incorporation of international standards into a state's law, the obligatory nature of law, the role of judicial scrutiny of the hitherto immunized internal jurisdiction, and the obligation to protect de jure and effectively stateless persons.

I have examined the implications of one of these features: a stateless person's 'country', which rests neither with a state nor with habitual residence on a territory but rather with the place social relationships are experienced through time and space. In such a context, executive decisions to expel or refuse to recognize the nationality of someone must be judicially scrutinized. And a law is neither a domestically enacted rule nor an international treaty or customary norm: it exists by virtue of the obligatory character entertained in the ethos of social relationships hitherto protected from external intervention by external sources. What is crucial more generally is the obligatory character of the content of such an identifiable law as well as of its reserved domain. Such an issue revolves around the lived reality of social relationships as experienced by natural persons.

I. THE TERRITORIAL KNOWLEDGE OF LEGAL SPACE

The enigma of statelessness in an international community that claims universality for its legal standards hinges upon a bounded residuary. The residuary of the international community has incorporated laws enacted and administered inside 'internal jurisdiction' as its own. This residuary manifests a spatial character, albeit the legal space is territorial-like rather than territorial.

A. The Legal Space of the Residuary

The residuary represents a mental map. The boundary is mapped as if it were a curved line encircling a legal space. The boundary of the space demarcates an 'inside' and an 'outside'. The bounded 'inside' constitutes the international community's legal reality of law-making and represents what has been considered the freedom of the state, just as it has described the natural person's freedom.[6] The boundary of the residuary cannot but have insiders and outsiders. Such a line inevitably excludes persons outside the line. The residuary is a bounded legal space that jurists have projected onto the map of legal knowledge. Laws are known if they can be 'located' inside the legal space. External to the legal space, an unknowable world of extra-legality or non-law pervades. The extra-legality is unknowable. A de jure or effectively stateless person lives in such a legally unknowable world. The challenge of the enigma, then, is to wonder whether the territorial-like boundary of the legal space is dissolving in favour of a knowledge that recognizes stateless persons.

---

[6] See above Introduction, s VII (27–28); ch 1, s II (39–41); ch 2, s III-B (76–77), s III-C (77–78); Conclusion, n 8 (307).

This challenge has usually been met by asserting a vertically higher system of legal norms in legal objectivity. Such a prospect, though, has risked a fusion of the state as subject with the objects of the state's expression. This fusion of subjectivity and objectivity has left natural persons as outsiders to international law. Put differently, the fused legal subjectivity/objectivity, represented by the state-centric international community, is reified vis-à-vis the social relationships of natural persons. That is, the fused subjectivity/objectivity thereby reifies the legal bond between a natural person on the one hand and the international community as a whole on the other.

International standards have been left in a heaven of concepts estranged from the experiential world. Such international standards can at best only supplement the domestic laws protected by the residuary, and then only if a state expressly or implicitly consents to them. The residuary of law-making is a hard fact of international law in the sense of an international community as the sum of the wills of its units. All sources outside the hard fact are 'oughts'. The foreclosed examination of the residuary has left tens of millions of natural persons without de jure or effective nationality.

The expectation of non-interference into the state's bounded legal space is not recent. Indeed, it was at the forefront of Anglo-American legal and political thought during the late eighteenth and early nineteenth centuries.[7] Both Immanuel Kant and John Stuart Mill, in particular, extended the moral and social freedom of natural persons to that of states in an international community.[8] This negative freedom of the state was institutionalized as a protected legal space that negatively excluded external norms and institutional structures. The internal jurisdiction of a state represented the individual natural person's 'inner sphere of life', as Mill put it. What matters for the construction of internal jurisdiction, as with territorial space, is its boundary.[9] The international community, as an aggregated wills of states, considers the jurisdiction content-independent.[10] The effect is the reification of the international community (and of the state) from the social ethos of the international community.

The reserved and protected jurisdiction became all-important in the legal issues and social consequences surrounding nationality. The conferment, withholding and withdrawal of nationality became an attribute of the legal space, known to jurists as the reserved domain, for the state.[11] By virtue of the impermeable boundary of the state's legal space, international organizations and their desired standards about nationality and

---

[7] See generally above ch 2, s IIIA (73–75).
[8] See above ch 2, ss IIIA & B (73–78).
[9] See above ch 2, ss III–V (73–94); ch 8, s I (236–40), sVB–D (265–68).
[10] See above ch I, s IIA; ch 2 s III-D (78).
[11] This was highlighted above chs 2 and 3.

statelessness have been projected as alien to 'law'.[12] The residuary has maintained its hold on the interpretation of human rights treaties and customary international norms.[13] Hence, international standards begin to play a role in the international law discourse only after states confer nationality onto a natural person.

B. The Boundary of the Protected Legal Space

The germ of the enigma of the international community rests upon the boundary of an essence or jurisdiction reserved for the state. Without the boundary to the jurisdiction, there is no privileged domain within which states are free to enact laws, to declare war or to choose who are their members and who are not. The pressing issue then is: what is the character of the boundary of a state's freedom?

To be sure, when one thinks about a boundary, one may intuitively imagine a territorial border. A territorial border can be seen on a map; it can be physically guarded. Foreigners can be stopped at the border; and inhabitants can be expelled from within the border. The border represents the physical situs where state officials inspect travel documents, legal identity papers, passports, border control cards, work visas and immigration papers. The border is a locus of control over the imposition of tax, economic sanctions and import or export of goods.[14] Such a territorial border physically differentiates insiders from outsiders.

The boundary within which a state is free to choose its members and to exclude others from legal recognition, however, is best described as territorial-like – not a physical border. Stateless people do not have to cross a territorial border to be stateless. Statelessness is the absence of a legal category posited inside the boundary of the reserved domain of a state. A stateless person is unknowable as a legal person. So long as the international legal community is presupposed to have a law-making residuary with a boundary around the state's legal space, there will be outsiders inside the international community. In other words, there will be natural persons without legal status in the international community.

C. Nationality as Entitlement to Membership in the Legal Space

The sign for the recognition of a natural person's membership in an international community is nationality. In the context of the community

---

[12] See above ch 2, s III (73–79).
[13] See esp chs 4 and 5.
[14] See esp S Goulbourne, 'Introduction' in S Goulbourne (ed), *Law and Migration*, vol 6 (Cheltenham, Elgar Reference Collection, 1998).

as an aggregate of legal spaces, nationality in turn becomes the legal sign for the authority of one state's privileged space against another's. Inside the space, the state possesses a freedom to confer, withhold or withdraw nationality. So too the state possesses the freedom to exclude, detain or expel non-members. In addition, the state retains uncontrolled discretion regarding whether to diplomatically protect a member. Social and legal consequences follow from the state's freedom inside its bounded legal space. And the state is reserved the freedom to withhold recognition of a natural person as a member of the international community by virtue of deference to another state's legal space. Unless the person is a member, the state will lack legal obligation to protect him/her.

A natural person needs nationality in order to escape from the legal vacuum in which s/he would otherwise find her/himself. I pointed out in chapter two that at one time, most notably in the writings of European jurists from the seventeenth and eighteenth centuries, the relationship between state and national was voluntarily chosen by natural persons. The state was said to protect a national in exchange for the national's allegiance to the state. But by the later nineteenth century, the state was determining who was loyal and who was not. In contrast with the European juridical opinions of the seventeenth and eighteenth centuries, the legal order and legal reasoning took on a conceptual or metaphysical character, displacing the former centrality of sociality.

As a consequence of this shift in focus, the state was reserved a bounded legal space within which the state could enact laws, make decisions and act without intervention by other entities. Not the will of God, not God's agents, not another state, not some imperial king, not an international organization, not inhabitants themselves could legitimately claim suzerainty over state laws, decisions and actions. This protected and bounded universality again was formerly represented by the Roman Church and, before it, the Roman Empire. Such a universality, enclosed in a state's territorial knowledge, rests in the state's claim to radical title to all territory and objects under its physical control. After all, if a state member could not choose the members of the international community, the state might be hard-pressed to be considered free or, for that matter, to possess a property interest in the territory under its control. Although an inhabitant could refuse to be a national of a state in an earlier day, an individual's voluntary consent has more recently dissipated in favour of the state's freedom over to confer, withdraw or withhold nationality. The legal bond between a natural person and the state has not been reciprocal as it was during the earlier epoch. This 'absolute' and unrestrained freedom of the state to choose its members reached its pinnacle in the international legal discourse from the period between the First and Second World Wars.

D. Nationality as the Sign of Legal Knowledge

Given the territorial-like boundary of legal space, nationality signifies who is knowable. Although the boundary of the space is imagined as a matter of legal consciousness rather than as geological fact, the boundary demonstrably encircles what is knowable. The boundary differentiates what we know as a law (the sources) from what we do not know. The boundary of our legal knowledge excludes and includes. The problem of the enigma of the modern international community then is not that states exist but that the sense of legal knowledge presupposes a solid boundary separating familiar knowledge from the unfamiliar. The residuary represents the familiar space of legal knowledge.

The international community as a whole has also functioned as the referent of legal knowledge. But in this case, the former boundary of the residuary is transparent as demarcating legal knowledge from extralegality. Social relationships may be located on territory owned by this state or that state. Although the relationships may draw from territory where one is habitually resident, this is not necessarily so. A natural person possesses nationality in terms of a referent independent of the state and independent of the state's territory. What has heretofore been taken as hard fact or as 'given' and uncontrollable by international legal norms – that is, one's residuary – is now recognized as contingently constructed by social factors independent of the state or a state's territory. With matters pertaining to de jure and effectively stateless persons, the boundary-line of legal knowledge is dissolving in favour of social knowledge.

This social knowledge goes hand in hand with the international community as a whole. For the community exists as a legal objectivity that is separate from its members. The separation raises the possibility that there are subjects of the international community. There cannot be a subject without such separation. Unlike the idealized community in a heaven of concepts estranged from the social relationships of natural persons, however, the international community as a whole is rooted in the actuality of social relationships. The legal bond of effective nationality can displace that of allegiance. The boundary of the residuary can be transparent, and nationality can be effective independent of the state. The socially buried international community is just as much a legal actuality as is an international legal discourse that has privileged the bounded legal space of the state. For effective nationality, jurisdiction is embodied by social relationships.

II. THE OBLIGATORY CHARACTER OF NATIONALITY LAW

Against the background of chapter six, legal knowledge emerges as social. Such social knowledge contrasts with territorial knowledge drawn from a reserved domain. Since the late eighteenth century, jurists have accepted de jure statelessness as an incident of such a reserved domain. Knowledge about who is stateless, that is, has presupposed territoriality as the object of knowledge. Such territorial knowledge focuses upon rules and rights as if they were bounded legal spaces, just as their ultimate sources – treaties, customary norms and judicial commentaries – have presupposed that legal knowledge represents the consent of the territorial-like reserved domain. Customary international rules and the rules in human rights treaties take for granted a territorial-like boundary of legal knowledge, and that boundary encircles a legal space that is protected from external scrutiny and intervention.[15] So long as a domestic rule authorizes the exclusion of certain natural persons from nationality, that exclusionary knowledge remains unknowable to external international or other state organizations. It also remains unknowable to domestic or international tribunals. The rule is legally valid and obligatory so long as the boundary of territorial knowledge – that is, the boundary of the residuary – is accepted by jurists. The social assumptions and expectations of stateless persons are extra-law or 'out of bounds' from legal knowledge. Even the legal knowledge inside the territorial-like boundary of the domestic legal space is unknowable except in terms of the justification of the rule through an institutional source of the state.

In contrast, effective nationality now grounds the legal bond, which is so necessary in order to understand why a law is obligatory. And the reserved domain, a legal space heretofore immune from external evaluation of its content, is now open to scrutiny. Such scrutiny encompasses the assumptions and expectations of the content of the legal space. The scrutiny is now constituted by social knowledge and in particular is concerned with the extent to which reciprocal social relationships are respected and protected. It is now a state obligation to protect the social relationships of de jure and effectively stateless persons. That state obligation changes what we mean by an international community. Once the bounded legal space is no longer free from external interference, an alternative understanding of the international community changes the issue before jurists.

For one thing, important consequences follow from such social knowledge. The most important effect in the context of statelessness is that the boundary of legal knowledge in the aggregated international community dissolves as the determining factor about nationality. With such dissolution of the boundary of legal space, domestic laws of nationality are in turn no longer exclusive of international standards. Both domestic and international standards become knowable objects of inquiry about a legal objectivity independent of the boundary of the legal space.

---

[15] See above Introduction chapter and chs 4 and 5.

It would be in error to suggest, though, that a sense of the international community as a whole, signified by a legal bond as effective nationality, has emerged as dominant over the sense of the community as the aggregated wills of states. As chapters four and five outlined, discursive ambiguity and struggle have characterized knowledge about nationality issues. The struggle is manifest in the decisions of human rights and refugee tribunals, the opinio juris of the International Law Commission (ILC) and the General Comments of the Human Rights Committee of the ICCPR, as well as in the Universal Declaration of Human Rights and the statelessness treaties and human rights treaties themselves.

To take an example, on the one hand, some texts by the ILC no longer accept the exclusivity of domestic and international legal orders with regard to nationality. The ILC 'First Report Concerning Nationality and the Succession of States' (1995), of which Václav Mikulka was the Raporteur, outlined how the state's discretionary authority is limited concerning nationality.[16] Chapter four of the First Report especially elaborated how effective nationality and human rights limited the freedom of a state in matters of nationality. A subsequent summary of an ILC meeting addressing the First Report stated, 'Seen from the perspective of international law, to the extent that individuals were not direct subjects of international law, nationality was the medium through which they could normally enjoy benefits from international law.'[17] In like vein, a subsequent ILC Report concerning 'State Succession and its Impact on Nationality of Natural and Legal Persons' (1995) raised the issue whether an act carried out under domestic law is null and void if resultant denaturalization has the effect of persecuting an ethnic minority.[18] In addition, the ILC 'Draft Articles on State Responsibility' especially hold out a legal obligation on the part of a state if the obligation 'is of such a character as radically to change the position of all other states to which the obligation is owed with the further performance of the obligation'.[19] Even if no state is injured, harm to stateless persons invokes the obligation of all states to protect the international community as a whole.[20]

On the other hand, the ILC reports on diplomatic protection have often suggested that international standards are to be used only in 'exceptional

---

[16] See ILC, 'State Succession and Its Impact on the Nationality of Natural and Legal Persons', *ILC Yearbook 1995* vol II(1) A/CN.4/464/Add.2, s F, A/CN.4/467, paras 57–74.

[17] ILC, 'Summary Record of the 2385th Meeting (17 May 1995)', A/CN.4/SR.2385, Agenda item 7, in *ILC Yearbook 1995*, vol I, 47 (para 34).

[18] ILC, 'Report on the Work of its Forty-Seventh Session', ch 3, UN Doc A/50/10, *ILC Yearbook 1995*, vol II(2), 37 (paras 183–85).

[19] ILC, 'Draft Articles on Responsibility of States for Internationally Wrongful Acts' (2001), *Report of the ILC on the Work of Its Fifty-third Session*, UN Doc A/56/10, legal.un.org/ilc/reports/2001/2001report.htm, reprinted in J Crawford (ed), *The International Law Commission's Articles on State Responsibility: Introduction, Text and Commentaries* (Cambridge, Cambridge University Press, 2002) vol II(2), Art 42 (Comm 1).

[20] ILC (ibid) esp Art 48 (Comm 9).

circumstances' – in other words, only when domestic law is silent as to the withdrawal, withholding or conferral of de jure nationality.[21] If the reserved legal space is *not* silent as to an identifiable internal standard, only the state's standard may bind or even guide domestic and international officials. Needless to say, nationality has not been such a silent matter of internal jurisdiction. Despite sustained appeals to the 'international community as a whole', that community is often presupposed to be the aggregate of atomistic legal entities called states.[22] As the ILC explained in one nationality study, 'In internal law, the function of nationality was different and there could be various categories of "nationals".'[23] As a consequence, any international standard concerning nationality has varied with the domestic laws protected by a bounded legal space. Such circularity continues into the present day.

Statelessness remains an enigma of the international legal order if and to the extent that nationality is considered an attribute of the residuary of the international community and to the extent that the residuary incorporates the reserved domain of the state. The residuary protects a state's freedom much as the natural person possesses self-regarding legal space as her/his freedom. And that freedom has heretofore presupposed that the international community is an aggregate of the wills of the state members. What is knowable as law is presupposed to be 'found' inside the territorial-like boundary of the legal space reserved for the state by the international community. The boundary of the reserved legal space, again, necessitates outsiders to the boundary. Stateless persons are unknowable as legal persons. They lack the sign that represents legal personhood.

Legal knowledge, in other words, has been traditionally presupposed to rest inside the very bounded legal space associated with the freedom of the state. From the standpoint of most jurists, the legal space is a brute fact. Being a legal fact, domestic nationality laws cannot be questioned or scrutinized by courts, as we saw in chapter eight. A national is any natural person who is knowable inside the bounded freedom. What rules and rights are nested inside the boundary of the state's space are knowable by jurists. The social-cultural content inside the space is immaterial from the standpoint of the observer. The content, inside and outside the boundary of the space, is unknowable and therefore extra-law. Legal space exists by virtue of the territorial-like boundary of legal consciousness. The very boundary of the state's freedom defines the legal space. Whether conferred by the state or attributed by habitual residence, the boundary forecloses any effort by another state or international organization to claim to know what is inside the residuary/legal space.

---

[21] ILC, 'State Succession and its Impact on the Nationality of Natural and Legal Persons' (above n 16) 48 (para 38).

[22] Ibid, 47 (para 34).

[23] Ibid.

Such a legal space is constitutive of legal reality in the international community as understood as the aggregated wills of states. Jurists just cannot know the identity of a stateless person as a legal person if and to the extent that the ultimate referent of legal knowledge about natural persons lies inside the territorial-like boundary of the state's legal space. The 'situs' of a stateless person in an extra-legal black hole brings to the fore the principle inherited from the Romans, *damnum absque injuria* ('loss without [legal] injury'). Even with treaties expressly focusing upon the stateless condition, it has been very difficult to question the boundary of the hard fact of legal space. Peremptory norms with customary norms have exemplified just such a sense of an aggregate of the international community. An international standard has not been considered obligatory unless it is the object of express or implicit consent of state members. International law and international organizations are excluded as external to the legal space except as objects of consent by the state. Even if all states were to agree to recognize a new legal personhood signified as 'a stateless person', the enforcement of the new category would be left to institutions of the internal jurisdiction. An international standard is considered non-obligatory. But what renders them non-obligatory is faith in the bounded residuary of the international community. And that is the distinguishing element of one sense of an international community.

The problem is that efforts to eradicate statelessness, whether in the form of stateless treaties or human rights treaties or international customary norms, have subtly conflated the universality of human rights into a territorial knowledge characterized by universalities inside each state's territorial-like boundary of legal space. Although 'both literature and jurisprudence [have] recognized the exclusive character of the competence of the state in determining which individuals [are] its nationals',[24] the ILC has raised the question whether 'acts carried out under internal law were null and void, such as the case where the decision to divest certain natural persons of their nationality was an element in the persecution of an ethnic minority'.[25] The boundary of the reserved legal space denotes the limit of legal knowledge as if its facticity, like nature, cannot be humanly changed, modified, revised or rendered void. This returns us to the initial question: does law always proceed through territorial-like partitions?

A certain logic colours the preoccupation with the boundary of the reserved domain incorporated into the international community. Once the justifying source of a right, rule or other concept has been identified as presupposing an institutional source of the state, the analytic challenge has been for jurists to dissect the concept into its minute parts, to revise the initial concept and then to enclose context-specific social-cultural

---

[24] ILC, 'Report on the Work of its Forty-Seventh Session' (above n 18) 37 (paras 183–84).
[25] Ibid, para 185.

events within the boundary of the revised concept. This project has especially been encouraged in that a right to nationality has been deemed
knowable inside a boundary. It has not been necessary to address the
social consequences of this logic. The idea of a line that demarcates legal
knowledge from non-knowledge evokes an image of the jurist's project as
one that is clear and straightforward. It is not surprising that *Flegenheimer*
and other judicial decisions examined in chapter six have accepted that
any inquiry into the binding character of the content of the reserved
domain would encourage a 'political' or 'ought' evaluation that obfus-
cates the legal situation.[26]

The simplicity of the identity issue is self-deceptive, however. Stateless
people do not always cross territorial borders. Even such crossing does
not ensure the protection of a stateless person. Nor are stateless persons
invariably newcomers to a domestic society. Some groups of stateless persons, as we have seen, have lived on the territory of a state for generations
or even centuries without being recognized as legal persons by any modern state. Mass migration from territories of birth has added a further
complication to the global consideration of statelessness. The stateless
condition causes especial suffering for women and children. The resultant
social, economic and psychological harm cannot be ignored. Yet states
remain blameless for the social and economic consequences, let alone for
the legal exclusion of natural persons from nationality. The boundary of
territorial knowledge protects these social consequences from external
scrutiny.

III. THE INTERNATIONAL COMMUNITY AS A WHOLE

The notion of the international community as a whole displaces the territorial-like residuary of state law-making and law administration. There have
been two international law discourses in this regard, the one concealed
inside the other. Each has had a different understanding of the nature of
legal bond in an international community. The one sense of an international
community has accepted allegiance as the legal bond; the second sense of a
community has taken for granted that the legal bond rests in the reciprocal
social relationships between natural persons. This latter understanding of
legal bond is dissolving of the residuary's boundaries, which has required
insiders and outsiders, nationals and stateless persons. Territorial knowledge is being displaced by law as social knowledge.

Different historically contingent epochs with different assumptions and
expectations on the part of jurists have characterized the two discourses.

---

[26] *Flegenheimer Claim (Decision No 182)* (1958) 16 RIAA 327, 25 ILR 91 (Italy–US Conciliation
Commission). See above ch 6, s I (178–81); s V (202–03); ch 7 (221–23).

During the seventeenth and eighteenth centuries, an individual's voluntary consent to nationality conditioned allegiance. A state agreed to protect a national if the national agreed to exhibit allegiance to the state. This allegiance of a natural person to the state justified any state enactment or act of its executive regarding whom would be protected by the international standards to which the state had consented. By the late nineteenth century, however, the international legal discourse had shifted in a way that no longer required an individual's voluntary consent to nationality. The effective control of territory by a state and the legal claim of radical title to the territory as property came to the fore. At first sight, the critical feature here was the geographical territorial border caused by cession or conquest. With the transformation of physical control over territory to the property interest of the state, however, nationality became a metaphysical condition of knowledge. Nationality signified a knowable person in such a metaphysical international community.

Within this framework, the residuary is not of physical territory studied by cartography. Rather, the residuary is a discursively constructed concept representing a territorial-like space in legal consciousness. The critical point is that the state-centric international legal discourse has been imagined as if a stateless person could be perceived as an object on a physical space. As a product of how jurists think, even the jurisdiction of the state, we have learned, is the product of a particular way of organizing international relations during a particular historical period that has differed seriously from international relations before, now and after. With such a sense of knowledge as a concept (of property), the international law discourse has taken on a sense of the national as if the national could be known inside a territorial-like bounded residuary of the international community. This 'as if' boundary encloses legal space, within which a state can enact laws, make decisions and impact upon social life without interference from state and international sources that are outside the boundary.

When efforts have been made to find a discrete right or rule protective of stateless persons, the right or rule has been either at the cost of ignoring the discursive contingency of the reserved domain or at the cost of excluding international standards as mere 'oughts' or as non-obligatory. In both contexts, the universality of human rights has been accepted as a 'given' without sufficient appreciation for the emptiness of the bounded residuary. Jurists who seek identifiable laws have frequently turned to Kant in search of a transcendent a priori concept signified in 'the league of states'. Such a league, though, fuses subjects and legal objectivity into a oneness. The fusion excludes universal norms as 'oughts' in a heaven of a priori concepts. The fusion excludes social bonding as (ironically) immaterial to law. Such a confederation of states is divorced from the social relationships of natural persons by Kant's own insistence. The emptiness of such an international community is reinforced by its residuary of law-making. The residuary is empty because an identifiable law inside the residuary exists by virtue of its justification with reference to a source on the boundary of the residuary.

One might turn, as an alternative, to Hans Kelsen, who described the foundation of law as neither a perceptible fact nor an ordinary norm but rather an invisible or inaccessible foundation of the legal structure.[27] Or one may return to HLA Hart's claim of a rupture between the 'pre-legal' or 'primitive' experiential world 'buried' in legal obligation on the one hand and the justification of a legal rule, right or other concept with reference to the rule/concept of recognition on the other hand.[28] Each of these efforts has appealed to discrete rules and rights, whether domestic or international, as if justified in terms of higher-ordered institutional sources of the state. Instead of un-concealing the social-cultural content of the state's reserved legal space, such traditional approaches abstract from the historically contingent social assumptions and expectations of the ethos of the state-centric international community. As a consequence, the international community has invariably become reified vis-à-vis the social ethos of the community. An appreciation that there might be two international legal communities might well seem destabilizing from the standpoint of a jurist immersed in the familiar knowledge concerning the boundary of the state's legal space.

The challenge of my effort, then, has been to analyse what we have taken for granted as legally knowable. Legal knowledge has presupposed its limit as a territorial-like boundary. Such a limit, however, dissolves once one appreciates the importance of the legal bond as social bonding. Such being the case, stateless persons are not necessarily outsiders to the international community. Indeed, a radically different international community with very different senses of legal bond, nationality and law comes to the fore. The discourse about the international community as a whole does not map out an ideal world of justice. Rather, the international community as a whole retrieves a sense of nationality nested in a discursive actuality of social relationships.

This emerging sense of nationality is dissolving the differentiation between nationals and stateless persons. A boundary-line no longer protects knowledge of the one from the other. As a result, statelessness is no longer a logically necessary feature of international law. And a series of issues and arguments, reviewed in my Introduction, come to the fore with respect to social conditions. Nationality, as the ILC has put it, is an attribute,

---

[27] H Kelsen, 'Sovereignty and International Law' (1960) 48 *Georgetown Law Journal* 627, 631. See also WE Conklin, *The Invisible Origins of Legal Positivism* (Dordrecht, Kluwer, 2001) 187–200.

[28] See HLA Hart, *Concept of Law*, L Green, J Raz and PA Bulloch (eds), 3rd edn (Oxford, Clarendon, 2012) 85–93.

not an object to be posited as if an uncontrollable fact. And I now add, it is an attribute of 'effective' social relationships of natural persons.

This social basis of nationality is independent of states as legal members of the international community. As such, statelessness, as the inverse of nationality, is also independent of a state-centric international community. This being so, stateless persons no longer exist, at least to the extent that the emerging international legal discourse is displacing the international legal protection of the reserved and bounded legal space of states in the context of nationality.

State obligations take on a very different meaning as a consequence. Asylum, security of the person, the right of return, the succession of states, refugee law, nomadic and traditional societies, and undocumented migrant groups – these exemplify very different social contexts but all share a state obligation to protect them. Indeed, what is taken as 'law' is shifting course from a rule or right conferred inside the bounded residuary. The residuary is no longer a bounded empty legal space protected from external interference. A law is obligatory because of the reciprocal social relationships presupposed in the content of the legal space. Such relationships have heretofore been inaccessible to legal analysis so long as it has been states that determine the allegiance of natural persons.

With the recognition of this alternative, inner international law discourse, the separation between domestic and international legal standards dissolves. It does not dissolve by virtue of some transcendent concept such as the humanity of beings, 'morality' or 'public policy', nor does it dissolve because of economic-social phenomena described as globalization. It dissolves because the boundary of the international community's residuary dissolves with the emergence of legal bond as social bonding. The reciprocal social relationships of inhabitants, we have seen, can trump de jure nationality and a state's declaration of a person's (dis)loyalty. International legal objectivity, as mirrored in the international community as a whole, no longer depends upon nor needs stateless outsiders as did the international community as the aggregated wills of state members of the community. Mandatory detention of stateless persons is brought into question. So too is a state's freedom to refuse admission, to expel, to internally displace or to detain stateless persons for a prolonged period. The denaturalization of stateless persons, the withholding of naturalization and the accompanying social consequences concerning employment, public education and public medical heath (identified in chapter three) must all be met with suspicion. Domestic legal structures, based as they have been on the foundation of a reserved legal space, can no longer be exclusionary of international legal standards. Each stateless person now has a country, embodied by iterant events experienced in a place. Judicial scrutiny of executive action such as denaturalization, detention and expulsion is now justifiable. And what is taken as 'lawfulness' is very different than the simple trace of a right to some institutional source protected by the bounded internal jurisdiction of a state.

With the powerful notion of the international community as a whole, a very different set of issues now comes to the surface. Legal officials and jurists who ignore the issues risk the production of de jure and effective statelessness. More than this, though, by not coming to terms with the enigma and the potentiality of dissolving the enigma in an international community as a whole, jurists further divorce domestic as well as international legal standards from social life. Such a silencing of social life in legal discourse in turn risks an empty peace.

Select Bibliography

Adams, C and Laurence, R (eds), *Travel and Geography in the Roman Empire* (London and New York, Routledge, 2001).

Agamben, G, *Homo Sacer: Sovereign Power and Bare Life*, D Heller-Roazen (trans) (Stanford, Stanford University Press, 1998).

——*State of Exception*, K Attell (trans) (Chicago, University of Chicago Press, 2005).

Albers PC, 'Changing Patterns of Ethnicity in the Northeastern Plains' in JD Hill (ed), *History, Power and Identity: Ethnogenesis in the Americas, 1492–1992* (Iowa City, University of Iowa Press, 1996) 90–118.

Albert, M and Brock, L, 'Debordering the World of States: New Spaces in International Relations' in M Albert, L Brock and K Dieter Wolf (eds), *Civilizing World Politics: Society and Community beyond the State* (Lanham, Rowman & Littlejohn, 2000) 19–68.

Albert, M, Brock, L and Dieter Wolf, K (eds), *Civilizing World Politics: Society and Community beyond the State* (Latham, Rowman & Littlefield, 2000).

Aleinikoff, AT, 'Theories of Loss of Citizenship' (1986) 84 *Michigan Law Review* 1471.

Aleinikoff, AT and Chetail, V (eds), *Migration and International Legal Norms* (The Hague, TMC Asser Press, 2003).

Aleinikoff, AT and Klusmeyer, D (eds), *From Migrants to Citizens: Membership in a Changing World* (Washington, Carnegie Endowment for International Peace, 2000).

Allain, J, 'The Jus Cogens Nature of Non-Refoulement' (2001) 13 *International Journal of Refugee Law* 533.

Allott, P, 'Book Review' (2009) 80 *British Yearbook of International Law* 409.

——'Boundaries and the Law in Africa' in CG Widstrand (ed), *African Boundary Problems* (Uppsala, Scandinavian Institute of African Studies, 1969).

——*Eunomia: New Order for a New World* (Oxford, Oxford University Press, 2002 [1990]).

——'Globalization from Above: Actualising the Ideal through Law' (2000) 26 *Review of International Studies* 61.

——*The Health of Nations: Society and Law beyond the State* (Cambridge, Cambridge University Press, 2002).

——'Law and the Re-Making of Humanity: The Challenge' in N Dorsen and P Gifford (eds), *Democracy and the Rule of Law* (Washington, DC, CQ Press, 2001) 1–31.

——'Mare Nostrum: A New International Law of the Sea' (1992) 86 *American Journal of International Law* 764.

van Alphen E, 'Symptoms of Discursivity: Experience, Memory, and Trauma' in M Bal, J Crewe and L Spitzer (eds), *Acts of Memory: Cultural Recall in the Present.* (Hanover, University Press of New England, 1999) 24–38.

Alston, P and Goodman, R, *International Human Rights* (Oxford, Oxford University Press, 2013).

Alvarez, JE, 'Crimes of States/Crimes of Hate: Lessons from Rwanda' (1999) 24 *Yale Journal of International Law* 365.

American Law Institute, *Restatement of the Law, Third: Foreign Relations Law of the United States* (St Paul, American Law Institute, 1987).

Anderson, B, *Imagined Communities: Reflections of the Origins and Spread of Nationalism* (London, Verso, 1991).

Anghie A, 'Finding the Peripheries: Sovereignty and Colonialism in Nineteenth-Century International Law' (1999) 40 *Harvard International Law Journal* 22.

—— 'Francisco de Victoria and the Colonial Origins of International Law' (1996) 5 *Society and Legal Studies* 321.

—— *Imperialism, Sovereignty and the Making of International Law* (Cambridge, Cambridge University Press, 2004).

An-Na'im AA, 'Human Rights in the Muslim World: Socio-Political Conditions and Scriptural Imperatives' (1990) 3 *Harvard Human Rights Journal* 13.

—— 'State Responsibility under International Human Rights Law to Change Religious and Customary Law' in R Cook (ed), *Human Rights of Women* (Philadelphia, University of Pennsylvania Press, 1994) 167–98.

Aquinas T, 'Treatise on Law, First Part of the Second Part' in AC Pegis (eds), *Basic Writings of Saint Thomas Aquinas*, as trans from *Theologica*, vol 2 (New York, Random House, 1945).

Arboleda E and Hoy, I, 'The Convention Refugee Definition in the West: Disharmony of Interpretation and Application' (1993) 5 *International Journal of Refugee Law* 66.

Archibugi, D, Held, D and Köhler, M (eds), *Re-imagining Political Community: Studies in Cosmopolitan Democracy* (Stanford, Stanford University Press, 1998).

Arendt, H, *Between Past and Future: Six Exercises in Political Thought* (London, Viking Press, 1961).

—— *Eichmann in Jerusalem* (New York, Penguin Books, 1977).

—— *Eichmann on Trial* (London, Penguin Books, 1963).

—— *The Origins of Totalitarianism* (New York, Harcourt Brace Jovanovich, 1973).

Armitage, D, *Foundations of Modern International Thought* (Cambridge, Cambridge University Press, 2013).

Armitage, D and Subrahmanyyam, S (eds), *The Age of the Revolutions in Global Context, c 1760–1840* (New York, Palgrave, 2010).

Arnold, C, 'Corrective Justice' (1980) 90 *Ethics* 180.

Arsanjani, MH, 'The Rome Statute of the International Criminal Court' (1999) 93 *American Journal of International Law* 22.

Bahdi, R, 'No Exit: Racial Profiling and Canada's War against Terrorism' (2003) 41 *Osgoode Hall Law Journal* 293.

Barboza, J, 'Legal Injury: The Tip of the Iceberg in the Law of State Responsibility' in M Ragazzi (ed), *International Responsibility Today: Essays in Memory of Oscar Schachter* (Leiden, Martinus Nijhoff, 2005) 7–22.

Bardenstein, CB, 'Trees, Forests, and the Shaping of Palestinian and Israeli Collective Memory' in M Bal, K Crewe and L Spitzer (eds), *Acts of Memory: Cultural Recall in the Present* (Hanover, University Press of New England, 1999) 148–68.

Blackstone, W, *Commentaries on the Laws of England*, vol 1 (Oxford, Clarendon Press, 1821).

Barber, P and Harper, T, *Magnificent Maps: Power, Propaganda and Art* (London, British Library, 2010).

Bartelson J, *A Genealogy of Sovereignty* (Cambridge, Cambridge University Press, 1995).

—— *Visions of World Community* (Cambridge, Cambridge University Press, 2009).

Bassiouni, MC, 'Policy Perspectives Favoring the Establishment of the International Criminal Court' (1999) 52 *Journal of International Affairs* 795.

Batchelor, CA, 'Statelessness and the Problem of Resolving Nationality Status' (1998) 10 *International Journal of Refugee Law* 156.

—— 'Stateless Persons: Some Gaps in International Protection' (1995) 7 *International Journal of Refugee Law* 232.

—— 'UNHCR and Issues related to Nationality' (1995) 14 *Refugee Survey Quarterly* 91.

Bates, DG, 'Differential Access to Pasture in a Nomadic Society: The Yörük of Southeastern Turkey' in W Irons and N Dyson-Hudson (eds), *Perspectives on Nomadism* (Leiden, Brill, 1972) 48–59.

Bayefsky, A (ed), *Human Rights and Refugees, Internally Displaced Persons and Migrant Workers: Essays in Memory of Joan Fitzpatrick and Arthur Helton* (Leiden, Martinus Nijhoff, 2006).

Beier, A, 'The Military Tribunals on Trial', *New York Review of Books* (14 February 2002) 11–15.

Bell, C, *Peace Agreements and Human Rights* (Oxford, Clarendon Press, 2000).

Benhabib S, *The Rights of Others: Aliens, Residents, and Citizens* (Cambridge, Cambridge University Press, 2004).

Benhabib, S and Resnik, J, 'Introduction: Citizenship and Migration Theory Engendered' in S Benhabib and J Resnik (eds), *Migrations and Mobilities: Citizenship, Borders, and Gender* (New York & London, New York University Press, 2009) 1–44.

Bennoune, K, 'Sovereignty versus Suffering? Re-examining Sovereignty and Human Rights through the Lens of Iraq' (2002) 13 *European Journal of International Law* 243.

Bentwich, N, 'International Aspects of Restitution and Compensation for Victims of the Nazis' (1955–56) 32 *British Yearbook of International Law* 204.

—— 'Nationality in Mandated Territories Detached from Turkey' (1926) 7 *British Yearbook of International Law* 97.

—— 'Statelessness through the Peace Treaties after the First World War' (1944) 21 *British Yearbook of International Law* 171.

Berland, JC and Rao, A, 'Unveiling the Stranger: A New Look at Peripatetic Peoples' in JC Berland and A Rao (eds), *Customary Strangers: New Perspectives on Peripatetic Peoples in the Middle East, Africa and Asia* (Westport, CT, Praeger, 2004).

Berlin, I, 'Two Concepts of Liberty' in *Four Essays on Liberty* (London, Oxford University Press, 1969) 118–72.

Berman, N, '"But the Alternative is Despair": European Nationalism and the Modernist Renewal of International Law' (1993) 106 *Harvard Law Review* 1792.

Bernasconi, R, 'Hegel at the Court of Ashanti' in S Barnett (ed), *Hegel after Derrida* (New York, Routledge, 1998) 41–63.

Bernasconi, R, 'Kant's Third Thoughts on Race' in S Elden and E Mendieta (eds), *Reading Kant's Geography* (New York, State University of New York, 2001) 291–318.

Besson, S, 'Theorizing the Sources of International Law' in S Besson and J Tsioulas (eds), *Philosophy of International Law* (Oxford, Oxford University Press, 2010).

Bhabba, J (ed), *Children without a State: A Global Human Rights Challenge* (Cambridge, MA, Massachusetts Institute of Technology Press, 2011).

Bienen, D, Rittberger, V and Wagner, W, 'Democracy in the United Nations System: Cosmopolitan and Communitarian Principles' in D Archibugi, D Held and M Kohler (eds), *Re-imagining Political Community: Studies in Cosmopolitan Democracy* (Stanford, Stanford University Press, 1998) 287–308.

Bilder, RB, 'Can Minorities Treaties Work?' (1991) 20 *Israel Yearbook on Human Rights* 71.

Blandy, S and Sibley, D, 'Law, Boundaries and the Production of Space' (2010) 19 *Social and Legal Studies* 275.

Blitz, BK, 'Advocacy Campaigns and Policy Development' (April 2009) 32 *Forced Migration* 25.

——'Neither Seen nor Heard: Compound Deprivation among Stateless Children' in J Bhabha (ed), *Children without a State: A Global Human Rights Challenge* (Cambridge, MA, Massachusetts Institute of Technology Press, 2011) 43–66.

——'Statelessness, Protection and Equality', Forced Migration Policy Briefing 3, Refugee Studies Centre (Oxford Department of International Development, 2009).

Blitz, BK and Lynch, M, 'Statelessness and the Deprivation of Nationality' in BK Blitz and M Lynch (eds), *Statelessness and Citizenship: A Comparative Study on the Benefits of Nationality* (Cheltenham, Edward Elgar, 2011) 1–22.

——(eds), *Statelessness and Citizenship: A Comparative Study on the Benefits of Nationality* (Cheltenham, Edward Elgar, 2011).

Blitz, BK and Sawyer, C, 'Statelessness in the European Union' in C Sawyer and BK Blitz (eds), *Statelessness in the European Union: Displaced, Undocumented, Unwanted* (Cambridge, Cambridge University Press, 2011) 3–21.

Bodin, J, *On Sovereignty*, JH Franklin (trans and ed) (Cambridge, Cambridge University Press, 1992 [1583]).

Bodlore-Penlaez, M, *Atlas of Stateless Nations in Europe: Minority Peoples in Search of Recognition*, S Finn and C Finn (trans) (Talybont, Y Lolfa, 2012).

Borchard, EM, *The Diplomatic Protection of Citizens Abroad; or, The Law of International Claims* (New York, Klaus Reprint, 1970 [1915]).

——'The Law of Responsibility of States for Damage Done in Their Territory to the Person or Property of Foreigners (The Harvard Code of Responsibility)' (1929) 23(2) *American Journal of International Law* 131.

Bowett, D, *Self Defence in International Law* (Manchester, Manchester University Press, 1988).

Bowring, B, 'The Tartars of the Russian Federation and National-Cultural Autonomy: A Contradiction in Terms?' (2007) 6 *Ethnopolitics* 417.

Boyle, K and Baldaccini, A, 'A Critical Evaluation of International Human Rights Approaches to Racism' in S Fredman (ed), *Discrimination and Human Rights* (Oxford, Oxford University Press, 2001) 135–91.

Bozeman, AB, 'An Introduction to Various Cultural Traditions of International Law: A Preliminary Assessment' in P-M Dupuy (ed), *The Future of International Law in a Multi-Cultural World* (Netherlands, Samson-Sijhoff, 1993) 85–104.

——*Politics and Culture in International History: From the Ancient Near East to the Opening of the Modern Age* (New Brunswick, NJ, Transaction Publishers, 1994).

Bradley, CA and Goldsmith, JL, '*Pinochet* and International Human Rights Litigation' (1999) 97 *Michigan Law Review* 2129.

Brennan, K, 'The Influence of Cultural Relativism on International Human Rights Law: Female Circumcision as a Case Study' (1989) 7 *Law and Inequality: A Journal of Theory and Practice* 367.

Breuilly, J, *Nationalism and the State* (New York, St Martin's Press, 1982).

Brierly, JL and Waldock, H (eds), *The Law of Nations: An Introduction to the International Law of Peace* (Oxford, Clarendon Press, 1963).

Briggs, H, *The Law of Nations: Cases, Documents and Notes*, 3rd edn (New York, Appleton-Century-Crofts, 1966).

Brilmayer, L, 'Secession and Self-Determination' (1991) 16 *Yale Journal of International Law* 177.

de Brito, A, Barrahonba, C, González, E and Aguilar, P (eds), *The Politics of Memory: Transitional Justice in Democratizing Societies* (Oxford, Oxford University Press, 2001).

Brunnée, J and Troupe, S, *Legitimacy and Legality in International Law: An International Account* (Cambridge, Cambridge University Press, 2012).

Brölmann, C, 'Deterritorialization in International Law: Moving Away from the Divide between National and International Law' in J Nijman and A Nollkaemper (eds), *New Perspectives on the Divide Between National and International Law* (Oxford, Oxford University Press, 2007) 84–109.

——'A Flat Earth? International Organizations in the System of International Law' (2001) 70 *Nordic Journal of International Law* 319.

Bromley, NK, *Law, Space and the Geographies of Power* (New York, Guilford Press, 1994).

Brown, C, 'Borders and Identity in International Political Theory' in M Albert, D Jacobson and Y Lapid (eds), *Identities, Borders, Orders: Rethinking International Relations* (Minneapolis, University of Minnesota Press, 2001) 117–36.

Brown, RJ and Ross, GF, 'The Battle for Acceptance: An Investigation into the Dynamics of Intergroup Behaviour' in H Tajfel (ed), *Social Identity and Intergroup Relations* (Cambridge, Cambridge University Press, 1982) 155–78.

Brownlie, I, *Principles of Public International Law*, 6th edn (Cary, NC, Oxford University Press, 2003).

——'The Relations of Nationality in Public International Law' (1963) 39 *British Yearbook of International Law* 284.

Brubaker, R, 'Myths and Misconceptions in the Study of Nationalism' in JA Hall (ed), *The State of the Nations* (Cambridge, Cambridge University Press, 1998) 272–307.

Brudner, A, 'The Domestic Enforcement of International Covenants on Human Rights: A Theoretical Framework' (1985) 35 *University of Toronto Law Journal* 219.

Buchanan, A, 'The Legitimacy of International Law' in S Besson and J Tsioulas (eds), *Philosophy of International Law* (Oxford, Oxford University Press, 2010).

——'Self-Determination, Secession, and the Rule of Law' in R McKim and J McMahan (eds), *The Morality of Nationalism* (Oxford, Oxford University Press, 1997) 301–23.

Bull, H, *The Anarchical Society: A Study of Order in World Politics* (London, Macmillan, 1977).

—— 'The Emergence of a Universal International Society' in H Bull and A Watson (eds), *The Expansion of International Society* (New York, Oxford University Press, 1984) 118–41.

Byers, M, *Custom, Power and the Power of Rules: International Relations and Customary International Law* (Cambridge, Cambridge University Press, 1999).

Callewaert, J, 'Is There a Margin of Appreciation in the Application of Articles 2, 3 and 4 of the Convention?' (1998) 16 *Human Rights Law Journal* 6.

Calvo, C and Gallaudet, EM (eds), *Le Droit International* (NY, Holt, 1892).

Caney, S, George, D and Jones, P (eds), *National Rights, International Obligations* (Boulder, Westview, 1996).

Casey, ES, *Getting Back into Place: Toward a Renewed Understanding of the Place-World*, 2nd edn (Bloomington, Indiana University Press, 2009).

—— *Remembering: A Phenomenological Study*, 2nd edn (Bloomington, Indiana University Press, 2000).

Casimir, MJ, '"Once upon a Time": Reconciling the Stranger' in JC Berland and A Rao (eds), *Customary Strangers: New Perspectives on Peripatetic Peoples in the Middle East, Africa and Asia* (Westport, CT, Praeger, 2004).

Chan, JMM, 'The Right to a Nationality as a Human Right' (1991) 12 *Human Rights Law Journal* 1.

Changani, RC, 'Expulsion of Ugandan Asians and International Law' (1972) *Indian Journal of International Law* 12.

Charlesworth, H, Chinkin, C and Wright, S, 'Feminist Approaches to International Law' (1991) 85 *American Journal of International Law* 613.

Cheng, B, 'Custom: The Future of General State Practice in a Divided World' in R St John Macdonald and DM Johnston (eds), *The Structure and Process of International Law: Essays in Legal Philosophy Doctrine and Theory* (Dordrecht, Martinus Nijhoff, 1986) 513–54.

—— *General Principles of Law as Applied by International Courts and Tribunals* (Cambridge, Grotius Publications, 1987).

Chesterton, S, 'Violence in the Name of Human Rights' in C Gearty and C Douzinas (eds), *Cambridge Companion to Human Rights* (Cambridge, Cambridge University Press, 2012) 134–49.

Chimni, BS, 'Legitimating the Rule of Law' in J Crawford and M Koskenniemi (eds), *Cambridge Companion to International Law* (Cambridge, Cambridge University Press, 2012) 290-308.

Chinkin, C, 'The Gender of Jus Cogens' (1993) 63 *Human Rights Quarterly* 63.

Cholewinski, R, Perruchoud, R and MacDonald, E (eds), *International Migration Law: Developing Paradigms and Key Challenges* (The Hague, Asser Press, 2007).

Chung, S, Lee, C, Lee, HT and Park, JH, 'The Treatment of Stateless Persons and the Reduction of Statelessness: Policy Suggestions for the Republic of Korea' (2010) 13 *Korea Review of International Studies* 7.

Cicero, MT, *On the Commonwealth and on the Laws*, JEG Zetzel (trans) (Cambridge, Cambridge University Press, 1999).

—— *On Duties*, MT Griffin and ET Atkins (trans) (Cambridge, Cambridge University Press, 1991).

Clapham, A, 'National Action Challenged: Sovereignty, Immunity and Universal Jurisdiction before the International Court of Justice' in M Lattimer and P Sands (eds), *Justice for Crimes against Humanity* (Oxford, Hart Publishing, 2003) 303–32.

Clark, I, *Legitimacy in International Society* (Oxford, Oxford University Press, 2005).

Clark, RS, 'Treaty and Custom' in L Boisson de Chazournes and P Sands (eds), *International Law, The International Court of Justice and Nuclear Weapons* (Cambridge, Cambridge University Press, 1999).

Cleveland, S, 'Embedded International Law and the Constitution Abroad' (2010) 110 *Columbia Law Review* 225.

Cohen, J (ed), *For Love of Country: Debating the Limits of Patriotism* (Boston, Beacon Press, 1996).

Cohen, R, 'Diasporas and the Nation-State: From Victims to Challengers' (1996) 72(3) *International Affairs* 507.

—— 'Strengthening International Protection for Internally Displaced Persons' in L Henkin and JK Hargrove (eds), *Human Rights: An Agenda for the Next Century* (Washington, DC, American Society of International Law, 1994) 17–48.

Colby, E, 'How to Fight Savage Tribes' (1927) 21 *American Journal of International Law* 279.

Coles, GJL, 'The Human Rights of Individuals Who are Not Nationals of the Country in which They Live' (1985) *Yearbook of the International Institute of Humanitarian Law* 126.

Conklin, A and Meir, BM, 'A "Vector of Rights" Approach for Public Health: Towards an Intersectional Human Rights Framework for Considering the Prevention and Treatment of Harms to Girl Child Soldiers' (2008) 13 *Australian Journal of Human Rights* 65.

Conklin, WE, 'The Exclusionary Character of the Early Modern International Community' (2012) 81 *Nordic Journal of International Law* 133.

—— 'The Ghosts of Cemetery Road: Two Forgotten Indigenous Women and the Crisis of Analytical Jurisprudence' (2011) *Australian Feminist Law Journal* 3.

—— 'Hegel and the Crisis of His Times' in J Lavery, L Groarke and W Sweet (eds), *Idea under Fire* (Madison, Fairleigh Dickinson University Press, 2013).

—— *Hegel's Laws: The Legitimacy of the Modern Legal Order* (Stanford, Stanford University Press, 2008).

—— *The Invisible Origins of Legal Positivism: A Re-Reading of a Tradition* (Dordrecht, Kluwer, 2001).

—— 'Kelsen on Norms and Language' (2006) 19 *Ratio Juris* 101.

—— 'Lon Fuller's Phenomenology of Language' (2006) 19 *International Journal for the Semiotics of Law* 93.

—— 'The Myth of Primordialism in Cicero's Theory of *Jus Gentium*' (2010) 23 *Leiden Journal of International Law* 479.

—— 'The Peremptory Norms of the International Community' (2012) 23 *European Journal of International Law* 837.

—— 'The Peremptory Norms of the International Community: A Rejoinder to Alexander Orakhelashvili' (2012) 23 *European Journal of International Law* 869.

—— 'A Phenomenological Theory of the Human Rights of the Alien' (2006) 13 *Ethical Perspectives* 245.

—— *The Phenomenology of Modern Legal Discourse* (Aldershot, Dartmouth, 1998).

Conklin, WE, 'The Role of Third World Courts during Alleged Emergencies' in ML Marasinghe and WE Conklin (eds), *Essays on Third World Perspectives in Jurisprudence* (Singapore, Malayan Law Journal, 1984).

——*Le savoir oublié de l'expérience des lois*, B Kingstone (trans) (Quebec, Laval University Press, 2011).

——'Statelessness and Bernhard Waldenfels' Phenomenology of the Alien' (2007) 38 *Journal of British Society for Phenomenology* 280.

——'The Transformation of Meaning: Legal Discourse and Canadian Internment Camps' (1996) 9 *International Journal for the Semiotics of Law* 227.

Connelly, W, 'The Complexity of Sovereignty' in J Edkins, N Persram and V Pin-Fat (eds), *Sovereignty and Subjectivity* (Boulder, Lynne Rienner, 1999) 23–39; also in J Edkins, V Pin-Fat and M Shapiro (eds), *Sovereign Lives: Power in Global Politics* (New York, Routledge, 2004) 23–40.

Copp, D, 'Democracy and Communal Self-Determination' in R McKim and J McMahan (eds), *The Morality of Nationalism* (Oxford, Oxford University Press, 1997) 277–300.

Corrigan, EC, 'The Legal Debate in Canada on the Protection of Stateless Individuals under the 1951 Geneva Convention' (2003) 23 *Immigtation Law Report* 196.

Cotler, I, 'International Decisions: *R v Finta*' (1996) 90 *American Journal of International Law* 460.

Courtois, S et al, *The Black Book of Communism: Crimes, Terror, Repression*, J Murphy and M Kramer (trans) (Cambridge, MA, Harvard University Press, 1999).

Couture, J, Nielsen, K and Seymour, M, *Rethinking Nationalism* (Calgary, University of Calgary Press, 1998).

Cove, RL, 'State Responsibility for Constructive Wrongful Expulsion of Foreign Nationals' (1988) 11 *Fordham International Law Journal* 802.

Crampton, JW and Elden, S, 'Introduction: Space, Knowledge and Power – Foucault and Geography' in JW Crampton, *Knowledge and Power: Foucault and Geography* (Surrey, Ashgate, 2007) 1–16.

Cranor, C, 'Toward a Theory of Respect for Persons' (1975) 12 *American Philosophical Quarterly* 309.

Craven, MCR, *International Covenant on Economic, Social and Cultural Rights: A Perspective of its Development* (Oxford, Clarendon Press, 1995).

Crawford, E and Rayfuse, R, 'Climate Change and Statehood' in R Rayfuse and SV Scott (eds), *International Law in the Era of Climate Change* (Cheltenham, Edward Elgar, 2012) 243–53.

Crawford, J, *The Creation of States in International Law*, 2nd edn (Oxford, Oxford University Press, 2006).

——'The Criteria for Statehood in International Law' (1976–77) 48 *British Yearbook of International Law* 93.

——'Introduction' in J Crawford (ed), *The International Law Commission's Articles on State Responsibility: Introduction, Text and Commentaries* (Cambridge, Cambridge University Press, 2002) 1–60.

——'The Original Status of Aboriginal Peoples in North America', Public Inquiry into the Administration of Justice and Aboriginal People (Manitoba, 1971).

——'The Right of Self-Determination in International Law: Its Development and Future' in P Alston and J Crawford (eds), *Peoples' Rights* (Oxford, Oxford University Press, 2001) 7–67.

——'Sovereignty as a Legal Value' in J Crawford and M Koskenniemi (eds), *Cambridge Companion to International Law* (Cambridge, Cambridge University Press, 2012) 117–33.

Crawford, J, (ed), *Brownlie's Principles of Public International Law*, 8th edn (Oxford, Oxford University Press, 2012).

——*International Law Commission's Articles on State Responsibility: Introduction, Text and Commentaries* (Cambridge, Cambridge University Press, 2002).

Crawford, J and Koskenniemi, M, (eds), *Cambridge Companion to International Law* (Cambridge, Cambridge University Press, 2012).

Crawford, J and Marks, S, 'The Global Democracy Deficit: An Essay in International Law and its Limits' in D Archibugi, D Held and M Kohler (eds), *Re-imagining Political Community: Studies in Cosmopolitan Democracy* (Stanford, Stanford University Press, 1998) 72–90.

Crawford, J with Pellet, A and Olleson, S (eds), *Law of International Responsibility* (Oxford, Oxford University Press, 2010).

Dakin, B, 'Islamic Community in *Bosnia and Herzegovina v Republika Srpska*: Human Rights in a Multi-Ethnic Bosnia' (2002) 15 *Harvard Human Rights Journal* 245.

Daly, M and Wilson, M, *Crime and Conflict: Homicide in Evolutionary Psychological Perspective* (Chicago, University of Chicago Press, 1997).

D'Amato, A, *The Concept of Custom in International Law* (Ithaca, Cornell University Press, 1971).

——'Is International Law Really "Law"?' (1985) 79 *Northwestern University Law Review* 1293.

Danilenko, GM, 'International Jus Cogens: Issues of Law-Making' (1991) 2 *European Journal of International Law* 42.

Darwell, S, 'Two Kinds of Respect' (1977) 86 *Ethics* 36.

Dauvergne, C, *Making People Illegal: What Globalization Means for Migration and Law* (Cambridge, Cambridge University Press, 2008).

——'Sovereignty, Migration and the Rule of Law in Global Times' (2004) 67 *Modern Law Review* 588.

David, E, 'Primary and Secondary Rules' in J Crawford, A Pellet and S Olleson (eds), *Law of International Responsibility* (Oxford, Oxford University Press, 2010) 27–33.

Davide, HG, 'Hostes Humani Generis: Piracy, Territory and the Concept of Universal Jurisdiction' in R St John Macdonald and DM Johnston (eds), *Towards World Constitutionalism: Issues in the Legal Ordering of the World Community* (Leiden, Martinus Nijhoff, 2005) 715–36.

Dawidowicz, L (ed), *The Holocaust Reader* (New York, Behrman, 1976).

De Berry, JP and Petrini, B, *Forced Displacement in Europe and Central Asia: Social Development Europe and Central Asia* (Washington, DC, World Bank, 2011).

Dekker, IF and Werner, WG, *Governance and International Legal Theory* (Leiden, Martinus Nijoff, 2004).

Dench, E, *Romulus' Astlum: Roman Identities from the Age of Alexander to the Age of Hadrian* (Oxford, Oxford University Press, 2005).

Derrida, J, 'Before the Law' in D Attridge (ed), *Acts of Literature* (London, Routledge, 1992) 181–220.

——'Force of Law: The Mystical Foundation of Law' in G Anidjar (ed), *Acts of Religion* (New York, Routledge, 2002) 230–98.

Derrida, J, *Of Hospitality: Anne Dufourmantelle Invites Jacques Derrida to Respond*, R Bowlby (trans) (Stanford, Stanford University Press, 2000).

——*Monolingualism of the Other; or, The Prosthesis of Origin*, P Mensah (trans) (Stanford, Stanford University Press, 1996).

Devine H, *The People Who Own Themselves: Aboriginal Ethnogensis in a Canadian Family, 1660–1900* (Calgary, University of Calgary Press, 2004).

Diez, T, Mathias, A and Stetter, S, *The European Union and Border Conflicts: The Power of Integration and Association* (Cambridge, Cambridge University Press, 2008).

Dillon, M, 'The Sovereign and the Stranger' in J Edkins, V Pin-Fat and MJ Schapiro (eds), *Sovereign Lives: Power in Global Politics* (Boulder, Lynne Rienner, 1999) 117–40.

Dobson, J (Queen's Advocate to the Foreign Secretary), 'Report on Admission to Louisiana, 4 August 1843' in Lord McNair (annotated), *International Law Opinions*, vol 2 (New York, Cambridge University Press, 1956) 105.

Doebbler, CF, 'A Human Rights Approach to Statelessness in the Middle East' (2002) 15 *Leiden Journal of International Law* 527.

Dolgopol, U, 'Women's Voices, Women's Pain' (1995) 17 *Human Rights Quarterly* 127.

D'Oliveira, HUJ, 'Union Citizenship: Pie in the Sky?' in A Rosas and E Antola (eds), *A Citizens' Europe: In Search of a New Order* (London, Sage Publications, 1995) 58–84.

Dolzer, R, 'Diplomatic Protection and Foreign Nationals' in R Bernhardt (ed), *Encyclopaedia of Public International Law*, vol 2 (Amsterdam, Elsevier, 1992–2000).

Doman, NR, 'Aftermath of Nuremberg: The Trial of Klaus Barbie' (1989) 60 *University of Colorado Law Review* 449.

Donnelly, J, 'Human Rights and Human Dignity: An Analytic Critique of Non-Western Conceptions of Human Rights' (1983) 76 *American Political Science Review* 303.

Donner, R, 'The Regulation of Nationality in International Law' (Societas Scientiarum Fennica, Finnish Society of Sciences and Letters, Commentationes Scientiarum Socialium, 1994 [1983]).

Douzinas, C, *The End of Human Rights* (Oxford, Hart Publishing, 2000).

——*Human Rights and Empire: The Political Philosophy of Cosmopolitanism* (Abington, Routledge-Cavendish, 2007).

——'The Poverty of (Rights) Jurisprudence' in C Gearty and C Douzinas (eds), *Cambridge Companion to Human Rights* (Cambridge, Cambridge University Press, 2012) 56–78.

Dubois, D, 'The Authority of Peremptory Norms in International Law: State Consent or Natural Law' (2009) 78 *Nordic Journal of International Law* 133.

Dubrovsky, G, *Six from Leipzig* (London, Frank Cass/Valentine Mitchell, 2002).

Duff, A, 'Authority and Responsibility in International Criminal Law' in S Besson and J Tsioulas (eds), *Philosophy of International Law* (Oxford, Oxford University Press, 2010) 589–604.

Dunoff, J, Ratner, SR and Wippman, D (eds), *International Law: Norms, Actors, Process*, 3rd edn (New York, Aspen, 2010).

Dupuy, P-M, 'Between the Individual and the State: International Law at a Crossroads' in L Boisson de Chazournes and P Sands (eds), *International Law,*

The International Court of Justice and Nuclear Weapons (Cambridge, Cambridge University Press, 1993) 449–61.

——(ed), *The Future of International Law in a Multi-Cultural World* (Netherlands, Samson-Sijhoff, 1993).

Dworkin, R, 'Equality, Luck and Hierarchy' (2003) 31(2) *Philosophy and Public Affairs* 190.

——'A New Philosophy for Law' (2013) 41(1) *Philosophy and Public Affairs* 2.

——'Objectivity: You'd Better Believe It' (1996) 25(2) *Philosophy and Public Affairs* 87.

Dyson-Hudson, N, 'The Study of Nomads' in W Irons and N Dyson-Hudson (eds), *Perspectives on Nomadism* (Leiden, Brill, 1972) 2–29.

Dyson-Hudson, R, 'Pastoralism: Self Image and Behavioral Reality' in W Irons and N Dyson-Hudson (eds), *Perspectives on Nomadism* (Leiden, Brill, 1972) 30–47.

Edkins, J and Pin-Fat, V, 'Introduction: Life, Power, Resistance' in J Edkins, V Pin-Fat and M Shapiro (eds), *Sovereign Lives: Power in Global Politics: Power in Global Politics* (New York, Routledge, 2004) 1–22.

Edwards, A, 'Displacement, Statelessness, and Questions of Gender Equality and the Convention on the Elimination of All Forms of Discrimination against Women', Background Paper, joint UN High Commissioner for Refugees and UN Committee on the Elimination of Discrimination against Women seminar (New York, 16–17 July 2009).

——'The "Feminizing" of Torture under International Human Rights Law' (2006) 19 *Leiden Journal of International Law* 349.

Edwards, A and Ferstman, C, 'Humanising Non-Citizens: The Convergence of Human Rights and Human Security' in A Edwards and C Ferstman (eds), *Human Security and Non-Citizens* (Cambridge, Cambridge University Press, 2010) 3–46.

Edwards, J, '"The Unity of All Places on the Face of the Earth": Original Community, Acquisition, and Universal Will in Kant's Doctrine of Right' in S Elden and E Mendieta (eds), *Reading Kant's Geography* (Albany, State University of New York Press, 2011) 233–66.

Elden, S, *Mapping the Present: Heidegger, Foucault and the Project of a Spatial History* (London, Continuum, 2001).

Evans, A, 'Union Citizenship and the Equality Principle' in A Rosas and E Antola (eds), *A Citizens' Europe: In Search of a New Order* (London, Sage, 1995) 85–112.

Falk, R, 'The United Nations and Cosmopolitan Democracy: Bad Dream, Utopian Fantasy, Political Project' in D Archibugi, D Held and M Kohler (eds), *Re-imagining Political Community: Studies in Cosmopolitan Democracy* (Stanford, Stanford University Press, 1998) 209–31.

Fawcett, J, 'The *Eichmann* Case' (1962) 38 *British Yearbook of International Law* 181.

Feller, E, Türk, V and Nicholson, F (eds), *Refugee Protection in International Law: UNHCR's Global Consultations on International Protection* (Cambridge, Cambridge University Press, 2003).

Figgis, JN, *Political Thought from Gerson to Grotius: 1414–1625* (New York, Harper, 1960).

Finley, MI, 'Empire in the Greco-Roman World' (1978) 25 *Greece and Rome* 1.

Fiss, OM, 'The Autonomy of Law' (2001) 26 *Yale Journal of International Law* 517.

Fitzmaurice, G, 'The General Principles of International Law Considered from the Standpoint of the Rule of Law' (1957) 92 *Recueil des Cours* 5.

Fitzpatrick, J, 'Flight From Asylum: Trends Toward Temporary "Refuge" and Local Responses to Forced Migrations' (1994–95) 35 *Virginia Journal of International Law* 13.

Fitzpatrick, P, 'Bare Sovereignty: Homo Sacer and the Insistence of Law' in A Norris (ed), *Politics, Metaphysics and Death: Essays on Giorgio Agamben's Homo Sacer* (Durham, NC, Duke University Press, 2005) 49–73.

——'Gods Would Be Needed...: American Empire and the Rule of (International) Law' (2003) 16 *Leiden Journal of International Law* 429.

——'Justice as Access' (2005) 23 *Windsor Yearbook of Access to Justice* 1.

——'Latin Roots: Imperialism and the Making of Modern Law' in P Fitzpatrick (ed), *Law as Resistance: Modernism, Imperialism, Legalism* (Burlington, VT, Ashgate, 2008) 275–91.

——'No Higher Duty: *Mabo* and the Failure of Legal Foundation' (2002) 13 *Law and Critique* 233.

——'"What Are the Gods to Us Now?" Secular Theology and the Modernity of Law' (2007) 8 *Theoretical Inquiries in Law* 161.

Fletcher, G, 'The Case for Linguistic Self-Defense' in R McKim and J McMahan (eds), *The Morality of Nationalism* (Oxford, Oxford University Press, 1997) 324–39.

Flournoy, RW and Hudson, MO, *A Collection of Nationality Laws of Various Countries as Contained in Constitutions, Statutes and Treaties* (New York, Oxford University Press, 1929).

Fogelson, S, 'Nuremberg Legacy: An Unfulfilled Promise' (1990) 63 *Southern California Law Review* 833.

Forcese, C, 'The Capacity to Protect: Diplomatic Protection of Dual Nationals in the "War on Terror"' (2006) 17 *European Journal of International Law* 369.

——'A Distinction with a Legal Difference: The Consequences of Non-ctizenship in the "War on Terror"' in A Edwards and C Ferstman (eds), *Human Security and Non-citizens* (Cambridge, Cambridge University Press, 2010) 421–58.

Fortin, A, 'The Meaning of "Protection" in the Refugee Definition' (2001) 12 *International Journal of Refugee Law* 548.

Fox-Decent, E and Criddle, EJ, 'The Fiduciary Constitution of Human Rights' (2009) 15 *Legal Theory* 301.

Fox, GH, 'Self-Determination in the Post-Cold War Era: A New Internal Focus?' (1995) 16 *Michigan Journal of International Law* 733.

Foucault, M, 'The Discourse on Language' in *The Archaeology of Knowledge*, AM Sheridan Smith (trans) (New York, Pantheon, 1972) 215–37.

——'Governmentality' in G Burchell, C Gordon and P Miller (eds), *The Foucault Effect: Studies in Governmentality* (Chicago, University of Chicago Press, 1991) 87–104.

——*I, Pierre Revierre, Having Slaughtered My Mother, My Sister and My Brother* (Lincoln, NB, University of Nebraska Press, 1975).

——'Questions on Geography' C Gordon (trans) in JW Crampton and S Elden (eds), *Space, Knowledge and Power: Foucault and Geography* (Surrey, Ashgate, 2007) 173–82.

——'What is an Author?' in P Rabinow (ed), *The Foucault Reader* (New York, Pantheon, 1984) 101–20.

Fraser, D, 'To Belong or Not to Belong: The Roma, State Violence and the New Europe in the House of Lords' (2001) 21 *Oxford Journal of Legal Studies* 569.

Freeman, M, 'The Philosophical Foundations of Human Rights' (1994) 16 *Human Rights Quarterly* 491.

Franck, TM, 'Legitimacy in the International System' (1988) 82 *American Journal of International Law* 705.

Friedlander, H, 'German Law and German Crimes in the Nazi Era' in FC DeCoste and B Schwartz (eds), *The Holocaust Ghost: Writings on Art, Politics, Law and Education* (Edmonton, University of Alberta Press, 2000) 283–89.

Frowein, J, 'Obligations Erga Omnes' in R Bernhardt (ed), *Encyclopaedia of Public International Law*, vol 2 (Amsterdam, Elsevier, 1997).

Fullerton, M, 'A Comparative Look at Refugee Status Based on Persecution Due to Membership in a Particular Social Group' (1993) 26 *Cornell International Law Journal* 505.

——'Hungary, Refugees, and the Law of Return' (1996) 8 *International Journal of Refugee Law* 499.

Gamboa, MJ, *A Dictionary of International Law and Diplomacy* (New York, Oceana, 1973).

Gans, C, 'National Self-Determination: A Sub- and Inter-Statist Conception' (2000) 13 *Canadian Journal of Law and Jurisprudence* 185.

Geissler, N, 'The International Protection of Internally Displaced Persons' (1999) 11 *International Journal of Refugee Law* 451.

Gelazis, N, 'An Evaluation of International Instruments that Address the Condition of Statelessness: A Case Study of Estonia and Latvia' in R Cholewinski, R Perruchoud and E MacDonald (eds), *International Migration Law: Developing Paradigms and Key Challenges* (The Hague, Asser Press, 2007) 291–309.

Gemünden, G, 'Nostalgia for the Nation: Intellectuals and National Identity in Unified Germany' in M Bal, J Crewe and L Spitzer (eds), *Acts of Memory: Cultural Recall in the Present* (Hanover, University Press of New England, 1999) 120–33.

Ghandi, PR, 'The Human Rights Committee and the Rights of Individual Communication' (1986) 57 *British Yearbook of International Law* 201.

Gierke, O, *Political Theories of the Middle Ages* (Boston, Beacon Hill, 1958).

Gill, TD, '*Elettronica Sicula SpA (ELSI) (United States v. Italy)* (1989) ICJ Rep 15, 28 ILM 1109 (1989)' (1990) 84 *American Journal of International Law* 249.

Glover, J, 'Nations, Identity, and Conflict' in R McKim and J McMahan (eds), *The Morality of Nationalism* (Oxford, Oxford University Press, 1997) 11–30.

Goble, GW, 'A Redefinition of Basic Legal Terms' (1935) 35 *Columbia Law Review* 535.

Goemans, H, 'Bounded Communities: Territoriality, Territorial Attachment, and Conflict' in M Kahler and BF Walker (eds), *Territoriality and Conflict in an Era of Globalization* (Cambridge, Cambridge University Press, 2006) 25–61.

Gofbarg, G and Gal, M, 'Hierarchies of Suffering in the Promised Land' in J Edkins, V Pin-Fat and MJ Shapiro (eds), *Sovereign Lives: Power in Global Politics* (New York, Routledge, 2004) 153–87.

Goldston, JA, 'Epilogue' in BK Blitz and M Lynch (eds), *Statelessness and Citizenship: A Comparative Study on the Benefits of Nationality* (Cambridge, Cambridge University Press, 2011) 209–15.

——'Legal Approaches to Combating Statelessness', discussion paper for UNHCR Executive Committee Panel Discussion on the 50th Anniversary of the 1954 Convention Relating to the Status of Stateless Persons (6 October 2004).

Gong, GW, *The Standard of 'Civilization' in International Society* (Oxford, Clarendon Press, 1984).

Goodman, R, 'Human Rights Treaties, Invalid Reservations, and State Consent' (2002) 96 *American Journal of International Law* 531.

Goodman, R and Jinks, D, 'Toward an Institutional Theory of Sovereignty' (2003) 55 *Stanford Law Review* 101.

Goodwin-Gill, GS, *International Law and the Movement of Persons between States* (Oxford, Clarendon, 1978).

——*The Refugee in International Law*, 2nd edn (Oxford, Clarendon Press, 1996).

Goodwin-Gill, GS and Newland, K, 'Forced Migration and International Law' in TA Aleinikoff and V Chetail (eds), *Migration and International Legal Norms* (The Hague, TMC Asser Press, 2003) 123–36.

Goris, I, Harrington, J and Köhn, S, 'Statelessness: What It Is and Why It Matters' (2009) 32 *Forced Migration* 4.

Gorlick, B, '(Mis)perception of Refugees, State Sovereignty, and the Continuing Challenge of International Protection' in A Bayefsky (ed), *Human Rights and Refugees, Internally Displaced Persons and Migrant Workers: Essays in Memory of Joan Fitzpatrick and Arthur Helton* (Leiden, Martinus Nijhoff, 2006) 65–89.

Goulbourne, S, 'Introduction' in S Goulbourne (ed), *Law and Migration*, vol 6 (Cheltanham, Elgar Reference Collection, 1998).

Graupner, R, 'British Nationality and State Succession' (1945) 6 *Law Quarterly Review* 161.

——'Nationality and State Succession – General Principles of the Effect of Territorial Changes on Individuals in International Law' (1946) 32 *Transactions of the Grotius Society* 87.

Grebe, S, 'Augustus' Divine Authority and Vergil's Aeneid' (2004) 50 *Vergilius* 35.

Green, LC and Dickason, OP, *The Law of Nations and the New World* (Edmonton, University of Alberta Press, 1989).

Greenfeld, L, 'The Modern Religion?' (1996) 8 *Utilitas* 169.

Gross, O and Ní Aoláin, F, *Law in Times of Crisis: Emergency Powers in Theory and Practice* (Cambridge, Cambridge University Press, 2006).

Grotius, H, *De Jure Belli ac pacis Libriri Tres*, F Kelsey (trans) (Oxford, Clarendon Press, 1925).

——*De Jure Praedae Commentarius*, GL Williams (trans), Classics of International Law Series (New York, Carnegie, 1950).

——*The Rights of War and Peace, Including the Law of Nature and of Nations*, AC Campbell (trans) (Washington, DC, M Walter Dunn, 1901).

Hackworth, GH, *Digest of International Law* (Washington, DC, US Government Print Office, 1940–44).

Hailbronner, K, 'Third-Country Nationals and EC Law' in A Rosas and E Antola (eds), *A Citizens' Europe: In Search of a New Order* (London, Sage, 1995) 182–206.

Halbwachs, M, *The Collective Memory*, F Ditter and VY Ditter (trans) (New York, Harper Colophon Books, 1980).

Hall, JA, *The State of the Nation: Ernest Gellner and the Theory of Nationalism* (Cambridge, Cambridge University Press, 1998).

Hall, S, 'Loss of Union Citizenship in Breach of Fundamental Rights' (1996) 21 *European Law Review* 129; reprinted in S Goulbourne (ed), *Law and Migration* (Cheltenham, Elgar Reference Collection, 1998) 54–68.

Hammer, S, 'The Neo-Kantian Dimension of Kelsen's Pure Theory of Law' (1990) 12 *Oxford Journal of Legal Studies* 311.
——'A Neo-Kantian Theory of Legal Knowledge in Kelsen's Pure Theory of Law' in S Paulson and BP Litschewski (eds), *Normativity and Norms* (Oxford, Clarendon Press, 1998) 177–94.
Hannikainen, L, *Peremptory Norms (Jus Cogens) in International Law: Historical Development, Criteria, Present Status* (Helsinki, Lakimesliiton Kustannus, 1988).
Hannum, H, *The Strasbourg Declaration on the Right to Leave and Return* (1987) 81 *American Journal of International Law* 432.
Harrington, J, 'Punting Territories, Assassins and Other Undesirables: Canada, the Human Rights Committee and Requests for Interim Measures of Protection' (2003) 48 *McGill Law Journal* 55.
Harris, DJ, *Cases and Materials on International Law*, 3rd edn (London, Sweet & Maxwell, 1983).
Harrison, C, 'Uganda: The Expulsion of the Asians' in WA Veenhoven (ed), *Case Studies on Human Rights and Fundamental Freedoms: A World Survey*, vol 4 (The Hague, Nijhoff, 1976) 210–18.
Hart, HLA, 'Commands and Authoritative Legal Reasons' in J Raz (ed), *Authority* (New York, New York University Press, 1990) 739–71.
——*The Concept of Law*, 3rd edn (Oxford, Clarendon Press, 2012).
——'Positivism and the Separation of Law from Morals' (1958) 71 *Harvard Law Review* 593.
Harvey, D, 'Cosmopolitanism in the *Anthropology* and *Geography*' in S Elden and E Mendieta (eds), *Reading Kant's Geography* (New York, State University of New York Press, 2001) 267–84.
——'The Kantian Roots of Foucault's Dilemmas' in JW Crampton and S Elden (eds), *Space, Knowledge and Power: Foucault and Geography* (Surrey, Ashgate, 2007) 41–47.
Hassner, P, 'Refugees: A Special Case for Cosmopolitan Citizenship?' in D Archibugi, D Held and M Kohler (eds), *Re-imagining Political Community: Studies in Cosmopolitan Democracy* (Stanford, Stanford University Press, 1998) 273–86.
Hathaway, J, 'The Evolution of Refugee Status in International law, 1920–1950' (1984) 33 *International and Comparative Law Journal* 348.
——'International Refugee Rights Regime' (1997) 8(2) *Collected Courses of the Academy of European Law* 91.
——*The Law of Refugee Status* (Toronto, Butterworths, 1991).
——*The Rights of Refugees under International Law* (Cambridge, Cambridge University Press, 2005).
Hathaway, JC and Foster, M, 'Internal Protection/Relocation/Flight Alternative as an Aspect of Refugee States Determination' in E Feller, V Türk and F Nicholson (eds), *Refugee Protection in International Law: UNCHR's Global Consultations on International Protection* (Cambridge, Cambridge University Press, 2003) 357–417.
Haughey, É, 'Gypsy Identity and Political Theory' in J Edkins, N Persram and V Pin-Fat (eds), *Sovereignty and Subjectivity* (Boulder, Lynne Rienner, 1999) 141–52.
Henckaerts, J-M, 'The Current Status and Content of the Prohibition of Mass Expulsion of Aliens' (1994) 15 *Human Rights Law Journal* 301.
——*Mass Expulsion on Modern International Law and Practice* (The Hague, Martinus Nijhoff, 1995).

Henckaerts, J-M, 'Study on Customary International Humanitarian Law: A Contribution to the Understanding and Respect for the Rule of Law in Armed Conflict' (2005) 87 *International Review of Red Cross* 175.

Henkin, L et al, 'The Constitution as Compact and as Conscience: Individual Rights Abroad and at Our Gates' (1985) 27 *William and Mary Review* 11.

——*International law: Cases and Materials* (St Paul, West, 1980).

Herz, JH, 'Rise and Demise of the Territorial State' (1957) 9 *World Politics* 473.

Higgins, R, *Problems and Process: International Law and How We Use It* (Oxford, Oxford University Press, 1994).

Hill, JD, 'Introduction' in JD Hill (ed), *History, Power and Identity: Ethnogenesis in the Americas, 1492–1992* (Iowa City, University of Iowa Press, 1996) 7–13.

Himmelfarb, G, 'The Illusions of Cosmopolitanism' in J Cohen (ed), *For Love of Country: Debating the Limits of Patriotism* (Boston, Beacon Press, 1996) 72–77.

Hinsley, FH, *Power and the Pursuit of Peace* (Cambridge, Cambridge University Press, 1967).

Hobbs, JJ, 'Speaking with People in Egypt's St Katherine National Park' (1996) 86 *Geographical Review* 1.

Hobbes, T, *Leviathan*, CB MacPherson (ed) (London, Penguin, 1968).

——*Leviathan, with Selected Variants from the Latin Edition of 1668*, E Curley (ed) (Indianapolis, Hackett, 1994).

Hoffman, PL, '*The Alvarez* Case and the Rule of Law' in A Bayefsky (ed), *Human Rights and Refugees, Internally Displaced Persons and Migrant Workers: Essays in Memory of Joan Fitzpatrick and Arthur Helton* (Leiden, Martinus Nijhoff, 2006) 321–47.

Hoffmann, R, 'Aliens' in R Bernhardt (ed), *Encyclopaedia of Public International Law*, vol 1 (Amsterdam, Elsvier Science Publishers, 1992) 102–7.

——'Denaturalisation and Forced Exile' in R Bernhardt (ed), *Encyclopaedia of Public International Law*, vol 1 (Amsterdam, Elsevier Science Publishers, 1992) 1001–7.

Hohfeld, WN, *Fundamental Conceptions as Applied to Judicial Reasoning*, WW Cook (ed), (New Haven, Yale University Press, 1923).

de Hoogh, AJJ, 'The Relationship Between Jus Cogens, Obligations Erga Omnes and International Crimes: Peremptory Norms in Perspective' (1991) 42 *Australian Journal of Public and International Law* 183.

Horwitz, M, 'Why is Anglo-American Jurisprudence Unhistorical?' (1997) 17 *Oxford Journal of Legal Studies* 551.

Horowitz, M and Rabbie, JM, 'Individuality and Membership in the Intergroup System' in H Tajfel (ed), *Social Identity and Intergroup Relations* (Cambridge, Cambridge University Press, 1982) 241–74.

Houle, F, 'Pitfalls for Administrative Tribunals in Relying on Formal Common Law Rules of Evidence' in R Creyke (ed), *Tribunals in the Common Law World* (Sydney, Federation Press, 2008) 102–21.

Hovannisian, RG, *The Armenian Genocide: History, Politics, Ethics* (New York, St Martin's Press, 1992).

——(ed), *The Armenian Genocide in Perspective* (Oxford, Transaction Books, 1986).

Howard, RE and Donnelly, J, 'Human Dignity, Human Rights, and Political Regimes' (1986) 80 *American Political Science Review* 802.

Hroch, M, 'Real and Constructed: The Nature of the Nation' in JA Hall (ed), *The State of the Nations* (Cambridge, Cambridge University Press, 1998).

Hudson, M (ed), *International Legislation: A Collection of Texts of Multipartite International Instruments of General Interest*, 9 vols (Washington, DC, Carnegie Endowment for International Peace, 1931–50).

Hughes-Jones, NC, 'Intergroup Aggression: Multi-Individual Organisms and the Survival Instinct' (2000) 25 *Interdisciplinary Science Reviews* 101.

Hume, D, *A Treatise of Human Nature*, PH Nidditch (ed), 2nd edn (Oxford, Oxford University Press, 1978).

Husserl, E, *Logical Investigations* (New York, Humanities Press, 1970).

Hutton, PH, *History as an Art of Memory* (Hanover, University Press of New England, 1993).

Huxley, M, 'Geographies of Governmentality' in JW Crampton and S Elden (eds), *Space, Knowledge and Power: Foucault and Geography* (Surrey, Ashgate, 2007) 185–204.

International Law Commission (ILC), 'Conclusions on the Reservations Dialogue Provisionally Adopted by the Working Group on Reservations to Treaties on 6, 12 and 14 July 2011, 63rd sess, UN Doc A/CN.4/L.779 (19 May 2011).

——'Conclusions of the Work of the Study Group on the Fragmentation of International Law: Difficulties Arising from the Diversification and Expansion of International Law' (2006), legal.un.org/ilc/texts/instruments/english/draft%20articles/1_9_2006.pdf, reprinted in *ILC Yearbook 2006*, vol II(2).

——'Draft Articles on Diplomatic Protection, with Commentaries', UN Doc A/61/10, reprinted in *ILC Yearbook 2006*, vol II(2).

——'Draft Articles on the Law of Treaties, with Commentaries' in *Report of the International Law Commission on the Work of its Eighteenth Session*, A/CN.4/SER. A/1966/Add.1, reprinted in *ILC Yearbook 1966*, vol II, 187–273.

——'Draft Articles on Nationality of Natural Persons in Relation to the Succession of States, with Commentaries' in *Report of the ILC on the Work of its Fifty-First Session*, UN Doc A/54/10, reprinted in *ILC Yearbook 1999*, vol II(2), 20–47.

——'Draft Articles on Responsibility of States for Internationally Wrongful Acts' in *Report of the ILC on the Work of Its Fifty-third Session*, UN Doc. A/56/10 (2001), reprinted in J Crawford (ed), *The International Law Commission's Articles on State Responsibility: Introduction, Text and Commentaries* (Cambridge, Cambridge University Press, 2002).

——'Expulsion of Aliens', 58th sess, UN Doc A/CN.4/ 565 (10 July 2006).

——'Fragmentation of International Law: Difficulties Arising from the Diversification and Expansion of International Law' ('Koskenniemi Report'), UN Doc A/CN.4/L.682 and Corr.1 (13 April 2006), daccess-dds-ny.un.org/doc/UNDOC/LTD/G06/610/77/PDF/G0661077.pdf?OpenElement.

——'Principles of International Law Recognised in the Charter of the Nurnberg Tribunal and in the Judgment of the Tribunal' in *Report of the ILC Covering its second session*, UN Doc A/1316, reprinted in *ILC Yearbook 1950*, vol II, 374.

International Law Association, 'Declaration of Principles of International Law on Mass Expulsion' (1986), reprinted in (1986) 20 *International Migration Review* 1048; and in A-M Henkaerts, *Mass Expulsion in Modern International Law and Practice* (The Hague, Martinus Nijtoff, 1995).

International Law Association, 'The London Declaration of International Law Principles on Internally Displaced Persons' (2000), reprinted in (2000) 12 *International Journal of Refugee Law* 672.

International Law Association (Committee on Feminism and International Law), 'Women's Equality and Nationality: Final Report' (2000).

Irons, W and Dyson-Hudson, N (eds), *Perspectives on Nomadism* (Leiden, Brill, 1972).

Jackson, IC, 'The 1951 Convention Relating to the Status of Refugees: A Universal Basis for Protection' (1991) 3 *International Journal of Refugee Law* 403.

Jackson-Preece, J, 'Ethnic Cleansing as an Instrument of Nation-State Creation: Changing State Practices and Evolving Legal Norms' (1998) 20 *Human Rights Quarterly* 820.

Jacobson, D, 'Multiculturalism, Gender, and Rights' in S Benhabib and J Resnik (eds), *Migrations and Mobilities: Citizenship, Borders, and Gender* (New York, New York University Press, 2009) 304–30.

Jayawickrama, N, *The Judicial Application of Human Rights Law: National Regional and International Jurisprudence* (Cambridge, Cambridge University Press, 2002).

Jenkins, D, Henricksen, A and Jacobson, A (eds), *The Long Decade: How 9/11 Has Changed the Law* (Oxford, Oxford University Press, 2012).

Jennings, R, *The Acquisition of Territory in International Law* (Manchester, Manchester University Press, 1963).

——'The Progress of International Law' (1958) 34 *British Yearbook of International Law* 334.

——'Statelessness through the Peace Treaties after the First World War' (1944) 21 *British Yearbook of International Law* 171.

Jessup, PC, *A Modern Law of Nations: An Introduction* (New York, Macmillan, 1968).

Jochnick, C and Normand, R, 'The Legitimation of Violence: A Critical History of the Laws of War' (1994) 35 *Harvard International Law Journal* 49.

Johansson, A, 'Third Party Involvement in Jerusalem's Future: An International Law Perspective' in E Watkins (ed), *The Middle East Environment: Selected Papers of the 1991 Conference of the British Society for Middle Eastern Studies* (Cambridge, St Malo Press, 1995) 118–25.

Johnson, DHN, 'Acquisitive Prescription in International Law' (1950) 27 *British Yearbook of International Law* 332.

——'Draft Code of Offences against the Peace and Security of Mankind' (1955) 4 *International and Comparative Law Quarterly* 445.

Johnson, DR and Post, D, 'Law and Borders: The Rise of Law in Cyberspace' 49 (1995–96) *Stanford Law Review* 1367.

Jolowicz, HF and Nicholas, B, *Historical Introduction to the Study of Roman Law*, 3rd edn (Cambridge, Cambridge University Press, 1972).

Jones, JM, *British Nationality Law*, revised edn (Oxford, Clarendon Press, 1956).

——*British Nationality Law and Practice* (Oxford, Clarendon Press, 1947).

——'The *Nottebohm* Case' (1956) 5 *International and Comparative Law Quarterly* 230.

Jones, S, *The Archaeology of Ethnicity: Constructing Identities in the Past and Present* (New York, Routledge, 2002).

de Jong, CD, 'The Legal Framework: The Convention Relating to the Status of Refugees and the Development of Law Half a Century Later' (1998) 10 *International Journal of Refugee Law* 688.

Joseph, S, Schultz, J and Castan, M, *The International Covenant on Civil and Political Rights: Cases, Materials and Commentary*, 2nd edn (Oxford, Oxford University Press, 2004).

Jung, K, 'The Concept of the Collective Unconscious' in WK Gordon (ed), *Literature in Critical Perspective* (New York, Appleton-Crofts, 1968) 504–8.

Kaeckenbeeck, G, *The International Experiment of Upper Silesia: A Study in the Working of the Upper Silesian Settlement, 1922–1937* (London, Oxford University Press, 1942).

Kahler, M and Walker, BF, *Territoriality and Conflict in an Era of Globalization* (Cambridge, Cambridge University Press, 2006).

Kaldor, M, 'Reconceptualizing Organized Violence' in D Archibugi, D Held and M Kohler (eds), *Re-imagining Political Community: Studies in Cosmopolitan Democracy* (Stanford, Stanford University Press, 1998) 91–110.

Kälin, W, 'Non-state Agents of Persecution and the Inability of the State to Protect' (2001) 15 *Georgetown Immigration Law Journal* 415.

Kälin, W et al (eds), *Incorporating the Guiding Principles on Internal Displacement into Domestic Law: Issues and Challenges*, Studies in Transnational Legal Policy, No 41 (Washington, DC, American Society of International Law/Brookings Bern, 2010).

Kant, I, 'On the Common Saying: "This May Be True in Theory, But It Does Not Apply in Practice"' in HS Reiss (ed), *Kant's Political Writings*, 2nd edn (Cambridge, Cambridge University Press, 1991).

——*Grounding of the Metaphysics of Morals*, JW Ellington (trans), 3rd edn (Indianapolis, Hackett, 1993).

——'Groundwork of the Metaphysics of Morals [1785]' in MJ Gregor (ed), *Practical Philosophy*, MJ Gregor (trans) (Cambridge, Cambridge University Press, 1999).

——*Metaphysical Elements of Justice*, J Ladd (trans), 2nd edn (Indianapolis, Hackett, 1999).

——'Perpetual Peace: A Philosophical Sketch Practice' in HS Reiss (ed), *Kant's Political Writings*, 2nd edn (Cambridge, Cambridge University Press, 1991).

Kassim, AF, 'Book Review and Note: *The Status of Palestinian Refugees in International Law* by Lex Talkenberg' (Oxford, Clarendon Press, 1998); (2000) 94 *American Journal of International Law* 215.

Keene, E, *Beyond the Anarchical Society: Grotius, Colonialism and Order in World Politics* (Cambridge, Cambridge University Press, 2002).

——*Global Civil Society* (Cambridge, Cambridge University Press, 2003).

Keller, AS, Lissitzyn, OJ and Mann, FJ, *The Creation of Rights of Sovereignty through Symbolic Acts, 1400–1800* (New York, Columbia Press, 1984).

Keller, P, 'Re-thinking Ethnic and Cultural Rights in Europe' (1998) 18 *Oxford Journal of Legal Studies* 29.

Kelly, JP, 'The Twilight of Customary International Law' (1999–2000) 40 *Virginia Journal of International Law* 449.

Kelsen, H, 'Recognition in International Law: Theoretical Observations' (1941) 35 *American Journal of International Law* 605.

——'Sovereignty and International Law' (1960) 48 *Georgetown Law Journal* 627.

Kennedy, D, 'A Case Study of Legal Architecture: The Hans Kelsen of the Oliver Wendell Holmes Lectures – Public International Law Pragmatist' (1995) 13 *Current Legal Theory* 33.

Kennedy, D, 'Lawfare and Warfare' in J Crawford and M Koskenniemi (eds), *Cambridge Companion to International Law* (Cambridge, Cambridge University Press, 2012) 158–84.

——'Reassessing International Humanitarianism: The Dark Sides' in A Orford (ed), *International Law and its Others* (Cambridge, Cambridge University Press, 2006) 131–55.

Kerber, LK, 'The Stateless as the Citizen's Other: A View from the United States' in S Benhabib and J Resnik (eds), *Migrations and Mobilities: Citizenship, Borders, and Gender* (New York, New York University Press, 2009) 76–123.

King-Irani, L, 'Exiled to a Liminal Legal Zone: Are We All Palestinians Now?' in R Falk, B Rajagopal and J Stevens (eds), *International Law and the Third World* (London, Routledge-Cavendish, 2008) 219–32.

Kirgis, FL, 'Custom as a Sliding Scale' (1987) 81 *American Journal of International Law* 146.

——'The Degrees of Self-Determination in the United Nations Era' (1994) 88 *American Journal of International Law* 304.

Klebes, H, 'The Council of Europe's Framework Convention for the Protection of National Minorities' (1995) 16 *Human Rights Law Journal* 92.

——'Draft Protocol on Minority Rights to the ECHR' (1993) 14 *Human Rights Law Journal* 140.

Klusmeyer, DB, 'Aliens, Immigrants, and Citizens: The Politics of Inclusion in the Federal Republic of Germany' (1933) 122 *Daedalus* 81.

Knop, K, 'Citizenship, Public and Private' (2008) 71 *Law and Contemporary Problems* 309.

Knox, JH, 'A Presumption against Extrajurisdictionality' (2010) 104 *American Journal of International Law* 351.

Kohler, M, 'From the National to the Cosmopolitan Public Sphere' in D Archibugi, D Held and M Köhler (eds), *Re-imagining Political Community: Studies in Cosmopolitan Democracy* (Stanford, Stanford University Press, 1998) 231–51.

Koselleck, R, *The Practice of Conceptual History: Timing History, Spacing Concepts*, TS Presner et al (trans) (Stanford, Stanford University Press, 2002).

Koskenniemi, M, 'Between Impunity and Show Trials' (2002) 6 *Max Planck Yearbook of UN Law* 1.

——'Empire and International Law: The Real Spanish Contribution' (2011) 61 *University of Toronto Law Journal* 1.

——*From Apology to Utopia: The Structure of International Legal Argument* (Cambridge, Cambridge University Press, 2005).

——*The Gentle Civilizer of Nations: The Rise and Fall of International Law, 1870–1960* (Cambridge, Cambridge University Press, 2001).

——'Lauterpacht: The Victorian Tradition in International Law' (1997) 8 *European Journal of International Law* 215.

——'National Self-Determination Today: Problems of Legal Theory and Practice' (1994) 43 *International and Comparative Law Quarterly* 241.

——'The Politics of International Law' (1990) 1 *European Journal of International Law* 4.

——'The Pull of the Mainstream' (1990) 88 *Michigan Law Review* 1946.

Kreß, C, 'Universal Jurisdiction over International Crimes and the Institut de droit International' (2006) 4 *Journal of International Criminal Justice* 1.

van Krieken, PJ, *Refugee Law in Context: The Exclusion Clause* (The Hague, Asser Press, 1999).

Kroes, R, *Them and Us: Questions of Citizenship in a Globalizing World* (Urbana, University of Illinois Press, 2000).

Kulka, OD and Jäckel, E (eds), *The Jews in the Secret Nazi Reports on Popular Opinion in Germany, 1933–1945* (New Haven, Yale University Press, 2010).

Kumm, M, 'The Legitimacy of International Law: A Constitutionalist Framework of Analysis' (2004) 15 *European Journal of International Law* 907.

Kuper, L, 'The Turkish Genocide of Armenians, 1915–1917' in RG Hovannisian (ed), *The Armenian Genocide in Perspective* (Oxford, Transaction Books, 1986).

Lake, DA and Rothschild, D, 'Containing Fear: The Origins and Management of Ethnic Conflict' (1996) 21 *International Security* 41.

Lalonde, S, *Determining Boundaries in a Conflicted World: The Role of Uti Possidetis* (Montreal, McGill-Queen's University Press, 2002).

Lâm, MC, *At the Edge of the State: Indigenous Peoples and Self-Determination* (New York, Transnational, 2000).

Lattimer, M and Sands, P (eds), *Justice for Crimes Against Humanity* (Oxford, Hart Publishing, 2003).

Lauterpacht, E and Bethlehem, D, 'The Scope and Content of the Principle of Non-refoulement: Opinion' in E Feller, V Türk and F Nicholson (eds), *Refugee Protection in International Law: The UNHCR's Global Consultations on International Protection* (Cambridge, Cambridge University Press, 2003) 87–177.

Lauterpacht, H, 'Allegiance, Diplomatic Protection and Criminal Jurisdiction over Aliens' (1947) 9 *Cambridge Law Journal* 330.

—— 'The Definition and Nature of International Law and its Place in Jurisprudence' in E Lauterpacht (ed), *International Law: The Collected Papers of Hersch Lauterpacht*, vol 1 (Cambridge, Cambridge University Press, 1970) 9–50.

—— 'In *re Friedrich Nottebohm*' in E Lauterpacht (ed), *International Law: The Collected Papers of Hersch Lauterpacht*, vol 4 (Cambridge, Cambridge University Press, 1978) 5–20.

—— *The Function of Law in the International Community* (Hamden, CT, Archon, 1966).

—— 'General Rules of the Law of Peace: The Sources of International Law' in E Lauterpacht (ed), *International Law: The Collected Papers of Hersch Lauterpacht*, vol 1 (Cambridge, Cambridge University Press, 1970) 232–60.

—— 'The Grotian Tradition in International Law' (1946) 23 *British Yearbook of International Law* 1; reprinted in E Lauterpacht (ed), *International Law: The Collected Papers of Hersch Lauterpach*, vol 2 (Cambridge, Cambridge University Press, 1975) 307–65.

—— *International Law and Human Rights* (New York, Garland, 1973).

—— 'International Law, the General Part: The Sources of International Law' in E Lauterpacht (ed), *International Law: The Collected Papers of Hersch Lauterpacht*, vol 1 (Cambridge, Cambridge University Press, 1970) 51–135.

—— 'The Law of Nations and the Punishment of War Crimes' (1944) 21 *British Yearbook of International Law* 58.

—— 'Nationality of Denaturalised Persons' (1948) *Jewish Yearbook of International Law* 164; reprinted in E Lauterpacht (ed), *International Law: The Collected Papers of Hersch Lauterpacht*, vol 3 (Cambridge, Cambridge University Press, 1977) 283–406.

Lauterpacht, H, 'Private Law Sources and Analogies of International Law' in E Lauterpacht (ed), *International Law: The Collected Papers of Hersch Lauterpacht*, vol 2 (Cambridge, Cambridge University Press, 1975) 173–212.

——'Westlake and Present Day International Law' (1925) 5 *Economica* 307; reprinted in E Lauterpacht (ed), *International Law: The Collected Papers of Hersch Lauterpacht*, vol 2 (Cambridge, Cambridge University Press, 1975) 385–403.

Lawland, K, 'The Right of Return of Palestinians in International Law' (1996) 8 *International Journal of Refugee Law* 532.

Lee, RW, 'Hugo Grotius, 1583–1645' (1946) 62 *Law Quarterly Review* 53.

Lee, TL, 'Chinese Nationality and the Republic of China (Taiwan)' (1995) 7 *International Journal of Refugee Law* 201.

——'Refugees from Bhutan' (1998) 10 *International Journal of Refugee Law* 118.

Lefebvre, H, *The Production of Space*, D Nicholson-Smith (trans) (Oxford, Blackwell, 1991).

——'Reflections on the Politics of Space' in N Brenner and S Elden (eds), *State, Space, World: Selected Essays of Lefebvre*, G Moore, N Brenner and S Elden (trans) (Minneapolis, University of Minnesota Press, 2009) 167–84.

——'Space and the State' in N Brenner and S Elden (eds), *State, Space, World: Selected Essays of Lefebvre*, G Moore, N Brenner and S Elden (trans) (Minneapolis, University of Minnesota Press, 2009) 223–53.

Lefkowita, D, 'The Sources of International Law: Some Philosophical Reflections' in S Besson and J Tsioulas (eds), *Philosophy of International Law* (Oxford, Oxford University Press, 2010) 187–203.

Lepard, BD, *Customary International Law: A New Theory with Practical Applications* (Cambridge, Cambridge University Press, 2010).

Levi-Strauss, L, *Totemism*, R Needham (trans) (London, Merlin Press, 1964).

Luban, D, 'Fairness to Rightness: Jurisdiction, Legality, and the Legitimacy of International Criminal Law' in S Besson and J Tsioulas (eds), *Philosophy of International Law* (Oxford, Oxford University Press, 2010) 569–88.

Lewa, C, 'North Arakan: An Open Prison for the Rohingya in Burma' 32 (April 2009) *Forced Migration* 11.

Lewis, B, *The Emergence of Modern Turkey*, 3rd edn (London, Oxford University Press, 2002).

Ley, D and Samuels, MS (eds), *Humanistic Geography: Prospects and Problems* (London, Croom Helm, 1978).

Liegeoris, J-P and Gheorghe, N, *Rome/Gypsies: A European Minority*, S ni Shinéar (trans) (London, Minority Rights Group, 1995).

Lillich, RB, 'The Current Status of the Law of State Responsibility for Injuries to Aliens' in RB Lillich (ed), *International Law of State Responsibility for Injuries to Aliens* (Charlottesville, University Press of Virginia, 1983) 1–60.

——*The Human Rights of Aliens in Contemporary International Law* (Washington, Pail Institute Publications, 1984).

——*International Human Rights: Problems of Law, Policy and Practice*, 2nd edn (Boston, Little Brown, 1991).

Lillich, RB and Hurstm, H, *International Human Rights: Problems of Law, Policy and Practice*, 3rd edn (Boston, Little Brown, 1995).

Lillich, RB and Newman, FC, *International Human Rights: Problems of Law and Policy* (Boston, Little Brown, 1979).

Lindblom, A-K, 'The Responsibility of Other Entities: Non-governmental Organizations' in J Crawford, A Pellet and S Olleson (eds), *The Law of International Responsibility* (Oxford, Oxford University Press) 343–54.

Lindahl, H, 'Breaking Promises to Keep Them: Immigration and the Boundaries of Distributive Justice' in H Lindahl (ed), *A Right to Inclusion and Exclusion? Normative Fault Lines of the EU's Area of Freedom, Security and Justice* (Oxford, Hart Publishing, 2009) 137–59.

——(ed), *A Right to Inclusion and Exclusion? Normative Fault Lines of the EU's Area of Freedom, Security and Justice* (Oxford, Hart Publishing, 2009).

Linderfalk, U, 'The Effect of Jus Cogens Norms: Whoever Opened Pandora's Box, Did You Ever Think about the Consequences?' (2008) 18 *European Journal of International Law* 853.

Linklater, A, 'Citizenship and Sovereignty in the Post-Westphalian European State' in D Archibugi, D Held and M Köhler (eds), *Re-imagining Political Community: Studies in Cosmopolitan Democracy* (Stanford, Stanford University Press, 1998) 113–37.

Lippman, M, 'Law, Lawyers and Legality in the Third Reich: The Perversion of Principle and Professionalism' (1997) 14 *Temple International and Comparative Law Journal* 199.

Locke, J, *Second Treatise of Government* in P Laslett (ed), *Two Treatises of Government* (Cambridge, Cambridge University Press, 1960]).

Loescher, G, 'Non-Refoulement Through Time: The Case for the Derogation Clause to the Refugee Convention in Mass Influx Emergencies' in A Bayefsky (ed), *Human Rights and Refugees, Internally Displaced Persons and Migrant Workers: Essays in Memory of Joan Fitzpatrick and Arthur Helton* (Leiden, Martinus Nijhoff, 2006) 211–31.

Lowe, V, 'Injuries to Corporations' in J Crawford, A Pellet and S Olleson (eds), *The Law of International Responsibility* (Oxford, Oxford University Press) 1005–21.

Luca, D, '"Questioning Temporary Protection" with Selected Bibliography on Temporary Refuge/Temporary Protection' (1994) 6 *International Journal of Refugee Law* 535.

MacDonald, RSJ, 'The International Community as a Legal Community' in RSJ Macdonald and DM Johnston (eds), *Towards World Constitutionalism: Issues in the Legal Ordering of the World Community* (Leiden, Martinus Nijhoff, 2005) 853–909.

——'The Margin of Appreciation' in RSJ Macdonald and D Johnson (eds), *The European System for the Protection of Human Rights* (Boston, Martinus Nijoff, 1993) 83–124.

MacIver, DN, 'Conclusion, Ethnic Identity and the Modern State' in CH Williams (ed), *National Separatism* (Vancouver, University of British Columbia Press, 1982) 299–307.

Macklin, A, 'Particularized Citizenship: Encultured Women and the Public Sphere' in S Benhabib and J Resnik (eds), *Migrations and Mobilities: Citizenship, Borders, and Gender* (New York, New York University Press, 2009) 276–303.

Macpherson, CB, 'Introduction' in J Locke (ed), *Second Treatise of Government* (Indianapolis, Hackett, 1980) vii–xxi.

——*The Political Theory of Possessive Individualism: Hobbes to Locke* (Oxford, Clarendon Press, 1962).

Mahalic, D and Mahalic, G, 'The Limitation Provisions of the International Convention on the Elimination of All Forms of Racial Discrimination' (1987) 9 *Human Rights Quarterly* 74.

Mahoney, P, 'Marvelous Richness or Diversity or Invidious Cultural Relativism?' (1998) 19 *Human Rights Kaw Journal* 1.

Malanczuk, P, *Akehurst's Modern Introduction to International Law*, 7th edn (New York, Routledge, 1997).

Malpas, J and Thiel, K, 'Kant's Geography of Reason' in S Elden and E Mendieta (eds), *Reading Kant's Geography* (Albany, State University of New York Press, 2011) 195–214.

Mamdani, M, 'Customary Law: The Theory of Decentralized Despotism' in SB Ortner, NB Dirks and G Eley (eds), *Citizen and Subject: Contemporary Africa and the Legacy of Late Colonialism* (Princeton, Princeton University Press, 1996) 109–37.

von Mangoldtm, H, 'Stateless Persons' in R Bernhardt (ed), *Encyclopaedia of Public International Law*, vol 4 (Amsterdam, Elsevier, 1992).

Manly, M and van Waas, L, 'The Value of the Human Security Framework in Addressing Statelessness' in A Edwards and C Ferstman (eds), *Human Security and Non-Citizens* (Cambridge, Cambridge University Press, 2010) 49–81.

Mann, CC, *1491: New Revelations of the Americas Before Columbus*, 2nd edn (New York, Vintage Books, 2011).

Mann, FA, 'The Effect of Changes of Sovereignty Upon Nationality' (1942) 5 *Modern Law Review* 218.

Manning, CAW, *The Nature of International Society* (London, Macmillan, 1975).

Mansbach, RW and Wilmer, F, 'War, Violence and the Westphalian State System as a Moral Community' in M Albert, D Jacobson, and Y Lapid (eds), *Identities, Borders, Orders: Rethinking International Relations* (Minneapolis, University of Minnesota Press, 2001) 51–71.

Margalit, A and Raz, J, 'National Self-Determination' (1990) 87 *Journal of Philosophy* 439.

Marks, S, 'Human Rights in Disastrous Times' in J Crawford and M Koskenniemi (eds), *Cambridge Companion to International Law* (Cambridge, Cambridge University Press, 2012) 309–26.

Marschil, A, 'Too Much Order? The Impact of Special Secondary Norms on the Unity and Efficacy of the International Legal System' (1998) 9 *European Journal of International Law* 212.

Martin, PM, 'Note: Temporary Protected Status and the Legacy of *Santos-Gomez*' (1991) 25 *George Washington Journal of International Law and Economics* 231.

Marx, K, 'On the Jewish Question' in RC Tucker (ed), *The Marx-Engels Reader*, 2nd edn (New York, WW Norton, 1978) 26–52.

Marx, R, '*Non-Refoulement*, Access to Procedures, and Responsibility for Determining Refugee Claims' (1995) 7 *International Journal of Refugee Law* 383.

Matscher, F, 'Methods of Interpretation of the Convention' in RSJ Macdonald and DM Johnson (eds), *The European System for the Protection of Human Rights* (Leiden, Martinus Nijhoff, 1993) 63–75.

McAdam, J, *Climate Change and Displacement Multilateral Perspectives* (Oxford, Hart Publishing, 2010).

——*Climate Change, Force Migration, and International Law* (Oxford, Oxford University Press, 2012).

——*Complementary Protection in International Refugee Law* (Oxford, Oxford University Press, 2007).

McDougal, M, 'The Hydrogen Bomb Tests and the International Law of the Sea' (1955) 49 *American Journal of International Law* 356.

McDougall, M, Lasswell, H and Chen, L-C, *Human Rights and World Public Order* (New Haven, Yale University Press, 1980).

——'Nationality and Human Rights: The Protection of the Individual in External Arenas' (1974) 83 *Yale Law Journal* 900.

——'The Protection of Aliens from Discrimination and World Public Order: Responsibility of States Conjoined with Human Rights' (1976) 70 *American Journal of International Law* 432.

McGoldrick, D, *The Human Rights Committee* (Oxford, Clarendon Press, 1991).

McIlwaine, C, 'The Gendered Exclusions of International Migration: Perspectives from Latin American Migrants in London' in S Chant (ed), *The International Handbook of Gender and Poverty* (Cheltenham, Edward Elgar, 2010) 260–65.

McKim, R, 'National Identity and Respect Among Nations' in R McKim and J McMahan (eds), *The Morality of Nationalism* (Oxford, Oxford University Press, 1997) 258–73.

McKim, R and McMahan, J (eds), *The Morality of Nationalism* (New York, Oxford University Press, 1997).

McNair Lord (ed), *International Law Opinions*, vol 2 (New York, Cambridge University Press, 1956).

Mégret, F, 'From "Savages" to "Unlawful Combatants": A Postcolonial Look at International Humanitarian Law's "Other"' in A Orford (ed), *International Law and its Others* (Cambridge, Cambridge University Press, 2012) 265–317.

——'International Law as Law' in J Crawford and M Koskenniemi (eds), *Cambridge Companion to International Law* (Cambridge, Cambridge University Press, 2012) 64–92.

Merleau-Ponty, M, *Phenomenology of Perception*, C Smith (trans) (London, Routledge & Kegan Paul, 1962).

Meron, T, 'On a Hierarchy of International Human Rights' (1986) 80 *American Journal of International Law* 1.

——'War Crimes in Yugoslavia and the Development of International Law' (1994) 88 *American Journal of International Law* 78.

Mgbeojim I, 'The Civilised Self and the Barbaric Other: Imperial Delusions of Order and the Challenges of Human Security' in R Falk, B Rajagopal and J Stevens (eds), *International Law and the Third World* (London, Routledge-Cavendish, 2008) 151–65.

Mill, JS, 'A Few Words on Non-Intervention' in Himmelfarb G (ed), *John Stuart Mill: Essays on Politics and Culture* (Garden City, Anchor Books, 1963) 368–84.

——'On Liberty' in M Warnock (ed), *Utilitarianism* (Glasgow, William Collins, 1962 [1869]).

——*Principles of Political Economy*, D Winch (ed) (London, Penguin, 1970 [1848]).

Mojtahed-Zadeh, P, *Security and Territoriality in the Persian Gulf: A Maritime Political Geography* (Surrey, Curzon, 1999).

Molloy, P, 'Killing Canadians: The International Politics of Capital Punishment' in J Edkins, N Persram and V Pin-Fat (eds), *Sovereignty and Subjectivity* (Boulder, Lynne Rienner, 1999) 125–40; also in J Edkins, V Pin-Fat, and M Shapiro (eds), *Sovereign Lives: Power in Global Politics* (London, Routledge, 2004) 125–40.

Moore, JB, *History and Digest of the International Arbitrations to which the United States has been a Party* (Washington, DC, US Government Printing Office, 1896).

Moran, M, 'Shifting Boundaries: The Authority of International Law' in J Nijman and A Nollkaemper (eds), *New Perspectives on the Divide between National and International Law* (Oxford, Oxford University Press, 2007) 163–90.

Morgenstern, F, 'The Right of Asylum' (1949) 26 *British Yearbook of International Law* 327.

Morsink, J, *The Universal Declaration of Human Rights: Origins, Drafting and Intent* (Philadelphia, University of Pennsylvania Press, 1999).

Mosler, H, 'International Legal Community' in R Bernhardt (ed), *Encyclopedia of Public International Law*, vol 2 (Amsterdam, Elsevier, 1997) 1251–55.

——'The International Society as a Legal Community' (1980) 140 *Recueil des Cours* 11.

Müller, I, *Hitler's Justice: The Courts of the Third Reich* (London, IB Tauris, 1991 [1967]).

Mushkat, R, 'Hong Kong as an International Legal Person' (1992) 6 *Emory International Law Review* 105.

Mutharika, PA, *The Regulation of Statelessness under International and National Law* (Dobbs Ferry, Oceana, 1977).

Nafziger, JAR, 'The General Admission of Aliens under International Law' (1983) 77 *American Journal of International Law* 804.

Nagy, B, 'The Frontiers of the Sovereign' in A Bayefsky (ed), *Human Rights and Refugees, Internally Displaced Persons and Migrant Workers: Essays in Memory of Joan Fitzpatrick and Arthur Helton* (Leiden, Martinus Nijhoff, 2006) 91–122.

Nancy, J-L, 'The Surprise of the Event' in S Barnett (ed), *Hegel after Derrida* (New York, Routledge, 1998) 159–76.

Nanz, P, 'Mobility, Migrants and Solidarity: Towards an Emerging European Citizenship Regime' in S Benhabib and J Resnik (eds), *Migrations and Mobilities: Citizenship, Borders, and Gender* (New York, New York University Press, 2009) 410–38.

Naylor, S, 'Spatial Regulation of British Emigration to Argentina' in J Edkins, N Persram and V Pin-Fat (eds), *Sovereignty and Subjectivity* (Boulder, Lynne Rienner, 1999) 71–87.

Newman, D, 'Boundaries, Borders, and Barriers: Changing Geographic Perspectives on Territorial Lines' in M Albert, D Jacobson and Y Lapid (eds), *Identities, Borders, Orders: Rethinking International Relations* (Minneapolis, University of Minnesota Press, 2001) 137–51.

——'The Resilience of Territorial Conflict in an Era of Globalization' in M Kahler and BF Walter (eds), *Territoriality and Conflict in an Era of Globalization* (Cambridge, Cambridge University Press, 2006) 85–110.

Newman, F and Weissbrodt, D, 'The Situation in Iran' in D Weissbrodt, J Fitzpatrick and F Newman (eds), *International Human Rights: Law, Policy, and Process* (Cincinnati, Anderson Publishing, 1996) 130–41.

Newman, GL, 'Anomalous Zones' (1995–96) 48 *Stanford Law Review* 1197.

Ng, SH, 'Power and Intergroup Discrimination' in H Tajfel (ed), *Social Identity and Intergroup Relations* (Cambridge, Cambridge University Press, 1982) 179–206.

Nora, P, 'Between Memory and History: Les Lieux de Mémorie, M Roudebush (trans) (1989) 26 *Representations* 7.

——*Realms of Memory*, LD Kritzman (ed), A Goldhammer (trans) (New York, Columbia University Press, 1996).

Nouwen, SMH, 'Justifying Justice' in J Crawford and M Koskenniemi (eds), *Cambridge Companion to International Law* (Cambridge, Cambridge University Press, 2012) 327–51.

Nowak, M, *UN Covenant on Civil and Political Rights: Commentary* (Strasbourg, NP Engel, 1993).

——'What's in a Name? The Prohibitions on Torture and Ill Treatment Today' in C Gearty and C Douzinas (eds), *Cambridge Companion to Human Rights Law* (Cambridge, Cambridge University Press, 2012) 307–28.

Nussbaum, M, 'Patriotism and Cosmopolitanism' in J Cohen (ed), *For Love of Country: Debating the Limits of Patriotism* (Boston, Beacon Press, 1996) 3–17.

Nyers, P, *Securitizations of Citizenship* (New York, Routledge, 2009).

Oakeshott, M, 'On History' in M Oakeshott, *On History and other Essays* (Indianapolis, Liberty Fund, 1999) 1–128.

O'Boyle, M, 'The Margin of Appreciation and Derogation Under Article 15: Ritual Incantation or Principle?' (1998) 19 *Human Rights Law Journal* 23.

Obregón, L, 'Between Civilisation and Barbarism: Creole Interventions in International Law' in R Falk, B Rajagopal and J Stevens (eds), *International Law and the Third World* (London, Routledge-Cavendish, 2008) 111–21.

O'Connell, DP, *International Law* (London, Stevens, 1965).

——*The Law of State Succession* (Cambridge, Cambridge University Press, 1956).

——'Nationality in "C" Class Mandates' (1954) 31 *British Yearbook of International Law* 458.

——*State Succession in Municipal Law and International Law* (Cambridge, Cambridge University Press, 1967).

O'Connell, DP and Lillich, RB, 'The Current Status of the Law of State Responsibility for Injuries to Aliens' in RB Lillich (ed), *International Law of State Responsibility for Injuries to Aliens* (Charlottesville, University Press of Virginia, 1983).

O'Keefe, R, 'The Grave Breaches Regime and Universal Jurisdiction" (2009) 7 *Journal of International Criminal Justice* 811.

——'Universal Jurisdiction' (2004) 2 *Journal of International Criminal Justice* 735.

O'Leary, B, 'Ernest Gellner's Diagnoses of Nationalism: A Critical Overview; or, What Is Living and What Is Dead in Ernest Gellner's Philosophy of Nationalism?' in JA Hall (ed), *The State of the Nations* (Cambridge, Cambridge University Press, 1998) 40–88.

Olick, JK, Vinitsky-Seroussi, V and Levy, D (eds), *The Collective Memory Reader* (Oxford, Oxford University Press, 2011).

O'Neill, O, 'Orientation in Thinking: Geographical Problems, Political Solutions' in S Elden and E Mendieta (eds), *Reading Kant's Geography* (Albany, State University of New York Press, 2011) 215–32.

Oppenheim, L, *International Law: Peace*, R Jennings and A Watts (eds), 9th edn (London, Longman Publishing, 1992).

——*International Law*, 8th edn, vol 1, H Lauterpacht (ed) (New York, David McKay, 1955).

Orakhelashvili, A, *Peremptory Norms of International Law* (Oxford, Oxford University Press, 2006).

Orentlicher, DF, 'Citizenship and National Identity' in D Wippman (ed), *International Law and Ethnic Conflict* (Ithaca, Cornell University Press, 1988), 296–325.

——'Separation Anxiety: International Responses to Ethno-Separatist Claims' (1998) 23 *Yale Journal of International Law* 1.

Orford, A, 'Constituting Order' in J Crawford and M Koskenniemi (eds), *Cambridge Companion to International Law* (Cambridge, Cambridge University Press, 2012) 271–89.

——*International Authority and the Responsibility to Protect* (Cambridge, Cambridge University Press, 2011).

——'A Jurisprudence of the Limit' in A Orford (ed), *International Law and its Others* (Cambridge, Cambridge University Press, 2006) 1–32.

——*Reading Humanitarian Intervention* (Cambridge, Cambridge University Press, 2003).

Orford, A (ed), *International Law and its Others* (Cambridge, Cambridge University Press, 2012).

Orridge, AW, 'Separatist and Autonomist Nationalisms: The Structure of Regional Loyalties in the Modern State' in CH Williams (ed), *National Separatism* (Vancouver, University of British Columbia Press, 1982) 43–74.

Parry, C, *Nationality and Citizenship Laws of the Commonwealth and of the Republic of Ireland* (London, Stevens, 1957).

——'Plural Nationality and Citizenship with Special Reference to the Commonwealth' (1953) 30 *British Yearbook of International Law* 244.

Paulson, S, 'Kelsen on Legal Interpretation' (1990) 10 *Oxford Journal of Legal Studies* 136.

Peers, L, *The Ojibwa of Western Canada: 1780 to 1870* (Winnipeg, University of Manitoba Press, 1994).

Pictet, J (ed), *Commentary to the 4th Geneva Convention Relative to the Protection of Civilian Persons in the Time of War* (Geneva, International Committee of the Red Cross, 1958).

Plender R, 'The Legal Basis of International Jurisdiction to Act with Regard to the Internally Displaced' (1994) 6 *International Journal of Refugee Law* 345.

——'The Ugandan Crisis and the Right of Expulsion Under International Law' (1972) 9 *The Review: International Commission of Jurists* 19.

Prebensen, SC, 'The Margin of Appreciation and Articles 9, 10 and 11 of the Convention' (1998) 19 *Human Rights Law Journal* 13.

Preece, JJ, 'Ethnic Cleansing as an Instrument of the Nation-State' (1998) 20 *Human Rights Quarterly* 820.

Preufs, UK, 'Citizenship in the European Union: A Paradigm for Transnational Democracy?' in D Archibugi, D Held and M Kohler (eds), *Re-imagining Political Community: Studies in Cosmopolitan Democracy* (Stanford, Stanford University Press, 1998) 138–51.

Proudfoot, MJ, *European Refugees: 1939–52* (Evanston, Northwestern University Press, 1956).

Pufendorf, S, *De Jure Naturae et Gentium Libri Octo*, CH Oldfather and WA Oldfather (eds) (Oxford, Clarendon Press, 1934 [1688]).

——*On the Duty of Man and Citizen According to Natural Law*, J Tully (ed), M Silverthorne (trans) (Cambridge, Cambridge University Press, 1991 [1673]).

—— *Elements of Universal Jurisprudence in Two Books*, CL Carr (ed and trans), in CL Carr (ed), *The Political Writings of Samuel Pufendorf*, MJ Seidler (trans) (New York, Oxford University Press, 1994 [1658]) 31–94.

—— *The Political Writings of Samuel Pufendorf*, MJ Seidler (trans) (Oxford, Oxford University Press, 1994 [1658]).

—— 'On the Law of Nature and of Nations in Eight Books' in CL Carr (ed), *The Political Writings of Samuel Pufendorf*, MJ Seidler (trans) (New York, Oxford University Press, 1994) 95–268.

Purvis, N, 'Critical Legal Studies in Public International Law' (1991) 32 *Harvard International Law Journal* 81.

Putnam, H, 'Must We Choose between Patriotism and Universal Reason?' in J Cohen (ed), *For Love of Country: Debating the Limits of Patriotism* (Boston, Beacon Press, 1996) 91–97.

Qeitzhanler, A, 'Temporary Protected Status: The Congressional Response to the Plight of Salvadorean Aliens' (1981) 64 *University of Colorado Law Review* 249.

Radin, M, 'A Restatement of Hohfeld' (1938) 41 *Harvard Law Review* 1141.

Ragazzi, M, *The Concept of International Obligations Erga Omnes* (Oxford, Oxford University Press, 1997).

Ramcharan, B, 'Equality and Non-discrimination' in L Henkin (ed), *The International Bill of Rights: The Covenant on Civil and Political Rights* (New York, Columbia University Press, 1981) 246–78.

Randall, KC, 'Universal Jurisdiction Under International Law' (1988) 66 *Texas Law Review* 785.

Raustiala, K, *Does the Constitution Follow the Flag? The Evolution of Territoriality in American Law* (Oxford, Oxford University Press, 2009).

—— 'The Evolution of Territoriality: International Relations and American Law' in M Kahler and BF Walker (eds), *Territoriality and Conflict in an Era of Globalization* (Cambridge, Cambridge University Press, 2006) 219–50.

—— 'The Geography of Justice' (2004–05) 73 *Fordham Law Review* 2501.

Raz, J, 'Authority, Law and Morality' (1985) 68 *Monist* 295; reprinted in J Raz, *Ethics in the Public Domain: Essays in the Morality of Law and Politics* (Oxford, Clarendon Press, 1994) 210–37.

—— *The Authority of Law* (Oxford, Clarendon Press, 1979).

—— *Between Authority and Interpretation* (Oxford, Oxford University Press, 2009).

Rezek, JF, 'Le droit international de la nationalité' (1986) 198 *Recueil des Cours* 333.

Ricoeur, P, *Memory, History, Forgetting*, K Blamey and D Pellauer (trans) (Chicago, University of Chicago Press, 2004).

Riggsby, AM, 'Space' in A Feldherr (ed), *The Roman Historians* (Cambridge, Cambridge University Press, 2009) 152–65.

—— 'Space and Geography' in A Barchiese and W Scheidel (eds), *Oxford Handbook of Roman Studies* (Oxford, Oxford University Press, 2010) 827–37.

Roberts, AE, 'Traditional and Modern Approaches to Customary International Law: A Reconciliation' (2001) 95 *American Journal of International Law* 757.

Robinson, D, 'Defining "Crimes against Humanity"' (1999) 93 *American Journal of International Law* 43.

van Roermund, B, 'Migrants, Humans and Human Rights: The Right to Move as the Right to Stay' in H Lindahl (ed), *A Right to Inclusion and Exclusion? Normative Fault*

Lines of the EU's Area of Freedom, Security and Justice (Oxford, Hart Publishing, 2009).

Rosand, E, 'The Right to Return under International Law Following Mass Dislocation: The Bosnia Precedent?' (1998) 19 *Michigan Journal of International Law* 1094.

Rosenstock, R, 'The Forty-Ninth Session of International Law Commission' (1998) 92 *American Journal of International Law* 107.

Roth, L, 'Transkei: A Tale of Two Citizenships' (1976) 9 *New York University Journal of International Law and Politics* 205.

Roucounas, E, 'The Idea of Justice in the Works of Early Scholars of International Law' in L Boisson de Chazournes and V Gowlland-Debbas (eds), *The International Legal System in Quest of Equity and Universality. Liber Amicorum Georges Abi Saab* (The Hague, Martinus Nijhoff, 2001) 77–99.

Rousseau, C, 'L'indépendance de l'état dans l'ordre international' (1948) 2 *Recueil des Cours* 167.

Rousseau, J-J, 'The Social Contract' in LG Crocker (ed), *The Social Contract and Discourse on Inequality* (London, Penguin, 1988) 5–147.

Rozzi, E, 'Undocumented Migrant and Roma Children in Italy: Between Rights Protection and Control' in J Bhabha (ed), *Children Without a State: A Global Human Rights Challenge* (Cambridge, MA, Massachusetts Institute of Technology Press, 2011) 177–216.

Rubin, A, 'International Law in the Age of Columbus' (1992) 39 *Netherlands International Law Review* 5.

Ruggie, JG, 'Territoriality and Beyond: Problematizing Modernity in International Relations' (1993) 47 *International Organization* 139.

Sahadevan, P, *India and the Overseas Indians: The Case of Sri Lanka* (New Delhi, Kalinga Publishers, 1995).

Said, E, *Orientalism* (New York, Vintage Books, 1979).

Salcedo, C and Juan, A, 'Reflections on Existence of a Hierarchy of Norms in International Law' (1997) 8 *European Journal of International Law* 583.

Salzman, PC, 'Multi-Recourse Nomadism in Iranian Baluchistan' in W Irons and N Dyson-Hudson (eds), *Perspectives on Nomadism* (Leiden, Brill, 1972) 48–59.

Samuels, MS, 'Existentialism and Human Geography' in D Ley and M Samuels (eds), *Humanistic Geography: Prospects and Problems* (London, Croom Helm, 1978) 22–40.

Sartre, JP, *Anti-Semite and Jew*, G Beck (trans) (New York, Schocken Books, 1976).

Sassen, S, *Territory, Authority, Rights: From Medieval to Global Assemblages* (Princeton, Princeton University Press, 2006).

Sawyer, C, 'Legal Frameworks of Statelessness in Europe' in BK Blitz and Sawyer (eds), *Statelessness in the European Union: Displaced, Undocumented, Unwanted* (Cambridge, Cambridge University Press, 2011) 69–107.

Scarry, E, 'The Difficulty of Imagining Other People' in J Cohen (ed), *For Love of Country: Debating the Limits of Patriotism* (Boston, Beacon Press, 1996) 98–110.

Schachter, O, *International Law in Theory and Practice* (The Hague, Martinus Nijhoff, 1991).

Scheffer, DJ, 'The United States and the International Criminal Court' (1999) 93 *American Journal of International Law* 12.

Scheinin, M, 'Resisting Panic: Lessons about the Role of Human Rights during the Long Decade after 9/11' in C Gearty and C Douzinas (eds), *Cambridge Companion to Human Rights* (Cambridge, Cambridge University Press, 2012) 293–306.

Schermers, H, 'General Course: European Convention of Human Rights' (1999) 7(2) *Collected Courses of the Academy of European Law* 1.

Schiffauer, W, 'Suspect Subjects: Muslim Migrants and the Security Agencies in Germany' in JM Eckert (ed), *The Social Life of Anti-Terrorism Laws: The War on Terror and the Classifications* (Bielefeld, Verlag, 2008) 56–77.

Schlütter, B, *Developments in Customary Law: Theory and the Practice of the International Court of Justice and the International Ad Hoc Criminal Tribunals for Rwanda and Yugoslavia* (The Hague, Martinus Nijhoff, 2010).

Schmitt, C, *The Nomos of the Earth in the International Law of the Jus Publicum Europaeum*, GL Ulmen (trans) (New York, Telos Press, 2006).

—— *Political Theology*, G Schwab (ed and trans) (Chicago, University of Chicago Press, 1985).

Schokkenbroek, J, 'The Basis, Nature and Application of the Margin-of-Appreciation Doctrine in the Case Law of the European Court of Human Rights' (1998) 19 *Human Rights Law Journal* 30.

—— 'The Prohibition of Discrimination in Article 14 of the Convention and the Margin of Appreciation' (1998) 19 *Human Rights Law Journal* 20.

Schutz, A, 'Concept and Theory Formation in the Social Sciences' in A Schutz, *Collected Papers*, H Wagner and G Psathas (eds), vol 1 (Dordrecht, Kluwer, 1996) 48–66.

—— *The Phenomenology of the Social World* (Evanston, Northwestern University Press, 1967).

—— 'The Problem of Social Reality' in A Schutz, *Collected Papers*, H Wagner and G Psathas (eds), vol 4 (Dordrecht, Kluwer, 1996) 71–74.

—— 'Scientific Model of the Social World' in A Schutz, *Collected Papers*, H Wagner and G Psathas (eds), vol 1 (Dordrecht, Kluwer, 1996) 3–47.

—— 'The Stranger' in A Schutz, *Collected Papers*, H Wagner and G Psathas (eds), vol 2 (Dordrecht, Kluwer, 1996) 91–105.

Schutz, A and Luckmann, T, *The Structure of the Life-World*, RM Zaner and TH Engelhardt (trans), 2 vols (Evanston, Northwestern University Press, 1973).

Schwarzenberger, G, 'International Jus Cogens', (1964) 43 *Texas Law Review* 455.

—— *International Law*, 3rd edn (London, Stevens, 1957).

Scobbie, I, 'Towards the Elimination of International Law: Some Radical Scepticism about Sceptical Radicalism' (1990) 61 *British Yearbook of International Law* 339.

Selinger, CM, 'Equality in the Relief of Destitution Abroad: A Test Case in Distinguishing Duties From Charity' (1982) 2 *Windsor Yearbook of Access to Justice* 53.

Sen, S, 'Stateless Refugees and the Right to Return: The Bihari Refugees of South Asia – Part 1' (1999) 11 *International Journal of Refugee* Law 625.

—— 'Stateless Refugees and the Right to Return: The Bihari Refugees of South Asia – Part 2' (2000) 12 *International Journal of Refugee Law* 41.

Seri, G, 'On the "Triple Frontier" and the "Borderization" of Argentina' in J Edkins, V Pin-Fat and M Shapiro (eds), *Sovereign Lives: Power in Global Politics* (New York, Routledge, 2004) 79–100.

Shabati, R (ed), *League of Nations Conference for the Codification of International Law (1930)* (Dobbs Ferry, Oceana Publ, 1975).

Shaw, J, 'Introduction' in J Shaw and G More (eds), *New Legal Dynamics of European Union* (Oxford, Clarendon Press, 1995) 1–14.

Shaw, K, 'Creating/Negotiating Interstices' in J Edkins, V Pin-Fat and M Shapiro (eds), *Sovereign Lives: Power in Global Politics* (New York, Routledge, 2004) 165–87.

Shaw, M, *International Law*, 5th edn (Cambridge, Cambridge University Press, 2003).

Shearer, I and Opeskin, B, 'Nationality and Statelessness' in B Opeskin, R Perruchoud and J Redpath-Cross (eds), *Foundations of International Migration Law* (Cambridge, Cambridge University Press, 2012) 93–122.

Shrijver, N, 'The Changing Nature of State Sovereignty' (1999) 70 *British Yearbook of International Law* 65.

Sik, KS, 'Nationality and (Public) International Law' (1982) 29 *Netherlands International Law Review* 100.

Simeon, JC, 'Introduction: The Research Workshop on Critical Issues in International Refugee Law and Strategies Towards Interpretative Harmony' in JC Simeon (ed), *Critical Issues in International Refugee Law: Strategies Toward Interpretative Harmony* (Cambridge, Cambridge University Press, 2010) 1–39.

Simma, B and Alston, P, 'The Sources of Human Rights Law: Custom, Jus Cogens, and General Principles' (1988–89) 12 *Australian Yearbook of International Law* 82.

Simmel, G, 'The Stranger' in KH Wolff (ed and trans), *The Sociology of Georg Simmel* (New York, Free Press, 1950) 402–8.

Simmons, AJ, 'Justification and Legitimacy' (1999) 109 *Ethics* 739.

Simpson, G, 'Atrocity, Law, Humanity: Punishing Human Rights Violators' in C Gearty and C Douzinas (eds), *Cambridge Companion to Human Rights* (Cambridge, Cambridge University Press, 2012) 114–33.

Singer, P, 'The Legal Rights Debate in Analytical Jurisprudence from Bentham to Hohfeld' (1982) *Wisconsin Law Review* 975.

——*Practical Ethics* (Cambridge, Cambridge University Press, 1994).

Sipkov, I, 'Introduction Note to Bulgarian Law on Citizenship' (1987) 26 *International Legal Materials* 422.

——'Introductory Note' (1990) 29 *International Legal Materials* 538.

Skinner, Q and Stråth, B (eds), *States and Citizens: History/Theory/Prospects* (Cambridge, Cambridge University Press, 2003).

Slaughter, A-M, *A New World Order* (Princeton, Princeton University Press, 2004).

——'Sovereignty and Power in a Networked World Order' (2004) 40 *Stanford Journal of International Law* 283.

Sloane, RD, 'Breaking the Genuine Link: The Contemporary International Legal Regulation of Nationality' (2009) 50 *Harvard International Law Journal* 1.

Smith, A, 'Report dated 1766' in RL Meek, DD Raphael and PG Stein (eds), *Lectures on Jurisprudence* (Indianapolis, Oxford University Press & Liberty Fund, 1978).

Smith, AD, 'The Ethnic Basis of National Identity' in AD Smith (ed), *National Identity/Ethnonationalism in Comparative Perspective* (Reno, University of Nevada Press, 1991) 19–42.

——'Nationalism, Ethnic Separatism and the Intelligentsia' in CH Williams (ed), *National Separatism* (Vancouver, University of British Columbia Press, 1982) 17–41.

—— 'The Rise of Nations' in AD Smith (ed), *National Identity/Ethnonationalism in Comparative Perspective* (Reno, University of Nevada Press, 1991) 43–70.

Smith, RW, 'The Armenian Genocide: Memory, Politics, and the Future' in RG Hovannisian (ed), *The Armenian Genocide: History, Politics, Ethics* (New York, St Martin's Press, 1992) 1–20.

Sohn, LB and Baxter, RR, 'Responsibility of States for Injuries to the Economic Interests of Aliens' (1961) 55 *American Journal of International Law* 545.

Sohn, LB and Buergenthal, T (eds), *International Protection of Human Rights* (New York, Bobbs-Merrill, 1973).

—— *The Movement of Persons across Borders, Studies in Transnational Legal Policy*, vol 23 (Washington, DC, American Society of International Law, 1992).

Somer, J, 'Acts of Non-State Armed Groups and Law Governing Armed Conflict' (2006) 10 *American Society of International Law Insights* 21.

Somers, MR, *Genealogies of Citizenship: Markets, Statelessness, and the Right to Have Rights* (Cambridge, Cambridge University Press, 2008).

Soysal, YN, *Limits of Citizenship: Migrants and Post National Membership in Europe* (Chicago, University of Chicago Press, 1994).

Spiermann, O, 'Lotus and the Double Structure of International Legal Argument' in L Boisson de Chazournes and P Sands (eds), *International Law, the International Court of Justice and Nuclear Weapons* (Cambridge, Cambridge University Press, 1999) 131–80.

Spinoza, B, 'Ethics' in E Curley (ed), *Collected Works of Spinoza*, E Curley (trans) (Princeton, Princeton University Press, 1985) 408–617.

Starke, J, *Introduction to International Law*, 7th edn (London, Butterworths, 1972).

Steiner, H, 'Ideals and Counter-Ideals in the Struggle Over Autonomy Regimes for Minorities' (1991) 66 *Notre Dame Law Review* 1529.

—— 'Individual Claims in a World of Massive Violations: What Role for the Human Rights Committee?' in P Alston and J Crawford (eds), *The Future of UN Human Rights Treaty Monitoring* (Cambridge, Cambridge University Press, 2000) 15–30.

Steiner, H, Alston, P and Goodman, R, *International Human Rights in Context: Law, Politics and Morals*, 3rd edn (Oxford, Oxford University Press, 2008).

Strayer, JR, *On the Medieval Origins of the Modern State* (Princeton, Princeton University Press, 1970).

Sugarman, D, 'Legal Theory, the Common Law Mind, and the Making of the Textbook Tradition' in W Twining (ed), *Legal Theory and the Common Law* (Oxford, Blackwell, 1986) 26–61.

Sunga, LS, *Individual Responsibility in International Law for Serious Human Rights Violations* (Dordrecht, Martinus Nijhoff, 1992).

Suy, E, 'The Concept of Jus Cogens in Public International Law' in *Lagonissi Conference on International Law: Papers and Proceedings*, vol 2 (Geneva, Carnegie Endowment for International Peace, 1967) 17–77.

Tajfel, H, *Human Groups and Social Categories: Studies in Social Psychology* (Cambridge, Cambridge University Press, 1981).

Talbot, RJA, 'Rome's Empire and Beyond: The Spatial Aspect' (1991) 26 *Cahiers des Études Anciennes* 215.

Talkenberg, L, *The Status of Palestinian Refugees in International Law* (Oxford, Clarendon Press, 1998).

Tasioulas, J, 'In Defence of Relative Normativity: Communitarian Values and the Nicaragua Case' (1996) 16 *Oxford Journal of Legal Studies* 85.

——'The Legitimacy of International Law' in S Besson and J Tasioulas (eds), *Philosophy of International Law* (Oxford, Oxford University Press, 2010) 97–116.

Taylor, C, 'Nationalism and Modernity' in R McKim and J McMahan (eds), *The Morality of Nationalism* (Oxford, Oxford University Press, 1997) 31–55.

——'Nationalism and Modernity' in JA Hall (ed), *The State of the Nations* (Cambridge, Cambridge University Press, 1998) 91–106.

Tesón, FR, 'International Human Rights and Cultural Relativism' (1984–85) 25 *Virginia Journal of International Law* 869.

——'The Kantian Theory of International Law' (1992) 92 *Columbia Law Review* 53.

Thirlway, H, 'Injured and Non-injured States before the International Court of Justice' in M Ragazzi (ed), *International Responsibility Today: Essays in Memory of Oscar Schacter* (Dorrecht, Martinus Nijhoff, 2005) 311–28.

Thompson, J, 'Community Identity and World Citizenship' in D Archibugi, D Held and M Kohler (eds), *Re-imagining Political Community: Studies in Cosmopolitan Democracy* (Stanford, Stanford University Press, 1998) 179–97.

Thornberry, P, *International Law and the Rights of Minorities* (Oxford, Clarendon Press, 1991).

Tiburcio, C, *The Human Rights of Aliens under International and Comparative Law* (The Hague, Martinus Nijhoff, 2001).

Tilly, C, 'The State of Nationalism' (1996) 10 *Critical Review* 299.

——'States and Nationalism in Europe, 1492–1992' (1994) 23 *Theory and Society* 131.

Tomuschat, C, 'Individuals' in J Crawford, A Pellet and S Olleson (eds), *The Law of International Responsibility* (Oxford, Oxford University Press) 985–91.

Torpey, J, *The Invention of the Passport: Surveillance, Citizenship and the State* (Cambridge, Cambridge University Press, 2000).

Tsagourias, N, 'The Will of the International Community as a Normative Source of International Law' in IF Dekker and WG Werner (eds), *Governance and International Legal Theory* (Leiden, Martinus Nijhoff, 2004) 97–121.

Tuck, R, *Natural Rights Theories: Their Origin and Development* (Cambridge, Cambridge University Press, 1979).

——*The Rights of War and Peace: Political Thought and the International Order from Grotius to Kant* (Oxford, Oxford University Press, 1999).

Turack, DC, *The Passport in International Law* (Lexington, MA, Lexington Books, 1971).

Tyrrell, M, 'Nation-States and States of Mind: Nationalism as Psychology' (1996) 10 *Critical Review* 233.

United Nations High Commission for Human Rights, *Human Rights Instruments, Volumes I and II: Compilation of General Comments and General Recommendations adopted by Human Rights Treaty Bodies* (most recent edition from 2008), available at www.ohchr.org/EN/HRBodies/Pages/TBGeneralComments.aspx.

United Nations High Commission for Human Rights, *Selected Decisions of the Human Rights Committee under the Optional Protocol: International Covenant on Civil and Political Rights*, 9 vols (New York, United Nations, 2008).

United Nations High Commissioner for Refugees (UNHCR), 'Commentary on the Refugee Convention 1951' (October 1997).

——'Conclusion on the Prevention and Reduction of Statelessness and the Protection of Stateless Persons', UN Doc A/AC.96/860 (23 October 1995).

——'Evaluation and Policy Analysis Unit, Evaluation of UNHCR's Role and Activities in Relation to Statelessness', RPAU/2001/09 (July 2001).

——'Final Report Concerning the Questionnaire on Statelessness Pursuant to the Agenda for Protection' (March 2004 [September 2003]).

——*Handbook on Procedures and Criteria for Determining Refugee Status*, revised edn (Geneva, 1992).

——'Does anyone want these people? The Problem of Statelessness Has Become a Live Issue Again' (1998) 112 *Protecting Refugees Magazine*.

——'Stateless: Prevention and Reduction of Statelessness and Protection of Stateless Persons', UN Doc EC/57/SC/CRP.6 (14 February 2006), reprinted in (2006) 25 *Refugee Survey Quarterly* 72.

——'Statelessness in the Canadian Context: A Discussion Paper' (Ottawa, 2003).

——'Statelessness Determination Procedures and the Status of Stateless Persons: Summary Conclusions' (December 2010).

——'UNHCR's Activities in the Field of Statelessness: Progress Report', UN Doc EC/55/SC/CRP.13/REV.1 (May 2001), reprinted in (2006) 25 *Refugee Survey Quarterly* 122.

UNHCR Executive Committee, 'Current UNHCR Activities on Behalf of Stateless Persons', UN Doc EC/1995/SCP/CRP.6 (21 September 1995).

UNHCR Regional Bureau for Europe, 'The Czech and Slovak Citizenship Laws and the Problem of Statelessness' in UNHCR (ed), *Citizenship in the Context of the Dissolution of Czechoslovakia*, European Series, vol 2(4) (1 September 1996) 1–48.

Vandenabeele, C, 'To Register or Not to Register? Legal Identity, Birth Registration, and Inclusive Development' in Bhabha J (ed), *Children without a State: A Global Human Rights Challenge* (Cambridge, MA, Massachusetts Institute of Technology Press, 2011) 307–30.

de Vattel, E, *The Law of Nations or the Principles of Natural Law*, G Fenwick (trans) (Washington, DC, Carnegie Institution, 1916).

Vaurs-Chaumette, A-L, 'Peoples and Minorities' in J Crawford, A Pellet and S Olleson (eds), *The Law of International Responsibility* (Oxford, Oxford University Press) 996–97.

Verdross, A, 'Jus Dispositivum and Jus Cogens in International Law' (1966) 60 *American Journal of International Law* 55.

Vermeer-Künzli, A, 'As If: The Legal Fiction in Diplomatic Protection' (2007) 18 *European Journal of International Law* 37.

Vertovec, S and Cohin, R, 'Introduction' in S Vertovec and R Cohin (eds), *Migration, Diasporas and Transnationalism* (Cheltenham, Elgar Reference Collection, 1999) xiii–xxviii.

Verzijl, JHW, *International Law in Historical Perspective* (Leiden, Sijthoff, 1972).

Vishniak, M, *The Legal Status of Stateless Persons*, AG Duker (ed) (New York, American Jewish Committee, 1945).

de Vitoria, F, 'On the American Indians' [1539] in A Pagden and L Jeremy (eds), *Political Writings* (Cambridge, Cambridge University Press, 1991) 233–92.

——'On Law' in A Pagden and L Jeremy (eds), *Political Writings* (Cambridge, Cambridge University Press, 1991) 153–205.

Vlastos, G, 'Justice and Equality' in RB Brandt (ed), *Social Justice* (New Jersey, Prentice-Hall, 1962) 31–72.

Vohra, S, 'Detention of Irregular Migrants and Asylum Seekers' in R Cholewinski, R Perruchoud and E MacDonald (eds), *International Migration Law: Developing Paradigms and Key Challenges* (The Hague, Asser Press, 2007) 49–69.

van Waas, L, 'Nationality and Rights' in BK Blitz and M Lynch (eds), *Statelessness and Citizenship: A Comparative Study on the Benefits of Nationality* (Northampton, MA, Edward Edgar, 2011) 23–44.

——*Nationality Matters: Statelessness under International Law* (Antwerp, Intersentia, 2008).

Waldenfels, B, *Order in the Twilight*, trans by Parent DJ (Athens, Ohio University Press, 1996).

——*The Question of the Other* (Albany, State University of New York, 2007).

——*Topographie des Fremden*, vol 1, Studien zur Phänomenologie des Fremden, 2nd edn (Frankfurt, Suhrkamp Verlag, 1997).

Waldock, H, 'General Course on Public International Law' (1962) 106 *Recueil des cours* 253.

——'The Plea of Internal Jurisdiction Before International Legal Tribunals' (1954) 31 *British Yearbook of International Law* 96.

Waldron, J, *Theories of Rights* (Oxford, Clarendon Press, 1984).

Walker, N, 'Citizenship and Deterrioralisation in the European Union' in H Lindahl (ed), *A Right to Inclusion and Exclusion? Normative Fault Lines of the EU's Area of Freedom, Security and Justice* (Oxford, Hart Publishing, 2009) 261–74.

Walzer, M, *Spheres of Justice: A Defense of Pluralism and Equality* (New York, Basic Books, 1983).

Ward, I, 'Identity and Difference: The European Union and Postmodernism' in J Shaw, and G More (eds), *New Legal Dynamics of European Union* (Oxford, Clarendon Press, 1995) 15–28.

Watson, A, *The Expansion of International Society* (Oxford, Clarendon Press, 1988).

Watts, A, *International Law Commission, 1949–1998* (Oxford, Oxford University Press, 1999).

——'The Legal Position in International Law of Heads of States, Heads of Government and Foreign Ministers' (1994) 247 *Recueil des cours* 10.

Weber, E, 'What Rough Beast?' (1996) 10 *Critical Review* 285.

Weil, P, 'Access to Citizenship: A Comparison of Twenty-Five Nationality Laws' in A Aleinikoff and D Klusmeyer (eds), *From Migrants to Citizens: Membership in a Changing World* (Washington, Carnegie Endowment for International Peace, 2000) 17–35.

——*La France et ses étrangers: L'aventure d'une politique de l'immigration* (Paris, Calmann-Lévy, 1993).

——'The Transformation of Immigration Policies: Immigration Control and Nationality Laws in Europe: A Comparative Approach' (1999) 7(2) *Collective Courses of the Academy of European Law* 87.

Weiner, M, 'Rejected Peoples and Unwanted Migrants in South Asia' in M Weiner (ed), *International Migration and Security* (Colorado, Westview, 1993) 149–78.

Weis, P, 'The Convention Relating to the Status of Stateless Persons' (1961) 10 *International and Comparative Law Quarterly* 255.

——'Diplomatic Protection of Nationals and International Protection of Human Rights' (1971) 4 *Human Rights Journal* 643.

——'The International Protection of Refugees' (1954) 48 *American Journal of International Law* 193.

——'Legal Aspects of the Convention of 25 July 1951 Relating to the Status of Refugees' (1953) 30 *British Yearbook of International Law* 478.

——*Nationality and Statelessness in International Law*, 2nd edn (London, Stevens, 1979).

——'Review of *A Study of Statelessness (UN Department of Social Affairs, 1949)*' (1950) 27 *British Yearbook of International Law* 510.

——'The United Nations Convention on the Reduction of Statelessness, 1961' (1962) 11 *International and Comparative Law Quarterly* 1073.

Weissbrodt, D, 'The Approach of the Committee on the Elimination of Racial Discrimination to Interpreting and Applying International Humanitarian Law' (2010) 19 *Minnesota Journal of International Law* 327.

——'Final Report on the Rights of Non-Citizens', UN Doc E/CN.4/Sub.2/2003/23 (2003).

——*The Human Rights of Non-Citizens* (Oxford, Oxford University Press, 2008).

——*International Human Rights: Law, Policy and Process* (Newark, LexisNexis, 2009).

——'The Protection of Non-citizens in International Human Rights' in R Cholewinski, R Perruchoud and E MacDonald (eds), *International Migration Law: Developing Paradigms and Key Challenges* (The Hague, Asser Press, 2007) 221–35.

Weissbrodt, D and Collins, C, 'The Human Rights of Stateless Persons' (2006) 28 *Human Rights Quarterly* 246.

Weissbrodt, D, Fitzpatrick, J and Newman, F (eds), *International Human Rights: Law, Rights, and Process*, 3rd edn (Cincinnati, Anderson, 2001).

Wells, PS, *The Barbarians Speak: How the Conquered Peoples Shaped Roman Europe* (Princeton, Princeton University Press, 1999).

Werner, WG, 'State Sovereignty and International Legal Discourse' in IF Dekker and WG Werner (eds), *Governance and International Legal Theory* (Leiden, Martinus Nijhoff, 2004) 125–57.

Westlake, J, 'Territorial Sovereignty, Especially with Relation to Uncivilized Regions' in L Oppenheim (ed), *The Collected Papers of John Westlake on Public International Law*, vol 1 (Cambridge, Cambridge University Press, 1914) 131–35.

Wheaton, H, *Elements of International Law*, GG Wilson (ed) (Oxford, Clarendon Press, 1936).

White, G, *Nationalism and Territory: Constructing Group Identity in Southeastern Europe* (Oxford, Rowman & Littlefield, 2000).

Whitecross, RW, 'Migrants, Settlers and Refugees: Law and the Contestation of "Citizenship" in I von Bhutan et al (eds), *Rules of Law and Laws of Ruling: On the Governance of Law* (Farnham, Ashgate, 2009) 57–74.

Wilkinson, JC, 'Traditional Concepts of Territory in South East Arabia' (1983) 149 *Geographical Journal* 301.

Williams, B, 'The Idea of Equality' in P Laslett and WG Runciman (eds), *Philosophy, Politics and Society*, 2nd Series (Oxford, Oxford University Press, 1972).

Williams, CH, *National Separatism* (Vancouver, University of British Columbia Press, 1982).

Williams, JF, 'Denaturalization' (1927) 8 *British Yearbook of International Law* 45.

Williams, RA, *The American Indian in Western Legal Thought: The Discourses of Conquest* (Oxford, Oxford University Press, 1990).

Williams, SA and de Maestral, ALC, *An Introduction to International Law: Chiefly as Interpreted and Adopted in Canada*, 2nd edn (Toronto, Butterworths, 1987).

Wilson, RJ, 'Prosecuting Pinochet: International Crimes in Spanish Domestic Law' (1999) 21 *Human Rights Quarterly* 927.

Wincott, D, 'Political Theory, Law, and European Union' in J Shaw and G More (eds), *New Legal Dynamics of European Union* (Oxford, Clarendon Press, 1995) 293–311.

Wing, AK, 'Legal Decision-Making during the Palestinian *Intifada*: Embryonic Self-Rule' (1993) 18 *Yale Journal of International Law* 299.

Wolf, ER, *Europe and the People without History* (Berkeley, University of California Press, 2010).

Wooldridge, F and Sharma, VD, 'International Law and the Expulsion of Ugandan Asians' (1975) 9 *International Lawyer (ABA)* 30.

Wright, J, 'Minority Groups, Autonomy, and Self-Determination' (1999) 19 *Oxford Journal of Legal Studies* 605.

Wright, Q, 'The Bombardment of Damascus' (1926) 20 *American Journal of International Law* 263.

—— 'The Law of the Nuremberg Tribunal' (1947) 41 *American Journal of International Law* 38.

Wyler, E and Papaux, A, 'The Search for Universal Justice' in RSJ Macdonald and DM Johnston (eds), *Towards World Constitutionalism: Issues in the Legal Ordering of the World Community* (Leiden, Martinus Nijhoff, 2005) 273–302.

Yack, B, 'The Myth of the Civic Nation' (1996) 10 *Critical Review* 193.

Yamada, C, 'Revisiting the International Law Commission's Draft Articles on State Responsibility' in M Ragazzi (ed), *International Responsibility Today: Essays in Memory of Oscar Schacter* (Leiden, Martinus Nijohoff, 2005) 117–23.

Yost, DS, 'Political Philosophy and the Theory of International Relations' (1994) 70 *International Affairs* 263.

Zappala, G and Castles, S, 'Citizenship and Immigration in Australia' in TA Aleinikoff and D Klusmeyer (eds), *From Migrants to Citizens: Membership in a Changing World* (Washington, DC, Carnegie Endowment for International Peace, 2000) 32–81.

Zemanek, K, 'New Trends in the Enforcement of *Erga Omnes* Obligations' (2000) 4 *Max Planck Yearbook of UN Law* 1.

Ziegler, KS, 'Domaine Réservé' in M Planck (ed), *Encyclopaedia of Public International Law*, www.mpepil.com (2013) 222.

Ziemele, I and Schram, GG, 'Article 15' in G Alfredsson and A Eide (eds), *The Universal Declaration of Human Rights: A Common Standard of Achievement* (The Hague, Martinus Nijhoff, 1999) 297–323.

Ziller, A, 'The Community is Not a Place and Why It Matters: Green Square' (2004) 22 *Urban Policy and Research* 465.

Zolo, D, 'Humanitarian Militarism' in S Besson and J Tsioulas (eds), *Philosophy of International Law* (Oxford, Oxford University Press, 2010) 549–65.

Index